When should I travel to get the best airfare?
Where do I go for answers to my travel questions?
What's the best and easiest way to plan and book my trip?

frommers.travelocity.com

Frommer's, the travel guide leader, has teamed up with **Travelocity.com**, the leader in online travel, to bring you an in-depth, easy-to-use resource designed to help you plan and book your trip online.

At **frommers.travelocity.com**, you'll find free online updates about your destination from the experts at Frommer's plus the outstanding travel planning and purchasing features of Travelocity.com. Travelocity.com provides reservations capabilities for 95 percent of all airline seats sold, more than 47,000 hotels, and over 50 car rental companies. In addition, Travelocity.com offers more than 2,000 exciting vacation and cruise packages. Travelocity.com puts you in complete control of your travel planning with these and other great features:

Expert travel guidance from Frommer's - over 150 writers reporting from around the world!

Best Fare Finder - an interactive calendar tells you when to travel to get the best airfare

Fare Watcher - we'll track airfare changes to your favorite destinations

Dream Maps - a mapping feature that suggests travel opportunities based on your budget

Shop Safe Guarantee - 24 hours a day / 7 days a week live customer service, and more!

Whether traveling on a tight budget, looking for a quick weekend getaway, or planning the trip of a lifetime, Frommer's guides and Travelocity.com will make your travel dreams a reality. You've bought the book, now book the trip!

Pueblito "Los Dominicos"

Argentina
& Chile

1st Edition

by Shane Christensen
& Kristina Schreck

HUNGRY MINDS, INC.
Best-Selling Books • Digital Downloads • e-Books •
Answer Networks • e-Newsletters • Branded Web Sites • e-Learning
New York, NY • Cleveland, OH • Indianapolis, IN

ABOUT THE AUTHORS

To do Argentina right, **Shane Christensen** (chapters 1, 2, 3, 4, 5, 7, and appendix A) moved in with a *Porteño* family, committed himself to a rigorous steak-only diet, searched Buenos Aires for the perfect tango partner, and added a rich Argentine accent to his Mexican-learned Spanish. With his nascent Argentine credentials, he roamed the country's far corners, finding that no place in South America offers such geographic diversity and cultural distinction. A California native, Shane has written extensively in South America, Western Europe, and the United States for the Berkeley Guides, Fodor's, and the *Wall Street Journal*. He is now a U.S. diplomat serving in the Middle East.

Kristina Schreck (chapters 1, 6, 8, 9, 10, 11, 12, 13, 14, 15, appendix A, and appendix B) has traveled extensively throughout South America and has lived and worked in Argentina and Chile for 5 years. She now resides in Chile; and though she fell in love with its magical rhythm and its magnificent landscapes, she'll never understand the country's fondness for marinated sea urchin, bad soap operas, and *cumbia* music. Kristina is the former managing editor of *Adventure Journal* magazine, and she currently works as a freelance writer, translator, and outdoor guide.

Published by:

HUNGRY MINDS, INC.

909 Third Ave.
New York, NY 10022

ISBN 0-7645-6260-6
ISSN 1532-9968

Editors: Kelly Regan and Matthew Garcia
Special Thanks to Myka Carroll
Production Editor: Tammy Ahrens
Design by Michele Laseau
Cartographer: Elizabeth Puhl
Photo Editor: Richard Fox
Production by Hungry Minds Indianapolis Production Services

Front cover photo: Llamas in the Andean Altiplano region, Chile

SPECIAL SALES

For general information on Hungry Minds' products and services please contact our Customer Care department; within the U.S. at 800-762-2974, outside the U.S. at 317-572-3993 or fax 317-572-4002. For sales inquiries and reseller information, including discounts, bulk sales, customized editions, and premium sales, please contact our Customer Care department at 800-434-3422.

Manufactured in the United States of America

5   4   3   2   1

Contents

List of Maps

ACKNOWLEDGMENTS

Shane Christensen would like to thank three people, all of whom helped on this mission: Marisa Plowden, Anand Selvarajan, and Chrystelle Lalanne.

    Kristina Schreck would like to thank: Sally Thomas for her utmost support in completing this book; the Fuenzalida family for the truck and the apartment in Santiago; Misty Pinson at Lan Chile; Miguel Yarut at Explora in San Pedro; Marí Inés Stipicic for the hospitality in Valdivia; Bertrand Deschamps for accompanying me in Argentina; Will Taylor for the photos and camaraderie on the Carretera Austral; Suzi Wortman, Anne Patterson, Jeremy Salter, and the gang at Bigfoot Expeditions for their unflagging support and friendship in Puerto Natales; Rodrigo Fuentes in Punta Arenas; Sebastian Maier for laughs in Ushuaia; Barbara Schmaltz for hanging in there with me; Javier Pinto-Duk for obvious reasons; and last but not least, thanks to Pedro Moita for accompanying me on the long, long journey north.

To Marisa, who is my favorite tango partner.

—Shane Christensen

This book is dedicated to the memory of Richard Thomas.

—Kristina Schreck

AN INVITATION TO THE READER

In researching this book, we discovered many wonderful places—hotels, restaurants, shops, and more. We're sure you'll find others. Please tell us about them, so we can share the information with your fellow travelers in upcoming editions. If you were disappointed with a recommendation, we'd love to know that, too. Please write to:

Frommer's Argentina & Chile, 1st Edition
Hungry Minds, Inc.
909 Third Ave.
New York, NY 10022

AN ADDITIONAL NOTE

Please be advised that travel information is subject to change at any time—and this is especially true of prices. We therefore suggest that you write or call ahead for confirmation when making your travel plans. The authors, editors, and publisher cannot be held responsible for the experiences of readers while traveling. Your safety is important to us, however, so we encourage you to stay alert and be aware of your surroundings. Keep a close eye on cameras, purses, and wallets, all favorite targets of thieves and pickpockets.

WHAT THE SYMBOLS MEAN

✪ **Frommer's Favorites**

Our favorite places and experiences—outstanding for quality, value, or both.

The following abbreviations are used for credit cards:

AE	American Express	EC	Eurocard
CB	Carte Blanche	MC	MasterCard
DC	Diners Club	V	Visa
DISC	Discover		

FIND FROMMER'S ONLINE

Now that you have the guidebook to a great trip, visit our Web site at **www.frommers.com** for travel information on nearly 2,000 destinations. With features updated regularly, we give you instant access to the most current trip-planning information available. At Frommers.com, you'll also find the best prices on air fares, accommodations, and car rentals—and you can even book travel online through our travel booking partners. At Frommers.com you'll also find the following:

- Daily Newsletter highlighting the best travel deals
- Hot Spot of the Month/Vacation Sweepstakes & Travel Photo Contest
- More than 200 Travel Message Boards
- Outspoken Newsletters and Feature Articles on travel bargains, vacation ideas, tips & resources, and more!

The Best of Argentina & Chile

Argentina and Chile—separated by the serrated peaks of the Andes Mountains—combine to blanket the southern half of South America; the distance from Chile's northern tip to the southern tail of Argentina's Tierra del Fuego spans almost 3,000 miles. And the scope of experience to be found here is no less grand: from the cosmopolitan bustle of Buenos Aires to the desolate moonscape of Chile's Atacama Desert; from the tropical jungles and thunderous falls of Iguazú to the tundra and glaciers of Torres del Paine National Park. Whether you've come to meander the quiet towns of Chile's Lake District or dance the night away in a smoky, low-lit tango bar, your trip to the southern hemisphere will never disappoint. In this chapter we've selected the best that Argentina and Chile have to offer—museums, outdoor adventures, hotels, and more. So read on and start planning!

1 The Most Unforgettable Travel Experiences

- **Learning to Dance Tango in Buenos Aires:** *Salones de baile,* as tango salons are called, blanket the city; the most famous are in San Telmo. In these salons you can watch traditional Argentine tango danced by all generations, and most offer lessons before the floor opens up to dancers. You won't find many novices on the dance floor after midnight, however. See chapter 3.
- **Visiting the Recoleta Cemetery:** The beautiful cemetery in Buenos Aires houses expensive mausoleums competing for grandeur—a place where people can remain rich, even after death. Among the only non-aristocrats buried here is Eva Perón, or "Evita." Some of Argentina's upper class still believe she has no right to be here. See chapter 3.
- **Wandering Caminito Street in La Boca:** Capture the flavor of early Buenos Aires on this short historic street, which is also considered an outdoor museum. The Caminito is famous for the brightly colored sheet-metal houses that border it and for the sculptures, paintings, and wall murals you'll find along the street. Performers and dancers are here every day. See chapter 3.
- **Visiting Iguazú Falls:** One of the world's most spectacular sights, Iguazú boasts over 275 waterfalls fed by the Iguazú River, which

can (and should) be visited from both the Argentine and Brazilian sides. In addition to the falls, Iguazú encompasses a marvelous subtropical jungle with extensive flora and fauna. See chapter 4.

- **Sailing Through the Andes Between Chile & Argentina:** Why fly or drive when you can sail through the Andes? Two companies work together to provide boat journeys from near Ensenada, Chile, to Bariloche, Argentina, or vice versa. It's a dazzling cruise—but worth the journey only on a clear day. Leaving from Vicente Pérez Rosales National Park in Chile, the cruise takes you across the emerald waters of Lago Todos los Santos, through rugged peaks and rainforest, and eventually to Puerto Blest in Argentina for a sail across Lake Nahuel Huapi and past gorgeous alpine scenery and the Llao Llao Peninsula. The trip can be done in 1 or in 2 days with an overnight at the Hotel Peulla. If Argentina (or Chile) isn't on your itinerary, each company offers a round-trip day ride. See chapters 6 and 12.

- **Visiting Punta del Este in Summer:** As *Porteños* (residents of Buenos Aires) will tell you, anyone who's anyone from Buenos Aires heads to Punta del Este for summer vacation. The glitzy Atlantic coast resort in Uruguay is packed with South America's jet set from December through February and offers inviting beaches and outstanding nightlife. See chapter 7.

- **Waking Up in Santiago After a Rainstorm:** Santiago is a magnificent city, but it's usually hidden under a blanket of smog so filthy it would make even Paris look like Detroit. If you're lucky enough to catch Santiago after a rainstorm has cleared the skies, try to make it to the top of Cerro San Cristóbal for a breathtaking view of the city spread below the towering, snowcapped Andes. Few cityscapes in the world compare. See chapter 9.

- **Watching the World Go by in the Plaza de Armas, Santiago:** Enjoy Santiago society the way they used to: on a park bench in the grand Plaza de Armas. Like a magnet, this square attracts all shapes and sizes of Chileans, and a half hour on a bench offers ample opportunity to study them all: businessmen racing to and fro, young couples at a more leisurely stride, shoeshiners, photographers, religious fanatics, painters, poets, chess players, and, of course, other tourists like yourself. The best time is during the lunch hour from 1 to 3pm, when the pace picks up. See chapter 9.

- **Exploring the Madcap Streets of Valparaíso:** The ramshackle, colorful, and sinuous streets of Valparaíso offer a walking tour unlike any other. Apart from the picturesque, Victorian mansions and tin houses that seem cut into every shape possible, terraced walkways wind around the various hills that shoot up from downtown, and there are plenty of antique funiculars to lift you to the top. Great restaurants and cafes can be found at every turn to rest aching feet. Valparaíso is like a diamond in the rough, and part of the fascination is touring the faded remains of this once-thriving port town. See chapter 10.

- **Catching a Full Moon in the Valle de la Luna:** Nothing could be more appropriate, or dreamier, than an evening under the glow of a full moon in the Valley of the Moon. This region of the Atacama Desert was named for its otherworldly land formations and salt-encrusted canyons that supposedly resemble the surface of the moon, a comparison that is hard to dispute, especially when these formations are cast under an eerie, nighttime glow. The full moon "experience" is popular enough that nearly all tour companies in San Pedro plan excursions. See chapter 11.

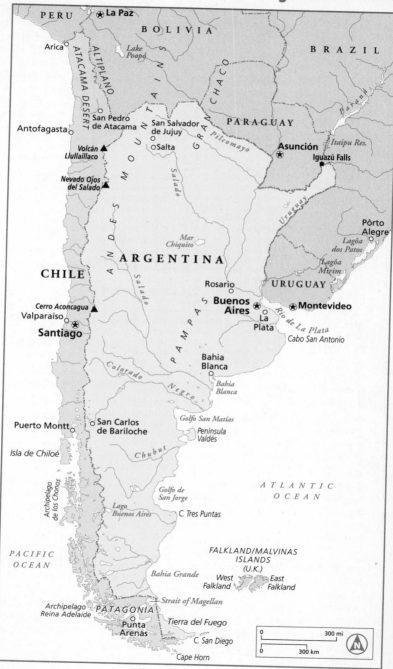

Argentina & Chile

PERU

La Paz ⊛

BOLIVIA

Arica ○

Lake Poopó

ALTIPLANO

ATACAMA DESERT

San Pedró de Atacama ○

Antofagasta ○

Volcán Llullaillaco ▲

Nevado Ojos del Salado ▲

BRAZIL

GRAN CHACO

Pilcomayo

PARAGUAY

San Salvador de Jujuy

○ Salta

Salado

Asunción ⊛

Itaipu Res.

Iguazú Falls ■

Uruguay

Paraná

ANDES MOUNTAINS

Mar Chiquito

A R G E N T I N A

Salado

CHILE

Rosario ○

Cerro Aconcagua ▲

Valparaíso ○

Santiago ⊛

Buenos Aires ⊛

La Plata

P A M P A S

Colorado

Negro

Bahia Blanca

Bahia Blanca

Rio de La Plata

Montevideo ⊛

URUGUAY

Pôrto Alegre ○

Lagôa dos Patos

Lagôa Mirim

Cabo San Antonio

Puerto Montt ○

San Carlos de Bariloche ○

Isla de Chiloé

Chubut

Golfo San Matías

Península Valdés

Golfo de San Jorge

Lago Buenos Aires

C. Tres Puntas

ATLANTIC OCEAN

Archipelago de los Chonos

PACIFIC OCEAN

FALKLAND/MALVINAS ISLANDS (U.K.)

Bahia Grande

West Falkland

East Falkland

Archipelago Reina Adelaide

PATAGONIA

Strait of Magellan

Punta Arenas ○

Tierra del Fuego

C. San Diego

Cape Horn

| 0 | 300 mi |
| 0 | 300 km |

3

- **Sailing the Fjords of Southern Chile:** Quietly sailing through the lush beauty of Chile's southern fjords is an experience that all can afford. There are two breath-taking trajectories: a 3-day ride between Puerto Natales and Puerto Montt, and a 1- to 6-day ride to the spectacular Laguna San Rafael Glacier. Backpackers on a shoestring as well as those who need spiffier accommodations all have options. These pristine, remote fjords are often said to be more dramatic than those in Norway, but the scenery isn't the only pleasure here—often the camaraderie that grows between passengers is what in the end makes for such a fulfilling trip. See chapter 12.

- **Soaking in Hot Springs:** The volatile Andes not only builds volcanoes; it also produces steaming mineralized water that is used to fill hot springs complexes from the desert north to the Aisén region. Chileans often take to these waters to relieve arthritis and rheumatism problems, but most take a soothing soak to relax. Virtually every region near the Andes mentioned in this book has either a rustic hole in the ground or a full-scale, luxury resort with a complete spa. Notably, these hot springs seem to have been magically paired by nature with outdoor adventure spots, making for a thankful way to end a day of activity. The Lake District is a noted "hot spot," especially around Pucón. See chapter 12.

- **Driving the Carretera Austral:** It's a tough, crunchy drive along 620 miles (1,000km) of gravel road, but that is precisely why Chile's "Southern Highway" has kept the crowds at bay. This natural wonderland, saturated in green and hemmed in by jagged, snowcapped peaks, offers a journey for those seeking to travel through some of Chile's most remote and stunning territory. It can be done in a variety of directions and segments, but you'll need a rental car. There are plenty of great stops along the way, including rainforest walks, the idyllic mountain valley of Futaleufú, the wet primeval forest of Parque Quelat, Puyuhuapi and its luxury thermal spas, and the city of Coyhaique. See chapter 14.

2 The Most Charming Small Towns

- **Salta, Argentina:** Salta sits in the Lerma valley of Argentina's Northwest with an eternal springlike climate; it's a town boasting Argentina's best-preserved colonial architecture, reflected in its churches, government buildings, and houses. It's surrounded by the fertile valley of the provincial capital, the polychrome canyons of Cafayate, and the desolate plateau of La Puña. See chapter 5.

- **San Martín de los Andes, Argentina:** City planners in San Martín had the smart sense to do what Bariloche never thought of: to limit building height to two stories and to mandate continuity in the town's alpine architecture. The result? Bariloche is crass whereas San Martín is class, and the town is a year-round playground to boot. The cornucopia of hotels, restaurants, and shops that line the streets are built of stout, cinnamon-colored tree trunks or are Swiss-style, gingerbread confections that all seem right at home in San Martín's blessed, pastoral setting. Relax, swim, bike, ski, raft, hunt, or fish—this small town has it all. See chapter 6.

- **Villa La Angostura, Argentina:** Villa La Angostura has everything its neighbor Bariloche has and more. This is where you go to escape the crowds and savor the sense of exclusivity. Great restaurants go hand in hand with cozy lodging. The town (whose name means "Narrow Town") is accordingly spread along one street and along the shore of Nahuel Huapi Lake, with plenty of hiking, biking, and boating nearby; there's a great little ski resort, too. The wood-heavy construction is eye-catching, and the location is sumptuous. See chapter 6.

- **Colonia del Sacramento, Uruguay:** Just a short ferry trip away from Buenos Aires, Colonia is Uruguay's best example of colonial life. The Old Neighborhood contains brilliant examples of colonial wealth and many of Uruguay's oldest structures. Dating from the 17th century, this beautifully preserved Portuguese settlement makes a perfect day trip. See chapter 7.
- **San Pedro de Atacama, Chile:** Quaint, unhurried, and built of adobe brick, San Pedro de Atacama has drawn *Santiaguinos* and expatriates the world over who have come to experience the mellow charm and new-age spirituality that wafts through the dusty roads of this town. San Pedro hasn't grown much over the past 10 years—it has simply reinvented itself. Its location in the driest desert in the world makes for starry skies and breath-taking views of the weird and wonderful land formations that are just a stone's throw away. See chapter 11.
- **Pucón, Chile:** Not only was Pucón bestowed with a stunning location at the skirt of a smoking volcano and the shore of a glittering lake, it's also Chile's self-proclaimed adventure capital, offering so many outdoor activities you could keep busy for a week. But Pucón also has plenty of low-key activities if your idea of a vacation is plopping yourself down on a beach, and that is the real attraction here. You'll find everything you want and need without forfeiting small-town charm (that is, if you don't come with the January and February crowds). Timber creates the downtown atmosphere, with plenty of wood-hewn restaurants, pubs, and crafts stores, blending harmoniously with the forested surroundings. See chapter 12.
- **Frutillar & Puerto Varas, Chile:** Built from the sweat of German immigrants who settled here in the early 1900s, these neighboring towns bear the clear stamp of Prussian order and workmanship, from the crisp lines of trees that line the country lanes to the picturesque, shingled homes and tidy plazas ringed with roses. If you're lucky, you can still catch a few old-timers chatting in German over coffee and *kuchen*. Both towns feature a glorious view of Volcán Osorno and a lakefront address, a postcard-picture–worthy location that makes for an excellent boardwalk stroll. If that isn't enough, both towns also offer above-par lodging and a few of the best restaurants in the country. See chapter 12.
- **Futaleufú, Chile:** Nestled in a green valley surrounded by an amphitheater of craggy, snow-encrusted peaks, Futaleufú is made of colorful, clapboard homes and unpaved streets, and is without a doubt one of the prettiest villages in Chile. The population of 1,000 swells during the summer when the hordes descend for rafting adventures on the nearby Class V river, but it hasn't changed the town's fabric too dramatically, and locals rarely saunter past a visitor without a tip of the hat and a *"buenos tardes."* See chapter 14.

3   The Best Outdoor Adventures

- **Discovering Iguazú Falls by Raft:** A number of tour companies operate rafts that speed toward the falls, soaking their awestruck passengers along the way. This is the best way to experience the sound and fury of Iguazú's magnificent *cataratas*. See chapter 4.
- **Traveling Beyond the Falls into the Iguazú Jungle:** This is a place where birds like the great dusky swift and brilliant morpho butterflies spread color through the thick forest canopy. You can easily arrange an outing into the forest once you arrive in Iguazú. See chapter 4.
- **Riding the "Train to the Clouds":** The *Tren a las Nubes* is one of the world's great railroad experiences. The journey through Argentina's Northwest takes you

269 miles (434km) through tunnels, turns, and bridges, culminating in the breathtaking La Polvorilla viaduct. You will cross magnificent landscapes, making your way from the multicolored Lerma valley through the deep canyons and rugged peaks of the Quebrada del Toro and on to the desolate desert plateau of La Puña. See chapter 5.

- **Rafting or Horseback Riding in the Cajon del Maipo:** Okay, it's not even close to rafting the Futaleufú, but the River Maipo whips up enough exciting rapids for a thrill and, best of all, it's just a 45-minute drive from Santiago. The Maipo River winds through the Cajon del Maipo, a hemmed-in, alpine valley that is so fragrant and pleasant it seems worlds away from the smoggy metropolis. To get deep into the Andes, saddle up for a full- or half-day horseback ride. Beginners and kids are welcome too. Contact **Cascada Expediciones** in Santiago at ☎ 2/234-2274. See chapter 10.

- **Skiing or Snowboarding Portillo:** It's been around for 50 years, and the steep chutes of **Centro de Ski Portillo** still raise fear in the hearts of those about to make the descent on a pair of skis or snowboard. This is where the speed-skiing record was broken, where Fidel Castro spent the night, and where a Who's Who of northern ski lovers come in search of the endless winter. The grand yet rustic hotel is a single, all-inclusive destination, much like a cruise ship in the sky: short lift lines, a spa, plentiful food, and lots for kids to do, too. Call ☎ **800/ 829-5325** in the United States, or 2/263-0606 in Santiago. See chapter 10.

- **Sunrise at the Geysers del Tatio:** It's 4:30am, the sky is dark and the air cold, and you're waiting for your shuttle ride to the Tatio Geysers to catch the world's highest fumaroles at their steaming peak of fury. You'll find comfort in the fact that this is the only physical effort you'll have to give today. The Tatio Geysers are as theatrical as a fireworks display, highlighted by a stark Andean landscape stained in hues of red, green, and orange. The return trip includes a stop in an oasis hot spring for a soak. Contact **Desert Adventure** (☎ **55/85-1067**) or **Cosmo Andino Expediciones** (☎ **55/85-1069**). See chapter 11.

- **Summiting a Volcano:** There's something intangibly more thrilling about summiting a volcano than any old mountain, especially when the volcano threatens to blow at any given time. Chile is home to a large share of the world's volcanoes, some of which are perfectly conical and entirely feasible to climb, such as Volcán Villarrica in Pucón and Volcán Osorno near Puerto Varas. Active Villarrica is a relatively moderate climb to the gaseous crater, followed by a fun slide on your rear down a human toboggan chute. Osorno offers a more technical climb, roping up for a crampon-aided walk past glacier crevasses and caves. Electrifying views are included with the package, from the ocean and into Argentina. For Volcán Villarrica, contact **Aguaventura** (☎ **45/444246**) or **Politour** (☎ **45/ 441373**); for Volcán Osorno, contact **Tranco Expediciones** (☎ **65/311311**). See chapter 12.

- **Rafting or Kayaking the Futaleufú River:** With churning river sections that are frightening enough to be dubbed "Hell" and "The Terminator," the Class V Futaleufú River, or the "Fu," as it's known, is solemnly revered by rafting and kayaking enthusiasts around the world as one of the most difficult to descend. A little too much excitement for your nerves? Rafting companies offer short-section rafting trips on the Futaleufú and down the tamer, crystalline waters of the neighboring Río Espolón—kayak schools use this stretch, too. The scenery here redefines mountain beauty. Contact **Expediciones Chile** in Futaleufú at ☎ **888/488-9082** in the U.S., or 65/721320 in Chile. See chapter 14.

- **Face to Face with the Perito Moreno Glacier:** Few natural wonders in South America are as magnificent or as easily accessed as the Perito Moreno Glacier. You can drive right up to it, park, and descend a series of walkways that take you directly to the 160-feet-plus wall of turquoise ice—an unforgettable experience. But to get really close, strap on a pair of crampons and take a walk across the glacier's surface to admire the sculpted walls and caves and changing tonal variety of blues, not to mention a scotch on the "millenary rocks." Nearly all travel agencies in Calafate book this excursion. See chapter 15.
- **Trekking in Torres del Paine:** This backpacking mecca just keeps growing in popularity, and it's no wonder. Torres del Paine is one of the most spectacular national parks in the world, with hundreds of kilometers of trails through ever-changing landscapes of jagged peaks and one-of-a-kind granite spires, undulating meadows, milky, turquoise lakes and rivers, and mammoth glaciers. The park has a well-organized system of *refugios* and campgrounds, but there are also several hotels, and visitors can access the park's major highlights on a day hike. See chapter 15.

4 The Best Hotels

- **Alvear Palace Hotel,** Buenos Aires (☎ **0800-44HOTEL,** local toll-free, or 11/4808-2100): Decorated in Empire and Louis XV–style furnishings, this is the most exclusive hotel in Buenos Aires. Luxurious guest rooms and suites have chandelier lighting, feather beds, silk drapes, and beautiful marble bathrooms; service is sharp and professional. See chapter 3.
- **Marriott Plaza Hotel,** Buenos Aires (☎ **11/4318-3000**): This historic hotel was the grande dame of Buenos Aires for much of the 20th century, a gathering place of Argentine politicians, foreign dignitaries, and international celebrities. It remains one of the city's most impressive hotels. See chapter 3.
- **Sheraton International Iguazú,** Puerto Iguazú (☎ **0800/888-9180,** local toll-free, or 3757/491-800): If you visit Iguazú Falls, the Sheraton International Iguazú enjoys the best location by far. The only hotel on the Argentine side situated within the national park, half the rooms overlook the falls, and guests are within easy walking distance of the waterfall circuits. See chapter 4.
- **Las Balsas,** Villa La Angostura (☎/fax **02944/494308**): This exquisite lakefront inn is part of the Relais & Châteaux hotel group, incorporating all the splendor of its natural alpine setting with generous service, country-chic interiors, first-class amenities, and rooms as individual as the guests themselves. The high-concept spa has a heated pool, and there's a bundle of equipment for biking or boating around the area. For dining, you can't surpass Las Balsas's intimate restaurant and gourmet cuisine. See chapter 6.
- **Llao Llao Hotel & Resort,** near Bariloche (☎ **02944/448530;** fax 02944/445789): If you're looking for a memorable evening and your pocketbook can afford it, this is your place. The world-renowned Llao Llao Hotel & Resort's style was influenced by Canadian-style mountain lodges, and the hotel's magnificent alpine setting is one of the best in the world. Antler chandeliers, pine-log walls, and Oriental rugs set the mood, and the "winter garden" cafe overlooking Lake Nahuel Huapi is divine. The hotel boasts every amenity imaginable, including its own golf course, and service is impeccable. See chapter 6.
- **Plaza Victoria Hotel,** Montevideo (☎ **2/902-0111**): Montevideo's best hotel is situated next to Plaza Independencia in the heart of downtown. Spacious guest

rooms boast French-style furnishings and upgraded amenities, and the hotel's restaurant Arcadia is outstanding. See chapter 7.

- **Conrad Resort & Casino,** Punta del Este (☎ **42/491-111**): This resort dominates social life in Punta del Este. Luxurious rooms have terraces overlooking the two main beaches, and there's a wealth of outdoor activities from tennis and golf to horseback riding and watersports. See chapter 7.

- **Hotel Carrera,** Santiago (☎ **2/698-2011;** fax 2/672-1083): This, the grande dame of Santiago hotels, has been a classic since it opened its revolving brass doors in 1940. The hotel's front rooms and glitzy rooftop pool overlook the historic Plaza Constitución, catty-corner from the Palacio de la Moneda. The hotel was for decades the social center of Santiago's elite, who met under the Bohemian crystal chandeliers of the hotel's lounge or the Copper Room restaurant. The English-style rooms are elegant, and the amenities and services are first-rate. Newer five-star hotels such as the Hyatt, the Radisson, and the Sheraton have given the Carrera a run for its money, but these North American chains can't match the Carrera's old-world glamour and history. See chapter 9.

- **Hotel Orly,** Santiago (☎ **2/231-8947;** fax 2/252-0051): The Hotel Orly is an ideal little inn for those who look for personal service and intimate accommodations to compensate for the overwhelming hustle and bustle of Santiago. The hotel is inside a converted, French-style mansion that has been tastefully renovated with contemporary style and art, and there's a compact interior garden patio and bar. Helpful, courteous service makes this inn shine, but it's all about location here, as the Orly sits smack-dab in the middle of everything in Providencia, and is just steps from the subway station for the 10-minute shuttle to downtown. See chapter 9.

- **Residencial Londres,** Santiago (☎/fax **2/638-2215**): The Residencial Londres is a budget hotel that merits mention for its lovely interiors—an ideal address for those really looking to spend as little as possible for lodging. The rooms are very modest, but parquet floors, antique furniture, and indoor balconies that wind around an interior patio lend a singular appeal—more appeal than many moderately priced hotels in Chile. The Residencial is located on a cobblestone street of the charming Barrio París-Londres. See chapter 9.

- **Hacienda Los Lingues,** near San Fernando (☎ **2/235-5446** in Santiago; fax 2/235-7604): Step back in time to the 17th century with a visit to one of Chile's oldest hotels, located in the rural heartland of the central valley south of Santiago. The incomparability of this hotel is such that Los Lingues is a destination within itself. Los Lingues has been in the same family hands for more than 400 years, and each venerable room has been lovingly and individually decorated with personal touches such as family antiques, photos, and other collectibles. Like all haciendas, Los Lingues wraps around a plant-filled patio and fountain, but you'll also find a small chapel, a stately main building, one of the country's finest horse breeding farms, clay tennis courts, and a grand outdoor swimming pool. If you can't spend a night or the price is too steep, the hotel offers day visits that include lunch in the hacienda's grand wine cellar. See chapter 10.

- **Hotel Explora in San Pedro de Atacama & Explora in Torres del Paine** (☎ **2/206-6060** in Santiago; fax 2/228-4655): Few hotels have generated as much press in Latin America as the two all-inclusive Explora lodges in San Pedro de Atacama and Torres del Paine. A dynamite location has helped, of course, but great service, cozy rooms with out-of-this-world views, interiors that are equally elegant and comfortable, and guided outdoor trekking, horseback riding, and biking excursions are what really put these hotels above par. The lodges were designed by several of Chile's top architects, built of native materials, and decorated with local art. All-inclusive packages are pricey, but you won't need to spend anything once you're there. See chapters 11 and 15.

- **Lodge Terrantai,** San Pedro de Atacama (☎ **55/85-1140;** fax 55/85-1037): This minimalist-style, small inn is virtually unrecognizable from the other adobe buildings that flank it, but once inside you know that great care went into the renovation of this 100-year-old building. The hotel's design effortlessly blends clean, contemporary lines and simple river-rock walls with the building's original antique adobe structure and thatched roof. Quiet, understated, and cheaper than Hotel Explora, Terrantai also offers packages that include excursions around the area. See chapter 11.

- **Hotel Antumalal,** Pucón (☎ **45/441011;** fax 45/441013): This low-slung, Bauhaus-influenced country inn is one of the most special places to lodge in Chile. Located high above the shore of Lake Villarrica and a sloping, terraced garden, the hotel literally sinks into its surroundings, offering a cozy ambience and number-one view of the evening sunset. A warm welcome and a room with no lock are all part of making you feel at home, and the chic, retro decor is a welcome relief from the cookie-cutter style of many hotels. Outstanding cuisine, too. See chapter 12.

- **Termas de Puyuhuapi Spa & Hotel,** near Puyuhuapi (☎/fax **2/225-6489** in Santiago): This is arguably the best hotel/thermal spa facility in Chile. Spread across a remote cove on the Ventisquero Sound, this one-of-a-kind resort is nestled in pristine rainforest and is reached only by boat. The hotel is so deluxe that it has become the region's top attraction, drawing as many day visitors who come for a soak in one of the handful of indoor or outdoor pools and a massage or session in the state-of-the-art spa. The accommodations are wonderfully comfortable and the food is, in a word, outstanding. Many overnighters include the hotel's package trips with an additional trip to the Laguna San Rafael Glacier. See chapter 14.

- **Los Notros,** Perito Moreno Glacier, near Calafate (☎ **11/4814-3934** in Buenos Aires; fax 11/4815-7645): Location is everything at the Los Notros hotel, in this case the view spanning one of Argentina's great wonders, the Perito Moreno Glacier. The hotel blends contemporary folk art with a range of colorful hues, and this, along with impeccable rooms that come with a dramatic view of the electric-blue tongue of the glacier, make this lodge one of the most upscale, unique lodging options in Argentina. The hotel arranges excursions around the area and occasional informative talks, and there are plenty of easy chairs and lounges for sitting and contemplating the glorious nature surrounding you. See chapter 15.

- **Hotel José Nogueira,** Punta Arenas (☎ **61/248840;** fax 61/248832): Originally the home of one of Punta Arenas's wealthiest families, the Nogueira offers the chance to spend the night in a historic landmark, the principal rooms of which have been preserved as a museum to give visitors a look at the outlandish luxury that must have seemed dramatically out of place in Patagonia of the early 1900s. The upper floors have been converted into handsome, classically designed rooms that come with marvelously high ceilings. The mansion's glass-enclosed patio now houses the hotel's excellent restaurant, La Pérgola, and the cellar is now an evening pub. See chapter 15.

5 The Best Dining Experiences

- **Cabaña las Lilas,** Buenos Aires (☎ **11/4313-1336**): Widely considered the best *parrilla* in Buenos Aires, Cabaña las Lilas is always packed. The menu pays homage to Argentine beef cuts, which come exclusively from the restaurant's private *estancia* (ranch). The steaks are outstanding. See chapter 3.

- **Catalinas,** Buenos Aires (☎ **11/4313-0182**): This is without doubt the best international restaurant in Buenos Aires, its kitchen a model of culinary diversity and innovation. In addition to Chef Pardo's enormous Patagonian toothfish steaks, his grilled lamb chops—sprinkled with rosemary and fresh savory—are famous throughout Argentina. See chapter 3.

- **De Olivas i Lustres,** Buenos Aires (☎ **11/4405-2714** or 11/4867-3388): This magical restaurant in Old Palermo serves Mediterranean cuisine in a small, rustic dining room where antiques, olive jars, and wine bottles are on display. Each candlelit table is individually decorated—one resembles a writer's desk, another is sprinkled with seashells. See chapter 3.

- **Arcadia,** Montevideo (☎ **2/902-0111**): Arcadia, an elegant restaurant atop the Plaza Victoria, is a quiet paradise in Montevideo. Tables are nestled in semi-private nooks with floor-to-ceiling bay windows in a dining room decorated with Italian curtains and crystal chandeliers. Executive chef Torsten Spies's culinary interpretations are light, fresh, and carefully presented. See chapter 7.

- **La Bourgogne,** Punta del Este (☎ **42/482-007**): Jean-Paul Bondoux is the top French chef in South America, splitting his time between La Bourgogne in Punta del Este and its sister restaurant tucked inside the Alvear Palace Hotel, Buenos Aires. A member of Relais & Châteaux, La Bourgogne serves exquisite cuisine inspired by Bondoux's Burgundy heritage. See chapter 7.

- **The Mercado Central,** Santiago: The chaotic, colorful central fish and produce market of Santiago should not be missed by anyone, even if you are not particularly fond of seafood. But if you are, you'll want to relish one of the flavorful concoctions served at one of the market's simple but excellent restaurants. Hawklike waitresses guard the market's passageways awaiting hungry diners and shouting "Hey, lady! Hey, sir! Eat here!"—but **Donde Augusto** is a good bet. See chapter 9.

- **Azul Profundo,** Santiago (☎ **2/738-0288**): The boom of gourmet restaurants in Santiago has revolutionized the dining scene, yet this moderately priced, intimate restaurant consistently serves fresh, tantalizing seafood and excellent, classic Chilean dishes like *ceviche* and *pastel de jaiva,* a savory crab casserole. Located in the quaint Bellavista neighborhood, the restaurant has a woodsy, nautical-themed decor that is warm and inviting, and the service is sharp. The enticing menu makes for tough ordering decisions, but try any fish *a la plancha* and hear it sail from the kitchen on a sizzling platter. See chapter 9.

- **Bar Liguria,** Santiago (☎ **2/235-7914**): This lively yet cozy restaurant is a Providencia hot spot, often filling before 10pm and spilling out onto tables on the sidewalk. The mix of actors, artists, businessmen, and locals ensures a vibrant crowd, and you can check out all the action from the Liguria's 19th-century–style wood bar, where a sharply dressed waiter delivers the restaurant's short bistro menu with a plate of fresh clams, on the house. See chapter 9.

- **Enoteca/Camino Real,** Santiago (☎ **2/232-1758**): If you've been graced with clear skies, you'll spend more time staring out the window of the Camino Real than concentrating on the food before you (you're paying more for the view than the food anyway). This restaurant sits high atop the Cerro San Cristóbal and affords a breath-taking eyeful of the sprawl of Santiago and the Andes that rise majestically behind it. If there's no time to dine, order a drink and admire the sunset as the city lights twinkle on. See chapter 9.

- **Aquí Está Coco,** Santiago (☎ 2/235-8649): Wildly popular with foreign visitors and with reason: The kitsch atmosphere is as fun as the food is mouth-watering. The restaurant is spread over two levels of a 140-year-old home and festooned with oddball and nautically themed trinkets, gadgets, and curios, but the best bet is to arrive a little early and enjoy an aperitif in the cavelike, brick cellar lounge. Seafood is the specialty here. See chapter 9.
- **Café Turri,** Valparaíso (☎ 32/259198): Regionally famous for superb cuisine paired with gorgeous views, this is a memorable dining experience whether at lunch or dinner. Housed in a converted Victorian home high on a cliff, the restaurant has three patios—where you'll want to sit for the "aerial" vista of the jumbled streets of Valparaíso. Of course, the specialty is seafood; this is a port town, isn't it? And this classic restaurant serves the best in town. See chapter 10.
- **Merlin,** Puerto Varas (☎ 65/233105): This little restaurant had the good sense to celebrate the bounty of fresh regional products available in the Lake District by offering creative, flavorful food that arrives at your table *prepared,* not just "cooked." Fresh fish and shellfish, meats, and vegetarian dishes are seasoned with flair, using fresh herbs and spices. The restaurant occupies the first floor of an old home, with cozy, candlelit tables. See chapter 12.
- **La Calesa,** Valdivia (☎ 63/225437): Don't overlook a Peruvian restaurant in Chile, especially La Calesa. The spicy, delectable cuisine brought to Valdivia by an immigrant family from Peru is as enjoyable as the architecture of the 19th-century home the restaurant is housed in. Soaring ceilings, antique furniture, great *pisco* sours at an old wooden bar, the river slowly meandering by . . . need I say more? See chapter 12.
- **Remezón,** Punta Arenas (☎ 61/241029): You'll have to come to the end of Chile for some of the country's best cuisine. This unassuming little restaurant consistently garners rave reviews by diners, many of whom come back night after night while in Punta Arenas. Sumptuous dishes prepared with local king crab, lamb, and goose are the highlight here, as are the incredible desserts. If that weren't enough, the warm welcome and personal contact with the chef (who often likes to explain specials to guests) leave you feeling happy and well fed. See chapter 15.
- **Kapué Restaurant,** Ushuaia (☎ 02901/422704): King crab features predominantly on the menu at the Kapué, in puff pastries, soufflés, and fresh-on-the-plate, but nearly every dish here is as refined and delectable. The gracious, family-run service is as pleasant as the view of the Beagle Channel, and the restaurant's new wine bar really sets it apart from other eateries in town. See chapter 15.

6 The Best Cafes, Confiterías & Tea Spots

- **Café Tortoni,** Buenos Aires (☎ 11/4342-4328): This historic cafe has served as the artistic and intellectual capital of Buenos Aires since 1858, serving personalities like Jorge Luis Borges, Julio de Caro, Cátulo Castillo, and José Gobello. Come here to glimpse the history, sip a coffee, or even catch an evening tango performance in the Tortoni's back room. See chapter 3.

- **Petit Paris Cafe,** Buenos Aires (☎ **11/4312-5885**): The Petit Paris offers marble-top tables with velvet upholstered chairs, crystal chandeliers, and bow tie–clad waiters. Large windows look directly on to Plaza San Martín, placing the cafe within short walking distance of some of the city's best sights. See chapter 3.
- **Plaza Dorrego Bar,** Buenos Aires (☎ **11/4361-0141**): Representative of a typical *Porteño* bar from the 19th century, Plaza Dorrego proudly displays portraits of Carlos Gardel, antique liquor bottles stored in cases along the walls, and anonymous writings engraved in the wood. Stop by during the day on Sunday, when you can also catch the colorful San Telmo antiques market on the plaza in front. See chapter 3.
- **Café Arrayán,** San Martín de los Andes (☎ **02972/425570**): A short cab ride takes you high up to this 70-year-old wooden home, now the site of daily afternoon teas that serve traditional sandwiches, cakes, and pastries amid scenic mountain and lake views. See chapter 6.
- **Confitería Torres,** Santiago (☎ **2/698-6220**): You're here for the atmosphere, not the food, so stick with an espresso and spend a half hour soaking up the old-world charm of this antique cafe. Yapping old-timers, wilting furniture, blackened mirrors—it's much more entertaining than a Starbucks. See chapter 9.
- **La Columbina,** Valparaíso (☎ **32/236254**): This multi-tiered restaurant, built out of a lovely old Victorian home, boasts a penthouse tea salon accented with colorful stained glass. The height and position above a steep cliff makes the salon feel like a promontory over the plunging city streets and bay of Valparaíso—in other words, fantastic views. There's outdoor patio seating, too, and lots of rich, creamy cakes and pastries to choose from. See chapter 10.
- **Café Bellavista,** road from Puerto Varas to Ensenada (☎ **65/212040**): This unlikely cafe is really the owner's home, and it sits back on a sloping, enormous lawn with grazing sheep and llamas. It's like a local secret; open on Saturday, Sunday, and holidays after 4pm only, and the best cakes, sandwiches, pastries, and homemade jams around. See chapter 12.
- **Café Mamusia,** Puerto Varas (☎ **65/237971**): The minute you step into this cafe, your sweet tooth is assaulted by long, glass-encased tiers of creamy fruit *kuchen,* apple strudel, and other German-influenced cakes and pastries, literally dozens upon dozens of sugary delights. It will take you a long time to get past this display case. See chapter 12.
- **La Cabaña,** Ushuaia (☎ **06/696-9511**): Chances are you'll want to grab a table outside on the deck: How else will you revel in the view of Glacier Martial and the surrounding forest? La Cabaña takes the tea hour to a new height, literally, well above Ushuaia, where they treat you to "tasty pastries" slathered with homemade jams, as well as cakes, chocolate, and other confectioneries. See chapter 15.

7 The Best Museums

- **Caminito,** Buenos Aires: At the center of La Boca lies the Caminito, a short pedestrian walkway that is both an outdoor museum and marketplace. Each day, tango performers dance alongside musicians, street vendors, and artists. Surrounding the street are shabby metal houses painted in dynamic shades of red, yellow, blue, and green, thanks to designer Benito Quinquela Martín. See chapter 3.
- **Museo Nacional de Bellas Artes,** Buenos Aires: This museum contains the world's largest collection of Argentine sculptures and paintings from the 19th

and 20th centuries. It also houses European art dating from the pre-Renaissance period to present day. The collections include notable pieces by Manet, Goya, El Greco, and Gaugin. See chapter 3.

• **Museo Arqueológico Provincial,** Jujuy: The Provincial Archaeological Museum displays archaeological finds representing over 2,500 years of life in the Jujuy region, including a 2,600-year-old ceramic goddess, a lithic collection of arrowheads, the bones of a child from 1,000 years ago, and two mummified adults. See chapter 5.

• **Casa Colorada & Museo de Santiago,** Santiago: The "Red House" not only houses the Santiago Museum; it is in itself a living museum: The building is widely regarded as the best-preserved colonial structure in Santiago. The Red House was initially built for the first president of Chile, Mateo de Toro y Zambrano; today its rooms house displays depicting the urban history of the city until the 19th century. There's a good bookstore here and a visitor's information center, too. See chapter 9.

• **Iglesia, Convento y Museo de San Francisco,** Santiago: One step into this museum and you'll feel like you've been instantly beamed out of downtown Santiago. This is the oldest standing building in Santiago and home to an impossibly serene garden patio where the only sounds are a trickling fountain and the cooing of a handful of white pigeons. The museum boasts 54 paintings depicting the life and death of San Francisco, one of the largest and best-conserved displays of 17th-century art in South America. If you look closely at the altar of the church, you'll see the famous *Virgen del Socorro,* the first Virgin Mary icon in Chile, brought here to Santiago by Pedro de Valdivia. See chapter 9.

• **Museo Chileno de Arte Precolombino,** Santiago: More than 1,500 gorgeously displayed objects related to indigenous life and culture throughout the Americas make the Precolumbian Museum one of the best in Latin America. Artifacts include textiles, metals, paintings, figurines, and ceramics from Mexico to Chile. All are handsomely lit and mounted throughout seven exhibition rooms that are divided into the Mesoamérica, Intermedia, Andina, and Surandina regions of Latin America. The museum is housed in the old Royal Customs House built in the ever-popular neoclassical design in 1807. If you need a break, there's a patio with a small cafe and a good bookstore to browse. See chapter 9.

• **Palacio de la Real Audencia/Museo Historico Nacional,** Santiago: The National History Museum holds a superb collection of more than 70,000 colonial-era pieces, from furniture to suits of armor to home appliances. This fascinating grab bag of artifacts is laid out in 16 display rooms within the lemon-colored, neoclassical Palacio de la Real, built in 1807 and the historic site of the first Chilean congressional session. The museum will give you insight into the history of the lives of Chileans, and it's conveniently located on the Plaza de las Armas. See chapter 9.

• **Casa Pablo Neruda,** Isla Negra: This was Nobel prize–winning poet Pablo Neruda's favorite home, and although his other residences in Valparaíso and Santiago are as eccentric and absorbing, this is the best preserved of the three. The home is stuffed with books by his favorite authors and the whimsical curios, trinkets, and toys he collected during his travels around the world, including African masks, ships in bottles, butterflies, and more. The museum can be found in Isla Negra, south of Valparaíso, and you need to plan a half-day trip to get there. See chapter 10.

- **Museo Arqueológico Padre Le Paige,** San Pedro de Atacama: This little museum will come as an unexpected surprise for its wealth of indigenous artifacts, such as "Miss Chile," a leathered mummy whose skin, teeth, and hair are mostly intact, as well as a display of skulls that show the creepy ancient custom of cranial deformation practiced by the elite as a status symbol. The Atacama Desert is the driest in the world, and this climate has produced some of the best-preserved artifacts in Latin America, on view here. See chapter 11.
- **Museo Regional de Ancud Audelio Bórquez Canobra,** Ancud, Chiloé: It's all crammed in pretty tight, but this museum is interesting more than anything for a glimpse into the wild variety of lifestyles that make Chiloé what it is today. The museum is perched high above the sea, with outdoor sculptures depicting the mythological characters of Chilote folklore, a replica of the ship *Ancud* that first took possession of the Strait of Magellan in 1843, and a replica of a thatched Chilote house. The interactive displays will hold even a kid's attention. See chapter 13.
- **Museo Marítimo y Presidio de Ushuaia,** Ushuaia: The United States used to send its worst criminals to Alcatraz, but Argentina took isolation to a whole new level and shipped its criminals to the end of the world. Ushuaia was virtually built from the forced labor of these prisoners, whose former penitentiary you can now tour. While walking the echoing halls of the prison, try imagining what it must have been like to know that any escape plan was futile: After all, where would you go? And where would you change out of your comical, black-and-white striped wool uniform (also on display)? See chapter 15.
- **Museo Regional Braun Menéndez,** Punta Arenas: The Braun Menéndez Regional Museum is the former home of one of Patagonia's wealthiest families, who believed that the best defense against their remote, wind-whipped location was to live "splendidly." Tapestries, furniture from France, Italian marble fireplaces, hand-painted wallpaper: This veritable palace is a testament to the Braun family's insatiable need to match European elite society, as a tour through the ornate rooms will illustrate. Several small salons are devoted to ranching and maritime history, but the grandeur of this museum is really the reason for a visit. See chapter 15.
- **Museo Salesiano Maggiorino Borgatello,** Punta Arenas: There's so much on display here that you could spend more than an hour wandering and marveling at the hodgepodge collection of archeological artifacts, photo exhibits, petroleum production interpretative exhibitions, ranch furniture, industrial gadgets, and, best of all, the macabre collection of stuffed and mounted regional wildlife gathered by a Salesian priest. See chapter 15.

8 The Best Historic Architecture

- **Cabildo,** Buenos Aires: The Cabildo was the original seat of city government, built in 1764. The old colonial building was significant in the events leading up to Argentina's declaration of independence from Spain in May 1810. It's the only remaining public building dating back to colonial times. See chapter 3.
- **Manzana de las Luces,** Buenos Aires: The Manzana de las Luces (Block of Lights) served as the intellectual center of the city in the 17th and 18th centuries. This land was granted in 1616 to the Jesuits, who built **San Ignacio**—the city's oldest church—still standing at the corner of Bolivar and Aslina streets. Worth a visit to see the beautiful altar. See chapter 3.

- **Teatro Colón,** Buenos Aires: The majestic Teatro Colón, completed in 1908, combines a variety of European styles, from the Ionic and Corinthian capitals and French–stained-glass pieces in the main entrance to the Italian marble staircase and exquisite French furniture, chandeliers, and vases in the Golden Hall. The Colón has hosted the world's most important opera singers. See chapter 3.
- **San Bernardo Convent,** Salta: This convent is the oldest religious building in Salta, declared a historical national monument in 1941. The entrance was carved from a carob tree by aborigines in 1762 and is the city's most impressive example of colonial art. See chapter 5.
- **Barrio Bellavista,** Santiago: The wonderfully eclectic homes that line the streets of Barrio Bellavista now form Santiago's bohemian quarter and restaurant alley, and residents have renovated and maintained the colorful enclave's architectural integrity with style. One of the more fanciful homes here is Pablo Neruda's former residence at the foot of the Cerro San Cristóbal, and it's open for tours. See chapter 9.
- **Calle Dieciocho,** Santiago: Dieciocho and Alameda Bernardo O'Higgins was a tony address for Santiago's elite during the turn-of-the-last-century, who built elegant, stately mansions of European, especially French, influence, each of which seems intent on outdoing the next in terms of size and grandeur. Most of these showpieces now house educational institutions, embassies, and social clubs, but the most extravagant of them all, the Palacio Cousiño, is open for tours. See chapter 9.
- **San Pedro de Atacama, Chiu Chiu & Caspana:** The driest desert in the world has one advantage: Everything deteriorates very, very slowly. This is good news for travelers in search of the architectural roots of Chile, where villages such as San Pedro, Chiu Chiu, and Caspana boast equally impressive examples of 17th-century–colonial adobe buildings and the sun-baked ruins of the Atacama Indian culture; some sites date back to 800 B.C. Highlights undoubtedly are the enchanting, crumbling San Francisco Church of Chiu Chiu and the labyrinthine streets of the indigenous fort **Pukará de Lasana**. See chapter 11.
- *Tejuelas* **& the German Influence,** Puerto Varas: The lovely, picturesque homes of the Lake District that are built of *tejuelas,* or shingles, are not just architectural fancies—more important, the overlapping design works to keep out the rain. Although German immigrants from Puerto Montt to the north were the first to develop this style, it spread throughout the Lake District and to Valdivia and Chiloé, but the best representations, from modest two-bedroom homes to barn-sized buildings, are concentrated in Puerto Varas. See chapter 12.
- **The Churches of Chiloé:** The singular beauty of the 17th- and 18th-century churches of Chiloé recently prompted UNESCO to designate 14 as World Heritage Monuments. That's 14 out of *300,* quite a sum for a tiny island, and each is as picturesque as the next. The churches follow the same architectural design, built entirely of wood—without nails—and triangular in shape, with humble shingled facades that belie the colorfully painted splendor within. See chapter 13.

9 The Best Markets

- **San Telmo Antiques Market,** Buenos Aires: The Sunday market is as much a cultural event as a commercial event, as old-time tango and *milonga* dancers take to the streets with other performers. Here you will glimpse Buenos Aires much as it was at the beginning of the 20th century. See chapter 3.

- **Mercado del Puerto,** Montevideo: The Mercado del Puerto (Port Market) takes place afternoons and weekends, letting you sample the flavors of Uruguay, from small empanadas to enormous barbecued meats. Saturday is the best day to visit, when cultural activities accompany the market. See chapter 7.

- **Mercado Central,** Santiago: It would be a crime to visit Chile and not sample the rich variety of fish and shellfish available here, and this vibrant market is the best place to experience the country's love affair with its fruits of the sea. Nearly every edible (and seemingly inedible) creature is for sale, from sea urchins to the alien-looking and unfamiliar *piure,* among colorful bushels of fresh vegetables and some of the most aggressive salesmen this side of the Andes. Inside the market you'll want to head to **Donde Augusto** for a bowl of the popular *paila marina,* a seafood stew sure to recharge the body. See chapter 9.

- **Pomaire,** near Santiago: The pottery business in Pomaire grew at such a pace that merchants decided to turn the entire downtown into one living market. The inexpensive, locally produced clay bowls, pots, vases, figurines, and anything else that can be made of clay are the show-stealer here, but a handful of restaurants have joined in the tourism fray, serving up delicious regional specialties and *cueca* dance performances. See chapter 10.

- **Fería Artesenal de Angelmó,** Puerto Montt: Stretching along several blocks of the Angelmó port area of Puerto Montt are rows and rows of stalls stocked with arts and crafts, clothing, and novelty items from the entire surrounding region, even Chiloé. This market is set up to buy, buy, buy! and it imparts little local color, but chances are you'll find yourself here before Temuco, which is more off the beaten path. Be sure to bargain for everything. See chapter 12.

- **Feria de Chillán in Chillán & Mercado Municipal in Temuco:** Two of the richest markets in Chile, these cluttered and diverse shopping meccas hawk everything from *huaso* chaps and spurs to jewelry to finely woven ponchos to baskets. The outdoor market in Chillán is bordered by 100 stands of fish and vegetables, but as many offer specialties such as exquisite dried fruits and bags of homemade *pebre* salsa. Temuco is the Mapuche Indian heartland, and much of the culture's crafts and traditional silver jewelry are sold here, but to really observe the indigenous group (who come to Temuco from the countryside), head to the city's "open market" 4 blocks up Manuel Rodríguez Street. See chapters 10 and 12.

- **Mercado Fluvial,** Valdivia: The bustling heart of Valdivia can be found along the waterfront at the city's fish and vegetable market. You won't find much to buy here, but you will find a spirited promenade of fishmongers and the enormous pelicans and sea lions that watch their every move. See chapter 12.

- **Castro & Dalcahue Markets,** Chiloé: Cold, wet winters in Chiloé have translated into lots and lots of sweater-making. The island's trademark handknit woolens are the thick, fuzzy kind, and they come in a rainbow of brilliant colors intended, one would suppose, to brighten up a gray day. You'll find these inexpensive and cozy duds and other woolen items, such as handknitted socks, gloves, and hats, alongside *artensanía* of carved wood and handwoven baskets in these two excellent markets. Sunday mornings are when things really get hopping. See chapter 13.

Planning a Trip to Argentina

A little advance planning can make the difference between a good trip and a great trip. What do you need to know before you go? When should you go? What's the best way to get there? How much should you plan on spending? What safety or health precautions are advised? All the basics are outlined in this chapter—the when, why, and how of traveling to and around Argentina.

1 The Regions in Brief

Argentina is the world's eighth largest country, covering 1,068,302 square miles. To the north, it is bordered by Bolivia, Paraguay, Brazil, and Uruguay, the latter situated directly northeast of Buenos Aires. The Andes cascade along Argentina's western border with Chile, where the continent's highest peaks stand. The polychromatic hills and desert plateau of the nation's Northwest are as far removed from the bustling activity of Buenos Aires as are the flat grasslands of Las Pampas from the dazzling waterfalls and subtropical jungle of Iguazú. The land's geographic diversity is reflected in the people, too: Witness the contrast between the capital's largely immigrant population and the indigenous people of the Northwest. For me, Argentina's cultural distinction and geographic diversity make this South America's most fascinating travel destination.

Many people who spend at least a week in Argentina choose between traveling to Iguazú Falls and the Northwest. To see the spectacular falls of Iguazú from both the Argentine and Brazil sides, you need at least 2 full days. A visit to the geographically stunning Northwest, where Argentine's history began and traces of Incan influence still appear, requires 3 or more days. If you choose to head south to the Lake District and Patagonia, you can do it in a week, but you'd spend a good chunk of that time just getting down there. Better to allot 2 weeks and allow time to savor the distinctive landscape.

BUENOS AIRES & THE PAMPAS   Buenos Aires, a rich combination of South American energy and European sophistication, requires at least several days (a week would be better) to explore. In addition to the city's impressive museums and architectural sites, take time to wander its grand plazas and boulevards, to stroll along its fashionable waterfront, and to engage in its dynamic culture and nightlife. A thick Argentine steak in a local *parrilla* (grill), a visit to a San Telmo antiques shop, a dance in a traditional tango salon—these are the small experiences that will connect you to the city's soul.

The heartland of the country is the *pampas,* an enormous fertile plain where the legendary *gaucho* roamed. It includes the provinces of Buenos Aires, southern Santa Fe, southeastern Córdoba, and eastern La Pampa. The *pampas* today contain many of the major cities, including the capital. One third of Argentines live in greater Buenos Aires. For more, see chapter 3, "Buenos Aires."

MISIONES   This small province of Mesopotamia enjoys a subtropical climate responsible for the region's flowing rivers and lush vegetation. The spectacular Iguazú Falls are created by the merger of the Iguazú and Parana rivers at the border of Argentina, Brazil, and Paraguay. For more, see chapter 4, "Iguazú Falls."

NORTHWEST   The Andes dominate the Northwest, with ranges between 16,000 and 23,000 feet. It is here that South America's tallest mountain, Aconcagua, stands at 22,831 feet above sea level. The two parallel mountain ranges are the Salto-Jujeña, cut by magnificent multicolored canyons called *quebradas.* This region is often compared with the Basin and Range region of the Southwestern United States, and can be visited from the historic towns of Salta and Jujuy. For more, see chapter 5, "The Northwest."

THE LAKE DISTRICT   Argentina's Lake District extends from Junín de los Andes south to Esquel—an Alpine-like region of snowy mountains, waterfalls, lush forest, and, of course, glacier-fed lakes. San Martín de los Andes, Bariloche, and Villa La Angostura are the chief destinations here; but this isn't an area where you stay in one place for long. Driving tours, boating, skiing—you'll be on the move from the moment you set foot in the region. For more, see chapter 6, "The Argentine Lake District."

Considering the enormous, flat *pampa* that separates Buenos Aires from the Lake District, and the region's proximity to the international border with Chile, many visitors opt to include a trip to Chile's Lake District while here. (For more information, see chapter 12, "The Chilean Lake District.") To avoid the crowds, I highly recommend that you plan a trip during the spring or fall (see "When to Go," below).

PATAGONIA   Also known as **Magallanes** or the **Deep South,** this dry, arid region at the southern end of the continent has soared in popularity over the past 5 years. We've grouped both Argentina and Chile in one Patagonia chapter because the majority of travelers visit destinations in both countries when here. Patagonia is characterized by vast, open *pampa,* the colossal Northern and Southern Ice Fields and hundreds of glaciers, the jagged peaks of the Andes as they reach their terminus, beautiful emerald fjords, and wind, wind, wind. Getting here is an adventure—it usually takes 24 hours if coming directly from the United States or Europe. But the long journey pays off in the beauty and singularity of the region. El Calafate is a tourist-oriented village adjacent to the Perito Moreno Glacier, which beckons visitors from around the world to come stand face-to-face with its tremendous wall of ice. El Chaltén is a tiny village of 200 whose numbers swell each summer with those who come to marvel the stunning towers of Mounts Fitz Roy, Cerro Torre, and Puntiagudo. This is the second most-visited region of Argentina's Los Glaciares National Park and quite possibly its most exquisite, for the singular nature of the granite spires here that shoot up, torpedolike, above massive tongues of ice that descend from the Southern Ice Field. For more, see chapter 15, "Patagonia & Tierra Del Fuego."

TIERRA DEL FUEGO   Even more south than the Deep South, this archipelago at the southern extremity of South America is, like Patagonia, shared by both Chile and

Argentina

BOLIVIA

BRAZIL

San Pedro
de Atacama

Antofagasta

ATACAMA DESERT

PARAGUAY

San Salvador
de Jujuy

Salta

GRAN CHACO

Pilcomayo

Paraná

Asunción

Chapter 4

Iguazú Falls

Chapter 5

A R G E N T I N A

Salado

La Serena

Mar
Chiquito

Córdoba

M O U N T A I N S

Rosario

Paraná

Chapter 3

Lagôa
dos Patos

Lagôa
Mirim

Uruguay

Valparaíso

Mendoza

A N D E S

Santiago

Buenos
Aires

La Plata

URUGUAY

Montevideo

Río de la Plata

Chapter 7

C H I L E

Colorado

Salado

P A M P A S

Bahia
Blanca

Cabo San Antonio

Bahia
Blanca

Negro

Chapter 6

Puerto Montt

San Carlos
de Bariloche

Golfo San Matías

Isla de
Chiloé

Esquel

Chubut

Península
Valdés

Archipelago
de los Chonos

Chico

Golfo de
San Jorge

ATLANTIC
OCEAN

Deseado

C. Tres Puntas

FALKLAND/MALVINAS
ISLANDS
(U.K.)

Bahia Grande

Puerto Natales

Río Gallegos

West
Falkland

East
Falkland

Archipelago
Reina Adelaide

PATAGONIA

Strait of Magellan

Punta
Arenas

Tierra del Fuego

PACIFIC
OCEAN

Ushuaia

C. San Diego

Chapter 15

Cape Horn

0   300 mi
0   300 km

N

Argentina. The main island, separated from the mainland by the Strait of Magellan, is a triangle with its base on the Beagle Channel. Tierra del Fuego's main town is Ushuaia, the southernmost city in the world. Many use the city as a jumping-off point for trips to Antarctica or sailing trips around the Cape Horn. As with the Argentine section of Patagonia, this region is outlined in chapter 15.

2 Visitor Information

IN THE U.S. The Argentina Government Tourist Office has offices at: 12 W. 56th St., New York, NY 10019 (☎ **212/603-0443;** fax 212/315-5545); 2655 Le Jeune Road, Penthouse Ste. F, Coral Gables, FL 33134 (☎ **305/442-1366;** fax 305/441-7029); and 5055 Wilshire Boulevard, Rm. 210, Los Angeles CA 90036 (☎ **213/930-0681;** fax 213/934-9076). For more detail, consult Argentina's Ministry of Tourism Web site (see "Web Sites of Note," below).

IN CANADA Basic tourist information can be obtained by the Consulate General of Argentina, 2000 Peel St., Ste. 600, Montreal, Quebec H3A 2W5 (☎ **514/842-6582;** fax 514/842-5797; www.consargenmtl.com); for more detail, consult Argentina's Ministry of Tourism Web site (see "Web Sites of Note," below).

IN THE U.K. For visitor information, contact the Embassy of Argentina in London (see "Entry Requirements & Customs," below) or consult Argentina's Ministry of Tourism Web site (see "Web Sites of Note," below).

IN AUSTRALIA & NEW ZEALAND For visitor information, contact the Embassy of Argentina in Canberra (see "Entry Requirements & Customs," below) or consult Argentina's Ministry of Tourism Web site (see "Web Sites of Note," below).

WEB SITES OF NOTE
- **www.embassyofargentina-usa.org** Up-to-date travel information from the Argentine embassy in Washington, DC.
- **www.sectur.gov.ar** This Ministry of Tourism site has travel information for all of Argentina, including a virtual tour of the country's tourist regions, shopping tips, links to city tourist sites, and general travel facts.
- **www.mercotour.com** A travel site focused on adventure and ecological excursions, with information on outdoor activities in both Argentina and Chile.
- **www.argentinatravel.com** This promotional site advertises vacation packages, accommodations, transportation, and *estancia* (ranch) stays.

3 Entry Requirements & Customs

ENTRY REQUIREMENTS
Citizens of the United States, Canada, the United Kingdom, Australia, New Zealand, and South Africa require a passport to enter the country. No visa is required for citizens of these countries for tourist stays of up to 90 days. For more information concerning longer stays, employment, or other types of visas, contact the embassies or consulates in your home country.

IN THE U.S. Contact the Consular Section of the Argentine Embassy, 1718 Connecticut Ave., NW, Washington, D.C. 20009 (☎ **202/238-6460**). Consulates are also located in California (☎ **213/954-9155**), Florida (☎ **305/373-7794**), Georgia (☎ **404/880-0805**), Illinois (☎ **312/819-2610**), New York City (☎ **212/603-0400**), and Texas (☎ **713/871-8935**). For more information, try www.uic.edu/orgs/argentina/.

IN CANADA   Contact the Embassy of the Argentine Republic, Suite 910, Royal Bank Center, 90 Sparks St., Ottawa, Ontario K1P 5B4 (☎ **613/236-2351;** fax 613/235-2659).

IN THE U.K.   Contact the Embassy of the Argentine Republic, 65 Brooke St., London W1Y 4AH (☎ **020/7318-1300;** fax 020/7318-1301; www.argentine-embassy-uk. org; e-mail: seruni@mrecic.gov.ar).

IN AUSTRALIA   Contact the Embassy of Argentina at John McEwan House, 7 National Circuit, Barton, ACT 2600 (☎2/6273-9111; fax 2/6273-0500).

IN NEW ZEALAND   Contact the Embassy of Argentina at Sovereign Assurance Building, Level 14, 142 Lambton Quay, P.O. Box 5430, Wellington (☎ **4/472-8330;** fax 4/472-8331; www.arg.org.nz).

CUSTOMS
WHAT YOU CAN BRING INTO ARGENTINA

Travelers entering Argentina can bring personal effects—including clothes, jewelry, and professional equipment—without paying duty. In addition they can bring in 21 liters of alcohol, 400 cigarettes, and 50 cigars duty free.

WHAT YOU CAN BRING HOME

FOR U.S. CITIZENS   Travelers returning to the **United States** are allowed to bring $400 worth of goods, per person, and family members who live in the same home may combine their exemptions. Travelers who stay less than 48 hours outside the country or who have left the United States more than once in 30 days are given a $200 exemption only. You may include up to 1 liter of alcohol (provided you are over 21 years of age), 100 cigars, and 200 cigarettes; any more and you'll pay a duty fee. Keep all your receipts handy. The legal limit for goods mailed home per day is no more than $20 for yourself; mark the package "for personal use." You may mail a gift to someone worth no more than $100 per person per day, marked "unsolicited gift." Packages must clearly describe the contents on the exterior. You may not mail alcohol, perfume that contains alcohol, or tobacco products, but a legitimate company such as a wine dealer can ship alcohol to you in the United States, usually for a prohibitively steep shipping fee. Foodstuffs must be tinned or professionally sealed; you may not bring fresh foodstuffs into the United States.

Duty tax is a flat 10% on the first $1,000 worth of goods over $400. Anything over is subject to an item-by-item basis. For more information, contact the **U.S. Customs Service** at P.O. Box 7407, Washington, DC 20044 (☎ **202/927-6724**), for their free booklet "Know Before You Go," or simply look it up on their Web site: **www. customs.ustreas.gov**.

FOR U.K. CITIZENS   Returnees to the United Kingdom may bring back up to 200 cigarettes, 50 cigars, or 250 grams of tobacco; 2 liters of still table wine; 1 liter of distilled spirits over 22% volume or 2 liters sparkling wine, fortified wine, or other liqueurs; 60cc/ml perfume; 250cc/ml toilet water; and £145 worth of all other gifts and souvenirs. Travelers must be over 17 to bring back tobacco and alcohol. For more information, consult the **HM Customs & Excise** at ☎ **020/8910-3744,** or their Web site at **www.hmce.gov.uk**.

FOR CANADIAN CITIZENS   If you've been out of the country for over 48 hours, you may bring back $200 Canadian worth of goods, and if you've been gone for 7 consecutive days or more, not counting your departure, the limit is $750. The limit for alcohol is up to $\frac{1}{5}$ liters of wine or $\frac{1}{14}$ liters of liquor, or 24 12-ounce cans or bottles of beer; and up to 200 cigarettes, 50 cigars, or 200 grams of tobacco. You may not ship tobacco or alcohol and you must be of legal age for your province to bring these items through customs. For more information, call the **Canada Customs and Review Agency** at ☎ **800/461-9999** or 204/9833500 outside Canada; or try their Web site for their document *I Declare:* **www.ccra-adrc.gc.ca.**

FOR AUSTRALIAN CITIZENS   The duty-free allowance in **Australia** is A$400 or, for those under 18, A$200. Upon returning to Australia, citizens can bring in 250 cigarettes or 250 grams of loose tobacco, and 1,125 ml of alcohol. If you're returning with valuable goods you already own, such as foreign-made cameras, you should file form B263. A helpful brochure, available from Australian consulates or Customs offices, is *Know Before You Go.* For more information, contact **Australian Customs Services**, GPO Box 8, Sydney NSW 2001 (☎ **02/9213-2000**).

FOR CITIZENS OF NEW ZEALAND   The duty-free allowance for **New Zealand** is NZ$700. Citizens over 17 can bring in 200 cigarettes, 50 cigars, or 250 grams of tobacco (or a mixture of all three if their combined weight doesn't exceed 250 grams); plus 4.5 liters of wine and beer, or 1.125 liters of liquor. New Zealand currency does not carry import or export restrictions. Fill out a certificate of export, listing the valuables you are taking out of the country; that way, you can bring them back without paying duty. Most questions are answered in a free pamphlet available at New Zealand consulates and Customs offices: *New Zealand Customs Guide for Travellers, Notice no. 4.* For more information, contact New Zealand Customs, 50 Anzac Ave., P.O. Box 29, Auckland (☎ **09/359-6655**).

4 Money

CASH & CURRENCY

The official Argentine currency is the **peso,** made up of 100 **centavos.** It is pegged to the U.S. dollar and fluctuates in value along with it. For this reason, prices in the Argentina chapters are given in U.S. dollars. Money is denominated in notes of 2, 5, 10, 20, 50, and 100 pesos and coins of 1, 2, and 5 pesos and 1, 5, 10, 25, and 50 centavos.

Many tourists find Argentina, and Buenos Aires in particular, very expensive—on par with prices in wealthy European countries. Hotels, domestic flights, and telephone calls are expensive when compared to similar items in the rest of Latin America. Is anything cheap here? City taxis are a bargain, as is public transportation. You can find good, inexpensive wine in stores and restaurants. And although dining is not automatically cheap in Buenos Aires, you can find places to enjoy an excellent meal at very reasonable costs. Cities outside Buenos Aires are less expensive, though considerably more expensive than other cities (except maybe in Brazil) in Latin America.

EXCHANGING MONEY

U.S. dollars are widely accepted in Buenos Aires and can be used to pay taxis, hotels, restaurants, and stores. (in fact, many ATMs in Buenos Aires dispense U.S. dollars as well as pesos.) Keep some pesos on hand, however, because you might run into spots where you'll need them. You'll find that U.S. dollars are less useful in rural areas (and places to exchange money less common), so plan ahead. You can convert your currency in hotels, *casas de cambio* (money exchanges), some banks, and at the Buenos Aires International Airport. Change American Express traveler's checks in Buenos Aires at **American Express,** Arenales 707 (☎ **11/4130-3135**). It is difficult to change traveler's checks outside the capital. Therefore, I recommend that you carry sufficient pesos (or purchase traveler's checks in pesos) when you venture into small-town Argentina. You can usually change money at their hotels, as well.

ATMS

Traveler's checks are something of an anachronism from the days when people wrote personal checks instead of going to an ATM. Because traveler's checks could be replaced if lost or stolen, they were a sound alternative to filling your wallet with cash at the beginning of a trip.

ATMs (automated-teller machines) are easy to access in Buenos Aires and other urban areas, but don't depend on finding them off the beaten path. Typically, they are connected to **Cirrus** (☎ 800/424-7787; www.mastercard.com/atm/) or **PLUS** (☎ 800/843-7587; www.visa.com/atms) networks. Check the back of your ATM card to see which network your bank belongs to. The 800 numbers and Web sites will give you specific locations of ATMs where you can withdraw money while on vacation. You can withdraw only as much cash as you need every couple of days, which eliminates the insecurity (and the pickpocketing threat) of carrying around a wad of cash. Many ATMs also accept Visa and MasterCard, less often American Express and Diners Club.

One important reminder: Many banks now charge a fee ranging from 50¢ to $3 whenever non–account-holders use their ATMs. Your own bank might also assess a fee for using an ATM that's not one of its branch locations. This means in some cases you'll get charged *twice* just for using your bank card when you're on vacation. And while an ATM card can be an amazing convenience when traveling in another country (put your card in the machine, and out comes foreign currency, at an extremely advantageous exchange rate), banks are also likely to slap you with a "foreign currency transaction fee" just for making them do the pesos-to-dollars conversion math. Given these sneaky tactics, it might just be cheaper (though certainly less convenient) to revert to the traveler's check policy when staying in a bigger city.

CREDIT CARDS

If you choose to use plastic instead of cash, Visa, American Express, MasterCard, and Diners Club are commonly accepted, and since the peso is fixed to the dollar, exchange rate fluctuations aren't a problem. However, bargain hunters take note: Some establishments—especially smaller businesses—don't like paying the fee to process your credit card and will give you a better price if you pay cash. Credit cards are accepted at most all hotels and restaurants, except the very cheapest ones. But note you cannot use credit cards in many taxis or at most attractions (museums, trams, etc.).

You can get **cash advances** off your credit card at any bank, and you don't even need to go to a teller; you can get a cash advance at the ATM if you know your PIN. If you've forgotten your PIN or didn't even know you had one, call the phone number on the back of your credit card and ask the bank to send it to you. It usually takes 5 to 7 business days, although some banks will do it over the phone if you tell them your mother's maiden name or some other security clearance.

Another hidden expense to contend with: Interest rates for cash advances are often significantly higher than rates for credit card purchases. More important, you start paying interest on the advance *the moment you receive the cash.* On an airline-affiliated credit card, a cash advance does not earn frequent-flyer miles.

5 When to Go

The seasons in Argentina are the reverse of those in the northern hemisphere. Buenos Aires is ideal in fall (March to May) and spring (September to November), when temperatures are mild. The beaches and resort towns are packed with vacationing Argentines in summer (December to March), while Buenos Aires becomes somewhat deserted (you decide if that's a plus or a minus—hotel prices usually fall here in summer). Plan a trip to Patagonia and the southern Andes in summer, when days are longer and warmer. Winter (June to August) is the best time to visit Iguazú and the Northwest, when the rains and heat have subsided; but spring (August to October) is also pleasant, as temperatures are mild and the crowds have cleared out.

CLIMATE   Except for a small tropical area in northern Argentina, the country lies in the temperate zone, characterized by cool, dry weather in the south, and warmer, humid air in the center. Accordingly, January and February are quite hot—often in the high 90s to over 100°F (35–40°C)—while winter (from about July to October) can be chilly.

HOLIDAYS   Public holidays are January 1 (New Year's Day); April 2 (Good Friday); May 1 (Labor Day); May 25 (First Argentine Government); June 10 (National Sovereignty Day); June 20 (Flag Day); July 9 (Independence Day); August 17 (Anniversary of the Death of General San Martín); October 12 (Columbus Day); December 8 (Immaculate Conception Day); and December 25 (Christmas).

FESTIVALS & SPECIAL EVENTS   Several holidays and festivals are worth planning a trip around; the best place to get information for these events is through your local Argentine tourism office (see "Visitor Information," above). **Carnaval** (Mardi Gras), the week before the start of Lent, is celebrated in many towns in Argentina, although to a much lesser extent than in neighboring Brazil. In Salta, citizens throw a large parade, including caricatures of public officials and "water bomb" fights. The **Gaucho Parade** takes place in Salta on June 16, with music by folk artists and gauchos dressed in traditional red ponchos with black stripes, leather chaps, black boots, belts, and knives.

Inti Raymi (Festival of the Sun) takes places in towns throughout the Northwest the night before the summer solstice (June 20) to give thanks for the year's harvest. **Dia de Independencia** (Independence Day) is celebrated in Tucumán on July 9. **Exodo Jujeño** (Jujuy Exodus) takes place August 23 and 24, when locals reenact the exodus of 1812. The **Batalla de Tucumán** (Battle of Tucumán) celebrates Belgrano's victory over the Spanish, on September 24. And the **Fiesta Provincial del Turismo** (Provincial Tourist Festival) takes place in December in Puerto Iguazú.

6 Health & Insurance

HEALTH

Life in Argentina presents few health issues. Argentina requires no vaccinations to enter the country, except for passengers coming from countries where cholera and yellow fever are endemic. Some people who have allergies (especially the ones related to the respiratory system) can be affected by the pollution in the city and the high level of pollen during spring. Because motor vehicle crashes are a leading cause of injury among travelers, walk and drive defensively. Avoid nighttime travel if possible and always use seat belts.

Most visitors find that Argentine food and water is generally easy on the stomach. Water and ice are considered safe to drink in Buenos Aires. Be careful with street food, especially in dodgy neighborhoods of Buenos Aires and in cities outside the capital. Beef is a staple of the Argentine diet (an understatement, to be sure), and as this book went to press, Argentinean cattle farmers had discovered traces of **foot-and-mouth disease** among their herds. As a result, the U.S. has banned importation of Argentine beef. It is unclear just what effect this outbreak will have on Argentina's beef industry—or what this means for travelers arriving in a country where beef items are the overwhelming menu choice in a majority of restaurants. For the most up-to-date information on this issue, consult the United States Department of Agriculture Web site (**www.usda.gov**) or the Centers for Disease control Web site (**www.cdc.gov**).

ALTITUDE SICKNESS   If you visit the Andes Mountains, ascend gradually to allow time for your body to adjust to the high altitude, to avoid contracting **altitude sickness.** Altitude sickness, known as *soroche* or *puna,* is a temporary yet often debilitating affliction that affects about a quarter of travelers to the northern *altiplano,* or the Andes at 7,872 feet (2,427m) and up. Nausea, fatigue, headaches, shortness of breath, and sleeplessness are the symptoms, which can last from 2 to 5 days. If you feel as though you've been affected, drink plenty of water, take aspirin or ibuprofen, and avoid alcohol and sleeping pills. To prevent altitude sickness, acclimatize your body by breaking the climb to higher regions into segments.

AUSTRAL SUN   The shrinking ozone layer in southern South America has caused an onset of health problems among the citizens who live there, including increased incidents of skin cancer and cataracts. If you are planning to travel to Patagonia, keep in mind that on "red alert" days (typically from September to November), it is possible to burn in *10 minutes.* If you plan to be outdoors, you'll need to protect yourself with strong sunblock, a long-sleeved shirt, a wide-brimmed hat, and sunglasses.

MALARIA & OTHER TROPICAL AILMENTS   The Centers for Disease Control (**www.cdc.gov**) recommends that travelers to northwestern Argentina take malaria medication, but I have not heard of any incidents of Malaria. Cholera has appeared from time to time in the Northwest, but such tropical diseases do not seem to be a problem in the sultry climate of Iguazu.

WHAT TO DO IF YOU GET SICK AWAY FROM HOME

The medical facilities and personnel in Buenos Aires and the other urban areas in Argentina are very professional and comparable to the United States standards. Argentina has a system of socialized medicine, where basic services are free. Private clinics are inexpensive by Western standards. If you worry about getting sick away from home, you may want to consider **medical travel insurance** (see the section on travel insurance below). In most cases, however, your existing health plan will provide all the coverage you need. Be sure to carry your identification card in your wallet.

INSURANCE

Nothing can spoil a vacation like losing your luggage or suffering a medical emergency. Planning ahead and making certain you're covered for any unforeseen catastrophes can save your trip. But before buying specific travel insurance, first investigate your **homeowner's insurance** policy to see if it covers lost luggage, as most policies often do. Airlines will reimburse travelers for up to $9.07 per pound up to $640, but the process is time-consuming. Second, check to see what kind of insurance your **credit card company** offers, and whether it is solely for tickets or goods purchased using the card. Some credit cards offer flight insurance in the event of a plane crash or other transportation accidents.

If you plan to take advantage of one of Argentina's many adventure travel opportunities, it is imperative that you protect yourself with **medical insurance,** even if all you plan to do is light trekking. Trip medical insurance appeals to travelers who do not have a current regular medical plan back home. Your regular medical plan should reimburse you for any costs incurred while out of the country, but be sure to check with the company for coverage details before traveling, especially if you're part of an HMO. Remember that Medicare only covers travelers to Mexico and Canada, not Argentina. Companies specializing in medical care include **MEDEX International** (☎ **888/MEDEX-00** or 410/453-6300; www.medexassist.com) and **Travel Assistance International** (☎ 800/821-2828). STA Travel offers low-cost medical coverage, which you can buy from any one of its many travel agencies, or by calling ☎ **800/777-0122.**

Trip cancellation insurance is a good idea, especially if you prepay some or all of your vacation expenses. Companies usually charge about 6 to 8% of the total price of your trip. The following companies offer a variety of insurance options: **Access America** (☎ **800/284-8300**); **Travel Guard** (☎ **800/826-1300**); **Travel Insured International, Inc.** (☎ **800/243-3172**); and **International SOS Assistance** (☎ **800/ 523-8930** or 215/244-1500), which offers 24-hour assistance for problems that arise while abroad.

7　Tips for Travelers with Special Needs

FOR TRAVELERS WITH DISABILITIES

Argentina is not a very accessible destination for travelers with disabilities. Four- and five-star hotels in Buenos Aires often have a few rooms designed for travelers with disabilities—check with the hotel in advance. But once you get out of the city, services dry up pretty quickly.

Fortunately, there are several organizations in the United States that can help. **Mobility International USA,** P.O. Box 10767, Eugene, OR 97440 (☎ **541/ 343-1284;** www.miusa.org), publishes a guide to travel and international exchange programs for travelers with disabilities called *A World of Options* for $35 ($30 for members). Another place to try is **Access-Able Travel Source** (www.access-able.com), a comprehensive database of travel agents who specialize in travel for those with disabilities; it's also a clearinghouse for information about accessible destinations around the world.

Travelers with disabilities might also want to consider joining a tour that caters specifically to them. One of the best operators is **Flying Wheels Travel,** P.O. Box 382, Owatonna, MN 55060 (☎ **800/535-6790;** fax 507/451-1685). They offer various escorted tours and cruises as well as private tours in minivans with lifts.

FOR SENIORS

Argentines treat seniors with great respect, making travel for them easy. Discounts are usually available; ask when booking a hotel room or before ordering a meal in a restaurant. **Aerolineas Argentinas** (☎ **800/333-0276** in the U.S.; www.aerolineas.com.ar/english.htm) offers a ten percent discount on fares to Buenos Aires from Miami and New York for passengers 62 and older; companion fares are also discounted. Both **American** (☎ **800/433-7300;** www.americanair.com) and **United** (☎ **800/ 241-6522;** www.united.com) also offer discounted senior fares.

Members of the **American Association of Retired Persons (AARP),** 601 E St. NW, Washington, DC 20049 (☎ **800/424-3410;** www.aarp.com), receive discounts at hotel chains such as Best Western, Holiday Inn, and the Marriott, as well as car rentals from companies like Avis and Hertz.

In addition, most of the major U.S.-based airlines, including American, United, Continental, US Airways, and TWA, all offer discount programs for senior travelers—be sure to ask whenever you book a flight.

The Mature Traveler, a monthly newsletter on senior travel, is a valuable resource. It is available by subscription ($30 a year); for a free sample, send a postcard with your name and address to GEM Publishing Group, Box 50400, Reno, NV 89513 (e-mail: maturetrav@aol.com). Another helpful publication is *101 Tips for the Mature Traveler,* available from Grand Circle Travel, 347 Congress St., Suite 3A, Boston, MA 02210 (☎ **800/221-2610;** www.gct.com).

Grand Circle Travel is also one of the literally hundreds of travel agencies that specialize in vacations for seniors. But beware: Many of them are of the tour-bus variety, with free trips thrown in for those who organize groups of 20 or more. Seniors seeking more independent travel should probably consult a regular travel agent. **SAGA International Holidays,** 222 Berkeley St., Boston, MA 02116 (☎ **800/343-0273**), offers inclusive tours and cruises for those 50 and older.

Probably the most interesting and well-respected senior organization is **Elderhostel,** 75 Federal St., Boston, MA 02110-1941 (☎ **800/426-8056;** www.elderhostel.org), which offers cultural and educational trips to Argentina with themes such as "Argentina's Many Faces" (which includes Buenos Aires, Salta, and Iguazú Falls) and "Patagonia: Land of Magnificent Contrasts."

FOR GAY & LESBIAN TRAVELERS

Argentina remains a very traditional, Catholic society, and is fairly closed minded about homosexuality. Buenos Aires is more liberal than the rest of the country; in particular, the Rosario neighborhood is gay- and lesbian-friendly.

A most helpful source is *Our World,* a magazine designed specifically for gay and lesbian travelers (10 issues a year, $35), at 1104 N. Nova Rd., Suite 251, Daytona Beach, FL 32117 (☎ **904/441-5367;** www.ourworldmagazine.com); it not only is full of ads for travel agencies and facilities that accommodate gays and lesbians, but also carries firsthand accounts of visits to locales all around the world. The **International Gay & Lesbian Travel Association (IGLTA),** 52 W. Oakland Park Blvd. #237, Wilton Manors, FL 33311 (☎ **800/448-8550** or 954/776-2626; www.iglta.org; e-mail: iglta@iglta.org), can advise you about travel opportunities, agents, and tour operators. The monthly newsletter *Out and About* also has information for gay and lesbian travelers (☎ **800/929-2268**).

FOR WOMEN TRAVELERS

Female beauty is idealized in Argentina, and women seem constantly on display—both for each other and for Argentine men. Any looks and calls you might get are generally more flirtatious than harassing in nature. If you seek to avoid unwanted attention, don't dress skimpily (as many *Porteñas* do) or flash jewelry. Women should not walk alone at night.

FOR STUDENTS

Student discounts are very common in Argentina, but usually only if one has appropriate ID. Both **STA Travel** (☎ **800/781-4040** in the U.S., 020/7361-6144 in the U.K., and 1300/360-960 in Australia; www.statravel.com) and **Council Travel** (☎ **800/2-COUNCIL** in the U.S.; www.counciltravel.com) specialize in affordable airfares, bus and rail passes, accommodations, insurance, tours, and packages for students and young travelers. Both issue **International Student Identity Cards (ISIC).** This is the most widely recognized proof that you really are a student. As well as getting you discounts on a huge range of travel, tours, and attractions, it comes with a 24-hour emergency help line and a global voice/fax/e-mail messaging system with discounted international telephone calls. Available to any full-time student over 12, it costs $22.

Council Travel has a partnership in Buenos Aires with **TIJE,** San Martín 674, 3rd Floor B (☎ **11/4326-5665**).

8 Getting There

BY PLANE

Argentina's main international airport is **Ezeiza Ministro Pistarini (EZE)** (☎ **11/4480-9538**), located 26 miles (42km) outside Buenos Aires. You will be assessed a departure tax of approximately $23.50 upon leaving the country. For flights from Buenos Aires to Montevideo (in Uruguay), the departure tax is $5. Passengers in transit and children under 2 years of age are exempt from this tax. However, visitors are advised to verify the departure tax with their airline or travel agent, as the exact amount changes frequently.

I have listed below the major airlines that fly into Argentina from North America, Europe, and Australia:

FROM THE U.S. & CANADA Argentina's national airline, **Aerolineas Argentinas** (☎ **800/333-0276** in the U.S., or 11/4340-3777 in Buenos Aires; www.aerolineas. com.ar/english.htm), flies nonstop from Los Angeles, Miami, and New York's JFK. **American Airlines** (☎ **800/433-7300** in the U.S. or 11/4318-1111 in Buenos Aires; www.americanair.com) flies nonstop from Miami. **United Airlines** (☎ **800/241-6522** in the U.S., or 0810/777-8648 in Buenos Aires; www.ual.com) flies nonstop from Miami, New York, and Chicago. Approximate flight time from Los Angeles to Buenos Aires is 16 hours, from Miami 9 hours, and from New York 14 hours. **Air Canada** (☎ **888/247-2262** in Canada, or 11-4327-3640 in Buenos Aires; www.aircanada.ca) flies from Toronto to Buenos Aires through São Paulo, Brazil.

FROM THE U.K. **British Airways** (☎ **0845/773-3377** in the U.K., or 11/4320-6600 in Buenos Aires) flies nonstop from London–Gatwick to Buenos Aires; approximate flight time is 13 hours. **Iberia** (☎ **0845/601-2854** in the U.K., or 11/4131-1000 in Buenos Aires) connects through Madrid.

FROM AUSTRALIA & NEW ZEALAND Aerolineas Argentinas (☎ **1800/22-22-15** in Australia) flies from Sydney, with a stop in Auckland. Approximate flight time from Sydney is 16 hours.

FLYING FOR LESS: TIPS FOR GETTING THE BEST AIRFARE

Passengers within the same airplane cabin are rarely paying the same fare for their seats. Passengers who can book their ticket long in advance, who don't mind staying over Saturday night, or who are willing to travel on a Tuesday, Wednesday, or Thursday after 7pm, usually pay a fraction of the full fare. Here are a few easy ways to save.

1. Check your newspaper for advertised discounts or call the airlines directly and ask if any **promotional rates or special fares** are available. You'll almost never see a sale during peak travel times (from December through February). If your schedule is flexible, ask if you can secure a cheaper fare by staying an extra day or by flying midweek. (Many airlines won't volunteer this information.) If you

already hold a ticket when a sale breaks, it might even pay to exchange your ticket, which usually incurs a $50 to $75 charge.

Note, however, that the lowest-priced fares are often nonrefundable, require advance purchase of 1 to 3 weeks and a certain length of stay, and carry penalties for changing dates of travel.

2. **Consolidators,** also known as bucket shops, are a good place to find low fares. Consolidators buy seats in bulk from the airlines and then sell them back to the public at prices below even the airlines' discounted rates. Their small, boxed ads usually run in the Sunday travel section at the bottom of the page. Before you pay, however, ask for a confirmation number from the consolidator, and then call the airline itself to confirm your seat. Be prepared to book your ticket with a different consolidator; there are many to choose from if the airline can't confirm your reservation. Also be aware that bucket shop tickets are usually nonrefundable or rigged with stiff cancellation penalties, often as high as 50% to 75% of the ticket price. (In addition, many airlines won't grant frequent-flier miles on consolidator tickets.)

   Council Travel (☎ 800/226-8624; www.counciltravel.com) and **STA Travel** (☎ 800/781-4040; www.sta.travel.com) cater especially to young travelers, but their bargain-basement prices are available to people of all ages. **Travel Bargains** (☎ 800/AIR-FARE; www.1800airfare.com) was formerly owned by TWA but now offers the deepest discounts on many other airlines, with a 4-day advance purchase. Other reliable consolidators include **1-800/FLY-CHEAP** (www.1800flycheap.com); **TFI Tours International** (☎ 800/745-8000 or 212/736-1140), which serves as a clearinghouse for unused seats; or "rebators" such as **Travel Avenue** (☎ 800/333-3335 or 312/876-1116) and the **Smart Traveller** (☎ 800/448-3338 in the U.S., or 305/448-3338), which rebate part of their commissions to you.

3. **Look into courier flights.** Companies that hire couriers use your luggage allowance for their business baggage; in return, you get a deeply discounted ticket. Flights are often offered at the last minute, and you might have to arrange a pretrip interview to make sure you're right for the job. **Now Voyager,** open Monday to Friday 10am to 5:30pm and Saturday noon to 4:30pm (☎ 212/431-1616), flies from New York. Now Voyager also offers non-courier discounted fares, so call the company even if you don't want to fly as a courier.

4. **Surf the Net and save.** It's possible to get some great deals on airfare, hotels, and car rentals via the Internet. Grab your mouse and surf before you take off; you could save a bundle on your trip. The Web sites highlighted below are worth checking out, especially since all services are free. Always check the lowest published fare, however, before you shop for flights online.

   Of course, we're a little biased, but we think **Arthur Frommer's Budget Travel** (www.frommers.com) is an excellent travel-planning resource. You'll find indispensable travel tips, reviews, destination information, monthly vacation giveaways, and online booking. Full-service sites like **Travelocity** (www.travelocity.com) and **Microsoft Expedia** (www.expedia.com) offer domestic and international flight booking; hotel and car rental reservations; late-breaking travel news; and personalized "fare watcher" e-mails that keep you posted on special deals for preselected routes. **The Trip** (www.thetrip.com) is really geared toward the business traveler, but vacationers-to-be can also use The Trip's exceptionally powerful fare-finding engine, which will e-mail you every week with the best city-to-city airfare deals for as many as 10 routes.

5. **You've got mail.** Most major airlines offer a free e-mail service known as **E-Savers,** via which they'll send you their best bargain airfares on a regular basis. Once a week (usually Wednesday), or whenever a sale fare comes up, subscribers receive a list of discounted flights to and from various destinations, both international and domestic. Here's the catch: These fares are usually available only if you leave the very next Saturday (or sometimes Friday night) and return on the following Monday or Tuesday. It's really a service for the spontaneously inclined and travelers looking for a quick getaway. For instance, American often has good last-minute deals on flights from the United States to Buenos Aires. *One caveat:* You'll get frequent-flier miles if you purchase one of these e-saver fares, but you can't use miles to buy the ticket.

If the thought of all that surfing and comparison shopping gives you a headache, try **Smarter Living** (www.smarterliving.com). Sign up for their newsletter service, and every week you'll get a customized e-mail summarizing the discount fares available from your departure city. Smarter Living tracks more than 15 different airlines, so it's a worthwhile timesaver. Another excellent way to take advantage of several Internet travel-booking services at once is to use **Qixo** (www.qixo.com). Qixo is a search engine that offers real-time airfare price comparisons for more than 10 online booking sites, including several airline sites, Expedia, Lowestfare, Travelocity, Cheap Tickets, Travelscape, and Trip.com.

9 Getting Around

BY PLANE

The easiest way to travel Argentina's vast distances is by air. **Aerolíneas Argentinas** (see above), which is affiliated with **Austral Líneas Aéreas** (☎ 11/4340-7777 in Buenos Aires), connects most cities and tourist destinations in Argentina, including Córdoba, Jujuy, Iguazú, and Salta. Its competitor, **LAPA** (☎ 11/4114-5272 in Buenos Aires; www.lapa.com.ar), serves roughly the same routes. By American standards, domestic flights within Argentina are expensive. In Buenos Aires, domestic flights and flights to Uruguay (see chapter 7) travel out of **Jorge Newbery Airport** (☎11/4514-1515), 15 minutes from downtown.

If you plan to travel extensively in Argentina, consider buying the **Airpass Visit Argentina,** issued by Aerolíneas Argentinas and Austral Líneas Aéreas. You must purchase the pass in your home country; it cannot be purchased once in Argentina. This pass offers discounts for domestic travel in conjunction with your international ticket. Purchase between one and three flight coupons (one coupon for each flight) for $299. Up to five additional coupons can be purchased for $105 each. If you arrive in Argentina on a eligible airline other than Aerolíneas Argentinas, the price for the first three coupons is $339. For more information, contact the Aerolíneas office in your home country or try **www.aerolineas.com.ar**. Those visiting more than one country in South America might want to buy the "Mercosur Airpass" for Argentina, Brazil, Paraguay, and Uruguay. The following airlines participate in this air pass program: Aerolíneas Argentinas, Austral, Dinar, LADE, LAER, LAPA, SW, and TAN.

BY BUS

Argentine buses are comfortable, safe, and efficient. They connect nearly every part of Argentina as well as bordering countries. In cases where two classes of bus service are offered (*comun* and *diferencial*), the latter is more luxurious. Most long distance buses offer toilets, air conditioning, and snack/bar service. Bus travel is usually considerably cheaper than air travel for similar routes. In almost every instance, I believe travelers would prefer a (slightly more) expensive two-hour flight to a 20-plus hour bus ride (see chart below). But taking a long-distance bus in South America is a singular cultural experience, so you might find it time well spent.

Among the major bus companies that operate out of Buenos Aires are: **La Veloz del Norte** (☎ 11/4315-2482), serving destinations in the Northwest including Salta and Jujuy; **Singer** (☎ 11/4315-2653), serving Puerto Iguazú as well as Brazilian destinations; and **T.A. Chevallier** (☎ 11/4313-3297), serving Bariloche.

Sample Times & Fares for Travel in Argentina from Buenos Aires

From Buenos Aires to	Length of bus trip	Cost of a one-way bus ticket	Length of plane trip	Cost of a one-way plane ticket
Bariloche	23 hr.	$76	2¼ hr.	$100–$220
Puerto Iguazú	21 hr.	$50	2 hr.	$90–$220
Salta	22 hr.	$80	2 hr.	$110–$220

BY CAR

Argentine roads and highways are generally in good condition, with the exception of some rural areas. Most highways have been privatized and charge nominal tolls. In Buenos Aires, drivers are aggressive and don't always obey traffic lanes or lights. Wear your seat belt, required by Argentine law. U.S. driver's licenses are valid in greater Buenos Aires, but you need an Argentine or international license to drive in most other parts of the country. Fuel is expensive at about $1 per liter (or $4 per gallon). A car that uses gasoil (as the name implies, a hybrid fuel of gas and oil) is the cheaper option fuel-wise, about 15% cheaper than regular unleaded gasoline.

The **Automovil Club Argentino (ACA),** Av. del Libertador 1850 (☎ 11/4802-6061), has working arrangements with International Automobile Clubs. The ACA offers numerous services, including roadside assistance, road maps, hotel and camping information, and discounts for various tourist activities.

CAR RENTALS   Many international car rental companies operate in Argentina with offices at airports and in city centers. Here are the main offices in Buenos Aires for the following agencies: **Hertz,** Paraguay 1122 (☎ 800/654-3131 in the U.S., or 11/4816-8001 in Buenos Aires); **Avis,** Cerrito 1527 (☎ 800/230-4898 in the U.S., or 11/4300-8201 in Buenos Aires); **Dollar,** Marcelo T. de Alvear 523 (☎ 800/800-6000 in the U.S., or 11/4315-8800 in Buenos Aires); and **Thrifty,** Av. Leandro N. Alem 699 (☎ 800/847-4389 in the U.S., or 11/4315-0777 in Buenos Aires). Car rental is expensive in Argentina, with standard rates beginning at about $90 per day for a subcompact with unlimited mileage (ask for any special promotions, especially on weekly rates). Check to see if your existing automobile insurance policy (or a credit card) covers insurance for car rentals; otherwise, purchasing insurance should run you an extra $15 a day.

BY TRAIN

Argentina's railroad network is very limited. There are trains from Buenos Aires to Bariloche and to Mar de la Plata, but they are neither as comfortable nor convenient as buses. One train service stands out, however. The tourist train called **Tren a las Nubes** (Train to the Clouds) begins in Salta and cuts an unforgettable swath through the Andes in northwest Argentina. The trip lasts approximately 14 hours and costs $100 per person. For more information, call ☎ 387/431-4984 in Salta, ☎ 11/4311-8871 in Buenos Aires, consult www.trenubes.com.ar (a Spanish-language site), or see chapter 5 for more information.

10 The Active Vacation Planner

Argentina encompasses so many climate zones, with such a wide variety of terrain, that it is a haven for outdoor activities of all kinds. There are numerous hiking and climbing opportunities in the Northwest. Activities around Iguazu Falls range from easy hiking along the waterfall circuits and on San Martín Island, speed rafting along the river, and trekking into the jungle. And of course, Argentine Patagonia is home to more kayaking, climbing, and trekking than you could possibly fit in one lifetime. Below I have listed some recommended tour operators specializing in outdoor-themed vacations in Argentina.

ORGANIZED ADVENTURE TRIPS   The advantages of traveling with an organized group are plentiful, especially for travelers who have limited time and resources. Tour operators take the headache out of planning a trip, and they iron out the wrinkles that invariably pop up along the way. Many tours are organized to include guides, transportation, accommodations, meals, and gear (some outfits will even carry gear for you, for example on trekking adventures). Independent travelers tend to view organized tours as antithetical to the joy of discovery, but leaving the details to someone else does free up substantial time to concentrate on something else. Besides, your traveling companions are likely to be kindred souls interested in similar things.

Remember to be aware of what you're getting yourself into. A 5-day trek in the remote Patagonian wilderness may look great on paper, but are you physically up to it? Tour operators are responsible for their clients' well-being and safety, but that doesn't let you off the hook in terms of personal responsibility. Inquire about your guide's experience, safety record, and insurance policy. Remember, no adventure trip is 100% risk-free.

RECOMMENDED OPERATORS   The following U.S.-based adventure operators offer solid, well-organized tours, and they are backed by years of experience. Most of these operators are expensive, a few are exorbitant (remember that prices do not include airfare), but that usually is because they include luxury accommodations and gourmet dining. Most offer trips to hot spots like Patagonia, and operators with trips to that region are listed here for both Argentina and Chile.

- **Abercrombie & Kent,** 1520 Kensington Rd., Oak Brook, IL 60521 (☎ **800/ 323-7308;** www.abercrombiekent.com), is a luxury tour operator that offers a "Patagonia: A Natural Playground" trip that heads from Buenos Aires to Ushuaia for a 3-day cruise around Tierra del Fuego, followed by visits to Torres del Paine park, Puerto Varas, and Bariloche. Cost is $6,980 per person, double occupancy. This trip also features a 4-day extension to Iguazu Falls.
- **Butterfield and Robinson,** 70 Bond St., Toronto, Canada M5B 1X3 (☎ **800/ 678-1147;** www.butterfieldandrobinson.com; e-mail: info@butterfield.com), is another gourmet tour operator, with a walking-oriented, 10-day trip to Patagonia starting in El Calafate, Argentina and finishing in Punta Arenas, Chile. In between, travelers visit national parks Los Glaciares and Torres del Paine, with visits to the Perito Moreno glacier and lodging in fine lodges and ranches. Cost is $5,975 per person, double occupancy.
- **Mountain-Travel Sobek,** 6420 Fairmount Ave., El Cerrito, CA 94530 (☎ **888/ MTSOBEK** or 510/527-8100; fax 510/525-7718; www.mtsobek.com; e-mail: info@mtsobek.com), are the pioneers of organized adventure travel, and they offer trips that involve a lot of physical activity. One of their more gung-ho journeys traverses part of the Patagonian Ice Cap in Fitzroy National Park for 21 days; a more moderate Patagonia Explorer mixes hiking with cruising. Prices run

from $1,500 to $3,000 and more. Sobek always comes recommended for their excellent guides.

- **Backroads Active Vacations,** 801 Cedar St., Berkeley, CA 94710-1800 (☎ **800/GO-ACTIVE** or 510/527-1555; www.backroads.com), offers a biking tour through the lake districts of Chile and Argentina, with stops in Villa La Angostura and San Martín de los Andes; an afternoon of rafting is included. There's also a hiking trip through the same region, and a 9-day hiking trip in Patagonia that begins in El Calafate and travels between the two countries. Guests lodge in luxury hotels and inns. Costs run from $3,798 to $5,298.

- **Wilderness Travel,** 1102 Ninth St., Berkeley, CA 94710 (☎ **800/368-2794** or 510/558-2488; www.wildernesstravel.com; e-mail: webinfo@wildernesstravel. com), offers a more mellow sightseeing/day hiking tour around Patagonia, including Los Glaciares, Ushuaia, El Calafate, and the Perito Moreno Glacier. The trip costs $4,495 to $5,095, depending on the number of guests (maximum 15).

- **Wildland Adventures,** 3516 NE 155th St., Seattle, WA 98155 (☎ **800/ 345-4453** or 206/365-0686; www.wildland.com), offers a few adventure tours of Argentina. The "Salta Trek Through Silent Valleys" tour takes in Salta, Jujuy, and the Andean plain. Two Patagonia tours are offered: "Best of Patagonia," which concentrates on Argentine Patagonia (including Peninsula Valdes, Rio Gallegos, Perito Moreno, and Ushuaia); and "Los Glaciares Adventure," which visits El Calafate, Fitzroy National Park, and Perito Moreno Glacier, among others. Accommodation ranges from hotels to camping to rustic park lodges. Eco-tourism is an integral part of Wildland tours. Prices start at $1,380 for the 8-day Salta tour and continue upwards of $3,000 for the 2-week Patagonia trip.

Fast Facts: Argentina

American Express   Offices are located in Buenos Aires, Bariloche, Salta, San Martín, and Ushuaia. In Buenos Aires, the Amex office is at Arenales 707 (☎ **11/4130-3135**).

Business Hours   Banks are open weekdays 10am to 3pm. Shopping hours are weekdays 9am to 8pm and Saturday 9am to 1pm. Shopping centers are open daily 10am to 8pm. Some stores close for lunch.

Climate   See "When to Go," earlier in this chapter.

Currency   See "Money," earlier in this chapter.

Documents   See "Entry Requirements & Customs," earlier in this chapter.

Driving Rules   In cities, Argentines drive exceedingly fast, and do not always obey traffic lights or lanes. Seat belts are mandatory, although few Argentines actually wear them. When driving outside the city, remember that *autopista* means motorway or highway, and *paso* means mountain pass. Don't drive in rural areas at night, as cattle sometimes overtake the road to keep warm and are nearly impossible to see.

Drugstores   Ask your hotel where the nearest pharmacy (*farmacia*) is; they are generally ubiquitous in city centers, and there is always at least one open 24 hours. In Buenos Aires, the chain Farmacity is open 24 hours, with locations at Lavalle 919 (☎ **11/4821-3000**) and Av. Santa Fe 2830 (☎ **11/4821-0235**). They will also deliver to your hotel .

Electricity   If you plan to bring a hair dryer, radio, travel iron, or any other small appliance, pack a transformer and a European-style adapter, since electricity in Argentina runs on 220 volts. Note that most laptops operate on both 110 and 220 volts. Luxury hotels usually have transformers and adapters available.

Embassies   These are all in Buenos Aires: **U.S. Embassy,** Av. Colombia 4300 (☎ 11/4774-5333); **Australian Embassy,** Villanueva 1400 (☎ 11/4777-6580); **Canadian Embassy,** Tagle 2828 (☎ 11/4805-3032); **New Zealand Embassy,** Echeverria 2140 (☎ 11/4787-0583); **South African Embassy,** Marcelo T. de Alvear (☎ 11/4317-2900); **United Kingdom Embassy,** Luis Agote 2412 (☎ 11/4803-6021).

Emergencies   The following emergency numbers are valid throughout Argentina. For an ambulance, call ☎ **107;** in case of fire, call ☎ **1100;** for police assistance, call ☎ **101.**

Information   See "Visitor Information," earlier in this chapter.

Internet Access   Cybercafes have begun to pop up on seemingly every corner in Buenos Aires, and are found in other cities as well, so it won't be hard to stay connected while in Argentina. Access is reasonably priced (usually averaging $2.50 to $5 per hour) and connections are reliably good.

Mail   Airmail postage for a letter 7 ounces or less from Argentina to North America and Europe is $1. Mail takes on average between 10 and 14 days to get to the U.S. and Europe.

Maps   Reliable maps can be purchased at the offices of the Automóvil Club Argentino, Av. del Libertador 1850, in Buenos Aires (☎ **11/4802-6061** or 11/4802-7071).

Newspapers & Magazines   The *International Herald Tribune* is widely available at news kiosks around the country. The *Buenos Aires Herald* is the (quite good) local English newspaper. Some hotels in Buenos Aires will deliver a *New York Times* headline news fax to your room; inquire when booking or checking in.

Safety   While Buenos Aires was once among the world's safest cities, petty crime (particularly pickpockets and purse snatching) has increased as Argentina's economy has stagnated. Tourist areas remain well patrolled, however, and you needn't be concerned if you take sensible precautions and avoid walking alone late at night. San Telmo, La Boca, Monserrat, and the suburbs of Buenos Aires are better avoided at night. Smaller towns in Argentina are safer; ask your hotel staff or the local visitor center for an update on safety issues.

Smoking   Smoking is a pervasive aspect of Argentinean society, and you will find that most everyone lights up in restaurants and clubs. You can, however, request a no-smoking table in a restaurant, and you will usually be accommodated.

Taxes   Argentina's value added tax (VAT) is 21%. You can recover this 21% at the airport if you have purchased local products totaling more than $200 (per invoice) from stores participating in tax-free shopping. Forms are available at the airport.

Telephone   The country code for Argentina is **54.** When making domestic long-distance calls in Argentina, place a 0 before the area code. For international calls, add 00 before the country code. Direct dialing to North America and

Europe is available from most phones. International, as well as domestic, calls are expensive in Argentina, especially from hotels (rates fall between 10pm and 8am). Holders of AT&T credit cards can reach the money-saving **USA Direct** from Argentina by calling toll-free ☎ **0800/555-4288** from the north of Argentina or 0800/222-1288 from the south. Similar services are offered by **MCI Worldcom** (☎ **0800/555-1002**) and **Sprint** (☎ **0800/555-1003** from the north of Argentina, or 0800/222-1003 from the south).

Public phones take either phone cards (sold at kiosks on the street) or coins (less common). Local calls cost 20 centavos to start and charge more the longer you talk. Telecentro offices—found everywhere in city centers—offer private phone booths where calls are paid when completed. Most hotels offer fax services, as do all telecentro offices. Dial **110** for directory assistance (most operators will speak English) and **000** to reach an international operator.

Time   Argentina does not adopt daylight savings time, so the country is 1 hour ahead of eastern standard time in the United States in summer and 2 hours ahead in winter.

Tipping   A 10% tip is expected at cafes and restaurants. Give at least $1 to bellboys and porters, 5% to hairdressers, and leftover change to taxi drivers.

Water   In Buenos Aires, the water is perfectly safe to drink. But if you are traveling to more remote regions of Argentina, it's best to stick with bottled water for drinking.

3 Buenos Aires

The elegance of Europe and the spirit of South America live side by side in Buenos Aires. Founded by immigrants along the shores of the Rio de la Plata, Buenos Aires built its identity on Spanish, Italian, and French influences, which appear in the grand boulevards, expansive parks, magnificent architecture, and ever-changing fashion of Argentina's beautiful capital. Take a walk through neighborhoods like Recoleta and Belgrano, for example, and you'll be convinced you're in the 16th district of Paris. Even *Porteños,* as residents of Buenos Aires are called, characterize themselves as more European than South American.

If Buenos Aires has a European face, its soul is intensely Latin. This is a city where the sun shines brightly, where people speak passionately, where family and friendship still come first. It is a city where locals go outside to interact, lining the streets, packing cafe terraces, and strolling in parks and plazas. Visit the historic neighborhoods of San Telmo and La Boca, where the first immigrants arrived, and you will find working-class Argentines living alongside the city's oldest tango salons. Stand in Plaza de Mayo, the historic center of Buenos Aires where citizens gather in pivotal moments, to gain a sense of the city's political and social dynamism. And walk along the revived harbor of Puerto Madero to see where Argentina reaches out to the rest of the world.

While exploring Buenos Aires, you will find a city of contradictions. Great wealth exists alongside considerable—if often hidden—poverty. The economy has been stagnant, but hotels and restaurants remain inexplicably full. *Porteños* seem self-assured, although the population is intensely image-conscious. And Buenos Aires defines Argentina, yet has little to do with the rest of the country. All these elements demonstrate the complexity of a city searching for identity among its South American and European influences. And they make Buenos Aires an unusual and fascinating place.

1 Orientation

ARRIVING

BY PLANE International flights arrive at **Ezeiza International Airport** (☎ **11/4480-6111**), located 21 miles (34km) west of downtown Buenos Aires. You can reach the city with several shuttle

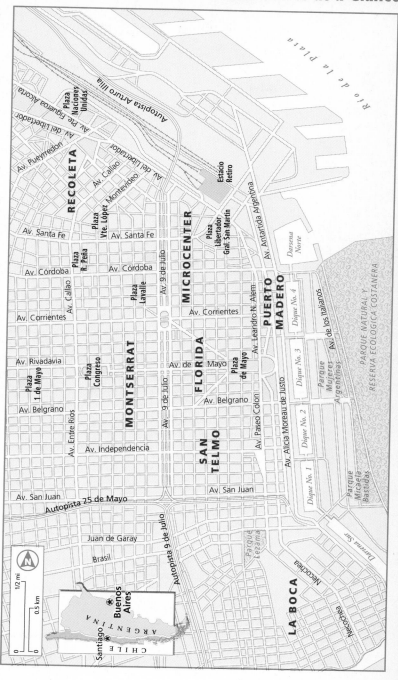

Río de la Plata

Autopista Arturo Illia

Plaza Naciones Unidas

Av. Pte. Figueroa Alcorta

Av. del Libertador

Plaza
Vte. López

Av. Callao

Montevideo

Av. Pueyrredón

RECOLETA

Av. del Libertador

Estádio
Retiro

Av. Santa Fe

Av. Santa Fe

Plaza
R. Peña

Av. Córdoba

Av. Córdoba

Plaza
Libertador
Gral. San Martín

Av. Antártida Argentina

MICROCENTER

Av. Callao

Plaza
Lavalle

Av. 9 de Julio

**PUERTO
MADERO**

*Dársena
Norte*

Av. Corrientes

Av. Corrientes

Av. Leandro N. Alem

Dique No. 4

Av. de los Italianos

Av. Rivadavia

FLORIDA

Av. de Mayo

Plaza
de Mayo

Dique No. 3

*Parque
Mujeres
Argentinas*

*PARQUE NATURAL Y
RESERVA ECOLÓGICA COSTANERA*

Plaza
Congreso

MONTSERRAT

Av. 9 de Julio

Plaza
1 de Mayo

Av. Belgrano

Av. Belgrano

Av. Paseo Colón

Dique No. 2

Av. Entre Ríos

Av. Independencia

**SAN
TELMO**

Av. Alicia Moreau de Justo

Dique No. 1

*Parque
Micaela
Bastidas*

Av. San Juan

Av. San Juan

Av. San Juan

Autopista 25 de Mayo

Juan de Garay

Brasil

Autopista 9 de Julio

*Parque
Lezama*

Dársena Sur

Necochea

LA BOCA

Necochea

1/2 mi

0.5 km

0

0

**Buenos
Aires**

CHILE

ARGENTINA

Santiago

Frommer's Favorite Buenos Aires Experiences

- **Have Coffee at Café Tortoni.** This historic cafe has served as the artistic and intellectual capital of Buenos Aires since 1858, serving personalities like Jorge Luis Borges, Julio de Caro, Cátulo Castillo, and José Gobello. Come for coffee or a light meal, or catch an evening tango show in the back room.

- **Visit Plaza de Mayo at Sunset.** Historic buildings surround the square, which has served as the political and social gathering spot for *Porteños* during the nation's most important moments. The changing of the guard takes place every hour on the hour in front of the Casa Rosada, the building from which Evita once addressed great crowds.

- **Go to the San Telmo Antiques Market.** The Sunday market is as much a cultural event as a commercial one, as old-time tango and *milonga* dancers take to the streets with other performers. Here you will glimpse Buenos Aires much as it was at the beginning of the 20th century.

- **Wander Caminito Street in La Boca.** Capture the flavor of early Buenos Aires on this short historic street, considered something of an outdoor museum. ✪ The Caminito is famous for the brightly colored sheet-metal houses that border it and for the sculptures, paintings, and wall murals lining it. Street performers and dancers are here every day.

- **Visit the Recoleta Cemetery.** This beautiful cemetery houses expensive mausoleums competing for grandeur—a place where people can remain rich, even after death. Among the only non-aristocrats buried here is Eva Perón, or Evita. Some of Argentina's upper class still believe she has no right to be here.

- **Peek Inside the Alvear Palace Hotel.** While you're in Recoleta, stop inside this exclusive boutique hotel, the most luxurious in the city. If you weren't convinced this was Paris before, you might change your mind. Pull the coattails of one of the bell boys and run.

- **Take a Stroll Along the Riverfront in Puerto Madero.** Revived 5 years ago by the local government, the old port has become the city's most fashionable dining area and has numerous bars and lounges. Everything is located along the waterfront.

companies and *remise* (airport taxi) services; you will see official stands with exact fares in the airport once you clear customs. Taxis from the airport to the center of town cost about $35.

Domestic flights and flights to Uruguay use **Jorge Newbery Airport** (☎ 11/4514-1515), located only 15 minutes from downtown. Inexpensive taxis and *remises* ($6 to $10) will get you to and from the city center.

BY BUS   The **Estación Terminal de Omnibus,** Av. Ramos Mejía 1680 (☎ 11/4310-0700), located near Retiro Station, serves all long-distance buses.

BY CAR   In Buenos Aires, travel by *subte* (subway) or taxi is easier and safer than driving yourself. Rush-hour traffic is chaotic, and parking difficult. If you do rent a car, park it at your hotel and leave it there.

- **Enjoy Opera at the Teatro Colón.** The majestic theater is considered to have some of the best acoustics of any theater on the globe. World-class opera singers perform here, and the Colón has its own opera, ballet, and symphony companies.

- **Watch a Tango Show.** The best clubs are in San Telmo, and the most famous is El Viejo Almacén. Most combine dinner and tango show, and have excellent musicians and dancers. Many five-star hotels offer afternoon tango shows in their lobbies, and you can catch a free tango show on the streets of San Telmo or La Boca.

- **Learn to Dance Tango.** *Salones de baile,* as tango salons are called, blanket the city. In these salons you can watch traditional Argentine tango danced by all generations, and most offer lessons before the floor opens up to dancers. You won't find many novices on the dance floor after midnight, however.

- **Shop at Galerías Pacífico.** This luxurious mall along the pedestrian walking street Florida is as nice as any you will find in America or Europe, and gives you a good taste of Argentine fashion.

- **Eat a Juicy Argentine Steak in a *Parrilla*.** This will not be difficult since every restaurant serves Argentine steaks and every other restaurant is a *parrilla.*

- **Catch a Polo Match.** Argentina has won more international polo tournaments than any other country, and the Argentine Open Championship, held each November, is the world's most important polo event. Polo season runs March through May and September through December.

- **See the Boca Juniors Play Soccer.** Argentines go crazy for soccer, and no team arouses more passion than the Boca Juniors, traditionally the team of the working class.

- **Try an Argentine Wine.** Argentine wines from Mendoza, San Juan, and Salta are exported across the world. Argentina is famous for its Malbec, but most of its other reds are actually quite good.

VISITOR INFORMATION

Obtain tourist information for Argentina from the **Tourism Secretariat of the Nation,** Av. Santa Fe 883, 1059 (☎ **11/4312-2232** or 0800/555-0016). There are branches at Ezeiza International Airport and Jorge Newbery Airport as well.

The **Information Office of the Tourism Department of Buenos Aires** can be reached weekdays 10am to 5pm by calling ☎ **11/4372-3612.** Tourist information centers for the city of Buenos Aires are located at Av. Sarmiento 1551, Calle Florida and Diagonal Norte, Galerías Pacífico, Puerto Madero, Café Tortoni, and Caminito Street. Most are open weekdays 10am to 5pm. The center on Caminito Street in La Boca is open weekends 10am to 5pm.

CITY LAYOUT

While Buenos Aires is a huge city, the main tourist neighborhoods are concentrated in a very small, comparatively wealthy section near the Río de la Plata. The "microcenter," which extends from Plaza de Mayo to the south and Plaza San Martín to the north, and from Plaza del Congreso to the west and Puerto Madero to the east, forms the city center. San Telmo, La Boca, Puerto Madero, Recoleta, and Palermo immediately surround the microcenter. The city layout is fairly straightforward, where *avenidas* signify two-way avenues and *calles* one-way streets, while *diagonales* cut streets and avenues at 45-degree angles. Each city block extends 100m (328 ft.), and building addresses indicate the distance on that street.

The **microcenter** includes Plaza de Mayo (the political and historic center of Buenos Aires), Plaza San Martín, and 9 de Julio Avenue (the widest street in the world). Most commercial activity is focused here, as are the majority of hotels and restaurants. Next to the microcenter, the revived riverfront area called **Puerto Madero** boasts excellent restaurants and nightlife as well as new commercial areas. A bit farther south, **La Boca, Monserrat,** and **San Telmo** are the historic neighborhoods of Buenos Aires where the first immigrants arrived and *milonga* and tango originated.

The city's most strikingly European neighborhood, **Recoleta,** offers fashionable restaurants, cafes, and evening entertainment amid rich French architecture. It's home to the city's main cultural center as well as the Recoleta Cemetery, where key personalities like Evita are buried. To the northwest, **Palermo** is a neighborhood of parks, mansions, and gardens—perfect for a weekend picnic or evening outing. Another similarly wealthy neighborhood, **Belgrano,** lies farther west.

STREET MAPS   Ask the front desk of your hotel for a copy of "The Golden Map" and "QuickGuide Buenos Aires" to help you navigate the city and locate its major attractions.

GETTING AROUND

The Buenos Aires metro—called the *subte*—is the fastest and cheapest way to navigate the city. Buses are also convenient, although less commonly used by tourists. Maps of metro and bus lines are available from tourist offices and most hotels (ask for the "QuickGuide Buenos Aires"). In addition, all metro stations and most bus stops have maps.

BY METRO   Five *subte* lines connect commercial and tourist areas in the city Monday to Saturday 5am to 10pm and Sunday and holidays 8am to 10pm. The flat fare is 60¢, with tickets purchased at machines or windows at every station. Line A connects Plaza de Mayo to Primera Junta. Line B runs from near Puerto Madero (Avenida Leandro N. Alem) to Federico Lacroze. Line C travels between the city's train stations, Retiro and Constitución. Line D runs from Juramento to Catedral. Line E links Bolívar with Plaza de los Virreyes. While the *subte* is the fastest and cheapest way to travel in Buenos Aires, it gets crowded during rush hours and hot in summer.

Please note that neither the Recoleta nor Puerto Madero neighborhoods have *subte* access. Most of Puerto Madero, however, can be reached via the L.N. Alem subte (anywhere from a 5- to a 20-minute walk, depending on which dock you're going to).

BY BUS   One hundred and forty bus lines operate in Buenos Aires 24 hours a day. Local buses, called *colectivos,* are mostly used by city workers. The minimum fare is 65¢ and goes up depending on distance traveled. Pay your fare inside the bus to an electronic ticket machine accepting coins only. Many bus drivers, provided you can communicate with them, will tell you the fare for your destination and help you with where to get off.

BY TAXI   Like little busy bees, thousands of black and yellow cabs crowd the streets of Buenos Aires. Fares are relatively inexpensive, with an initial meter reading of $1.10 increasing 15¢ every 200m (218 yds.) or each minute. Radio taxis are safer than street taxis and only marginally more expensive (usually an additional $1.50). To request a cab by phone, call **Radio Taxi Pidalo** at ☎ **11/4956-1200.** These are sample prices from downtown Buenos Aires: to La Plata, $50; to Ezeiza International Airport, $35; to Tigre, $25; and to San Isidro, $20.

BY CAR   Driving in Buenos Aires is like jungle warfare: Never mind the lane, disregard the light, and honk your way through traffic. It's far safer, and cheaper, to use public transportation, hail a taxi, or hire a private driver (usually about $25 per hour) with the help of your hotel or travel agent. If you must drive, international car rental companies abound—but it's not cheap. A subcompact with only 50 free kilometers (31 miles) starts at over $50 per day, while a similar car with unlimited mileage runs about $90. Most hotels offer parking for a fee—usually between $15 and $20 per day.

Car Rentals   Rental cars are available from **Hertz** (☎ **800/654-3131** in the U.S.), Paraguay 1122 (☎ 11/4816-8001); **Avis** (☎ **800/230-4898** in the U.S.), Cerrito 1527 (☎ 11/4300-8201); **Dollar** (☎ **800/800-6000** in the U.S.), Marcelo T. de Alvear 523 (☎ 11/4315-8800); and **Thrifty** (☎ **800/847-4389** in the U.S.), Av. Leandro N. Alem 699 (☎ 11/4315-0777).

ON FOOT   Buenos Aires is a walker's city, and you'll find far more pedestrians than vehicles. The microcenter is small enough to navigate by foot, and you can quickly connect to adjacent neighborhoods by catching a taxi or using the *subte*. If you have several days in Buenos Aires, it makes sense to slice your time into segments for walking tours—so you spend a day in the microcenter, for example, an evening in Puerto Madero, another day in La Boca and San Telmo, and another day in Recoleta and Palermo. Plazas, parks, and pedestrian walkways are omnipresent in the city center.

Fast Facts: Buenos Aires

American Express   The enormous American Express building is located next to Plaza San Martín, at Arenales 707 (☎ **11/4130-3135**). The travel agency is open Monday to Friday 9am to 6pm, while the bank is open Monday to Friday 9am to 5pm. In addition to card-member services, the bank offers currency exchange (dollars only), money orders, check cashing, and refunds.

Area Code   The area code for Buenos Aires is **11.** The country code for Argentina is **54.**

Business Hours   Banks are generally open weekdays 10am to 3pm. Shopping hours are Monday to Friday 9am to 8pm and Saturday 9am to 1pm. Shopping centers are open daily 10am to 8pm. Some stores close for lunch.

Currency Exchange   You can typically use American dollars just as easily as pesos in Buenos Aires (although torn or damaged dollars aren't accepted), and credit cards are widely used. If you must change money or cash traveler's checks, it's easier to do so at the airport, your hotel, or an independent exchange house rather than an Argentine bank. **American Express** (see above) offers the best rates on its traveler's checks and charges no commission. It offers currency exchange for dollars only, and is open Monday to Friday 9am to 5pm. ATMs are plentiful in Buenos Aires. You can have money wired to **Western Union,** Av. Córdoba 917 (☎ **11/4322-7774**).

Embassies/Consulates   See "Fast Facts: Argentina" in chapter 2, "Planning a Trip to Argentina."

Emergencies   For an ambulance, call ☎ **107;** in case of fire, call ☎ **100;** for police assistance, call ☎ **101;** for an English-speaking hospital, call ☎ **11/4304-1081.**

Language   Shops, hotels, and restaurants are usually staffed by at least one or two fluent English speakers, and many people speak at least a few words of English.

Newspapers/Magazines   The *Buenos Aires Herald* is published daily and includes a brief but well-written summary of events in Argentina and abroad. Many luxury hotels deliver it to your room, or it can be purchased at newsstands for $1. Many streetside kiosks sell the *International Herald Tribune, New York Times,* and *Financial Times,* but are often a day or two behind. You can sometimes find current editions of major American and European magazines, but they are likely to be dated as well.

Police   Dial ☎ **101** or 11/4346-7000.

Post Office   You never have to venture more than a few blocks to find a post office, open weekdays 9am to 6pm and Saturday until 1pm. The main post office, or *Correo Central,* is at Av. Sarmiento 151 (☎ **11/4311-5040**).

Safety   Crime in Buenos Aires—especially pickpocketing, robberies, and car thefts—has increased steadily in recent years as the economy has stagnated, although it's generally safe to walk around the microcenter both day and evening. Some tourist areas deemed safe by day, like San Telmo, La Boca, and Monserrat, are better avoided at night. Tourists should take care not to be overly conspicuous, walking in pairs or groups when possible.

Taxes   The sales tax, or VAT, is 21% and is already included in the sales price. At the airport, you can recover this 21% if you have purchased local products amounting to more than $200 per invoice from participating shops.

Taxis   See "Getting Around," earlier in this chapter.

Telephone   Unless you are calling from your hotel (which will be expensive, whether international or domestic), the easiest way to place calls in Buenos Aires is by going to a branch of *telecentro,* the country's telecommunications company, found on nearly every city block. Private booths allow you to place as many calls as you like, after which you pay an attendant. A running meter gives you an idea what the call will cost. Most *telecentros* also have fax and Internet machines.

While there are some coin-operated public phones in Buenos Aires, most require a calling card, available at kiosks. Local calls, like all others, are charged by the minute. Dial ☎ **110** for information, ☎ **000** to reach an international operator. To dial another number in Argentina from Buenos Aires, dial the area code first, then the local number. *Note:* If you call someone's cellular phone in Argentina, the call is also charged to you, and can cost over $1 per minute.

Tipping   A 10% tip is expected at cafes and restaurants. Give at least $1 to bellboys and porters, 5% to hairdressers, and leftover change to taxis.

2 Where to Stay

Hotels in Buenos Aires are almost always full in high season, so be sure to book ahead. The best hotels are found in Recoleta and the microcenter; the new Hilton in Puerto Madero is close to the center. Recoleta is more scenic and not quite as noisy as the microcenter. Prices listed below are rack rates in high season; discounts are often available for weekends and low season. Check-in time is generally 3pm; checkout is at noon. Most hotels charge $15 to $20 per night for valet parking. (Self-parking is not really an option; I definitely do *not* recommend trying to park on the street.)

By comparison with hotels in major American and European cities, accommodations in Buenos Aires are overpriced for the quality. Many are older and in need of renovation. We have chosen the best hotels for each price category, but you should not expect modernity in every case.

All five-star and most four-star hotels in Buenos Aires offer in-room safes, cable TV, direct dial phones with voice mail, and in-room modem access. Most of the hotels named in this guide, except the least expensive options, are designated four or five stars.

PUERTO MADERO

There are no convenient metro stops to this neighborhood.

EXPENSIVE

✪ **Hilton Buenos Aires.** Av. Macacha Guemes 351, 1107 Buenos Aires. ☎ **11/ 4891-0000.** Fax 11/4891-0001. www.hilton.com. 430 units. A/C MINIBAR TV TEL. From $260 double. AE, DC, MC, V.

The Hilton has been the talk of the town since its opening in April 2000. As the first major hotel and convention center in Puerto Madero, it promises to contribute markedly to the growth of this redesigned port area. A shopping center, sea museum, and cinemas are being built near the hotel, which also lies within easy walking distance of some of the best restaurants in Buenos Aires. The strikingly contemporary hotel—a sleek silver block hoisted on stilts—features a seven-story atrium with over 400 guest rooms and an additional number of private residences.

Guest rooms are large, modern, and functional. They feature two telephone lines with modem connections, large-screen televisions, big closets, and spacious bathrooms with separate bathtubs and showers. Those staying on the executive floors get complimentary breakfast and have access to a private concierge. A large hotel staff means that all guest needs are prioritized, and you can expect this hotel to become a favorite of both business travelers and tourists in Buenos Aires.

Dining/Diversions: There is a lobby bar and a restaurant serving California cuisine, with a focus on seafood.

Amenities: Corporate meeting facilities, two ballrooms, exhibition center, executive floors, business center and secretarial services, concierge, modern gym facility with open-air pool deck and a service of light snacks and beverages, room service, dry cleaning and laundry service, newspaper delivery, nightly turndown.

RECOLETA

There are no convenient metro stops to this neighborhood.

VERY EXPENSIVE

✪ **Alvear Palace Hotel.** Av. Alvear 1891, 1129 Buenos Aires. ☎ **0800-44HOTEL** (local toll-free), or 11/4808-2100. Fax 11/4804-0034. www.alvearpalace.com. E-mail: alvear@ satlink.com. 200 units, 12 salons. A/C MINIBAR TV TEL. From $410 double; from $475 suite. Rates include buffet breakfast. AE, DC, MC, V.

Located in the center of the upscale Recoleta district, the Alvear Palace Hotel sits at the apex of the city's luxury hotel market. It's decorated with beautiful flower arrangements, Empire- and Louis XV–style furniture, original oil paintings, and carefully

Buenos Aires Accommodations & Dining

DINING ◆
Bistro Galani **44**
Bonpler **15**
Broccolino **32**
Cabaña las Lilas **8**
Café de la Paix **50**
Café Tortoni **7**
Café Victoria **54**
Catalinas **20**
Clark's **52**
Club Español **6**
The Coffee Store **31**
De Olivas i Lustres **55**
Harry Cipriani **47**
Katrine **12**
La Brigada **2**
La Casa de Esteban
  de Lucas **1**
La Chacra **34**
Las Nazarenas **26**
Ligure **43**
Lola **53**
Massey **45**
Morizono **23**
Parilla al Carbon
  Eva y Roberto **3**
Petit Paris Café **42**
The Pier Café **10**
Plaza Hotel Grill **29**
Primera Plana **46**
Restaurante y Bar
  Mediterraneo **5**
Schlotzsky's Deli **13**
Sorrento del Puerto **11**

ACCOMMODATIONS ■
Amerian Buenos Aires **19**
Alvear Palace **49**
Best Western Embassy **35**
Bisonte Palace **38**
Caesar Park **48**
Claridge Hotel **18**
Clarion Aspen Towers **39**
Comfort Inn &
  Suites Esmeralda **40**
Courtyard Marriott **30**
El Conquistador **36**
Etoile Hotel **51**
Goya Hotel **33**
Gran Hotel Dora **16**
Grand King Hotel **17**
Hilton Buenos Aires **9**
Holiday Inn Express **22**
Hotel Crillon **41**
Hotel Nogaro **4**
InterContinental **5**
Lancaster Hotel **21**
Liberty Hotel **14**
Marriott Plaza Hotel **28**
Melia Confort **24**
Park Hyatt **44**
Park Tower **27**
Regente Palace **37**
Sheraton **28**
Tulip Inn **25**

chosen objets d'art. Spacious guest rooms combine modern technical conveniences, like multiple phone lines and in-room Internet access, with traditional comforts like chandelier lighting, feather beds, plush carpeting, and silk drapes. Half of the hotel rooms are suites, perfect for business or entertaining.

Guests are pampered with fresh flowers and fruit baskets in their rooms upon arrival, daily newspaper delivery, complimentary shoeshine and clothes pressing, and personal butler service on request. Large marble bathrooms offer Hermès toiletries, terrycloth robes, and in some cases whirlpool baths. Hotel service is sharp and professional, but the elite clientele also makes the staff a bit standoffish. Ask for a toothbrush or other amenity and it will arrive at your room within minutes, but don't expect to have a conversation with the person who brings it. Likewise, the lobby is a place to impress clients, not to make them feel at home (note the semiformal dress code).

Dining: There are two excellent restaurants, **L'Orangerie** and **La Bourgogne.** The former is a popular spot for power breakfasts and business lunches during the week, while the latter serves refined and expensive French cuisine under the direction of acclaimed chef Jean Paul Bondoux. A wonderful buffet breakfast is served in the **Jardin d'Hiver,** a sunlit atrium room filled with plants and flowers. Afternoon tea is served there too.

Amenities: Elegant health club with an indoor pool, exercise room, massage service, and sauna; business center; conference rooms; concierge; room service; dry cleaning and laundry service; newspaper delivery; nightly turndown; executive business services.

Caesar Park. Posadas 1232, 1014 Buenos Aires. ☎ **11/4819-1100.** Fax 11/4819-1121. www.caesar.com.ar. 170 untis. A/C MINIBAR TV TEL. From $347 double. AE, DC, MC, V. Free valet parking.

This classic hotel sits opposite Patio Bullrich, the city's most exclusive shopping mall. Guest rooms vary in size and amenities, but all have been tastefully appointed with fine furniture and elegant linens, marble bathrooms with separate bathtubs and showers, entertainment centers with TVs and stereos, and desks with dual-line phones and Internet connections. Larger rooms come with a fresh fruit basket on the first night's stay. The Caesar Park boasts four restaurants and bars, including a Japanese steak and sushi house.

Dining/Diversions: Restaurants include **Café de la Plate, Midori Japanese,** and **Cheers** (an English-style bar); there's also a lobby piano bar.

Amenities: Indoor pool, fitness center, massage service, and sauna; business center; conference rooms; concierge; room service; dry cleaning and laundry service; newspaper delivery; nightly turndown; beauty salon; executive business services.

Park Hyatt Buenos Aires. Posadas 1086/88, 1011 Buenos Aires. ☎ **11/4321-1234.** Fax 11/4321-1235. www.buenosaires.hyatt.com. E-mail: hotel@parkhyatt.com.ar. 158 units, 7 suites in La Mansion. A/C MINIBAR TV TEL. $340–405 double; from $435 suite (from $750 in La Mansion). AE, DC, MC, V.

One of the most luxurious—and expensive—hotels in Argentina, the Park Hyatt caters to business executives and international celebrities visiting Buenos Aires. There are two parts to the hotel—the 12-story "Park" tower housing the majority of guest rooms, and the turn-of-the-last-century French-Rococo "La Mansion" with seven elegant suites and a handful of private event rooms. This is where Madonna stayed during the filming of *Evita,* and it's where the Rolling Stones lodge when they're in town. A French-style garden and a lovely pool separate the two buildings, and there's a well-equipped health club offering spa treatments.

Spacious guest rooms offer atypical amenities like walk-in closets, wet and dry bars, stereo systems, and cellular phones. Large bathrooms, with separate bathtubs and showers, display so much marble you'll wonder if it took an entire Italian quarry to furnish them. People staying on the executive floors enjoy even larger rooms, additional amenities, complimentary breakfast and afternoon tea, and access to a private concierge.

Dining/Diversions: A lobby bar, **Le Dome,** is a popular spot for business lunches, afternoon tea (featuring live piano music and a tango show), and evening cocktails. The hotel's restaurant, **Bistro Galani,** serves Mediterranean cuisine in a casual environment.

Amenities: Health club "Olympus" with a heated outdoor pool, exercise room, massage service, and sauna; business center; conference rooms; concierge; room service; dry cleaning and laundry service; newspaper delivery; nightly turndown; executive business services.

EXPENSIVE

Etoile Hotel. Pte. Roberto M. Ortiz 1835, 1113 Buenos Aires. ☎ **11/4805-2626.** Fax 11/4805-3613. www.etoile.com.ar. E-mail: hotel@etoile.com.ar. 96 units. A/C MINIBAR TV TEL. From $200 double. Rates include buffet breakfast. AE, DC, MC, V.

Located in the heart of Recoleta just steps away from the neighborhood's fashionable restaurants and cafes, the 14-story Etoile is an older hotel with a Turkish flair. If it's not as luxurious as the city's other five-star hotels, it is not as expensive either—making it a good value for Recoleta. The common areas remind you of a visit to the Middle East; notice the wall rugs depicting scenes reminiscent of Arabian nights. Colored in gold and cream, guest rooms are fairly large—although they're not really "suites," as the hotel describes them. Executive rooms have separate sitting areas, large tile-floor bathrooms with whirlpool baths, and balconies. Rooms facing south offer balconies overlooking Plaza Francia and the Recoleta Cemetery.

Dining: Pigalle Restaurant serves international cuisine accompanied by soft piano music.

Amenities: Rooftop health club with indoor pool, exercise room, Turkish bath, and sauna; conference rooms; concierge; room service; dry cleaning and laundry service; nightly turndown; executive business services.

MONSERRAT
VERY EXPENSIVE/EXPENSIVE

Hotel Nogaro. Av. Pte. Julio A. Roca 562, 1067 Buenos Aires. ☎ **11/4331-0091/99.** Fax 11/4331-6791. www.nogarobue.com.ar. E-mail: reservas@nogarobue.com.ar. 140 units. A/C MINIBAR TV TEL. $125–145 double; from $189 suite. Rates include buffet breakfast. AE, DC, MC, V. Metro: Monserrat.

One of the best finds in the neighborhood, Hotel Nogaro's grand marble staircase leads to a variety of guest rooms noteworthy for their comfort and quietness. Deluxe rooms boast hardwood floors and high ceilings, small but modern bathrooms with hair dryers, and whirlpool tubs in the suites. Standard rooms, while smaller, are pleasant too, with red carpet, large closets, and a bit of modern art.

Dining/Diversions: There is a handsome international restaurant and bar.

Amenities: Business center, conference rooms, 24-hour room service, laundry service. The staff will also arrange sightseeing tours, car rentals, and baby-sitting.

Inter-Continental. Moreno 809, 1091 Buenos Aires. ☎ **11/4340-7100.** Fax 11/4340-7119. www.buenos-aires.interconti.com. E-mail: buenosaires@interconti.com. 315 units. A/C MINIBAR TV TEL. $225–$375 double; from $515 suite. AE, DC, MC, V. Valet parking $20. Metro: Piedras Bolivar.

The Inter-Continental is one of the capital's newest five-star hotels. Despite its modernity, this luxurious tower hotel was built in the city's oldest district, Monserrat, and decorated in the Argentine style of the 1930s. The marble lobby is colored in beige and apricot tones, with handsome furniture and antiques inlaid with stones and agates. The lobby's Café de las Luces, in which you might catch a glimpse of an evening tango performance, resembles the colonial style of the famous Café Tortoni. An inviting courtyard and fountain leads from the lobby, looking out to one of the oldest churches in the city.

Guest rooms continue the 1930s theme, with elegant black woodwork, comfortable king beds, marble-top nightstands, large desks, and black and white photographs of Buenos Aires. Marble bathrooms have separate showers and bathtubs and feature extensive amenities. Business rooms, "Six Continents" rooms, and various suites offer even more luxuries. The hotel caters to generous expense accounts: It's expensive and few items are included in the regular room rates.

Dining/Diversions: The lobby bar and **Café de las Luces** are popular places to entertain, and an outdoor terrace is a wonderful spot for breakfast or an afternoon snack. The **Restaurante y Bar Mediterraneo** (see "Where to Dine," below) serves healthy, gourmet Mediterranean cuisine. Stop by the **Brasco & Duane** wine bar for an extensive selection of Argentine vintages.

Amenities: Excellent health club with an indoor pool, exercise room ($10 charge for guests; $50 for non-guests), massage service, sauna, and sundeck; business center; conference rooms; concierge; room service; dry cleaning and laundry service; executive business services.

MICROCENTER
VERY EXPENSIVE

✪ **Marriott Plaza Hotel.** Calle Florida 1005, 1005 Buenos Aires. ☎ **11/4318-3000.** Fax 11/4318-3008. E-mail: marriott.plazahotel@marriott.com.ar. 325 units. A/C MINIBAR TV TEL. $300 double; from $400 suite. Rates include buffet breakfast. AE, DC, MC, V. Valet parking $23. Metro: San Martín.

The historic Plaza was the grande dame of Buenos Aires for most of the 20th century, and the Marriott management has maintained much of its original splendor (the hotel still belongs to descendants of the first owners from 1906). The elegant lobby, decorated in Italian marble, crystal, and Persian carpets, is a virtual revolving door of Argentine politicians and foreign diplomats. The hotel hosts numerous international conferences and is equally popular with business executives. The veteran staff offers sharp, professional service, and the concierge will address needs ranging from executive business services to sightseeing tours. Although the quality of guest rooms varies widely (some still await renovation), all are spacious and well-appointed. Twenty-six overlook Plaza San Martín, some with beautiful bay windows.

Dining/Diversions: The Plaza Hotel Grill is a favorite lunch spot for Argentine politicians and international executives and offers a reasonably priced multi-course dinner menu as well. Stop in for a cigar and after-dinner drink at the **Plaza Bar.** A tango buffet with music and dancers takes place every Thursday and Saturday evening in **La Brasserie,** the hotel's casual restaurant. Wine-tasting seminars are held here once a month.

Amenities: Newly designed health club with a pretty outdoor pool, exercise room, massage service, and sauna; business center; conference rooms; concierge; room service; dry cleaning and laundry service; beauty salon; newspaper delivery; nightly turndown; executive business services; gift shops.

Park Tower Buenos Aires (The Luxury Connection). Av. Leandro N. Alem 1193, 1104 Buenos Aires. ☎ **11/4318-9100.** Fax 11/4318-9150. www.luxurylatinamerica.com. 181 units. A/C MINIBAR TV TEL. From $450 double. AE, DC, MC, V. Valet parking $18. Metro: Retiro.

One of the most beautiful, and expensive, hotels in Buenos Aires, the Park Tower is connected to the Sheraton next door. The hotel combines traditional elegance with technological sophistication and offers impeccable service. Common areas as well as private rooms feature imported marble, Italian linens, lavish furniture, and impressive works of art. The lobby, with its floor-to-ceiling windows, potted palms, and Japanese wall screens, contributes to a sense of the Pacific Rim rather than South America. Tastefully designed guest rooms are equipped with 29-inch color TVs, stereo systems with CD players, and dual-line telephones with Internet connections. Guests also have access to 24-hour private butler service.

Dining/Diversions: Chrystal Garden serves elegant international food, **El Aljibe** serves Argentine beef from the grill, and **Cardinale** offers Italian specialties; a lobby lounge features piano music, a cigar bar, tea, cocktails, and special liqueurs.

Amenities: Corporate meeting facilities, business center and secretarial services, concierge, "Neptune" pool and fitness center with gymnasium, wet and dry saunas, message therapy, indoor and outdoor pools, two lighted tennis courts, putting green, snack bar, room service, dry cleaning and laundry service, newspaper delivery, nightly turndown.

Sheraton Buenos Aires Hotel and Convention Center. Av. San Martín 1225, 1104 Buenos Aires. ☎ **11/4318-9000.** Fax 11/4318-9353. www.sheratonlatinamerica.com. 739 units. A/C MINIBAR TV TEL. $300 double; from $360 suite. AE, DC, MC, V. Valet parking $18. Metro: Retiro.

The enormous Sheraton has, at least until the recent opening of the Hilton in Puerto Madero, been the main convention center of Buenos Aires. Situated in the heart of the business, shopping, and theater district, it's an ideal location for business travelers and tourists. Guest rooms are typical of a large American chain—well equipped, but lacking in particular charm. What the hotel lacks in intimacy, however, it makes up for in the wide range of services offered to guests. The hotel's pool and fitness center is the best in the city.

Dining/Diversions: Sharing with its neighbor the Park Tower, **Chrystal Garden** serves elegant international food, **El Aljibe** serves Argentine beef from the grill, and **Cardinale** offers Italian specialties; a lobby lounge features piano music, a cigar bar, tea, cocktails, and special liqueurs.

Amenities: Corporate meeting facilities, business center and secretarial services, concierge, executive floors, "Neptune" pool and fitness center with gymnasium, wet and dry saunas, message therapy, indoor and outdoor pools, two lighted tennis courts, putting green, snack bar, room service, car rental, theater and concert ticket service, beauty parlor, currency exchange, travel agency, dry cleaning and laundry service, newspaper delivery, nightly turndown.

EXPENSIVE

Amerian Buenos Aires Park Hotel. Reconquista 699, 1003 Buenos Aires. ☎ **11/4317-5100.** Fax 11/4317-5101. www.amerianhoteles.com.ar. E-mail: reservas@amerianhoteles.com.ar. 151 units. A/C MINIBAR TV TEL. $200 double; from $260 suite. Rates include buffet breakfast. AE, DC, MC, V. Metro: Florida.

Without question one of the finest four-star hotels in the city, the modern Amerian is a good bet for tourists as well as business travelers. The warm atrium lobby looks more California than Argentina, and the highly qualified staff offers personalized service.

Soundproof rooms are elegantly appointed with wood, marble, and granite, and all boast comfortable beds, chairs, and work areas. The Argentine-owned hotel is just blocks away from Calle Florida, Plaza San Martín, and the Teatro Colón.

Dining/Diversions: The Amerian Golden Restaurant and Traditional Pub, a relaxing spot with English-style decor, features regional, national, and international dishes. There is also a wide selection of beers and cocktails.

Amenities: Well-equipped exercise room and sauna, business center, conference rooms, concierge, room service, dry cleaning and laundry service.

Claridge Hotel. Tucamán 535, 1049 Buenos Aires. ☎ **11/4314-7700.** Fax 11/4314-8022. www.claridge.com.ar. E-mail: reservations@claridge-hotel.com. 160 units. A/C MINIBAR TV TEL. $235–$250 double; from $350 suite. Rates include buffet breakfast. AE, DC, MC, V. Metro: Florida.

The Claridge has topped the city's hotel market for 50 years, and if it's no longer the capital's most luxurious hotel, it certainly remains among the most well-known. From the grand entrance with its imposing Roman columns to the elegant lobby with its English hunt-club theme, the Claridge seems far removed from the bustling city life outside. Wood paneling, wrought-iron lamps, and dark furniture lend the hotel a sense of tranquillity, if not modernity. Even the staff moves at a more relaxed pace, although service remains attentive and professional. Guest rooms are spacious, tastefully decorated, and equipped with all the amenities expected of a five-star hotel. Because it occasionally hosts conventions, the Claridge can become very busy.

Dining/Diversions: The Claridge Restaurant offers a good-value executive menu for those with little time to linger over a meal. This country-style restaurant serves carefully prepared international food and has a nice breakfast buffet. An adjacent bar is a popular business meeting spot.

Amenities: First-rate health club with a heated outdoor pool, exercise room, massage service, and sauna; business center; conference rooms; concierge; room service; dry cleaning and laundry service; newspaper delivery; nightly turndown; executive business services.

✪ **Clarion Aspen Towers.** Paraguay 857, 1057 Buenos Aires. ☎ **11/4313-1919.** Fax 11/4313-2662. www.aspentowers.com.ar. E-mail: hotel@aspentowers.com.ar. 105 units. A/C MINIBAR TV TEL. $225–$295 double. Rates include buffet breakfast. AE, DC, MC, V. Metro: San Martín.

Built in 1995, the Aspen Towers (part of the Clarion chain) is one of the city's newest and more luxurious hotels. Its 13-floor tower is contemporary in design, with a light-filled atrium lobby, elegant restaurant, and inviting rooftop pool. Guest rooms are small but classically decorated, with faux-antique furniture and soft colored linens. All rooms enjoy marble bathrooms with whirlpool baths—something you're unlikely to find anywhere in the city at this price. The hotel is especially popular with Brazilians, Chileans, and Americans, and lies within easy walking distance of downtown's main attractions.

Dining/Diversions: Restaurant Orleans offers national and international dishes in a refined ambience. **Café La Tour,** just off the lobby, is an appealing spot for casual meetings and evening drinks.

Amenities: Rooftop pool, exercise room, and sauna; business center; conference rooms; concierge; room service; dry cleaning and laundry service.

Meliá Confort. Reconquista 945, 1003 Buenos Aires. ☎ **11/4891-3834.** Fax 11/4891-3834. E-mail: meliabue@confort.com.ar. 125 units. A/C MINIBAR TV TEL. $230 double; from $270 suite. Rates include buffet breakfast. AE, DC, MC, V. Metro: San Martín.

Within easy walking distance of Plaza San Martín and Calle Florida, this modern hotel compares favorably with the city's five-star hotels yet costs considerably less. Spacious guest rooms colored in soft earth tones feature overstuffed chairs and comfortable beds, sound-proof windows, and marble bathrooms. Large desks, two phone lines, data ports, and available cell phones make this a good choice for business travelers; there is also a well-equipped business center downstairs. The hotel staff offers friendly, relaxed service.

Dining/Diversions: The Meliá has a small Spanish restaurant and bar.

Amenities: Concierge, conference rooms, exercise room, dry cleaning and laundry service, evening turndown.

MODERATE

Bisonte Palace Hotel. Marcelo T. de Alvear 910, 1058 Buenos Aires. ☎ **11/4328-4751.** Fax 11/4328-6476. www.hotelesbisonte.com. E-mail: bispal@iname.com. 72 units. A/C TV TEL. $135 double; from $185 suite. Rates include buffet breakfast. AE, DC, MC, V. Metro: San Martín.

The better of the two Bisonte hotels (the other is located at Paraguay 1207), the sleek Bisonte Palace attracts a large Brazilian business clientele and is popular with travelers looking for four-star comfort at reasonable rates. Rooms are spacious and well lit and were recently renovated—those on the upper floors hear less street noise, and all have marble bathrooms. The staff is attentive to guest needs, and various business services are offered. Plaza San Martín is a 3-block walk from the hotel.

Comfort Inn & Suites Esmeralda. Marcelo T. de Alvear 842, 1058 Buenos Aires. ☎ **11/4311-3929.** Fax 11/4312-1472. www.loisuites.com.ar. E-mail: edemare@loisuites.com.ar. 103 units. A/C MINIBAR TV TEL. $138 double. Rates include buffet breakfast. AE, MC, V. Metro: San Martín.

What the hotel lacks in sophistication it makes up for in value. One-, two-, or three-bedroom suites with kitchens or kitchenettes are good bets for families with children. They are sparsely decorated but comfortable, with cable TV and central air-conditioning—don't be alarmed by the bright floral patterns consuming the linens in certain rooms. The bilingual staff will help you plan a tour in town, and the hotel offers access to a swimming pool and gymnasium. Laundry service is available.

✪ Courtyard Marriott. Calle Florida 944, 1005 Buenos Aires. ☎ **11/4891-9200.** Fax 11/4891-9208. E-mail: courtyard.floridastreet@marriott.com.ar. 77 units. A/C MINIBAR TV TEL. $175 double. Rates include buffet breakfast. AE, DC, MC, V. Metro: San Martín.

The new Courtyard—the first in Latin America—is an excellent choice for business travelers, with a perfect location off Calle Florida near Plaza San Martín. Guest rooms resemble studio apartments, with king- or queen-size beds, sleeper chairs, large desks and dressers, and well-appointed bathrooms. There are two phones in each room, and local calls are free—a rarity in Buenos Aires. Hotel service is prompt and friendly, although room service is not yet offered (there's a small, airy cafe adjacent to the lobby). Guests have access to the business center and health club at the Marriott Plaza Hotel, just steps away. There are four function rooms available for business and social events.

El Conquistador Hotel. Suipacha 948, 1008 Buenos Aires. ☎ **11/4328-3012.** Fax 11/4328-3252. www.elconquistador.com.ar. E-mail: mailhotel@elconquistador.com.ar. 140 units. A/C MINIBAR TV TEL. $187 double; from $218 suite. AE, DC, MC, V. Metro: San Martín.

There is something of *Saturday Night Fever* in the low ceilings, wood paneling, and brass fixtures of the hotel lobby. Even the rooms are 1970s in style, although they are also clean and comfy, with firm mattresses and ample desk space with Internet connections. El Conquistador is located in the city's financial district and lies within easy walking distance of Plaza San Martín. The professional staff caters to most business traveler needs. There's a restaurant, a lobby piano bar, and room service.

Holiday Inn Express. Av. Leandro N. Alem 770, 1057 Buenos Aires. ☎ **11/4311-5200.** Fax 11/4311-5757. www.holiday-inn.com. E-mail: reserva@holiday.com.ar. 116 units. A/C TV TEL. $110–$140 double. Children under 18 stay free. Rates include buffet breakfast. AE, DC, MC, V. Metro: L.N. Alem.

This new Holiday Inn Express enjoys a perfect location next to Puerto Madero. Although there is no room service, concierge, or bellboys, the small hotel is friendly, modern, and inexpensive. Guest rooms have large, firm beds, ample desk space, and 27-inch cable TVs; half of them boast river views. Coffee and tea are served 24 hours, and the buffet breakfast is excellent. Amenities include a business center with free fax and local calls, exercise room, sauna, whirlpool tub, meeting rooms, and a deli.

Hotel Crillon. Av. Santa Fe 796, 1059 Buenos Aires. ☎ **0800/888-4448** (local toll free) or 11/4310-2000. Fax 11/4310-2020. www.hotelcrillon.com.ar. E-mail: hotcri@movi.com.ar. 96 units. A/C MINIBAR TV TEL. $180–$215 double; from $245 suite. Rates include buffet breakfast. AE, DC, MC, V. Metro: San Martín.

This 50-year-old French-style hotel enjoys an outstanding location adjacent to Plaza San Martín, next to some of the city's best sights and shops. Undergoing a slow renovation, the Crillon is becoming a more comfortable hotel as well, as guest rooms are refitted with nicer furniture and better linens. A pool, health club, and business center are in the works. The hotel is popular with European and Brazilian business travelers, and offers such in-room conveniences as Internet access, cell phones, in-room safes, and hair dryers in bathrooms. Deluxe rooms enjoy views of Santa Fe and Esmeralda streets, while the suites overlook Plaza San Martín. Stay away from interior rooms, which have no views. There is an international restaurant and a lobby bar. The hotel staff is extremely helpful.

Lancaster Hotel. Av. Córdoba 405, 1054 Buenos Aires. ☎ **11/4311-3021/26.** Fax 11/4312-4068. E-mail: lancast@infovia.com.ar. 114 units. A/C MINIBAR TV TEL. $135 double; from $160 suite. Rates include buffet breakfast. AE, DC, MC, V. Metro: San Martín.

The character of this old-fashioned hotel remains unchanged as the city modernizes around it. Situated next to Plaza San Martín, it's ideal for business travelers working in the microcenter and tourists who don't want to pay the extravagant costs of a five-star hotel (the Lancaster has four stars). A Russian countess opened the hotel in 1938, and the new owners have kept her paintings and furnishings on display; the style is old traditional British. Guest rooms retain the feeling of antiquity, although they are being renovated to give them nicer bathrooms and sound-proof windows. The staff is extremely polite, and the hotel enjoys many repeat customers. There is a restaurant and a bar.

Regente Palace. Suipacha 964, 1008 Buenos Aires. ☎ **11/4328-6800.** Fax 11/4328-7460. 140 units. A/C MINIBAR TV TEL. $125 double. AE, DC, MC, V. Metro: San Martín.

This hotel was designed by the same architect responsible for the El Conquistador Hotel next door; you will notice the abundance of 1970s disco brass in the lobby as well as original artwork from Argentina's northwest. Rooms are fairly standard and not overly modern, but they are quiet and comfortable. The hotel features a business center, meeting rooms, a fitness room, a restaurant, and a bar.

Tulip Inn. Paraguay 481, 1057 Buenos Aires. ☎ **11/4313-3022.** Fax 11/4313-3952. www.principado.com.ar. E-mail: hotel@principado.com.ar. 88 units. A/C MINIBAR TV TEL. $130 double. Rates include buffet breakfast. AE, MC, V. Free parking. Metro: San Martín.

This is the best three-star hotel you're likely to find in the microcenter, just a block away from Plaza San Martín. With its dim lights, dark furniture, and low ceilings, you'll feel more like you're in rural Argentina than in the nation's capital. Cozy guest rooms are better equipped than at some of the city's four-star hotels, and the hotel offers 24-hour room service, same-day laundry service, and a multilingual staff.

INEXPENSIVE

Best Western Embassy. Av. Córdoba 860, 1054 Buenos Aires. ☎ **11/4322-1228.** Fax 11/4322-2337. www.bestwestern.com. E-mail: bestwesternembassy@arnet.com.ar. 66 units. A/C MINIBAR TV TEL. $76–$150 double. Rates include buffet breakfast. AE, DC, MC, V. Metro: Lavalle.

While the owners may be exaggerating when they call this an "all suites" hotel, guest rooms (available in five categories) do have kitchenettes and balconies, and some have separate living areas and bedrooms. Renovated in 1998, the hotel is convenient and comfortable, offering decent if limited service. Don't be alarmed by the talking elevators. There's a small cafe, 24-hour room service, a business center, concierge service, a fitness room, and a sauna.

Goya Hotel. Suipacha 748, 1008 Buenos Aires. ☎/fax **11/4322-9269.** 40 units. A/C TV TEL. $55–$70 double. AE, MC, V. Metro: San Martín.

Popular with European travelers, this Mediterranean-style hotel lies 6 blocks from Plaza San Martín and only 3 from the pedestrian walking street Calle Florida. Bright, quiet superior rooms have rose-colored bedspreads and marble bathrooms; classic rooms are a bit smaller and older. The 14 largest guest rooms feature whirlpool baths. The hotel offers few services, except 24-hour room service and breakfast for $4.

Gran Hotel Dora. Maipú 963, 1006 Buenos Aires. ☎/fax **11/4312-7391.** 96 units. A/C TV TEL. $100 double. MC, V. Metro: San Martín.

It would be misleading to steer you to this hotel for luxury, but the Gran Hotel Dora does offer a few frills with its central location, inexpensive rates, and European styling. This old hotel features clean but sparsely decorated rooms with cable TV, marble bathrooms, and a bit of local artwork. A small business center and conference rooms have been added.

Grand King Hotel. Lavalle 560, 1047 Buenos Aires. ☎ **11/4393-4012.** Fax 11/4393-4052. E-mail: granking@hotelnet.com.ar. 100 units. A/C MINIBAR TV TEL. $100 double. Rates include traditional breakfast buffet. MC, V. Metro: Florida.

The recently renovated Grand King lies equidistant between the Colón Theater, Puerto Madero, Plaza de Mayo, and Plaza San Martín. What the hotel lacks in charm, it makes up for in location and value. Guest rooms, decorated in light blue and yellow tones, are small but in good taste. An experienced staff offers warm, personalized service.

Liberty Hotel. Av. Corrientes 632, 1043 Buenos Aires. ☎/fax **11/4325-0261.** www. liberty-hotel.com.ar. E-mail: info@liberty-hotel.com.ar. 94 units. A/C TV TEL. $88 double. Rates include buffet breakfast. AE, MC, V. Metro: Florida.

The recently renovated Liberty Hotel is among the least expensive options in the microcenter. A series of international flags fly proudly outside; inside, the first-floor sitting area is decorated with old photographic equipment and has large windows overlooking Avenida Corrientes. Many of the guest rooms have small sitting areas, period furniture, and tacky red bedspreads; bathrooms have hair dryers. The hotel offers few additional amenities.

3 Where to Dine

Buenos Aires offers world-class dining, with a fantastic variety of Argentine, Italian, and international restaurants. You've heard that Argentine beef is the best in the world; *parrillas* (grills) serving the choicest cuts are ubiquitous in this town (it is said that when Argentines go on a diet, they limit themselves to eating only meat). Many kitchens have an Italian influence, and you'll find pasta on most menus. The city's most fashionable restaurants line the docks of Puerto Madero—with the majority focused on seafood. The microcenter and Recoleta offer many outstanding restaurants and cafes as well. Cafe life is as sacred to *Porteños* as it is to Parisians.

Porteños eat breakfast until 10am, lunch between noon and 2:30pm, and dinner late—usually after 9pm. Many restaurants require reservations, particularly on weekends. There is usually a "cover" charge for bread and other accouterments placed at the table. In those restaurants that serve pasta, the pasta and its sauce are priced separately. Standard tipping is 10% in Buenos Aires, more for exceptional service. When paying your bill by credit card, you will often be expected to leave the *propina* (tip) in cash, since many credit card receipts don't provide a place to include it.

PUERTO MADERO

There are no convenient metro stops to this neighborhood.

VERY EXPENSIVE

○ **Cabaña las Lilas.** Av. Dávila 516. ☎ **11/4313-1336.** Reservations recommended. Main courses $15–$30. AE, DC, V. Daily noon–midnight. Metro: L.N. Alem. ARGENTINE.

Widely considered the best *parrilla* in Buenos Aires, Cabaña las Lilas is always packed. The menu pays homage to Argentine beef, which comes from the restaurant's private *estancia* (ranch). The table "cover"—which includes dried tomatoes, mozzarella, olives, peppers, and delicious garlic bread—nicely whets the appetite. Clearly you're here to order steak: The best cuts are the rib-eye, baby beef, and thin skirt steak. Order sautéed vegetables, grilled onions, or Provençal-style fries separately. Service is hurried but professional; ask your waiter to match a fine Argentine wine with your meal. And make reservations well in advance.

Katrine. Av. Alicia Moreau de Justo 138. ☎ **11/4315-6222.** Reservations recommended. Main courses $15–$30. AE, DC, MC, V. Daily noon–1am. Metro: L.N. Alem. INTERNATIONAL.

One of the best, and most expensive, restaurants in Buenos Aires, Katrine serves exquisite cuisine. Yet for such an exclusive restaurant, the dining room is surprisingly loud and festive. You won't go wrong with any of the menu choices, but a couple of suggestions include the terrine of shrimp served with avocado, fillet of sole with mashed potatoes, jumbo shrimp in bread crumbs and Thai sauce, and the thinly sliced beef tenderloin over arugula. Black sea bass with mashed fava beans and citrus vinaigrette is another adventuresome choice. Katrine's modern dining room and outdoor terrace overlook the water. Service is outstanding.

EXPENSIVE

Sorrento del Puerto. Av. Alicia Moreau de Justo 410. ☎ **11/4319-8731.** Reservations recommended. Main courses $10–$25. AE, DC, MC, V. Daily noon–3am. Metro: L.N. Alem. SEAFOOD/ITALIAN.

The only two-story restaurant in Puerto Madero enjoys impressive views of the water from both floors. When the city decided to reinvigorate the port in 1995, this was one of the first five restaurants opened (today there are 55). The sleek modern dining room boasts large windows, modern blue lighting, and tables and booths decorated with white linens and individual roses. While an outdoor patio accommodates only 15 tables, the inside is enormous. Upstairs, you will see some of the brick columns and steel beams that formed part of the original dock house.

People come here for two reasons: great pasta and even better seafood. Choose your pasta and accompanying sauce—seafood, shrimp scampi, pesto, or four cheeses. Among the best seafood are the lobster thermidor, Galician octopus, grilled trout, and tuna steak. King crab prepared with scallions, sweet peppers, button mushrooms, Parmesan cheese, cream, and cognac, is superb. A three-course menu with a drink is offered for $23.

INEXPENSIVE

The Pier Cafe. Av. Alicia Moreau de Justo 530. ☎ **11/4313-4133.** Main courses $2–$5. No credit cards. Mon–Thurs 8am–8pm; Fri 8am–3am; Sat 6pm–3am. Metro: L.N. Alem. CAFE.

This beautiful English-style cafe at Dock 4 in Puerto Madero has only one table and a few bar stools at which to sit, but it's probably the most refined cafe in the city. Stop in for a gourmet coffee or take away; the drinks—including exotic teas—are delicious.

RECOLETA

There are no convenient metro stops to this neighborhood.

VERY EXPENSIVE

Harry Cipriani. Posadas 1229. ☎ **11/4813-4291.** Reservations recommended. Main courses $26–$36. AE, DC, MC, V. Daily noon–3:30pm and 8pm–1am (tea time 3:30–8pm). ITALIAN.

Among the city's many outstanding Italian restaurants, Harry Cipriani sits near the top. An exact replica of the famous Harry Ciprianis in Venice and New York, the Buenos Aires version attracts a wealthy clientele from the Recoleta neighborhood. Everything here is from Venice—the furniture, the marble, the photographs. People come primarily for pastas and risotto, although the antipasti, soups (especially minestrone), and seafood dishes are also excellent. Many diners begin their meals with a bellini (champagne and peach cocktail) and continue the celebration with an Italian sparkling wine. The hours between lunch and dinner are reserved for teatime.

Lola. Pte. Roberto M. Ortiz 1805. ☎ **11/4802-3023** or 11/4804-3410. Reservations recommended. Main courses $17–$30; fixed-price lunch menu $25. AE, DC, MC, V. Daily 12:30–3:30pm and 7pm–1am. INTERNATIONAL.

Among the best known and most recommended international restaurants in Buenos Aires, Lola is undergoing a substantial makeover to make its dining room one of the city's brightest and most contemporary (it should be done by the time this book is printed). A French-trained chef offers creative, complicated dishes, like stuffed quails with herb mousse over a small ratatouille, or Peking duck fillet with terrine of eggplant accompanied by duck confit, pears, and a crisp hazelnut pastry. If you've failed to exhaust your craving for Argentine beef, tenderloin medallions with mushrooms, cream potatoes, and gourmet vegetables are delicious. The chef will prepare dishes for those with special dietary requirements.

Prices are high because of outstanding product quality, including the best beef and fish on the market. The staff, accustomed to an older, distinguished crowd, offers impeccable service. Expect your waiter to be friendly and engaging if this is the style you enjoy, or quiet and reserved if you prefer more private dining. On weekends, live music accompanies lunch on the refined outdoor patio.

Massey. Posadas 1089. ☎ **11/4328-4104.** Reservations recommended. Main courses $18–$26; fixed-price lunch menu $21. AE, MC, V. Mon–Fri 11:30am–4pm and 8pm–1am; Sat. 8pm–1am. MEDITERRANEAN/THAI.

This chic restaurant in Recoleta combines classic Mediterranean cuisine with an Asian flair. Although it's a popular business lunch spot, come here for dinner when tables are candlelit and the room fills with the city's beautiful people. On the walls hang sexually suggestive photographs of what the staff swears are vegetables; expect your lettuce to taste a little better this night. The staff is young and interactive, contributing to the dining room's hip feel. In the center extends a long marble table where clients are seated close to each other, and there are a number of individual tables surrounding it.

For an appetizer, order the coconut-crusted prawns served on a bed of crunchy spinach—the chef refuses to reveal the ingredients in the spicy sauce, but rest assured they will likely be the best shrimp you've ever tasted. For main dishes, try the Thai shamani rice with chicken and shrimp caramelized with soy sauce in honey. Or maybe the marinated lamb with Oriental vegetables and papaya chutney. It doesn't really matter what you order: You're here for a sensual experience and everything tastes delicious.

EXPENSIVE

Bistro Galani. Posadas 1086 (Park Hyatt Hotel). ☎ **11/4321-1234.** Reservations recommended. Main courses $12–$25. AE, DC, MC, V. Mon–Sat 7–11am, 12:30–3pm, and 8pm–1am; Sun 1–4pm. MEDITERRANEAN.

This casual bistro inside the spectacular Park Hyatt Hotel serves Mediterranean cuisine with a French flair. It offers live harp music during breakfast, an executive buffet for lunch, and an à la carte menu at dinner. Entrees include braised rabbit in olive sauce, salmon with fruit couscous, and an outstanding New York strip steak. Enjoy an after-dinner drink in *Le Dôme*, the split-level bar adjacent to the lobby featuring live piano music and occasional tango shows.

Clark's. Pte. Roberto M. Ortiz 1777. ☎ **11/4801-9502.** Reservations recommended. Main courses $13–$25. AE, DC, MC, V. Daily 12:30–3:30pm and 7:30pm–12:30am. ARGENTINE.

The dining room here is an eclectic mix of oak wood, yellow lamps, live plants, and deer horns. A slanted ceiling descends over the English-style bar; in back, a 10-foot-high glass case showcases a winter garden. Comfortable booths and tables are covered with green-and-white checkered tablecloths and are usually occupied by North Americans. Opt for the three-course lunch or dinner menu, or order à la carte. Specialties include pink salmon with a mustard sauce, rack of lamb served with herbs and au gratin potatoes, and a giant omelet stuffed with king crab. There are a number of pasta and rice dishes as well. A large outside terrace attracts a fashionable crowd in summer.

MODERATE

Café de la Paix. Calle Quintana 595. ☎ **11/4804-6820.** Main courses $8–$15. AE, MC, V. Sun–Thurs 8am–3am; Fri–Sat 8am–5am. CAFE.

This peaceful cafe has a lovely sun-drenched terrace with red umbrellas and a two-level indoor dining room. If seated outside, you'll notice the bright red English telephone booth to the patio's right side—this is the northernmost cafe on Pte. Roberto M. Ortiz. Linger over coffee or another drink as long as you like, or order snacks from the simple menu. Omelets, sandwiches, and salads are offered, as well as pastries and numerous desserts. The house "café de la Paix" comes with cream, cinnamon, and cloves.

Café Victoria. Pte. Roberto M. Ortiz 1865. ☎ **11/4804-0016.** Main courses $7–$15. AE, DC, MC, V. Sun–Thurs 7am–2am; Fri 7am–4am; Sat 7am–5am. INTERNATIONAL.

Perfect for a relaxing afternoon in Recoleta, the cafe's outdoor patio is surrounded by flowers and shaded by an enormous *romero de India* tree. Sit and have a coffee or enjoy a complete meal. The three-course menu ($12, cash only) offers a salad, main dish, and dessert, with a drink included. Try the Ales salad, with sliced carrots, beets, white asparagus, lettuce, and *palmitos* (hearts of palm), followed by grilled chicken and potatoes or a pasta dish. The cafe is equally popular in the evening, when live music serenades the patio and people-watching abounds. This is a great value for the area—the Recoleta Cemetery and cultural center are located next door.

INEXPENSIVE

Primera (1re) Plana. Posadas 1011. ☎ **11/4326-4499.** Main courses $5–$15. AE, MC, V. Daily 8am–2am (Fri until 3am). PIZZA/SNACKS.

Located in the part of Recoleta known as "La Recova de Posadas," Primera Plana is an inviting spot for a quick meal or drink on the outdoor terrace. The restaurant takes its name from a newspaper published in Buenos Aires decades ago: the restaurant's entire decor—even the staff's uniforms—reflects front pages of the country's numerous periodicals. Come for one of the delicious pizzas, or try the $7 lunchtime buffet. Salads are also large and tasty. Arrive in time for the two-for-one beers offered daily 5 to 10pm.

PALERMO
MODERATE

✪ **De Olivas i Lustres.** Gascón 1460. ☎ **11/4405-2714** or 11/4867-3388. Reservations recommended. Main courses $9–$16; fixed-price menu $25. AE, V. Tues–Sat 8:30pm–1am. Metro: Scalabrini Ortiz. MEDITERRANEAN.

Located in Palermo Viejo, this magical restaurant is worth the short taxi ride. The small, rustic dining room displays antiques, olive jars, and wine bottles, and each candlelit table is individually decorated—one resembles a writer's desk, another is sprinkled with sea shells. The reasonably priced menu celebrates Mediterranean cuisine, with light soups, fresh fish, and sautéed vegetables the focus. The breast of duck with lemon and honey is mouth-watering; there are also a number of *tapeos*—appetizer-size dishes that let you sample a variety of the chef's selections. For $25 each, you and your partner can share 13 such dishes brought out individually (a great option provided you have at least a couple of hours). Open only for dinner, this is a romantic spot with soft, subtle service.

MONSERRAT
VERY EXPENSIVE

Club Español. Bernardo de Irigoyen 180. ☎ **11/4334-4876.** Reservations recommended. Main courses $15–$33. AE, DC, MC, V. Daily noon–3pm and 7pm–midnight. Metro: Piedras Bolívar. SPANISH.

This art nouveau Spanish club, with its high, gilded ceiling and grand pillars, bas-relief artwork, and original Spanish paintings, boasts the most magnificent dining room in Buenos Aires. Despite the restaurant's architectural grandeur, the atmosphere is surprisingly relaxed and often celebratory—don't be surprised to find a table of champagne-clinking Argentines next to you. Tables have beautiful silver place settings, and tuxedo-clad waiters offer formal service.

While the menu is a tempting mix of Spanish cuisine—including excellent paella and Spanish omelets—the fish dishes are the chef's best. Consider the fillet of sole topped with béchamel and shrimp and served with sliced potatoes and spinach. Codfish with garlic cream and trout flamed in whisky are equally delicious. Top off your meal with crêpes suzette or profiteroles served with hot, rich chocolate and vanilla ice cream. Club Español lies within easy walking distance of the Inter-Continental Hotel.

Restaurante y Bar Mediterraneo. Moreno 809. ☎ **11/4340-7200.** Reservations recommended. Main courses $18–29. AE, DC, MC, V. Daily 7:30am–3:30pm and 7pm–midnight. Metro: Piedras Bolivar. MEDITERRANEAN.

The Inter-Continental Hotel's exclusive Mediterranean restaurant and bar were built in colonial style, resembling the city's famous Café Tortoni. The downstairs bar, with its hardwood floor, marble-top tables, and polished Victrola playing a forgotten tango, takes you back to Buenos Aires of the 1930s. A spiral staircase leads to the elegant restaurant, where subdued lighting and well-spaced tables create an intimate atmosphere. French chef Thierry Grodet has designed a menu that is light, healthy, and delicious: Mediterranean herbs, olive oil, and sun-dried tomatoes are among the chef's usual ingredients. Carefully prepared dishes might include shellfish bouillabaisse; black hake served with ratatouille; chicken casserole with morels, fava beans, and potatoes; or duck breast with cabbage confit, wild mushrooms, and sautéed apples. Express menus (ready within minutes) are available at lunch, while a three-course, prix fixe menu is offered at dinner.

MICROCENTER
VERY EXPENSIVE

✪ **Catalinas.** Reconquista 850. ☎ **11/4313-0182.** Reservations recommended. Main courses $20–$30; fixed-price menu $40. AE, DC, MC, V. Mon–Fri 11:30am–4pm and 8pm–1am; Sat. 8pm–1am. Metro: San Martín. MEDITERRANEAN/INTERNATIONAL.

It's no secret that this is Argentina's best international restaurant. Since 1979, Galician-born Ramiro Rodriguez Pardo has impressed the most exacting gourmands from Argentina and abroad, his kitchen defined by culinary diversity and innovation. The colorful, yet classic dining room—now adjacent to the Lancaster hotel—has three open salons, each painted by one of Argentina's most famous "plastic" artists: Polesello, Beuedit, and Rovirosa. A breathtaking Venetian crystal chandelier shines on the center dining room, created by the same artist who arranged the chandeliers in the lobby of the Plaza Hotel in New York. Tables are large and comfortable, decorated with white linens, fresh flower arrangements, and bone china and porcelain from Villeroy & Boch.

For lunch, expect to see an elite business crowd, which comes more to eat—and eat well—than to conduct meetings. Evenings inspire a more romantic ambience. A three-course, prix fixe menu, including two bottles of Argentina's finest wines, is offered at lunch and dinner—an excellent value for such an elegant restaurant. The menu changes seasonally, but always includes impeccable lobsters, T-bone steaks, and steaks of Patagonian toothfish (which grow to over 200 lbs). Pardo's grilled lamb chops, sprinkled with rosemary and fresh savory, are famous throughout Argentina. The dessert selection will make your mouth water.

EXPENSIVE

La Chacra. Av. Córdoba 941. ☎ **11/4322-1409.** Main courses $12–$25. AE, DC, MC, V. Daily noon–1am. Metro: San Martín. ARGENTINE.

Your first impression will be either the perfectly stuffed cow begging you to go on in and eat some meat or the open fire spit grill glowing through the window. Professional waiters clad in black pants and white dinner jackets welcome you into what is otherwise a casual environment, with deer horns and wrought-iron lamps adorning the walls. This is what the management calls "Buenos Aires's most typical restaurant." Maybe they're right.

Timeless dishes from the grill include sirloin steak, T-bone with red peppers, and tenderloin. Barbecue ribs and suckling pig call out from the open-pit fire, and there are a number of hearty brochettes on the menu. Steaks are thick, juicy, and served hot. Get a good beer, or at least an Argentine wine, to wash it all down.

Las Nazarenas. Reconquista 1132. ☎ **11/4312-5559.** Reservations recommended. Main courses $12–$25. AE, DC, MC, V. Daily noon–1am. Metro: San Martín. ARGENTINE.

This is not a restaurant, an old waiter will warn you; it's an *asador*. More specifically, it's a steakhouse with meat on the menu, not a pseudo-*parrilla* with vegetable plates or some foofy international dishes slipped in for the faint of heart. You have two choices: cuts grilled on the *parrilla,* or meat cooked on a spit over the fire. Argentine presidents and foreign ministers have all made their way here, a pilgrimage to Argentina's great culinary tradition. The two-level dining room is handsomely decorated with cases of Argentine wines and abundant plants. Service is unhurried, offering you plenty of time for a relaxing meal.

Ligure. Juncal 855. ☎ **11/4393-0644** or 11/4394-8226. Reservations recommended. Main courses $10–$25. AE, DC, MC, V. Daily noon–3pm and 8–11:30pm. Metro: San Martín. FRENCH.

Painted mirrors of Buenos Aires look over the long rectangular dining room, which for over 75 years has drawn ambassadors, artists, and business leaders by day and a more romantic crowd at night. A nautical theme prevails, with fishnets, dock ropes, and masts decorating the room; captains' wheels substitute for chandeliers.

Portions are both huge and meticulously prepared—an unusual combination for French-inspired cuisine. Among the seafood options, consider the Patagonian toothfish sautéed with butter, prawns, and mushrooms, or perhaps the trout glazed with an almond sauce. If you're in the mood for beef, the chateaubriand is outstanding, and the *bife de lomo* (filet mignon) can be prepared seven different ways (pepper sauce with brandy is delightful, and made right at your table). The diverse menu also includes dishes like chicken kiev, crêpes with béchamel sauce, and homemade pastas. Order vegetables separately.

Plaza Hotel Grill. Marriott Plaza Hotel, Calle Florida 1005. ☎ **11/4318-3000.** Reservations recommended. Main courses $10–$25. AE, DC, MC, V. Daily noon–4pm and 7pm–midnight. Metro: San Martín. INTERNATIONAL.

For nearly a century, the Plaza Hotel Grill dominated the city's power lunch scene, and it remains the first choice for government officials and business executives. The exclusive dining room is decorated with dark oak furniture, 90-year-old Dutch porcelain, Indian fans from the British Empire, and Villeroy & Boch china place settings. Tables are well-spaced, allowing for intimate conversations.

Order à la carte from the international menu or off the *parrilla*—the steaks are perfect Argentine cuts. Marinated filet mignon, thinly sliced and served with gratinéed potatoes, is superb. The "po parisky eggs" form another classic dish—two poached eggs in a bread shell topped with a rich mushroom and bacon sauce. In the evening, a three-course "Bonne Fourchette Menu" is offered for $40, taxes included. The restaurant's wine list spans seven countries, with the world's best Malbec coming from Mendoza.

MODERATE

Broccolino. Esmeralda 776. ☎ **11/4322-7652.** Reservations recommended. Main courses $8–$15. No credit cards. Daily noon–4pm and 7pm–1am. Metro: Lavalle. ITALIAN.

Taking its name from New York's Italian immigrant neighborhood—notice the Brooklyn memorabilia filling the walls and the backlit mural of Manhattan's skyline—this casual trattoria near Calle Florida is extremely popular with North Americans (Robert Duvall has shown up three times). Many of the waiters speak English, still a rarity in much of the city, and the restaurant has a distinctly New York feel. Three small dining rooms are decorated in quintessential red-and-white checkered table-cloths, and the smell of tomatoes, onions, and garlic fills the air. The restaurant is known for its spicy pizzas, fresh pastas, and above all its sauces (called *salsas* in Spanish). Two of the best *salsas* are *profumo de mare,* made with a variety of seafood, and *caligula,* combining pesto (garlic, basil, and nuts) and black mushrooms from Chile. For a fish plate, try the grilled sole with a rich shrimp sauce. The restaurant serves 2,000 pounds per month of baby calamari sautéed in wine, onions, parsley, and garlic.

✪ **Café Tortoni.** Av. de Mayo 825/9. ☎ **11/4342-4328.** Reservations not necessary. Main courses $8–$25. AE, DC, MC, V. Mon–Thurs 8am–2am; Fri–Sat 8am–3am; Sun 8am–1am. Metro: Av. de Mayo. CAFE.

This historic cafe has served as the artistic and intellectual capital of Buenos Aires since 1858, serving personalities like Jorge Luis Borges, Julio de Caro, Cátulo Castillo, and José Gobello. Waiters gaze over the cafe's antique tables and their momentary occupants with sphinx-like serenity, just as the eyes of the great poets whose photographs line the walls have watched so many diners come and go. Come in for coffee, or even a simple meal, and feel Argentine history surround you. The Tortoni is more a cultural tradition than a cafe; there are a number of social events planned here, including evening tango shows held in the back room.

Morizono. Reconquista 899. ☎ **11/4314-0924.** Reservations recommended. Main courses $10–$22. AE, DC, MC, V. Mon–Fri noon–3pm and 8pm–midnight; Sat 8pm–1am. Metro: San Martín. JAPANESE.

A casual Japanese restaurant and sushi bar, Morizono offers such treats as dumplings stuffed with pork, shrimp and vegetable tempuras, salmon with ginger sauce, and a variety of sushi and sashimi combination platters. At lunch, a three-course *menú del día* is $20. Morizono also has locations in Palermo at Paraguay 3521 (☎ **11/4314-0924**) and Belgrano at F. Lazroze 2173 (☎ **11/4773-0940**).

INEXPENSIVE

Bonpler. Calle Florida 481. ☎ **11/4325-9900.** Main courses $3–$5. No credit cards. Daily 7:30am–11pm. Metro: Florida. FRENCH SNACKS.

For fast food other than burgers, Bonpler offers a healthy alternative. This French eatery serves croissant and baguette sandwiches, hot *paninis* (toasted Italian sandwiches), a salad bar, and fresh fruit. There are two levels of seating, if you opt not to take away.

The Coffee Store. Calle Florida 825. ☎ **11/4313-2314.** Main courses $5–$10. AE, V. Mon–Fri 8am–9pm; Sat–Sun 10am–9pm. Metro: Florida. CAFE.

A chic, artsy cafe on the busy pedestrian street Calle Florida, The Coffee Store is Buenos Aires's answer to Starbuck's. Although a few snacks are served, people come almost exclusively to sip coffee and read the newspaper—a number of English editions are available. Twenty-two varieties of coffee are served, from classics like Columbian Supremo (suave) and Ethiopian Harrar (strong), to more exotic almond amarettos, hazelnut creams, and French vanillas. Artwork filling the cafe changes every 15 days, and there are couches in back for prolonged rest and relaxation.

Filo. San Martín 975. ☎ **11/4311-0312.** Main courses $6-$12. AE, MC, V. Daily 12pm–2am. Metro: San Martín. PIZZA.

Popular with young professionals, artists, and anyone looking for cause to celebrate, Filo presents its happy clients with mouth-watering pizzas and potent cocktails. The crowded bar has occasional live music, and tango lessons are offered a few evenings per week downstairs.

✪ Petit Paris Cafe. Av. Santa Fe 774. ☎ **11/4312-5885.** Main courses $5–$15. AE, DC, MC, V. Daily 6am–1am. Metro: San Martín. SNACKS/AFTERNOON TEA.

Marble-top tables with velvet upholstered chairs, crystal chandeliers, and bow tie–clad waiters give this cafe a distinctly European flavor. Large windows look directly onto Plaza San Martín, placing the cafe within short walking distance of some of the city's best sights. The menu offers a selection of hot and cold sandwiches, pastries, and special coffees and teas. Linger over your coffee as long as you like—nobody will pressure you to move.

Schlotzsky's Deli. Viamonte 170. ☎ **11/4576-7222.** Main courses $2–$8. No credit cards. Daily 8am–6pm. Metro: L.N. Alem. DELI.

This New York–style deli makes great sandwiches, salads, and pizzas. Subs, made to order, are stacked high with meats, cheeses, and vegetables, like the "Park Avenue" with roast beef, three cheeses (mozzarella, cheddar, and Parmesan), lettuce, tomatoes, onions, and black olives. Lighter fare is available for the health conscious. Eat in or take away.

SAN TELMO
EXPENSIVE

La Brigada. Estados Unidos 465. ☎ **11/4361-5557.** Reservations recommended. Main courses $7–$28. AE, DC, MC, V. Daily noon–4pm and 8pm–1am. Metro: Constitución. ARGENTINE.

The best *parrilla* in San Telmo is reminiscent of the *pampas,* with memorabilia of *gauchos* (Argentine cowboys) filling the restaurant. White linen tables and tango music complement the rustic atmosphere, with an upstairs dining room that faces an excellent walled wine rack. The large, professional staff makes sure diners are never disappointed.

Meats are carefully selected by chef-owner Hugo Echevarrieta, known locally as *el maestro parrillero.* The best choices include the *asado* (short rib roast), *lomo* (sirloin steak, here prepared with a mushroom or pepper sauce), baby beef (an enormous 850g [30 oz.], served for two), and the *mollejas de chivito al verdero* (young goat sweetbreads in a scallion sauce). Less glamorous—but equally recommended—selections from the *parrilla* include young kid tripes and blood sausage. The Felipe Rutini merlot goes perfectly with baby beef and chorizo.

MODERATE

La Casa de Esteban de Lucas. Calle Defensa 1000. ☎ **11/4361-4338.** Main courses $15–$20. AE, DC, MC, V. Tues–Sun 9am–2am. Metro: Constitución. ARGENTINE.

This historic house, once inhabited by Argentina's beloved poet and soldier Esteban de Luca (who wrote the country's first national anthem, the *Marcha Patriotica*), was built in 1786 and declared a National Historic Monument in 1941. Today, it's a popular restaurant serving pasta and meat dishes. Come on Thursday, Friday, or Saturday night after 9pm for the fun-spirited piano show.

INEXPENSIVE

Parrilla al Carbon Eva y Roberto. Estados Unidos 407. ☎ **11/4300-7062.** Main courses $3–$12. No credit cards. Daily noon–4pm and 8pm–2am. Metro: Constitución. ARGENTINE.

This inexpensive, no-nonsense *parrilla* resembles the run-down neighborhood it calls home. A few old records scattered on the walls form the decor, and tables are so tightly spaced that you'll have no choice but to eavesdrop. But during peak times every table is full, as locals slice through thick, juicy steaks sprinkled with *chimichurri* salsa and munch on huge portions of *papas fritas.* Service is friendly and very casual.

4 What to See & Do

Buenos Aires is a wonderful city to explore and fairly easy to navigate. The most impressive historical sites are located around Plaza de Mayo, although you will certainly experience Argentine history in neighborhoods like La Boca and San Telmo, too. Don't miss a walk along the riverfront in Puerto Madero, or an afternoon among the plazas and cafes of Recoleta or Palermo. Numerous sidewalk cafes offer respite for weary feet, and there's good public transportation to carry you from neighborhood to neighborhood.

Your first stop should be to one of the city tourism centers (see "Visitor Information," above) to pick up a guidebook, city map, and any advice you might require. You can also ask at the front desk of your hotel for a copy of "The Golden Map" and "QuickGuide Buenos Aires" to help you navigate the city and locate its major attractions.

NEIGHBORHOODS TO EXPLORE
LA BOCA

La Boca, on the banks of the Riachuelo River, developed originally as a trading center and shipyard. Drawn to the river's commercial potential, Italian immigrants—mainly from Genoa—moved in, giving the neighborhood the distinct flavor it maintains today.

At the center of La Boca lies the ✪ **Caminito,** a short pedestrian walkway (as well as a famous tango song) that is both an outdoor museum and a marketplace. Surrounding the street are shabby metal houses painted in dynamic shades of red, yellow, blue, and green, thanks to designer Benito Quinquela Martín. Today, many Argentine artists live or set up their studios in these vivid sheet-metal houses. Along the Caminito, art and souvenir vendors work side by side with tango performers—this is one place you won't have to pay to see Argentina's great dance. Sculptures, murals, and engravings—some with political and social themes—also line the street.

La Boca's Fine Arts Museum of Argentine Artists, Av. Pedro de Mendoza 1835 (☎ **11/4301-1080**), captures the works of some of the city's best artists. To catch an additional glimpse of La Boca's spirit, walk 4 blocks from the Caminito to the corner of Del Valle Iberlucca and Brandsen streets. **Estadio de Boca Juniors**—the stadium for Buenos Aires's most popular *club de futbol* (soccer club), the Boca Juniors—is here. Go on game day when street parties and general debauchery take over the area. Use caution in straying too far from the Caminito, however, as the less patrolled surrounding areas can be unsafe. Avoid La Boca at night.

SAN TELMO

San Telmo was originally an aristocratic neighborhood, home to Buenos Aires's elite. When yellow fever struck in the 1870s—aggravated by substandard health conditions in the area—these aristocratic families moved north to escape. Poor immigrants soon filled the neighborhood, and the large houses were converted to tenements, called *conventillos*. In 1970, the city passed a number of regulations to restore some of San Telmo's important architectural landmarks. With new life injected into it, the neighborhood has taken on a bohemian flair, attracting artists, dancers, and numerous antiques dealers.

After Plaza de Mayo, **Plaza Dorrego** is the oldest square in the city. Originally the site of a Bethlehemite monastery, the plaza is also where Argentines met to reconfirm their Declaration of Independence from Spain. On Sundays from 10am to 5pm, a wonderful antiques market, along with tango and *milonga* dancers, crowds the square. You can buy leather, silver, and other products here along with antiques.

San Telmo is full of tango clubs, one of the most notable being the **El Viejo Almacén.** During the day you can appreciate the club as a historic landmark: An example of colonial architecture, it was built in 1798 and was a general store and hospital before its reincarnation as the quintessential Argentine tango club. But make sure to go back for a show at night (see "Buenos Aires After Dark," below). If you get the urge for a quick beginner or refresher tango course while you're in San Telmo, look for signs advertising lessons in the windows of clubs—it's a great way to spend the afternoon. (For more, see "Where to Go for Tango Lessons," later in this chapter.)

PALERMO

Palermo is a neighborhood of parks filled with magnolias, pines, palms, and weeping willows, a place where families picnic on weekends and couples stroll at sunset. Take the metro to Plaza Italia, which lets you out next to the **Botanical Gardens** (☎ 11/4831-2951) and **Zoological Gardens** (☎ 11/4806-7412), both open dawn to dusk. Stone paths wind their way through the Botanical Garden, where a student might escape hurried city life to study on a park bench. Flora from throughout South America fills the garden, and fountains bubble at every turn. Next door, the city zoo features an impressive diversity of animals, including indigenous birds and monkeys.

Parque Tres de Febrero, a 1,000-acre paradise of trees, lakes, and walking trails, begins just past the Rose Garden off Avenida Sarmiento. In summer, paddleboats are rented by the hour. Nearby, small streams and lakes meander through the **Japanese Garden** (☎ 11/4804-4922; open daily 9am to 6pm, admission $2), where children can feed the fish (*alimento para peces* means "fish food") and watch the ducks. A small Japanese restaurant offers tea, pastries, sandwiches, and a few Japanese dishes like sushi and teriyaki chicken.

RECOLETA

The city's most fashionable neighborhood, Recoleta, boasts excellent restaurants, cafes, shops, and evening entertainment. French architecture abounds, and Recoleta has a distinctly European feel. Much of the activity takes place along the pedestrian walkway Pte. Roberto M. Ortiz and in front of the Cultural Center and cemetery. Recoleta is a neighborhood of plazas and parks, a place where tourists and wealthy Argentines spend their leisure time outside. Weekends bring street performances, art exhibits, fairs, and sports.

The ✪ **Recoleta Cemetery** (no phone), open daily 10am to 5pm, is a grand tribute to some of Argentina's greatest historical figures and a place where the elite can

Buenos Aires Attractions

Basilica y Convento de San Francisco **2**
Biblioteca Nacional **17**
Botanical & Zoological Gardens **19**
Cabildo **9**
Caminito La Boca **1**
Casa Rosada (Pink House) **6**
Centro Cultural La Recoleta **14**
Congreso (Congress) **10**
El Museo de la Ciudad **3**
Galerías Pacifíco **12**
Iglesia San Ignacio **4**
Japanese Garden **19**
Manzana de las Luces (Block of Lights) **5**
Metropolitan Cathedral **8**
Museo Nacional de Arte Decorativo **18**
Museo Nacional de Bellas Artes **16**
Palacio San Martín **13**
Piramide de Mayo **7**
Recoleta Cemetery **15**
Teatro Colón **11**

show off its wealth. Once the garden of the adjoining white-faced church, the cemetery was created in 1822 and is the oldest in the city. You can spend hours wandering the grounds that cover 4 city blocks and are adorned with works by local and international sculptors. Over 6,400 mausoleums form an architectural free-for-all, including Greek temples and elaborate pyramids. Some are big enough to be small churches. The most popular site of the cemetery is the tomb of Eva Perón (Evita), which is always heaped with flowers and letters from adoring fans. To prevent her body from being stolen again, she has been buried in a concrete vault 27 feet underground. Many rich or famous Argentines are buried here as well, including numerous Argentine presidents of the 20th century, various literary figures, and heroes of the war for independence. As any Argentine will tell you, it's important to live in Recoleta while you're alive, but even more important to stay here in death. How to get a space? You're in luck if your family already owns a plot; otherwise, you can buy space for about $20,000 per square meter—if someone is willing to sell. Guided tours of the cemetery take place the last Sunday of each month at 2:30pm from the cemetery's entrance.

Adjacent to the cemetery, the **Centro Cultural La Recoleta** (Recoleta Cultural Center; see "Buenos Aires After Dark," below) holds permanent and touring art exhibits along with theatrical and musical performances. Designed in the mid–18th century as a Franciscan convent, it was reincarnated as a poorhouse in 1858, serving that function until becoming a cultural center in 1979. The first floor houses an interactive children's science museum.

Biblioteca Nacional (National Library). Calle Aguero 2502. ☎ **11/4806-6155.** Free admission. Mon–Sat 10am–7pm.

Opened in 1992, this modern architectural oddity stands on the land of the former Presidential Residence in which Eva Perón died. With its underground levels, the library can store up to five million volumes. Visit the reading room—occupying two stories at the top of the building—to enjoy an awe-inspiring view of Buenos Aires. The library also hosts special events in its exhibition hall and auditorium.

✪ PLAZA DE MAYO

The historic core of Buenos Aires, the Plaza de Mayo was founded by Juan de Garay in 1580. The plaza's prominent buildings create an architectural timeline: the Cabildo, *Piramide de Mayo* (Pyramid of May), and Metropolitan Cathedral are vestiges of the colonial period (18th and early 19th centuries), while the seats of national and local government reflect the styles of the late 19th and early 20th centuries. In the center of the plaza you'll find palm trees, fountains, and benches. Plaza de Mayo remains the political heart of the city, serving as a forum for protests. The mothers of the *desaparecidos,* victims of the military dictatorship's war against leftists, have demonstrated here since 1976.

The Argentine President, whose actual residence is located in a suburb, goes to work every day at the elegant **Casa Rosada** (Pink House). It is from a balcony of this mansion that Eva Perón addressed adoring crowds of Argentine workers. You can watch the changing of the guards in front of the palace every hour on the hour, and around back is a small museum with information on the history of the building and of the nation. It's open Monday to Friday 10am to 6pm; admission is free.

The original structure of the **Metropolitan Cathedral** (☎ **11/4331-2845**) was built in 1745; it was given a new facade depicting Jacob and his son Joseph and was designated a cathedral in 1836. Inside lies a mausoleum containing the remains of General Jose San Martín, South American liberator regarded as the "Father of the

Evita Perón: Woman, Wife, Icon

Eva Duarte de Perón, widely known as Evita, captured the imagination of millions of Argentines because of her social and economic programs for the working classes. A mediocre stage and radio actress, she married Colonel Juan Perón, a widower, in 1945 and helped in his charismatic presidential campaign. Her own rags-to-riches story endeared her to the people, whom Evita greeted as *los descamisados* (the shirtless ones).

Once Perón took office, she created the Eva Perón Foundation, which redirected funds traditionally controlled by Argentina's elite to programs benefiting hospitals, schools, elderly homes, and various charities. In addition, she raised wages for union workers, established nationwide religious education, and successfully fought for women's suffrage. When Evita died of cancer in 1952, the working classes tried to have her canonized. This effort was blocked, however, by anti-Perónists and members of the nation's elite. Her body was stolen in 1955 following a coup against Juan Perón, and for the next 19 years was hidden in Italy and Spain. Her remains returned to Argentina in 1974 thanks to efforts by Juan Perón's third wife, Isabel, who hoped to be repaid in support from the masses. Evita finally landed next to Juan Perón in the Recoleta Cemetery, one of the only bodies allowed there from a non-elite family.

You will find that even today there is considerable disagreement among Argentines over Evita's legacy. Members of the middle and lower classes tend to see her as a national hero, while many of the country's upper classes believe she stole money from the wealthy and used it to embellish her own popularity.

Nation" (San Martín fought successfully for freedom in Argentina, Peru, and Chile). The tomb of the unknown soldier of Argentine independence is also here. Guided tours take place Monday to Saturday at 11:30am.

The ✪ **Cabildo,** Bolívar 65 (☎ **11/4334-1782**), was the original seat of city government, built in 1764. The old colonial building was significant in the events leading up to Argentina's declaration of independence from Spain in May 1810. Parts of the Cabildo were demolished to create space for Avenida de Mayo and Diagonal Sur. However, the remainder of the building was lovingly restored in 1939 and is worth a visit today. It's the only remaining public building dating back to colonial times.

A striking neoclassical facade covers the **Legislatura de la Ciudad** (City Legislature Building), at Calle Peru and Hipólito Irigoyen, which houses exhibitions in several of its recently restored halls. The building's watchtower has more than 30 bells. In front of the Legislatura, you'll see a bronze statue of Julio A. Roca, considered one of Argentina's greatest presidents.

Farther down Calle Peru stands the enormous ✪ **Manzana de las Luces** (Block of Lights), Calle Peru 272, which served as the intellectual center of the city in the 17th and 18th centuries. This land was granted in 1616 to the Jesuits, who built **San Ignacio**—the city's oldest church—still standing at the corner of Bolivar and Aslina streets. San Ignacio has a beautiful altar. Also located here is the **National School of Buenos Aires,** the most prestigious school in the city. Argentina's best-known intellectuals have gathered and studied here, and the name "block of lights" recognizes the contributions of the National School's graduates, especially in achieving Argentina's independence in the 19th century. Tours (☎ **11/4342-6973**) are usually led on weekends at 3 and 4:30pm and include a visit to the Jesuits' system of underground tunnels, which connected their churches to strategic spots in the city (admission $7). In addition to weekend tours, the Comisión Nacional de la Manzana de las Luces organizes a variety of cultural activities during the week, including folkloric dance lessons, open-air theater performances, art expositions, and music concerts. Call ☎ 11/4331-9534 for information.

Basilica y Convento de San Francisco (San Francisco's Church and Convent, San Roque Parish). Calle Defensa and Alsina. ☎ **11/4331-0625.**Free admission. Metro: Plaza de Mayo.

The San Roque parish is one of the oldest in the city. A Jesuit architect designed the church in 1730, but a final reconstruction in the early 20th century added a German baroque facade, along with statues of Saint Francis of Assisi, Dante, and Christopher Columbus. Inside you'll find a tapestry by Argentine artist Horacio Butler along with an extensive library.

PUERTO MADERO

Puerto Madero became Buenos Aires's first major gateway to trade with Europe when it was built in 1880. But by 1910 the city had already outgrown the port. The Puerto Nuevo (New Port) was established to the north to accommodate growing commercial activity, and Madero was abandoned for almost a century. Urban renewal saved the original port in the 1990s with the construction of a riverfront promenade, apartments, and offices. Bustling and businesslike during the day, the area attracts a fashionable, wealthy crowd at night. It's lined with elegant restaurants serving Argentine steaks and fresh seafood specialties, and there is a popular cinema showing Argentine and Hollywood films.

Calle Florida is the main pedestrian thoroughfare of Buenos Aires and a shopper's paradise. The busiest section, extending south from Plaza San Martín to Avenida Corrientes, is lined with boutiques, restaurants, and record stores. You'll also find the upscale Galerías Pacífico fashion center here (see "Shopping," below).

Plaza San Martín, a tranquil park at the base of Calle Florida in the Retiro neighborhood, is a nice place to take a break. In summer months Argentine businesspeople flock to the park on their lunch hour, loosening their ties, taking off some layers, and sunning for a while. A monument to General Jose San Martín on horseback towers over the scene. The San Martín Palace, one of the seats of the Argentine Ministry of Foreign Affairs, and the elegant Plaza Hotel face the square.

Avenida Corrientes is a living diary of Buenos Aires's cultural development. Until the 1930s, Avenida Corrientes was the favored hangout of tango legends. When the avenue was widened in the mid-1930s, it made its debut as the Argentine Broadway. Today Corrientes, lined with cinemas and theaters, pulses with activity day and night.

MUSEUMS

El Museo de la Ciudad (Museum of the City of Buenos Aires). Calle Alsina 412. ☎ **11/4331-9855** or 11/4343-2123. Admission $1. Mon–Fri 11am–7pm; Sun 3–7pm. Metro: Plaza de Mayo.

The museum pays tribute to the history of the city with its collection of artifacts, documents, and household objects associated with city life. A 19th-century neighborhood pharmacy preserved in its original condition takes up the first floor.

El Museo Histórico Nacional (National History Museum). Calle Defensa 1600. ☎ **11/4307-1182.** Free admission. Tues–Fri noon–6pm; Sat–Sun 3–7pm. Closed in January. Metro: Constitución.

Argentine history from the 16th through the 19th centuries comes to life in the former Lezama family home. The expansive Italian-style mansion houses items saved from Jesuit missions, paintings illustrating clashes between the Spaniards and Native Americans, and relics from the War of Independence against Spain. The focal point of the museum's collection is artist Candido Lopez's series of captivating scenes of the war against Paraguay in the 1870s.

✪ **Museo Nacional de Bellas Artes (National Museum of Fine Arts).** Av. del Libertador 1473. ☎ **11/4803-0802.** Free admission. Tues–Sun 12:30–7:30pm.

This building that formerly pumped the city's water supply metamorphosed into Buenos Aires's most important art museum in 1930. The museum contains the world's largest collection of Argentine sculptures and paintings from the 19th and 20th centuries. It also houses European art dating from the pre-Renaissance period to the present day. The collections include notable pieces by Manet, Goya, El Greco, and Gaugin.

Museo Nacional de Arte Decorativo (National Museum of Decorative Art). Av. del Libertador 1902. ☎ **11/4801-8248.** Admission $2. Mon–Fri 2–8pm; Sat–Sun 11am–7pm.

French architect Rene Sergent, who designed some of the grandest mansions in Buenos Aires, envisioned and developed this museum. The building's 18th-century French design provides a classical setting for the diverse decorative styles represented within. Breathtaking sculptures, paintings, and furnishings round off the collection. The **Museo de Arte Oriental** (Museum of Eastern Art) displays art, pottery, and engravings on the first floor of the building.

OTHER ATTRACTIONS

Among the other notable attractions in town is the historic **Café Tortoni,** long a meeting place for *Porteño* artists and intellectuals. For a full review, see "Where to Dine," above, and for information on the cafe's tango shows, see "Buenos Aires After Dark," below.

Congreso (Congress). Plaza del Congreso. Not open to the public.

The National Congress towers over Avenida de Mayo, with its occupants presumably keeping a watchful eye on the President's Casa Rosada down the street. The capitol building, built in 1906, combines elements of classic Greek and Roman architecture and is topped with an immense central dome modeled after its counterpart in Washington, DC. Today, the building cannot hold all its congressional staff, who have spilled over into neighboring structures.

Plaza Congreso was designed in 1910 to frame the congress building and memorialize the centennial of a revolutionary junta that helped overthrow Spanish rule in Argentina. Stroll around the square and its surroundings to see a number of architectural landmarks, theaters, sidewalk cafes, and bars.

✪ **Teatro Colón (Colón Theater).** Calle Libertad 621 or Calle Toscanini 1180. ☎ **11/4378-7100.** Admission $5. Metro: Tribunales.

Buenos Aires's golden age of prosperity gave birth to this luxurious opera house, which has hosted, among others, Luciano Pavarotti, Julio Bocca, Maria Callas, Placido Domingo, Arturo Toscanini, and Igor Stravinsky. The project took close to 80 years to complete, but the result is spectacular. The majestic building, completed in 1908, combines a variety of European styles, from the Ionic and Corinthian capitals and French stained-glass pieces in the main entrance to the Italian marble staircase and exquisite French furniture, chandeliers, and vases in the Golden Hall. In the main theater—which seats 2,500 people among the orchestra, stalls, boxes, and four rises—an enormous chandelier hangs from the domed ceiling painted by Raúl Soldi. The theatre's acoustics are world renowned. In addition to hosting visiting performers, the Colón has its own philharmonic orchestra, choir, and ballet company. Opera and symphony seasons last from April to November. **Guided tours,** which let you view the main theater, backstage, and costume and stage design workshops, were suspended at the time of publication, but may be resumed at any time. Call ☎ **11/4378-7130** for information.

SPECTATOR SPORTS & OUTDOOR ACTIVITIES

GOLF   Argentina boasts over 200 golf courses. The following are closest to downtown: **Cancha de Golf de la Cuiduad de Buenos Aires,** Av. Torquinst 1426 and Olleros (☎ **11/4772-7261**), is 10 minutes from downtown with great scenery and a 71-par course; **Jockey Club Argentino,** Av. Márquez 1700 (☎ **11/4743-1001**), offers two courses (71 and 72 par) designed by Allister McKenzie.

HORSE RACING   Over much of the 20th century, Argentina was famous for its thoroughbreds. It continues to send prize horses to competitions around the world, although you can watch some of the best right here in Buenos Aires. Races take place at two tracks: **Hipódromo de San Isidro,** Av. Márquez 504 (☎ **11/4743-4010**), and **Hipódromo Argentino,** Av. del Libertador 4205 (☎ **11/4777-9001**), in Palermo. Check the *Buenos Aires Herald* for race information.

POLO   Argentina has won more international polo tournaments than any other country, and the **Argentine Open Championship,** held each November, is the world's most important polo event. There are two seasons for polo in Buenos Aires: March through May and September through December, held at the **Campo Argentino de Polo,** Avenida del Libertador and Avenida Dorrego (☎ **11/4774-4517**). Tickets can be purchased at the gate. Contact the **Asociación Argentina de Polo,** Hipólito Yrigoyen 636 (☎ **11/4331-4646** or 11/4342-8321) for information on polo schools and events. **La Martina Polo Ranch** (☎ **11/4576-7997**), located 37 miles (60km) from Buenos Aires near the town of Vicente Casares, houses over 80 polo horses, as well as a guesthouse with a swimming pool and tennis courts.

SOCCER   One cannot discuss soccer in Argentina without first paying homage to Diego Armando Maradona, Argentina's most revered player and one of the best ever to play the sport. If Argentines unite around Maradona, their solidarity dissolves when they watch their favorite clubs—River Plate, Boca Juniors, Racing Club, Independiente, and San Lorenzo—battle for goals on Sundays. Passion for soccer could not run hotter, and you can catch a game at the **Estadio Boca Juniors,** Brandsen 805 (☎ **11/4362-2050**), in San Telmo, followed by raucous streetside parties. Tickets range from $20 to $100 and can be purchased in advance or at the gate.

5 Shopping

Porteños like to consider their city one of the fashion capitals of the world and, even if it's not Milan, Buenos Aires boasts many of the same upscale stores you would find in New York or Paris (the wealthiest Argentines still fly to Miami for their wardrobes, however). Do not expect to find a city full of indigenous textiles and crafts as you would elsewhere in Latin America; Hermès, Louis Vuitton, Versace, and Ralph Lauren are more on the mark in wealthy districts like Recoleta or Palermo. The European boutiques also sell much better quality clothes than their Argentine counterparts, with the exception of furs, wool, and some leather goods, which are excellent across the country.

STORE HOURS & SHIPPING

Most stores are open weekdays 9am to 8pm and Saturday 9am to 1pm. You might find some shops open Sunday along Avenida Santa Fe, but few will be open on Calle Florida. Shopping centers are open daily 10am to 10pm.

Certain art and antiques dealers will crate and ship bulky objects for an additional fee; others will tell you it's no problem to take that new sculpture directly on the plane. If you don't want to take any chances, contact **UPS** at ☎ **11/4314-5321** or **Federal Express** at ☎ **11/4325-6551.** Whatever your purchase, keep your receipts for invoices over $200; you should be able to get a refund of the 21% tax (VAT) when you leave the country.

GREAT SHOPPING AREAS

MICROCENTER   Calle Florida, the pedestrian walking street in the microcenter, is home to wall-to-wall shops stretching from Plaza San Martín past Avenida Corrientes. The **Galerías Pacífico** mall is located at Calle Florida 750 and Avenida Córdoba (☎ **11/4319-5100**), with a magnificent dome and stunning frescoes painted by renowned local artists. As you approach Plaza San Martín, you find a number of well-regarded shoe stores, jewelers, and shops selling leather goods.

RECOLETA   Avenida Alvear is Argentina's response to the Champs-Elysée and—without taking the comparison too far—it is indeed an elegant, Parisian-like strip of renowned European boutiques and cafes. Start your walk from Plaza Francia and continue from Junín to Cerrito. Along Calle Quintana, French-style mansions share company with additional upscale shops. Nearby **Patio Bullrich,** Av. del Libertador 750 (☎ **11/4815-3501**), is one of the city's best malls. *Caution:* The prices in Recoleta are Parisian as well.

AVENIDA SANTA FE   Popular with local shoppers, Avenida Santa Fe—which the city tourist office likens to Madrid's Gran Vía—offers a wide selection of clothes stores and more down-to-earth prices. You will also find bookstores, ice cream shops, and cinemas along this avenue. The **Alto Palermo Shopping Center,** Av. Santa Fe 3250 (☎ **11/4821-6030**), is another excellent shopping center, with over 160 stores.

SAN TELMO AND LA BOCA   These traditional neighborhoods offer excellent antiques as well as arts and crafts celebrating tango. Street performers and artists are omnipresent. Both of these areas should be visited during the day and avoided at night.

OUTDOOR MARKETS

The ✪ **antiques market in San Telmo,** which takes place every Sunday 10am to 5pm at Plaza Dorrego, is a vibrant, colorful experience. As street vendors sell their heirlooms, singers and dancers move amid the crowd to the music of tangos and *milongas.* Among the vendor stands you will find antique silversmith objects, porcelain, crystal, and other antiques.

Plaza Francia's Fair, at Avenidas del Libertador and Pueyrredón, offers ceramics, leather goods, and other local products. It takes place Sunday 10am to 5pm.

SHOPPING A TO Z

Almost all shops in Buenos Aires accept credit cards. However, you will often get a better price if you offer to pay with cash. You won't be able to use credit cards at outdoor markets.

Shopping Tip

Most antiques stores will come down 10% to 20% from the listed price if you try to bargain, but staff members have a final price from which they can go no lower.

ANTIQUES

Throughout the streets of San Telmo, you will find the city's best antique shops; don't miss the antiques market that takes place all day Sunday at Plaza Dorrego (see "Outdoor Markets," above).

America Antigüedades. Calle Libertad 1591. ☎ **11/4815-4472.**

Set up like an art gallery, this store offers an eclectic mix of antiques, from European and Argentine furniture and paintings, to marble, bronze, and ivory sculptures and 17th-century chandeliers. Open weekdays 10am to 8pm and Saturday 10am to 1pm.

Galería El Solar de French. Calle Defensa 1066. Metro: Constitución.

Built at the beginning of the 20th century in a Spanish colonial style, this is where Argentine patriot Domingo French lived. Today, it's a bustling commercial gallery, with antiques shops, art galleries, and photography stores depicting San Telmo of yesteryear. Hours vary.

ART GALLERIES

Galería Ruth Benzacar. Calle Florida 1000. ☎ **11/4313-8400.** Metro: San Martín.

This contemporary art gallery, located in a hidden underground space at the start of Calle Florida next to Plaza San Martín, hosts temporary exhibitions of local and national interest and gives a good indication of art trends in the country. Among the best-known Argentines who have exhibited here are Alfredo Prior, Miguel Angel Rios, Daniel Garcia, Graciela Hasper, and Pablo Siguier. Open Monday to Friday 11:30am to 8pm, Saturday 10:30am to 1:30pm.

FASHION & APPAREL

Most Argentine clothing stores do not offer the same quality as European names. You will find the city's top fashion stores along Avenida Alvear and Calle Quintana in Recoleta.

Cravall. Calle Quintana 497. ☎ **11/4804-5135.**

Cravall follows the latest trends from New York, Paris, and Milan. Its selections include Brioni, Canali, Gianfranco Ferre, Mila Schön, Roberto Cavalli, Versace, and Dolce & Gabbana.

Ermenegildo Zegna. Alvear Ave. 1920.

The famous Italian chain sells outstanding suits and jackets made of light, cool fabrics. If you've landed in Buenos Aires without your suit, this is among your best options.

Escada Sport. Alvear Ave. and Montevideo. ☎ **11/4815-0353.**

This innovative women's clothing store offers both casual and elegant selections combining quality and comfort.

Yves Saint Laurent. Galerías Pacífico, Calle Florida 753 (metro: Florida) and Alto Palermo, Av. Santa Fe, at Av. Colonel Diaz (metro: Bulnes).

Both branches of YSL (downtown or in Palermo) house excellent suits, shirts, ties, and sportswear for men.

JEWELRY

The city's finest jewelry stores are located in Recoleta and inside many five-star hotels. You can find bargains on gold jewelry along Calle Libertad, near Avenida Corrientes.

Cartier. Alvear Ave. 1898. ☎ **11/4804-2422.**

The famous French jeweler turns up in the elegant Recoleta neighborhood offering a limited selection of dazzling but expensive jewelry.

Cousiño Jewels. In the Sheraton Buenos Aires Hotel, Av. San Martín. ☎ **11/ 4318-9000, ext. 2687.** Metro: Retiro.

Located along the Sheraton hotel's shopping arcade, this Argentine jeweler features a brilliant collection of art made of the national stone, the rhodochrosite, or Inca Rose.

H.Stern. Branches in the Alvear Palace, Inter-Continental, Marriott Plaza, and Park Hyatt hotels.

This upscale Brazilian jeweler, with branches in major cities around the world, sells beautiful stones, including emeralds and the unique imperial topaz. It's the top jeweler in South America.

LEATHER

Argentina is famous for its leather—particularly raw leather—and there are a number of excellent quality shops in Buenos Aires selling everything from clothes, wallets, and purses to luggage, saddles, and shoes. You can usually find better values on leather goods here than abroad, although you should pay close attention to the quality of craftsmanship—especially in less well-known stores—before making your purchase.

El Nochero. Posadas 1245, in the Patio Bullrich Mall. ☎ **11/4815-3629.**

All the products sold at El Nochero are made with first-rate Argentine leather and manufactured by local workers. Shoes and boots, leather goods and clothes, and native silverware (including *mate*) decorate the store. El Nochero is found in the Patio Bullrich mall in Recoleta.

Louis Vuitton. Alvear Ave 1751. ☎ **11/4813-7072.**

The famous Parisian boutique sells an elite line of luggage, purses, and travel bags. It's located alongside Recoleta's most exclusive shops. Open Monday to Friday 10am to 7:30pm and Saturday 10am to 1:30pm.

Rossi & Caruso. Av. Santa Fe 1601. ☎ **11/4811-1965.** Metro: Bulnes.

This store offers the best leather products in the city and is the first choice for visiting celebrities—the King and Queen of Spain and Prince Phillip among them. Products include luggage, saddles and accessories, leather and chamois clothes, purses, wallets, and belts. There is another branch in the Galerías Pacífico mall.

Welcome. Alvear Ave. 500. ☎ **11/4312-8911.**

Open since 1930, this *marroquineria* (leather goods shop) in Recoleta specializes in briefcases, purses, luggage, and other leather goods. It's open Monday to Friday 10am to 2pm and 3 to 7:30pm, Saturday 10am to 2pm.

Tango: A Dance of Seduction and Despair

Argentine tango. The words are so inseparable that it seems impossible to imagine Argentina without thinking of its greatest export to the world. What is this sad soulful melody that captures the hearts of musicians and poets and makes dancing such a seductive art form? Tango originated with a guitar and violin toward the end of the 19th century and was first danced by working-class men in La Boca, San Telmo, and the port area. Combining African rhythms with the *habanera* and *candombe,* it was not the sophisticated dance you know today— rather, the tango originated in brothels and was accompanied by obscene lyrics, not unlike the origins of early American jazz.

Increasing waves of immigrants meant the tango soon made its way to Europe, however, and the dance was internationalized in Paris. With a sense of European approval, Argentine middle and upper classes began to accept the newly refined dance as part of their cultural identity, and the form blossomed under the extraordinary voice of Carlos Gardel. Gardel, who brought tango to Broadway and Hollywood, is nothing short of legendary among Argentines, and you will find his portrait hanging in cafes and tango salons across town.

Tango involves not one but three forms of expression: music, poetry, and dance. While tango may be played by two musicians or a complete orchestra, a piano and *bandoneon*—a German instrument akin to an accordion—are usually included. If there is a singer, the lyrics might come from one of Argentina's great poets, like Jorge Luis Borges, Homero Manzi, or Horacio Ferrer. The words usually concern the connectedness and separateness of man and woman. The dance itself is improvised rather than standardized, although it consists of a series of long walks and intertwined movements, usually in eight-step. In the tango, the man and woman glide across the floor as an exquisitely orchestrated duo with early flirtatious movements giving way to dramatic leads and heartfelt turns. Depending on the music, the dance might proceed slowly and sensually or with furious splendor.

6 Buenos Aires After Dark

From the world-famous Teatro Colón (Colón Theater) to a dimly lit tango salon, Buenos Aires offers an exceptional variety of evening entertainment. *Porteños* eat late and play even later, with theater performances starting around 9pm, bars and nightclubs opening around midnight, and no one showing up until after 1am. Thursday, Friday, and Saturday are the big going-out nights, with the bulk of activity in Recoleta, Palermo, and Costanera. Summer is quieter, since most of the town flees to the coast.

Performing arts in Buenos Aires are centered on the highly regarded Teatro Colón, home to the National Opera, National Symphony, and National Ballet. In addition, there are nearly 40 professional theaters around town showing Broadway and off-Broadway–style hits, Argentine plays, and music reviews. Buy tickets for most productions at the box office or through **Ticketron** (☎ **11/4321-9700**) or **Ticketmaster** (☎ **11/4326-9903**).

For current information on after-dark entertainment during your visit, consult the *Buenos Aires Herald* (in English) or any of the major local publications. The "Quick-Guide Buenos Aires" also has information on shows, theaters, and nightclubs.

THE PERFORMING ARTS
OPERA, BALLET, AND CLASSICAL MUSIC

Luna Park. Av. Corrientes and Bouchard. ☎ **11/4311-1990.** Metro: L.N. Alem.

Once the home of international boxing matches, the Luna is the largest indoor stadium in Argentina and hosts the biggest shows and concerts in Buenos Aires. Many of these are classical music concerts, and the National Symphonic Orchestra often plays here.

Teatro Colón. Calle Libertad 621. ☎ **11/4378-7100.** Metro: Tribunales.

Known across the world for its impeccable acoustics, the Colón has attracted the world's finest opera performers—Luciano Pavarotti, Julio Bocca, Maria Callas, Placido Domingo, and Arturo Toscanini among them. Opera season lasts April to November and, in addition to opera, the Colón has its own philharmonic orchestra, ballet, and choir companies. The main theater seats 2,500 people among the orchestra, stalls, boxes, and four rises.

THEATERS & EXHIBITIONS

The city's best dramatic plays take place at the **Teatro Nacional Cervantes,** Calle Libertad 815 (☎ **11/4816-4224**). **Teatro Opera,** Av. Corrientes 860 (☎ **11/4326-1335**), has been adapted for Broadway-style shows. The **Teatro Municipal General San Martín,** Av. Corrientes 1530 (☎ **0800/333-5254**) has three theaters showing drama, comedy, ballet, music, and children's plays. In Recoleta, **Teatro Coliseo,** Av. Alvear 1125 (☎ **11/4816-5943**), puts on classical music productions. **Teatro Presidente Alvear,** Av. Corrientes 1659 (☎ **11/4374-6076**), features tango and other music shows. The majority of foreign and national music concerts are held at the **Teatro Gran Rex,** Av. Corrientes 857 (☎ **11/4322-8000**).

Centro Cultural Recoleta (Recoleta Cultural Center). Junín 1930. ☎ **11/4803-1041.**

The distinctive building—originally designed as a Franciscan convent—hosts Argentine and international art exhibits, experimental theater works, occasional music concerts, and an interactive science museum for children. The Hard Rock Cafe is located behind the Cultural Center.

THE CLUB AND MUSIC SCENE
TANGO CLUBS

In Buenos Aires, you have the option of *watching* the tango or *dancing* the tango. The former might well lend inspiration to the latter—we recommend a few lessons before you take to the floor (see "Where to Go for Tango Lessons," below). You'll have numerous opportunities to see the dance performed during your visit: Tango and *milonga* dancers frequent the streets of La Boca and San Telmo, many five-star hotels offer afternoon tango shows in their lobbies and bars, and tango salons blanket the city. The most famous salons (except Café Tortoni) are found in San Telmo and combine dinner and show.

Café Tortoni. Av. de Mayo 829. ☎ **11/4342-4328.** Metro: Plaza de Mayo.

High-quality yet inexpensive tango shows are held in the back room of the Café Tortoni and do not include dinner. Show every day but Tuesday at 9pm. Tickets are $9 plus a minimum per-person charge (for food or beverage) of $6.

El Viejo Almacén. Independencía and Balcarce. ☎ **11/4307-7388.** Metro: Constitución.

The most famous of all the city's tango salons, the Almacén has exquisite dancers and a dedicated crowd. Shows involve traditional Argentine—rather than international—style tango. Sunday through Friday with dinner at 8:30pm, show at 9:30pm, Saturday shows at 9:30pm and 11:30pm. Dinner and show $60, show with two drinks $40. Transportation offered to and from some downtown hotels.

La Ventana. Balcarce 425. ☎ **11/4331-0217.** Metro: Constitución.

Some people swear that La Ventana offers the best package in the city—a good meal of Argentine beef and wine with an excellent and varied tango show. Open nightly with dinner at 8pm, show at 10pm. Dinner and show $70, show with two drinks $45.

Michelangelo. Balcarce 433. ☎ **11/4331-5392.** Metro: Constitución.

Michelangelo has its own tango academy and offers exceptional performances. In addition to the dinner and tango show, there is a "tango bar" open at midnight. Open nightly with dinner at 9pm, show at 10:15pm. Dinner and show $75, show with two drinks $50. Transfers to and from hotels included.

Tangoteca. Av. Alicia Moreau de Justo 1728. ☎ **11/4311-1988.** Metro: L.N. Alem.

This tango pavilion in Puerto Madero combines seven tango performances with a restaurant, virtual library, art gallery, dance academy, and multimedia theme bar. Nightly shows at 10pm. Dinner and show $45, show with two drinks $30.

OTHER DANCE CLUBS

Contrary to what you may think, dancing in Buenos Aires is not just about tango. In fact, a surprisingly small number of residents can actually dance tango, with the majority of the younger population preferring clubs with salsa and European beats. Of course, nothing in life changes quite so fast as the "in" discos, so you will want to ask around for the latest hot spots. Here are some that have been holding steady: **El Devino,** Cecilia Grierson 225 (☎ **11/4315-2791**), in Puerto Madero, boasts the top spot among the city's clubs, attracting an affluent and fashionable crowd. Built along the waterfront and resembling the Sydney opera house, El Divino features a good international restaurant, jazz club, and discotheque. There's usually a long line after midnight and a $15 cover; advance reservations at the restaurant will ease your entrance. The city's best salsa dancers head to **Salsón,** Av. Alvarez Thomas 1166 (☎ **11/4637-6970**), which offers lessons on Wednesdays and Fridays at 9pm. In Palermo, **Buenos Aires News,** Av. del Libertador 3883 (☎ **11/4778-1500**), is a rocking late-night club with Latin and European mixes. **Tequila,** Costanera Norte and La Pampa (☎ **11/4788-0438**), is packed every night of the week. There are a number of popular discos nearby as well.

THE BAR SCENE

There is no shortage of popular bars in Buenos Aires, and *Porteños* need little excuse to party. The following are only a few of the many bars and pubs worthy of recommendation.

Chandon Bar. Av. Alicia Moreau de Justo 152. ☎ **11/4315-3533.** Metro: L.N. Alem.

This intimate champagne lounge serves bottles and flutes of Chandon, produced both in France and Argentina. Located in Puerto Madero adjacent to some of the city's best restaurants, Chandon is perfect for a before- or after-dinner drink. Light fare is offered as well.

Where to Go for Tango Lessons

Entering a tango salon—called a *salon de baile*—can be a bit intimidating for the novice. *Porteños* move with such grace and precision it seems they were born with a special tango gene. The style of tango danced in salons is considerably different from, and more subdued than, "show tango." Most respectable dancers would not show up before midnight, giving you the perfect opportunity to sneak in for a group lesson, offered at most of the salons starting around 8 or 9pm. They usually cost between $5 and $10 for an hour; you can request private instruction for between $40 and $70 per hour, depending on the instructor's skill level.

For information on places to dance and learn tango, get a copy of *B.A. Tango* or *El Tangauta,* the city's dedicated tango magazines. One of the best-known spots is **Club Almagro,** Medrano 522 (☎ **11/4774-7454**), which offers evening lessons before opening up the dance floor on Tuesday, Friday, Saturday, and Sunday. **La Galería,** Boedo 722 (☎ **11/4957-1829**), is open Thursday, Saturday, and Sunday and attracts excellent dancers, many of whom compete professionally. **Ideal,** Suipacha 384 (☎ **11/4605-8234**), is open Monday, Wednesday, and Friday. The dancers here come in all ages and have varied abilities. Ongoing evening lessons are also offered at the **Academia Nacional de Tango,** Av. de Mayo 833 (☎ **11/4345-6967**), which is an institute rather than a tango salon.

Henry J. Beans. Junín 1749. ☎ **11/4801-8477.**

A favorite of the expatriate American community and visiting foreigners, this casual Recoleta bar and grill serves burgers, sandwiches, and nachos, along with cocktails and pitchers of beer. Old Coca-Cola ads, Miller and Budweiser neon signs, and model airplanes hang from the ceilings. The waiters do occasional impromptu dances, and the place is packed after midnight. There are a number of other popular restaurants, bars, and discos along Junín.

The Kilkenny. Marcelo T. de Alvear 399. ☎ **11/4312-7291.** Metro: San Martín.

This trendy cafe-bar is more like a rock house than an Irish pub, although you will still be able to order Guinness, Kilkenny, and Harp Irish draft beers. Packed with both locals and foreigners, you are as likely to find people with suits and ties as with jeans and T-shirts. The Kilkenny offers happy hour from 7 to 9pm and live bands every night after midnight; it stays open until 5am.

Ñ Bar & Lounge. Calle Libertad 1082. ☎ **11/816-7508.**

This chic cocktail lounge attracts a fashionable crowd lounging around comfortable tables and couches. Dimly lit studio lighting reveals old album covers on the walls. Try one of the martinis or vodka and whisky cocktails. The bar is open Monday to Thursday 6pm to 3am, Friday 6pm to 5am, and Saturday 8pm to 5am.

Plaza Bar. Marriott Plaza Hotel, Calle Florida 1005. ☎ **11/4318-3000.** Metro: San Martín.

Nearly every Argentine president and his cabinet members have come here, as well as visiting celebrities like the Queen of Spain, the Emperor of Japan, Luciano Pavarotti, and David Copperfield. The English-style bar features mahogany furniture and green velvet upholstery, where guests sip martinis and smoke Cuban cigars. Tuxedo-clad waiters recommend a fine selection of whiskies and brandies.

Feel Like a Movie?

Buenos Aires has over 250 movie theatres showing Argentine and international films. One of the best is the 16-theatre **Village Recoleta,** V. López and Junín (☎ **11/4805-2220**). There are also cinemas at the **Alto Palermo,** Av. Santa Fe 3251 (☎ **11/4827-8000**), and **Galerías Pacífico,** Calle Florida 753 (☎ **11/4319-5357**), shopping malls.

✪ **Plaza Dorrego Bar.** Calle Defensa 1098. ☎ **11/4361-0141.** Metro: Constitución.

Representative of a typical *Porteño* bar from the 19th century, Plaza Dorrego proudly displays portraits of Carlos Gardel, antique liquor bottles stored in cases along the walls, and anonymous writings engraved in the wood. Stop by during the day on Sunday, when you can also catch the colorful San Telmo antiques market on the plaza in front.

The Shamrock. Rodriguez Peña 1220. ☎ **11/4812-3584.** Metro: Callao.

The city's best-known Irish pub is somewhat lacking in authenticity, betrayed by the hot Latin rhythms rather than soft Gaelic music. That said, it's hugely popular with both Argentines and foreign visitors, and is a great spot to begin the night.

Iguazú Falls 4

Las Cataratas del Iguazú—Iguazú Falls—refers to the spectacular canyon of 275 waterfalls in Argentina's Misiones province—falls shaped by over 120 million years of geological history. What UNESCO declared a World Heritage Area in 1984 has become one of South America's most important tourist attractions, a dazzling panorama of cascades that overwhelm the sounds of the surrounding jungle. Fed by the Iguazú River, these perpetual falls were discovered in 1542 by Spanish explorer Alvar Nuñes Cabeza de Vaca and are shared by both Argentina and Brazil—the views are equally impressive from both sides. Although a five-star hotel overlooking the falls exists in both the Argentine and Brazilian national parks, many visitors stay in Puerto Iguazú in Argentina or Foz do Iguaçu in Brazil.

Although Iguazú is best known for its waterfalls, the surrounding subtropical jungle is well worth including in your itinerary. Here, Cupay (a South American hardwood) trees tower over the various layers of life that compete for light, and the National Park is known to contain 200 species of trees, 448 species of birds, 71 species of mammals, 36 species of reptiles, 20 species of amphibians, and over 250 species of butterflies. Spray from the waterfall keeps the humidity levels at over 75%, which promotes a tremendous growth of epiphytes (plants that grow on other plants without taking nutrients from their hosts). Iguazú's climate also provides for the flowering of plants year-round, lending brilliant color to the forest.

You can visit the waterfalls on your own, but you will most certainly need a tour operator to explore the jungle. Allocate at least 1 day to explore the waterfalls on the Argentine side, another day to visit the Brazilian side, and perhaps half a day for a jungle tour.

1 Puerto Iguazú

825mi (1330km) NE of Buenos Aires

This sedate town serves as the main base from which to explore Iguazú National Park, 11 miles (18km) away. It is smaller and safer than its Brazilian counterpart, Foz do Iguaçu, and the hotels and restaurants here are commendable. Nights are generally very quiet.

ESSENTIALS

GETTING THERE

BY PLANE   **Aerolíneas Argentinas** (☎ **3757/420-168**) and **LAPA** (☎ **3757/420-390**) have multiple flights daily from Buenos Aires to **Aeropuerto Internacional Cataratas del Iguazú;** the trip takes 1½ hours. Round-trip fares range between $200 and $400, depending on whether any specials are offered. Catch a taxi or one of the shuttle buses from the airport to town, a 20-minute drive.

BY BUS   The fastest bus service from Buenos Aires is with **Vía Bariloche** (☎ **11/4315-4456** in Buenos Aires), which takes 16 hours for $75 one-way. Less expensive but longer (21 hours) are **Expreso Singer** (☎ **11/4313-3927** in Buenos Aires) and **Expreso Tigre Iguazú** (☎ **11/4313-3915** in Buenos Aires).

VISITOR INFORMATION

Dirección General de Turismo, Victoria Aguirre and Brasil (☎ **3757/420-722**), distributes maps and brochures with excursion and service information. It's open weekdays 8am to noon and 3 to 8pm, weekends 8am to noon and 4:30 to 8pm. Visitor information is also available near the National Park entrance (see below).

In Buenos Aires, get information about Iguazú from **Casa de la Provincia de Misiones,** Av. Santa Fe 989 (☎ **11/4322-0686**), open weekdays 10am to 5pm.

GETTING AROUND

El Práctico local buses run every hour from 8am to 8pm between Puerto Iguazú and the national park, and cost $2. **Parada 10** (☎ **3757/421-527**) provides 24-hour taxi service.

You can rent a car at the airport for the exuberant fee of $150 per day, although this is much more a luxury than a necessity. Try **A1 Ansa Rent a Car** (☎ **3757/420-100**).

VISITING THE NATIONAL PARK

Your first stop is likely to be the **visitor center,** where you can get maps and information about the area's flora and fauna. Although the main National Park visitor center is located near the park entrance, a major project is underway to create a new, environmentally friendly visitor center about one mile further into the park that will house a restaurant and shops. New footbridges are being constructed for the waterfall circuits, and a natural gas train will soon take visitors to the path entrance for the Upper and Lower Circuits and to the footbridge leading to the Devil's Throat (footpaths will remain open for walkers). The visitor center will be staffed with a number of English-speaking guides, available for individual and private tours—you may opt to see the falls on your own or with an experienced local guide. There is a $5 entrance fee to enter the National Park.

The two main paths to view the waterfalls are the ✪ **Circuito Superior** (Upper Circuit) and ✪ **Circuito Inferior** (Lower Circuit), which both begin within walking distance of the visitor center. There's a small snack stop near the beginning of the trails. The Upper Circuit winds its way along the top of the canyon, allowing you to look down the falls and see the area's rich flora, including cacti, ferns, and orchids. The Lower Circuit offers the best views, however, as magnificent waterfalls come hurtling down before you in walls of silvery spray. The waterfalls are clearly marked by signs along the way.

The best time to walk the **Upper Circuit** is early in the morning or late afternoon, and rainbows often appear near sunset. This 3,000-foot (900m) path takes 1 to 2 hours, starting at the viewing tower and leading past **Dos Hermanos, Bossetti,**

The Iguazú Falls Region

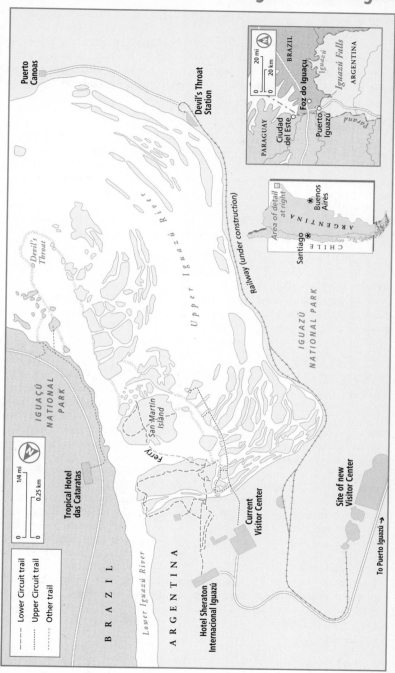

Lower Circuit trail
Upper Circuit trail
Other trail

N

0   1/4 mi
0   0.25 km

BRAZIL

IGUAÇÚ NATIONAL PARK

Tropical Hotel das Cataratas

Devil's Throat

Lower Iguazú River

ARGENTINA

Ferry

San Martin Island

Hotel Sheraton Internacional Iguazú

Current Visitor Center

Site of new Visitor Center

To Puerto Iguazú →

IGUAZÚ NATIONAL PARK

Upper Iguazú River

Railway (under construction)

Devil's Throat Station

Puerto Canoas

N

20 mi
0
20 km
0

BRAZIL

Iguaçu

Iguazú Falls

ARGENTINA

Foz do Iguaçu

Ciudad del Este

PARAGUAY

Puerto Iguazú

Paraná

Area of detail at right

Buenos Aires

ARGENTINA

Santiago

CHILE

Chico, Ramírez, and **San Martín** (the park's widest) waterfalls. You can come right to the edge of these falls and look over them as they fall up to 200 feet below. Along your walk, you can also look across to San Martín Island and the Brazilian side, and you pass a number of small streams and creeks.

The 1.8km (1-mile) **Lower Circuit** takes 2 hours to walk, leading you past **Salto Lanusse** and **Salto Alvar Núñez,** along the Lower Iguazú River past the raging **Salto Dos** and **Tres Mosqueteros** (Two and Three Musketeers) falls. The trail then winds its way toward **Salto Ramírez, Salto Chico** (Small Falls), and **Salto Dos Hermanos** (Two Brothers Falls). Here you'll find an inspiring view of the Devil's Throat and **Salto Bossetti** as well. From the vista point of Salto Bossetti, a small pathway leads down to a small pier where you can catch a free boat to **San Martín Island.**

Once on the island, climb the stairs and walk along clearly marked trails for remarkable views of the surrounding *cataratas*—to the left you see **Garganta del Diablo** (Devil's Throat), **Saltos Brasileros** (Brazilian Falls), and **Ventana;** to the right you overlook the mighty **Saltos San Martín,** which sprays 100 feet (30m) high after hitting the river below. This panoramic view looks out at dozens of falls forming an arch before you. San Martín Island also has a small, idyllic beach perfect for sunbathing and swimming.

Garganta del Diablo is the mother of all waterfalls in Iguazú, visible from vantage points in both the Brazilian and Argentinan parks. Cross the walking bridge to the observation point, at the top of Diablo: The water is eerily calm as it makes its way down the Iguazú River, although it begins to speed up as it approaches the gorge ahead. In front of you, Mother Nature has created a furious avalanche of water and spray that is the tallest waterfall in Iguazú and one of the world's greatest natural spectacles. You might want to bring a raincoat—you *will* get wet.

TOUR OPERATORS

The main tour operator is **Iguazú Jungle Explorer** (☎ 3757/421-600), located both inside the National Park and in the Sheraton International Iguazú. This company offers a "Nautical Adventure" ($15) that visits the falls by inflatable raft, an "Ecological Tour" ($15) that takes you to Devil's Throat and lets you paddle rubber boats along the Upper Iguazú Delta, and the *Gran Aventura* (Great Adventure) tour ($33). This last tour begins with a 5-mile (8km) safari ride along the Yacoratia Path, the original dirt road that led through the forest and on to Buenos Aires. During the ride, you'll view the jungle's extensive flora and might glimpse some of the region's indigenous wildlife (see box below). You will be let off at Puerto Macuco, where you then hop in an inflatable boat with your tour group and navigate 4 miles (6½km) along the lower Iguazú River, braving 1 mile of rapids as you approach the falls in Devil's Throat Canyon. After a thrilling and wet ride, the raft lets you off across from San Martín Island—you can then catch a free boat to the island where there's a small beach for swimming and sunbathing as well as excellent hiking trails. You can combine the Ecological Tour and Great Adventure by buying a full-day Passaporte Verde ($45).

If you want to arrange a private tour for your specific interests, the best outfit is **Explorador Expediciones,** with offices in the Sheraton International Iguazú and in Puerto Iguazú at Puerto Moreno 217 (☎ 3757/421-632). The guides are experts on life in the Iguazú jungle.

WHERE TO STAY

Peak season for hotels in Iguazú is January and February (summer holiday), July (winter break), Semana Santa (Holy Week, the week before Easter), and all long weekends. On the Argentine side, the Sheraton International Iguazú is the only hotel located

Behind the Falls and into the Iguazú Jungle

Dawn in Iguazú brings the first rays of light through the thick forest canopy, as orchids, butterflies, frogs, lizards, parrots, and monkeys wake from their slumber and spread color and life through the forest. Binoculars in hand, step softly into this wonderland, where most sounds are masked by the roar from the falls.

One sees parakeets long before entering the confines of the jungle. Their green bodies and loud song make them rather easy to spot; macaws, parrots, and toucans are other obvious feathered residents. Look closely and listen carefully for the great dusky swift, which nests near the waterfalls, and the great kiskadee, whose family name—*Tyrannidae*—tells much about this yellow-breasted bird's hunting prowess. Cast your eyes below the canopy to observe other flying wonders of the park—an enormous population of butterflies. Brilliant blue flyers known as morpho butterflies flit between deciduous trees and above orderly lines of leaf-cutter ants, along with beautiful red, black, and yellow species of butterflies.

It's close to impossible to walk through the park without running across some of the area's indigenous reptiles. The ubiquitous tropidurus lizards, which feed off birds' eggs, scamper everywhere, while colorful tree frogs hop and croak the nights away. Larger and rarer creatures, like the 1.5m (5-ft.) long tegu lizard and the caiman, a crocodilelike reptile, are discovered only by the patient and persistent visitor.

Warm-blooded creatures share the forest as well. Coatis—aardvark-esque mammals who travel in groups searching for insects and fruit—are frequent and fearless visitors to the trails. Swinging above the footpaths are brown capuchin monkeys, social creatures whose chatter and gestures make them seem more human than most primates. The predators of this warm-blooded group are unusual creatures, from vampire bats to endangered jaguars and pumas. Stay on the walking paths and, when in the jungle, with your tour operator.

An array of subtropical flora surrounds Iguazú's resident animals and insects. Bamboo, ficus, fig, and ancient rosewood trees—up to 1,000 years old—are but a few of the trees that grow abundantly near the river and compete for light, and there is an extraordinary proliferation of epiphytes (plants growing on others) such as bromeliads, güembés, and orchids. In fact, 85 species of orchid thrive in the park, mostly close to the damp and well-lit waterfalls.

inside the National Park; the rest are in Puerto Iguazú, 11 miles (18km) away. On the Brazilian side, the Tropical das Cataratas Hotel and Resort is also within the National Park (see "Where to Stay," under "The Brazilian Side: Foz do Iguaçu," below). Rates are often substantially discounted in the off-season.

EXPENSIVE

Hotel Cataratas. Ruta 12, Km4, 3370 Misiones. ☎ **3757/421-100.** Fax 3757/421-090. www.fnn.net/hoteis/cataratas-ar. E-mail: hotel.cataratas@fnn.net. 100 units. A/C MINIBAR TV TEL. $120–$140 double; from $160 suite. Rates include buffet breakfast. AE, DC, MC, V.

What sets Hotel Cataratas apart from other top hotels in Iguazú is its commitment to service: Staff members go out of their way to make you feel at home, from the helpful receptionists to the meticulous housekeepers. None of the stuffiness you sometimes feel at luxury hotels is in evidence. Despite the hotel's unimpressive exterior, rooms are among the most modern and spacious in the area—especially the 30 new "master rooms" that feature two double beds, handsome wood furniture, color-ful artwork, large bathrooms with separate toilet rooms, in-room safes, and views of the pool or gardens (these rooms are only $20 more than the standard rooms—called "superior"—and the staff is often willing to offer promotional rates). The hotel's many facilities, including outdoor pool, spa, tennis and volleyball courts, putting green, playroom, and gymnasium make this a great choice for families. Restaurant Cataratas offers a fine selection of regional and international dishes, and you can dine inside or out. The hotel lies 2½ miles (4km) from the center of Puerto Iguazú and 10½ miles (17km) from the national park entrance. Bus service is available.

Amenities: Pool, Jacuzzi, sauna, tennis court, game room, conference room, concierge, room service 7am to midnight, laundry service, massage, twice-daily maid service, secretarial services.

✪ **Sheraton International Iguazú.** Parque Nacional Iguazú, 3370 Misiones. ☎ **0800-888-9180** local toll free, or 3757/491-800. Fax 3757/491-810. www.sheraton.com. 180 units. A/C MINIBAR TV TEL. $150–$185 double. AE, DC, MC, V.

Sheraton bought the famous Internacional Cataratas de Iguazú and was in the middle of a major renovation as this book went to press. Guest rooms and facilities were still under construction, so it's not possible to comment on facilities or the quality of ser-vice. Sheraton does plan to maintain the hotel's five-star status. Yet without knowing the specifics, location is obviously the primary reason to stay here. This is the only hotel that sits within the Argentine national park, placing it steps away from the Upper and Lower Circuit trails. Half of the guest rooms will enjoy direct views of the *Garganta del Diablo* (Devil's Throat) and the surrounding falls.

Dining: The hotel's main restaurant has, in the past, enjoyed an excellent reputation.

Amenities: Pool, three tennis courts, conference rooms, activities desk that orga-nizes tours of the park, shopping arcade, room service 7am to 2am, laundry service.

MODERATE

Hotel Saint George. Av. Córdoba 148, 3370 Puerto Iguazú. ☎ **3757/420-633.** Fax 3757/420-651. 60 units. A/C MINIBAR TV TEL. $80 double. Rates include buffet breakfast. AE, DC, MC, V.

A modest hotel in the heart of Puerto Iguazú, the Saint George features colorful rooms with single beds, an inviting pool surrounded by lush vegetation, and a commendable international restaurant that serves tasty fish from the local river. The friendly and enthusiastic staff will answer questions about the National Park and help arrange tours if requested.

INEXPENSIVE

Los Helechos. Paulino Amarante 76, 3370 Puerto Iguazú. ☎/fax **3757/420-338.** 54 units. A/C TV (in some rooms). $35–$45 double. AE, DC, MC, V.

Los Helechos is a great bargain for those seeking comfortable, inexpensive accommo-dations in Puerto Iguazú. Located in the city center, this intimate hotel offers simple rooms with firm mattresses, private bathrooms, and fans or air-conditioning (rooms with air-conditioning and television cost an additional $10). Most rooms surround a plant-filled courtyard, giving you a sense of sleeping near the jungle. There's also a small pool and restaurant.

WHERE TO DINE

Dining in Puerto Iguazú is casual and inexpensive, provided you're looking for a meal outside your hotel. Argentine steaks, seafood, and pasta are common on most menus. The Sheraton, inside the National Park, has the area's best restaurant.

MODERATE

El Charo. Av. Córdoba 106. ☎ **3757/421529.** Main courses $5–$15. No credit cards. Daily 11am–3pm and 7pm–midnight. ARGENTINE.

El Charo is a shambles of a restaurant: Its sagging roof is missing a number of wood beams, pictures hang crooked on the walls, and the bindings on the menus are falling apart. Consider it part of the charm. The casual, cozy restaurant offers cheap, delicious food and is tremendously popular with both tourists and locals. Among the main dishes you'll find breaded veal, sirloin steaks, pork chops, catfish, and items from the *parrilla.* There is also a healthy selection of salads and such pastas as ravioli and cannelloni.

La Rueda. Av. Córdoba 28. No phone. Main courses $4–$13. MC, V. Daily 11am–3pm and 8pm–12:30am. ARGENTINE.

Nothing more than a small A-frame house with an outdoor patio, La Rudea is a delightful place to eat. Despite the casual atmosphere, tables have carefully prepared place settings, waiters are attentive and friendly, and the food—served in large portions—is very good. The diverse menu features pastas, steaks, and fish dishes. Try the *serubi brochette,* a local whitefish served with bacon, tomatoes, onions, and peppers, served with green rice and potatoes.

INEXPENSIVE

La Martina. Av. San Martín 146. ☎ **3757/420-673.** Main courses $6–$10. AE, DC, MC, V. Mon–Sat noon–1am. ARGENTINE.

Young, eager waitresses dressed in white and purple uniforms seat you under the covered patio or on the outdoor terrace. For the duration of your meal—whether you're out of salt or in need of another dish—they will practically sprint across the restaurant to assist you. At lunch, people lounge around the pool ordering sandwiches and snacks; come evening, diners choose the all-you-can-eat *parrilla,* which includes a salad bar, grilled meats and fish (the seasoned dorado is outstanding), and dessert.

PUERTO IGUAZÚ AFTER DARK

Puerto Iguazú offers little in the way of nightlife, although the major hotels often have live music and other entertainment during peak seasons. Try the **Cambalache Tango Bar,** located at Paraguay 546, or **Disco Azaro** at Av. Misiones 110. **Casino Iguazú,** Ruta 12, Km1640 (☎ **3757/498-000**), attracts a well-dressed Argentine and Brazilian crowd and is open nightly 6pm to 5am. Foz do Iguaçu, on the Brazilian side, offers more evening entertainment than Puerto Iguazú (see "Foz do Iguaçu After Dark," below).

2 The Brazilian Side: Foz do Iguaçu

A visit to the Brazilian side of the Iguazú Falls affords a dazzling perspective of the waterfalls. While the trails here are not as extensive as on the Argentine side, the views are no less spectacular. In fact, many people find Brazil's unobstructed panoramic view of Iguazú Falls even more inspiring.

If you decide to stay on the Brazilian side, the Tropical das Cataratas Hotel and Resort (see "Where to Stay," below) is a spectacular hotel at the foot of the National Park, overlooking the falls. Alternatively, you could stay in Foz do Iguaçu—the Brazilian counterpart to Puerto Iguazú. Foz is a slightly larger town 15½ miles (25km) from Iguaçu National Park with numerous hotels, restaurants, and shops (along with a slightly larger incidence of poverty and street crime).

ESSENTIALS

GETTING THERE

BY PLANE **Varig** (☎ **0455/741-424**), **Transbrasil** (☎ **0455/742-029**), and **Vasp** (☎ **0455/742-999**) fly from Rio de Janeiro and other major Brazilian cities to Foz do Iguaçu Airport. The airport lies 7 miles (11km) from Foz do Iguaçu. Public buses make frequent trips to the national park and into town for a small fee.

FROM THE ARGENTINE SIDE Crossing the border is fairly easy (make sure you bring your passport). The most convenient way to get from the Argentine to the Brazilian side is by taxi (about $50 round-trip). Buses are considerably less expensive, but less convenient, too. **Tres Fronteras** (no phone) makes the half-hour trip to Foz do Iguaçu 15 times per day ($3) from the Puerto Iguazú bus terminal; to visit the National Park, ask the bus driver to let you off just after the border check and then catch the national park bus.

BY CAR To avoid border hassles and international driving issues, it's best to take a bus or taxi to the Brazilian side (see "From the Argentine Side," above).

VISITOR INFORMATION

The **Secretaria Municipal de Turismo,** Rua Almirante Barroso 1300 (☎ **045/ 523-0222**), is in Foz do Iguaçu.

SEEING THE BRAZILIAN SIDE OF THE FALLS

The National Park entrance to the **Cataratas do Iguaçu** is at Km17, Rodovia das Cataratas (☎ **045/523-8383**), and the entrance fee is $4. However, the waterfall path begins just in front of the Tropical das Cataratas Hotel and Resort, which is 7 miles (11km) from the National Park entrance (if you are taking a taxi, have your driver bring you directly to the Tropical das Cataratas Hotel and jump onto the trail from here). The trail winds for about 1¼ miles (2km) past **Salto Santa Maria, Deodoro,** and **Floriano.** The last catwalk plants you directly in front of the awesome **Garganta do Diablo** (Devil's Throat) and, once again, you will get wet (there's a small store in front where you can buy rain gear and film). Back on the main trail, a tower beckons visitors to take an elevator to the top for an even broader panoramic view of the falls. The circuit takes about 2 hours.

WHERE TO STAY

As with the hotels on the Argentina side, peak season is January and February (summer holiday), July (winter break), Semana Santa (Holy Week, the week preceding Easter Sunday), and all long weekends. Rates are often substantially discounted in the off-season. The Tropical das Cataratas Hotel and Resort is located within the National Park.

EXPENSIVE

✪ **Tropical das Cataratas Hotel and Resort.** Parque Nacional do Iguaçu, 85863 Foz do Iguaçu. ☎ **045/521-7000.** Fax. 045/574-1688. www.tropicalhotel.com.br. E-mail: gegctr@tropicalhotel.com.br. 200 units. A/C MINIBAR TV TEL. $230–$320 double; suite from $460. AE, DC, MC, V.

The Portuguese colonial hotel (called Hotel das Cataratas for most of its existence), built in 1958 and ideally located in the Brazilian national park, is a UNESCO-declared national heritage site. The meticulously kept pink and white buildings on a cliff above the Brazilian falls have hosted an impressive list of princes and princesses, presidents and ministers, artists and celebrities. While the hotel is often fully booked, its spacious corridors and quiet courtyards promise guests a relaxing vacation. Deluxe and superior rooms, fitted with two-poster beds, granite or marble-top tables, and hardwood floors, are far better than standard rooms; make sure you ask for one that's been refurbished so you don't get stuck with a 45-year-old bathroom. Only the Presidential suite has direct views of the falls; other rooms stare at trees. The trail to the Brazilian falls is just steps from the hotel entrance; when it's a full moon, magical night hikes are arranged for a limited number of guests. An in-house tour operator arranges ecological tours through the National Park and shopping excursions to nearby Paraguay.

Dining/Diversions: The hotel has two commendable restaurants serving Brazilian and international food. **Restaurante Itaipu** is the more formal choice, while the outdoor **Ipe Bar & Grill** offers evening entertainment. Although the national park closes to the public after 7pm, people wanting to come for dinner at the hotel can get a special after-hours pass at the park entrance.

Amenities: Large outdoor pool; tennis court; game room; business center; conference rooms; activities desk; shopping arcade, including a branch of the famous Brazilian jeweler, H. Stern (note that U.S. citizens don't have to pay taxes on Brazilian stones); concierge; room service; laundry service.

WHERE TO DINE

You will find a number of pleasant restaurants in Foz do Iguaçu. **Avenida Brasil,** a main artery of town, is a good place to start for food stalls, coffee bars, and hearty homestyle Brazilian fare.

FOZ DO IGUAÇU AFTER DARK

The **Teatro Plaza Foz,** BR (National Road) 277, Km726 (☎ **045/526-3733**), offers folkloric music and dance shows celebrating Brazilian, Argentine, and Paraguayan cultures. The program starts nightly at 9:30pm and costs $35 with dinner, $25 show only.

5 The Northwest

Far removed from the urban noise of Buenos Aires, Argentina's Northwest feels like a different country altogether. Here you'll find a land rich in history, influenced by an age of pre-Hispanic civilization—a place more culturally similar to Chile and Bolivia (which border the region) than to the federal capital. The Northwest's wildly diverse terrain ranges from the cold peaks of the Andes to the subtropical air of the fertile valleys. You will approach a different pace of life among the old country houses and farms scattered across the area.

The Northwest is considered one of Argentina's oldest settled regions, inhabited largely by Quechuan Indians, an Inca-influenced tribe who descended from Peru in 1450. The Spanish arrived in the early 16th century under explorers Pizarro and Diego de Almagro and colonized the area with forts in Salta, San Salvador de Jujuy, Tucumán, and San Luis. The Diaguita tribes (living here before the Quechuans arrived) were agricultural people whom the Spanish forced into slavery as they extended their empire into the New World. Archaeological sites throughout the region reveal traces of pre-colonial life, including Indian settlements with terraced irrigation farming in the subtropical valleys.

EXPLORING THE REGION

There is no more fascinating way to discover the Northwest than aboard the ✪ **Tren a las Nubes** (Train to the Clouds), an all-day trip that takes you from Salta toward the Chilean border, climbing through breath-taking Andean landscapes and on to the magnificent La Puña Desert. For more, see "Riding the Train to the Clouds," below.

Even if you don't find time for that 15-hour locomotive adventure, you'll still witness the rich history and flavor of the Northwest in its principal towns of **Salta** and **San Salvador de Jujuy.** Keep your eyes open for cultural festivals or religious celebrations to glimpse just how alive the Northwest's traditions remain. Three days at a minimum and 5 days on the outside should allow you to thoroughly experience the flavor of the region.

The easiest way to visit the Northwest is to rent a car, take a bus, or hire a tour guide. Renting a car in this region, however, is very expensive. A subcompact with unlimited mileage costs a minimum of $90 per day. A car that uses gasoil (a hybrid gas/oil fuel) is the cheaper option, though it pollutes the air horribly.

Northwestern Argentina

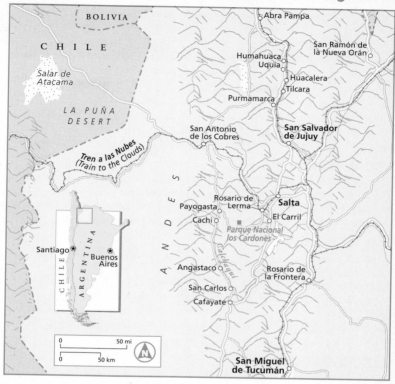

1 Salta

56mi (90km) S of San Salvador de Jujuy

One of Argentina's largest provinces, Salta is bordered by Chile, Bolivia, and Paraguay and is characterized by vastly diverse terrain, ranging from the fertile valley of the provincial capital to the polychrome canyons of Cafayate and the desolate plateau of La Puña. The provincial capital, also called Salta, sits in the Lerma valley with an eternal springlike climate, a town boasting Argentina's best preserved colonial architecture reflected in its churches, government buildings, and houses. Wandering its narrow streets and charming plazas, you will get a sense of how Salta has existed for centuries—quiet, gracious, and reserved. Salta loses its quietude during *Carnival* (Mardi Gras), when thousands of *Salteños* come out for a parade of floats celebrating the region's history and poking fun at public figures; water balloons are also tossed from balconies with great aplomb. Without doubt, the Tren a las Nubes is Salta's main attraction, a 15-hour journey into the sky that takes you across the Northwest's magnificent landscapes. (See "Riding the Train to the Clouds," below.)

ESSENTIALS
GETTING THERE

I don't recommend making the long-distance drive to Argentina's northwest; it's safer and much easier to either fly or take the bus.

BY PLANE   Flights land at **Aybal Airport,** Ruta Nacional 51 (☎ **387/424-1215**). **Aerolíneas Argentinas** (☎ **387/431-1331**), **Southern Winds** (☎ **387/421-1188**), and **LAPA** (☎ **387/431-7080**) fly from Buenos Aires. Flights from Buenos Aires cost between $85 and $300, depending on the season and availability. A shuttle bus travels between the airport and town for about $3 one way; a taxi into town will run about $10.

BY BUS   The **Terminal de Omnibus,** or central bus station, is at Avenida H. Yrigoyen and Abraham Cornejo (☎ **387/431-5227**). Buses arrive from Buenos Aires (20 hours, $64) and travel to San Salvador de Jujuy (2½ hours, $7) and other cities in the region. **Chevalier** and **La Veloz del Norte** are the main bus companies.

VISITOR INFORMATION

The tourism office, **Secretaria de Turismo de la Provincia de Salta,** Buenos Aires 93 (☎ **387/431-0950**), will provide you with maps and information on dining, lodging, and sightseeing in the region. It can also help you arrange individual or group tours. It's open Monday to Friday 9am to 9pm and weekends 9am to 8pm.

FAST FACTS: SALTA

Currency Exchange   Exchange money at the airport or at **Banco de La Nación,** Balcarce 66 (☎ **387/421-3553**).
Emergency   Dial ☎ **377/431-9000** for police, ☎ **377/421-2222** for fire.
Hospital   Saint Bernard Hospital, Tobias 69 (☎ **387/422-4255**).
Tour Operators   Arrange a tour of the region with **Saltur Turismo,** Caseros 525 (☎ **387/431-2012**). The tourist office can also recommend English-speaking tour guides.

GETTING AROUND

Salta is small and easy to explore by foot. The **Peatonal Florida** is Salta's pedestrian walking street—a smaller version of Calle Florida in Buenos Aires—where most of the city's shops are. The main sites are centered on **Plaza 9 de Julio,** where a monument to General Arenales stands in the center and a beautiful baroque cathedral stands at its edge. Built in 1858, the **Cathedral** is considered Argentina's best-preserved colonial church. All the other attractions—except the **Salta Tram** and the **Tren a las Nubes**—are within easy walking distance.

RENTING A CAR   One of the cheapest (and "cheap" is a relative term in these parts) car rental agencies is **Luteral Renta Car,** Buenos Aires 94 (☎ **387/431-4721**), which has subcompacts and four-wheel drives. More expensive, **Hertz** is at Buenos Aires 88 (☎ **387/431-7270**) and **Dollar** is at Buenos Aires 1 (☎ **387/431-8049**).

SEEING THE SIGHTS

Note that museums in the Northwest don't have formal admission fees. Most request small contributions, usually $1 or less.

El Cabildo. Caseros 549. ☎ **387/421-5340.** Museum open Tues–Sun 9:30am–1:30pm and 3:30–7:30pm.

First erected in 1582 when the city was founded, the Cabildo has since reinvented itself a number of times. The latest town hall was completed in 1783 and is typical of Spanish construction—two levels and a tower built around interior patios. The building houses the **Museo Histórico del Norte** (Historic Museum of the North), with 15 exhibition halls related to the Indian, colonial, and liberal periods of *Salteña* history.

Riding the Train to the Clouds

The ✪ **"train to the clouds"** is one of the world's great railroad experiences—a breath-taking ride that climbs to 13,842 feet (4,220m) without the help of cable tracks. The journey takes you 269 miles (434km) through tunnels, turns, and bridges, culminating in the stunning La Polvorilla viaduct. You will cross magnificent landscapes, making your way from the multicolored Lerma valley through the deep canyons and rugged peaks of the Quebrada del Toro and on to the desolate desert plateau of La Puña. The train stops at the peak, where your tour guide will describe the region's topography and verify that everyone is breathing fine and not suffering from altitude sickness. In the small town of San Antonio de los Cobres, you'll have a chance to buy handicrafts, ponchos, and other textile goods from the indigenous people. The 14½-hour ride includes a small breakfast, lunch (additional), and folkloric show with regional music and dance. A restaurant, post office, communications center, and infirmary are among the first-class passenger cars. The ride makes for a fascinating experience, but be prepared for a very long day.

The ticket office for *Tren a las Nubes* (Train to the Clouds) is at Caseros 431 (☎ **387/431-4984**; www.trenubes.com). The train departs Salta's General Belgrano Station most Saturdays at 7:10am and returns that night at 9:50pm, making one stop. The cost is $100, not including lunch.

Here you will see religious and popular art, as well as works from the Jesuit period and from Upper Peru.

Iglesia San Francisco (San Francisco Church). Córdoba and Caseros. Museum open Tues–Fri 10:30am–12:30pm and 4:30–6:30pm; Sat 10:30am–12:30pm.

Rebuilt in 1759 after a fire destroyed the original building, the Iglesia San Francisco is Salta's most prominent postcard image. The terra-cotta facade with its 174-foot tower and tiered white pillars was designed by architect Luis Giorgi. The belfry—the tallest in the Americas—holds the *Campaña de la Patria,* a bronze bell made from the cannons used in the War of Independence's Battle of Salta. A small museum exhibits a variety of 17th- and 18th-century religious images.

Museo Histórico José Evaristo Uriburo. Caseros 417. ☎ **387/421-5340.** Tues–Sun 9:30am–1:30pm and 3–8pm.

José Evaristo Uriburo's family—who produced two of Argentina's presidents—bought this simple adobe house with a roof of reeds and curved tiles in 1810. An entrance from the street leads directly to the courtyard, characteristic of homes of this era. Exhibits include period furniture and costumes, as well as documents and objects belonging to the Uriburos and General Arenales.

Museo Provincial de Bellas Artes de Salta (Museum of Fine Arts). Florida 20. ☎ **387/421-4714.** Mon–Sat 9am–2pm and 4–9pm.

Colorfully decorated tapestries and other regional works fill this 18th-century Spanish house, which houses a permanent collection of colonial art upstairs and religious and contemporary art downstairs. Noteworthy pieces include a portrait of Francisco de Uriburo by Spanish painter Joaquín Sorolla y Bastida and a painting of Salta by Italian Carlo Penutti.

Salta Tram. At the intersection of H. Yrigoyen and San Martin aves. Admission $6 adults, $3 children. Daily 10am–7:45pm.

The Swiss-made cable car has been in operation since 1987 and takes tourists to the top of San Bernardo Hill, 1,000 feet (300m) over Salta. There is not much to do other than enjoy the panoramic view of the Lerma valley and grab a snack at the casual restaurant. If you miss the last tram, a $5 taxi will return you to the city center.

✪ **San Bernardo Convent.** Caseros near Santa Fe.

The oldest religious building in Salta was declared a Historical National Monument in 1941. It's worth a walk by to admire the city's most impressive example of colonial and indigenous art. The entrance was carved from a carob tree by aborigines in 1762.

WHERE TO STAY

Salta's hotels leave luxury to the imagination—hard to believe, given the 21% tax on lodging. That said, a five-star **Hotel Internacional de Salta** is being built on Balcare, near Avenida de Belgrano, which will outshine all other hotels in the region. However, as this book went to press, the hotel's exact opening date had not been determined.

EXPENSIVE

Gran Hotel Presidente. Av. de Belgrano 353, 4400 Salta. ☎ /fax **387/431-2022.** E-mail: granhotelpresidente@salnet.com.ar. 96 units. A/C MINIBAR TV TEL. $138 double; $185 suite. Rates include buffet breakfast. AE, DC, MC, V.

The best hotel in Salta has attractive guest rooms splashed in rose and apple green with comfortable white tile bathrooms. The hotel's modernity stands in stark contrast to other accommodations in Salta: The chic lobby features black and white marble with art deco furniture and leopard-skin upholstery. The international restaurant can be seen on the upstairs mezzanine, and the Presidente has a great spa with a heated indoor pool, sauna, fitness room, and solarium. The hotel also offers 24-hour room service, meeting rooms, laundry, and dry cleaning.

Portezuelo Hotel. Av. Turística 1, 4400 Salta. ☎ **387/431-0104.** Fax 387/431-4654. www.portezuelohotel.com. E-mail: info@portezuelohotel.com.ar. 63 units. A/C MINIBAR TV TEL. $95 double; $175 suite. Rates include buffet breakfast. AE, DC, MC, V.

Remodeled in 1998, the Portezuelo Hotel stands on top of Cerro San Bernardo, a hill just outside the city center. Local artwork decorates the lobby, adjacent to which is Santana—Salta's most elegant restaurant, boasting panoramic views of the Lerma valley (see "Where to Dine," below). Guest rooms have A-frame ceilings and simple wood decor; expect to sleep peacefully since you're away from downtown. Amenities include an outdoor pool, meeting rooms, travel agency, room service, and laundry facilities.

MODERATE

Hotel Salta. Buenos Aires 1, 4400 Salta. ☎ **387/431-0740.** Fax 387/431-0740. E-mail: hotelsalta@arnet.com.ar. 98 units. A/C TV TEL. From $100 double. Rates include buffet breakfast. AE, DC, MC, V.

Popular with Europeans, this neoclassical hotel sits in the heart of Salta—next to Plaza 9 de Julio—and makes a good base from which to explore the city. Opened in 1890, it is hardly the most modern accommodation you'll find, but the hotel's wood balconies and arabesque carvings, peaceful courtyard and refreshing pool, and beautiful dining room considerably increase its appeal. The hotel also features a small business center, 24-hour room service, and laundry facilities.

INEXPENSIVE

Hotel Victoria Plaza. Zuviría 16, 4400 Salta. ☎ **387/431-8500.** Fax 387/431-0634. www.usuarios.arnet.com.ar/vplaza. E-mail: vplaza@arnet.com.ar. 96 units. A/C MINIBAR TV TEL. From $80 double. Rates include buffet breakfast. AE, DC, MC, V.

If your purpose in Salta is sightseeing rather than hotel appreciation, then the Victoria Plaza should do just fine. Rooms are stark and simple but also clean, comfortable, and cheerfully maintained. The hotel is also well located, next to the main plaza, the cabildo (town hall), and the cathedral. The cafeterialike restaurant is open 24 hours, and the hotel offers free airport transfers and laundry service.

WHERE TO DINE

The Northwest has its own cuisine influenced by indigenous cooking. *Locro* (a corn and bean soup), *humitas* (a sort of corn and goat cheese soufflé), tamales (meat and potatoes in a ground corn shell), empanadas (a turnover filled with potatoes, meat, and vegetables), *lechón* (suckling pig), and *cabrito* (goat) occupy most menus. Traditional Argentine steaks and pasta dishes are usually available, too.

MODERATE

Jockey Club. Av. de Belgrano 366. ☎ **387/315-612.** Reservations recommended. Main courses $7–$16. AE, DC, MC, V. Daily noon–3:30pm and 8:30pm–1am. INTERNATIONAL.

For refined dining in the city center, the Jockey Club's small dining rooms feature stone floors, rose-colored tablecloths, soft lighting, and jazz playing in the background. The menu is light and healthy: The chicken with vegetables and the beef Wellington are both recommended, although the trout stuffed with shrimp is the best choice on the menu.

Restaurante Portezuelo. Av. Turística 1. ☎ **387/431-0104.** Reservations recommended. Main courses $8–$15. AE, DC, MC, V. Daily 6am–midnight. INTERNATIONAL.

This restaurant in the Portezuelo Hotel is Salta's most elegant. The intimate dining room, set aside large windows overlooking Lerma valley, is decorated with regional artwork and tables topped with white linens and silver candles. You won't go wrong with any of the creative entrees, such as trout stuffed with shrimp and cheese, sirloin steak with scalloped potatoes, or grilled chicken with mustard and tarragon. Jazz music occasionally accompanies dinner, and tables on the veranda are available in warm weather.

✪ **Santana.** Mendoza 208. ☎ **387/320-941.** Reservations recommended. Main courses $8–$14. AE, DC, MC, V. Daily noon–3:30pm and 8pm–midnight. INTERNATIONAL.

One of the few international restaurants in Salta with a classic rather than rustic style, Santana's refined atmosphere is slightly offset by a beautifully framed caricature of the Mona Lisa. Da Vinci's masterpiece notwithstanding, the enticing menu features chicken with white-wine cream sauce, lobster with chimichurri sauce, and homemade ravioli with various cheeses. There is a rich selection of Argentine wines; ask for a bottle from San Juan or Mendoza. At lunch, a three-course menu is offered for $10.

INEXPENSIVE

Café van Gogh. España 502. No phone. Main courses $4–$6. AE, DC, MC, V. Mon–Thurs 7am–2am; Fri–Sat 24 hours; Sun 7am–1am. CAFE.

"Our mission is to make everyone feel at home, no matter where they're from," says one staff member, who proudly displays a collection of coffee cups from Argentina, Europe, and North America. The comfortable cafe, surrounded by little white lights on the outside and decorated with van Gogh prints inside, serves pizzas, sandwiches, meats, hot dogs, and empanadas. Come evening, the cafe-turned-bar becomes the center of Salta nightlife, with live bands playing Wednesday through Saturday after midnight.

✪ **El Solar del Convento.** Caseros 444. ☎ **387/421-5124.** Main courses $5–$10. AE, DC, MC, V. Daily 11am–3pm and 8pm–midnight. ARGENTINE.

Ask locals to point you to Salta's best "typical" restaurant—the word used to describe places serving traditional Argentine fare—and they won't hesitate with their answer. The former Jesuit convent has long been an outstanding *parrilla* serving quality steaks (the mixed grill for two is a deal at $15) and regional specialties like empanadas, tamales, and *humitas.* The 10-page menu also includes beef brochettes, grilled salmon, chicken with mushrooms, and large, fresh salads. There are two dining rooms connected by an A-frame thatched roof, and a medieval-style chandelier hangs from the front ceiling. Red and green tables give the restaurant an aura of Christmas, and the atmosphere is indeed festive: Even late on a Sunday night, expect the restaurant to be packed.

La Posta. España 456. ☎ **387/421-7091.** Main courses $4–$6. DC, MC, V. Daily noon–4pm and 8pm–1am. ARGENTINE.

An inexpensive local *parrilla* in the town center, La Posta serves succulent steaks and fresh pastas. There's a garden courtyard and a rustic indoor dining room lined with paintings of provincial life. The encircled brick grill in back lets you watch the *parrilla* in action.

2 A Driving Tour of the Calchaquíes Valley via Cachi & Cafayate

The landscape surrounding Salta resembles the southwestern United States, with polychromatic hills keeping watch over the Lerma valley. Tobacco, tropical fruits, and sugar cane are the main agricultural products, and you will see tobacco "ovens" off the side of the road (Marlboro grows Virginia tobacco here through a subsidiary). Heading south from Salta on Ruta Nacional 68 for 23½ miles (38km) will bring you to **El Carril,** which is a typical small town of the valley, with a central plaza and botanical garden displaying 70% of the region's flora.

Although you can reach **Cafayate** more quickly by continuing south on Ruta Nacional 68, it is far more interesting to go west on Ruta Provincial 33 for about 1½ miles (2.7km) after El Carril. You'll come across **Cabaña de Cabras, La Flor del Pago** (☎ 387/684-3960), one of the principal goat farm and cheese factories in Argentina. Ducks, geese, and hundreds of goats roam the scenic property, and there is a small dining room and cheese shop in the proprietors' home where you can sample the delicious chèvre. (The kind owners will prepare a multicourse lunch or dinner with advance reservations.) All cheese production on the farm is natural.

While the region surrounding El Carril is characterized by dense vegetation, the land quickly becomes dry as you climb Ruta Provincial 33 toward **Piedra del Molino** (Mill Rock). The road narrows from pavement to dirt 6 miles (10km) west of El Carril—watch closely for oncoming cars. A small shrine to Saint Raphael (a patron saint of travelers) indicates your arrival at Mill Rock (11,873 ft/3,620m) and the entrance to **Parque Nacional los Cardones,** a semi-arid landscape filled with cacti, sage, and limestone rock formations.

Six miles (10km) before Cachi lies **Payogasta,** an ancient Indian town on the path of the Inca Road that once connected an empire stretching from Peru. **Cachi** (see below) is another pre-colonial village worth a visit for its Indian ruins. From Cachi, take Ruta Nacional 40 south past Brealito to Molinos, a 17th-century town of adobe homes and dusty streets virtually unchanged from how it must have appeared 350 years ago. Continuing south, consider stopping 5½ miles (9km) before Angastaco at the **Estancia Carmen** (☎ **368/15693005**), which boasts spectacular views of the Calchaquíes valley and its long mountain canyon. Between 9am and 6pm you can visit the ranch's Inca ruins, rent horses, and peek inside the private church in back—inside, two 300-year-old mummies rest in peace.

Continue south on Ruta Nacional 40 to **Angastaco**—depending on where you are along the circuit, this may be a good place to spend the night. **Hostería Angastaco,** Avenida Libertad (☎ **3868/15639016**), lies 0.6 miles (1km) west of the village and is popular with European travelers. The simple hotel offers live folkloric music each evening and help arranging regional excursions and horseback riding. From Angastaco to San Carlos, you will pass the **Quebrada de las Flechas** (Arrows Ravine) with stunning rock formations that appeared in *The Empire Strikes Back*. People often stop their cars at the side of the road and climb a bit. Jesuits settled in **San Carlos,** and the church is a national historic monument. **Cafayate** (see below) marks the southern end of this circuit.

Return to Salta along Ruta Nacional 68 heading north, which takes you through the **Río Calchaquíes valley** and on to the **Quebrada del Río de las Conchas** (Canyon of the River of Shells). Among the most interesting crimson rock formations you should stop at are the Garganta del Diablo (Devil's Throat), El Anfiteatro (the Ampitheater), and Los Castillos (the Castles), which are all indicated by road signs. Salta is 120 miles (194km) from Cafayate along Ruta Nacional 68, and it shouldn't take more than a few hours to drive.

CACHI

Home of the Chicoanas Indians before the Spanish arrived, Cachi is a tiny pueblo of about 5,000 people, interesting for its Indian ruins, colonial church, and archaeological museum. The Spanish colonial **church,** built in the 17th century and located next to the main plaza, has a floor and ceiling made from cactus wood. The **archaeological museum** is the most impressive museum of its kind in the Northwest, capturing the influence of the Incas and Spanish on the region's indigenous people. Located next to the main plaza, its courtyard is filled with Incan stone engravings and pre-Columbian artifacts. Wall rugs, ponchos, and ceramics are sold at the **Centro Artesanal,** next to the tourist office, on the main plaza (the people of Cachi are well respected for their weaving skills, and the ponchos they sell are beautiful). **La Paya,** 6mi (10km) south of Cachi, and **Potrero de Payogasta,** 6 mi (10km) north of Cachi, hold the area's most important archaeological sites.

GETTING THERE   Cachi lies 97 miles (157km) west of Salta on Ruta Provincial 33. **Empresa Marcos Rueda** offers two buses daily from Salta; the trip takes 5 hours and costs $15.

VISITOR INFORMATION   You can pick up maps, excursion information, and tips on restaurants and hotels at the **Oficina de Turismo,** Avenida General Güemes (☎ **3868/491053**), open Monday to Saturday 9am to 9pm.

WHERE TO STAY

Hostal La Paya. 8km from Cachi, on RN 40 to Molinos. ☎ **3868/491139.** E-mail: hostallapaya@ish.com.ar. 10 units. From $48 double. Rates include breakfast. AE, MC, V.

Opened in 2000 on a 19th-century *estancia* (ranch), this rustic inn looks out to the Calchaquíes valley and is a quiet place to walk, read, and relax. Guest rooms have adobe walls and wood beam ceilings, floor blankets made from llama wool, and mattresses laid on stone frames. You can have each of your meals here if you like—all the produce (except the meat) comes from this farm. The owners will also arrange excursions to the nearby mountains, valley, and river upon request.

WHERE TO DINE

Confitería y Comedor del Sol. Ruiz de los Llanos. ☎ **387/156055149.** Main courses $3–6. No credit cards. Daily 8am–1am. REGIONAL.

When you walk into this village restaurant, locals are likely to cease their conversations and stare for a minute. Not to worry—they will quickly return to their business ònce you sit down; many are engaged in the afternoon's current soap opera. The menu is simple, consisting of pastas, *milanesas* (breaded meat cutlets), empanadas, and tamales. This is a great place to have lunch on your way to Molinos.

CAFAYATE

Cafayate is a picturesque colonial town nestled in the Río Calchaquíes valley and famous for its wine production. Popular with Argentine tourists, Cafayate's streets are lined with baroque-style houses built in the late 19th century. The main tourist attractions, in addition to the two major vineyards just outside town, are the Regional and Archeological Museum and the Museum of Grapevines and Wine (see below). You can find regional arts and crafts of excellent quality at shops surrounding the main plaza.

GETTING THERE   Cafayate lies 120 miles (194km) southwest of Salta on Ruta Nacional 68. **Empresa El Indio** (☎ **387/421-9519**) offers three buses daily from Salta; the trip takes 3½ hours and costs $13.

VISITOR INFORMATION   The **tourist office** (☎ 3868/21206) is located on the main plaza and provides maps, bus schedules, and lodging recommendations. Open hours are Monday through Saturday from 10am to 6pm.

SEEING THE SIGHTS

Museo Regional y Arqueologíco Rodolfo Bravo (Regional and Archaeological Museum). Colón 191. Hours vary.

This small museum displays ceramics, textiles, and metal objects discovered over a 66-year period by Rodolfo Bravo. These archaeological finds celebrate the heritage of Diaguita-Calchaquíes and Incan tribes in the region and cover a period between the 4th and 15th centuries.

Museo de la Vid y el Vino (Museum of Grapevines and Wine). Ruta Nacional 40, at Av. General Güemes. ☎ **3868/421125.** Daily 8am–8pm.

Part of the Bodega Encantada winery, this museum tells the story of grape-growing and wine-making in and around Cafayate. The 19th-century building houses old-fashioned machinery and more modern equipment, as well as agricultural implements and documentary photographs.

Michel Torino Bodega La Rosa. Finca La Rosa, 2 miles (3km) from Cafayate on Ruta Nacional 40. No phone. Hours vary.

This medium-sized *bodega,* opened since 1892, produces roughly 10 million liters of wine per year (10,000 bottles per hour), with Malbec (a dry red), Cabernet Sauvignon, Merlot, Chardonnay, and "Michael Torino" Torrontes (a Riesling-like white) the main products. The Don David reserve is the vineyard's top selection. Guided tours in Spanish only are offered Monday to Thursday 8am to 5pm, and Friday 8am to 4pm.

Bodegas Etchart. Finca La Rosa, 2 miles (3km) from Cafayate on Ruta Nacional 40. ☎ **3868/421310.** Hours vary.

This is one of the region's most important vineyards, with 6,000 bottles per hour—including Chardonnay (for which this *bodega* is best known), Cabernet Sauvignon, Torrontes, and Malbec—exported to more than 30 countries. One-hour guided tours and wine tastings are offered Monday to Friday 8am to noon and 3 to 6pm, and Saturday 8am to noon.

WHERE TO STAY

The tourist office can help you with lodging in Cafayate and the surrounding area. Inquire about a new luxury property (not completed at press time) called **La Casa,** a colonial-style inn that promises to be the best accommodation in the region, with double rooms starting at $250.

Gran Real. Av. General Güemes 128, 4427 Cafayate. ☎ **3868/421231.** Fax 3868/421016. 34 units. A/C TV TEL. From $60 double. MC, V.

This modest hotel has quiet rooms and simple furnishings. Popular with Argentine visitors, it also has a pool and barbecue area, cafe, and bar. Service is friendly.

WHERE TO DINE

La Carreta de Don Olegario. Av. General Güemes 2. ☎ **3868/421004.** Main courses $3–7. MC, V. Daily noon–3pm and 8–11pm. REGIONAL.

Of the couple of restaurants surrounding the main plaza, this is the best. The large dining room, furnished with green tables and strobe lighting, lacks elegance but has an authentic selection of regional dishes from the northwest. Service is unhurried, so plan to enjoy a leisurely lunch or dinner if you come here.

3 San Salvador de Jujuy

1,004mi (1,620km) NW of Buenos Aires, 56mi (90km) N of Salta

The regional capital of Jujuy, San Salvador—commonly called Jujuy—was established by the Spanish in 1592 as their northernmost settlement in Argentina. In 1812 during the wars of independence, General Belgrano evacuated residents of the city before Spanish troops arrived—an event celebrated each July known as *Éxodo Jujueño* (Jujuy Exodus). The well-preserved colonial town is smaller than Salta and doesn't have a great deal to offer, although there are a few interesting museums and a beautiful cathedral surrounding Plaza Belgrano. The Indian market across from the bus terminal offers a good sense of daily life here, with many vendors dressed in traditional costumes selling food, indigenous crafts, and textiles. Jujuy is also the best base from which to explore the Quebrada de Humahuaca (Humahuaca Gorge), which extends to the north (see "Driving the Quebrada de Humahuaca (Humahuaca Gorge)," below). The circuit includes the Cerro de los Siete Colores (Hill of the Seven Colors), the artists' haven Tilcara, and La Garganta del Diablo (Devil's Throat) gorge.

ESSENTIALS

GETTING THERE   Jujuy's airport (☎ **388/491505**) is 15½ miles (25km) from town. **Aerolíneas Argentinas** (☎ **388/422-5414**) and **LAPA** (☎ **387/423-0839**) fly from Buenos Aires. Flights from Buenos Aires cost between $85 and $300, depending on the season and availability.

The **Terminal de Omnibus,** or main bus station, is located at Dorrego and Iguazú (☎ **388/426229**). Buses arrive from Buenos Aires and travel to Salta, Tucumán, Catamarca, and other cities in the region. **Empresa Balut** (☎ **387/432-0608**) makes the 2½-hour trip to Humahuaca (see "Driving the Quebrada de Humahuaca (Humahuaca Gorge)," below).

If you opt to rent a car, expect to pay about $80 per day with 124 miles (200km) included, $90 per day with 186 miles (300km) included. Try **Avis** at Belgrano 715 (☎ **388/422-5880**) or one of the rental agencies at the airport.

VISITOR INFORMATION & FAST FACTS   The small **visitor information center** is located at Belgrano 690 (☎ **388/422-1326**). It is open weekdays 7am to 1pm and 3 to 9pm, and weekends 9am to 9pm.

You can arrange regional tours at **Grafitti Turismo,** Belgrano 601 (☎ **388/423-4033**). They will change money here, too.

Citibank, located at the corner of España and Balcare, has a 24-hour ATM and change machine. The bank is open weekdays 9am to 2pm.

GETTING AROUND   Easy to explore on foot, Jujuy is more compact than Salta, and its major attractions can be visited in a few hours. The bulk of commercial activity takes place around **Plaza Belgrano,** where the Casa de Gobierno, the cabildo (town hall), and the cathedral are located. Built in 1750, the **cathedral** has a baroque pulpit carved in wood by the indigenous people and should not be missed. Shopping in Jujuy is concentrated along **Calle Belgrano.**

SEEING THE SIGHTS

Most museums in this area are free or request a small donation, usually no more that $1.

✪ **Museo Arqueológico Provincial (Provincial Archaeological Museum).** Lavalle 434. ☎ **388/422-1343.** Daily 9am–noon and 3–8pm.

Archaeological finds represent over 2,500 years of life in the Jujuy region, including a 2,600-year-old ceramic goddess, a lithic collection of arrowheads, the bones of a child from 1,000 years ago, and two mummified adults. Objects from the Yavi and Humahuaca cultures are also exhibited.

Museo Histórico Provincial "Juan Galo Lavalle" (Provincial Historical Museum). Lavalle 252. ☎ **388/422-1355.** Mon–Fri 8am–1pm and 4–8pm; Sat–Sun 9am–noon and 4–8pm.

This was the house in which General Lavalle was killed in 1841, and the large door through which he was shot is on display, right next to an enormous bust of the Argentine hero. Other exhibits include war materials and documents used during the 25-year struggle for independence in Jujuy.

Museo Histórico en Maquetas y Miniaturas "Victor Morales" (Historical Museum in Miniatures and Models). Gordaliza 1511. ☎ **388/422-4243.** Mon–Fri 8am–12:30pm and 4–10pm; Sat–Sun 9am–noon and 3–8pm.

This unique museum recounts the history of Argentina in miniature, using tiny lead and tin models to depict the English invasions, the founding of Jujuy, and the country's independence movement, including the Battle of Salta. Miniature weapons, uniforms, and carriages are also on display.

WHERE TO STAY

Accommodations in the Northwest are overpriced, given their mediocre quality. The places we list are the best you will find, but in many cases that's not saying much. But you're here to see the sights, not to linger in the confines of your hotel. Note that accommodations in San Salvador quickly fill up in July during the *Éxodo Jujeño* (Jujuy Exodus) celebration.

Altos de la Viña. Av. Pasquini López 50, 4600 Jujuy. ☎ **388/426-2626.** E-mail: lavina@imagine.com.ar. 70 units. A/C MINIBAR TV TEL. From $95 double; $160 suite. AE, DC, MC, V.

This is the best hotel in Jujuy, located on a hill 2 miles (3km) from the city center. A wealth of outdoor activities on the sprawling property include volleyball, miniature golf, tennis, and swimming in the outdoor pool. Half of the guest rooms have balconies with terrific views of the city; bathrooms have phones, hair dryers, and good amenities. The best rooms are "VIPs" (only $15 more)—they feature classic furniture, impressive woodwork, and linens decorated with country French colors. The hotel has an excellent restaurant and a very friendly staff. Meeting rooms, room service, and laundry facilities are available.

Augustus Hotel. Calle Belgrano 715, 4600 Jujuy. ☎ **388/423-0203.** Fax 388/423-0209. 81 units. TV TEL. From $68 double; $132 suite. Rates include buffet breakfast. AE, DC, MC, V.

Don't expect too much from this simple hotel, located on Jujuy's one shopping street. Standard rooms have uninspiring red carpet, small bathrooms, and twin beds. For only $10 more, "VIP" rooms are slightly larger and have better furniture and air conditioning. This is your best option if the nicer hotels are already booked.

Jujuy Palace Hotel. Calle Belgrano 1060, 4600 Jujuy. ☎/fax **388/423-0433.** E-mail: jupalace@imagine.com.ar. 54 units. A/C TV TEL. $80 double; $120 suite. Rates include buffet breakfast. AE, DC, MC, V.

If lobbies are any indication of a hotel's quality, then the modern and comfortable furnishings you'll find upon entering the Jujuy Palace prove that the management is committed to maintaining a good face. And for a 30-year-old property, the hotel isn't bad—guest rooms have in fact been remodeled to make them more inviting. They are clean, small, and sparsely decorated—definitely overpriced, though. The friendly hotel, centrally located in front of the cathedral, has meeting rooms, 24-hour room service, a restaurant, a gym, and a sauna.

WHERE TO DINE

Altos de la Viña. Av. Pasquini López 50. ☎ **388/426-2626.** Reservations recommended. Main courses $9–$11. AE, DC, MC, V. Daily 11:30am–4pm and 8:30pm–midnight. INTERNATIONAL.

This is as elegant as Jujuy gets. You'll have to leave the city center to reach this hilltop hotel restaurant, with splendid views of the town below. Folkloric groups occasionally serenade the dining room at dinner, and there are candlelit tables outside in summer. The extensive menu focuses on seafood and homemade pastas: The *trucha rellena*—trout stuffed with shrimp, mushrooms, cognac, and white wine—is among the best choices. Plan to stay for a long meal, as you'll want to linger over one of the mouthwatering desserts. A weekend buffet is offered for $10.

Krysys. Balcarce 272. ☎ **388/423-1126.** Main courses $6–$10. AE, DC, MC, V. Daily noon–3pm and 8pm–midnight. ARGENTINE.

A giant Coke sign outside marks the entrance to Jujuy's best *parrilla*, serving juicy Argentine steaks. The international menu also has a number of pasta and chicken

> ### Need a Break?
>
> **Heladeria Pinguino,** Belgrano 718 (☎ **388/422-7247**), has 50 flavors of ice cream and frozen yogurt to cool you down. The small cafe is open daily 10am to midnight.

selections as well. This is a festive restaurant, where locals come to celebrate good times and special occasions.

La Royal Confitería. Calle Belgrano 766. ☎ **388/422-6202.** Main courses $2–$6. MC, V. Daily 7:30am–midnight. SNACKS.

One of the few places you can eat any time of day, La Royal offers pizzas, empanadas, sandwiches, and other light snacks. An old grandfather clock goes undisturbed by the modern American rock playing over speakers. Black-and-white photos of American actors decorate the walls of this casual but popular cafeteria.

Manos Jujeñas. Senador Pérez 222. ☎ **388/422-2368.** Main courses $4–$8. No credit cards. Mon–Sat noon–3pm and 8pm–midnight. REGIONAL.

Tables are normally packed at this delightful restaurant specializing in regional dishes like empanadas, *humitas,* and tamales. The small, two-level dining room is decorated with local crafts and costumes, and soft Andean music plays in the background. You will have an excellent and very inexpensive meal here: Consider the trout from the nearby Yala River, or one of the homemade pastas served weekends only. A tall glass of orange juice is only a peso. When it's crowded, be prepared to wait a bit for your food.

4 Driving the Quebrada de Humahuaca (Humahuaca Gorge)

For the first 30 or 40 minutes as you head north on Ruta Nacional 9 from San Salvador de Jujuy, undulating hills reveal fields rich with tobacco and corn and expose the rural economy of Argentina's Northwest. Quechuan women wearing colorful ponchos walk with babies strapped to their backs while horses, cows, and goats graze on the surrounding vegetation. Look closely and you might spot a gaucho charging after his herd.

As you climb along the Río Grande to Purmamarca, 44 miles (71km) from the region's capital, the land becomes increasingly dry and gives way to striking rock formations. When you arrive at the junction of Ruta Provincial 52 and Ruta Nacional 9, head west for a few kilometers to reach the small colonial hamlet. Framing Purmamarca like a timeless painting, the **Cerro de los Siete Colores** (Hill of the Seven Colors) reflects its beauty onto the pueblo's quiet streets and dusty adobe homes. Try to arrive early—9am is best—when the morning sun shines brightly on the hill's facade and reveals its tapestry of colors.

Heading back to Ruta Nacional 9 and continuing 12 miles (20km) north, you will arrive at the artist's haven of **Tilcara,** with a pre-Hispanic fortress called a *pucará.* Here you will find spectacular panoramic views of the Humahuaca valley as well as a trapezoid-shaped monument marking the Tropic of Capricorn. To visit **La Garganta del Diablo** (Devil's Throat)—a steep gorge with a small walkway leading along the rock's edge—leave Ruta Nacional 9 and head east of Tilcara for a short distance. Be careful walking here, as there is only a small rope separating you from the depth below.

Continue north along Ruta Nacional 9, where you will pass the small adobe villages of Huacalera and Uquia. About 26 miles (42km) north of Tilcara lies **Humahuaca,** a sleepy yet enchanting village of only a couple of thousand Indian residents. Its relaxed pace will make Buenos Aires seem light years away. Note that at an elevation of 9,000 feet (2,700m), you will feel a little out of breath here, and nights are quite cold. Although the nearby Inca ruins of **Coctaca** are best explored with a tour guide, you can visit them on your own or with a taxi ($15 round-trip, including driver wait time) by following a dirt road about 6 miles (10km) out of Humahuaca. Coctaca is a large Indian settlement that the Spaniards discovered in the 17th century. Although the ruins are hard to distinguish from the rocks and debris, you can make out outlines of the terraced crop fields for which the Incas were famous. The site is surrounded by cactus and provides excellent photo opportunities.

From San Salvador de Jujuy, you can travel this circuit by bus or by car. If you decide you'd like to stay the night in Humahuaca (78 miles/126km north of San Salvador), a simple but hospitable option is the **Hostería Camino del Inca,** Calle Ejército del Norte s/n (☎ **887/421-1136**). Otherwise, the circuit can easily be completed in a day.

6 The Argentine Lake District

The Lake District is Argentina's premier vacation destination, a ruggedly beautiful jewel of a region characterized by snowcapped mountains, waterfalls, lush forest, the area's namesake lakes and trout-filled, crystalline rivers. The region stretches from north of Junín de los Andes to the south of Esquel, incorporating small villages, ranches, several spectacular national parks, and the thriving city of Bariloche. Visitors here often liken the Lake District to Alpine Europe, as much for the landscape as for the clapboard architecture influenced by Swiss and German immigration. Although it is considered part of Patagonia, the Lake District has little in common with its southern neighbors, especially now that increased migration from cities such as Buenos Aires continues to urbanize the region.

The allure of the Lake District is that it offers something for everyone year-round, from hiking to biking, fishing to hunting, sightseeing to sunbathing, summer boating to winter skiing. The region is also well known for its food—venison, wild boar, trout, smoked cheeses, wild mushrooms, sweet marmalades, chocolates, and more. Tourism is the principal economic force here, which means that prices soar as the swarming masses pour into this region from December to March and during the month of July. I highly recommend that you plan a trip during the off-season, especially in November or April, when the weather is still pleasant, although it is possible to escape the crowds even during the middle of summer.

Considering the enormous, flat *pampa* that separates Buenos Aires from the Lake District, and the region's proximity to the international border with Chile, many visitors opt to include a trip to Chile's Lake District while here. (For more on Chile's Lake District, see chapter 12, "The Chilean Lake District.") This can be done by boat aboard the popular "Lake Crossing" through Puerto Blest to Lago Todos los Santos near Ensenada, or by vehicle. For general information about this region on the Web, try **www.7lagos.com**.

EXPLORING THE REGION

Although the Lake District extends from Junín de los Andes south to Esquel, I have focused in this chapter on the most scenic and accessible destinations in the region: Junín de los Andes, San Martín de los Andes, San Carlos de Bariloche (usually called simply Bariloche), and Villa La Angostura. This coverage includes the area's many national parks as well as driving tours and boat trips that take in the best of that

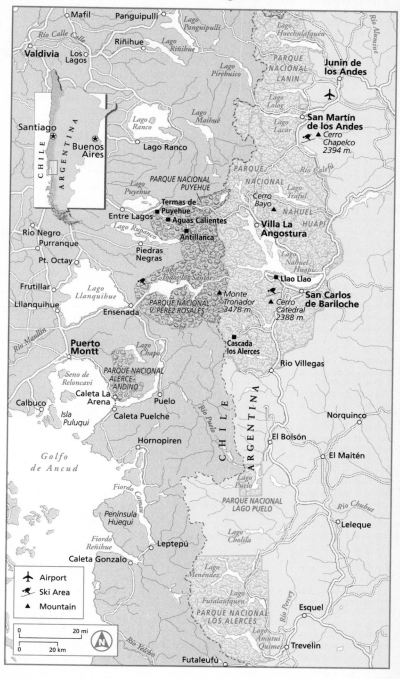

Mafil
Panguipulli
Lago Panguipulli
Río Calle Calle
Río Alumine
Lago Huechulafquen

Riñihue
Lago Riñihue

Valdivia
Los Lagos

PARQUE NACIONAL LANIN

Junín de los Andes

Lago Pirehuico

Lago Lolog

Santiago

Lago Ranco

Lago Maihué

Lago Lacar

San Martín de los Andes

▲ Cerro Chapelco 2394 m.

Buenos Aires

Lago Ranco

PARQUE NACIONAL PUYEHUE

PARQUE NACIONAL

Río Calefu

CHILE
ARGENTINA

Lago Puyehue

Termas de Puyehue
■ Aguas Calientes

Cerro Bayo ▲

NAHUEL

Lago Traful

Entre Lagos

Lago Rupanco

■ Antillanca

Villa La Angostura

HUAPI

Río Negro
Purranque

Piedras Negras

Lago Nahuel Huapi

Pt. Octay

Lago Todos los Santos

● Llao Llao

Frutillar

Lago Llanquihue

PARQUE NACIONAL V. PEREZ ROSALES

▲ Monte Tronador 3478 m.

▲ Cerro Catedral 2388 m.

San Carlos de Bariloche

Llanquihue

Ensenada

■ Cascada los Alerces

Puerto Montt

Lago Chapo

Río Villegas

PARQUE NACIONAL ALERCE-ANDINO

Seno de Reloncavi

Norquinco

Caleta La Arena

Puelo

Calbuco

Isla Puluqui

Caleta Puelche

El Bolsón

El Maitén

Hornopiren

CHILE
ARGENTINA

Río Puelo

Golfo de Ancud

Fiordo Comau

Lago Puelo

PARQUE NACIONAL LAGO PUELO

Río Chubut

Península Huequi

Leleque

Fiordo Reñihue

Leptepú

Lago Cholila

Caleta Gonzalo

Lago Menéndez

Lago Futalaufquen

PARQUE NACIONAL LOS ALERCES

Río Percey

Esquel

✈ Airport

⛷ Ski Area

▲ Mountain

Río Yelcho

Lago Amutui Quimei

Trevelin

0 ——— 20 mi

0 ——— 20 km

Futaleufú

stunning lakeside scenery. The best way to view this region is to base yourself in one of these towns and strike out and explore the surrounding wilderness. All of the towns described in this chapter offer enough outdoor and sightseeing excursions to fill one or even two weeks, but four to five days in one location is ample time for a visit. An interesting option for travelers is to make a detour into Chile via the lake crossing from Bariloche, or to organize a boat-bus combination that loops from Bariloche and Villa La Angostura in Argentina, then crosses the border into Chile and stops in Puyehue, continuing on south to Puerto Varas or Puerto Montt, then crossing back into Argentina and Bariloche via the Lake Crossing. This takes some planning; see chapter 12, "The Chilean Lake District," for more information.

1 San Martín de los Andes

1,017 miles (1,640km) SW of Buenos Aires; 124 miles (200km) N of San Carlos de Bariloche

San Martín de los Andes is a charming mountain town of 15,000 nestled on the tip of Lago Lácar between high peaks. The town is considered the tourism capital of the Neuquen region, a claim that's hard to negate considering the copious arts and crafts shops, gear rental shops, restaurants, and hotels that constitute much of downtown. San Martín has grown considerably in the past 10 years, but thankfully hasn't succumbed to the whims of developers as Bariloche has, owing to city laws that limit building height and regulate architectural styles. The town is quieter than Bariloche, and decidedly more picturesque, thanks to its timber-heavy architecture and Swiss Alpine influence. San Martín overflows with activities, from biking to hiking to boating to skiing, but it is also very popular for hunting and fishing, and some do come just to relax. The tourism infrastructure here is excellent, with every lodging option imaginable and plenty of great restaurants.

ESSENTIALS
GETTING THERE
BY PLANE   **Aeropuerto Internacional Chapelco** (☎ **02972/428388**) sits halfway between San Martín and Junín de los Andes (see below), and therefore serves both destinations. **Austral,** Capitán Drury 876 (☎ **02972/427003**), has flights from Buenos Aires and Córdoba; **TAN,** Belgrano 760 (☎ **02972/427872**), has service from Buenos Aires, Córdoba, Mendoza, and Bariloche. **LADE,** Av. San Martín 915 (☎ **02972/427672**), has service to Buenos Aires, Córdoba, and Bariloche. A taxi to San Martín costs about $18; there are also transfer services available at the airport for $5 per person. A taxi to Junín de los Andes costs $15; transfer services are $5 per person. By Mich Rent a Car and Avis both have auto rental kiosks at the airport.

BY BUS   The **Terminal de Ómnibus** is at Villegas and Juez del Valle (☎ **02972/ 427044**). Daily bus service to San Martín de los Andes from Buenos Aires is offered by **El Valle** (☎ **02972/422800**). **Ko-Ko Chevalier** (☎ **02972/427422**) also offers service to and from Buenos Aires, and serves Villa La Angostura and Bariloche by the paved or by the scenic Siete Lagos route. **Centenario** (☎ **02972/427294**) has service to Chile, and also offers daily service to Buenos Aires; Villarrica- and Pucón-bound buses leave Monday to Saturday, and those for Puerto Montt, Tuesday to Thursday. **Albus** (☎ **02972/428100**) has trips to Bariloche via the Siete Lagos route. Bus service can vary due to season, and it's best to evaluate a coach's condition and services before buying a ticket, especially for trips to and from Buenos Aires.

BY CAR   San Martín de los Andes can be reached from San Carlos de Bariloche following one of three routes. The popular 124-mile (200km) Siete Lagos route takes Routes 234-231-237, and sometimes closes during the winter. The 99-mile (160km) Paso Córdoba route takes Routes 234-63-237; the longest, yet entirely paved 161-mile (260km) Collón Curá route follows routes 234-40-237. If driving at night, take the paved route. To get to Neuquén (260 miles/420km), take Routes 234-40-22. From Chile, take the Tromen Pass (82 miles, or 132km, from Pucón) to Route 62, taking you to Route 234 and through Junín de los Andes.

GETTING AROUND

San Martín is compact enough to explore by foot. For outlying excursions, tour companies can arrange transportation. **Avis** car rental has an office at Av. San Martín 998 (☎ **02972/427704;** fax 428500) as well as a kiosk at the airport; **ICI Rent-A-Car** is at Villegas 590 (☎ **02972/427800**); **Nieves Rent-A-Car** is at Villegas 725 (☎ **02972/428684**); **Localiza/El Claro** is at Villegas 977 (☎ **02972/428876**); and **By Mich Rent a Car** is at Av. San Martín 960 (☎ **02972/427997**) and at the airport.

Note that two main streets have similar names and can be confusing: Perito Moreno and Mariano Moreno.

VISITOR INFORMATION

San Martín's excellent **Oficina de Turismo** offers comprehensive accommodation listings with prices and other tourism-related info, and the staff is friendly and eager to make your stay pleasurable. They can be found at Rosas and Avenida San Martín at the main plaza and are open Monday to Sunday 8 to 11am (☎/fax **02972/427347** and 02972/427695). The **Asociación Hotelero y Gastronomía** (☎ **02972/427166**) also offers lodging information, including photographs of each establishment. It's open Monday to Sunday 9am to 1pm and 3 to 7pm, and during high season Monday to Sunday 9am to 10pm, but this service is not as efficient as the Oficina de Turismo.

FAST FACTS: SAN MARTÍN DE LOS ANDES

Banks/Currency Exchange   **Andina International** at Capitán Drury 876 exchanges money; banks such as **Banco de la Nacion** at Av. San Martín 687, **Banco de la Provincia Neuquen** at Belgrano and Obeid, and **Banco Rio Negro** at Perito Moreno and Elordi have automatic tellers and money exchange. All banks are open Monday to Friday 10am to 3pm.

Emergency   Dial **107.**

Hospital   **Hospital Regional Ramon Carrillo** is at Avenida San Martín and Coronel Rodhe (☎ **02972/427211**).

Laundry   **Marva** at Capitán Drury and Villegas (☎ **02972/428791**); **Laverap Plus** at Villegas 972 (☎ **02972/427500**); **Lácar** at Elordi 839 (☎ **02972/ 427317**).

Police   For emergencies, dial **101.** The federal police station is at Av. San Martín 915 (☎ **02972/428249**); the provincial police station is at Belgrano 635 (☎ **02972/ 427300**).

Post Office   **Correo Argentino** is at the corner of General Roca and Coronel Pérez (☎ **02972/427201**).

Telephone & Internet   Try logging on at **Cooperativa Telefoníca** at Capitán Drury 761; open 9am–11pm.

WHAT TO SEE & DO

San Martín de los Andes is heavily geared toward tourism, and accordingly its streets are lined with shops selling arts and crafts, wonderful regional specialties such as smoked meats and cheeses, outdoor gear, books and more. Visitors will find most of these shops on **Av. San Martín** and **General Villegas,** but suffice to say that you could lose an afternoon wandering the general downtown area and poking your head into these well-stocked shops. For regional specialties and/or chocolates try **Ahumadero El Ciervo,** General Villegas 724 (☎ **02972/427450**); **El Turista,** Belgrano 845 (☎ **02972/428524**); or **Su Chocolate Casero** Villegas 453 (☎ **02972/427924**). For arts and crafts try **Artesanís Neuquinas,** J.M. de Rosas 790 (☎ **02972/428396**).

San Martín is a mountain town geared toward outdoor activities. If you're not up to exercising a lot of physical activity, take a stroll down to the lake and kick back on the beach. Alternatively, rent a bike and take a slow pedal around town. Pack a picnic lunch and head to Hua Hum (described below).

TOUR OPERATORS & TRAVEL AGENCIES

Both **Tiempo,** Av. San Martín 950 (☎/fax **02972/427113;** e-mail: tiempopatagonico@usa.net), and **Pucará,** Av. San Martín 943 (☎ **02972/427218;** e-mail: pucara@smandes.com.ar), offer similar tours and prices, and also operate as travel agencies for booking plane tickets. Excursions to the village Quila Quina, via a sinuous road that offers dramatic views of Lago Lácar, cost $14; a longer excursion including Chapelco and Arrayán is $22. Excursions to the hot springs Termas de Lahuenco are $30; scenic drives through the Siete Lagos route are $30 (to Villa La Angostura) and $35 (to Bariloche). A gorgeous circuit trip to Volcán Lanín and Lago Huechulafquen goes for $30. Tours do not include lunch, which must be brought along or arranged ahead of time.

OUTDOOR ACTIVITIES

BIKING San Martín is well suited for biking, and shops offer directions and maps. Bike rentals are available at **Enduro Kawa & Bikes** at Belgrano 845 (☎ **02972/427093**), **HD Rodados** at Av. San Martín 1061 (☎ **02972/427345**), and **Mountain Snow Shop** at Av. San Martín 861 (☎ **02972/427728**).

BOATING **Naviera Lacar & Nonthue** (☎ **02972/428427**) at the Costanera and main pier offers year-round boat excursions on Lago Lácar. A full-day excursion to Hua Hum includes a short navigation through Lago Nonthué. The cost is $35 adults, $20 kids 6 to 12 and seniors, plus park entrance fees; there's a restaurant in Hua Hum, or you can bring a picnic lunch. Naviera also operates a ferry service to the beautiful, but packed during the summer, beaches of Quila Quina for $10 adults, $7 kids 6 to 12 and seniors. Naviera also rents kayaks for $6 per hour.

To raft the Hua Hum River, get in contact with Tiempo Tours or Pucará (see "Tour Operators & Travel Agencies," above).

FISHING INFORMATION & LICENSES **Jorge Cardillo Pesca** at General Roca 636 (☎ **02972/428372;** e-mail: cardillo@smandes.com.ar) is a well-stocked fly-fishing shop that organizes day and overnight fishing expeditions to the Meliquina, Chimehuín, and Malleo rivers, among other areas. The other local fishing expert is **Jorge Bisso** (☎ **02972/421453;** e-mail: jbissoflyfishing@smandes.com.ar), who will arrange fishing expeditions around the area. You can pick up a fishing guide at the **Oficina Guardafauna** at General Roca 849 (☎ **02972/427091**).

MOUNTAINEERING Victor Gutiérrez and his son Jano Gutiérrez are the top climbing and mountaineering guides in the region (Victor has more than 40 years' experience in the region), and offer climbing and orientation courses, ascents of Volcán Lanín and Volcán Domuyo, and treks, climbs and overnight trips in Lanín and Nahuel Huapi national parks. Both have cell phones; Victor can be reached at ☎ **02944/15-61-0440;** e-mail: victorg11@latinmail.com. Jano can be reached at ☎ **02944/15-63-3260;** e-mail: janoclif@latinmail.com.

SKIING   The principal winter draw for San Martín de los Andes is **Cerro Chapelco,** one of the premier ski resorts in South America. Just 12 miles (20km) outside town, Cerro Chapelco is known for its plentiful, varying terrain and great amenities. Although popular, the resort isn't as swamped with skiers as Bariloche is. The resort sports one gondola (which takes skiers and visitors to the main lodge), five chair lifts, and five T-bars. The terrain is 40% beginner, 30% intermediate, and 30% advanced/expert. Chapelco offers excellent, bilingual ski instruction, ski and snowboard rental, and special activities such as dog-sledding. The resort has open-bowl skiing and tree skiing, and numerous restaurants. To get here without renting a car, ask your hotel to arrange transportation or hire a *remise* (private taxi).

To drive to the resort from town, follow Ruta 234 south along Lago Lácar; it's paved except for the last 3 miles (5km). Lift tickets are quite reasonable, and vary from low to high season. A 3-day ticket runs $63 to $113 for adults, and $54 to $90 for kids. During the summer the resort is open for hiking and sightseeing, with lift access. For more information, call ☎ **02972/427460** or visit www.7lagos.com/skienchapelco. The road is usually passable, but you may need chains during heavy snowfall; check chain conditions before heading up to the resort.

WHERE TO STAY

Accommodations in San Martín have either private parking or ample free street parking.

EXPENSIVE

Hostería del Chapelco. Almirante Brown 297, San Martín de los Andes. ☎ **02972/ 427610.** Fax 02972/427097. www.hosteríadelchapelco.com.ar. E-mail: hcchapelco@ smandes.com.ar. 14 units, 22 cabañas. TV TEL. $65 double. AE, MC, DC, V.

Just about every kind of unit is available at this hostería, including new hotel rooms and cabañas, and cheaper, older duplex and A-frame units. Although it sits on the lakeshore, the rooms do not benefit from the view, but a bright lobby takes advantage of the location with giant picture windows. The hotel rooms and the six attached cabañas are spanking new, with stark, modern furnishings and tile floors; the cabañas have open living/kitchen areas. The duplex units are more economical, but they feel like family rumpus rooms, and the interiors could use new carpet and fresh paint. Las Alpinas houses the oldest units, six small but decent A-frame detached cabañas. The wood and whitewashed walls of the hotel are pleasant, but lend little character to the place. The lobby's fireside chairs and wraparound banquette are a nice place to watch the rippling lake.

As quality, size, and character differ, it's best to view all units if you have the opportunity to do so before booking.

Amenities: Room service, a pretty little dining area for breakfast, bar, and baby-sitting.

Hostería La Posta del Cazador. Av. San Martín 175, San Martín de los Andes. ☎ **02972/ 427501.** Fax 02972/422231. E-mail: laposta@satlink.com. 19 units. TV TEL. $77–$109 double. AE, DC, MC, V.

The hostería that bills itself as "the only lodge with a view of the lake" actually affords views to only half the guests; the other half have a view of a leafy parking lot. Either way, proximity to the lakeshore is a bonus during the summer months, and the street on which the hotel sits is quiet and wooded. La Posta del Cazador (The Hunting Lodge) comes with the de rigueur deer antlers and the like, but it feels more like a castle, due to an enormous circular iron chandelier that casts an eerie yellow light, a floor-to-ceiling stone fireplace, stained glass, and walls adorned with battle swords and cross-of-arms. Rooms are slightly cramped, but they are comfortable; interiors feature wavy white plaster walls, dark wood, and chiffon curtains. The Hostería is owner-run and patrolled by a friendly cat.

Dining: There's a pleasant bar and dining area for breakfast and a reasonably priced menu of snacks and sandwiches.

Hotel Sol de los Andes. Cerro Commandante Díaz s/n, San Martín de los Andes. ☎/fax **02972/427460.** www.wam.com/tourism/hoteles/demor. E-mail: soldelosandes@smandes. neuquen.com.ar. 117 units. TV TEL. $60–$120 double; $110–$220 suite. AE, DC, MC, V.

San Martín's first grand hotel has taken a nosedive during the past decade, going from a five-star rating to just three stars—and with good reason. It's still the only hotel with the capacity for conventions (and it continues to host a multitude of business events, fashion shows, and other gala parties), but few upgrades since the 1970s make for tired, funky interiors. Double rooms are spacious but older; the same can be said for the bathrooms. The beds are low to the ground and average in quality. The suites come with cracked white leather sofas, a dining table, and a sliding door that opens to the bedroom, and they are quite large. The Sol de los Andes sits high above the San Martín, with great views—half look toward the city, half toward the mountain that abuts the hotel—but you'll have to hoof it or take a cab to get to downtown. The hotel is popular with families for its ski and summer package deals and kid's activities, including a penthouse swimming pool, video game, and Ping-Pong room. It might take a little work getting past the Kelly green AstroTurf that blankets the deck and pool area, however.

Dining: The hotel has a restaurant that serves international cuisine, and a spacious bar/lounge with great views.

Amenities: Laundry, room service, outdoor pool, massage, sauna, minigym, game room, conference rooms.

✪ **La Cheminée.** General Roca and Mariano Moreno, San Martín de los Andes. ☎ **02972/ 427617.** Fax 02972/427762. www.7lagos.com/lacheminee. E-mail: lacheminee@smandes. com.ar. 19 units. MINIBAR TV TEL. $120–$175 double, including breakfast. AE, DC, MC, V.

Warm, attentive service and snug accommodations make La Cheminée a top choice, which is why so many foreign travel groups book a few nights here. The Alpine-Swiss design popular in San Martín is in full swing here, with carved and stenciled woodwork and other touches that have been meticulously well-maintained since the hotel's opening 15 years ago. Spacious rooms are carpeted and feature wood ceilings and a pastel, country design with thick cotton floral bedspreads and striped wallpaper. Be sure to book the room they call a double *hogar*—for 10 dollars more, it includes a fireplace. The fern-filled lobby's wooden floors are softened by fluffy rugs, and the walls are adorned with oil paintings rendered by local artists; there's even a small gallery with paintings for sale. La Cheminée has one of the area's few swimming pools, and there's a whirlpool and sauna too. Conveniently located, but 1 block up from the hubbub. Ask for multiple-day discounts.

Dining: The hotel is known for its delicious breakfast, adding trout pâté, caviar, and fresh bread to the usual offerings; a restaurant also serves lunch and dinner.

Amenities: Laundry, room service, outdoor pool, whirlpool, sauna.

✪ **Le Chatelet.** Villegas 650, San Martín de los Andes. ☎ **02972/428294.** E-mail: lechatelet@smandes.com.ar. 32 units. TV TEL. $100–$160 double; $120–$185 suite, including breakfast. AE, DC, MC, V.

Le Chatelet's spacious bedrooms, charming Swiss design, and full-service amenities are its strength. The classically designed lobby/lounge area is not as cozy as other hotels are, but the bedrooms are wonderful, with fireplaces and queen-size beds. All rooms have atticlike wooden ceilings and triangular windows, lace curtains, and a tremendous amount of walking room; suites are twice the size of doubles. There's free use of video cassette players, and the hotel stocks a video and book library in the lobby. The location is 2 blocks from downtown on a quiet residential street, and there's a grassy, enclosed backyard with an outdoor pool. Le Chatelet often offers ski and summer package deals; inquire when making a reservation. They'll also help you organize excursions around the area.

Dining: Le Chatelet serves an abundant breakfast, adding excellent meats and smoked cheeses to the morning menu; a restaurant sports a roaring fire in the evenings and makes a good place to unwind after a day of outdoor activity.

Amenities: Laundry, 24-hour room service, business center, outdoor pool, sauna, minigym, stereo, VCR, library, kid's area.

Le Village. General Roca 816, San Martín de los Andes. ☎/fax **02972/427698.** www. 7lagos.com/levillage. E-mail: levillage@smandes.com.ar. 23 units, 5 cabañas. MINIBAR TV TEL. $80–$160 double; $100–$220 cabaña for 4, including breakfast. AE, DC, MC, V.

This Alpine Swiss–style hotel is similar to La Cheminée and Le Chatelet in design, and is popular during the off-season for its slightly lower prices. The ambience leans toward family style; the staff is extremely friendly, knowledgeable, and eager to help you plan activities. Rooms are average-sized and carpeted, each with a small balcony, the usual carved wooden beams, and chiffon curtains. There are several lounge areas, including a reading area and library, felt-covered game table, and TV/VCR. Le Village also has five cabañas with queen and twin beds and spacious living areas, although they are not particularly bright. Also, cabañas for six mean two will sleep on sofa beds in the living room. All guests have use of the sauna, and the staff will help plan excursions.

Dining: An ample breakfast features specialties such as deer and trout and comes served in a pleasant eating area. There is also a *quincho,* a separate barbecue/dining area for groups; guests are allowed to throw dinners for friends not staying at the hotel.

Amenities: Sauna, library, game room.

✪ **Rincón de los Andes.** Juez de Valle 611, San Martín de los Andes. ☎ **02972/428583.** www.rinconclub.com. E-mail: rincon@smandes.com.ar. 100 units. TV TEL. Apartments $120–$200 double. AE, DC, MC, V.

Rincón de los Andes is part of the timeshare operation Interval; however, it rents a large percentage of the apartments to travelers who are not part of the program. The sizeable resort abuts a steep, forested mountain slope, and is recommended both for the smartly decorated apartments and the wealth of activities offered—especially for families. Set up like a townhouse complex and centered on a large, airy restaurant with outdoor deck, the 100 apartments range in size to accommodate two to eight guests. All come with fully stocked, earthy, wooden kitchens and spacious bedrooms. The new units are set up for two guests; one features a large living room and kitchen, the neighboring unit has a breakfast nook and kitchenette—both have different prices and come with a door that can connect the two to form a larger apartment. The grassy grounds include a golf driving range and paddle court, and there's a heated pool in a steamy, glass-enclosed building. One of the prize amenities is a travel office that rents bicycles and plans excursions for individual guests and for kids.

Dining: Atop the cliff behind Rincon de los Andes is the restaurant **Downtown Matias** (see "Where to Dine," below), reached by climbing a walkway. The complex is about a 5-block walk to downtown.

Amenities: Laundry, room service, tour office, indoor pool, sauna, massage, paddle court, driving range, kid's game area, baby-sitting.

MODERATE

Hostería Anay. Capitán Drury 841, San Martín de los Andes. ☎/fax **02972/427514.** www.7lagos.com/anay. E-mail: anay@smandes.com.ar. 23 units. TEL. $45–$72 double. No credit cards.

A convenient location, economical price, and simple yet comfortable accommodations make the Anay a good value in San Martín. The rooms come with a double bed or two twins, and there are triples and apartments for four and five guests. All rooms come with wooden ceilings and ruby-red bedspreads, a lamp here and there, and nothing else, and all are clean and neat. The bathrooms are older, yet they have huge showers. Downstairs, the lobby has a wraparound banquette for a seating area, a large fireplace, a felt-covered game table, and plenty of plants. The sunny, pleasant eating area is a nice spot for breakfast, but they also have room service, as well as laundry and baby-sitting services. The hotel is owner-operated, with direct and professional service.

La Raclette. Coronel Pérez 1170, San Martín de los Andes. ☎/fax **02972/427664.** E-mail: aspen@smandes.com.ar. 9 units. TV TEL. $50–$75 double. MC, V.

The design of this funky yet appealing hotel is a cross between Morocco and Switzerland—molded white stucco interiors set off by carved wooden shutters and eaves. More accurately, it might be described as a Hobbit House—anyone over 6 feet tall might have to stoop, the ceilings upstairs are so low. On a quiet street, La Raclette has a cozy seating area and an ample bar and restaurant downstairs with molded white stucco banquettes and cushions. The public areas and the rooms themselves have nooks and crannies and a haphazard design; lots of charisma, but slightly cramped (especially the attic apartments), and the beds are nothing more than thick foam mattresses, some suitable for children only. The hotel exudes a lot of warmth in the evening, but the service can be harried and distracted during the day.

Residencial Italia. Coronel Pérez 799 (at Obeid), San Martín de los Andes. ☎ **02972/ 427590.** 7 units. TV TEL. $40 double, including breakfast. No credit cards.

This little *residencial,* run by a sweet, elderly woman, is simple and kept scrupulously clean; indeed, it is doubtful you'll find a speck of dust anywhere. A good value, given that the double price does not fluctuate during the year. Rooms are modestly decorated in 1950s style; downstairs rooms are slightly darker—book the sunnier upstairs double or one of the two apartments. The apartments are for four and six people, with fully stocked kitchens. One comes with a living room for $110, the other without for $70; both have large dining tables. There's a tiny eating area for breakfast (for guests only). The sole single room ($20) is not recommended for its Lilliputian size. In the spring and summer, beautiful roses rim the perimeter of the *residencial.*

CABAÑAS

There are about three dozen cabaña complexes in San Martín, ranging from attached units to detached A-frames. The quality varies somewhat; generally, the real difference between each is size, so always ask if a cabin for four means one bedroom and two fold-out beds in the living room. Cabañas are a great deal for parties of four to six, as they're usually less expensive and come with small kitchens. During the off-season, couples will find reasonably priced cabañas; however, many places charge a full six-person price during the high season.

On the upscale end (with doubles priced at around $60, high season at $220) try the following. **Claro del Bosque,** Belgrano 1083 (☎ **02972/427451;** fax 02972/428434; www.smandes.gov.ar/clarodelbosque; e-mail: clarodelbosque@smandes.com.ar), is a Swiss Alpine–style building tucked away at the end of a street on a wooded lot. If you'd like to get out of town, try **Paihuen**'s beautiful stone-and-mortar, attached cabañas in a forested lot at Ruta Nacional 234, Km48 (☎/fax **02972/428154;** www.paihuen.com.ar; e-mail: info@paihuen.com.ar). **Aldea Misonet,** Los Cipreses 1801 (☎/fax **02972/421821;** www.smandes.gov.ar/aldeamisonet; e-mail: aldeamisonet@smandes.com.ar), has wood-and-stone attached units that sit at the edge of town; some units look out onto a gurgling stream, as does a pleasant terrace. **Terrazas del Pinar,** Juez de Valle 1174 (☎/fax **02972/429316;** www.7lagos.com/terrazasdelpinar), is near the lakeshore, and it has a children's play area.

Cabañas with doubles ranging from a low-season price of $30 to $150 in the high season include the following: **El Ciervo Rojo,** Almirante Brown 445 (☎/fax **02972/427949;** e-mail: cabanaselciervorojo@smandes.com.ar), has nice, wooden cabins; cheaper units have open second-story sleeping areas. **Del Lácar,** Coronel Rohde 1144 (☎/fax **02972/427679;** ww.7lagos.com/dellacar; e-mail: cabanasdellacar@smandes.com.ar), has several large, detached wooden cabins. **Las Rosas,** Almirante Brown 290 (☎/fax **02972/422002;** www.smandes.gov.ar/lasrosas; e-mail: lrosas@ciudad.com.ar), has pretty whitewashed units one-half block from the shore. **Hostería del Chapelco** and **Le Village** both offer cabañas in addition to their regular hotel rooms (see "Where to Stay," above).

WHERE TO DINE

For sandwiches and quick meals, try **Peuma Café** at Av. San Martín 851 (☎ **02972/428289**); for afternoon tea and delicious cakes and pastries, try **La Casa de Alicia** at Capitán Drury 814, #3 (☎ **02944/1561 6215**). The best tea salon in town, ✪ **Café Arrayán** (☎ **02972/425570**), open daily 4 to 8pm off-season, 5 to 9pm during summer, is a short cab ride away, high above the city at Km5 Mirador Arrayán, past the Sol de los Andes hotel. This 70-year-old wooden house serves the region's traditional sandwiches, cakes, and pastries that have long since replaced the more *criollo* tastes downtown. The cafe sits in one of the last remaining stands of *arrayán* trees in the area and offers beautiful views of the lake.

EXPENSIVE

✪ **Avataras.** Teniente Ramayón 765. ☎ **02972/427104.** Reservations recommended. Main courses $12–$22. AE, DC, MC, V. INTERNATIONAL.

I can't praise this relatively new restaurant enough. Exceptionally warm, friendly service and a marvelous variety of international dishes from Hungary to China to Egypt make it shine. The chefs, transplants from Buenos Aires, whip up exquisite items, such as Indian lamb curry, wild boar with juniper berry sauce, Malaysian shrimp sambal, and filet mignon with four-pepper sauce. The appetizer menu features Scandinavian gravlax and Caribbean citrus shrimp, and the herbs and specialty items used to flavor such dishes are imported from Buenos Aires and abroad. What stands out, however, is Avataras's willingness to please its guests. Although they officially do not serve dinner until 8:30pm, give them 15 minutes' notice and they'll open earlier for parties as small as two, a bonus for foreigners not accustomed to the late dining hours here (they'll also open for lunch if you call ahead).

The design leans toward light beechwood, ferns, Japanese paper lanterns, and an acoustic ceiling made of beige linen. There are smoking and nonsmoking sections; the restaurant even sells cigars, which diners may smoke on the premises. If this weren't enough, Avataras creates special theme menus for holidays or whenever the whim takes them, and hosts live jazz music.

✪ **La Tasca.** Mariano Moreno 866. ☎ **02972/428663.** Reservations recommended. Main courses $16–$22. AE, DC, MC, V. Daily noon–3:30pm and 7pm–1am. REGIONAL.

La Tasca is one of the best restaurants in San Martín for its fresh, superb cuisine and extensive wine offerings, the best in town. Regional specialties are the focus, such as venison flambéed in cognac and blueberries, saffron trout, and raviolis stuffed with wild boar. All meats are hand-picked from various ranches in the area by the chef-owner, and the organic cheese is made at a German family farm. Mushroom lovers will savor the fresh, gourmet varieties served with appetizers and pasta. La Tasca opened 12 years ago as a *picada,* a place to snack on smoked fish, cheese, and meats and pick-led conserves, and appetizer platters are still a specialty here. The cozy restaurant is festooned with hanging hams, bordered with racks of wine bottles, and warmed by a few potbellied iron stoves. Each week the owners feature a special wine at lower-than-usual prices.

MODERATE

Downtown Matias. S. Calderon and Juez de Valle. ☎ **02972/421699.** Reservations not required. Main courses $7–$16. MC, V. Tues–Sun 6pm–3am during summer; daily noon–3am rest of year. IRISH PUB.

This new restaurant atop a cliff offers great views of the lake and the rooftops of San Martín, and although it's billed as an "Irish pub," the wood interiors, deer antlers, and roaring fire give it the feel of a hunting lodge. The menu is brief, featuring pub fare such as steak-and-kidney pie, lamb cooked in Guinness beer, and Irish stew; dessert follows the same line with items such as plum pudding. The sandwiches are good, but pricey at $6 to $13, as are cocktails; apparently the view comes with a price. Downtown Matias is a popular nightspot for the 30 to 60 crowd, who come for a drink and an appetizer selection of smoked trout, cheese, and wild boar. And when the restaurant hosts live music, the place can get packed. A lengthy cocktail menu features mostly American concoctions, such as Long Island Iced Tea, that can be enjoyed at the heavy wood bar, at the tables, or fireside. They also have darts.

Picis Restaurante. Villegas 598. ☎ **02972/427601.** Reservations not required. Main courses $6–$15. AE, DC, MC, V. Daily noon–3pm and 8pm–midnight. REGIONAL.

This place is very popular with locals and consistently draws in packs of diners—the reason it often stays open past midnight until the last diner leaves. The *parrilla* is decent (meats sizzling on the barbecue rack can be observed through a picture window), and a giant assortment of grilled meats, organ meats, and sausages can be ordered for up to six people for $57. Picis sports an extensive menu, including a kid's menu, and serves regional specialties, such as venison in herb sauce. Homemade pastas come with a choice of nine sauces, from pesto to béchamel to bolognese, but they can be somewhat heavy and uninspiring, especially considering the price. The dining area exudes warmth with brick and mustard-colored walls and wooden floors. A daily fixed menu for two goes for $55, and includes appetizer, main course, wine, and coffee.

Pura Vida. Villegas 745. ☎ **02972/429302.** Reservations not required. Main courses $6–$14. MC. Daily 12:30–3:30pm and 8:30pm–midnight. VEGETARIAN.

San Martín's only vegetarian restaurant serves a few chicken and trout dishes too. The vegetarian offerings are not really extensive, but what they offer is fresh and good. This homespun, tiny restaurant has about seven tables, and features meatless dishes such as vegetable chop suey, soufflés, soy and eggplant *milanesas,* and rich flan. Pura Vida serves substantial slices of vegetable-and-egg tarts, and salads can be ordered for an additional price. Pastas are not only homemade, but are made from scratch the moment you order, which can mean a long wait. Pura Vida offers four daily menus that range in price from $7 to $10, including appetizer, main course, and dessert. There are also pizzas, but you'd do better at a pizzeria.

INEXPENSIVE

El Tata Jockey. Villegas 657. ☎ **02972/427585.** Reservations not required. Main courses $6–$13. AE, MC, V. Daily noon–2:30pm and 8pm–midnight. *PARRILLA*/PASTA.

This semi-casual restaurant is popular for its grilled meats and pastas at reasonable prices, as well as its funny name ("The Grandfather Jockey"). It's possible to order a *parrilla* of assorted barbecued meats and sausages for two; the price is $20 for enough food for three diners. The homemade pastas are also a good bet, as is the trout Al Jockey, served with seasonal vegetables and a smoked bacon and cream sauce. Owned and operated by a friendly, enthusiastic mountaineer, the restaurant is decorated with photos and tidbits taken from his various exploits around the area; the long, family-style tables have checkered tablecloths. El Tata Jockey offers special menus for groups and serves a daily fixed-price menu with appetizer, main dish, and dessert for $7. Slightly less formal than the popular Picis up the street (see above), but substantially more economical.

La Costa del Pueblo. Av. Costanera and Obeid. ☎ **02972/429289.** Reservations not required. Main courses $5–$10. AE, DC, MC, V. Daily 10am–2am. INTERNATIONAL.

A lake view and an extensive menu with everything from pastas to *parrilla* make this restaurant a good bet. The establishment operated as a cafe for 20 years until new owners expanded to include a dozen more tables, a cozy fireside nook, and a children's eating area separate from the main dining room, complete with mini tables and chairs. La Costa offers good, homemade pasta dishes such as cannellonis stuffed with ricotta and walnuts, grilled meats and dishes, pizzas, sandwiches, and a $5 daily special. There's also a kid's menu and vegetarian sandwiches. Popular with locals and families, the restaurant is also a good spot for a cold beer and an appetizer platter of smoked cheeses and venison while watching the lake lap the shore.

La Nonna Pizzería. Capitán Drury 857. ☎ **02972/422223.** Reservations not required. Pizzas $4–$9 small, $6–$13 large. MC, V. Daily noon–3:30pm and 7:30pm–midnight. PIZZA.

La Nonna's pizza, calzones, and empanadas are so good, they're sold packaged and ready-to-bake at the supermarket. There's nothing like a crusty pizza or *fugazza* made by La Nonna and baked in an authentic stone oven, so don't miss a stop here. Toppings unfortunately run the repetitive gamut of ham and onion, ham and pineapple, ham and hearts of palm, but there are a few deviations, such as anchovy, Roquefort, and Parmesan and, oddly enough, mozzarella with chopped egg. There are also specialty regional pizzas with the usual trout, boar, and deer, and calzones with fillings such as chicken, mozzarella, and bell pepper. La Nonna also delivers.

2 Junín de los Andes

25 miles (41km) N of San Martín de los Andes

The tiny town of Junín de los Andes does not hold much interest unless you're a fanatic for fly-fishing. The sport has caught on so well here that now even the street signs are shaped like fish. Junín is spread out in a grid pattern, a fertile little oasis along the shore of the Río Chimehuín, surrounded by dry *pampa*. You'll pass through Junín if you're crossing into Argentina from the Pucón area in Chile.

GETTING THERE   By Plane   See "Getting There" under "San Martín de los Andes," above.

By Bus   Ko-Ko Chevalier (☎ 02972/427422) has service from San Martín de los Andes and Buenos Aires. Koko also has service to Lago Huechulafquen.

GETTING AROUND   Most visitors find that the only real way to get around is to rent a car, especially if you've come to fly-fish. Car rental agencies can be found at the airport and in San Martín (see "Getting Around" under San Martín de los Andes, above).

VISITOR INFORMATION   The **Secretaría Municipal de Turismo** is located at Padre Milanesio 596 (☎ **02972/491160;** www.junin.com); it's open daily 8am to 9pm, 8am to 11pm during the summer.

WHAT TO SEE & DO

Puerto Canoa is the central entrance to the splendid **Parque Nacional Lanín,** 19 miles (30km) from Junín. Here you'll find a 30-minute interpretive trail and the departure spot for catamaran excursions across the park's largest lake, Lago Huechulafquen, which looks out onto the snowcapped, conical Volcán Lanín. Río Chimehuín begins at the lake's outlet and offers outstanding fishing opportunities. There are several excellent hiking and backpacking trails in the area, as well as a few rustic backcountry huts; you can pick up information at the ranger station at Puerto Canoa. If you're in San Martín de los Andes, stop by the park's headquarters, the **Intendencia Parque Nacional Lanín,** Emilio Frey 749 (☎ **02972/427233**).

Visitors can book a tour or rent a car for the 82-mile (132km) drive to the hot springs **Termas de Epulafquen,** winding through volcanic landscape and past Lake Curruhue. The hot springs are rustic; however, plans are in progress to develop its infrastructure in 2001. For tours, try Huiliches Turismo, Padre Milanesio 570, Local B (☎ **02972/491670**), or ask at the visitor's center.

FISHING INFORMATION & LICENSES   Licenses can be obtained at the **Tourism Office,** the office of the Guardafauna (☎ **02972/491277**), open Monday to Friday 8am to 3pm; The Fly Shop (☎ **02972/491548**); Bambi's Fly Shop (☎ **02972/491167**); or Casa Los Notros Fly Shop (☎ **02972/492157**). All of these shops can arrange fishing guides as well as sell gear.

WHERE TO STAY & DINE

There are a few lodges that specialize in fly-fishing, such as the **Hostería de Chimehuín** at Suarez and Avenida 21 de Mayo, on the shore of the Chimehuín River (☎ **02972/491132;** $25 double). Accommodations are basic, including rooms with balconies and apartments, but the atmosphere is friendly and homey and there's a good breakfast. Quite possibly the region's best fly-fishing lodge is the **San Humberto Lodge,** located on a privately owned stretch of the Malleo River (☎ **02972/491238**), which charges $280 for a double. The San Humberto consists of six chalets with twin beds, units that are separate from an enormous rustic lodge. The restaurant is excellent and so are the fishing guides. **Cerro los Pinos,** Brown 420 (☎ **02972/427207**), is a charming family ranch with close access to the Chimehuín River. Doubles are $30 to $50; they'll arrange a fishing guide. Dining options are limited here; try the **Ruca Hueney** at Milanesio 641 (☎ **02972/491113**), which serves pasta dishes and, of course, trout. These accommodations have either private parking or ample free street parking.

3 San Carlos de Bariloche

1,005 miles (1,621km) SW of Buenos Aires; 112 miles (180km) S of San Martín de los Andes

San Carlos de Bariloche, or simply Bariloche, is the winter and summer playground for vacationing Argentines and the second most-visited destination in the country. The city sits in the center of Nahuel Huapi National Park and is fronted by an enormous, irregularly shaped lake of the same name. Bariloche's grand appeal are the many outdoor activities, sightseeing drives, boat trips, great restaurants, and shopping opportunities here. Visitors could occupy themselves for a week regardless of the season.

Bariloche began as an ill-fated mission in 1670 that was founded by Jesuits from Chiloé, Chile. In the late 1800s, immigrants from Europe and migrants settled in the region and based their economy primarily on sheep and cattle ranching. The city was incorporated in 1902, and at that time tourism was already showing signs of becoming an economic force. As the city grew it replaced Europe as the top vacation destination for wealthy families from Buenos Aires, who built grand houses along the Avenida Bustillo out toward the Llao Llao Peninsula—a crowd eventually replaced by middle-class and student travelers during the 1950s.

The city itself embodies a strange juxtaposition: an urban city plopped down in the middle of beautiful wilderness. Unfortunately, Argentine migrants fleeing Buenos Aires, an ever-growing tourism industry, and 2 decades of unchecked development have left a cluttered mess in what once was an idyllic mountain town. Bits and pieces of the charming architecture influenced by German, Swiss, and English immigration are still in evidence. But visitors to Bariloche are sometimes overwhelmed by the hodgepodge of ugly apartment buildings, clamorous discos, and the crowds that descend on this area, especially from mid-December until the end of February and during ski season in July. Yet drive 15 minutes outside town, and you'll once again be surrounded by thick forests of pine, beech, and cypress, rippling lakes, and mammoth, snowcapped peaks that rival those found in alpine Europe. If you're looking for a quiet destination, you'd be better off lodging in the town of Villa La Angostura or along the road to the peninsula Llao Llao (see below). On the flip side, Bariloche offers a wealth of services.

ESSENTIALS
GETTING THERE

BY PLANE The **Aeropuerto Bariloche** (☎ **02944/426162**) is 8 miles (13km) from downtown. Buses to the city center are timed with the arrival of flights, and can be found outside at the arrival area; some are run by the airlines themselves. A taxi costs about $10. **Aerolíneas Argentinas/Austral,** Quaglia 238 (☎ **02944/422425;** www.aerolineasargentinas.com.ar), has daily flights from Buenos Aires and Calafate, among many other destinations. **LAPA,** Villegas 121 (☎ **02944/423714**), serves Buenos Aires, Neuquén, and Trelew. **KAIKEN,** Palacios 266 (☎ **02944/4281181**), serves Calafate, Mendoza, Río Gallegos, and Ushuaia. **Southern Winds,** Villegas 147 (☎ **02944/423704**), serves Córdoba, Mendoza, Salta, and Tucumán. **TAN,** Quaglia 262 #11 (☎ **02944/427889**), has flights to Puerto Montt, Chile. **LADE,** Quaglia 238 #8 (☎ **02944/423562**), serves small destinations in the area such as San Martín and Esquel.

BY BUS   The Terminal de Ómnibus (☎ **02944/432860**) is at Av. 12 de Octubre 2400; there are a dozen companies that serve most major destinations in Argentina and Chile. **TAC** (☎ **02944/431521**) has three daily departures for Buenos Aires and daily service to El Bolsón, Esquel, Mendoza, and Córdoba. **Via Bariloche** (☎ **02944/435770**) has three daily departures for Buenos Aires and one daily trip to Mar de Plata. **Andesmar** (☎ **02944/422140**) has service to Mendoza, Río Gallegos, and Neuquén, and service to Osorno, Valdivia, and Puerto Montt in Chile. To get to San Martín de los Andes via the scenic Siete Lagos (Seven Lakes) route (only during the summer) or any other route to that city or Villa La Angostura, try **Ko-Ko** (☎ **02944/423090**). For more on the Siete Lagos route, see chapter 12.

BY CAR   Bariloche can be reached from San Martín via several picturesque routes. The 124-mile (200km) scenic Siete Lagos route from San Martín de los Andes follows routes 234-231-237; the 99-mile (160km) Paso Córdoba takes routes 234-63-237; the longest, yet entirely paved, 161-mile (260km) Collón Curá route follows routes 234-40-237 and is recommended for night driving or when the weather is crummy. To get to El Bolsón, follow Route 258 south; continue down 40 to get to Esquel. To cross into Chile, take the Puyehue Pass via Route 231 (through Villa La Angostura); during periods of heavy snowfall, chains are required.

TRAVELING BY BOAT TO CHILE   Catedral Turismo offers a spectacular journey to the Lake District in Chile that operates as a boat-and-bus combination that terminates in Lago Todos los Santos near Ensenada and Puerto Varas. If you're planning to visit Chile, this is a superb option that really allows you to take in the beauty of the Andes and the volcanoes, rivers, and waterfalls in the mountain range; however, this journey is not recommended on days with heavy rain. The trip can be done in 1 long day or in 2 days, with an overnight in the Hotel Peulla in Chile (see Parque Nacional Vicente Pérez Rosales, in chapter 12 for more information). The trip costs $120 per person for the boat trip, and an average of $75 double for an overnight at the Hotel Peulla. Book at any travel agency or from Catedral Turismo's offices in Bariloche at Moreno 238 (☎ **02944/425443;** www.crucedelagos.cl; e-mail: crucelag@rdc.cl).

Getting Around

BY FOOT   The city is compact enough to explore by foot. However, most visitors spend just a few hours touring the city, and instead use Bariloche as a base to explore surrounding areas.

BY CAR   If you can fit a rental car into your budget, you'll really want one here to spend several afternoons driving through the region's sinuous roads that pass through exceptionally scenic landscapes, such as the Circuito Chico. All travel agencies offer excursions to these areas, which is another option. Rental agencies, including Budget, Dollar, Hertz, and Avis, have kiosks at the airport, and many downtown offices: **Budget** at Mitre 106 (☎ **02944/422482**), **AI Rent a Car** at Av. San Martín 235 (☎ **02944/422582**), **Dollar** at Villegas 285 (☎ **02944/430333**), **Hertz** at Quaglia 165 (☎ **02944/434543**), **Baricoche Rent A Car** at Moreno 115 (☎ **02944/427638**), **Localiza** at Av. San Martín 463 (☎ **02944/424767**), and **A Open Rent a Car** at Mitre 171 #15 (☎ **02944/426325**).

ACCOMMODATIONS ■
Hostería la Pastorella **6**
Hotel Aconcagua **4**
Hotel Edelweiss **5**
Hotel Nevada **13**
Hotel Panamericano **3**
Hotel Tres Reyes **17**
La Caleta Bungalows **1**
Residencial Piuké **16**
Villa Huinid **1**

DINING ◆
Casita Suiza **9**
Caza y Pesca **18**
Días de Zapata **8**
El Boliche de Alberto **11**
El Patacón **2**
Familia Weiss **15**
Friends **14**
Jauja Restaurante **10**
La Marmita **12**

ATTRACTIONS ●
Museo de la Patagonia **7**

When navigating the streets of Bariloche, do not confuse two streets with similar names: V.A. O'Connor runs parallel to the Costanera, and J. O'Connor bisects it.

VISITOR INFORMATION

The **Secretaría de Turismo,** in the stone-and-wood Civic Center complex between Urquiza and Panzoni streets (☎ **02944/426784;** e-mail: securturismo@bariloche. com.ar), has general information about Bariloche, and it is an indispensable source for accommodation listings, especially during the high season. It also operates an information stand in the bus terminal. It's open Monday to Friday 8am to 9pm, Saturday and Sunday 9am to 9pm. For information about lodging and attractions surrounding Bariloche, try the **Secretaría de Turismo de Río Negro,** Av. 12 de Octubre 605, at the waterfront (☎ **02944/426644**); it's open Monday to Friday 9am to 2pm.

The **Club Andino Bariloche,** Av. 20 de Febrero 30 (☎ **02944/422266;** fax 02944/424579; e-mail: transitando@bariloche.com.ar), provides excellent information about hiking, backpacking, and mountaineering in the area. They sell maps and provide treks, mountain ascents, and ice walks led by guides from the Club Andino, as well as rafting, photo safaris, and horseback rides; open daily 9am to 1pm and 6 to 9pm during winter, daily 8:30am to 3pm and 5 to 9pm during summer. For general info about Nahuel Huapi National Park, head to the park's headquarters in the Civic Center (☎ **02944/424111**), open Monday to Friday 8:30am to 12:30pm.

FAST FACTS: BARILOCHE

Banks/Currency Exchange   Most banks exchange currency, including Banco de Galicia, at Moreno and Quaglia (☎ **02944/7127**), or Citibank, Mitre 694 (☎ **02944/436301**). Try also Cambio Sudamerica, Mitre 63 (☎ **02944/434555**).

Hospital   Hospital Privado Regional, 20 de Febrero 594 (☎ **02944/423074**).

Internet Access   Cybermac Café, Rolando 217, #12 (no phone), or Net & Cappuccino, Quaglia 220 (☎ **02944/426128**).

Laundry   Marva Lavematic, San Martín 325 (☎ **02944/426319**); or Lavematic, Beschtedt 180 (☎ **02944/433022**).

Pharmacy   Angel Gallardo at A. Gallardo 701 (☎ **02944/427023**), Zona Vital at Moreno and Rolando (☎ **02944/420752**) or Nahuel at Moreno 238 (☎ **02944/422490**).

Police   For emergencies, dial **101.** For other matters call ☎ **02944/423434.**

Post Office   The central post office is in the Civic Center, next to the tourist office.

WHAT TO SEE & DO IN & AROUND BARILOCHE

Bariloche's **Civic Center,** Avenida Juan Manuel de Rosas and Panzoni, is a charming stone-and-wood complex that houses most municipal offices and tourism services, such as the information center and national park headquarters. The complex, built in 1940, was inspired by the architecture of Bern, Switzerland. Here you'll find the **Museo de la Patagonia Perito Moreno** (☎ **02944/422309**), open Tuesday to Friday 10am to 12:30pm and 2 to 7pm, Monday 10am to 1pm; closed Sunday. Admission is $2.50. The museum has five salons dedicated to the natural science, history, and ethnography of the Bariloche region. The well-tended displays here are intriguing, notably the stuffed and mounted local fauna, such as *pudú* (miniature deer), puma, condor, and more. The second floor has displays of Mapuche artifacts, such as weapons, art, and jewelry, and other artifacts from the colonial period. A small gift shop sells postcards, books, and crafts.

SHOPPING   You'll find everything and anything along Bariloche's main street, Mitre, including shops selling souvenirs and Argentine products such as *mate* gourds and leather goods. For the region's famous smoked meats and cheese, and other regional specialties such as trout pâté, try the renowned **Familia Weiss** at Mitre 360 (☎ **02944/424829**) or **Del Turista** at Av. San Martín 252 or Mitre 239 (no phone). Del Turista also has an enormous array of chocolates and candy, as do other confectioneries up and down Mitre Street, such as **Abuela Goye** at Mitre 258 (☎ **02944/423311**) and Quaglia 221 (☎ **02944/422276**), **Bari** at Mitre 339 (☎ **02944/422305**), **Mexicana** at Mitre 288 (☎ **02944/422505**), and **Mamuschka** at Mitre 216 (☎ **02944/423294**). Stop by the visitor's center for a map of Avenida Bustillo and the Llao Llao Peninsula, along which are dozens of shops selling regional specialties. Note that food items such as smoked meats wrapped in plastic are not generally not permitted outside Argentina.

TOUR OPERATORS

A plethora of travel agencies offer everything under the sun along the streets of Bariloche. Most tours do not include lunch, and some charge extra for a bilingual guide. The best of the lot include **Catedral Turismo** at Moreno 238 (☎ **02944/425443**), with a wide variety of land excursions to El Bolsón, Cerro Tronador, and circuit sightseeing routes. **Tom Wesley Viajes de Aventura** at Mitre 385 (☎ **02944/435040**)

Jugglers, dancers and an assortment of acrobats fill the street.

She shoots you a wide-eyed look as a seven-foot cartoon character approaches.

What brought you here was wanting the kids

to see something magical while they still believed in magic.

America Online Keyword: Travel

With 700 airlines, 50,000 hotels and over 5,000 cruise and vacation getaways, you can now go places you've always dreamed of.

Travelocity.com
A Sabre Company
Go Virtually Anywhere.

"WORLD'S LEADING TRAVEL WEB SITE, 5 YEARS IN A ROW" WORLD TRAVEL AWARDS

I HAVE TO CALL THE TRAVEL AGENCY AGAIN. DARN, OUT TO LUNCH. NOW HAVE TO CALL THE AIRLINE. I HATE CALLING THE AIRLINES. I GOT PUT ON HOLD AGAIN. "INSTRUMENTAL TOP 40" … LOVELY. I HATE GETTING PUT ON HOLD. TICKET PRICES ARE ALL OVER THE MAP. HOW DO I DIAL INTERNATIONALLY? OH SHOOT, FORGOT THE RENTAL CAR. I'M STILL ON HOLD. THIS MUSIC IS GIVING ME A HEADACHE. WONDER IF SOMEONE ELSE HAS CHEAPER FLIGHTS. FORGET IT, CAN'T TAKE IT ANYMORE … I'M HANGING UP

YAHOO! TRAVEL
100% MUZAK-FREE

Booking your trip online at Yahoo! Travel is simple. You compare the best prices. You click. You go have fun. Tickets, hotels, rental cars, cruises & more. Sorry, no muzak.

specializes in horseback riding, but offers everything else too, even sightseeing tours and an adventure camp. **Cumbres Patagonia,** Villegas 222 (☎ **02944/423283;** e-mail: cumbres@bariloche.com.ar), has easy sightseeing trips and more adventurous excursions, including trekking, fishing, and 4×4 trips. Also try **Ati Viajes** at V.A. O'Connor 335 (☎ **02944/426782**), **Barlan Travel** at Mitre 340 #68 (☎ **02944/ 426782**), or **Viajes Danneman** at Mitre 86 (☎ **02944/428793**).

PARQUE NACIONAL NAHUEL HUAPI

Nahuel Huapi is Argentina's oldest and most popular national park, offering just about everything for any interest or physical level. The park's main feature is the 3,500m (11,480-ft.) extinct volcano **Tronador,** or Thunderer, named for the rumbling produced by ice falling from the mountain's peak. But the park is also known for the glacial-formed Lake Nahuel Huapi and its lovely forested peninsulas and waterways that often provoke comparison to the channels of southern Patagonia or the fjords of Norway. During summertime visitors can take part in day hikes or backpacking trips along one of the park's several trails or boat out to one of the lake's islands.

There are also plenty of other outdoor activities such as rafting, horseback riding, and fishing, and during the winter the park's other dominant peak, **Cerro Catedral,** converts into a popular ski resort. Easy access to all regions of the park make Nahuel Huapi popular with visitors seeking mellower activities, such as sightseeing drives and cable cars to magnificent lookout points. The following information is for all attractions within Nahuel Huapi and around Bariloche.

CERRO OTTO

Walk, bike, drive, or ride a cable car to the top of **Cerro Otto** for sweeping views of Lake Nahuel Huapi, the Llao Llao Peninsula, and the high peaks of Catedral and Tronador, as well as for an assortment of diversions, including paragliding, trekking, rock climbing, and, during the winter, skiing and dog-sledding. The road up to Cerro Otto takes visitors through a thick forest of pine, beech, and *alerce* (larch) populated with charming chalets. To walk (2 to 3 hours) or bike, take Avenida Los Pioneros for about 1km (about one-half mile) and follow the signs to Cerro Otto. The cable car (☎ **02944/441035;** www.bariloche.com.ar/cerrotto) costs $20 per person and runs January to February and July to August 9:30am to 6pm; the rest of the year it runs 10am to 6pm. Riders are offered a free shuttle bus that leaves from Mitre and Villegas. Atop the summit you'll also find a revolving restaurant (☎ **02944/441035**), as well as a cafe run by the Club Andino situated about a 20-minute walk from the restaurant.

A DRIVING TOUR: CERRO TRONADOR, LOS ALERCES WATERFALL & VENTISQUERO NEGRO

This wonderful, full-day excursion takes visitors through lush forest and past hidden lakes such as the picturesque Lago Mascardi, waterfalls, and beaches to a trailhead that leads to the face of the Ventisquero Negro (Black Glacier). You'll need a vehicle to drive the 133-mile (215km) round-trip road, but most tour agencies do offer this excursion for about $25 per person. The 133 miles/215km includes a detour to the Cascada Los Alerces (Los Alerces Waterfall); it's 105 miles/170km without. Plan to stop frequently at the various lookout points along the road.

Leaving Bariloche on Onelli Street headed south, continue along Route 258 toward El Bolsón, passing Lake Gutierrez and several teahouses and smokeries that sell regional specialties. After about 22 miles (35km), you'll reach Villa Mascardi. From here it is possible to take a full-day sailing excursion aboard the *Victoria II* that takes riders across Lake Mascardi to the Hotel Tronador for lunch, followed by a bus ride up the valley to Pampa Linda and Los Ventisqueros for a trail walk. Visitors return the same way. This excursion can be booked at any travel agency and usually includes transportation from Bariloche leaving at 9am and returning at 8pm (from November to March only), or you can leave directly from the dock if you have your own vehicle. The cost, including transportation from Bariloche, is $35 per person.

Continue on the tour, past Villa Mascardi, and a road branches off to the right. At the Río Manso bridge a road heads left to the Los Alerces Waterfall. A 984-ft. (300m) walk takes you to a vista point looking out at the waterfall. After doubling back, you reach the bridge again, where you head left, continuing along the shore of Lake Mascardi until reaching the Hotel Tronador. The charming log cabin hotel, built in 1929 by a Belgian immigrant family, is backed by high peaks and makes a good spot for lunch. The road continues up the valley of the Río Manso Superior, winding through alpine scenery until arriving at Pampa Linda and eventually ending at a stunning cirque (a steep valley containing a lake) draped with vegetation and waterfalls. From here there's a trail that leads to the Black Glacier, named for the debris that colors the ice at its terminus. The return to Bariloche takes the same road.

BOAT EXCURSIONS

Another enjoyable full-day excursion takes you to **Isla Victoria** and the **Bosque Arrayánes** (see "Villa La Angostura," below) by boat, and leaves at 10:30am from Puerto San Carlos or Puerto Pañuelo at Llao Llao. The excursion begins with a 30-minute sail to Isla Victoria, where passengers can disembark for a walk through a conifer forest or ascent to a lookout point atop Cerro Bella Vista via chair lift. The second stop is Península Quetrihué and the Bosque Arrayánes, famous for its concentration of the unusual terra-cotta–colored *arrayán* tree. These handsome trees (which are really bushes) have an odd, slick trunk that is cool to the touch. From Puerto Pañuelo to Isla Victoria, trips leave at 10am and return at 5:30pm (cost is $22); from Puerto San Carlos, trips leave at 9am and return at 6:30pm (cost is $30).

There are also boat trips to **Puerto Blest.** These excursions leave from Puerto Pañuelo at Llao Llao, sailing through classic fjords and exuberant vegetation known as the Valdivian Forest, until reaching Puerto Blest. From this point there is an optional bus ride to Laguna Frías followed by a boat ride to Puerto Frías, returning to Puerto Blest for the return trip to Puerto Pañuelo, stopping first at Los Cántaros waterfall.

Note that the lake crossing from Bariloche to Chile follows the same trajectory, and is redundant for anyone planning to partake in that journey. There is a restaurant at Puerto Blest, or you can bring a picnic lunch. Both sailing trips are very crowded in the summer. From Puerto Pañuelo, trips to Puerto Blest leave at 10am and return at 5pm (cost is $22); trips from Puerto San Carlos leave at 9am and return at 6pm (cost is $30). The additional boat ride to Puerto Pañuelo costs $9 per person.

The new sailing trip to the well-organized, auto-guided trail at Isla Huemul gives visitors a chance to walk through native forest and visit a now-abandoned nuclear fusion study center. There are six sailings daily; the round-trip journey takes 3 hours and the cost is $16 per person. For all boat excursions, make a reservation at any travel agency, or call for more information (☎ **02944/426109**).

OUTDOOR ACTIVITIES

BIKING   Mountain bike rental for paved roads and information about bike trails and guided trips in Nahuel Huapi are available from **Bike Way** at V.A. O'Connor 867 (☎ **02944/424202**), **Bariloche Mountain Bike** at Gallardo 375 (☎ **02944/462397**), and **Dirty Bikes** at V.A. O'Connor 681 (☎ **02944/425616**).

FISHING   This region provides anglers with excellent fly-fishing on the Rivers Manso, Traful, and Machico and trolling on Lake Nahuel Huapi for introduced species such as brown trout, rainbow trout, and landlocked salmon. You can pick up information and fishing licenses at the **Club Caza y Pesca** on the coast at Onelli and Avenida 12 de Octubre (☎ **02944/421515**), open Monday to Friday 9am to 1pm, or the office of the Parque Nacional Nahuel Huapi in the Civic Center. The **Patagonia Fly-Shop** and its owner-guide Ricardo Ameijeiras offer great fly-fishing expeditions, multiple-day programs in lodges, and day tours with bilingual guides. They can be found at Quichahuala 200 (☎ **02944/441944;** e-mail: flyshop@bariloche.com.ar). Tour agencies such as **Cumbres Patagonia,** at Villegas 222 (☎ **02944/423283**), offer half-day and full-day fly-casting and trolling fishing excursions.

HIKING   The Nahuel Huapi National Park has a well-developed trail system that offers day hikes, multiple-day hikes, and loops that connect several backcountry *refugios,* some of which offer rustic lodging. The national park office in the Civic Center provides detailed maps and guides to difficulty levels of trails. Another great source for information is the **Club Andino,** at Av. 20 de Febrero 30 (☎ **02944/422266;** e-mail: transitando@bariloche.com.ar), which also has trails, guided trekking, ice walks, and climbing trips on Cerro Tronador.

HORSEBACK RIDING   Horseback rides in various areas of the park are offered by **Tom Wesley Viajes de Aventura** at Mitre 385 (☎ **02944/435040**), which also has a kid-friendly adventure camp. Rides cost an average of $20 for 2 hours and $30 for 3 hours. **Cumbres Patagonia** at Villegas 222 (☎ **02944/423283**) has trips to Fortín Chacabuco for $45 per half day and $65 per full day, including lunch.

RAFTING   Various companies offer river rafting on the Río Manso in both Class III and Class IV sections, either half-day or full-day trips. The average cost for a half day is $70 and full day, $90. Easier floats down the Class I Río Limay are also available, for about $38 for a half day. Excursions include all equipment, transportation, and a snack or lunch (full-day trips). Try **Cumbres Patagonia** at Villegas 222 (☎ **02944/423283**), **Transitando lo Natural** at Mandisoví 72 (☎ **02944/423918**), or **Rafting Adventure** at Mitre 161 (☎ **02944/432928**).

SKIING & SNOWBOARDING   Bariloche's main winter draw is the ski resorts at Cerro Catedral. The resort is divided in two, with separate tickets (it's possible to buy a more expensive ticket accepted by both resorts) for Robles and Catedral. Robles's bonus is that it is typically less crowded, with excellent open bowl skiing. Catedral offers more advanced lift services, but its runs are usually packed. Lift tickets cost between $22 and $40 for adults and $19 and $32 for kids, depending on high and low seasons. An electronic ticket system deducts each lift ride so that you pay only for what you use, a deal for multiple-day skiers and snowboarders. Bariloche suffers from a continually ascending snowline level, so the bottom portion is often patchy or bald. Both resorts are well liked by families and beginners for their abundance of intermediate terrain, but there's plenty of advanced terrain, too.

The season runs from about June 15 to September 30. Every August the resorts host the **National Snow Party,** with torchlight parades and other events (contact the Catedral ski resort for more information). The bustling Villa Catedral is at the base of the resorts with a jumble of shops, rental stores, and several lodging options. **Alp Apart Hotel** has fully furnished apartments for two to six guests, with lodging and ticket combinations that run about $70 per person, per evening (☎ **02944/460105;** e-mail: alp_uno@bariloche.com.ar). **Cabañas Autu Pukem** has cabins for six to eight guests; consult them directly for prices (☎ **02944/460074;** e-mail: norconde@ ciudad.com.ar).

WHERE TO STAY

A handful of hotels in and around Bariloche are owned by unions and offer discounts to members. These hotels, such as Argentina Libre, Curu Leuvu, Puente Peron, and the larger hotels on Avenida Bustillo toward Llao Llao, including the Amancay and Panamericano (not to be confused with the Panamericano that's downtown), can take on a clubby worker's atmosphere not usually desired by most visitors. Avoid completely hotels owned by the several tour groups that bring thousands of energetic teens to Bariloche from June to December every year (these hotels are identifiable by the blue logo AUSTONIA). A few hotels are subcontracted to lodge students, such as the Hotel Bella Vista. During the high season (December 15 to February 28 and Easter week), prices double. Many hotels consider the months of July and August to be midseason, with mid-range prices to match, but some hotels charge high-season rates.

The cheapest rates are from March 1 to June 30 and September 1 to December 15. Dates vary; inquire before booking and always ask for promotions or discounts for multiple-day stays. For lodging closer to the Llao Llao Peninsula, see "The Road to the Llao Llao Peninsula," later in this chapter.

EXPENSIVE

Hotel Edelweiss. Av. San Martín 202, San Carlos de Bariloche. ☎ **02944/426165;** in the U.S. 800/207-6900; in the U.K. 08705/300-200; in Australia 800/221-176. Fax 02944/ 425655. www.edelweiss.com.ar. E-mail: reservas@edelweiss.com.ar. 100 units. MINIBAR TV TEL. $155–$205 double superior; $240–$320 suite. AE, DC, MC, V. Valet parking.

This hotel offers reliable service and huge double bedrooms, and is really the best hotel in downtown Bariloche in this price category. Double superiors come with two fullsize beds, bay windows, and lake views, as do the suites; the double standards are less desirable for their smaller size, single full-size bed or two twins, and view of a building in the back, but they are just as comfortable and $20 cheaper. All rooms have recently been updated with fresh wallpaper and carpets. The design is pleasant but run-of-the-mill for a hotel that deems itself five-star. There is a striking penthouse pool with glass walls affording views of Lake Nahuel Huapi, a bar, and a lounge area, although it doesn't open until 2:30pm. The suites deserve mention for their gargantuan size, with separate living areas and small bars; suite bathrooms have hydromassage tubs. The lounge has polished floors and leather couches, and is scented with freshly cut flowers from a private garden.

Dining: La Taviola, the hotel's upscale restaurant, serves international and regional cuisine; there is also a bar and snack area, **El Patio.**

Amenities: Laundry, room service, business center, indoor pool, sauna, beauty salon, gift/sundry shop, conference room, baby-sitting.

Hotel Nevada. Rolando 250, San Carlos de Bariloche. ☎ **02944/422778.** Fax 02944/427914. www.nevada.com.ar. E-mail: hnevada@bariloche.com.ar. 81 units. MINIBAR TV TEL. $103–$115 double standard; $125–$150 junior suite. AE, DC, MC, V. Private parking.

Centrally located and welcoming with an appealing mint green and wood facade, the Nevada underwent a complete renovation in 1993, a date it now posts in large numbers outside in contrast to its real age, 1952, when it was one of the few hotels in the city. The hotel is billed as traditional although its rooms and lobby are slick and modern. A cream-and-maroon restaurant/lounge has a bar offset with pillars painted to appear marble, and there is often loud music playing in the background. The rooms are agreeable, with varnished wood paneling, but are average-size for the price.

Two rooms can be connected to make an apartment, but there isn't really any advantage, apart from giving parents an open door to their kids' bedroom. For $15 to $20 more, you can book a brighter, double superior with a tiny seating area and large windows that overlook the street. The Nevada is planning to complete an additional floor, with rooms that are more spacious, as well as space for a gym, sauna, and whirlpool—inquire as to the status when calling.

Hotel Panamericano. Av. San Martín 536, San Carlos de Bariloche. ☎/fax **02944/ 425846.** E-mail: panatel@bariloche.com.ar. 300 units. MINIBAR TV TEL. $150 double; $225 suite. AE, DC, MC, V. Valet parking.

The Hotel Panamericano has long coasted on its reputation as one of Bariloche's premier accommodations, boasting a casino, a lake view, a range of amenities, and an excellent Italian restaurant. Its five-star rating is exaggerated, however, especially when compared to rivals such as the Llao Llao Hotel & Resort (see "Where to Stay on the Llao Llao Peninsula," below). The rooms are spacious and comfortable, but the slick bedspreads and design in general need a face-lift. One has the suspicion the maids do overtime on the shag carpet, vacuuming it stiff with a pungent lemon cleanser that permeates the halls and rooms. The lake views are available only above the fifth floor; in fact, the hotel rarely books rooms on the bottom floors unless they're hosting a convention.

The back rooms face an ugly building, but are cheaper. The junior suites are quite nice, and really a better deal than the regular suites—although just a tad smaller, they come with plant-filled balcony patios and outdoor table and chairs, as well as a fireplace and a living area setup the staff will arrange to your liking. A double comes with two full-size beds or a king. Inside the lobby, a faux waterfall trickles in the background, and a bar/lounge regularly has live piano music. There is a steamy penthouse pool and a glass-enclosed gym where you can work out while savoring the lake view; a personal trainer is on hand to offer special ski-oriented workouts in the winter. The hotel has another 100 or so rooms and a casino on the other side of the street, connected by an aerial walkway.

Dining: La Rondiné serves excellent homemade pasta and meats (see "Where to Dine," below).

Amenities: Laundry, 24-hour room service, indoor pool, sauna, gym, massage, beauty salon, convention hall, car rental, travel agency, gift shop, child-care center, and, according to their brochure, "canned music."

✪ **Villa Huinid.** Av. Bustillo, Km2.5. ☎/fax **02944/5235234.** . E-mail: villahuinid@bariloche. com.ar. 16 units. TV TEL. $72–$120 suite; $120–$200 4-person cabaña. AE, DC, MC, V. Private parking.

The country-style, luxurious cabins and suites that make up the brand-new Villa Huinid are top-notch choices for travelers looking for independent accommodations outside town. The complex faces the lake, where it has a private beach, and is backed by a thick forest with a walking trail. Each room is handcrafted of knotty cypress, with stone fireplaces, decks with a full-size barbecue, and a handsome decor of floral wallpaper, plaid bedspreads, craftsy furniture, and other accents such as dried flowers and iron lamps. The rooms come as four-, six- and eight-person cabañas with fully stocked kitchens and living areas; however, there are also five suites with minibar and coffeemaker, but no kitchen or separate seating area. The suites might seem a bit lonely as there is no lobby to relax in. All rooms have daily maid service. The bathrooms are sumptuous, with wooden sinks and hydromassage baths, and the cabins come with one and a half bathrooms.

The service provided by the gracious owners of the Villa Huinid is one of this hotel's highlights, as are the property's well-manicured grounds, which are offset by a trickling stream that meanders through the property. Behind the rooms are several aromatic gardens and a dense forest (the quiet location is 1½ miles [2½km] from the city center). The Huinid has its own transfer van to get you into town when you need to or to take you to destinations such as Cerro Catedral.

Amenities: Hydromassage baths, airport transportation, shuttles to downtown and ski resorts, barbecues.

MODERATE

Hotel Aconcagua. Av. San Martín 289, San Carlos de Bariloche. ☎ **02944/424718.** Fax 02944/424719. www.hotelnet.com.ar. E-mail: aconcagua@infovia.com.ar. 32 units. TV TEL. $50–$100 double. AE, MC, V. Private parking.

This small, well-kept hotel is one of the best values in Bariloche. The establishment runs like clockwork, a carry-over from the German immigrant who built the hotel and whose design influence can be found throughout the lobby and lounge area. The rooms are nothing to go wild over, with average beds and a late 1960s design, but a few have lake views, and doubles with a full-size bed are spacious (doubles with two twins are not, however). The bathrooms are older but impeccable; the showers do not have stalls, just a shower curtain. Within the lounge is a cowhide bar with leatherette chairs surrounding a fireplace. The included "American" breakfast is quite good, and the dining area is pleasant and sunny. Surprisingly, the hotel offers 24-hour room service. It's popular with Americans during the November to December hunting/fishing season.

Hotel Tres Reyes. Av. 12 de Octubre 135, San Carlos de Bariloche. ☎ **02944/426121.** Fax 02944/424230. www.hoteltresreyes.com. E-mail: reservas@hoteltresreyes.com. 75 units. TV TEL. $78–$139 double garden view; $97–$169 lake view. AE, DC, MC, V. Private parking.

Located directly on the Costanera, this venerable hotel is often overlooked, but it's difficult to understand why. It has a tremendous amount of stark, Scandinavian style preferred by the Belgian immigrant who built the hotel in 1950, and perhaps that does not appeal to everyone. Nevertheless, the hotel has been superbly maintained, with architectural details such as wood ceilings and beechwood paneling, and the vast lounge area has dozens of chairs and a velvet couch to sink into to gaze out over the lake. A small room off the lounge is embellished with a set of antiques shipped over from Europe, and the backyard has a path that meanders through a pleasant garden. All the rooms have been renovated within the past year, with new bedding, paint, curtains, and carpet, and all are warm and come with sparkling bathrooms. Lake-view rooms are more expensive, but they might not be as desirable as loud traffic speeds by well into the night.

During the 1960s, the hotel's red leather bar was the "in" spot for Bariloche's fashionable set, and it hasn't been altered in the slightest. A restaurant serves a buffet breakfast and afternoon tea only, in a bright dining area that doubles as an excellent viewpoint for watching the sunset. The service is very friendly.

La Caleta Bungalows. Av. Bustillo 1900, San Carlos de Bariloche. ☎/fax **02944/441837.** E-mail: bungalows@bariloche.com.ar. 13 units. TV. $30 cabaña for 2; $80 for 2 high season. No credit cards. Private parking.

These two- to seven-person bungalows are a deal for those seeking the independence of kitchen facilities and a location close to town, without actually being in it. Run by an amicable British expatriate, the rooms are not the most luxurious on the shore, but they are entirely comfortable and have knockout views of Nahuel Huapi. Each room is nestled among winding, flower-filled walkways, and the principal room has a large dining table and a basic, open kitchen. The interiors are made of white stucco and feature a combination of one full-size bed and bunk beds, depending on the size. The bedrooms that sit behind the dining area have large, one-way mirrored windows that allow guests to see out toward the view. Each room comes with a central fireplace. La Caleta has a private beach across the road, and the owner has a wealth of tourist information and offers excursions. Downtown is a 20-minute walk or $3 taxi ride away.

INEXPENSIVE

Hostería La Pastorella. Belgrano 127, San Carlos de Bariloche. ☎ **02944/424656.** Fax 02944/424212. 12 units. TEL. $45–$60 double. AE, MC, V. Ample street parking. Children not accepted.

This cozy little hotel was one of the first in Bariloche, built in the 1930s. Its gingerbread style hearkens back to the German family who first ran the establishment. The Pastorella is entirely comfortable, with a dining area and a sunny lounge and bar that open up onto a lush garden. The rooms are a bit tired, but for the price they're a good value here in Bariloche. Some rooms have an extra seating area, although the funny futonlike chairs do nothing to beckon you to take a seat. Try to get a room that looks out over the garden. The hotel is run by a friendly Argentine couple who have recently installed a sauna ($10 extra). Note that this hotel does not accept children.

Residencial Piuké. Beschtedt 136, San Carlos de Bariloche. ☎ **02944/423044.** 20 units. TV TEL. $40–$50 double. No credit cards.

The budget hotel Residencial Piuke (Piuke means "heart" in Mapuche) is a good deal for its spotless accommodations and pleasing common area, not to mention the charming Swiss-styled exterior framed with ruby rose bushes and two towering blue pines. The elderly Hungarian owner takes great pride in providing quality, clean rooms with enough space to move about in and a table and chair for writing out postcards (not common in budget hotels in the area). The rooms are very simple, with beds of intermediate caliber. It's an older establishment, but it is refreshing to find that nothing is faded, ripped, or dirty. Several downstairs doubles are very large. The Piuké caters primarily to Europeans traveling on a budget and is located on a quiet street near the cathedral, just 2 blocks from the heart of downtown.

WHERE TO DINE
EXPENSIVE

✪ **El Patacón.** Av. Bustillo, Km7. ☎ **02944/442898.** Reservations recommended on weekends. Main courses $7–$17. AE, DC, MC, V. Daily noon–3pm and 8pm–midnight. ARGENTINE/REGIONAL.

This superb restaurant merits a visit even though it is a 4-mile (7km) drive from the city center. El Patacón's unique architecture and mouth-watering cuisine are so appealing that it was chosen as the dining spot for Bill Clinton and Argentina's Carlos Menem during a presidential meeting several years back, a fact the restaurant is more than happy to advertise. The building is made of chipped stone inlaid with polished, knotty tree trunks and branches that have been left in their natural shape, forming zany crooked beams and pillars. The tables and chairs were handcrafted from cypress driftwood also kept in its natural form.

Start your meal with a platter of five provolone cheeses served crispy warm off the grill, and follow it with venison ravioli or goulash, trout in a creamy leek sauce with puffy potatoes, wild boar in wine, or mustard chicken. There is also a *parrilla* with grilled meats, daily specials, and a *bodega* with an excellent selection of wines. The restaurant recently inaugurated an adjoining bar, a fascinating, medieval-style lounge with iron chandeliers and a tremendous fireplace with a tree-trunk mantel. This restaurant unfortunately sticks to the disappearing custom of charging a $2 service fee for each diner, which is not considered a tip.

La Rondiné. Carlos Pellegrini 551. ☎ **02944/425846.** Reservations recommended on weekends. Main courses $12–$17. AE, DC, MC, V. Wed–Mon 12:30 –3pm and 8:30pm– midnight. ARGENTINE/ITALIAN.

This restaurant is part of the Hotel Panamericano and is a more upscale option in town. A plant-filled dining area has leather booths and well-appointed tables draped in white linen. The strength of La Rondiné is pasta, made fresh daily by an Italian family. Selections include rich chicken lasagna in a bolognese sauce or fettucine with local wild mushrooms, bacon, and cream. There are also meats such as herb-baked filet mignon, and several seafood dishes that are based predominately around trout. Fine wines and freshly baked desserts can be expected nightly. During the weekends it's best to call ahead for a reservation.

MODERATE

Casita Suiza. Quaglia 342. ☎ **02944/426111.** Reservations not required. Main courses $8.50–$13. AE, DC, MC, V. Daily 8pm–midnight. SWISS.

The Casita Suiza lives up to its name with a menu of Swiss dishes, such as smoked pork, sauerkraut, and apple strudel, but also offers a wide variety of international meat and fish dishes. The restaurant is owned by the children of Swiss immigrants; the owner's mother still bakes fresh cakes and tarts daily using old family recipes. The Casita Suiza's ambience is slightly more cozy than its competitor, the Rincón Suiza, and the service is impeccable. Fondue and *raclette* are a bit pricey at $17 per person, considering the so-so quality of the cheeses used. If you're interested in a diner-participation meal, choose instead the *pierrade* for $22 per person, which is a platter of various meats, sauces, and potatoes that you grill at the table. Call ahead to see if they're open for lunch.

Caza y Pesca. Av. 12 de Octubre and Onelli. ☎ **02944/435963.** Reservations not required. Main courses $13–$16. AE, MC, V. Daily 7pm–2am year-round; Nov–Feb open for lunch daily 11am–4pm. REGIONAL.

Like the name ("Hunting and Fishing") suggests, this new restaurant on the waterfront has a hunting lodge atmosphere with rough-hewn interiors made of knotty cypress tree trunks, a crackling fireplace, and deer antler chandeliers. The chef here whips up tasty regional specialties and international dishes such as trout in garlic, tomatoes, and wine, salmon ravioli, or steak with a pepper sauce, but the restaurant also makes a suitable spot for a drink and an appetizer platter. The restaurant has great views during the day and a warm, candle-lit ambience in the evening, at least until around 11pm when they drop a giant TV screen and begin playing music videos and concerts. It's unnerving and inappropriate for this kind of restaurant, but nobody seems bothered enough to complain.

Días de Zapata. Morales 362. ☎ **02944/423128.** Reservations not required. Main courses $10–$13. MC, V. Daily noon–3pm and 7pm–midnight. MEXICAN.

Bariloche's only Mexican restaurant is surprisingly good. You'll find the usual tacos, fajitas, and nachos on the menu, but you'll also find dishes that stay true to Mexican cooking, such as chicken *mole* (cooked in a spicy sauce made with chocolate), Veracruz conger eel, and spicy enchiladas. Every evening from 7 to 9pm the restaurant has a happy hour: If you order one of the large margaritas or any other drink, the second one's free. The warm brick walls and Mexican folk art make for a cozy atmosphere; the service is very friendly too. Make a reservation on weekend evenings because Días de Zapata tends to fill up quickly.

✪ Familia Weiss. Corner of Palacios and V.A. O'Connor. ☎ **02944/435789.** Reservations not required. Main courses $7–$13. AE, DC, MC, V. Daily 10am–2am. REGIONAL.

The Weiss family is well known all over the region for their outstanding smoked meats and cheeses, which they've been selling from their shop at Mitre 360 for decades. They've also run a tiny restaurant up the street for years, and a year ago they opened this new restaurant near the waterfront that is so architecturally unique you really should at least stop in for one of the locally brewed beers and to view the handsome interiors. The decor includes cypress trunks that form pillars rising from a mosaic floor also made of cypress. Each wall is a patchwork of wood, brick, and ceramic, except the front area, which has large picture windows looking out onto the lake. Details such as papier-mâché lamps and folk art lend character.

As for the food, there's a lot on offer here, all very good (and the menu features photos of nearly every dish available). Start off with an appetizer of the smoked meats, seafood, and cheese the Familia Weiss is known for. There's cheese and beef fondue with five dipping sauces, large leafy salads, stewed venison with spaetzle, grilled meats with fresh vegetables, homemade pastas, and local trout, among much, much more. A good wine list and a kid's menu make the Familia Weiss hard to beat.

✪ Jauja. Quaglia 366. ☎ **02944/422952.** Reservations not required. Main courses $6–$18. AE, DC, MC, V. Daily 11:30am–3pm and 7:30pm–midnight. REGIONAL.

Jauja is one of the best restaurants in Bariloche, both for its extensive menu and woodsy atmosphere. You'll find just about everything on offer here, from regional to German-influenced dishes, including grilled or stewed venison, goulash with spaetzle, stuffed crêpes, homemade pastas, barbecued meats, and trout served 15 different ways. The semi-casual dining area is made entirely of wood, with wooden tables and lots of glass, plants, basket lamps, and candles. A glass-and-wood wall divides smoking and nonsmoking sections. The Jauja's fresh salads and desserts are quite good, especially the poached pears and apple mousse. If you don't have time to dine, you can order food to go.

La Marmite. Mitre 329. ☎ **02944/423685.** Reservations not required. Main courses $7–$17. AE, DC, MC, V. Daily noon–3:30pm and 7:30–11:30pm. SWISS.

La Marmite is very similar to the Casita Suiza, although not as cozy in the evening but with more on the menu. Once you step inside you'll feel as though you've traveled to Switzerland because of the decor: ruby-red tablecloths and carved wooden beams stained black and stenciled with flowers. The menu offers fondue ($28 to $32 for two) and *raclette,* but the main dishes are a better bet, especially regional specialties such as hunter's hare stew or wild boar steeped in burgundy wine with mushrooms. There's a wide variety of more standard fare, such as grilled tenderloin beef, which comes sizzling on a platter, as well as exquisite tarts and cakes.

INEXPENSIVE

✪ El Boliche de Alberto. Villegas 347. ☎ **02944/431433.** Reservations not required. Main courses $6–$10. AE, MC, V. Daily noon–4pm and 8pm–midnight. STEAKHOUSE.

If you're in the mood for steak, this is your place. El Boliche de Alberto is my favorite *parrilla* in Bariloche, and everyone else's too, it seems. Some regulars have been coming back for 20 years. The quality of meat here is outstanding, and the prices are very reasonable. The cowhide menu is very brief: several cuts of beef, chicken, and sausages, with salads and side dishes such as french fries. The newish dining area is unpretentious and brightly lit, with wooden tables. The charismatic owner, Alberto, has plastered an entire wall with photos of regulars and luminaries who have paid a visit, along with notes thanking him for a wonderful meal. Alberto will usually take your order himself and even lead you to the grill to show off the high quality of his cuts. A typical *bife de chorizo* steak is so thick you'll need to split it with your dining partner; if you're alone, they can do a half-order for $6. The Boliche de Alberto has another location on the road to Llao Llao at Bustillo 8800 (☎ **02944/462285**) and a very good pasta restaurant at Elflein 163 (☎ **02944/431084**).

El Mundo. Mitre 759. ☎ **02944/423461.** Reservations not required. Main courses $6–$15. AE, DC, MC, V. Daily noon–midnight. PIZZERIA.

El Mundo serves up crispy pizza in more than 100 varieties, as well as empanadas, pastas, and salads. There are so many kinds of pies on offer that the menu gets a little overwhelming. The pasta is fresh, and they deliver. A large downstairs and upstairs seating area makes El Mundo a good spot for groups.

Friends. Corner of Mitre and Rolando. ☎ **02944/423700.** Reservations not required. Main courses $5–$13. AE, MC, V. Daily 24 hours. CAFE.

Friends is worth a mention more than anything because it is open 24 hours a day and is popular with families with kids. The cafe is embellished with hundreds of antique toys and trinkets, which hang from the ceiling and fill every corner. The menu serves grilled meats and fish, crêpes, sandwiches, soups, and salads, and offers a daily fixed-price menu for about $7, which is usually something like pan-fried trout and french fries. There is a huge selection of rich, sugary desserts too.

BARILOCHE AFTER DARK

Bariloche is home to a handful of discos catering to the 20- to 30-year-old crowd. These discos adhere to Buenos Aires nightlife hours, beginning about midnight to 12:30am, with the peak of the evening at about 3 or 4am. The cover charge is usually $10 per person, and often women enter for free. Try **Roket** at J.M. de Rosas 424 (☎ **02944/431940**) or **Cerebro** at J.M. de Rosas 405 (☎ **02944/424965**). The Hotel Panamericano runs Bariloche's **Casino** at Av. San Martín 570 (☎ **02944/425846**), open 9am to 5am. The Casino hosts live shows every evening. Guests must be over 18 years old; entrance is free. The local cinema can be found at Moreno 39 (☎ **02944/422860**).

THE ROAD TO THE LLAO LLAO PENINSULA
CIRCUITO CHICO & THE CERRO CAMPANARIO

The Cerro Campanario provides possibly the best lookout point in the region, with exceptional views of Lakes Nahuel Huapi and Perito Moreno, as well as the ravishing beauty of the Llao Llao Peninsula and the peaks surrounding it. The lookout point is accessed by a 7-minute cable car ride located 10.5 miles (17km) outside Bariloche on the road to Llao Llao, meaning you'll have to arrange transportation with a tour, drive a rental car, or take a bus. You can also check in the Cerro Campanario cable car company's Bariloche office for transfer shuttles from downtown. There's also a restaurant with panoramic views. The office is at Belgrano 41 #B (☎ **02944/427274;** http://campanario.bariloche.net.ar), and is open daily 9am to noon and 2 to 6pm; the cost for the cable car is $10.

The Cerro Campanario is along a popular, 37-mile (60km) drive around the Llao Llao Peninsula, commonly known as the **Circuito Chico**. This drive offers spectacular views of Lakes Nahuel Huapi and Perito Moreno and the snowcapped peaks of Cerro Otway and Catedral that tower over them. The drive begins 11 miles (18km) from Bariloche on Avenida Bustillo, which changes into Route 237, loops around the peninsula as Route 77 and meets back at Route 237 and eventually Bustillo, all the while meandering through dense forest and picturesque bays with outstanding lookout points. Visitors will find *parrilla* and fondue-style restaurants along the way, as well as the world-renowned **Llao Llao Hotel & Resort** (see below). Stop by the visitor's center to pick up a detailed Circuito Chico map highlighting restaurants and shops along the way. Again, most tour operators offer this excursion.

WHERE TO STAY ON THE LLAO LLAO PENINSULA

✪ **La Cascada Hotel.** Av. Bustillo, Km6. ☎ **02944/441088.** Fax 02944/441076. www. lacascada.com. E-mail: lacascada@infovia.com.ar. 25 units. TV TEL. $100 double; $161 suite. AE, DC, MC, V.

La Cascada's prize feature is a lovely garden with a frothing waterfall that gives the hotel its name. Part of the Best Western chain, La Cascada has an uneven style but is exceptionally comfortable and pleasant, and its location 4 miles (6km) from town ensures a quiet connection with nature. The hotel has hosted its share of luminaries, notably Argentine ex-president Carlos Menem and more recently Sarah Ferguson, the Duchess of York.

The hotel seems like someone's stately home. Although the property was totally renovated in 1988, many design details hearken back to the hotel's founding in 1950, such as the stark, Scandinavian-style dining area and the classic English "Imperial" suites. Each guest room and common area seems to come from a different era or school of design, such as the early '80s purple disco or the country-style, wood-walled standard doubles with gingham bedspreads. The "Gris" suites are perhaps the best in the hotel, with fresh, clean interiors and two glass-enclosed nooks and an abundance of sunlight. A double with a lake view costs $35 more than rooms with a view of the surrounding vegetation. Doubles have bay windows and a few have king-size beds, but you'll have to ask for one. The hotel does not have transportation; a taxi to town costs about $5. Outside is a grassy slope that leads to a private beach, and there is a short nature trail that winds around the hotel's 3-hectare (7-acre) property.

Dining/Diversions: La Cascada's on-site restaurant serves international cuisine.

Amenities: Laundry, room service, heated pool, gym, sauna, game room.

✪ **Llao Llao Hotel & Resort.** Av. Bustillo Km25. ☎ **02944/448530.** Fax 02944/445789. Reservations (in Buenos Aires): ☎ 11/4311-3434; fax 11/4314-4646. www.llaollao.com. E-mail: llaollao@datamarkets.com.ar. 162 units. TV TEL. $266–$381 double; $399–$560 suite. AE, DC, MC, V.

The internationally renowned Llao Llao Hotel & Resort is one of the finest hotels in Latin America, as much for its magnificent location as its sumptuous, elegant interiors. Situated on a grassy crest of the Llao Llao Peninsula and framed by rugged peaks, this five-star hotel was modeled after the style of Canadian mountain lodges, taking cues such as cypress and pine-log walls, stone fireplaces, antler chandeliers, and barn-sized salons. This is the place to spend the night if you're willing to splurge for a special evening. The hotel was first built in 1934, but burned to the ground and was rebuilt again in 1938; since its inception it has been scrupulously maintained and was last updated in 1993. A driveway winds up to the hotel where a discreet security guard monitors traffic: The hotel tries to keep gawkers at a distance, although visitors may come for a drink or lunch. The lounge has glossy wood floors carpeted with oriental rugs, coffee-colored wicker furniture, and soft lights, and is the site of frequent teas and special appetizer hours, as is the nearby Club House, which has a daily tea at 4pm.

From the lobby, every turn leads to another remarkable room, including a "winter garden" cafe whose expansive glass walls look out onto a large patio, the hotel's golf course, and Lake Nahuel Huapi beyond. A monumental hallway adorned with paintings from local artists leads to the rooms, all of which have been decorated in a rustic country design and come with luxury bathrooms and feather-soft beds—nice, but the style is not as exceptional as one would expect from a hotel of this caliber. Superior suites are split into bedroom and living areas and come with a wraparound deck and fireplace; there's also one two-bedroom cabin. The presidential suite is so costly that typically only presidents can afford to book it. The hotel is reluctant to advertise its cheapest prices for doubles without a view, so inquire thoroughly and do not hesitate to bargain for an upgrade.

Dining: There is a cozy coffee shop for casual fare and quick snacks; this is also the location for an enormous breakfast buffet. The hotel also has a more formal dining room that serves excellent international and regional fare. The lounge and winter garden have revolving teas, appetizers, and salad bars.

Amenities: Laundry, room service, game room, business center, health and fitness center, heated pool, whirlpool, sauna, gift shop, travel agency, child-care center, library, beauty salon, canoes, windsurfing, archery, golf course, paddle tennis, guided excursions.

4 Villa La Angostura

50 miles (81km) N of Bariloche; 27 miles (44km) E of the Chilean border

Villa La Angostura (Narrow Village) takes its name for the slender isthmus that connects the town's center with the Peninsula Quetrihué. The town was founded in 1934 when it was a collection of simple farmers with small plots of land. These farmers were eventually usurped by out-of-towners who chose this lovely location for their summer homes. Increased boating activity, the paving of the road to Bariloche, increased tourism with Chile (whose border crossing is just 20 minutes from town), and the inauguration of several exclusive hotels and a handful of bungalow complexes has converted Villa La Angostura into a popular tourist destination—although the tiny enclave still sees only a fraction of visitors to the region, unlike Bariloche. This picturesque village is for visitors seeking to get away from the crowds. Most lodging options are tucked away in the forest on the shore of the Lake Nahuel Huapi, providing beautiful views and quiet surroundings.

GETTING THERE   By Plane   For airport and flight information, see "Getting There," under San Carlos de Bariloche, above. To get to Villa La Angostura from the airport, take a taxi or transfer service.

By Bus   Algarrobal Buses (☎ 02944/494360) leaves for Villa La Angostura from Bariloche about every 3 hours from 8am to 9pm, from the Terminal de Omnibus.

VISITOR INFORMATION   The Secretaría de Turismo is at Av. Siete Lagos 93 (☎ 02944/494124), open daily 8am to 8pm. It offers accommodation listings and prices, and information about excursions around the area. For information about Nahuel Huapi National Park or Parque Nacional Bosque Arrayánes, try the **Bosques y Parques Provincials Oficína de Turismo** at the pier (☎ 02944/494157), open Monday to Friday 11am to 4pm, Wednesday until 2pm, Saturday and holidays 2:30 to 5pm; closed Sunday.

WHAT TO SEE & DO

PARQUE NACIONAL BOSQUE ARRAYÁNES   The Parque Nacional Bosque Arrayánes is home to the only two *arrayán* forests in the world (although the *arrayán* can be found throughout this region, including in Chile), one of which can be visited at the tip of Península Quetrihué. This fascinating bush grows as high as 20m (66 ft.) and to the untrained eye looks like a tree, with slick cinnamon-colored trunks that are cool to the touch. They are especially beautiful in the spring when in bloom.

The peninsula itself offers a pleasant, 15-mile (24km) round-trip moderate hiking and biking trail to the *arrayán* forest. Most visitors either walk (2 to 3 hours) or bike (1 to 2 hours) half of the trail and boat to or back from the park; you can also take the boat both ways (trip time 2½ hours). **Paisano** (☎ **02944/494459**) has an 18-passenger launch with a cafeteria and daily trips leaving at 3pm. They offer four to five trips during the summer depending on demand; adults are $15 round-trip, kids 6 to 12 $12 round-trip; all ages are $10 one-way. **Bettanso Excursiones** has a 50-person boat with daily departures at 2:30pm, and six to seven trips during the summer for the same price as Paisano (☎ **02944/495024**). Bettanso also offers excursions to Isla Victoria and Puerto Blest, a trip which is described in "What to See & Do In & Around Bariloche," above.

BIKING   Ian Bikes, Topa Topa 102 (☎ **02944/495047;** e-mail: ianbikes@ hotmail.com), has a large selection of rental bikes for $3 per hour, $10 up to 6 hours, and $15 for a full day. They also supply information about trails in the area.

FISHING   Anglers typically head to the renowned Río Correntoso for rainbow and brown trout, reached just before crossing the bridge just outside town on Ruta Nacional 231, from the Siete Lagos road. **Banana Fly Shop,** at Arrayánes 282 (☎ **02944/494634**), sells flies and gear, and they have information and can recommend guides. You may pick up a **fishing license** here or at the Bosques y Parques Provinciales office at the port (☎ **02944/494157**); Monday to Friday 11am to 4pm, Wednesday until 2pm, Saturday and holidays 2:30 to 5pm; closed Sunday.

SKIING   Villa La Angostura is home to a little gem of a ski resort, **Cerro Bayo,** located about 5.5 miles (9km) from downtown. It's a smaller resort than the one at Cerro Catedral, but the crowds are thinner and the view is wonderful—for those reasons I almost prefer it. There are 250 skiable acres, with 40% of the terrain intermediate and about 35% advanced. To get to it, you'll need to take a long lift from the base up to the summit; during the summer this same chair lift provides access to an excellent short hike and lookout point. Cerro Bayo has ski and snowboard rental and instruction; the season runs from mid-June to mid-September, although it can get fairly patchy toward the end of the season.

To get to Cerro Bayo, ask your hotel to arrange transportation or hire a taxi for the short ride. Tickets run from low to high season $19 to $27 for adults, $13 to $21 for kids, and kids under 6 and adults over 65 ski free. For more information, call ☎ **02944/494189** or visit www.7lagos.com/cerrobayo.

WHERE TO STAY

Accommodations have either private parking or ample free street parking.

✪ **La Posada.** Ruta Nacional 231. ☎/fax **02944/494368.** www.hosterialaposada.com. E-mail: laposada@bariloche.com.ar. 20 units. TV TEL. $107–$140 double with view; $82–$107 double without view. AE, DC, MC, V. Closed June.

This attractive country inn packs a punch with a magnificent view of the rippling waters of Lago Nahuel Huapi—so be sure to request a west-facing room that boasts that view. La Posada's cozy country decor features plaid and oak-wood furnishings and opens directly onto a pretty sloping garden that leads to a beach and private dock—the garden has, in fact, won numerous awards over the years. To the untrained eye, the junior suites are no larger than the doubles. Doubles that face the lake come with bay windows, and they are substantially better than the other half that don't, but this might not be much of an issue if you plan to spend the entire day outdoors.

The beds are very comfortable, and the decor handsome, with striped furnishings and wooden ceilings. Outside, a terraced walkway leading to the dock has tables and lounge chairs set among fragrant flowers. Another walkway leads to the hotel's outdoor pool overlooking the lake, which is closed during the winter. The hotel has its own private deck, and during the summer sets out kayaks and small boats for guests; in the evening, the dock is lit up with twinkling lights. If you're doing any fishing, the hotel is near the Río Correntoso.

Dining: La Posada's chef whips up tasty international food; guests spending more than a night typically dine here at least once.

Amenities: Laundry, room service, outdoor pool, Jacuzzi, private dock.

✪ **Las Balsas.** Bahía Las Balsas. ☎/fax **02944/494308.** www.lasbalsas.com.ar. E-mail: balsas@satlink.com. 15 units. TEL. $280 double; $480 suite. AE, DC, MC, V.

Part of the Relais & Châteaux group, this exquisite country inn sits directly on the shore of Lago Nahuel Huapi, with its own private dock, spa, and superb gourmet restaurant. Guests are treated with generous, warm-hearted service and made to feel as though they are in their own elegant yet comfortable home. Rooms come with views of the lake and the evening sunset, and each is thematically different. One has a romantic decor, with mauve walls, iron beds, antique lamps, and thick white cotton drapes; another is appointed with folk art and a tweedy bedspread. There's also a cozy attic loft popular with honeymooning couples. The suites are sumptuous, with polished wood floors, larger-than-king-sized beds, rectangular desks with fax and stereo, bathrooms nearly as large as the standard doubles, and wraparound floor-to-ceiling windows that allow the sun to cascade in. Gleaming bathrooms come with fluffy terrycloth robes and peek-a-boo windows leading to views of the room and the lake. The lounge area abounds with couches and chairs to sink into for reading, gazing at the roaring fire, or enjoying conversation among guests.

Next door, a minimalist river rock–and–wood "spa" has an indoor/outdoor heated pool separated by a wall of windows, and a massage room built like a temple of relaxation. This is one of the few Relais & Châteaux hotels to welcome children; and although kids are required to dine upstairs, they usually love it, as the room doubles as a play/TV area. The hotel takes advantage of the lake by offering inflatable rafts, paddle boats, and kayaks to guests, as well as a fleet of mountain bikes. The only regretful thing about Las Balsas is that the price may be prohibitive to many.

Dining/Diversions: Las Balsas features an outstanding restaurant serving international and regional dishes from a set daily menu ($40 per person). They also have a small lounge/bar.

Amenities: Laundry, room service, business center, gift shop, conference room, gym, indoor/outdoor pool, whirlpool, sauna, massage, mountain bikes, paddle boats, kayaks, inflatable rafts, evening turndown.

WHERE TO DINE

For sweeping views of Lake Nahuel Huapi and the region, you can't beat the El Mirador confitería and restaurant at Av. Siete Lagos 5018 (☎ **02944/1555 0847**).

✪ **La Macarena.** Cerro Bayo 65. ☎ **02944/495120.** Reservations not necessary. Main courses $12–$22. MC, V. Tues–Sun noon–3pm and 8–11:30pm. CONTEMPORARY ARGENTINE.

Don't be fooled by the semi-casual atmosphere at La Macarena—the food is divine. Chef Pablo Tejeda whips up a creative take on regional cooking, with mouth-watering cuisine such as polenta with a ragout of wild mushrooms, venison goulash, and rack of lamb steeped in merlot and sautéed vegetables. His recipe for wild hare in a sauvignon blanc sauce was chosen as northern Patagonia's representative dish in the Certamen Nacional Cucarón cooking competition in 2000. There's also fresh pasta with a choice of 10 different sauces, as well as several Chinese and Mexican dishes.

Rincón Suiza. Av. Arrayánes 44. ☎/fax **02944/494248.** Reservations not necessary. Main courses $10–$20. AE, MC, V. Daily noon–11:30pm. Apr–Sept closed Wed. SWISS/REGIONAL.

This little restaurant comes with all the usual trappings of a Swiss-style restaurant, from Alpine interiors to a menu offering everything from fondue to pork chops with sauerkraut. The owner, a Swiss descendant, strives to "rescue the traditional flavors of the Swiss and regional Argentine kitchens." Also on the menu are venison marinated in beer and served with spaetzle, lamb brochettes, and a trout dish served with sauces of capers, Roquefort cheese, and almonds. Some of the richest, most flavorful items on the menu are the desserts, including the *Torta Rincón Suiza* made of chocolate, peaches, and cream, as well as the apple strudel.

✪ **Waldhaus.** Ruta Nacional 231, Km61. ☎ **02944/495123.** Reservations not necessary. Main courses $10–$18. MC, V. Daily noon–3:30pm and 8pm–12:30am. SWISS/REGIONAL.

If you think the Rincón Suiza has gone overboard with the Swiss theme, try this little restaurant, whose gingerbread eaves, notched furniture, and woodsy location will make you feel like you're dining in the Black Forest. The location 4 miles (6km) from downtown makes the Waldhaus less convenient than the Rincón Suiza, but the food is slightly better here. There are nightly specials, and typical menu offerings include wild mushroom soup, beef fondue, venison marinated in burgundy wine, and typical Tyrolean dishes such as spaetzle with ham.

7

Uruguay

The second smallest nation in South America, Uruguay is a little place that makes a big impression. With a healthy economy, impressive living standard, high literacy rate, and excellent social services—including the best medical care system in South America—it has become a model for other developing countries in the region. Despite its homogeneous population (mostly of European descent), Uruguay reveals splendid contrasts. This is a land of dusty colonial towns and sparkling beach resorts, of rough-and-ready gauchos and subtle artists, of pious homes and festive plazas. Uruguay is a place where God and football are worshipped without reserve, where the sun shines brightly and the air stays warm, where few question the dignity of their homeland.

Uruguay's origins as a country rest firmly in Europe; the indigenous people inhabiting the region were displaced by the colonizing Portuguese and Spanish in the late 17th and early 18th centuries. You will find their influence most evident among the historic treasures of Colonia, where the Portuguese first entrenched themselves, and amid the rich architecture of Montevideo, where the Spanish landed. Montevideo is the cultural heartland of the country, a place where you will discover the bold accomplishments of Uruguay in music, arts, and literature. Among the several internationally accomplished artists are Pedro Figari, who inspired a school of painters; José Enrique Rodó, Uruguay's famed essayist from the early 20th century; and Mauricio Rosencof, the politically active playwright from recent decades. Outside the capital, miles of tilled fields and rolling hills draw your attention away from the capital's urban existence to a softer, quieter life. But this rural lifestyle stops at the coast, where world-class resorts centered on Punta del Este lure the continent's rich and famous.

1 Uruguay Essentials

ENTRY REQUIREMENTS & CUSTOMS

American, British, Canadian, and New Zealand citizens need only a passport to enter Uruguay (for tourist stays of up to 90 days). Australian citizens must get a tourist visa before arrival.

A customs information guide for Uruguay can be found at **www. euro-trans.com/customs/uruguay.asp**.

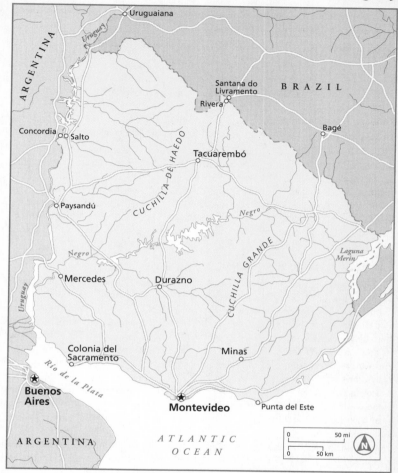

VISITOR INFORMATION

The Web is an excellent source of information on Uruguay. Try **www.turismo.gub.uy** for country-wide visitor information. Another excellent site, **www.uruguaywebdirectory. com**, has a host of Uruguay-related links.

The Uruguayan embassy in your home country is a good source of information. At **www.embassy.org/uruguay**, the Uruguayan Embassy site in Washington, D.C., you'll find a description of tourist activities in Montevideo, Punta del Este, and Uruguay's northwest, as well as travel tips and a hostel list.

MONEY

The official currency is the **Uruguayan peso** (designated NP$, $U, or simply $); each peso is comprised of 100 **centavos.** Uruguayan pesos are available in $10, $20, $50, $100, $200, $500, $1,000, and $5,000 notes; coins come in 10, 20, and 50 centavos, and 1 and 2 pesos. The exchange rate as this book went to press was approximately

12½ pesos to the dollar. The value of the peso fluctuates greatly with inflation, so prices here are quoted in U.S. dollars.

WHEN TO GO

The best time to visit Uruguay is October through March, when the sun shines and temperatures are mild. Punta del Este overflows with tourists from Argentina in January and February; if you're seeking a more relaxed time to visit the beaches of the coast, consider going between October and December.

Average temperatures are spring, 62°F, summer 73°F, autumn 64°F, and winter 53°F (remember that seasons are reversed from the northern hemisphere).

SPECIAL EVENTS The country's biggest festival is **Carnival,** which takes place during the week leading up to Ash Wednesday, the first day of Lent. It's celebrated across the country, although Montevideo is the center for the main events, including parades, dance parties, and widespread debauchery. **Semana Criolla,** a Uruguayan-style rodeo performed by traditional gauchos, is celebrated 1 week before Easter in the Carrasco neighborhood of Montevideo. Uruguay celebrates its **Independence** on August 25. For more information on these activities, contact the **municipal tourist office,** Explanada Municipal, in Montevideo (☎ **2/903-0649**).

GETTING THERE & GETTING AROUND

International flights land at **Carrasco International Airport** (☎ 2/601-4855), located 12 miles (19km) from downtown Montevideo. A taxi to downtown costs about $20. Uruguay's national carrier is **PLUNA,** Colonia and Julio Herrera (☎ 2/903-0273), serving domestic and international destinations. **United** (☎ 800/247-6522 in the U.S., 2/902-5630 in Uruguay) and **American** (☎ 800/433-7300 in the U.S., 2/916-3929 in Uruguay) offer connecting service from the United States. **Aerolíneas Argentinas** (☎ 2/901-9466) connects Buenos Aires and Montevideo; the flight takes 50 minutes.

Punta del Este has its own international airport; the majority of flights arrive from Buenos Aires. From Montevideo, the easiest way to reach Colonia and Punta del Este is by bus (see the "Getting There" sections under "Montevideo" and "Punta del Este," below).

For information on driving in Uruguay, contact the Automovil Club de Uruguay, Colonia 1251 (☎ 2/902-5792), or the Centro Automovilista del Uruguay, E.V. Haedo 2378 (☎ 2/408-2091).

Fast Facts: Uruguay

ATM Networks   ATMs on the Cirrus network are widely available in Montevideo and Punta del Este. If you travel to Colonia or elsewhere outside these cities, you should bring Uruguayan pesos.

Customs   See "Entry Requirements & Customs," above.

Electricity   Electricity in Uruguay runs on 220 volts, so bring a transformer and adapter along with any electrical appliances. Note that most laptops operate on both 110 and 220 volts. Some luxury hotels may supply transformers and adapters.

Embassies & Consulates   United States Embassy, Lauro Muller 1776, Montevideo 11100 (☎ 2/408-7777); British Embassy, Marco Bruto No. 1073, P.O.

Box 16024, Montevideo 11300 (☎ **2/622-3630**); and Australian Consulate, Cerro Largo 1000, Montevideo 11100 (☎ **2/901-0743**).

Holidays   January 1 (New Year), January 6 (Dia de los Niños), Carnival (the days leading up to Ash Wednesday), Easter, April 19 (Desembarco de los 33 Orientales), May 1 (Labor Day), May 18 (Batalla de las Piedras), June 19 (Natalicio de Jose Artigas), July 18 (Jura de la Constitucion), August 25 (Independence Day), October 12 (Dia de las Americas), November 2 (Dia de los Difuntos), December 25 (Christmas).

Internet Access   Many hotel business centers have Internet access, as do guest rooms of five-star hotels. See "Internet Access" under "Fast Facts: Montevideo," for a listing of cybercafes in town.

Mail   International airmail postage for a letter weighing up to 22g is 22 pesos ($1.75); from 22g to 100g costs 55 pesos ($4.40).

Safety   Uruguay is one of the safest countries in the world, although street crime in Montevideo has risen in recent years. Outside the capital, cities and beach resorts like Punta del Este are considered extremely safe.

Taxes   Value-added tax is called *IVA* in Spanish. IVA is 14% for hotels and restaurants and 24% for general sales tax; the tax is almost always included in your bill.

Telephones   The country code for Uruguay is **598.** Uruguay's national telephone company is called ANTEL. You can buy a telephone card from any kiosk or ANTEL *telecentro* location. You can also make domestic and international calls from *telecentro* offices—they are located every few blocks in major cities—but be warned that international calls are very expensive, especially during peak hours. To call home using AT&T, dial ☎ **000-410;** for MCI Worldcom, dial ☎ **000-412;** for Sprint, dial ☎ **000-417.**

Time Zone   Uruguay is 1 hour ahead of EST (4pm in New York is 5pm in Uruguay).

Toilets   It's permissible to use the toilets in restaurants and bars without patronizing the establishment; offer a nice smile on the way in. Nobody should bother you, unless they're having a bad day.

Water   Locals swear that the drinking water in Uruguay is perfectly healthy. If you are concerned, stick with bottled water.

2 Montevideo

Montevideo, the southernmost capital on the continent, is home to half the country's population. Born on the banks of the Rio de la Plata, Montevideo first existed as a fortress of the Spanish empire and developed into a major port city in the mid-18th century. European immigrants, including Spanish, Portuguese, French, and British, influenced the city's architecture, and a walk around the capital reveals architectural styles ranging from colonial to art deco. Indeed, the richness of Montevideo's architecture is unrivaled in South America.

While Montevideo has few must-see attractions, its charm lies in wait for the careful traveler. A walk along La Rambla, stretching from the Old City to the neighborhood of Carrasco, takes you along the riverfront past fishermen and their catch to parks and gardens where children play and elders sip *maté* (a tealike beverage).

Restaurants, cafes, bars, and street performers populate the port area, where you will also discover the flavors of Uruguay at the afternoon and weekend Mercado del Puerto, or Port Market. Many of the city's historic sites surround Plaza Independencia and can be visited in a few hours.

ESSENTIALS
GETTING THERE

BY PLANE   To get to Montevideo by plane, see "Getting There & Getting Around," above. A taxi from the airport to downtown costs about $20.

BY BOAT OR HYDROFOIL   Buquebus, Calle Río Negro 1400 (☎ **2/4316-6550** or 2/4316-6500), operates three to four hydrofoils per day between Montevideo and Buenos Aires; the trip takes about 2½ hours and costs under $100 round-trip. Montevideo's port is just over a mile from downtown. If you have taken a ferry to Colonia, you can get connecting bus service to Montevideo.

BY BUS   Terminal Omnibus Tres Cruces, General Artigas 1825 (☎ **2/408-8601**), is Montevideo's long-distance bus terminal, connecting the capital with cities in Uruguay and throughout South America. Buses to Buenos Aires takes about 8 hours. **COT** (☎ **2/409-4949**) offers the best service to Punta del Este, Maldonado, and Colonia.

For information on driving in Uruguay, contact the **Automovil Club de Uruguay,** Colonia 1251 (☎ **2/902-5792**), or the **Centro Automovilista del Uruguay,** E.V. Haedo 2378 (☎ **2/408-2091**).

VISITOR INFORMATION

Uruguay's **Ministerio de Turismo** is at Av. Libertador 1409 and Colonia (☎ **2/908-9105**). It's open weekdays 11:30am to 6:30pm. There's also a branch at Carrasco International Airport. The **municipal tourist office,** Explanada Municipal (☎ **2/903-0649**), offers city maps and brochures of tourist activities, and is open daily 10am to 8pm. It also organizes cultural city tours on weekends.

GETTING AROUND

Montevideo has the second lowest crime rate of any big city (after Tokyo), and it's easy to navigate on foot or by bus. You can easily walk between sites in the Old City and along Avenida 18 de Julio. Safe, convenient buses criss-cross Montevideo if you want to venture farther (for less than $1 per trip). Taxis, while plentiful, can be difficult to flag down during rush hour.

ORIENTATION

Montevideo is surrounded by water on three sides, a testament to its earlier incarnation as an easily defended fortress for the Spanish Empire. The Old City begins near the western edge of Montevideo, found on the skinny portion of a peninsula between the Rambla Gran Bretaña and the city's main artery, Avenida 18 de Julio. Look for the Plaza Independencia and the Plaza Constitucion to find the center of the district. Many of the city's museums, theaters, and hotels reside in this historic area, although a trip east on Avenida 18 de Julio reveals the more modern Montevideo with its own share of hotels, markets, and monuments. Along the city's long southern coastline runs the Rambla Gran Bretaña, traveling from the piers of the Old City past the Parque Rodó and on to points south and east, passing fish stalls and street performers along the way.

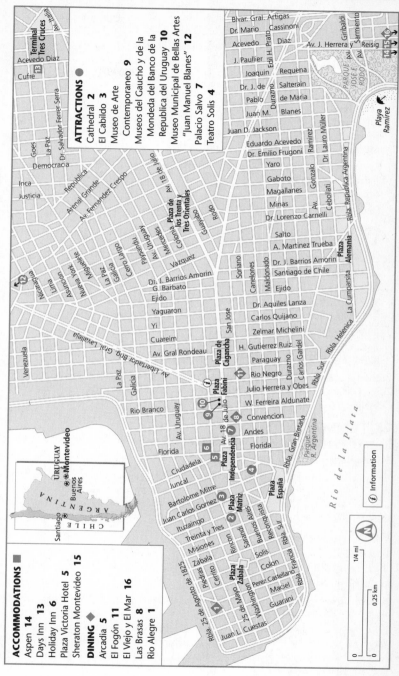

ACCOMMODATIONS
Aspen **14**
Days Inn **13**
Holiday Inn **6**
Plaza Victoria Hotel **5**
Sheraton Montevideo **15**

DINING
Arcadia **5**
El Fogón **11**
El Viejo y El Mar **16**
Las Brasas **8**
Río Alegre **1**

ATTRACTIONS
Cathedral **2**
El Cabildo **3**
Museo de Arte
Contemporaneo **9**
Museos del Gaucho y de la
Mondeda del Banco de la
Republica del Uruguay **10**
Museo Municipal de Bellas Artes
"Juan Manuel Blanes" **12**
Palacio Salvo **7**
Teatro Solis **4**

Playa Ramírez

Río de la Plata

ⓘ Information

Fast Facts: Montevideo

Area Code   The country code for Uruguay is **598;** the city code for Montevideo is **2.**

ATMs   ATMs are plentiful; look for **Bancomat** and **Redbrou** banks. Most have access to the Cirrus network.

Car Rental   Hertz is located at the Carrasco International Airport (☎ **2/604-0006**) and Av. Monte Caseros 3355 (☎ **2/507-6844**). **Avis** rents vehicles at the International Airport (☎ **2/604-0334**) and at Yaguarón 1527 (☎ **2/903-0303**).

Currency Exchange   Try **Cambio Martiz,** Av. Rincón 487 (☎ **2/915-0800**), **Gales Casa Cambiaria,** Av. 18 de Julio 1046 (☎ **2/902-0229**), or one of the airport exchanges.

Drugstores   Try **Campus,** Av. Gorlero 920 (☎ **2/444-4444**).

Emergencies   For police, dial ☎ **109** or **1909;** for first aid, dial ☎ **105;** for the fire department, dial ☎ **104.**

Hospital   The **British Hospital** is located at Av. Italia 2420 (☎ **2/487-1020**) and has emergency room services.

Internet Access   Reliable cybercafes include **El Cybercafe,** Calle 25 de Mayo 568 (☎ **2/915-4816**), **Arroba del Sur,** Guayabo 1858 (☎ **2/402-3049**), and **El Cybercafe Softec,** Santiago de Chile 1286 (☎ **2/900-6010**). Average cost is $5 per hour of usage.

Post Office   The main post office is at Calle Buenos Aires 451 (☎ **2/916-0200**) and is open weekdays 9am to 6pm.

Safety   While Montevideo remains very safe for big city standards, street crime has risen in recent years. As always, travelers should exercise caution when walking outside tourist areas and at night.

EXPLORING MONTEVIDEO
THE TOP ATTRACTIONS

Plaza Independencia. Bordered by Av. 18 de Julio, Florida, and Juncal.

Originally the site of a Spanish citadel, Independence Square marks the beginning of the Old City and is a good point from which to begin your tour of Montevideo. An enormous statue of General Gervasio Artigas, father of Uruguay and hero of its independent movement, stands in the center.

Palacio Salvo (Salvo Palace). Plaza Independencia.

Often referred to as the symbol of Montevideo, the Salvo Palace was once the tallest building in South America. While its 26 stories might not impress you, it remains the city's highest structure.

Palacio Taranco (Taranco Palace). Calle 25 de Mayo 376. ☎ **2/915-1101.** Free admission. Tues–Sun 10am–6pm.

Now the decorative arts museum, the Taranco Palace was built in the early 20th century and represents the trend toward French architecture during that period. The museum displays an assortment of Uruguayan furniture, draperies, clocks, paintings, and other cultural works.

El Cabildo (Town Hall). Juan Carlos Gómez 1362. ☎ **2/915-9685.** Free admission. Tues–Sun 2:30–7pm.

Uruguay's constitution was signed in the old town hall, which also served as the city's jailhouse in the 19th century. Now a museum, the Cabildo houses the city's historic archives as well as maps and photos, antiques, costumes, and artwork.

Cathedral. Calle Sarandí at Ituzaingó. Free admission. Mon–Fri 8am–8pm.

Also known as Matriz Church, the cathedral was the city's first public building, erected in 1804. It houses the remains of some of Uruguay's most important political, religious, and economic figures, and is distinguished by its domed bell towers.

Teatro Solís. Calle Buenos Aires 652. ☎ **2/916-0908.** Free admission. Museum Mon–Fri 2–6pm.

Montevideo's main theater and opera house, opened in 1852, has just completed an extensive renovation. It hosts Uruguay's most important cultural events and is the site of the **Museo Nacional de Historia Natural** (National Museum of Natural History).

Museos del Gaucho y de la Mondeda del Banco de la Republica del Uruguay (Mint Collection and Gaucho Museum of the National State Bank). Av. 18 de Julio 998. ☎ **2/900-8764.** Free admission. Tues–Fri 9:30am–noon and 1:30–6pm; Sat–Sun 4–7pm.

The neoclassic building houses two museums—one focused on work of Uruguayan cowboys and ranchers, the other on the national mint. The gaucho museum highlights life on the range with spurs, stirrups, saddles, horse whips, knives, daggers, and fancy harnesses representing tools used by these South American cowboys. The money museum displays national coins dating from 1840 as well as colonial coins, essays, and documents.

Museo de Arte Contemporaneo (Museum of Contemporary Art). Av. 18 de Julio 965, 2nd floor. Free admission. Daily noon–8pm.

Opened in 1997, this museum is dedicated to contemporary Uruguayan art and exhibits the country's biggest names. To promote cultural exchange across the region, a section of the museum has been set aside for artists who hail from countries belonging to the MERCOSUR trading block.

Museo Municipal de Bellas Artes "Juan Manuel Blanes" (Municipal Museum of Fine Arts). Av. Millan 4015. ☎ **2/336-2248.** Free admission. Tues–Sun 2–7pm.

The national art history museum displays Uruguayan artistic styles from the beginning of the nation to today. Works include oils, engravings, drawings, sculptures, and documents. Among the great Uruguayan artists exhibited are Juan Manuel Blanes, Pedro Figari, Rafael Barradas, José Cúneo, and Carlos Gonzales.

SHOPPING

Shopping in Montevideo is concentrated in a few downtown shops and in three major shopping centers. Expect to find Uruguayan stores focused on leather goods, jewelry, and local crafts and textiles—including sweaters, cardigan jackets, ponchos, coats, and tapestries made of high-quality wool. International stores carry American and European products. Montevideo's most fashionable mall is the **Punta Carretas Shopping Center,** Calle Ellauri and Solano, located on the site of a former prison next to the new Sheraton hotel. Downtown, the **Montevideo Shopping Center,** Av. Luis Alberto de Herrera 1290, is the city's original mall with over 180 stores and a 10-screen theater. **Portones de Carrasco,** Avenidas Bolíva and Italia, is another recommended shopping center in the Carrasco neighborhood.

MARKETS   The **Villa Biarritz fair** at Parque Zorilla de San Martín-Ellauri takes place Saturday 9:30am to 3pm and features handicrafts, antiques, books, fruit and vegetable vendors, flowers, and other goodies. The ✪ **Mercado del Puerto** (Port Market) happens afternoons and weekends at Piedras and Yacaré, letting you sample the flavors of Uruguay, from small empanadas to enormous barbecued meats. Saturday is the best day to visit, when cultural activities accompany the market. **Tristan Narvaja,** Avenida 18 de Julio in the Cordón neighborhood, is the city's Sunday flea market (9am to 3pm), originated over 50 years ago by Italian immigrants. **De la Abundancia/Artesanos** is a combined food and handicrafts market. It takes place Monday to Saturday 10am to 8pm at San José 1312.

WHERE TO STAY

Montevideo's hotel infrastructure is improving, and you will pay less money here than for a room of similar quality in Buenos Aires. Prices are jacked up during Carnival time in February and when major conventions come to town. A 14% tax will be added to your bill. Parking is included in the rates of most Uruguay hotels.

EXPENSIVE

✪ **Plaza Victoria Hotel.** Plaza Independencia, 11100 Montevideo. ☎ **2/902-0111.** Fax 2/902-1628. www.victoriaplaza.com. E-mail: radisson@adinet.com.uy. 256 units. A/C MINI-BAR TV TEL. $150 double. AE, DC, MC, V. Free parking.

Now part of the Radisson chain, the Plaza Victoria has long been Montevideo's finest hotel. The European-style hotel stands in the heart of the financial district (next to Plaza Independencia) and makes a good base from which to do business or explore the capital. Its convention center and casino also make it the center of business and social activity. Ask for a room in the new tower, built in 1995 adjacent to the original Plaza Victoria Hotel, housing spacious guest rooms and a number of executive suites with classic French-style furnishings and panoramic city views. All have electric trouser presses, hair dryers, in-room safes, ample desk space with computer and fax hookups, and voicemail. The busy hotel has a large, multilingual staff that is very attentive to guest needs. If you plan to stay on a weekend, inquire about one of the special spa packages.

   Dining/Diversions: The Plaza Victoria is famous for its casino, with French roulette tables, blackjack, baccarat, slot machines, horse races, and bingo. There are two lobby bars, in addition to the casino bars. **Arcadia Restaurant** (see "Where to Dine," below) on the 25th floor is the city's most elegant dining room. **La Pérgola Restaurant,** on the lobby level, serves an excellent and reasonably priced lunch buffet ($11 plus tax).

   Amenities: Convention center; corporate meeting facilities; ballroom; executive floors; business center and secretarial services; concierge; excellent health club with skylit indoor pool, fitness center, aerobics classes, Jacuzzi, sauna, massage service, and jogging track; room service; dry cleaning and laundry service; newspaper delivery; nightly turndown; hairdresser and barber shop; travel agency.

Sheraton Montevideo. Calle Víctor Soliño 349, 11300 Montevideo. ☎ **2/710-2121.** Fax 2/712-1262. www.sheraton.com. 207 units. A/C MINIBAR TV TEL. $195 double. Rates include buffet breakfast. AE, DC, MC, V. Free parking.

Opened in 1999, the Sheraton Montevideo is likely to replace the Plaza Victoria as Montevideo's most luxurious hotel. Spacious guest rooms have imported furniture, king beds, sleeper chairs, marble bathrooms with vanity mirrors and hair dryers, 25-inch televisions, and works from Uruguayan artists. Choose between views of the

Río de la Plata, Uruguay Golf Club, or downtown Montevideo, with views from the 20th through 24th floors the most impressive. Rooms on the top two executive floors feature Jacuzzi bathtubs and individual sound systems. Hotel service is excellent, particularly for guests with business needs. A walkway connects the hotel to the Puntas Carretas Shopping Center next door, formerly a jail during the military dictatorship. The hotel was actually built on the grounds of the old jail's football field—but you won't detect any of this today. The hotel lies just a few kilometers from downtown.

Dining/Diversions: Las Carretas Restaurant serves continental cuisine with a Mediterranean flair—don't miss the dining room's spectacular murals by contemporary Uruguayan artist Carlos Vilaro. Next door, the lobby bar is a popular spot for casual business meetings and afternoon cocktails. The Sheraton sits next to the Punta Carretas Shopping Center, one of the city's better malls with additional restaurants and cinemas.

Amenities: Corporate meeting facilities; ballroom; executive floors; business center and secretarial services; concierge; deluxe health club with fitness center, indoor pool, sauna, massage service, and sundeck; room service; dry cleaning and laundry service; newspaper delivery; nightly turndown; emergency medical service; baby-sitting service; hairdresser and barber shop; car rental.

MODERATE

Aspen. Pedro Berro 875, 11100 Montevideo. ☎ **2/711-3369.** Fax 2/712-0545. www.aspen.com.uy. E-mail: aspenhotel@netgate.com.uy. 20 units. A/C MINIBAR TV TEL. From $98 double. Rates include buffet breakfast. AE, DC, MC, V.

This small boutique hotel lies less than 10 minutes from downtown and the port area. Although colors are rather mismatched, guest rooms are well appointed with kitchenettes, two telephone lines, in-room safes, and radios with CD players. There are few hotel amenities besides a small fitness center, but the hotel staff is friendly and will help orient you to the area. This is a good choice if you don't like large hotels.

Holiday Inn. Colonia 823, 11100 Montevideo. ☎ **2/902-0001.** Fax 2/902-1242. www.holidayinn.com.uy. 134 units. A/C MINIBAR TV TEL. From $90 double. Rates include buffet breakfast. AE, DC, MC, V.

This colorful Holiday Inn is actually one of the city's best hotels, popular with tourists and business travelers. It's situated in the heart of downtown, next to Montevideo's main square. A bilingual staff greets you in the marble lobby, attached to a good restaurant and bar. Guest rooms have simple, contemporary furnishings typical of an American chain, with red the dominant color. Because the hotel doubles as a convention center, it can become very busy. Among other amenities here are a business center, heated indoor pool, fitness center, solarium, sauna, room service, and dry cleaning and laundry service.

INEXPENSIVE

Days Inn. Acevedo Diaz 1821/23, 11100 Montevideo. ☎ **2/400-4840.** Fax 2/402-0229. www.daysinn.com.uy. E-mail: daysinn@adinet.com.uy. 60 units. A/C MINIBAR TV TEL. From $80 double. Rates include buffet breakfast. AE, DC, MC, V. Free parking.

The recently opened Days Inn caters to business travelers looking for good-value accommodations. The hotel is located next to "Tres Cruces" bus station and not far from downtown or the airport. Rooms are comfortable and modern, if not overly spacious. The hotel has a small health club, coffee shop, business center, and meeting rooms. Also, 24-hour room service is available.

WHERE TO DINE

Restaurants in Montevideo serve steak—just as high quality as Argentine beef—and usually include a number of stews and seafood selections as well. You will find the native barbecue, in which beef and lamb are grilled on the fire, in any of the city's *parrilladas*. Sales tax on dining in Montevideo is a whopping 23%. As in Argentina, there's usually a table cover charge, called *cubierto*, as well—usually about 25 pesos ($2) per person. Reservations are not necessary unless otherwise noted.

MODERATE

✪ **Arcadia.** Plaza Independencia 759. ☎ **2/902-0111.** Main courses $9–$15. AE, DC, MC, V. Daily 7pm–midnight. INTERNATIONAL.

Virgil and Homer wrote that Arcadia was a quiet paradise in ancient Greece; this elegant restaurant atop the Plaza Victoria is a quiet paradise in Montevideo. Tables are nestled in semiprivate nooks with floor-to-ceiling bay windows. The classic dining room is decorated with Italian curtains and crystal chandeliers; each table has a fresh rose and sterling silver place settings. For such grandeur, however, dishes are priced very reasonably: A $20 chef's tasting menu lets you sample three courses. Creative plates like terrine of pheasant marinated in cognac are followed by grilled rack of lamb glazed with mint and garlic, or duck confit served on a thin strudel pastry with red cabbage. Executive chef Torsten Spies's culinary interpretations are light, fresh, and carefully presented. You won't find a better restaurant in Montevideo.

El Fogón. San Jose 1080. ☎ **2/900-0900.** Main courses $7–$12. AE, DC, MC, V. Daily noon–4pm and 7pm–1am. URUGUAYAN.

The brightly lit *parrillada* and seafood restaurant is popular with Montevideo's late-night crowd. The extensive menu includes calamari, salmon, shrimp, and other fish, as well as generous steak and pasta dishes. Food here is inexpensive and prepared with care. The $11 lunch menu comes with steak or chicken, dessert, and a glass of wine. Waiters, dressed in long white shirts, look suspiciously like medical doctors, and service is fairly reserved. Giant mirrors covering the walls give you an opportunity to inspect yourself; the large painting of two horses and a deserted wagon might spark a new table conversation.

El Viejo y El Mar. Rambla Gandhi 400. ☎ **2/710-5704.** Main courses $8–$13. MC, V. Daily noon–4pm and 8pm–1am. SEAFOOD.

Resembling an old fishing club, El Viejo y El Mar is located on the riverfront near the new Sheraton hotel. The bar is made from an abandoned boat, while the dining room is decorated with docklines, sea lamps, and pictures of 19th-century regattas. You'll find every kind of fish and pasta on the menu, and the restaurant is equally popular for evening cocktails. An outdoor patio is open most of the year.

Las Brasas. San Jose 909. ☎ **2/900-2285.** Main courses $8–$13. AE, DC, MC, V. Daily 11:45am–3:30pm and 7:30pm–midnight. URUGUAYAN.

When Hillary Clinton visited the restaurant in 1999, her photographer took 220 pictures of her with the staff. One of the images hangs proudly on the wall, and the waiters talk about her visit as though it happened yesterday. This casual *parrillada* resembles one you'd find in Buenos Aires—except that this restaurant also serves an outstanding range of *mariscos* (seafood) like the Spanish paella or *lenguago Las Brasas* (a flathead fish) served with prawns, mushrooms, and mashed potatoes. From the *parrilla*, the *filet de lomo* is the best cut—order it with Roquefort, mustard, or black pepper sauce. The restaurant's fresh produce is displayed in a case near the kitchen.

INEXPENSIVE

Río Alegre. Calle Pérez Castellano and Piedras, at the Mercado del Puerto, Local 33. ☎ **2/ 915-6504.** Main courses $2–$6. No credit cards. Daily 11am–3pm. SNACKS.

This cheap, inventive lunch stop specializes in quick steaks off the grill. Ribs, sausages, and most cuts of beef are cooked on the *parrilla* and made to order. Order a tall beer to wash it all down.

MONTEVIDEO AFTER DARK

Like Buenos Aires, nightlife in Montevideo means drinks after 10pm and dance after midnight. For earlier entertainment, ask at your hotel or call directly for performance information at the **Teatro Solis,** Calle Buenos Aires 652 (☎ 2/916-0908), the city's center for opera, theater, ballets, and symphonies. **SODRE,** Av. 18 de Julio 930 (☎ 2/901-2850), is the city's "Official Radio Service," which hosts classical music concerts from May to November. Gamblers should head to the **Plaza Victoria casino,** Plaza Independencia (☎ 2/902-0111), a fashionable venue with French roulette tables, blackjack, baccarat, slot machines, horse races, and bingo. It opens at 2pm and keeps going through most of the night. **Mariachi,** Gabriel Pereira 2964 (☎ 2/709- 1600), is one of the city's top bars and discos, with live bands or DJ music Wednesday to Sunday after 10pm. **Café Misterio,** Costa Rica 1700 (☎ 2/600-5999), is another popular bar, while **New York,** Calle Mar Artico 1227 (☎ 2/600-0444), mixes a restaurant, bar, and dance club under one roof and attracts a slightly older crowd. Montevideo's best tango clubs are **La Casa de Becho,** Nueva York 1415 (☎ 2/400-2717), where composer Gerardo Mattos Rodriguez wrote the famous "La Cumparsita," and **Cuareim,** Zelmar Michelini 1079 (☎ 2/900-8227), which offers both tango and *candombe,* a lively dance indigenous to the area. La Casa de Becho is open Friday and Saturday after 10:30pm; Cuareim, Wednesday, Friday, and Saturday after 9pm. The tourist office can give you schedule information for Montevideo's other tango salons.

3 Punta del Este

87 mi (140km) E of Montevideo

Come late December, Punta del Este transforms from a sleepy coastal village into a booming summer resort. For the next 2 months, there seem to be more *Porteños* (as residents of Buenos Aires are called) in "Punta" than in Buenos Aires itself, and anyone left in Argentina's Federal Capital is deemed to be clearly *declassé.* Without doubt, this coastal strip jetting into the southern Atlantic is the favorite summer getaway for Argentines, a resort with beautiful white-sand beaches and perfect swimming, world-class hotels and restaurants, and an inexhaustible list of outdoor activities—including golf, tennis, horseback riding, biking, bird watching, and numerous watersports. Browsing Punta's elegant boutiques offers the one respite from an endless sun, and the shopping here is world class. You'll have no problem finding an excellent restaurant for dinner, and nightlife in Punta del Este beats just about anywhere else in South America in summer.

ESSENTIALS
GETTING THERE

BY PLANE   International flights arrive at **Aeropuerto Internacional de Laguna del Sauce,** 15 miles east of Punta del Este. **PLUNA** (☎ 42/45292), **LAPA** (☎ 42/ 90840), and **Aerolineas Argentinas** (☎ 42/444-343) fly between Buenos Aires and

Punta. The flight takes 50 minutes. There is regular bus service from the airport into the bus station in town; cost is about $5. A taxi from the airport into town will run about $25.

BY BUS   The **Terminal de Buses Punta del Este,** Rambla Artigas and Calle Inzaurraga (☎ **42/89467**), has buses connecting to Montevideo, Colonia, and other cities throughout Uruguay. **COT** (☎ **42/86810** or 2/409-4949 in Montevideo) offers the best service to Montevideo. The trip takes 1½ to 2 hours and costs about $15 round trip.

BY CAR   If you are driving from Montevideo, you can reach Punta in an hour and a half by taking Route 1 east past Atlántida and Piriápolis to the turn-off for Route 93.

VISITOR INFORMATION

The **Oficina de Turismo** is at Parada 24 (☎ **42/46510**). You should also be able to obtain visitor information from your hotel staff and from the **Centro de Hoteles y Restaurantes de Punta del Este,** Plaza Artigas on Avenida Gorlero (☎ **42/440-512**).

GETTING AROUND

If you want to explore the region by car, you can visit **Avis** at the airport (☎ **42/559-065**), or Calle 31 and Calle Gorlero (☎ **42/442-020**). **Budget** also has a branch at the airport and at Calle 27 and Calle Gorlero (☎ **42/446-363**). **Hertz** rents cars at the airport (☎ **42/59032**), and in the Conrad Hotel (☎ **42/492-109**).

ORIENTATION

Punta del Este is both the name of the famous resort city and the broader region taking in Punta Ballena and Maldonado. The Rambla Artigas is the coastal road that winds its way around the peninsula past the enticing beaches (see "Outdoor Activities," below). Calle Gorlero is the main street running through the center of Punta, where you find most of the restaurants, cafes, and boutiques.

OUTDOOR ACTIVITIES

In Punta itself, the main beaches are **Playa Mansa** (on the Río de la Plata) and **Playa Brava** (on the Atlantic). The two beaches are separated by a small peninsula only a few blocks wide. **La Barra del Maldonado,** a small resort 3 miles (5km) east of Punta del Este, also boasts clean, beautiful beaches.

In summer, you will find vendors offering watersports from parasailing and windsurfing to water-skiing and snorkeling on both Playa Mansa and Playa Brava. If you're staying at the Conrad Resort & Casino (see "Where to Stay," below), a full-time staff is dedicated to helping you arrange outdoor activities. For boating or fishing expeditions, contact the **Yacht Club Punta del Este,** Puerto de Punta del Este (☎ **42/440-219**).

Golf courses include **Club de Golf** (☎ **42/482-127**) in Punta itself, and **Club del Lago** (☎ **42/578-423**) in Punta Ballena. Horseback riding can be arranged through **Hípico Burnett,** Camino a La Laguna, Pinares 33 (☎ **42/230-675**). Tennis fans should call **Médanos Tennis,** Avenida Mar del Plata and Avenida Las Delicias (☎ **42/484-299**).

SHOPPING

Punta has world-class shopping, with Uruguayan shops and European boutiques lining **Calle Gorlero,** the principal street bisecting this resort town. **Punta Shopping**

Mall, Avenida Roosevelt at Paradas 6 and 7, has 100 stores on three levels and a 12-screen cinema. A weekend crafts market takes place from 5pm to midnight at Plaza Artigas.

WHERE TO STAY

Prices listed below are for summer peak season and are often half that in the off-season. **Semana Santa** (December 24 to 31) is the busiest, most expensive week. Reserve well ahead of your visit, as all of Buenos Aires seems to flee to Punta del Este during summer vacation. Parking is free and available at all hotels in Punta.

VERY EXPENSIVE

✪ **Conrad Resort & Casino.** Parada 4, Playa Mansa, 20100 Punta del Este. ☎ **42/491-111.** Fax 42/489-999. www.conrad.com.uy. E-mail: conradpde@conrad.com.uy. 302 units. A/C MINIBAR TV TEL. From $300 double. AE, DC, MC, V.

The spectacular Conrad dominates social life in Punta del Este. It's the first choice of the international jet set—mostly from Argentina—that descends on this Atlantic resort in summer. The hotel's elegance stands in stark contrast to the city's other hotels, and guests look like they've dressed for an afternoon on Rodeo Drive rather than the beach. Luxurious rooms have terraces overlooking La Brava or La Mansa beaches, and the professional staff is highly attentive to guest needs. Personal trainers can assist you with your favorite sport, from tennis to golf to horseback riding. The outdoor pool and gardens are gorgeous, and there's an excellent health club for the truly motivated. The Conrad's casino and showrooms are focal points for Punta nightlife, and the hotel boasts five restaurants to choose from. If you're going to spend the money to visit Punta del Este, you might as well stay here.

Dining/Diversions: The Conrad is a year-round party with nonstop entertainment, from fashion shows and Las Vegas–style reviews to music, dance, and magic shows. The enormous casino has 450 slots and 63 tables for baccarat, roulette, blackjack, poker, dice, and fortune wheel. There are five restaurants, from refined dining to poolside barbecues. Two excellent beaches are located in front of the resort.

Amenities: Corporate meeting facilities; ballroom; executive floors; business center and secretarial services; concierge; deluxe health club with fitness center, temperate-water pool, sauna, and massages; two lit tennis courts; golf; water-skiing; horseback riding; scuba diving; room service; dry cleaning and laundry service; newspaper delivery; nightly turndown.

EXPENSIVE

L'Auberge. Barrio Parque del Golf, 20100 Punta del Este. ☎ **42/482-601.** Fax 42/483-408. www.lauberge.com.uy. E-mail: lauberge@punta.com.uy. 40 units. A/C MINIBAR TV TEL. From $160 double. AE, DC, MC, V.

This exclusive boutique hotel lies in the quiet residential neighborhood of Parque de Golf and is 2 blocks from the beach. A former water tower used in the 18th century, the hotel today houses beautiful guest rooms decorated with antiques and a dedicated staff committed to warm, personalized service. The colorful gardens and pool will draw you outside, and the staff can help you arrange horseback riding, golf, tennis, or other outdoor sports. The sophisticated resort has a delightful tea room, and an evening barbecue takes place by the pool.

Amenities: Corporate meeting facilities; business center and secretarial services; concierge; outdoor pool, spa, and fitness center; tennis court; golf; horseback riding; room service; dry cleaning and laundry service; newspaper delivery; nightly turndown.

MODERATE

Best Western La Foret. Calle La Foret, Parada 6, Playa Mansa, 20100 Punta del Este. ☎ **42/481-004.** Fax 42/481-004. www.bestwestern.com. 49 units. A/C MINIBAR TV TEL. From $120 double. Rates include buffet breakfast. AE, DC, MC, V.

One of the newest arrivals in Punta, La Foret offers spacious guest rooms 1 block from La Mansa beach. The amenities are impressive given the price—rooms feature safes, hair dryers, and Internet connections, and the hotel has a swimming pool, exercise room, and hot tub. There's also a good international restaurant and coffee shop, concierge, business services, and a multilingual staff.

Days Inn. Rambla Willman, Parada 3, Playa Mansa, 20100 Punta del Este. ☎ **42/484-353.** Fax 42/484-683. www.daysinn.com.uy. E-mail: daysinn@adinet.com.uy. 38 units. A/C MINI-BAR TV TEL. From $125 double, including buffet breakfast. AE, DC, MC, V.

Opened in 1999, this modern Days Inn sits on the waterfront. It's an excellent value for its location and amenities, including a health club with a solarium, Jacuzzi, and fitness center; 24-hour snack bar and room service. The Conrad Resort & Casino is next door, along with restaurants, cinemas, and excellent beaches. Rooms are simple but modern, many with ocean views. This is the best mid-range–priced hotel in Punta.

INEXPENSIVE

Hotel Ajax. General Artigas at Parada 2, 20100 Punta del Este. ☎ **42/481-798.** Fax 42/484-550. 40 units. TV TEL. From $100 double. Rates include buffet breakfast. AE, DC, MC, V.

Located 1 block from the beach, the modest Ajax is somewhat eclipsed by the giant Conrad Hotel next door. That said, staying here is much cheaper than at the Conrad (or most anywhere else in town), and you can easily wander over to your neighbor's world-class restaurants and casino when needed. The cozy lobby of the Ajax is filled with leather couches, plants, and surreal paintings completed by the hotel owner. The simple rooms have unattractive red and orange carpet, but are clean and comfortable. A few rooms on the first floor enjoy ocean views.

WHERE TO DINE

Punta's dining scene is seasonal, with restaurants packed in summer and fairly dead in winter. Not surprisingly, restaurant hours vary depending on the season, and some establishments close altogether from April to October. Expect considerably higher prices here than elsewhere in Uruguay, a consequence of Punta's jet-set clientele. Reservations are not necessary unless otherwise noted.

EXPENSIVE

✪ **La Bourgogne.** Pedragosa Sierra (Maldonado). ☎ **42/482-007.** Main courses $15–$30. AE, DC, MC, V. Open for lunch and dinner. Closed Mar 31–Oct 15. FRENCH.

Jean-Paul Bondoux is the top French chef in South America, splitting his time between La Bourgogne in Punta del Este and its sister restaurant tucked inside the Alvear Palace Hotel, Buenos Aires. A member of Relais & Châteaux, La Bourgogne serves exquisite cuisine inspired by Bondoux's Burgundy heritage. Traditional dishes like rack of lamb, breast of duck, and veal cutlet are chef's favorites, while fresh vegetables, fruits, herbs, and spices from the owner's private farm accentuate the menu. Delicious French bread, baked in-house, is available for take-away from the restaurant's small bakery. Ask for a table inside the elegant dining room or amid the jasmine-scented garden. Service is impeccable.

MODERATE

Andres. Edificio Vanguardia, Parada 1. ☎ **42/481-804.** Main courses $12–$20. AE, MC, V. Open Thurs–Sun Dec–Mar. INTERNATIONAL.

This father-son establishment enjoys an excellent reputation across the board. Its setting along the Rambla, with most tables outside, makes for a perfect summer night out. Dishes, ranging from grilled meats to baked fish and fresh vegetable soufflés, are prepared with considerable care. Service is friendly and professional; ask for assistance matching a South American wine with your meal.

Lo de Tere. Rambla del Puerto and Calle 21. ☎ **42/440-492.** Main courses $8–$20. AE, DC, MC, V. Summer daily 12:30–6pm and 9pm–3am; winter daily noon–3:30pm and 8pm–midnight. URUGUAYAN.

Among the first restaurants in Punta del Este, this cozy establishment has a staff that makes you feel at home, offering graceful, cheerful service. Lo de Tere sits right on the water, with a beautiful view of the harbor. The specialties are fresh fish and pastas, which vary depending on the catch and the chef's inspiration. The restaurant transforms from festive and relaxed at lunch to more refined at dinner. Three-course menus are available for $16 to $32.

Yacht Club Uruguayo. Rambla Artigas and Calle 8. ☎ **42/441-056.** Main courses $12–$25. AE, DC, MC, V. Summer daily noon–2am; winter daily noon–3:30pm and 7:30pm–midnight. URUGUAYAN.

This popular restaurant, with tables inside and on the outdoor terrace, looks across the water to Gorriti Island. The dining room's marine theme prepares you for an evening of seafood, with octopus, hake, and swordfish among the favorites. Waiters, dressed in proud white shirts, offer attentive service.

INEXPENSIVE

Los Caracoles. Calle Gorlero 20. ☎ **42/440-912.** Main courses $7–$12. AE, DC, MC, V. Summer daily noon–6pm and 8pm–3am; winter daily noon–4pm and 7pm–1am. URUGUAYAN.

The town's most recommended *parrillada* also serves excellent seafood, including Spanish-style paella. A good salad bar accompanies the hearty selection of meats and fish, and there are a number of homemade pastas to choose from as well. Packed with 70 tables, the rustic dining room is casual and boisterous.

PUNTA DEL ESTE AFTER DARK

The **Conrad Resort & Casino,** Parada 4, Playa Mansa (☎ 42/491-111), is the focal point for evening entertainment in Punta, featuring Las Vegas–style reviews and other music, dance, and magic shows—sometimes around the torch-lit swimming pools. The enormous casino has 450 slots and 63 tables for baccarat, roulette, blackjack, poker, dice, and fortune wheel.

Bars and discos come and go with considerable frequency in Punta, often changing names from one season to the next. The concierge at Conrad Resort & Casino (see "Where to Stay," above) is a good source for what's hot in town. A few clubs that have remained highly popular in the past couple of years are **Space,** in the La Barra neighborhood, and **Gitane La Plage** on Rambla Brava, Parada 12. **Chacras,** Ruta 10 La Barra, is one of the few restaurant-bars open year-round.

4 Colonia del Sacramento

150mi (242km) W of Montevideo

The tiny gem of Colonia del Sacramento, recently declared a World Heritage City by UNESCO, appears untouched by time. Dating from the 17th century, the old city boasts beautifully preserved colonial artistry down its dusty streets. A leisurely stroll from the Puerta de Campo into the **Barrio Histórico** (old, or historic, neighborhood) leads under flower-laden windowsills to churches dating from the 1680s, past exquisite single-story homes from Colonia's time as a Portuguese settlement and on to local museums detailing the riches of the town's past. The Barrio Histórico contains brilliant examples of colonial wealth and many of Uruguay's oldest structures. Yet while the city resides happily in tradition, a mix of lovely shops, delicious cafes, and thoughtful museums make the town more than a history lesson.

ESSENTIALS
GETTING THERE

Many people make Colonia a day trip from Buenos Aires, catching a morning ferry and returning late afternoon. The easiest way to reach Colonia from Buenos Aires is by ferry. **FerryLineas** (☎ 11/4314-5100) runs a fast boat that arrives in 45 minutes and costs $34 one-way; the slower 3-hour bus costs $21. **Buquebus** (☎ 11/4316-6500) also offers two classes of service for similar prices. You can then catch a bus connection to Montevideo for $8 or to Punta del Este for $16.

Colonia can also easily be visited from Montevideo, and is a good stopping-off point if you're traveling between Buenos Aires and Montevideo. **COT** (☎ 2/409-4949 in Montevideo) also offers bus service from Montevideo and from Punta del Este.

VISITOR INFORMATION

The **Oficina de Turismo,** General Flores and Rivera (☎ 52/2182), is open weekdays 8am to 7pm and weekends 9am until noon. To arrange a guided tour of the city, contact **Antiguo Sur,** Calle Misiones de los Tapes 143 (☎ 52/20654).

A WALK THROUGH COLONIA'S BARRIO HISTÓRICO

Your visit to Colonia will be concentrated in the **Barrio Histórico** (Old Neighborhood), located on the coast at the far southwestern corner of town. The sights, which are all within a few blocks, can easily be visited on foot in a few hours. Museums and tourist sites are open daily (except Wednesday) from 11:30am to 5:30pm. A $1 ticket pass, available at the Portuguese or Municipal museum, will get you into all the sights.

Start your tour at the **Plaza Mayor,** the principal square that served as the center of the colonial establishment. To explore Colonia's Portuguese history, cross the Calle Manuel Lobo on the southeastern side of the plaza and enter the **Museo Portugués** (Portuguese Museum), exhibiting European customs and traditions that influenced the town's beginnings. Upon exiting the museum, turn left and walk to the **Iglesia Matriz** (Church of Matriz del Santísimo Sacramento), among the oldest churches in the country and an excellent example of 17th-century architecture and design.

Next, exit the church and turn left to the **Ruinas Convento San Francisco** (Ruins from the San Francisco Convent). Dating from 1696, the San Francisco convent was once inhabited by Jesuit and Franciscan monks, two brotherhoods dedicated to preaching the gospel to indigenous people. Continue up Calle San Francisco to the **Casa de Brown** (Brown House), which houses the **Museo Municipal** (Municipal

Museum). Here you will find an impressive collection of colonial documents and artifacts, a must-see for history buffs.

For those with a more artistic bent, turn left on Calle Misiones de los Tapes, walking 2 blocks to the **Museo del Azuelo** (Tile Museum), a unique museum of 19th-century European and Uruguayan tiles housed in a gorgeous 300-year-old country house. Then stroll back into the center of town along Calle de la Playa, enjoying the shops and cafes along the way, until you come to the **Ruinas Casa del Gobernador** (House of the Viceroy). The House of the Viceroy captures something of the glorious past of the city's 17th- and 18th-century magistrates, when the city's port was used for imports, exports, and smuggling. After exploring the opulent lifestyle of colonial leaders, complete your walk with a visit to the **UNESCO–Colonia** headquarters, where exhibits on the city's newly acquired Historic Heritage of Humanity status will place your tour in the larger context of South American history.

WHERE TO STAY & DINE

Few people stay in Colonia, making it a day trip from Buenos Aires or a stop along the way to Montevideo. If you prefer to get a hotel, however, your best bets are the colonial-style **Hotel Plaza Mayor,** Calle del Comercio 111 (☎ **52/23193**), and the **Hotel La Misión,** Calle Misiones de los Tapes 171 (☎ **52/26767**), whose original building dates from 1762. Both hotels charge from $90 for a double. Parking is included in the rates of most Uruguay hotels. For dining, **Mesón de la Plaza,** Vasconcellos 153 (☎ **52/24807**), serves quality international and Uruguayan food in a colonial setting, while **Pulpería de los Faroles,** Calle Misiones de los Tapes 101 (☎ **52/25399**), in front of Plaza Mayor, specializes in beef and bean dishes and homemade pastas.

8 Planning a Trip to Chile

Pristine landscapes and an improved tourism infrastructure have made Chile, especially Patagonia and the Lake District, a hot destination for international travelers. Even Chileans themselves have begun to forgo the usual beach vacation to get to know their own country. A well-defined high season dictates price jumps in lodging and more, leaving the question, when should you go? *Where* should you go? How expensive is it, and what level of value can you expect? The following information should answer all the questions you might encounter when planning your trip to Chile.

1 The Regions in Brief

Chile's lengthy, serpentine shape incorporates nearly every kind of landscape and temperate zone imaginable. (In fact, the only zone not found in mainland Chile is tropical.) From tip to tail Chile stretches 2,684 miles (4,329km)—about the same distance as from the Hudson Bay to Panama. Conversely, traveling from the Pacific Coast to the border of Argentina in the Andes takes an average of only 3 hours. In this respect, Chile is somewhat uniform in that its citizens are perpetually "squeezed in" by the Pacific Ocean and the Andes; nevertheless, the scenery changes so dramatically from north to south that it is often hard to believe it's all within the same country.

Chile is bordered by Peru in the north, Bolivia in the northeast, and Argentina along the eastern spine of the Andes down to Tierra del Fuego. The country also claims a portion of Antarctica as well as Easter and Robinson Crusoe islands as part of its own. Chile is divided into 12 numbered *regiones,* or states, but the country could essentially be divided into four broad regions: the North, the Central Valley, the Lake District, and Patagonia.

NORTHERN CHILE This region claims the world's driest desert, a beautiful "wasteland" set below a chain of purple and pink volcanoes and high-altitude salt flats. The most popular destinations here, including the Atacama Desert, sit at altitudes of 6,560 feet (2,000m) and up. The extreme climate and the geological forces at work in this region have produced far-out land formations and superlatives such as the highest geyser field in the world. The earth here is parched, sun-baked, and unlike anything you've ever seen, but it thankfully gives

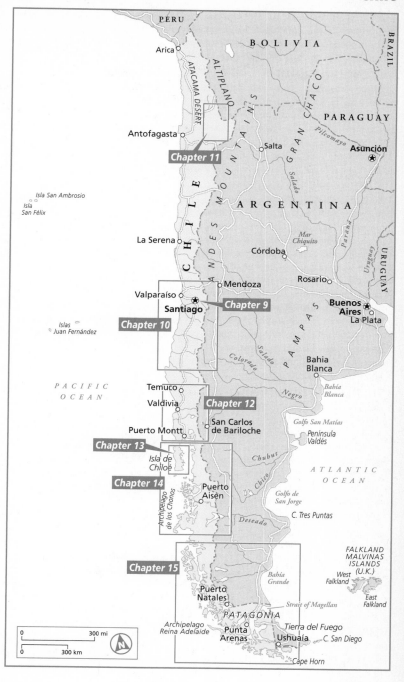

Chile

PERU

BOLIVIA

BRAZIL

Arica

ATACAMA DESERT

ALTIPLANO

PARAGUAY

Antofagasta

Salta

GRAN CHACO

Pilcomayo

Asunción ★

Chapter 11

Isla San Ambrosio

Isla
San Félix

Salado

ARGENTINA

La Serena

Córdoba

Mar
Chiquito

Paraná

URUGUAY

Uruguay

Islas
Juan Fernández

Valparaíso

Mendoza

Rosario

Buenos
Aires ★

Santiago ★

Chapter 9

La Plata

Chapter 10

PAMPAS

Colorado

Salado

Bahía
Blanca

PACIFIC
OCEAN

Temuco

Valdivia

Chapter 12

Negro

Bahía
Blanca

Puerto Montt

San Carlos
de Bariloche

Golfo San Matías

Chapter 13

Isla de
Chiloé

Península
Valdés

Chubut

ATLANTIC
OCEAN

Chapter 14

Archipiélago
de los Chonos

Puerto
Aisén

Chico

Golfo de
San Jorge

Deseado

C. Tres Puntas

FALKLAND
MALVINAS
ISLANDS
(U.K.)

Chapter 15

Bahía
Grande

West
Falkland

Puerto
Natales

East
Falkland

0   300 mi

0   300 km

PATAGONIA

Archipiélago
Reina Adelaide

Punta
Arenas

Strait of Magellan

Tierra del Fuego

Ushuaia

C. San Diego

Cape Horn

N

relief through many of its tiny emerald oases, such as San Pedro de Atacama. At Antofagasta on the coast, Chile's notorious Humboldt Current veers east, warming the sea from here up through Peru. See chapter 11, "The Desert North & San Pedro de Atacama."

SANTIAGO & CENTRAL CHILE   The central region of Chile, including Santiago and its environs, features a mild, Mediterranean climate. Many North American visitors say that this region reminds them of California. This is Chile's breadbasket, with fertile valleys and rolling fields that harvest a large share of the country's fruit and vegetables; it also is the site of world-famous Chilean wineries. Santiago's proximity to ski resorts, beach resorts, and the idyllic countryside with its campestral and ranching traditions and colonial estates offers a distinct variety of activities that make the Central Valley an excellent destination. See chapters 9, "Santiago," and 10, "Around Santiago & the Central Valley."

LAKE DISTRICT   Few destinations in the world rival the magnificent scenery of Chile's Lake District, and for that reason it's the most popular destination for foreigners visiting Chile. This region is packed with a chain of conical, snowcapped volcanoes, glacier-scoured valleys, several national parks, thick groves of native forest, hot springs, jagged peaks, and, of course, many shimmering lakes. Temperatures during the summer are idyllic, but winter is characterized by months of drizzling rain, much like the Pacific Northwest of the United States. It's an outdoor-lover and adventure-seeker's paradise, especially in Pucón and Puerto Varas, offering biking, hiking, kayaking, rafting, fly-fishing, and more, but it is also a low-key destination for those who just want to kick back and enjoy the marvelous views. The wealth of lakes high in the Andes makes for a wildly popular cruise to Bariloche, Argentina, from Ensenada, Chile, on Lago Llanquihue, and it's possible to do a circuit by beginning in Pucón, entering Argentina, and finishing in Puerto Varas via the lake crossing. See chapter 12, "The Chilean Lake District."

CHILOÉ   The island of **Chiloé** is as attractive for its emerald, rolling hills, and colorful wooden churches as it is for the unique culture that developed after 300 years of geographic isolation. During this period, a religion based on a mix of Catholicism and native customs created a strong belief in mythical figures; at the same time the island's cuisine, speech, and architectural style (the latter employing the area's abundance of wood) developed differently from that of mainland Chile. Beautiful fishing hamlets and views that stretch from the Pacific to the Andes make for fine sightseeing drives, and Chiloé National Park offers ample opportunity for hiking along the island's untamed coastal rain forest. See chapter 13, "Chiloé."

THE CARRETERA AUSTRAL   Across the sound from Chiloé sits Chile's "frontier" highway, commonly known as the **Carretera Austral,** a dirt road that stretches nearly 620 miles (1,000km) from Puerto Montt in the north to beyond Coyhaique in the south. Along the way, this relatively new road passes through virgin territory visited by few travelers: tiny villages separated by thick, untouched rainforest, rugged peaks that rise from crystal-clear lakes, and more waterfalls than one can reasonably count. This could be one of Chile's best-kept secrets. See chapter 14, "The Carretera Austral."

PATAGONIA   Also known as the **Magallanes Region,** this dry, arid region at the southern end of the continent has soared in popularity over the past 5 years, drawing visitors from all over the world to places such as Torres del Paine National Park in

Chile and Argentina's Perito Moreno Glacier. We've grouped both Argentina and Chile in one Patagonia chapter because the majority of travelers visit destinations in both countries when here. Patagonia is characterized by vast, open *pampa,* the colossal Northern and Southern Ice Fields and hundreds of mighty glaciers, the jagged peaks of the Andes as they reach their terminus, beautiful emerald fjords, and wind, wind, wind. Getting here is an adventure—it usually takes 24 hours if coming directly from the United States or Europe. But the long journey pays off in the beauty and singularity of the region. Cruise the fjords, walk across a glacier, stroll through frontier-like immigrant towns such as Puerto Natales, and, without a doubt, visit Chile's national jewel, Torres del Paine. For more, see chapter 15, "Patagonia & Tierra del Fuego."

TIERRA DEL FUEGO   Even more south than the Deep South, this archipelago at the southern extremity of South America is, like Patagonia, shared by both Chile and Argentina. The main island, separated from the mainland by the Strait of Magellan, is a triangle with its base on the Beagle Channel. See chapter 15 for more information.

2 Visitor Information

VISITOR INFORMATION

You'll find a municipal tourism office in nearly every city and a **Sernatur** (National Tourism Board) office in major cities. The quality of service and availability of printed matter, such as maps and brochures, varies from office to office. Unfortunately, the lion's share of these tourism offices hire stone-faced representatives who seem to have arrived at the destination no sooner than you, but typically you can count on receiving basic information. A good place to begin your research is Sernatur's helpful Web site at **www.sernatur.cl**, which has general regional information in Spanish and English. Outside of Chile, you won't find a tourism promotion board, but Chile's consulates do provide printed material and visitor information. Other helpful sites are listed below.

GENERAL INFORMATION AND HOTEL & LODGING LINKS

- **www.gochile.cl**   This well-designed, comprehensive site not only lists hotel, transportation, dining, and excursion information, but will allow you to search for flights and hotel and car-rental promotions and package deals.
- **www.chiptravel.com**   See "Recommended Web Sites for Chile," below.
- **www.ciudad.net**   This site offers general information and has dozens of links to other Chile-related sites. It's ad-heavy; however, the site allows travelers to make flight, car, and cruise reservations.
- **www.chile-hotels.com**   This site features full-length descriptions of hotels and online reservations. Be cautious of the showcased hotels or "best" hotels, as they are not objective opinions. It also has brief regional information.
- **www.samexplo.org**   The South American Explorer's Club produces an excellent Web site that includes up-to-date information about health and political crises, as well as frequently asked questions, travelogues, and catalogs and books for sale.
- **www.chileaustral.com**   See "Recommended Web Sites for Chile," below.
- **www.andesweb.com** and **www.southamericaskiguide.com**   Offer information about skiing and snowboarding in Chile and Argentina.

Recommended Web Sites for Chile

- **www.chiptravel.com**   Start your internet search here. This site offers great travel ideas and information, but the informed reviews and essays are especially enlightening. Good first-timer's guide to history, politics, and cultural issues.

- **www.labrujula.cl**   This Yahoo-like site is a search engine specifically for Chile, covering every category from soup to nuts. It's entirely in Spanish, but a search could yield bilingual Web sites.

- **www.gochile.com**   Well-designed and chock full of information, you'll find virtually everything here, including city and national park descriptions, information about tour packages, and a selective guide to hotels and restaurants (though these establishments presumably pay to be listed). You can also book rental cars and flights.

- **www.andesweb.com**   This great Web site offers complete information about skiing and snowboarding in Chile and Argentina. Full descriptions of resorts and related information such as weather conditions, ski rental, and general travel information.

- **www.chilevinos.com**   Every aspect of the Chilean wine industry is covered at this Web site, such as winemaker and winery profiles, grape-growing updates, a glossary, chat room, and on-line ordering. The only thing this site doesn't have is an English edition. If you can't get through the lingo, head to **www.winesofchile.com**. (Also, consult "A Select Tour of Chile's Vineyards" later in this chapter.)

- **www.chileaustral.com**   This is your one-stop site for Chilean Patagonia, with a telephone book–like listing of virtually everything—even land for sale. Links take you to the independent Web pages of businesses such as hotels, restaurants, tour operators, clubs, news and media, sheep wool . . . the list goes on.

- **www.elmercurio.com**   Chile's Spanish-language, and decidedly conservative, publication is the largest in the country, and their Web site contains weather and comprehensive events listings in addition to regular reporting.

3 Entry Requirements & Customs

ENTRY REQUIREMENTS

Citizens of the United States, Canada, the United Kingdom, Australia, and New Zealand need a valid passport to enter Chile. Citizens of these countries must pay an entrance fee upon arrival: U.S. $45, Canada $55, and Australia $25. You need pay the fee only once, so keep the payment stub stapled onto a page in your passport if you plan to leave Chile and return. Before entering Chile, either at the border or in the plane, you'll be asked to fill out a tourist card that allows visitors to stay for 90 days. You'll need to present this tourist card to customs when leaving the country. Also, many hotels waive Chile's 18% sales tax applied to rooms when the guest shows this card and pays with U.S. dollars. If you plan on staying longer than 90 days, the easiest (and free) way to renew your tourist card is to simply cross the border and return. However, tourist cards can be renewed for another 30 days in Santiago at **Extranjería**, Moneda 1342 (☎ **2/672-5320**), open Monday to Friday 8:30am to 3:30pm, or at any Gobernación Provincial office in the provinces; but it's expensive at $100.

LOST DOCUMENTS

If you lose your tourist card outside Santiago, any police station will direct you to the Extranjería police headquarters for that province (usually the nearest principal city). In Santiago, go to the **Policía Internacional,** Departamento Fronteras, General Borgoña 1052 (☎ **2/737-1292**), open Monday to Friday 8:30am to 12:30pm and 3 to 6pm. If you lose your passport, contact your embassy for a replacement. If you are an American and your passport is lost or stolen, you can only get a replacement at the U.S. embassy in Santiago, Av. Andrés Bello 2800 (☎ **2/232-2600**), which is open Monday to Friday 8:30am to 5pm. The fee is $60. It is imperative that you carry a photocopy of your passport with you and another form of ID to facilitate the process.

CUSTOMS

Any travel-related merchandise brought into Chile, such as personal effects or clothing, is not taxed. Visitors entering Chile may also bring in no more than 400 cigarettes, 500 grams of pipe tobacco, or 50 cigars, and 2.5 liters of alcoholic beverages per adult.

FOR U.S. CITIZENS   Travelers returning to the United States are allowed to bring $400 worth of goods, per person, and family members who live in the same home may combine their exemptions. Travelers who stay less than 48 hours outside the country or who have left the United States more than once in 30 days are given a $200 exemption only. You may include up to 1 liter of alcohol (provided you are over 21 years of age), 100 cigars, and 200 cigarettes; any more and you'll pay a duty fee. Keep all your receipts handy. The legal limit for goods mailed home per day is no more than $20 for yourself; mark the package "for personal use." You may mail a gift to someone worth no more than $100 per person per day, marked "unsolicited gift." Packages must clearly describe the contents on the exterior. You may not mail alcohol, perfume that contains alcohol, or tobacco products, but a legitimate company such as a wine dealer can ship alcohol to you in the United States, usually for a prohibitively steep shipping fee. Foodstuffs must be tinned or professionally sealed; you may not bring fresh foodstuffs into the United States.

Duty tax is a flat 10% on the first $1,000 worth of goods over $400. Anything over is subject to an item-by-item basis. For more information, contact the **U.S. Customs Service** at P.O. Box 7407, Washington, DC 20044 (☎ **202/927-6724**), for their free booklet "Know Before You Go," or simply look it up on their Web site: **www.customs.ustreas.gov**.

FOR U.K. CITIZENS   Returnees to the United Kingdom may bring back up to 200 cigarettes, 50 cigars, or 250 grams of tobacco; 2 liters of still table wine; 1 liter of distilled spirits over 22% volume or 2 liters sparkling wine, fortified wine or other liqueurs; 60cc/ml perfume; 250cc/ml toilet water; and £145 worth of all other gifts and souvenirs. Travelers must be over 17 to bring back tobacco and alcohol. For more information, consult the **HM Customs & Excise** at ☎ **020/8910-3744,** or their Web site at **www.hmce.gov.uk**.

FOR CANADIAN CITIZENS   If you've been out of the country for over 48 hours, you may bring back $200 Canadian worth of goods, and if you've been gone for 7 consecutive days or more, not counting your departure, the limit is $750. The limit for alcohol is up to ⅕ liters of wine or ¹⁄₁₄ liters of liquor, or 24 12-ounce cans or bottles of beer; and up to 200 cigarettes, 50 cigars, or 200 grams of tobacco. You may not ship tobacco or alcohol and you must be of legal age for your province to bring these items through customs. For more information, call the **Canada Customs and Review**

Agency at ☎ **800/461-9999,** or 204/9833500 outside Canada; or try their Web site for their document *I Declare:* www.ccra-adrc.gc.ca.

FOR AUSTRALIAN & NEW ZEALAND CITIZENS Excluding alcohol and tobacco, travelers to Australia who are 18 and over may bring $A400 worth of goods tax-free, and those under 18 may bring back $A200 worth of goods tax-free. Travelers 18 and older may bring 1,125ml of alcohol (including wine, beer, or spirits), 250 cigarettes, or 250 grams of cigars or tobacco products other than cigarettes. Personal goods owned and used for at least 12 months are not taxed (proof of date of purchase may be required). For more information, call ☎ **2/6275 6666** in Santiago.

Travelers entering New Zealand may bring goods up to a total combined value of $700 tax-free, and passengers traveling together may not combine their $700 concessions. Travelers 17 and over may bring 200 cigarettes, 250 grams of tobacco, 50 cigars, or a mix of all three totaling up to 250 grams; 4.5 liters of wine or 4.5 liters of beer (the equivalent of six 750ml bottles); and one bottle containing not more than 1,125ml of spirits.

4 Money

CASH & CURRENCY

The unit of currency in Chile is the **peso.** The value of the peso slowly declined last year and is, at press time, 560 pesos to the U.S. dollar, and it keeps going down—bad news for the country but good news for travelers with U.S. dollars. Bills come in denominations of 500, 1,000, 2,000, 5,000, 10,000 and a new 20,000. There are currently five coins in circulation, in denominations of 1, 5, 10, 50, and 100; however, it's unusual to be issued 1 peso or even 5. In slang, Chileans often call 1,000 a *luca,* as in, "it cost me *cinco luca"* (5,000). Try to carry an ample amount of coins and smaller bills because most shops seem plagued by a chronic shortage of change.

Chile levies a steep, 18% **sales tax** on all goods and services called IVA (*Impuesto al Valor Agregado*). Foreigners are supposedly exempt from the IVA tax when paying in dollars for hotel rooms, car rentals, and some tourism-oriented shops; however, you might find this is not the case with inexpensive hotels. Always verify if the price quoted to you is without IVA. The prices given in this book are listed in dollars (adjusted per a 550-pesos-to-the-dollar rate), due to the ambiguous nature of the IVA tax.

EXCHANGING MONEY

Dollars and traveler's checks can be exchanged at a *casa de cambio* for a small charge, and they are generally open 9am to 6pm Monday to Friday (closing from 1 to 3pm for lunch), and Saturdays until 1pm. A *casa de cambio* can be found near the center of every major city, but note that they are scarce in small towns. Some banks exchange money, although most charge a steep fee. Hotels tow the line with laughably poor exchange rates. By far the best exchange rates are given when retrieving money from an **ATM,** identifiable by the name "Redbanc" posted on a maroon and white sticker. These Redbancs use a variety of networks, including Cirrus and Plus, as well as Visa and MasterCard (if your bank card uses that system or should you need a cash advance). Really, the ATM card has replaced the **traveler's check** as the preferred way to deal with money when abroad, but be sure to investigate your bank's policies as to whether they charge a fee for each withdrawal. Also, you might consider traveling with an ATM card and a few traveler's checks in U.S. dollars as a backup in the event of a lost or stolen card. American Express traveler's checks in U.S. dollars are a good choice, and you can buy them over the phone by calling ☎ **800/221-7282.**

CREDIT CARDS

Most hotels and restaurants in Chile accept credit cards such as Visa, MasterCard, Diners Club, and American Express. In the event of a lost or stolen credit card, call the following numbers (in Santiago): Visa/MasterCard at ☎ **2/698-2465,** American Express at ☎ **2/672-2156,** and Diner's Club at ☎ **2/232-0000.**

5 When to Go

High season for Chilean, Brazilian, and Argentine vacationers is during the summer from December 15 to February 31, as well as the month of July and during Holy Week (*Semana Santa*), the week preceding Easter Sunday. The sheer volume of travelers to popular destinations such as Pucón or Viña del Mar during the high season is overwhelming, complete with traffic, crowded restaurants, screaming kids, and nature trails that begin to resemble an avenue. If that weren't enough, consider that hotels nearly double in price, and some businesses quietly jack up their prices in anticipation of the masses who come with money to burn. If being in Chile from December to February during the peak of the austral summer is still what you'd prefer, then by all means book a room for that season, but do it *well* in advance. Or you can do as most North American and Europeans do and come during late September to early December for the spring bloom, or March to mid-May when the trees turn color; both seasons have pleasant weather and the views are less crowded. In fact, it's preferable to be in the extreme regions of Chile during these "off seasons." In northern regions, such as San Pedro de Atacama, the searing heat is a killer and will zap your midday energy. In the deep south, the fierce Patagonian wind blows from October to April, but is most consistent in December and January.

CLIMATE

Chile's tremendous length incorporates a variety of climates, and in many areas there are microclimates, pockets of localized weather that can completely alter the vegetation and landscape of a small area. As well, weather and temperature can vary greatly the short distance from Andes to the coast.

The northern region of Chile is home to the driest desert in the world—so dry, in fact, that some areas in the Atacama Desert have never recorded rain. Summer temperatures from early December to late February in this region can top 100°F, then drop dramatically at night to 30°F. Winter days, from mid-June to late August, are crisp, but sunny and pleasant, but as soon as the sun drops it gets bitterly cold. Along the coast, the weather is mild and dry, ranging from 60°F to 90°F.

The central zone that stretches to Puerto Montt has seasons that are better defined. Temperatures in this region range from 32°F to 55°F in the winter, and 60°F to 95°F during the summer. Santiago and the Central Valley feature a more Mediterranean climate, whereas the Carretera Austral and the Lake District are home to very wet winters, especially in the regions around Valdivia and Puerto Montt. Last year the Lake District was hit hard by flooding as Chile underwent an unusually stormy winter, followed by a wet summer.

Below Puerto Montt, temperatures drop the farther you travel south. The Patagonia region is unpredictable with its weather patterns, especially during the summer. The Magellanic Region sees extraordinary, knockout windstorms that can reach upwards of 74 m.p.h. (120kmph), and it's not unusual to experience heavy rain during the summer. The windiest months are mid-December to early February, but it can hit any time between October and April. Winters are calm, with irregular snowfall and temperatures that can dip to 5°F.

HOLIDAYS

Chile's major celebrations are Christmas, New Year's, Easter Week, and Independence Day, the latter of which can carry on for days and days of dancing, drinking, and military parades. During official holidays, Chilean towns can take on the appearance of a ghost town. Transportation services might be reduced in some areas, government offices and banks close, and the majority of stores and markets follow suit.

It's important to note that national and local elections bring about a virtual standstill from midnight to midnight as Chileans cast their obligatory votes. Alcohol is not sold on this day.

The following are official holidays: **January 1** (New Year's Day), **Semana Santa** (Holy Week, but just Good Friday is considered a holiday), **May 1** (Labor Day), **May 21** (remembrance of the War of the Pacific victory), **June 29** (Corpus Christi), **August 15** (Asunción de la Virgen), **September 11** (commemoration of the 1973 military coup), **September 18 and 19** (Independence Day and Armed Forces Day), **October 12** (Indigenous Day), **November 1** (All Saint's Day), **December 8** (Feast of the Immaculate Conception), and **December 25** (Christmas Day).

CALENDAR OF EVENTS   The following are some of Chile's major events and festivals that take place during the year. For 1 week in early **February,** the city of Castro in Chiloé hosts a celebration of the culture, history, and mythical folklore that makes the island unique, including regional cooking, in the **Festival Costumbrista Chilote** (see chapter 13). During late **February,** Viña del Mar hosts its gala **Festival de la Canción,** or the Festival of Song, that showcases Latin American performers during a 5-day festival of concerts held in the city's outdoor amphitheater (see Viña del Mar, chapter 10). The spectacle draws thousands of visitors to an already packed Viña del Mar, so plan your hotel reservations accordingly. In **mid-February,** Valdivia hosts a grand, weeklong event called the **Semana Valdiviana.** A variety of maritime-theme activities, contests, expositions, and more takes place during the week, but the highlight takes place the third Saturday of February, the **Noche Valdiviana,** when the Río Valdivia fills with festively decorated boats and candles, and the skies fill with fireworks. This is a very crowded event, and advance hotel reservations are essential (see chapter 12). Between **March and mid-April,** Chilean wineries celebrate the grape harvest with a **Festival de Vendimia,** with food, wine-making exhibitions, grape-crushing, and more. Each winery celebrates according to the date of its harvest (the farther south, the later the date), so call ahead for each winery's exact festival date (see chapter 10). The **first Sunday** after Easter is the **Fiesta del Cuasimodo,** an event typically held throughout central Chile, in which *huaso* cowboys parade through the streets, accompanied by Catholic priests who often pay visits to the infirm and disabled. On **May 29,** fishermen celebrate the **Fiesta de San Pedro** in towns along the coast of Chile, to bring about good fortune, weather, and bountiful catches. Fishermen decorate their boats, light candles, arm themselves with an image of their patron saint, and drift along the coast. A great place to check out this event is in Valparaíso. **July 16** sees the celebration of the **Virgin del Carmen,** the patron saint of the armed forces. On this day, military parades take place throughout the country, especially near Maipú, where O'Higgins and San Martín defeated Spanish forces in the fight for independence. Chile's rodeo season kicks off on Independence Day, **September 18,** and culminates with a championship in the city Rancagua around late March or early April. There are a variety of rodeo dates throughout the Central Valley, but September 18 and the championships are festivals in their own right, with food stalls, lots of *chicha* (a fermented fruit cider) drinking and traditional *cueca* dancing. Contact the Federación de Rodeos in Santiago at ☎/fax **2/699-0115.**

6 Health & Insurance

HEALTH

Chile poses few health risks to travelers. There are no diseases such as malaria or dysentery, so no special vaccinations are required. In fact, there are no poisonous plants or animals in Chile to worry about, either. Nevertheless, standard wisdom says that travelers should drop in the doctor's office for tetanus and hepatitis boosters.

DIARRHEA & INTESTINAL PROBLEMS   Few visitors to Chile experience anything other than run-of-the-mill traveler's stomach in reaction to unfamiliar foods and any microorganisms in them. Chile's tap water is clean and safe to drink; however, a small percentage of travelers with delicate stomachs report having experienced intestinal upsets from tap water. You'll often hear that the water has a "high mineral content," but by and large most experience nothing at all. If you are sensitive to changes in food and water, by all means drink bottled mineral water, which is widely available throughout Chile.

Chile's love of shellfish has its consequences, and each year there are a dozen reports of intoxication due to the *marea roja,* or "red tide." This toxic alga poisons shellfish and is due to a rise in the temperature of the sea. Your chances of intoxication by the *marea roja* are nil, unless you plan to collect shellfish yourself and are oblivious to the signs posted by the government that caution you otherwise. All fish and shellfish in restaurants and markets are safe.

ALTITUDE SICKNESS   Altitude sickness, known as *soroche* or *puna,* is a temporary yet often debilitating affliction that affects about a quarter of travelers to the northern *altiplano,* or the Andes at 7,872 feet (2,400m) and up. Nausea, fatigue, headaches, shortness of breath, and sleeplessness are the symptoms, which can last from 2 to 5 days. If you feel as though you've been affected, drink plenty of water, take aspirin or ibuprofen, and avoid alcohol and sleeping pills. To prevent altitude sickness, acclimatize your body by breaking the climb to higher regions into segments.

AUSTRAL SUN   The shrinking ozone layer in southern Chile has caused an onset of health problems among the citizens who live there, including increased incidents of skin cancer and cataracts. Last year the ozone hole opened *completely* for several days in the southern town Punta Arenas—the first time it had ever happened. If you are planning to travel to Patagonia, keep in mind that on "red alert" days (typically from September to November), it's possible to burn in *10 minutes.* If you plan to be outdoors, you need to protect yourself with sunblock, a long-sleeved shirt, a wide-brimmed hat, and sunglasses.

WHAT TO DO IF YOU GET SICK AWAY FROM HOME

Medical attention in private hospitals and clinics throughout Chile is up to international standards, but you may find limited or nonexistent service in tiny villages. *Clinicas* are always better than a town's general hospital; in fact, some general hospitals are downright appalling. Most health insurance policies cover incidents that occur in foreign countries; check to see if yours does, and be sure to gather all receipts and information

Do not under any circumstances drink tap water while in San Pedro de Atacama (see chapter 11). It contains trace amounts of arsenic.

---

so that you can make a claim back home. The cost of medicine and treatment is expensive, but most hospitals and pharmacies accept credit cards. Many doctors, especially in Santiago, speak basic English; for a list of English-speaking doctors, call your embassy.

PHARMACIES   Chile is rife with pharmacies, and you'll find them in odd locations, such as shopping malls and gas stations—and, strangely enough, they always seem to be packed with ailing clientele. Many stay open 24 hours a day, and a few chains will deliver for a small fee. Chilean pharmacies sell numerous kinds of prescription drugs over the counter, including antibiotics and birth control pills. In fact, many Chileans skip the doctor altogether and head to the pharmacy for a dose of whatever the pharmacist deems is a suitable remedy. It goes without saying that this form of health care is not entirely recommended, so use your own discretion.

INSURANCE

Nothing can spoil a vacation like losing your luggage or suffering a medical emergency. Planning ahead and making certain you're covered for any unforeseen catastrophes can save your trip. But before buying specific travel insurance, first investigate your **homeowner's insurance** policy to see if it covers lost luggage, as most policies often do. Airlines will reimburse travelers for up to $9.07 per pound up to $640, but the process is time-consuming. Second, check to see what kind of insurance your **credit card company** offers, and whether it's solely for tickets or goods purchased using the card. Some credit cards offer flight insurance in the event of a plane crash or other transportation accidents.

If you plan to take advantage of one of Chile's many adventure travel opportunities, it's imperative that you protect yourself with **medical insurance,** even if all you plan to do is light trekking. Trip medical insurance appeals to travelers who do not have a current regular medical plan back home. Your regular medical plan should reimburse you for any costs incurred while out of the country, but be sure to check with the company for coverage details before traveling, especially if you're part of an HMO. Remember that Medicare only covers travelers to Mexico and Canada, not Chile. Companies specializing in medical care include **MEDEX International** (☎ 888/ **MEDEX-00** or 410/453-6300; www.medexassist.com) and **Travel Assistance International** (☎ 800/821-2828). **STA Travel** offers low-cost medical coverage, which you can buy from any one of its many travel agencies, or by calling ☎ 800/ **777-0122.**

Trip cancellation insurance is a good idea, especially if you prepay some or all of your vacation expenses. Companies usually charge about 6 to 8% of the total price of your trip. The following companies offer a variety of insurance options: **Access America** (☎ 800/284-8300); **Travel Guard** (☎ 800/826-1300); **Travel Insured International, Inc.** (☎ 800/243-3172); and **International SOS Assistance** (☎ 800/ **523-8930** or 215/244-1500), which offers 24-hour assistance for problems that arise while abroad.

7 Tips for Travelers with Special Needs

FOR TRAVELERS WITH DISABILITIES   There are relatively few handicapped-accessible buildings in Chile, apart from supermarkets and major hotels, which come equipped with ramps and wide doorways. It's best to call ahead and inquire about an establishment's facilities. For more information on resources for travelers with disabilities, see chapter 2, "Planning a Trip to Argentina."

FOR SENIORS   Seniors traveling in Chile are usually offered discounts for attractions such as museums (seniors here are called *tercer edad,* or "third age"). Probably the most interesting and well-respected senior organization is **Elderhostel,** 75 Federal St., Boston, MA 02110-1941 (☎ **800/426-8056;** www.elderhostel.org), which offers cultural and educational trips to Chile with themes such as "Land of Poets" and "The Perfect Desert: North Chile." For more information on resources for senior travelers, see chapter 2.

FOR GAY & LESBIAN TRAVELERS   Gays and lesbians visiting Chile will most likely not encounter any prejudice or outward intolerance. However, public displays of affection between same sexes are rare, even in metropolitan cities such as Santiago. In general, attitudes, especially those of Chilean men, toward gays and lesbians are not very liberal, owing in part to the Catholic, conservative nature of their society. Homosexual relationships have only recently been declared officially legal, and many gays and lesbians are not actively open about their orientation outside their own circles.

The best source for information is the Web site **www.gaychile.com**, a resource directory that covers gay issues and provides information about travel, gay-oriented businesses and bars, employment and more. The magazine *Follies* covers the gay scene in Chile; if you can't find a copy, call ☎ **2/233-6324** in Santiago. For more information on resources for gay and lesbian travelers, see chapter 2.

FOR FAMILIES   Chile is family-friendly, and parents will not have a problem finding lodging suitable for kids. Many hotels feature playgrounds, swimming pools, child care, and attached rooms or space for additional beds. Some larger resort hotels even arrange activities for kids. Parents might consider renting an apart-hotel or a cabaña (found in resort areas), which are self-catering units with living areas and kitchens; they are frequently less expensive. Many hotels offer discounts or grant a free stay for kids traveling with parents, so be sure to inquire when making a reservation. For more information on resources for families, see "Tips on Accommodations," later in this chapter, and chapter 2.

FOR WOMEN TRAVELERS   Women traveling in Chile will not encounter harassment other than a sporadic catcall or a few taps on the car horn. More than anything, Chilean men tend to stare intensely, which can be annoying or make some women feel uncomfortable. Staring back or ignoring the situation usually works. Hitchhiking is a well-accepted form of transportation in Chile, and you will occasionally see a woman hitchhiking on her own, especially on country lanes with poor public transportation. Although hitchhiking in Chile is safer than in most countries, exercise judgment if contemplating hitchhiking solo. A lift up to a ski resort or into a national park that does not have public transportation will probably result in nothing more than a free ride, but longer trips up and down the Panamericana Highway are best undertaken aboard one of the country's cheap and plentiful long-distance buses. It's the safest way to protect you from any serious problems.

FOR STUDENTS Many Chilean businesses and hostels recognize the International Student Identity Card issued by **The Council on International Educational Exchange (CIEE)** (☎ 800/2COUNCIL; www.ciee.org). The card offers discounts and a 24-hour help line for travel emergencies to anyone 26 and under and to full-time teachers. Their **Council Travel** agencies, located in most major cities, offer rock-bottom prices for flights. **American Youth Hostels,** P.O. Box 37613, Washington, DC 20013-7613 (☎ 202/783-6161; www.hiayh.org), offers a directory of youth hostels around South America and other travel-related publications.

8 Getting There

BY PLANE

Several major airlines serve Santiago's Arturo Merino Benítez airport with nonstop flights from Miami, Los Angeles, Atlanta, New York, and Dallas–Fort Worth. The flight time from Miami is approximately 8 hours; from Los Angeles, 13 hours; and from New York, 10 hours. A typical APEX flight (advance purchase excursion fares) from the United States costs around $1,000 to $1,300. Most APEX flights require a 7- to 21-day advance purchase, with a minimum stay of 1 week and maximum of 3 months, and date changes are costly. Airlines wage intermittent fare wars, so shop around before buying.

THE MAJOR AIRLINES The following airlines serve Chile from the United States and Canada (where noted). **Lan Chile** (☎ 800/735-5526; www.lanchile. com), the country's national air carrier, has direct flights to Santiago from New York, Los Angeles, and Miami. **American Airlines** (☎ 800/433-7300; www.americanair-lines.com) has daily nonstop flights from Miami and Dallas–Fort Worth, with connections from Vancouver, Toronto, and Montréal. **Delta** (☎ 800/221-1212; www. delta.com) offers nonstop daily flights from Atlanta. **United Airlines** (☎ 800/241-6522; www.ual.com) has nonstop daily flights from Miami, with connections from Canada (may include one other U.S. stop).

American Airlines (☎ 0345/789789) serves London with daily flights to Santiago via Miami. **Aerolíneas Argentinas** (☎ 020/7494-1001; www.aerolineas.com.ar) offers daily flights from London via Madrid and Buenos Aires. **Iberia** (☎ 800/772-4642 in the U.S., or 020/7830-0011 in London; www.iberia.com) offers flights via Madrid four times a week.

Qantas (☎ 1300/650729 in Australia, and ☎ 800/0014-0014 in New Zealand; www.qantas.com) works in conjunction with Lan Chile, offering two flights per week from Sydney and Auckland to Santiago via Papeete or Easter Island. **Air New Zealand** (☎ 13-2476 in New Zealand, 61/132476 in Australia; www.airnewzealand.com) also combines service with Lan Chile to offer two flights per week from Australia and New Zealand, with a stop in Papeete. **Aerolineas Argentinas** (☎ 1800/222-215 in Australia, 0800/650-881 in New Zealand; www.aerolineas.com.ar) has three weekly direct flights from Sydney and Auckland to Buenos Aires, Argentina, with a connecting flight to Santiago aboard Lan Chile.

OTHER GOOD-VALUE CHOICES

CONSOLIDATORS Consolidators are clearinghouses that buy blocks of tickets from airlines and sell them at a discounted price; they're the companies that advertise with those little boxes in the travel section of the Sunday paper. Heavy restrictions apply to consolidator tickets, so they are not recommended for travelers who need a great deal of flexibility. Also, always call your airline to verify your seat as a precaution.

Several large consolidators are **STA Travel** (☎ **800/781-4040;** www.statravel.com), which typically caters to younger travelers, but it offers low, low prices for any age; **TFI Tours International,** 34 W. 32nd St., New York, NY 10001 (☎ **800/745-8000**), which sells unused seats; **Travel Avenue,** 10 S. Riverside Plaza, Suite 1404, Chicago, IL 60606 (☎ **800/333-3335;** www.travelavenue.com); and **Travel Bargains** (☎ **800/AIR-FARE;** www.1800airfare.com), which offers discounts that vary depending on the date. Other outfits that specialize in finding the cheapest flights possible are **Cheap Tickets** (☎ **800/377-1000**), **1-800/FLY-4-LESS,** and **1-800/FLY-CHEAP.**

INTERNET   When shopping around for a ticket, it never hurts to see what the Internet has to offer. You might want to first start at **Arthur Frommer's Budget Travel** (www.frommers.com), where you'll find the Encyclopedia of Travel, a travel magazine and daily newsletter, and detailed information on up-to-the-minute ways to save dramatically on flights, hotels, car reservations, and cruises. Sites such as **Microsoft's Expedia** (www.expedia.com) and **Travelocity** (www.travelocity.com) use their search engines to find a plane ticket for you, based on your needs. Both offer rental car booking, cruises, and vacation packages; Expedia also has destination features. And they frequently offer last-minute deals, such as last October's Take a Friend for $10 to Santiago or Buenos Aires, offered by Aerolíneas Argentinas and Travelocity. Sites such as **www.lowestfare.com** and **www.travelforless.com** search for cheap flights. Another great site is **www.smarterliving.com**, which lists discounts, package deals, links to other helpful sites, and weekly e-mail newsletters with deals and information. For frequent flyer information and last-minute deals, try **www.webflyer.com**. Once you've found a great deal, always compare with a quote from a travel agent.

BY CRUISE SHIP

There are several 11- to 15-day cruises that sail around the Cape Horn, beginning in Buenos Aires and ending in Valparaíso, Chile, or vice versa. Ports of call include Chile's Puerto Montt, Punta Arenas, and the Strait of Magellan; Argentina's Ushuaia and Puerto Madryn; and a stop in Montevideo, Uruguay. Several cruise operators that provide this trip are **Norwegian Cruises** (☎ **800/206-1599;** www.ncl.com), **Celebrity Cruises** (☎ **800/466-8440;** www.celebrity-cruises.com), and **Princess Cruises** (☎ **800/PRINCESS;** www.princesscruises.com), who offers the Cape Horn trip in both directions, as well as a cruise along the Pacific Coast of South America that includes a stop in Arica and La Serena.

9 Getting Around

BY PLANE

The drawn-out geography of Chile makes flying the most reasonable way to get around: Even flying from Santiago to Punta Arenas takes about 3½ hours. Two domestic airlines serve major cities: **Ladeco,** a relatively new subsidiary of Lan Chile (☎ **800/735-5526** in the U.S., 600/600-4000 in Santiago; www.lanchile.com), and **Avant** (☎ **600/500-7000**), which offers lower prices, and lower quality, than Ladeco or Lan Chile. Avant is in partnership with TurBus, and you can buy tickets at any one of their offices (addresses and telephone numbers for TurBus are listed under each city it serves). **Aero Continente** (☎ **2/204-2424** in Santiago; www.aerocontinente.com.pe) is a Peruvian airline and newcomer on the scene, offering the cheapest fares, with two daily flights to Antofagasta and Iquique from Santiago, and four daily flights (only two on Saturdays) from Santiago to Concepción, Puerto Montt, and Punta Arenas. To get to smaller cities using an air taxi such as Aero Sur, see information in individual destination chapters.

Lan Chile offers foreigners a **Visit Chile Pass** good for three flights within the country. The price is $250 if you choose Lan Chile as your international carrier, and $60 for any additional flights; the cost is $350 if you use another carrier to Chile, and $80 for each additional flight. A maximum of six flights is permitted per Visit Chile Pass. Travelers have a maximum of 1 month to use the tickets, and they must be used within 14 days of your arrival. Lan Chile requires travelers to book their routes when buying, but they allow date and time changes. A pass can only be purchased before arriving to Chile, directly from Lan Chile or a travel agent.

To get into town from any major airport, take one of the numerous taxis, or take a shuttle (called a "transfer"). It's more economical, but you might make several stops before your destination. Drivers usually approach you at the airport, but they always have a main desk at arrivals.

BY BUS

Traveling by bus is very common in Chile, and there are many companies to meet the demand. Fortunately, most Chilean buses are clean and efficient and a good way to travel shorter distances, from Santiago to Valparaíso, for example. Think long and hard before booking a 30-hour ride to the desert north, or any comparable distance; it's an excruciatingly long time to be on the highway.

If you decide to travel for more than a few hours by bus, it helps to know your options. Standard buses go by the name *clásico* or *pullman* (no relation to the giant bus company Pullman). An *ejécutivo* or *semi-cama* is a little like business class: lots of leg room, and seats that recline farther. At the top end of the scale is the *salon cama,* which features seats that fold out into beds. Fares are typically inexpensive, and seats fill up fast, so buy a ticket with as far in advance as possible. Ask what is included with your fare, and whether they serve meals or if they plan to stop at a restaurant along the way.

BY CAR

Travelers seeking the independence to explore at their own pace might consider renting a car. Unfortunately, freedom to roam about at one's will does not come cheap, and some rental agencies charge up to $600 weekly for an intermediate car, rented from and returned to the Santiago airport. This is not including the high cost of gas. If you shop around, you can find rates around $350 per week, or even lower if you have a company deal or find a deal on the Internet. Most major American rental car companies have offices in Chile, which are listed under the appropriate chapter for each company's location. To make a reservation from the United States, call **Alamo** (☎ **800/GO ALAMO;** www.alamo.com), **Avis** (☎ **800/331-1084;** www.avis.com), **Budget** (☎ **800/527-0700;** www.budget.com), **Dollar** (☎ **800/800-6000;** www. dollar.com), or **Hertz** (☎ **800/654-3001;** www.hertz.com). If renting once you're already in Chile, don't overlook a few of the local car rental agencies for cheaper prices; you sometimes find better quality with the smaller operations.

To rent a car, you need to bring your current driver's license; car rental agencies and the police will accept an international driver's license, but it is not mandatory. Be forewarned that in Chile, the police, or *carabineros,* are allowed to stop motorists without reason, which they frequently do under the guise of "traffic control." They usually just ask to see your driver's license, and then let you pass through their checkpoint.

Driving in Chile is fairly straightforward. Drivers use their indicators constantly to signal where they're going, and you should too, even if there's no one close to you. On

A Note on Hitchhiking

Hitchhiking is common in Chile and mostly carried out along country roads with infrequent public transportation. In fact, you often see fed-up Chileans hitchhiking from a bus stop, especially in the southern regions of Chile. Hitchhiking is popular with students, workers, families, elderly folks without cars—in short, *everyone*. You stand a good chance of being picked up near the entrances to national parks or ski resorts. Hitching is never entirely recommended for obvious reasons, but if you feel comfortable with your ride, you might consider it.

---

the highway, car and especially truck drivers signal to show that it's safe ahead to pass, but don't put your entire faith in the other driver's judgment, and give yourself ample space, as many drivers tend to speed. Right turns on red are forbidden unless otherwise indicated. It's simply auto chaos in the confines of Santiago, with congested streets and speedy, aggressive drivers—*especially* bus drivers. Outside Santiago, especially on roads off the Panamericana Highway, your major concern will be keeping an eye out for the occasional farm animal grazing near the road. The Panamericana is undergoing an expansion from two to four lanes, and you might experience road-work delays south of Santiago to Puerto Montt in the near future. Few roads off the Panamericana are paved, and the condition of unpaved roads can be smoothly graveled or horrible washboard and Swiss cheese, conditions demanding that you drive very, very slowly. Gasoline is called *bencina,* and Chile sells both the leaded and unleaded varieties; unleaded gas is sold in varying grades as 93, 95, and 97.

The **Automovil Club Chileno** offers services, including emergency roadside service, to its worldwide members. For more information, contact their offices in Santiago at Av. Vitacura 8620 (☎ **2/212-5602**). Pick up a road map at any Sernatur office or visitor's center, or consider buying one of the several **Turistel** guidebooks from any kiosk; even though it's in Spanish, it provides detailed road maps, city maps, and visitor information. Many gas stations sell maps; try to get Auto Mapa's *Rutas de Chile.* Rental car agencies provide emergency road service. Be sure to obtain a 24-hour number before leaving with your rental vehicle.

BY FERRY

A superb way to get around the southern regions of Chile is by ferry. **Navimag** offers a trip that leaves from Puerto Montt and cruises along the shore of the Carretera Austral; the other is an exceptionally popular 3-day trip through the fjords from Puerto Montt to Puerto Natales, or vice versa, stopping along the way at Puerto Eden. This is not a luxury liner, but it's not bad either, and the views are breathtaking. There's also **Skorpios,** which offers more upscale 4- and 7-day cruises aboard one of their three boats from Puerto Chacabuco, stopping at Castro and Quellón in Chiloé. **Transmarchilay** has services similar to Navimag and Skorpios, and provides most ferry service around the gulf south of Puerto Montt. **Andina del Sud** provides countless visitors with a picturesque cruise across the emerald Lago Todos los Santos in Vicente Pérez Rosales National Park near Puerto Varas, and they also connect with the company Cruce de Lagos, which continues across Lago Nahuel Huapi to Bariloche, Argentina. The **Terra Australis** offers absolutely superb one-way and round-trip cruises from Punta Arenas to Ushuaia, as well as day excursions from Punta Arenas. For more information, see "Ferry Journeys Through the Fjords to Laguna San Rafael," near the end of chapter 14, and chapter 15.

10 Spanish-Language Programs

Spanish-language programs are not only an excellent way to pick up the local tongue, they are also indispensable introductions to Chilean culture for students who choose to stay with a host family. Surprisingly, there are relatively few options, but the following are good bets.

- **Linguatec Language Center,** Los Leones 439, Providencia, Santiago (☎ **2/233-4356;** fax 2/234-1380; www.linguatec.cl), has received praise for its intensive private tutoring and group programs (three to eight students). Classes run 15 to 20 hours per week (there's also a 30-hour weekly, private program). A 2-week group course costs $740; 4 weeks cost $1,200. Private classes for 20 hours per week are $840 per week for 1 to 2 weeks or $750 per week for 3 or more weeks; 15-hour weekly classes cost $560 per week. Room and board with a Chilean host family costs $120 per week, or you can arrange your own lodging. Note that they charge a $95 registration fee and $50 for books. Linguatec offers excursions and university credit.

  If Linguatec Language Center doesn't have what you're looking for, in Santiago try calling the **Instituto Chileno-Norteamericano,** Moneda 1467 (☎ **2/696-3215**), or the **Instituto de Idiomas Polyglot** at Villavicencio 361 (☎ **2/639-8078**).

- **Casa Aventura,** Pasaje Gálvez 11, Cerro Alegre, Valparaíso (☎/fax **32/75-5963**), is a three-bedroom hostel that offers language courses; classes are held in a pretty Victorian house in Valparaíso. There are beginner, intermediate, and advanced levels, privately or in groups. There aren't rigid end and start dates, but typically classes cost about $180 for 2 weeks and 20 hours of instruction for one person; about $160 per person when there are two students; and $110 per person when there are three to five students. You might even work out a package deal for lodging; e-mail casatur@ctcinternet.cl for reservations and information.

11 Tips on Accommodations

Chile's high season is from December 15 to the end of February, as well as Easter week and, in resort areas, the month of July. Hotels generally heed these blocks of time, but the start and end dates could vary slightly, and they might charge a "mid-season" rate during November and March. Rates during the high season are often sky-high in resort areas such as Pucón or Viña del Mar; however, reasonable or downright cheap accommodations can be had the rest of the year. Some hotels drop their prices by as much as 50%. **Price ranges listed in hotel write-ups reflect low to high season;** for example, $50 to $75 double would mean $50 from March to November and $75 from December to February. Always verify high-season dates with your hotel.

The past year was stagnant for the hotel industry in Chile, and many establishments are maintaining or even dropping prices in an effort to draw in business. The prices listed in this book are **rack rates,** that is, a hotel's standard rate offered to guests who simply walk in off the street. Hotels might be willing to offer a special price for multiple-day stays during the high season, but during the low season you're almost guaranteed they'll drop the price, so don't be afraid to ask when making a reservation. Some hotels might also be offering a promotion or package deal that you're not aware of, so inquire about that, too.

Almost every hotel in Chile includes **breakfast** in the price. In fact, of all the hotels I've seen throughout Chile, only about five did not, and I've stated this in the hotel's review. Expect a continental breakfast at inexpensive and moderately priced hotels and an "American" or buffet breakfast at larger, four- and five-star hotels.

ROOM RATES

Price categories in this guide are listed according to **Very Expensive,** $125 and up; **Expensive,** $80 to $125; **Moderate,** $40 to $80; and **Inexpensive,** under $40. All prices are for double occupancy, and Moderate to Very Expensive hotel prices shown do not include the 18% IVA tax (inexpensive hotels rarely accept dollars, always including the IVA tax in their set prices).

HOTEL OPTIONS

HOTELS & *HOSTERÍAS*   A *hostería* is a hotel attended by its owner, typically found in a country setting. The Chilean tourism board rates hotels using one to five stars, but the system is dubious because it concentrates too much on a checklist of services and amenities that may or may not be important to a guest. For example, a luxurious nature lodge that caters to fly-fishermen might receive three stars because it chooses not to equip its rooms with TV or because it does not offer 24-hour room service.

Mid-range hotels that charge $40 to $80 for a double vary in quality and size—and price isn't necessarily a good indicator. Generally, all come with in-room cable TV, a private bathroom, and a restaurant (or at least a dining area for breakfast and snacks), and some amplify their offerings with room service, a minibar, or even a sauna or pool. Some of the older hotels that enchant you with their picturesque facades can disappoint you with interiors the owners seem loathe to upgrade—but then so do a fair share of their more modern counterparts. Nevertheless, most offer a minimum level of comfort. If high quality is important to you, ask to see a room. Upscale hotels at $90 and more for a double are, obviously, the most dependable, and feature smart service and a long list of amenities.

APART-HOTEL   The amalgam is exactly what it implies: an "apartment-hotel," or a hotel room with an additional living area and kitchen. Found primarily in Santiago and other large cities, they offer a wider range of services than a cabaña. Some are bargains for their price and the independence they give its occupants, and they come with maid service. However, some are nothing more than a hotel room with a kitchenette tucked into a random corner.

CABAÑAS   Cabañas are a great lodging option. They are commonly found in resort areas and are popular with families and travelers seeking an independent unit. Each establishment will have between two and ten cabañas on its property, some hidden in wooden groves and some in a more "suburban" atmosphere. They resemble cabins or chalets and range from bare bones to the deluxe, although all come with fully equipped kitchens and most have maid service. During the high season, owners sock it to couples, who must pay a full-cabin price (usually six people), but low-season deals at some places can be negotiated down to $30 for two.

***RESIDENCIALES* & HOSTELS**   These lodging options are for budget travelers. *Residenciales* are private homes whose owners rent out rooms, and they range from simple, clean rooms with a private or shared bathroom to ugly flats with creepy bathrooms. In towns that see more tourists, a hostel can be a hip and very comfortable place run by foreigners or Chileans, typically from Santiago. Some hostels are private homes that use their living area as a common area, and some of them can be very comfortable.

12 The Active Vacation Planner

Chile is a veritable paradise for adventure and active travel, offering a tremendous diversity of activities such as trekking through lush forests and rugged peaks, kayaking blue lakes, rafting white water, mountain biking country lanes and desert canyons, horseback riding and skiing in the Andes, ascents to the top of smoking volcanoes . . . the list is endless.

There are several ways to go about planning an active vacation in Chile. Several full-service lodges have popped up throughout the country that offer limited or all-inclusive packages that include transportation, guides, and equipment.

ORGANIZED ADVENTURE TRIPS

The advantages of traveling with an organized group are plentiful, especially for travelers who have limited time and resources. Tour operators take the headache out of planning a trip, and they iron out the wrinkles that invariably pop up along the way. The language is less of a barrier when you have a guide to translate for you, and a guide can interpret the culture and history of Chile and the natural surroundings of your destination. Many tours are organized to include guides, transportation, accommodations, meals, and gear (some outfitters even carry gear for you—for example, on trekking adventures). Independent travelers tend to view organized tours as antithetical to the joy of discovery, but leaving the details to someone else does free up substantial time to concentrate on something else. Besides, your traveling companions are likely to be kindred souls interested in similar things.

Be careful of tour operators who try to pack 20 people or more into a trip. The personal attention just isn't there, nor is that bit of breathing room you might find yourself needing after a week on the road. Also, be sure you know what you're getting yourself into. A 5-day trek through a national park might look great on paper, but are you physically up to it? Tour operators are responsible for their clients' well-being and safety, but that doesn't let you off the hook in terms of your own personal responsibility. Inquire about your guide's experience, safety record, and insurance policy. Remember, no adventure trip is 100% risk-free.

U.S.-BASED ADVENTURE TOUR OPERATORS

These companies offer solid, well-organized tours, and they are backed by years of experience. Most of these operators are expensive, and a few are exorbitant (remember that prices do not include airfare), but that usually is because they include luxury accommodations and gourmet dining. Most offer trips to hot spots like Patagonia, and operators with trips to that region are listed here for both Argentina and Chile.

- **Abercrombie & Kent,** 1520 Kensington Rd., Oak Brook, IL 60521 (☎ **800/ 323-7308;** www.abercrombiekent.com), is a luxury tour operator that offers a Patagonia Paradise trip that heads from Buenos Aires to Ushuaia for a 3-day cruise around Tierra del Fuego, followed by visits to Torres del Paine National Park, Puerto Varas, and Bariloche. Cost is $6,980 per person, double occupancy.

- **Butterfield and Robinson,** 70 Bond St., Toronto, Canada M5B 1X3 (☎ **800/ 678-1147;** www.butterfieldandrobinson.com; e-mail: info@butterfield.com), is another gourmet tour operator that offers a walking-oriented, 10-day trip to Patagonia starting in El Calafate, Argentina, and finishing in Punta Arenas, Chile. In between, travelers visit the national parks Los Glaciares and Torres del Paine, with visits to the Perito Moreno Glacier and lodging in fine lodges and ranches. Cost is $5,975 per person, double occupancy.

- **Mountain-Travel Sobek,** 6420 Fairmount Ave., El Cerrito, CA 94530 (☎ **888/MTSOBEK** or 510/527-8100; fax 510/525-7718; www.mtsobek.com; e-mail: info@mtsobek.com), are the pioneers of organized adventure travel, and they offer trips that involve a lot of physical activity. One of their more gung-ho journeys traverses part of the Patagonian Ice Cap in Fitz Roy National Park in Argentina—for 21 days; a 10-day rafting adventure takes travelers down the Futaleufú River; a more moderate Patagonia Explorer mixes hiking with cruising. Prices run from $1,500 to $3,000 and more. Sobek always comes recommended for its excellent guides.

- **Backroads Active Vacations,** 801 Cedar St., Berkeley, CA 94710-1800 (☎ **800/GO-ACTIVE** or 510/527-1555; www.backroads.com), offers a biking tour through the lake districts of Chile and Argentina, with stops in Puerto Varas and the Llao Llao Peninsula; an afternoon of rafting is included. There's also a hiking trip through the same region, and a 9-day hiking in Patagonia trip. Guests lodge in luxury hotels and inns. Costs run from $3,798 to $5,298.

- **Wilderness Travel,** 1102 Ninth St., Berkeley, CA 94710 (☎ **800/368-2794** or 510/558-2488; www.wildernesstravel.com; e-mail: webinfo@wildernesstravel.com), offers a mellower sightseeing/day hiking tour and a more involved hiking/sea kayaking tour around Patagonia, including Torres del Paine; a hiking tour through the Futaleufú River area; cruises to Easter Island; and hiking in Fitz Roy National Park. The hiking trip around Patagonia costs $4,495 to $5,095, depending on the number of guests (maximum 15).

- **Wildland Adventures,** 3516 NE 155th St., Seattle, WA 98155 (☎ **800/345-4453** or 206/365-0686; www.wildland.com), offers several adventure tours of Chile: trekking in Patagonia, sea kayaking in Chiloé and Tierra del Fuego, and an 11-day "Chile Adventure: Land of Contrast" overview tour that stretches from the Atacama Desert down to Torres del Paine National Park. Accommodations range from hotels to camping to rustic park lodges. Ecotourism is an integral part of Wildland tours. Prices start at $695 for a 4-day kayaking tour and continue upward of $3,000 for a 2-week Patagonia trip.

- **REI Adventures,** P.O. Box 1938, Sumner, WA 98390 (☎ **800/622-2236;** www.rei.com/travel; e-mail: travel@rei.com), has a 12-day hiking trip to Torres del Paine National Park, for $2,395 per person, combining camping with overnights in comfortable *hosterías*.

- **PowderQuest Tours** (☎ **888/565-7158** toll-free in the U.S. or 804/285-4961; www.powderquest.com) offers complete ski and snowboard tour packages that take guests to a variety of ski resorts in both Chile and Argentina.

CHILEAN TOUR AGENCIES

Chilean tour agencies typically offer a wider variety of tours in Chile—after all, they operate within their own country. The following active travel operators are good bets.

- **Cascada Expediciones,** Orrego Luco 040, Providencia, Santiago (☎ **2/234-2274;** fax 2/233-9768; www.cascada-expediciones.com/ch; e-mail: webmaster@cascada-expediciones.com), offers a very wide variety of active trips around Chile but is particularly active in Cajon de Maipo, where the company is based. However, they offer excursions all over Chile, including rafting, kayaking, mountaineering, horseback riding, trekking in Torres del Paine, 1- to multiple-day climbing trips, and more.

A Select Tour of Chile's Vineyards

Most Chilean wines come from grapes grown in one of four valleys   Maipo (near Santiago), Rapel, Curicó, and Maule. The practice of "tasting" Chilean wine is slowly catching on, and few wineries apart from the large producers schedule tours. This book covers in detail only the wineries near Santiago; while I am highlighting other wineries and tours here, their distance from the city and any real destinations of interest mean they make for a full-day excursion (plus a rental car for the drive down the Panamericana Highway).

- **Cousiño-Macul** (Peñalolen, near Santiago; ☎ 2/284-1011). If you have time to visit just one winery while in Chile, make it the Cousiño-Macul. This winery is more traditional than eating empanadas on Sunday; in fact, the first vines in Chile were planted here in 1546. The beautiful estate and its lush, French-designed gardens are as impressive as the winery's Antiguas Reservas traditional red, and it's just a cab ride away from Santiago.

- **Concha y Toro** (Pirque, near Santiago; ☎ 2/853-0042). Chile's most popular winery produces the lion's share of wines, from inexpensive table reds to some of Chile's priciest Cabernet Sauvignons, as well as Chile's top traditional red Don Melchior. Like Cousiño Macul, the winery itself is part of the attraction, with gardens large enough to require eight full-time gardeners, and antique bodegas whose interiors are part of your tour. Concha y Toro is also close enough to Santiago to get there by cab.

- **Viña Santa Rita** (Buin, near Santiago; ☎ 2/362-2100). Santa Rita will not only let you sample their wine, they'll let you spend the night in their former estate house, which has been converted into an elegant inn. Because this winery is about an hour's drive from Santiago, it makes for a pleasant day

---

- **Altué Expediciones,** Encomenderos 83, 2nd floor, Las Condes, Santiago (☎ 2/233-6799; www.altue.co.cl; e-mail: altue@entelchile.net), is a well-organized, excellent Chilean outfitter that specializes in kayaking and rafting. Altué offers kayak trips around the island of Chiloé and the Andean fjords, horseback riding on the Army of Liberation trail through the Andes, rafting the Futaleufú, hiking in the Lake District, climbing the Ojos del Salado, and more.

OTHER GENERAL-INTEREST TOUR OPERATORS & PACKAGE DEALS

- **Discover Chile Tours/Ponce de Leon Travels,** 7325 W. Flager St., 2nd floor, Miami, FL 33144 (☎ **800/826-4845** or 305/266-5827; www.poncedeleontravel.com; e-mail: tours@discover-chile.com), is an excellent resource, offering complete trip planning and set packages, custom tours, and low-cost deals on transportation. There's a wide variety here, from 3-day/2-night tours of Santiago, Viña del Mar, and Valparaíso to 3-day tours of the Atacama Desert, with an option to add on any one of a dozen extra excursions.

- **Ladatco Tours,** Aviation Avenue #4C, Coconut Grove, FL 33133 (☎ **800/327-6162;** www.ladatco.com; e-mail: tailor@ladatco.com), organizes dozens of set and custom tours in all regions of Chile, including theme-oriented tours such as wine-tasting, fly-fishing, glaciers, and more. Ladatco has operated as a Central and South America tour operator for 30 years.

trip and a good base for exploring the Central Valley. The wine-tasting room where you'll sample your Casa Real Cabernet Sauvignon is a national monument.

- **Veramonte** (Casablanca, near Valparaíso; ☎ **32/742421**; www.veramonte. com). The Casablanca region is relatively new to wine-making, yet it is an ideal location for growing Chardonnay and Sauvignon Blanc grapes. One slick new winery has invested heavily in Casablanca's potential with a state-of-the-art, 63,000-foot facility capable of crushing 75 tons of grapes per day. The winery prides itself on its "Napa Valley-style" winetasting facilities, with a service-oriented staff and an impressive tasting room with a soaring rotunda and glass walls that let you peek into the barrel caves below. The winery makes for a perfect stop on the road from Santiago to Valparaíso. Groups of more than six should reserve by faxing Rodrigo Tapia at **32/742420.**
- **La Ruta del Vino del Valle de Colchagua** (Santa Cruz, Central Valley; ☎ **72/823199**). West of San Fernando, near Santa Cruz, four wineries have come together to promote their offerings with a half-day or full-day tour that includes lunch, wine tasting and tours of up to three wineries, including the delightful winery Santa Laura. Tours are conducted every day except Sundays and holidays. Transportation to Santa Cruz requires renting a car or taking a bus to San Fernando for a connecting bus to Santa Cruz. Tours are bilingual and reservations must be made 24 hours in advance; the cost is, per person, full-day $70 and half-day $60 for parties of two, and full-day $40 and half-day $30 for a maximum of 11 guests. Every March, these wineries organize the Fiesta de la Vendima, a festival that celebrates the grape harvest, with tastings and wine-making demonstrations.

- **PanAmerican Travel,** 320 E. 900 South, Salt Lake City, Utah 84111 (☎ **801/364-4300** or 800/364-4359; fax 801/364-4330; www.panam-tours.com; e-mail: info@panam-tours.com), arranges custom trips for its clients for most destinations in Chile.
- **4th Dimension Tours,** 7101 SW 99th Ave., Suite 106, Miami, FL 33173 (☎ **800/343-0020;** www.4thdimensiontours.com; e-mail: reserv@4thdimension. com), arranges packages as well, and tours throughout Chile and in combination with other South American destinations.

Fast Facts: Chile

Business Hours   Banks are open Monday to Friday 9am to 2pm, and are closed on Saturdays and Sundays. Commercial offices close for a long lunch hour, which can vary from business to business. Generally, hours are Monday through Friday 10am to 7pm, closing for lunch around 1 or 1:30pm and reopening at 2:30 or 3pm.

Cameras/Film   Most types of film are available in Chile, as are print-developing services. Slide-developing services are almost nonexistent except in Santiago.

Currency Exchange   See "Money" earlier in this chapter.

Drug Laws   Possession and use of dangerous drugs and narcotics are subject to heavy fines and jail terms.

Electricity   Chile's electricity standard is 220 volts/50Hz. Electrical sockets have two openings for tubular pins, not flat prongs, so you'll need an plug adapter available from most travel stores.

Embassies/Consulates   The only United States representative in Chile is the **U.S. Embassy** in Santiago, located at Av. Andrés Bello 2800 (☎ 2/232-2600). The **Canadian Embassy** is at Paseo Ahumada 11 (☎ 2/696-2256). The **British Embassy** can be found at El Bosque Norte 0125 (☎ 2/231-3737). The **Australian Embassy** is at Gertrudis Echenique 420 (☎ 2/228-5065); the **New Zealand Embassy** is at Av. Isidora Goyenechea 3516 (☎ 2/290-0802).

Emergencies   Obviously you'll want to contact the staff if something happens to you in your hotel. Otherwise, for a police emergency, call ☎ **133.** For fire, call ☎ **132.** To call an ambulance, dial ☎ **131.**

Internet   No matter where you are in Chile, chances are there is an Internet station, either in a cafe or at the telephone centers CTC or Entel. Most hotels, even hostels, have their own Internet service; if they don't, they'll be able to point out where to find one. Expect to pay $2 to $4 per hour.

Language   Spanish is the official language of Chile. Many Chileans in the tourism industry and in major cities can speak basic English, but don't count on it. Try to learn even a dozen basic Spanish phrases before arriving; there are several excellent phrasebooks on the market and they will facilitate your trip tremendously. See also appendix B, "Useful Spanish Terms & Phrases," at the back of this book.

Liquor Laws   The legal drinking age in Chile is 18. Alcohol is sold every day of the year, except during elections.

Newspapers & Magazines   The largest and most respected newspaper in Chile is the right-leaning *El Mercurio,* although *La Tercera* and the "news lite" paper *El Metropolitano* are popular. *La Epoca,* born out of the Pinochet dictatorship, is still hobbling along, while *La Segunda* and *El Cuarto,* two tabloid newspapers with photos of girls in bikinis despite the season, are good for a laugh. Newspapers and magazines are sold from kiosks and in smaller towns from *librerías.* Kiosks in major cities usually carry *Time* and *Newsweek* in English editions.

Police   Police officers wear olive-green uniforms and are referred to as *carabineros* or colloquially as *pacos.* Dial ☎ **133** for an emergency. A law is currently being passed to make it illegal for a policeman to stop you without cause, but until then *carabineros* can ask for your ID at checkpoints on the road.

Rest Rooms   Most establishments, apart from upscale hotels and restaurants, will ask that you deposit used toilet paper in a wastebasket and not in the toilet itself, because of poor plumbing. *Always* carry with you a small stash of toilet paper because 9 times out of 10 an establishment will not supply any.

Safety   Santiago is probably the safest major city in South America. Serious violent crime is not unheard of, but it's not common either. A visitor's principal concern will be pickpockets, tire slashers, and vandals, but even then your chances of being a victim are rare.

Showers   If you're staying in an inexpensive or moderately priced hotel, you'll probably have a shower whose water is heated by a *calafont.* They don't function as well as they should, and the trick is to turn on the hot water tap only, turning it on higher for cooler temperatures and lower for hotter temperatures.

Taxes   See "Cash & Currency" under "Money" earlier in this chapter.

Telephone   The competition between the several phone companies in Chile hasn't done much to lower prices. Each carrier has its own prefix, which you must dial when placing national and international long distance calls. Telephone centers use their own prefix, and there is a list of prefixes in telephone booths—all offer virtually the same rates. The prefixes are CTC (188), Entel (123), BellSouth (181), and Chilesat (171) among others. To place a collect call, dial a prefix and then 182 for an operator. The country code for Chile is **56.** A local phone call requires 100 pesos, and better rates are had with a phone card sold from kiosks, but verify that a particular company's phone card works with any phone and not only with its own public phone. Cellular phones are prefixed by 09, and are more expensive to call. To reach an **AT&T** operator while in Chile, dial ☎ **800/ 800-288.** The access numbers for **MCI** are ☎ **800/207-300** (using CTC) and ☎ **800/360-180** (using Entel). The access number for **Sprint** is ☎ **800/ 360-777.**

Time   Chile is 4 hours behind Greenwich mean time from the first Saturday in October and until the second Saturday in March; the country is 6 hours behind during the rest of the year. I prefer to think of it as on the same time zone as New York from the second Saturday in October to the second Saturday in March and 2 hours ahead the rest of the year.

Tipping   Diners leave a 10% tip in restaurants. In hotels, tipping is left to the guest's discretion. Taxi drivers are not tipped.

9 Santiago

Santiago, one of South America's most sophisticated cities, is a thriving metropolis that's home to five million people, or nearly a third of Chile's entire population. On a clear day, Santiago's main attraction is its spectacular location at the foot of the snowcapped Andes, which rise majestically over the city's eastern limits. It's a breathtaking sight, but the opportunity to view it is unfortunately rare due to a dense layer of smog that usually shrouds the city. The smog is at its eye-burning, throat-scratching worst in the winter, unless a rainstorm comes along and washes the air clean. During the summer, light breezes and an exodus by vacationers out of the city combine to alleviate the condition somewhat, but there's always a whiff of diesel in the air.

Nevertheless, Santiago is an intriguing city, and there's certainly plenty to see and do here. It is the historic, economic, and cultural center of Chile, and its restaurants, art centers, and theaters are the best in the country. It also makes a convenient base for exploring a number of great destinations outside the city limits—including beaches, ski resorts, and wineries. If you're planning a visit to Chile, you'll inevitably spend at least 1 night here on your way into or out of the country, but if you have the time you should try to spend 2 or 3 days here, more if you plan to visit those outlying areas.

The city is a curious mix of old and new; a glitzy glass skyscraper towers over a 2,000-year-old stone building, and a charming cobblestoned street dead-ends at a tacky 1970s shopping gallery. Santiago's unchecked development has led to a decided lack of architectural uniformity, and the contrasts can often be amusing—or shocking. Some neighborhoods look as though they belong to entirely different cities. Bear in mind that your opinion of Santiago can easily be shaped by the neighborhood you're staying in.

A BRIEF HISTORY

Pedro de Valdivia, an ambitious, dogged conquistador sent from Peru to colonize the south, founded "Santiago de la Nueva Extremadura" for the Spanish crown on February 12, 1541, at the foot of Cerro Santa Lucía. A surveyor laid out the city's plan, dividing blocks into lots for soldiers and the main Plaza de Armas, which was to be surrounded by civic buildings, a church, and the residences of high-ranking officers. Six months later, the native Mapuche Indians sacked the settlement. The Spanish were not discouraged, and immediately

Santiago at a Glance

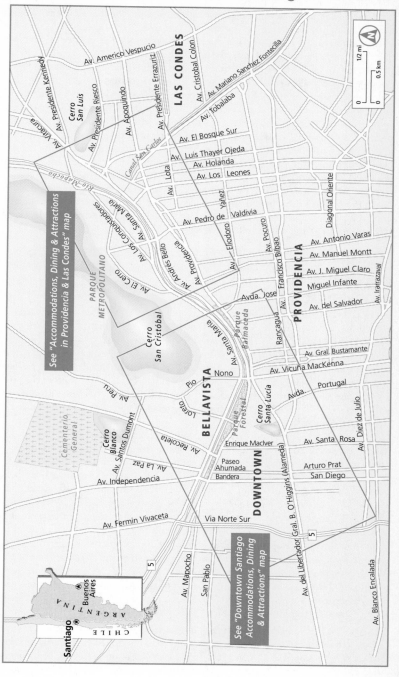

177

rebuilt. But starvation, devastating earthquakes, seasonal flooding from the Mapocho River, shifting interest to the war for colonial settlement in southern Chile, and a relative disinterest in Santiago by the Spanish crown meant the city would not grow much beyond a frontier town until the late 18th century.

But grow it did. The Mapocho River was outfitted with a series of dikes to prevent flooding, and a well-established route was set up between the city and the port town Valparaíso, promoting trade. By the 19th century the city had already begun building grand civic edifices, such as the Palacio de la Real and the Congress building. Wealthy landowners and merchants followed suit by trying to outdo each other with magnificent palaces that mimicked European styles down to the imported tapestries and furniture (although few of these residences still exist). The government invested in the city's culture with the Municipal Theater, parks, boulevards, and other beautification projects, and by the late 19th century, Santiago was a city that demanded attention.

Around the 1930s, Santiago's well-heeled residents began moving away from downtown, first to Bellavista, then on to Providencia and Las Condes. As the population grew the city expanded, and now Santiago's tentacles reach up into the Andes and sprawl over the fertile valleys to the south.

1 Orientation

ESSENTIALS
GETTING THERE

BY PLANE   Santiago's **Comodoro Arturo Merino Benítez Airport** (☎ 2/ 676-3000) is served by the Chilean national carrier Lan Chile, as well as by most major international carriers. The relatively new international wing is unmistakable next to the old terminal, now used for domestic flights. Once you pass through customs there is a small **currency exchange** kiosk, but it is recommended that you exchange larger sums downtown at a bank for better rates. Men in olive jumpsuits at the arrival and the outdoor departure curb work as airport bellhops, and they will assist you with your luggage for a 300 to 500 peso tip (50¢ to 90¢); if you're okay on your own, just shoo them away with a *no, gracias.*

Depending on traffic, your Santiago destination, and how you get there, the city can be reached in 20 minutes to an hour. When making hotel reservations, ask about transfers because most hotels offer private car or van pickup for around $20 or for free. A **taxi** to Santiago costs between $20 and $30, but always negotiate a price before accepting a ride. Another option is one of the several minivan **transfers** that charge around $8, such as Delfío or Tour Express. The transfer reps eagerly await passengers at the gate, but their desks are at the arrival area. You can also make a reservation for a transfer service to pick you up for the return trip to the airport. Keep in mind that your transfer might stop several times for other passengers before arriving at your destination. Cheaper yet are **bus** services that depart from the arrival area every 15 to 30 minutes; they'll drop you off downtown where you can catch a taxi or the Metro to your final destination. Tour Express has a bus that leaves every 15 minutes, dropping passengers off at Moneda 1529 (their pickup point as well); there's also a blue bus called Centropuerto; both cost $1.50 to $2.

BY BUS   There are three principal **bus stations** in Santiago. For international arrivals and departures to and from destinations in southern Chile: **Terminal Santiago,** Alameda O'Higgins 3850 (☎ 2/376-1755; Metro: Univ. de Santiago). The **Terminal Alameda** next door at Alameda O'Higgins 3712 is the terminal for the Pullman and Tur Bus companies, two well-respected, high-quality services. For departures to northern and central Chile: **Terminal San Borja,** Alameda O'Higgins 3250 (☎ **2/ 776-0645;** Metro: Estación Central). The smaller **Terminal Los Heroes,** Tucapel Jiménez 21 (☎ **2/420-0099;** Metro: Los Leones), has service to a variety of destinations in both northern and southern Chile.

VISITOR INFORMATION

There are several outlets offering information about Santiago and Chile in general, such as Chile's **National Tourism Service's (Sernatur)** main office, which can be found at Av. Providencia 1550 (☎ **2/236-1416;** www.sernatur.cl) and is open Monday to Friday 9:30am to 6:30pm, Saturday and Sunday 1:30 to 6:30pm. To get there, take the Metro to Manuel Montt. Sernatur also has an information center at the airport. Although somewhat helpful, Sernatur is plagued by inconsistent service and often depleted of brochures after the high season in March. It does, however, have a bilingual staff who will most likely be able to answer any question you might have about all of Chile, not just Santiago. Another option is the **Oficina de Turismo** with two locations: inside the Casa Colorada at Merced 860, and at the entrance to Cerro Santa Lucía on Alameda O'Higgins (☎ **2/632-7783**). The Oficina de Turismo offers brochures about Santiago and its nearby destinations only. A private concession operates a good tourism **kiosk** conveniently located at the intersection between Paseo Ahumada and Paseo Huérfanos pedestrian walkways in the city center; the kiosk provides brochures and relevant information, and you can book city tours there.

CITY LAYOUT

Santiago incorporates 32 *comunas,* or neighborhoods, although most visitors will find they spend their time in just one to five of these areas. **Downtown,** or *el centro,* is the thriving financial, political, and historic center of Santiago, although it has been losing clout as more and more companies opt to locate their offices in burgeoning neighborhoods, such as **Providencia** and **Las Condes.** These two upscale, attractive neighborhoods are residential areas centered on a bustling area with shopping galleries, restaurants, and office buildings. Farther east sit the residential communities Ñuñoa and **La Reina,** which, apart from a few attractions, offer little interest to the visitor. Santiago is bisected by the muddy Río Mapocho, a brown stream that trickles down from the Andes and is bordered through most of the city by the grassy Parque Forestal. On one side of the Mapocho rises the hill Cerro San Cristóbal, a large, forested park with lookout points over the city. Below the hill is the artists' neighborhood **Bellavista,** which has exploded in popularity for its fashionable bars and restaurants.

2 Getting Around

Heavy traffic in Santiago makes the Metro the preferred mode of intercity transportation. The Metro is cheap, clean, and efficient, and many stations are artfully designed with enormous murals and other attractive works.

BY METRO   There are three Metro lines. Line 1 runs from Providencia to west of downtown along Avenida O'Higgins; this is the most convenient trajectory that will take you to most major attractions. Line 2 runs from Cal y Canto (near the Franklin market and the Mercado Central) to Lo Ovalle (convenient for Palacio Cousiño). Line 5 runs from La Florida to Baquedano. Fares change during the day according to peak travel times, but expect to pay between 30¢ and 50¢ (fares are posted in the ticket window). The Metro runs from 6am to 10:30pm. The Metro is very safe, but normal precautions against pickpockets should be taken.

BY BUS **City buses,** or *micros,* are tricky in Santiago because there aren't any printed route maps available. A particular bus route might be mapped out on a sign inside the bus, but you have to guess its general path by reading the sign posted inside the windshield highlighting its principal destinations.

BY TAXI **Taxis** are identifiable by their black exterior and yellow roof; there's also a light in the corner of the windshield that displays a taxi's availability. Taxis are plentiful and moderately priced. Drivers do not expect tips, but you might find it convenient to round off a fare rather than grapple with change. Do not confuse taxis with *colectivos,* which are similar in appearance but without the yellow roof. They are local, shared taxis with fixed routes that are too confusing to the average visitor to merit taking a ride.

BY RENTAL CAR It is totally unnecessary to rent a car in Santiago unless you plan to drive to any of the peripheral areas, such as Viña del Mar or the Andes—and even then public transportation, such as direct buses and transfers, is very convenient. If you must have a car, be forewarned that driving in Santiago can be a hair-raising experience due to maniacal, swerving buses, drivers who do not confine their cars to one lane, and absolutely phenomenal traffic jams, especially between 5:30 and 7:30pm. The commuter gridlock is dreadful anywhere around Santiago but especially bad in Providencia and Las Condes.

Car Rentals At the airport you'll find most international rental agencies, such as **Alamo** (☎ 2/690-1370), **Avis** (☎ 2/690-1382), local agency **Bert** (☎ 2/601-8418), **Budget** (☎ 2/601-9421), **Dollar** (☎ 2/601-9262), **Hertz** (☎ 2/601-9262), and **Localiza** (☎ 2/362-3200). All agencies also have downtown or Providencia offices.

DRIVING HINTS Chileans use their horn and their indicators habitually to warn other motorists or advise them of their next move. Right turns on red lights are forbidden unless otherwise indicated. Ask your rental car company for a list of rules you may be unfamiliar with.

PARKING Most hotels offer parking on their own property or in a nearby lot. Forget trying to find a downtown parking space during the day, although you should have luck after everyone has gone home after work. Very few streets are metered; however, Chile is home to a peculiar phenomenon known as parking *cuidador,* where unofficial, freelance meter maids stake out individual blocks and watch your car for you while you go about your business. You'll see them everywhere, even at grocery store lots. They are not people who are hired by the city parking authority or a particular business, but residents treat them almost as though they were. You're expected to give them whatever change you have (from 50 to 200 pesos, or 10¢ to 50¢) when you leave your parking space. *Cuidadores* in the Suecia neighborhood of Providencia are very aggressive.

ON FOOT With a map in hand, Santiago is fairly easy to figure out, especially if you stick close to major streets. The problem with walking in Santiago is that most streets are a loathsome mess, with screeching buses expelling huge, gray plumes of exhaust into the already polluted air (which is especially foul from late fall to early spring). Saturday and Sunday afternoons are typically calmer days for a stroll, and the summer usually blesses its residents with cleaner air. You might consider taking shorter walks or at least breaking periodically in a quiet museum or park. Pedestrians should be alert at all times and should not stand on curbs, as buses roar by dangerously close to sidewalks. Also, drivers do not always give the right of way to pedestrians, and therefore you should get across the street as quickly as possible.

Fast Facts: Santiago

American Express   Operates out of **Turismo Cocha,** Av. El Bosque Norte 0430, in Las Condes (☎ **2/464-1000;** open Mon–Fri 9:30am–5pm; for 24-hour bilingual service ☎ **800/361002**).

Baby-sitting   Many hotels offer baby-sitting service; inquire when making a reservation.

Banks   Open 9am to 2pm, closed on Saturdays and Sundays. ATMs are referred to as "RedBancs" and can be identified by the maroon-and-white logo sticker. These machines accept Cirrus, PLUS, Visa, and MasterCard.

Business Hours   Commercial offices close for a long lunch hour, which can vary from business to business. Generally, hours are Monday to Friday 10am to 7pm, closing for lunch between 1 and 1:30pm and reopening between 2:30 or 3pm.

Cinema   English-language films are shown with Spanish subtitles, as are all foreign-language films in Chile. You'll find listings in nearly every newspaper, and both major shopping malls have megaplex theaters.

Currency Exchange   All major banks exchange currency, but only a few do so without charging commission; ask first. There are quite a few *casas de cambio* throughout downtown (try Paseo Huérfanos or Agustinas), such as Exprinter or Afex. In Providencia, exchange houses are around Avenida Pedro de Valdivia and Avenida Providencia. (Generally open Monday to Saturday 9am to 2pm and 4 to 6pm.)

Emergencies   For a police emergency, call **133.** For fire, call **132.** To call an ambulance, dial **131.**

Hospital   The American Embassy can provide a list of medical specialists in Santiago. The best hospitals in Santiago are private: **Clínica Las Condes** at Lo Fontecilla 441 (☎ **2/210-4000**) and **Clínica Alemana** at Vitacura 5951 (☎ **2/ 212-9700**).

Internet Access   Virtually every hotel in Santiago has Internet access available to guests. Try also **Café Phonet** (www.phonet.cl/), General Holley 2312, Providencia (☎ **2/335-6106**), and San Sebastian 2815, Las Condes; hours are daily 9am to 11pm.

Language   Many Chileans in the tourism industry and in major cities can speak basic English, but don't count on it. Try to learn even a dozen basic Spanish phrases before arriving; there are several excellent phrasebooks on the market and they will facilitate your trip tremendously.

Newspapers/Magazines   Easily identifiable kiosks throughout the city sell a variety of publications, including magazines in English. The kiosks at Huérfanos and Banderas streets offer a wide range of newspapers, including the *New York Times.* Libro's, Pedro de Valdivia 039 (☎ **2/232-8839**), in Providencia, sells hundreds of current magazines from English-speaking countries, and most bookstores have at least a small selection of English-language publications.

Pharmacies   Pharmacies are plentiful; you'll even find them at highway gas stations. Strangely, they are always packed, so be sure to take a number or have the pharmacy deliver at little or no cost. **Farmacias Ahumada** branches are open 24 hours a day, and there are dozens of locations. Try the one at the corner of Ahumada and Huérfanos streets; or at El Bosque 164, in Las Condes; call ☎ **2/ 222-4000** for information and ordering.

Downtown Santiago Accommodations, Dining & Attractions

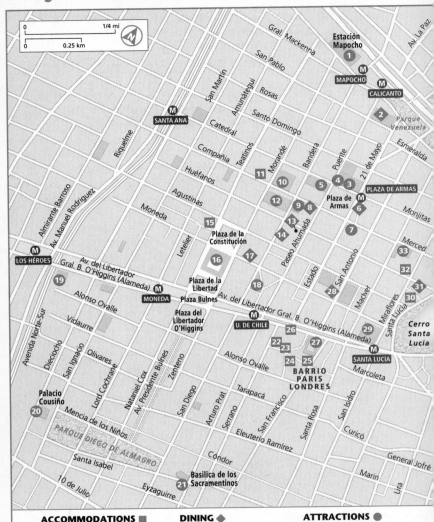

ACCOMMODATIONS ■
Apart Hotel Carlton **30**
City Hotel **11**
Hostal del Parque **37**
Hotel Carrera **15**
Hotel Foresta **34**
Hotel Fundador **22**
Hotel París **25**
Hotel Plaza San Francisco **26**
Hotel Riviera **32**
Hotel Vegas **23**
Residencial Londres **24**

DINING ◆
Bar Nacional **14**
Chez Henry **6**
Don Vitorino **36**
El Novillero **17**
Gatopardo **35**
Govindas **8**
Le Due Torri **28**
Mercado Central **2**
Restaurant Jacaranda **31**
San Marcos **13**

ATTRACTIONS ●
Basilica de la Merced **33**
Basilica del Santisimo
 Sacramento **21**
Biblioteca Nacional **29**
Bolsa de Comercio **18**
Casa Colorada/
 Museo de Santiago **7**
Catedral Metropolitana/
 Museo de Arte Sagrado **5**
Correo Central/
 Museo Postal **4**

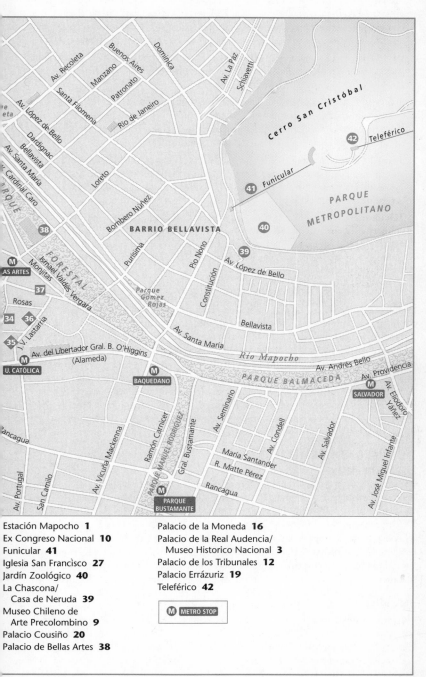

M METRO STOP

Police   Police officers wear olive-green uniforms and are referred to as *carabineros* or colloquially as *pacos*. Dial **133** for an emergency. A law is currently being passed to make it illegal for a policeman to stop you without cause, but until then *carabineros* can ask for your ID at checkpoints on the road.

Post Office   The main post office is on Plaza de Armas (Mon–Fri 8am–7pm and Sat 8am–2pm). There are other branches at Moneda 1155 in downtown and Av. 11 de Septiembre 2239 in Providencia.

Safety   Santiago is probably the safest major city in South America. A visitor's principal concern should be pickpockets operating in public places such as the Plaza de Armas or at night in Bellavista. Keep alert if you're crowded suddenly on the street, but in general, normal caution should suffice.

Taxes   Chile charges an 18% value-added tax (IVA) that is automatically integrated into most prices. Foreigners paying in dollars for hotels, rental cars, etc., however, are exempt from this charge. Smaller hostals and those who do not accept dollars might not be set up to offer foreigners this discount.

Telephone   Santiago's area code is **2;** cellular numbers are prefixed by **09.** The country code for Chile is **56.** Unless you've prepared yourself with a calling plan, expect to pay about $1 a minute to the United States when calling from a phone center. Many phone centers, such as Entel or CTC, have fax service and Internet access.

3 Where to Stay

Santiago accommodations are a mixed bag, and price is not always the best indicator of quality. Many hotels in the $90 to $110 range from bland boxes to quaint hotels in renovated mansions. Santiago is now home to several five-star hotels, but it's the city's smaller boutique hotels that usually offer the most personal service. Downtown is the obvious choice if proximity to major sites of interest is what's important to you, but keep in mind that an efficient metro quickly links visitors with areas such as the bustling residential neighborhoods of Providencia and Las Condes. If price is a factor, you'll find the most economical lodging downtown. Parking at Santiago hotels is free unless otherwise indicated in the review.

DOWNTOWN SANTIAGO
VERY EXPENSIVE

✪ **Hotel Carrera.** Teatinos 180. ☎ **2/698-2011.** Fax 2/672-1083. www.carrera.cl. E-mail: hotel.carrera@chilnet.cl. 281 units, 26 suites. A/C MINIBAR TV TEL. $260 double; $340 Carrera Club junior suite; $480 executive suite. AE, DC, MC, V. Parking available. Metro: Estación Moneda.

This is the grande dame of Santiago hotels. Although the city now hosts several five-star hotels, the history and old-fashioned splendor of the Carrera make it one of the more unique choices in the city. Built between 1937 and 1940, and for decades the social center of Santiago's elite, the building's lobby features crystal chandeliers from Bohemia and an enormous glass mural depicting the arrival of the Spanish to the New World. The hotel sits directly on the Plaza Constitución, catty-corner from the presidential building Palacio de la Moneda, and features a facade with mounted flags and brass revolving doors. Rooms are spacious, and the recently remodeled, executive Carrera Club rooms on the fifth and sixth floor are the best in the hotel; they are larger and come complete with marble sinks and mahogany furniture. Most rooms have a richly textured English decor with classic floral and striped wallpaper, oriental carpets, and heavy drapes. Some guests have remarked that rooms facing the neighboring Ministero de Hacienda are too dark; instead, opt for a room facing Agustinas Street or the plaza. A highlight at the Carrera is its glitzy rooftop pool, where you can gaze out above the rooftops and watch the hustle and bustle of businessmen and politicians below. Note that standard rooms do not include breakfast. Also, always ask for promotions because prices here vary and can often drop as low as $198 for a Carrera Club room, $150 for a standard.

Dining: There are two restaurants: the **Copper Room,** serving international cuisine, and the **Roof Garden Restaurant** on the 17th floor, next to the pool. The Copper Room Bar is a great spot for a cocktail.

Amenities: Concierge, 24-hour room service, business center, laundry, gift and floral shops, photo service, baby-sitting, conference rooms, gym, racquetball court, outdoor pool, sauna, whirlpool tub, massage, beauty salon, house doctor.

Hotel Fundador. Paseo Serrano 34. ☎ **2/387-1200.** Fax 2/387-1300. www.hotelfundador. cl. E-mail: hotelfundador@hotelfundador.cl. 150 units. A/C MINIBAR TV TEL. $170 double; $230 junior suite. AE, DC, MC, V. Parking available. Metro: Univ. de Chile.

The Fundador is similar to the Plaza (see below) in its classic decor, though ever-so-slightly less elegant. But never mind: The Fundador's attractive, English-style rooms are comfortable and bright, and its wonderful swimming pool is housed in a sunny penthouse. The hotel also has a great central location on a quiet street in the charming París-Londres neighborhood. Many doubles come with two full-size beds instead of twins; inquire before booking. The Fundador expanded 2 years ago when it bought the building next door, adding rooms and renovating every one of its older guest rooms (the buildings are connected by a fourth-floor interior walkway). The suites are compact but exceptionally cozy, and all come with cherrywood armoires to separate the bedroom from a sitting area. The small lobby has a bouserie ceiling and wooden pillars offset with Gobelin tapestry; adjoining the lobby is a wood-and-leather-walled bar that's great to hole up in for a drink.

Dining: The **Winter Garden** patio restaurant is lit by ceiling windows and offers a basic menu. The more formal **Calicanto Restaurant** serves international food.

Amenities: 24-hour room service, business center, laundry, gift shop, conference rooms, gym, indoor pool and sauna, baby-sitting, valet parking.

✪ **Hotel Plaza San Francisco.** Alameda O'Higgins 816. ☎ **2/639-3832.** Fax 2/639-7826. www.hotelsanfrancisco.cl. E-mail: fcohotel@entelchile.net. 160 units. A/C MINIBAR TV TEL. $150–$180 double; $210–$290 executive suite. AE, DC, MC, V. Parking available. Metro: Univ. de Chile.

This exceptional hotel, with an elegant, clubby design, offers smart service, impeccable rooms, and a central location—which explains its popularity with the traveling executive crowd. The decor is traditional and somewhat dark, with low, wood ceilings supported by pillars, richly colored fabric wallpaper, oriental rugs, and subdued light. The lobby makes you want to sink into it and relax to the sound of the tinkling indoor fountain—or enjoy one of the best happy hours in town. Guest rooms are spacious, with sparkling bathrooms and classic furniture buffed to a shine. Not a single thread is out of place, and even the carpets have been vacuumed in perfect strokes. The hotel is conveniently located on busy O'Higgins Avenue, but you won't hear the din of traffic due to double-paned windows. On the bottom floor is an annex for temporary art exhibits, and there is a wine shop and an on-site Lan Chile office. The pool area has been recently renovated, although it is hidden downstairs in a windowless room. Apart from executives, plenty of travelers choose the Plaza when visiting Santiago, including the Dalai Lama, who has stayed here twice and even gave a public benediction in the hallway outside his room. When booking a reservation, do so through the Web site; you'll find substantially lower prices offered as "Dollars and Cents" and "Hot Chile" deals.

Dining/Diversions: The award-winning **Restaurant Bristol** serves superb international cuisine (a fixed menu for $30 includes wine); the lounge has an open bar from 7 to 9pm for $10, including appetizers.

Amenities: Concierge, 24-hour room service, business center, laundry, Lan Chile office, gift shop, conference rooms, art gallery, gym, indoor pool and whirlpool, massage.

EXPENSIVE

✪ **Hostal del Parque.** Merced 294. ☎ **2/639-2694.** Fax 2/639-2754. 30 units, 14 suites, 2 penthouses. A/C MINIBAR TV TEL. $126 double; $160 junior suite. AE, DC, MC, V. Parking available. Metro: Univ. Católica.

A great location and kitchenettes in every spacious, comfortable room make the Hostal del Parque an excellent choice. This compact hotel sits around the corner from the charming cobblestoned streets off the Plaza Gil de Castro neighborhood, near several restaurants and close to downtown attractions. The rooms are warmly decorated in rose, beige, and navy, and kept very clean. They're all spacious enough for a table and two chairs; folding doors reveal a counter and stove. The eighth and ninth floors feature suites with floor-to-ceiling windows and fireplaces, and unfortunately they are really the only floors to receive maximum sunshine. Service is attentive, gracious, and personal.

Dining: A tiny indoor garden restaurant has skylights and potted ferns, and serves basic Chilean and international cuisine; there's also a bar.

Amenities: 24-hour room service, kitchenettes, laundry, conference rooms.

MODERATE

Apart Hotel Carlton. Máximo Humbster 574. ☎ **2/638-3130.** Fax 2/638-2930. 33 units, 22 suites. TV TEL $42 double; $52 suite with kitchenette. AE, DC, MC, V. Parking $4.50 per day. Metro: Santa Lucía.

This no-frills hotel is boxier and older than the Foresta or Riviera; however, the rooms are neat and crisp and their 1950s and '60s furniture has been fitted with fresh gingham slipcovers. It is highly recommended that guests opt for a suite, as they come with older but complete kitchenettes and fairly large common areas; those facing the street have sunny terraces. The gloomier doubles face a parking garage and are not as much of a value. Although the Carlton is as simple as it gets, it sits on a quaint, quiet street near the Cerro Santa Lucía.

✪ **Hotel Foresta.** Victoria Subercaseaux 353. ☎ **2/639-6261** or 2/639-4862. Fax 2/632-2996. 35 units. MINIBAR TV TEL. $40 double; $50 junior suite. AE, DC, MC, V. Parking available. Metro: Santa Lucía.

If you can get past the dungeonlike lobby, the Hotel Foresta offers comfortable, spacious rooms with leafy views of Cerro Santa Lucía, as well as a rooftop restaurant with panoramic windows. Doubles that face Subercaseaux Street are large enough to be suites, and each room is decorated with an eclectic mix of furniture from seemingly every era and design—one room has floral bedspreads, the next, jade-colored wallpaper and smoked glass tables. It's an older hotel, and its funkiness makes for a fun place to stay. Singles with interior views are disappointingly dark and cramped. A plant-filled restaurant serves Chilean fare, and there is a bar.

Hotel Riviera. Miraflores 106. ☎ **2/633-1176.** Fax 2/633-5988. 40 units. A/C TV TEL. $48 double; $59 suite. AE, DC, MC, V. Parking available. Metro: Santa Lucía.

This hotel is a great deal for its reasonable prices and convenient downtown location. The corner it occupies is loud on weekdays, but it won't be a problem if you're out sightseeing all day thanks to your proximity to a wealth of attractions. Bright corner rooms have wide, floor-to-ceiling windows overlooking a plaza, and the suite on the top floor has a panoramic view of Cerro Santa Lucía. Although somewhat older, the Riviera was recently renovated with fresh paint and carpets, and its Spanish decor features textured walls and iron chandeliers. There's a small restaurant for breakfast and snacks near the lobby.

Hotel Vegas. Londres 49. ☎ **2/632-2498.** Fax 2/632-5084. 20 units. TV TEL. $60 double. AE, DC, MC, V. Metro: Univ. de Chile.

The Hotel Vegas overlooks a cobblestoned street in an antique stone mansion in the París-Londres neighborhood. The price is economical, but rooms can be a bit drab, especially if you end up with one of the rooms with interior light. Rooms in the back are sunnier, but they don't have the street view. Dark-wood paneling, diamond-paned yellow windows with heavy shutters, iron chandeliers, and '70s-style furniture set the atmosphere. The price and the age of the hotel make for bathrooms that look a little tired and carpet that's a bit thin, but they're all generally neat and clean, and the service is friendly. There's a tiny restaurant and bar in the lobby and a wedged-in patio in the back.

INEXPENSIVE

City Hotel. Compañía 1063. ☎ **2/695-4526.** Fax 2/695-6775. 72 units. TV TEL. $40 double; $50 quadruple. Parking available. Metro: Plaza de Armas.

This 1925 relic has needed an update for many years, and it's surprising given the beauty of its stone exterior that the owners have not seen fit to do so. A hint of the old-world charm still shines through somehow, perhaps because of the manual elevator, creaky floors, and heavy room keys. It's an interesting place to spend the night if you don't mind spartan accommodations, and the price is right. Rooms are fairly spacious, and the beds and the bathrooms a bit battered, but clean. The location near the Plaza de Armas is ideal if you're looking to be in the thick of things, and there's an adjoining restaurant that harks back to the same era, with dark wood and iron banisters.

El Castillo Hotel. Pío Nono 420 (Bellavista). ☎ **2/735-0243.** Fax 2/777-3607. 12 units. TV TEL. $44 double; $60 spacious double with couch. DC, MC, V. Parking available. Metro: Baquedano.

This hotel is in Bellavista, near Providencia and downtown. El Castillo is as funky as the neighborhood that surrounds it and is the only hotel in the neighborhood. Originally built for an eccentric, well-heeled businessman in 1925, as the name implies the hotel is modeled after a *castillo* (castle), complete with wood panels carved with designs of lions, serfs, and crossed arms, and diamond-paned stained-glass windows and soaring ceilings. The Castillo opened 2 years ago and has been completely remodeled with very comfortable rooms. Be forewarned that the owners offer a discreet, by-the-hour room upstairs (with a mirrored ceiling and red satin bedspread), but it does not corrupt the atmosphere in any noticeable way. It's a smaller hotel with lots of character, and it sits at the foot of forested Cerro San Cristóbal, just blocks from great restaurants and nightlife. If you reserve by fax, be sure to specify "El Castillo," as the company owns other properties in town.

✪ **Hotel París/Nuevo Hotel París.** París 813. ☎ **2/664-0921.** Fax 2/639-4037. 40 units. TV TEL. $36 double (new wing); $26 double (old wing). AE, DC, MC, V. Parking across the street, $2–$3 per day. Metro: Univ. de Chile.

This is another good budget hotel with a central location and charming interiors, especially within the newer annex's antique rooms. Budget backpackers from all over the world usually bunk in one of the simple, older rooms (be sure to ask for a room with a TV because they tend to be larger). It's recommended that guests pay a little extra here and opt for a room in what's referred to as the Hotel Nuevo París, as rooms are quieter and include oriental rugs and mahogany molding. These rooms are darker, though not unappealingly so, and a few rooms even come with a glass-enclosed alcove or tiny outdoor terrace; they are the same price and worth asking for. Continental breakfast costs $2.

✪ **Residencial Londres.** Londres 54. ☎/fax **2/638-2215.** 25 units. $28 double with private bathroom; $24 double with shared bathroom. No credit cards. Metro: Univ. de Chile.

Residencial Londres is simply the best choice for travelers on the cheap in Santiago and is, accordingly, wildly popular in the summer. There are four floors of basic rooms that wrap around an interior patio; some rooms have French doors that open onto Paris Street. Residencial Londres is stuffed with period antiques; some rooms come with armoires, tables, and chairs. The beds are not the best, but the furnishings and architecture make up the difference. Golden light floats through the lobby in the afternoon, and there's a TV lounge off to the side. During the summer this hotel is frequented more by backpackers and younger travelers, and many use the interior terrace to dry tents and store bicycles. A toast-and-coffee breakfast is available for $1.50.

PROVIDENCIA
VERY EXPENSIVE

✪ **Santiago Park Plaza Hotel.** Ricardo Lyon 207. ☎ **2/372-4000.** Fax 2/233-6668. www.parkplaza.cl. E-mail: bookings@parkplaza.cl. 104 units. A/C MINIBAR TV TEL. $240 standard double; $330 junior suite. Parking available. Metro: Los Leones.

The Park Plaza is easily confused with the Plaza Hotel downtown, and indeed their styles are quite similar. This exclusive brick hotel also caters predominately to traveling executives and diplomats, although its discreet location tucked away on Lyon Street in Providencia is quieter. The Park Plaza is a boutique hotel designed in the European style, with classically designed rooms, rich fabrics, and wing-back chairs. The lobby has dark paneled walls, burgundy and green furniture, marble floors, and polished brass; adjoining is a small restaurant serving French cuisine. All 92 standard rooms have plenty of space and good light. The hotel is conveniently near shops and a block from the Metro, a quarter block up from busy Avenida 11 de Septiembre. But what really stands out is the Park Plaza's impeccable service; they even issue each room a binder packed with information about Santiago. The Park Plaza has a second hotel around the corner, with 20 fully furnished guest rooms featuring spacious kitchenettes and living areas in standard and superior sizes.

Dining/Diversions: The **Park Lane Restaurant** serves excellent French and Chilean cuisine and features a nightly appetizer and dessert buffet. The **Lobby Bar** has a happy hour 6:30 to 8pm.

Amenities: 24-hour room service, business center, laundry, gift shop, conference rooms, gym, indoor pool and sauna, baby-sitting, valet parking, city tours and transfers to tennis and golf courts.

✪ **Sheraton Santiago.** Av. Santa María 1742. ☎ **800/335-3535** in the U.S., or 2/233-5000. Fax 2/234-1066. www.sheraton.cl. 379 units. A/C MINIBAR TV TEL. $255 double; $310 executive suite. AE, DC, MC, V. Metro: Pedro de Valdivia.

The magnificent, gala Sheraton Santiago offers more room sizes and amenities than are possible to list in this description, especially now that they've added on the San Cristóbal Tower with conference centers and luxury executive rooms. The Sheraton sits apart from the city, facing the Río Mapocho and backing the Cerro San Cristóbal mountain, which is unfortunate because to get anywhere you have to cross the river, and it psychologically cuts you off from the city even though it is just 5 blocks from downtown Providencia. However, the Sheraton is such a full-service hotel that you won't find yourself running out to buy anything anyway. The glittering lobby can at once seem grand and stark, but a lengthy crossing leads to several couches and a comfortable restaurant. The rooms at the Sheraton vary according to their location within the hotel, but all are well appointed with the same high-quality linens and attractive furnishings. The new executive guest rooms and suites in the Towers complex are truly top-notch; each floor has its own butler, and there's a private lounge for breakfast or tea on the 21st floor. The Sheraton often offers weekend promotions for these rooms for as low as $400 for a double for 2 nights. Unfortunately, standard doubles do not come with breakfast, but all others do. The hotel gently curves around an outdoor circular pool fringed with lawn chairs. The Grecian-styled, state-of-the-art Neptune Pool & Fitness Center is unbelievable, with a turquoise pool surrounded by murals and softly lit by skylights. With its crystal chandeliers and marble floors, the Sheraton is all about glamour whereas the Park Plaza is low-key elegance. The constant action makes for an exciting play to stay.

Dining/Diversions: The Sheraton has three restaurants: **El Cid,** with fine dining and an international menu; **El Bohio,** a poolside cafe open during the summer; and **El Jardín,** a casual restaurant open 24 hours. There's also a bar, **El Quixote,** with live music.

Amenities: Laundry, concierge, rental car agency, shopping gallery, travel agency, business center, florist, beauty salon and barber, outdoor and indoor pools, sauna, whirlpool, massage, tennis courts, baby-sitting, conference centers.

EXPENSIVE

✪ **Hotel Orly.** Av. Pedro de Valdivia 027. ☎ **2/231-8947.** Fax 2/252-0051. 30 units, 2 suites. A/C MINIBAR TV TEL. $84 double; $95 suite. AE, DC, MC, V. Parking available. Metro: Pedro de Valdivia.

This irresistible boutique hotel is one of my favorites in Santiago. The Orly is housed in a renovated mansion with French-influenced architecture; the lobby door is between the hotel's hip cafe and an Internet site that occupy the bottom floor. The lobby is compact, but has a few nooks with reading lights for relaxing and a small, glass-covered patio; there's also a bar and an eating area for breakfast. The interiors are white and accented with contemporary art and glowing light. Because it is an old home, rooms vary in size. Doubles come with two twins or a full-size bed and are of average size; singles are claustrophobic. All rooms have desks, and suites have a sitting area within the same room. If you need peace and quiet, request a room in the back because the street is busy at all times. One of the high points here is the hotel's sharp service.

Los Españoles Hotel. Los Españoles 2539. ☎ **2/232-1824.** Fax 2/233-1048. www.cepri. cl/hotelespa. E-mail: hotelesp@cepri.cl. 48 units, 2 suites. A/C MINIBAR TV TEL. $90 double; $100 suite. AE, DC, MC, V. Parking available. Metro: Pedro de Valdivia.

Los Españoles is part of the Best Western chain, although it has been independently run by the same family for 26 years. In fact, the hotel was once their family home, and the owners want guests to feel as though they are in their own home. The rooms are sized differently and laid out in a maze. Top floor suites have attached terrace patios, and all rooms are comfortable, modern, and neat. A restaurant/bar near the lobby serves a good breakfast, and the hotel will arrange airport transportation. This is a good hotel for travelers seeking dependable, familiar comfort, and for that reason it is popular with Americans. It sits beside the Mapocho River in a quiet residential area, and is a 10-minute walk to the commercial center of Providencia and the closest Metro station. The hotel also has an apartment hotel down the street that isn't highly recommended due to its noisy locale and lousy design (the kitchenettes seem to have been thrown in at the last moment).

Sheraton Four Points. Santa Magdalena 111. ☎ **2/244-3344.** Fax 2/244-2442. www.sheraton.cl. 128 units. A/C MINIBAR TV TEL. $110 double. AE, DC, MC, V. Parking available. Metro: Los Leones.

Four Points is a brand-new Sheraton with rooms that cost far less than the Santiago (see above), but offer the same standard amenities. A bland exterior is virtually indistinguishable from the office buildings that surround it, but the location ensures quiet evenings. The hotel is a safe bet for anyone used to American chains: prompt, professional service and an attractive, shabby-chic design that nevertheless feels store-bought. The rose and cream decoration gives off warmth in the rooms, and along with simple yet fine furnishings creates an exceptionally comfortable place to spend the night. Corner suites come with walk-in closets. A great detail here is the rooftop pool and solarium, which can be a welcome relief on a hot day.

Dining: There's a bistro-style restaurant on the bottom floor serving international food.

   Amenities: Laundry, conference centers, outdoor pool, sauna, whirlpool, gym, business center.

MODERATE

✪ **Hotel Aloha.** Francisco Noguera 146. ☎ **2/233-2230.** Fax 2/233-2230. www.panamericanahoteles.cl. E-mail: resaloha@entelchile.net. 66 units. A/C MINIBAR TV TEL. $80 double; $140 suite. AE, DC, MC, V. Parking available. Metro: Pedro de Valdivia.

Perhaps the best feature of the Hotel Aloha is its outdoor pool. The pool is surrounded by greenery and fronted by a seating area covered by a white fabric awning with curtains; it's such a refreshing, tranquil place that you almost won't believe you're on a busy street in Providencia. The lobby entrance crosses a trickling pond shrouded in leafy plants, viewable from the inside thanks to glass panels. The rooms are identical, and all are smartly furnished, colorful, and filled with natural light, as is the rest of the hotel. True to its name, the Aloha does have a certain tropical feel, with its only defect being the orange carpet, which needs to be replaced. The hotel recently built a new salon and expanded its restaurant, which features a menu primarily of seafood, pastas, and meat. The Aloha, part of the Panamericana chain, offers frequent promotional prices.

✪ **Hotel Club Presidente.** Av. Eliodoro Yañez 867. ☎ **2/235-8015.** Fax 2/235-9148. www.presidente.cl. 50 units. A/C MINIBAR TV TEL. $70–90 double; $140 suite. Parking available. Metro: Salvador.

The Hotel Club Presidente is one of the best values in this category. The rooms here are fresh, tidy, and immensely comfortable, although a little on the small side and slightly dark due to the hotel's position between two tall buildings. But if you're out all day, you'll never notice. The Presidente is a small hotel but doesn't skimp on friendly, professional service. The compact, white foyer is decorated with Peruvian gold mirrors; from here a hall leads to a restaurant and a great patio draped in foliage and serenaded by a bubbling fountain. The hotel is located on a residential street just a 3-minute walk away from the subway, about halfway between Providencia and downtown. This is another hotel that offers airport transfer service and occasional promotions. The Club Presidente also owns **Apart-Hotel Club Presidente,** Luis Thayer Ojeda (☎ **2/233-5652**), with double rooms of the same quality as this hotel, plus a full kitchen, for $90 double.

Hotel Eurotel. Guardia Vieja 285. ☎/fax **2/251-6111.** E-mail: eurotel@ctc-mundo.net. 25 units. A/C TV TEL. $75 double. AE, DC, MC, V. Metro: Los Leones.

The Eurotel is just that, a European-style hotel frequented by French travelers; the owners themselves are French. It's in the hub of Providencia, near shopping and transportation, and is part of the Best Western chain. The style is decidedly 1980s, with a neon strip around the middle of the building, dark furniture, low light, and smoked-glass furnishings. Standards are called executives, and junior suites come with a sitting area and desk; there are also five apartments, each with two bedrooms and a kitchenette, that go for $125. The restaurant is particularly agreeable, with a cheery atmosphere and a daily changing menu.

Hotel Santa María. Av. Santa María 2050. ☎ **2/232-3376.** Fax 2/231-6287. 23 units. MINIBAR TV TEL. $75 double. AE, DC, MC, V. Parking available. Metro: Los Leones.

This hotel is located across the Río Mapocho but just blocks from central Providencia. It's another hotel within an old home, but unlike the Orly, the Santa María has not updated its interior, which some travelers prefer for its antiquated style. The rooms are darker, and probably too humble for the price, but there are three rooms facing the back that are exceptional for their enormous French doors that lead out onto the back patio. You might ask to see several rooms if you can, because each is sized differently. The front rooms are noisy due to fast-moving traffic down Avenida Santa María. Past the reception desk are two salons with couches for relaxing, and a modest eating area for breakfast.

LAS CONDES
VERY EXPENSIVE

✪ **Hyatt Regency Santiago.** Av. Kennedy 4601. ☎ **2/218-1234.** Fax 2/218-3155. www.santiago.hyatt.com. E-mail: info@hyatt.cl. 310 units, 26 suites. A/C MINIBAR TV TEL. $225–320 double; $375–$670 suite. AE, DC, MC, V.

In 1992, the Hyatt brought to Santiago a whole new concept in five-star luxury: 310 spacious, opulent rooms, hip restaurants, a plethora of services, and sky-high prices. The Hyatt is a 24-story atrium tower with two adjacent wings and four glass elevators that whisk guests up to their split-level rooms and terraced suites. It sits alone at a busy junction and can be seen from many places around Santiago; inside it feels as spacious as an airport hanger. Unfortunately, for this reason the Hyatt can't help feeling somewhat antiseptic, a fact exacerbated by bland, uniform brown stone interiors. Nevertheless, guests are usually wowed by this behemoth. The palm-and-fern–fringed pool and fully staffed gym are superb. The Hyatt's standard rooms are accented with weathered blond wood and richly colored furnishings. They're as large as average suites, meaning the executive suites are enormous. Guests in suites enjoy their own 16th-floor private lounge for lingering over breakfast and soaking up the spectacular view. All have sumptuous bathrooms. A complete business center rents out computers and cell phones. When visiting luminaries come to town, many of them stay here; in fact, the Iberoamerican Summit chose the Hyatt to host 23 heads of state in 1996. The lounge hosts daily tea, complete with a buffet of mouth-watering cakes, that is open to the public. You'll always need to take a taxi, because the location at the head of a crazy traffic loop makes it difficult to walk anywhere from here.

Dining/Diversions: There are four excellent restaurants: **Crostini,** featuring northern Italian cuisine; **Anakena,** with international steak and seafood grills and Thai food; **Matsuri,** a chic Japanese restaurant with a sushi bar and teppanyaki tables; and **Duke's Bar,** an English pub with live music and light snacks. The lobby lounge serves continental breakfast and afternoon English tea.

Amenities: Concierge, valet service, 24-hour room service, business center, laundry, florist and shopping arcade, conference rooms, gym, tennis courts, outdoor pool, sauna, whirlpool, solarium, massage, beauty salon, Hertz car rental office, American Airlines office, baby-sitting, house doctor, billiards room (suites only).

EXPENSIVE

✪ **Hotel Montebianco.** Av. Isidora Goyenechea 2911. ☎ **2/232-5034.** Fax 2/233-0420. www.montebianco.co.cl. E-mail: montebia@entelchile.net. 33 units. A/C MINIBAR TV TEL. $97 double; $109 suite; $125 suite with patio. AE, DC, MC, V. Parking available. Metro: El Golf.

This boutique hotel is another favorite, often of guests who have seen the Hyatt but opt for the Montebianco's more personalized attention and cheaper prices. Located in the midst of restaurant alley in the El Bosque area of Las Condes, the Montebianco has handsomely decorated, Mediterranean-style interiors with white stucco walls and a cozy restaurant. The rooms are average-size with large bathrooms, but if you need elbow space, book a Montebianco Pieza suite for an additional $15, which comes complete with a walk-in closet. The best rooms in the house are the suites with attached patios. The hotel also has a bar, 24-hour room service, and a business center. One of the perks here is the Montebianco's private minibus, which it uses for city tours, tours to outlying destinations, and airport pickup, all at an extra charge.

✪ **Hotel Rugendas.** Callao 3121. ☎ /fax **2/655-1881.** www.rugendas.cl. E-mail: hotel@rugendas.cl. 48 units. $125 double. AE, DC, MC, V. Parking available. Metro: El Golf.

The recently opened Hotel Rugendas is another superb choice in Las Condes for its cozy accommodations and excellent amenities that seem too good to be true for the price. The hotel is housed in a tall brick building whose top floor is encased with glass; here you'll find a game room with card tables and a billiards table, not to mention a pretty spectacular view. If an on-site gym is important to you, the Rugendas's state-of-the-art facility is open 24 hours a day. Thick, golden curtains and bedspreads, a country decor, and large wooden headboards accent each room, as do well-positioned lights. Rooms on the upper floors have great views of the Andes, and a few have terraces. The suites come with a CD player and an angled sitting area with a couch. A Tuscan-style restaurant serves flavorful food and a great breakfast buffet; there's also outdoor seating under large canvas umbrellas. Professional service and frequent promotions (such as $125 for any room with dinner) round out this premium hotel.

4 Where to Dine

Santiago's gastronomic scene is currently undergoing a revolution, and hungry diners can expect to find dozens upon dozens of innovative restaurants that serve updated Chilean cuisine. Ethnic restaurants, led by a growing sushi craze, have slowly made their way into the market. It's a welcome relief to be able to step out of the typical baked/fried fish and meat plates so popular up and down the length of Chile. Santiago's downtown caters to business folk and most restaurants are open for lunch only. It is possible to eat quite cheaply in the downtown area; most restaurants have a *menu del día* or *menu ejecutivo,* a fixed-price lunch for $4 to $7 that includes an appetizer, main course, beverage or wine, coffee, and dessert. *Autoservicios,* or self-service restaurants, abound, and most restaurants advertise their prices on sandwich boards or on signs posted near the front door. These restaurants are a dime a dozen, and quality is about the same. Around Plaza de Gil are several restaurants that do serve dinner in the evening.

Bellavista is perhaps the gastronomic center of Santiago. This artistic and intellectual haven has bred a mind-boggling number of chic restaurants. It seems as if the

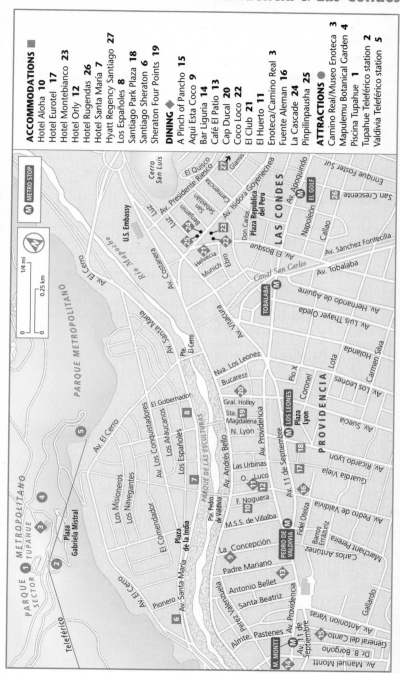

ACCOMMODATIONS ■
Hotel Aloha **10**
Hotel Eurotel **17**
Hotel Montebianco **23**
Hotel Orly **12**
Hotel Rugendas **26**
Hotel Santa María **7**
Hyatt Regency Santiago **27**
Los Españoles **8**
Santiago Park Plaza **18**
Santiago Sheraton **6**
Sheraton Four Points **19**

DINING ◆
A Pinch of Pancho **15**
Aquí Esta Coco **9**
Bar Liguria **14**
Café El Patio **13**
Cap Ducal **20**
Coco Loco **22**
El Club **21**
El Huerto **11**
Enoteca/Camino Real **3**
Fuente Aleman **16**
La Cascade **24**
Pinpilinpausha **25**

ATTRACTIONS ●
Camino Real/Museo Enoteca **3**
Mapulemu Botanical Garden **4**
Piscina Tupahue **1**
Tupahue Teleférico station **2**
Valdivia Teleférico station **5**

moment you turn your back another eatery is opening its doors, from Chilean to Cuban to Mediterranean. A few of the local favorites are listed below, but you could really just stroll the streets until something strikes your fancy. The same could be said for El Bosque Norte in the Las Condes district. Both El Bosque and its parallel street Avenida Isidora Goyenechea are lined door to door with a potpourri of flavorful offerings. Don't forget that most major hotels, notably the Hyatt and the Hotel Plaza San Francisco, have outstanding restaurants open to the public. Remember that Chile is to seafood what Argentina is to beef; don't miss out on the wonderful varieties it has to offer.

DOWNTOWN
EXPENSIVE
✪ **Le Due Torri.** San Antonio 258. ☎ **2/639-7609.** Main courses $11–$20. AE, DC, MC, V. Mon–Fri 12:30–11pm. ITALIAN.

Set back from busy San Antonio Street, the classic Le Due Torri serves more than 20 kinds of pasta and other Italian favorites, as well as international fish and meat entrees. It offers excellent service and great food to match. For a light lunch, try the colorful antipasto bar that offers one trip around for $12. A warm atmosphere has walls made of wood and river rock, and there are a few booths with crisp white linen seats. This is an expensive, semiformal setting that sees many executives during the lunch hours, usually wining and dining clients.

✪ **Squadritto.** Rosal 332. ☎ **2/632-2121.** Reservations recommended. Main courses $8–$12. AE, DC, MC, V. Daily 1–3pm and 7:30–11pm. ITALIAN.

The Squadritto is on a pretty street near the Plaza Mulatto de Gil, and its plant-filled, Tuscan-style dining room is a preferred setting for businesspeople in the area. It's a semiformal affair and a choice restaurant if you're looking for fine cuisine and a special place to dine. The fresh pastas are superb, with items such as salmon ravioli in a bay shrimp sauce, but there's lots else to offer, including grilled fish, beef, and chicken seasoned with herbs or a light sauce. Although the restaurant serves primarily Italian food, the fare is truly international. The wine list offers varietals ranging from $8 to $70 a bottle.

MODERATE
Bar Nacional. Bandera 317. ☎ **2/695-3368.** Main courses $7–$12; sandwiches $3–$4. DC, MC, V. Mon–Sat 8am–11pm. Closed Sun. CHILEAN.

This traditional, dinerlike restaurant has been a hit with downtown workers for decades, despite being slightly overpriced. Typical Chilean fare is served, such as *empanadas, cazuela* (a hearty chicken soup), and steak and fries, as well as surprisingly good fresh juices. There is a fixed-price lunch, which is typically gone by 3:30pm. The atmosphere is colorful, with a dated interior that serves as a great backdrop for the characters who come in to eat, gossip, and smoke, in no particular order. Although there are two Bar Nacionals (another at Paseo Huérfanos), go to the one on Bandera.

✪ **Don Vitorino.** Lastarria 138. ☎ **2/639-5263.** Main courses $9–$14. DC, MC, V. Mon–Fri 12:30–4pm and 7:30pm–1am; Fri and Sat open until 2am. Closed Sun. INTERNATIONAL/ CHILEAN.

This cozy, brick-and-wood restaurant is housed in a 16th-century annex of the neighboring Iglesia de la Veracruz and features a tiny ceramic patio with a bubbling fountain. Don Vitorino serves simply prepared fish, meat, and homemade pastas: Try the Peri-Peri fillet of beef marinated in the chef's 26 secret ingredients, and finish it off with a slice of fresh raspberry cheesecake. A good fixed-price lunch is $8, and offers more than just one option. In the evening, candlelit tables exude romance.

El Novillero. Moneda 1145. ☎ **2/699-1544.** Main courses $6–$11; $18 for *parrillada* for two. AE, DC, MC, V. Mon–Sat noon–11:30pm. STEAKHOUSE.

Meat lovers need only take the stairs down from Moneda street to the El Novillero for its ample servings of beef, chicken, pork, sausage, and liver. For a fun alternative, try the classic Chilean *parrillada,* a variety of grilled meats served on a mini-barbecue and brought sizzling to the table. You'll need to pair it with a side order, so tack on several dollars more.

✪ **Gatopardo.** Lastarria 192. ☎ **2/633-6420.** Main courses $8–$15. AE, DC, MC, V. Mon–Fri 12:30–3:30pm and 7:30pm–midnight; Sat 7:30pm–1am. Closed Sun. MEDITERRANEAN/ CHILEAN.

Excellent nouvelle cuisine has made this restaurant a local favorite. During lunch, executives head over for a fixed-price menu that can include pork loin in herb and curry sauce or for a run through the fresh salad bar, which, with the wine and dessert included, makes $9 seem like a steal. Gatopardo mixes Chilean, Mediterranean, and Bolivian specialties that might include spinach-ricotta ravioli with chopped walnuts in a Roquefort sauce. Bar appetizers are varied, from tacos and quesadillas to steamed mussels. The light, airy interior has mustard-colored walls and an atrium supported by giant oak trunks felled by an earthquake in the south of Chile.

Restaurant Jacaranda. Paseo Huérfanos 640 (set back from street). ☎ **2/639-3754.** Main courses $5.50–$12. AE, DC, MC, V. Mon–Sat 11am–10pm. FRENCH/CHILEAN.

The Norwegian immigrant who opened Jacaranda more than 30 years ago initially wanted to serve Norwegian food, but he didn't think it would fly with downtown customers. So he chose French, and found success with a menu that has repeatedly attracted customers for the coq au vin. Jacaranda's menu also features Chilean fare such as *osso buco,* or meat stewed in wine, and wild hare in a sherry sauce. The restaurant is tiny and somewhat dark during lunch; seat yourself at one of the few tables outdoors.

San Marcos. Paseo Huérfanos 618. ☎ **2/633-6880.** Reservations recommended. Main courses $7–$12. AE, DC, MC, V. Mon–Sat 8am–midnight. Metro: Univ. de Chile. ITALIAN.

For more than 50 years the San Marcos has been the preferred spot for homemade pastas. Among the wealth of raviolis, fettuccini, gnocchi, and spaghetti are highlights such as the rich *tris de pasta San Marcos* and the *lasagna alla Bolognesa,* as well as a wine list that features Chilean and Italian varieties. For dessert, try the sugary sweet *suspiro de limeño* or a classic tiramisu.

INEXPENSIVE

Chez Henry. Plaza de Armas. ☎ **2/696-6612.** Deli items vary in price. AC, DC, MC, V (restaurant only). Daily 9am–11pm. CHILEAN.

Chez Henry's cornucopia of a delicatessen offers sandwiches, hot meals, salads, soups, empanadas, pastries, even ice cream, all at very low prices. This is a great place to pick up food to go, either to eat back in the hotel room, in a park, or on one of the benches in the Plaza de Armas. At the back of the deli, you'll find the entrance to Chez Henry's restaurant, a pricier option but with good traditional Chilean dishes such as *pollo al cognac* that run $6 to $12. The restaurant's so-so atmosphere could use some improvement, but it seems less of an issue when the place is filled with diners.

✪ **Confitería Torres.** Bernardo O'Higgins 1570. ☎ **2/698-6220.** Main courses $6–$10. AE, MC, V. Daily 10:30am–1am. CHILEAN.

The Confitería Torres is recommended more for the turn-of-the-century ambience than for the food. Once you spy the mirrors fogged black around the edges and droopy chairs, you'll know that this is indeed Santiago's oldest restaurant. Old-timers will rave about the cuisine, but really it's just the same old mix-and-match menu of fries and pan-cooked meat and fish, not bad but not necessarily exciting, either. Drop in for a look if you're in the neighborhood.

Govindas. Compañía 1489. ☎ **2/673-0892.** Main courses $3–$5. No credit cards. Mon–Sat 12:30–5pm. VEGETARIAN.

This 4-year-old restaurant is a favorite among downtown office workers, both vegetarians and non-vegetarians alike. Govindas serves creative, delicious Chilean and Indian-influenced dishes, such as curried stir-fry. You'll sometimes find crêpes stuffed with seasoned vegetables, and there are always soups and sandwiches. It's mostly open only for lunch, but sometime will stay open for dinner late in the week. You'll have to call ahead.

✪ **Mercado Central.** Enter on Ismael Valdés Vergara between 21 de Mayo and Puente. No phone. Main course prices vary. AE, DC, MC, V. Sun–Thurs 6am–4pm; Fri 6am–8pm; Sat 6am–6pm. Metro: Cal y Canto. SEAFOOD.

Throughout the Mercado (see "Seeing the Sights," below) are restaurants and booths where you can savor traditional favorites such as *paila marina,* a seafood stew cooked with cilantro, *ceviche,* fish cooked in lemon juice, or the much-adored abalone *loco.* The most well-known, easiest to find, and most expensive restaurant here is Donde Augusto; however, several smaller and more economical outfits sit just at the edge of the central market. This is not a place to come for a quiet lunch, but to take part in an experience.

BELLAVISTA
EXPENSIVE

Como Agua Para Chocolate. Constitución 88. ☎ **2/777-8740.** Main courses $11–$18. DC, MC, V. Daily 1–4pm and 8pm–midnight. MEXICAN.

This newer restaurant opened to rave reviews for its innovative Mexican dishes and hip design, including terra-cotta ceramic floors, an indoor fountain, brass bed frames, and other trimmings influenced by the movie that gave this restaurant its name. You will find fajitas on the menu, but most dishes reflect authentic and revised traditional Mexican fare rather than Tex-Mex, with exotic entrees such as pheasant in mango sauce. It's a great place to go with friends for the plentiful variety of shared platters. Dishes are given offbeat names such as the salad *Suspiro de Amor,* or "sigh of love."

✪ **El Otro Sitio.** Antonia López de Bello 53. ☎ **2/777-3059.** Main courses $11–$14. AE, DC, MC, V. Daily 1–4pm and 8pm–midnight (Fri–Sat until 1:30am). PERUVIAN.

One of the best Peruvian restaurants in Santiago, this restaurant serves a savory menu of spicy, flavorful dishes, such as the *lomo saltado,* sliced beef with sautéed onions, tomatoes, and french fries. An extensive menu features a wealth of appetizers, including tangy *ceviche* and *choclo a la Huancaina,* and entrees such as lamb cooked in beer, cilantro, and herbs. The pleasant, airy interior is filled with plants and features an indoor patio lit by a skylight in the back. There's also a great old wood bar where you can sit and drink one of the excellent *pisco* sour cocktails (whose origin is still debated among Chileans and Peruvians).

✪ **San Fruttoso.** Mallinkrodt 102. ☎ **2/777-1476.** Main courses $8–$20. AE, DC, MC, V. Mon–Sat 1:15–3:30pm and 8–11:30pm; Sun open for lunch only. ITALIAN.

After earning acclaim in Asia, Peru, and the United States for his fine Italian restaurants, Roberto Revello moved to Chile and continued to find success with his restaurant San Fruttoso. Elegant dining and superb cuisine are guaranteed within the warm brick walls of this Bellavista favorite. The menu serves up highlights such as risotto, porcini mushrooms, tiramisu, and wild hare tortellini in cream. Expect to find creative takes on fish, meats, and pastas, sharp service, and an extensive wine list.

MODERATE

✪ **Azul Profundo.** Constitución 111. ☎ **2/738-0288.** Main courses $7–$13. DC, MC, V. Daily 1–4pm and 8:30pm–midnight. SEAFOOD.

If you love seafood, the "Deep Blue" is the place to come. Salmon, conger eel, swordfish, sea bass, and more come grilled or *a la plancha* (recommended, as it comes sizzling out of the kitchen on a cast-iron plate), and are served alone or with tantalizing sauces. Everything on the menu is appealing; therefore, decisions are not easily made, so try getting started with an appetizer of one of eight different kinds of *ceviche*. The cozy, nautical-themed ambience includes a wooden siren hanging from a mock ship's bow, as well as bathroom doors that look like they lead to a sailor's bunk.

✪ **Etniko.** Constitución 172. ☎ **2/732-0119.** Main courses $7–$14. AE. Daily noon–4pm and 8pm–midnight (until 2am Fri–Sat). ASIAN.

Etniko is one of Santiago's newest and hippest restaurants, serving Asian-influenced cuisine to the modern beat of house music played by resident DJs. The place is chic, sophisticated, and frequented by Santiago's fashion set. The menu offers a diverse selection, but the mainstay is the 16 varieties of sushi. Also on offer are Japanese tempura, Chinese and Vietnamese stir-frys, and Arabic dishes such as tabouli and seafood shish kabobs. The bar is a great place for a cocktail should you decide not to eat, and there is an extensive wine and champagne menu.

✪ **Kilometre 11680.** Dardignac 0145. ☎ **2/777-0410.** Main courses $10–$17. AE. Mon–Thurs and Sat 8pm–1am; Fri lunch only noon–4pm. FRENCH BISTRO.

The two French wine lovers who own Kilometre came to Chile to sample its varietals and ended up opening this bistro to offer what is possibly the best wine list in town. There are nearly 150 varieties of Chilean wine on the menu, including export varieties you won't find in stores. Each week they choose a special, expensive wine by the glass to try so you won't have to buy an entire bottle. The dining area is made of wood and brick and accented with cork-bottle walls and other wine motifs. The food includes Santiago's only fresh foie gras, as well as baked goat cheese, duck confit, tarte tatin, fish, and meats. The only day it's open for lunch is Friday, when there is a fixed-price menu for $11.

La Tasca Mediterreana. Purísima 165. ☎ **2/735-3901.** Main courses $5–$11. AE, DC, MC, V. Mon–Fri noon–1:30am; Sat noon–3am. MEDITERRANEAN.

La Tasca is part restaurant, part cafe, and dinner or lunch may be served at either side from the same menu. The cozy restaurant has long, dark wood tables, wood beams, and white stucco walls; the cafe's tiny, candlelit tables, with red tablecloths and its nook in the back stuffed with literature and poetry, are an ideal place for a light dinner and good conversation. The simple Mediterranean dishes include meats and fish seasoned with homemade ingredients, and there is a good selection of wine by the glass. The waitstaff is friendly, and there is jazz piano in the cafe starting at midnight on Saturdays.

INEXPENSIVE

El Caramaño. Purísima 257. ☎ **2/737-7043.** Main courses $3–$9. AE, DC, MC, V. Daily 1–4pm and 7pm–12:30am. CHILEAN.

They call themselves the "anti-restaurant," and they're probably right. The Caramaño is totally anonymous from the street, and diners might miss it because there isn't a sign—but just ring the front bell to enter. Inside, graffiti-scrawled walls are something of a contrast to the tables filled with men and women in suits. Service is casual, and the food simple, inexpensive, and very good, which is reason enough to check out this oddball restaurant.

Galindo. Dardignac 098. ☎ **2/777-0116.** Main courses $3.50–$9; fixed lunch $5. AE, DC, MC, V. Mon–Sat noon–3am. CHILEAN.

This local favorite is a hit for its cheap prices and its *comida casera:* simple, hearty dishes like your mother used to make, if your mother were Chilean, that is. Virtually any kind of typical meal served in Chilean homes can be found here, including *pastel de choclo, cazuela,* and *porotos con chorizo.* The atmosphere is very casual; in the evening the restaurant serves as a meeting place for writers, artists, and other local folk to share a bottle of wine and good conversation. There's additional seating outside on the sidewalk, and it's open late into the evening.

PROVIDENCIA

Avenida Suecia in Providencia and the several streets that surround it are commonly referred to as *gringolandia,* or "little America," for its eerie resemblance to a commercial center in the United States. Happy hours and a couple of restaurants serving typical American food, including Cajun, can be found here, but opinions about the neighborhood are mixed. After all, this is Chile, isn't it? Either way, there are a few gems to be rooted out here, and a few bars good for a nightcap. The best way to find them is to simply head over and take a look.

EXPENSIVE

✪ **Aquí Está Coco.** La Concepción 236. ☎ **2/235-8649.** Main courses $9–$16. AE, DC, MC, V. Mon–Sat 1–3pm and 8–10:30pm. SEAFOOD.

This one-of-a-kind restaurant not only serves superb seafood, it's also a fun place to dine. Housed in a 140-year-old home with more nooks and crannies than one can reasonably navigate, including a brick cellar bar lined with dusty bottles, the restaurant is owned by one charismatic Jorge "Coco" Pacheco, who gave the place its name: "Here's Coco." Jorge traveled the world for 3 years and brought back boxes of crazy knickknacks and a wealth of tantalizing recipes, both of which give Aquí Está Coco its unique flavor. Nearly every kind of seafood is offered, including trout stuffed with crab, hake, swordfish, cod, sea bass, and more, served with sauces such as caper, black butter, or tomato-wine. The appetizers are mouth-watering, such as crab cakes or broiled scallops in a barnacle sauce. Every inch of the place is decorated with kooky, nautically themed curios.

✪ **Enoteca/Camino Real.** Parque Metropolitano, Cerro San Cristóbal. ☎ **2/232-1758.** Main courses $15–$25; fixed lunches/dinners $20. AE, DC, MC, V. Daily 12:30–3:30pm and 8pm–midnight. INTERNATIONAL/CHILEAN.

There's nothing quite like dining in Santiago with the city lights twinkling at your feet. This restaurant/wine bar and museum is located atop Cerro San Cristóbal, affording sweeping views across the valley and up to the Andes. The restaurant takes full advantage of its location by spreading its tables about an L-shaped dining area enclosed in glass. The old smog factor is an issue if you come for lunch, but even bad air can't mask the thousands of lights at night. The cuisine is good, although one could certainly find more outstanding restaurants in the *barrios* below. What you're here for is the view. The menu serves a wide mix of international cuisine, including beef, chicken, seafood, and pasta. An on-site wine museum and cellar guarantees an excellent selection.

MODERATE

A Pinch of Pancho. General de Canto 45. ☎ **2/235-1700.** Main courses $6–$13. AE, DC, MC, V. Daily 1–3:30pm and 8–11:30pm. NORTH AMERICAN.

This restaurant serves American fare, such as barbecue ribs, Cajun chicken, and Caesar salads, in a rather odd crossover atmosphere between comfortable elegance and American kitsch. The place is hidden behind a white, plant-covered metal fence, and there is no sign apart from the door. Impeccable service and a menu that is 100% recognizable by Americans are the reasons you usually see a few U.S. businessmen having lunch here on weekdays. Don't miss the mouth-watering desserts, even apple pie à la mode.

Café El Patio. Av. Providencia 1670. ☎ **2/236-1251.** Main courses $5.50–$9. DC, MC, V. Mon–Thurs noon–midnight; Fri–Sat noon–1:30am; Sun 12:30–4pm. VEGETARIAN.

A welcome break from hectic Avenida Providencia, the location at the back of a tranquil little plaza is just one thing that makes this vegetarian restaurant great. Fresh salads include Greek, chef, Chinese, and more, and all vegetables come from the owner's organic farm. The slightly bohemian atmosphere is cozy, and food is served by good-looking waiters dressed in black. This restaurant is especially nice when jazz musicians play on Thursdays and Fridays. There are a few tables outside in the darkwood-and-glass-walled patio.

Cap Ducal. Av. Suecia 281. Reservations recommended on weekends. ☎ **2/231-1400.** Fax 2/334-7679. Main courses $6–$12. AE, DC, MC, V. Daily 1–3:30pm and 8:30pm–2am. SEAFOOD/CHILEAN.

As with the Cap Ducal's other location in Viña del Mar, this version serves fresh seafood shipped in daily from the Pacific coast. Although this is their specialty, the Cap Ducal also serves grilled meats, chicken, and a small selection of pasta. Two floors of tables draped with white linen tablecloths, polished wood floors, and soft light create a refined atmosphere. The food is good, but perhaps the best thing about the Cap Ducal is that it is open every day of the year and it's open late—sometimes until 3am. The restaurant is located in the Suecia neighborhood.

✪ **El Huerto.** Orrego Luco 054. ☎ **2/233-2690.** Main courses $4–$10. AE, DC, MC, V. Mon–Thurs 12:30pm–midnight; Fri–Sat 12:30pm–1am. Cafe opens at 9am. VEGETARIAN.

Some call the popular El Huerto the best vegetarian restaurant in Santiago, and with reason: The chefs whip up creative, appetizing dishes, from burritos to pasta to Chinese stir-frys. Add one of their fresh apple, raspberry, or peach juices, and it makes for a wonderful meal. Prices have risen slightly recently, and the owners have opened up a more economical cafe, *La Huerta,* next door (at the left), with a limited but good menu and fixed-price lunch. The softly lit, mellow dining room of El Huerto is a cool place to relax on a summer day. The restaurant also has a shop that sells books, postcards, and arts and crafts.

INEXPENSIVE

✪ **Bar Liguria.** Av. Providencia 1373 . ☎ **2/235-7914.** Main courses $4–$9. No credit cards. Mon–Wed 10am–noon; Thurs–Sat 10am–2am; Closed Sun. Metro: Pedro de Valdivia. CHILEAN BISTRO.

This is one of my favorite places in Santiago. It's vibrant and warm and is the "in" spot in Providencia for actors, businesspeople, and young people in the area. It's a great restaurant with tiny alcoves and corners to hide in, and a long wooden bar for dining and drinking. The menu is bistro-style, with about 15 entrees and a selection of soups and sandwiches. At lunch, every order is preceded by an appetizer of fresh clams on the house. The walls are adorned with Chilean kitsch, including movie posters, street signs, pictures of soccer stars, advertisements, and so on. Good service is provided by plentiful waiters in black bow ties. In the evening, the Bar Liguria is tremendously popular, especially for the potent *pisco* sours, and you might have to wait for a table. Outdoor seating is available on the sidewalk, but the occasional whoosh of air from the subway grate is unsettling.

Fuente Aleman. On Av. Pedro de Valdivia at Av. 11 de Septiembre. No phone. Sandwiches $3–$5; main dishes $3–$6.50. No credit cards. Mon–Sat 10am–11pm. DINER.

Popular for huge, delicious sandwiches, these German soda fountains can be found throughout the middle and southern half of Chile. They're similar to diners: lots of fluorescent light, counter seating, and waitresses in plain uniforms and hairnets. This new location of Fuente Aleman serves hefty *churrasco* sandwiches, sliced beef on freshly baked bread, with cheese, avocado, or sauerkraut. The chicken sandwich with red pepper is good, too, and all require a knife and fork. Main dishes are standard *escalopas,* deep-fried fish, and a daily lunch special (but no fixed-price menu).

LAS CONDES/EL BOSQUE

Around El Bosque and Goyenechea streets you'll find everything and anything, from upscale French cuisine to fast-food courts. The majority of sit-down restaurants here are pricey, but you'll find bagels at **New York Bakery,** Roger de Flor 2894 (no phone), and a **Friday's,** Goyenechea 3275 (no phone), with a sports bar and beefy hamburgers.

EXPENSIVE

Coco Loco. El Bosque Norte 0215. ☎ **2/231-3082.** Main courses $9–$15. AE, DC, MC, V. Daily noon–4pm and 7pm–midnight. SEAFOOD.

Out-of-towners flock to this restaurant in droves for its fresh seafood and attractive dining area (which has a fishing boat indoors that is armed with tables). It's all here: sea bass, hake, conger eel, and more, grilled and prepared with a variety of tasty sauces. If you can't decide, opt for the *parrillada* Coco Loco, with a medley of fruits of the sea. The menu is overpriced, as are most restaurants in this neighborhood.

✪ **El Club.** El Bosque Norte 0380. ☎ **2/246-1222.** Main courses $7–$15. AE, DC, MC, V. Daily noon–12:30am. CHILEAN.

The Club feels like one, especially during the day when businesspeople, politicians, and the odd sports star come to lunch and cut a deal. The restaurant is especially appealing on a summer evening when it opens its giant glass walls and lets tables spill onto the street. The inexhaustible menu features shellfish, meats, pastas, and Chilean classics such as *pastel de jaiba* (snow-crab casserole) and *niñitos revueltos* (rolled meats filled with eggs and vegetables). The varied wine list is surprisingly cheap and although the interior is a bit bland, with maroon tablecloths and plastic chairs, it's a great spot to sit and people-watch.

✪ **La Cascade.** Av. Isidora Goyenechea 2930. ☎ **2/232-2798.** Reservations recommended. Main courses $7–$15. AE, DC, MC, V. Mon–Sat noon–4pm and 8pm–midnight. FRENCH.

This traditional French restaurant has been on the scene since 1962, drawing Santiago's elite to savor traditional dishes such as coq au vin, duck à l'orange, escargot, and goose liver pâté. The menu is varied and includes meat, fowl, and seafood entrees, as well as an extensive wine list. Waiters in white waistcoats deliver outstanding personal attention, and the atmosphere is elegant and stylish, with attractive paintings and white linen tablecloths.

Pinpilinpausha. Av. Isidora Goyenechea 2900. ☎ **2/232-5800.** Main courses $10–$15. AE, DC, MC, V. Mon–Sat 12:30–11:30pm; Sun 12:30–4pm. SPANISH.

The long name means "butterfly" in Basque, the heritage of the Sanz family who has owned this restaurant since the 1940s. Pinpilinpausha operated downtown for 55 years and relocated here in Las Condes in an effort to upgrade the atmosphere, menu, and service. The essential menu hasn't deviated too much, and they still serve paella. The shellfish, fish, and meat dishes are all excellent, especially the conger eel stuffed with shrimp and served with a tart lemon sauce. The newer design strives for a rustic, Mediterranean feel, with terra-cotta walls and green-and-white checkered tablecloths. There are pleasant, quiet tables in a side hall along a row of windows.

5 Seeing the Sights

Visitors to Santiago should allow at least 2 or 3 days to get to know the city. But even if you have just 1 day in Santiago, you should be able to pack in a sizeable amount of the city's top attractions. It's a push, but nearly all attractions lie within a short walk or taxi ride from each other, which makes it easy to pick and choose according to your interests.

The best place to begin is in *el centro,* the city's historic downtown and home to museums, cathedrals, cultural centers, and civic institutions housed within handsome, neoclassical-style buildings. If you're an architecture buff or simply enjoy marveling at stately mansions, you'll want to spend a half hour exploring the sinuous streets of the Barrio París-Londres and then head to Calle Dieciocho, a street whose stone palaces convey the wealth of Santiago's elite at the turn of the 20th century.

If you're lucky enough to have a smog-free day, you won't want to miss heading to the top of one of the city's hilltop parks for a sweeping view of the rugged, snowcapped Andes that rise dramatically behind the city. If you have a little more time and just feel like strolling the city streets and watching *Santiaguinos* go about their daily business, you'll want to spend an afternoon in the residential and commercial neighborhoods of Providencia and Las Condes.

DOWNTOWN HISTORIC & CIVIC ATTRACTIONS
PLAZA DE ARMAS

Begin your tour of Santiago at the historic heart of the city, the ✪ **Plaza de Armas,** which can be reached by taking the Metro to Estación Plaza de Armas. The plaza was founded by Pedro de Valdivia in 1541 as the civic nucleus of the country, and its importance was such that all distances to other parts of Chile were, and still are, measured from here.

The impressive plaza was surrounded by the Royal Court of Justice (now the Natural History Museum), the Governor's Palace (now the Central Post Office), the Metropolitan Cathedral, and the grand residences of principal conquistadors, including Valdivia himself. In the mid-1800s, the plaza was fitted with gardens and trees, creating a promenade that became a social center for fashionable society. Towering trees from that era and billowy Chilean palms still shade park benches, although the plaza was remodeled again during the building of a new Metro station 2 years ago. The plaza is not only a wonderful place to sit, relax, or read, but is also a great place to watch the colorful characters milling about—old street photographers with box cameras, men lingering over chess games, shouting religious fanatics, office workers having their shoes shined, young couples strolling hand in hand, and artists hawking paintings.

There are several monuments here: a giant chiseled-stone sculpture dedicated to indigenous peoples; an equestrian statue of Pedro de Valdivia; a monument to the first Chilean Cardinal José María Caro; and *A la Libertad de América,* a marble statue commemorating independence from Spain, near the center of the plaza.

Catedral Metropolitana & Museo de Arte Sagrado. Paseo Ahumada, on the west side of the plaza. No phone. Free admission. Mon–Sat 9am–7pm; Sun 9am–noon. Metro: Plaza de Armas.

The Metropolitan Cathedral occupies nearly an entire city block, and it is the fifth cathedral to have been erected at this site. The cathedral began construction in 1748 but was completed in 1780 by the Italian architect Joaquín Toesca, who gave the building its neoclassical-Baroque facade. Toesca virtually launched his career with this cathedral, and he went on to design many important buildings in colonial Chile, including La Moneda and the Governor's Palace. Tremendous doors made of cypress carved by Jesuits open into three interior naves with pews made of carved wood. The central nave holds the cathedral's ornate alter, brought from Munich in 1912 and made of marble, bronze, and lapis lazuli. Just off the main body of the church is the cathedral's religious museum, the Museo de Arte Sagrado, where you'll find a collection of paintings, furniture, antique manuscripts, and silverwork handcrafted by Jesuits.

Correo Central & Museo Postal. Calle Puente, north side of the plaza. ☎ **2/601-0141.** Free admission. Mon–Fri 9am–5pm. Metro: Plaza de Armas.

The pink, Renaissance-style Central Post Office was built in 1882 on the remains of what was once the colonial Governor's Palace and the post-independence Presidential Palace. After the building succumbed to fire in 1881, workers rebuilt, incorporating several of the old building's walls. In 1908, architect Ramón Feherman added a third floor and a gorgeous, metal-framed glass cupola. On the second floor, you'll find a small museum whose main interest is its stamp collection.

✪ Palacio de la Real Audencia/Museo Historico Nacional. Plaza de Armas 951. ☎ **2/681-4095.** Admission 80¢ adults, 40¢ under 18; free Sun and holidays. Tues–Sat 10am–5:30pm; Sun and holidays 10am–1pm. Metro: Plaza de Armas.

Sandwiched between the post office and Santiago's municipal building is the Palacio de la Real, built between 1804 and 1807 by a student of architect Toesca who followed his preference for neoclassical design. The building has undergone several transformations, but the facade is still intact. The Palacio functioned for 2 years as a Supreme Court under Spanish rule, and then became the historic site of the first Chilean congressional session following independence. Today, the Palacio holds the fascinating National History Museum, which displays a grab bag of more than 70,000 items from the colonial period, including antiques, clothing, suits of armor, weapons, home appliances, industrial gadgets, flags, you name it. There are 16 display rooms, some devoted to the colonial period and one devoted entirely to Bernardo O'Higgins. There is also a collection of money and medallions through the years, including tokens used at salt mines, and an interpretive timeline and photo montage of Chilean history.

NEAR THE PLAZA DE ARMAS

At the southwest corner of the plaza you'll find **Ahumada Street,** which bisects **Huérfanos** a block away; both are lively pedestrian walkways lined with every imaginable shop and dozens of inexpensive lunch restaurants. The streets can get frenzied during the lunch hour when downtown workers scramble from place to place, but it's a fun spot to watch *Santiaguinos* go about their business. This is also where you'll find a few of the city's renowned cafes that serve "coffee with legs," meaning waitresses in skimpy ensembles serving ogling businessmen from behind a stand-up bar. **Café Haiti** (☎ **2/697-1810**) and **Café Caribe** (☎ **2/639-5041**) are two of the more well-known cafes, and because both are fairly tame compared to the raunchier versions with darkened windows, these two cafes are patronized by women as well as men.

۞ Casa Colorada & Museo de Santiago. Merced 860. ☎ **2/633-0723**. Admission $1. Tues–Fri 10am–6pm; Sat 10am–5pm; Sun 10am–1pm. Metro: Plaza de Armas.

The Casa Colorada is a half block from the Plaza de Armas, an antique structure made of stone whose color gives it its name—"The Red House." It's widely regarded as the best-preserved colonial structure in Santiago, built between 1769 and 1779 as a residence for the first president of Chile, Mateo de Toro y Zambrano. Today, the Casa Colorada operates as the Santiago Museum, depicting the urban history of the city until the 19th century. The museum is small but interesting and worth the visit to marvel at the architecture and browse through the museum's bookstore. A **visitor's center** with information about Santiago is also located in the Casa Colorada.

Basilica de la Merced. Mac Iver 341, corner of Merced. No phone. Admission 75¢ adults, 25¢ students. Tues–Fri 10am–1pm and 3–6pm; Sat 10am–1pm. Metro: Plaza de Armas.

One block from the Casa Colorada on Merced at the corner of MacIver sits this intriguing, neo-Renaissance–style church and museum. Built in 1735, the church boasts a magnificent Bavarian Baroque pulpit and arched naves. The museum, surprisingly, has an excellent collection of Easter Island art, including wooden Moai sculptures. There are also 78 wood and ivory Christ Child figures, among other religious artifacts.

۞ Museo Chileno de Arte Precolombino. Bandera 361. ☎ **2/688-7348**. Admission $1.75 adults, free for students; free Sat, Sun, and holidays for everyone. Tues–Fri 10am–6pm; Sun and holidays 10am–2pm.

Heading back on Merced and past the plaza to Bandera, you'll find the excellent Museo Chileno de Arte Precolombino, housed in the old Royal Customs House that was built in neoclassical design in 1807. This is one of the best museums in all of Chile, both for its collection of pre-Columbian artifacts and its inviting design. There are more than 1,500 objects on display here, including textiles, metals, paintings, figurines, and ceramics spread through seven exhibition rooms. It's not a stuffy old museum, but a vivid exhibition of indigenous life and culture before the arrival of the Spanish. The material spans from Mexico to Chile, incorporating all regions of Latin America divided into four areas: Mesoamérica, Intermedia, Andina, and Surandina. Each display is attractively mounted and infinitely absorbing—you'll really be missing out if you don't plan a stop here. Downstairs there's a patio cafe and a well-stocked bookstore that also sells music, videos, and reproductions of Indian art, textiles, and jewelry.

Ex Congreso Nacional & Palacio de los Tribunales. Morandé and Compañía. No phone. Palacio: Mon–Fri 1–7pm.

Two blocks from Plaza de Armas you'll find these two grand civic buildings across the street from each other on Compañía. The ex-Congress Building, with its French neoclassical design and Corinthian pillars, is a handsome edifice inaugurated in 1901. The National Congress convened here until the coup d'état on September 11, 1973, which dissolved Congress; Pinochet eventually moved the Congress to Valparaíso. The dove-white building is surrounded by lush gardens with a couple of benches, and is now occupied by a branch of the Ministry of Foreign Affairs. Across the street, the Palace of the Courts of Justice stretches the entire city block. The Palace is home to the Supreme Court, the Appeals Court, and the Military Court, and historically it was the site of the birth of the First National Government Assembly. The building's stern exterior belies the beauty found once you step inside. Leave your ID at the front, and take a stroll through the exquisite hallway whose vaulted metal and glass ceiling runs the length of the building, dappling the walls with light.

PLAZA CONSTITUCIÓN & THE COMMERCE CENTER

The Plaza Constitución, located between streets Agustinas, Morandé, Moneda, and Teatinos, is an expansive plaza used primarily as a pedestrian crossway. It's also the site of the famous ✪ **Palacio de la Moneda,** the Government Palace that was first built as headquarters of the Royal Mint (hence its name). The largest building erected by the Spanish government during the 18th century, the Palace was the focus of much criticism for being too ostentatious, but today it's considered one of the finest examples of neoclassical architecture in Latin America.

Joaquín Toesca, the Italian architect responsible for setting the neoclassical tone of civic buildings in Santiago, directed the design of the Palace until his death in 1799. From 1846 to 1958 it was the official presidential residence, and continued as presidential headquarters until the infamous coup d'état on September 11, 1973, when Pinochet's troops shelled and bombed the building until ex-President Allende surrendered by suicide. The military has since patched up the damage they inflicted.

Tours of the Palacio are difficult to arrange, and must be done so nearly a month in advance by contacting Oscar Pizarro (☎ 2/690-4000; fax 2/690-4096); you must give names of those in your party and their addresses, telephone numbers, and passport numbers. A better option would be to try to catch the impressive **changing of the guard,** when hundreds of soldiers march in step in front of the Palace, every other day at 10am. Across Alameda is the **Plaza Bernardo O'Higgins.** His remains are buried under the monument dedicated to him in the center of the plaza.

One block from the plaza at Moneda and Bandera is the **Bolsa de Comercio** (☎ 2/695-8077), Santiago's stock market exchange, housed in a 1917 national monument building with a beautiful metal dome roof. Inside, traders group around *La Rueda* (The Wheel), a circular railing where they conduct hectic transactions—you can even watch the action Monday to Friday 10:30 to 11:20am, 12:30 to 1:20pm, and 4 to 4:30pm. The Bolsa de Comercio is a triangular building set among several picturesque, cobblestoned streets that make for an intriguing short stroll: New York, La Bolsa, and Club de la Unión.

ATTRACTIONS OFF THE ALAMEDA

Hectic Avenida Bernardo O'Higgins is commonly referred to as *la Alameda,* and it's the main artery that runs through downtown Santiago. It's a roaring muddle of cars and buses and has only a few well-defined crosswalks. Nevertheless, you'll find some of the city's interesting attractions along this avenue.

✪ **Calle Deiciocho & Palacio Cousiño.** Dieciocho 438. ☎ **2/698-5063.** Admission $2 adults, $1 children under 12. Bilingual tours given Tues–Fri 9:30am–1:30pm and 2:30–5pm; Sat–Sun 9:30am–1:30pm.

Heading west on Alameda, past the giant Entel tower, will put you at Deiciocho Street, an elegant neighborhood of ornate mansions built by wealthy families at the turn of the century. The first few homes are on the corners of Deiciocho and Alameda, including the 1873 Palacio Errázuriz, now home to the Brazilian Embassy; the 1917 Palacio Arieztía; and the Iglesia San Vicente de Paul. These palaces were designed using beautiful European architectural styles, especially French.

The crème de la crème is the Palacio Cousiño, located several blocks down Deiciocho Street, today a museum and testament to the obscene wealth of one of Chile's most successful entrepreneurial dynasties, the Goyenechea-Cousiño family. In addition to their well-known wine business and ownership of the Lota coal mines, the family had interests in copper, thoroughbred horses, shipping, and railways. Inside, visitors are typically taken aback by the opulent interiors lavished with parquet floors, tapestries, ceramics, Bohemian crystal chandeliers, and furniture imported from Europe—along with European craftsmen to handcraft the interiors.

To get here, you'll have to walk (it's 8 blocks from the Plaza Bernardo O'Higgins), take a taxi, or ride the Metro to Estación Toesca. If you're walking back to downtown from here, head through the Parque Diego de Almagro near Palacio Cousiño and turn left up to Alameda via Paseo Bulnes until you reach O'Higgins. At the end of the Parque Diego de Almagro is the grand **Basilica del Santisimo Sacramento,** constructed between 1919 and 1931 and modeled after the church in Montmartre, France. If you've gone this far, you might want to continue to the row of **rare bookstores** located just beyond the church.

✪ **Barrio París-Londres.** The streets between Prat and Santa Rosa, walking south of Alameda O'Higgins.

This charming, singular neighborhood with its narrow cobblestoned streets was built between the 1920s and '30s on the old gardens of the Monastery of San Francisco. The neighborhood consists of small mansions, each with a different facade, that today house artists, students, and cultural centers. The neighborhood was designated a national monument in 1982, and its streets are now pedestrian walkways.

✪ **Iglesia, Convento y Museo de San Francisco.** Avenida Bernardo O'Higgins. ☎ **2/638-3238.** Admission Convent and Museum: 50¢ adults, 25¢ children. Tues–Sat 10am–1pm and 3–6pm; Sun and holidays 10am–2pm.

The Church of San Francisco is the oldest standing building in Santiago, and although this landmark has been renovated over the years, the main structure has miraculously survived three devastating earthquakes. At the altar sits the famous *Vírgen del Socorro,* the first Virgin Mary icon in Chile, brought here to Santiago by Pedro de Valdivia. The highlights, however, are the museum and the convent, the latter with its idyllic patio planted with flora brought from destinations as near as the south of Chile and as far away as the Canary Islands. The garden is so serene, you'll find it hard to believe you're in downtown Santiago. The museum boasts 54 paintings depicting the life and death of San Francisco, one of the largest and best-conserved displays of 17th-century art in South America.

Biblioteca Nacional. Avenida Bernardo O'Higgins 651. ☎ **2/360-5259.** Mon–Fri 9am–6:30pm; Sat 9am–1pm.

The venerable National Library is housed in a French neoclassical stone building that occupies an entire city block. Inside its handsomely painted interiors are over six million works as well as historical archives and a map room. Don't miss the classic leather and wood splendor of the Jose Medina reading room, with antique books stacked in tiers, leather-topped reading desks, and a giant spinning globe.

CERRO SANTA LUCÍA & PLAZA MULATO GIL DE CASTRO

Cerro Santa Lucía is a hilltop park located steps from the Biblioteca Nacional on Alameda and Santa Lucía. It's open Monday to Sunday 9am to 8pm from September to March, 9am to 7pm from April to August; free admission. The Mapuches called this rocky hill *Huelén* (curse) until Pedro de Valdivia renamed it Santa Lucía in 1540. In 1872, the area was expanded to create walkways and small squares for the public's entertainment, and now office workers, tourists, couples, schoolchildren, and solitary thinkers can be seen strolling along leafy terraces to the Caupolicán Plaza for a sweeping view of Santiago. The plaza also serves as the site of theater and concerts in the summer.

Continue along the garden walk to Castle Hidalgo, built in 1820 and now an event center. To get to the top, begin at the stone monument staircase on Santa Lucía and O'Higgins, or take the glass elevator up a bit farther on Santa Lucía. Although there have been reports that safety has improved, keep an eye open for suspicious characters if you choose to climb up at sunset. At the staircase you'll also find the **Centro de Exposición de Arte,** with a large assortment of Indian-influenced crafts, clothing, and jewelry on display and for sale. Across the street is a bustling crafts and junk market, the **Centro Artesanal de Santa Lucía,** with handicrafts, T-shirts, and more.

Behind the park, at José Victorino Lastarria 307, you'll find the **Plaza Mulato Gil de Castro** (closed Sundays). Named for the 18th-century Peruvian Army captain and portrait painter José Gil, who lived in the neighborhood, this quaint plaza is a great place to explore, grab a cup of coffee, or have lunch (there are a handful of good restaurants in the area). The plaza sits in the middle of rows of beautiful stone mansions and features a crafts shop and bookstore. On Lastarria Street near La Alameda is an art-film cinema and another bohemian cafe, **El Biógrafo** (☎ 2/633-4435).

PARQUE FORESTAL

This slender, well-manicured park, built in 1900 and lined with rows of native and imported trees, skirts the perimeter of the Río Mapocho from Vicuña Mackenna at the Metro station Baquedano to its terminus at the Mapocho station. Along the way the winding path takes walkers past several great attractions, and it makes for a pleasant 1- to 2-hour stroll, especially on a sunny afternoon when the air is clear. If you plan to walk the entire park, try to finish at the Mercado Central for lunch.

Palacio de Bellas Artes. Parque Forestal, by way of Jose Miguel de la Barra. ☎ **2/632-7760.** Admission Museum of Fine Arts 75¢ adults, 35¢ students; Museum of Contemporary Art 55¢ adults, 30¢ students. Museum of Fine Arts daily 10am–7pm; Museum of Contemporary Art Tues–Fri 11am–7pm, Sat–Sun 11am–2pm.

The Palacio de Bellas Artes houses both the Fine Arts and Contemporary Art museums (with separate entrances and admissions) in a regal, neoclassical building inaugurated on the eve of Chile's centennial independence day in 1910. The Palace has a noteworthy glass cupola that softly lights the vast lobby. The importance of the permanent installations in the Fine Arts museum may be debatable (an uneven mix of Chilean and international artists' works since the colonial period), but they occasionally host great temporary exhibitions. The Contemporary Museum features more than 2,000 paintings, sculptures, and other works by well-known Latin artists.

✪ **Mercado Central.** Vergara and Av. 21 de Mayo. No phone. Daily 7am–3pm. Metro: Calicanto.

Just before reaching the Estación Mapocho, you'll pass the colorful, chaotic world of the Mercado Central. This lively market sells fruits and vegetables, handicrafts, and rows and rows of slippery fish and shellfish displayed on chipped ice, some familiar, others odd fruits of the sea that can be found only off the shores of Chile. Depending on your perspective, the barking fishmongers and waitresses who harangue you to choose *their* zucchini, *their* sea bass, *their* restaurant, can be entertaining or somewhat annoying. Either way, don't miss it, especially for the market's lofty, steel structure that was fabricated in England and assembled here in 1868; it was originally intended as a gallery for national artists. Try to plan your visit during the lunch hour, for a rich bowl of *caldillo de congrio* or a tangy *ceviche* at one of the many typical restaurants (see "Where to Dine," above).

Estación Mapocho. Bandera and Río Mapocho. ☎ **2/361-1761.** www.estacionmapocho. cl. Daily 9am–5pm; other hours according to events.

Built in 1912 on reclaimed land formed by the canalization of the Río Mapocho, this behemoth of a building served as the train station for the Santiago–Valparaíso railway. In 1976 it was abandoned, and 15 years later repaired and converted into a cultural center that hosts events such as the yearly International Book Fair. It's worth a stop to admire the tremendous structure, which has a copper roof made of 40 tons of metal, as well as marble and glass. You'll also find a bookstore, restaurants, and theaters.

BARRIO BELLAVISTA & PARQUE METROPOLITANO (CERRO SAN CRISTÓBAL)

These two attractions lie next to one another, so it makes sense to see both in one visit. But here's a word of caution: The extensive views that come with an ascent to the top of Cerro San Cristóbal can be ruined if it is a particularly smoggy day. But if the air is clear, this attraction rates as one of the best in the city, offering a breathtaking panorama of sprawling Santiago and its city limits that stop just short of the craggy Andes. The Cerro San Cristóbal and its Metropolitan Park rise high above Santiago's bohemian hamlet ✪ **Bellavista.**

One of the more interesting neighborhoods in the city, its streets are lined with trees and colorful antique homes, many of which have been converted into great restaurants and studios for artists and musicians. It's a pleasant place for an afternoon stroll; in the evening, Bellavista pulses to the sound of music pouring from its many discos and bars.

You might begin your visit with a trip to Bellavista's prime attraction, ✪ **La Chascona,** near the zoo and the entrance point to the Parque Metropolitano on Fernando Márquez de la Plata 0192 (☎ **2/777-8741**); admission is $2 adults, $1 students and seniors, and it's open Tuesday to Sunday 10am to 1pm and 3 to 6pm. This is one of three homes once owned by the brilliant, Nobel Prize–winning poet Pablo Neruda. It was built for his third wife, Matilde, and its name refers to her unruly hair. As with Neruda's other two homes, La Chascona was built to resemble a ship, with oddly shaped rooms that wind around a compact courtyard. It's fascinating to wander through Neruda's quirky home and observe his collection of precious antiques and whimsical curios collected during his travels. Neruda's library is especially interesting, and it holds the antique encyclopedia set he purchased with a portion of his earnings from the Nobel Prize. The home is headquarters for the Fundación Pablo Neruda, which provides the guided tours.

The **Parque Metropolitano** is a 730-hectare (1,803-acre) park and recreation area with swimming pools, walking trails, a botanical garden, a zoo, picnic grounds, restaurants, and children's play areas. It's the lungs of Santiago, and city dwellers use the hill's roads and trails for jogging, biking, or just taking a stroll. The park is divided into two sectors, Cumbre and Tupahue, both of which are accessed by car, cable car, funicular, or foot. In Bellavista, head to the end of Pío Nono Street to Plaza Caupolican, where you'll encounter a 1925 **funicular** that lifts visitors up to a lookout point, open Monday to Friday 10am to 7:30pm, Saturday and Sunday 10am to 8pm; tickets cost $1.50 adults, $1 children. Along the way, the funicular stops at the **Jardín Zoológico,** open Monday to Sunday 10am to 6pm; admission is $3 adults, 75¢ children. This zoo features more than 200 species of mammals, reptiles, and birds, but it's a rather outmoded, sad affair, and many animals are confined to tiny cages. The lookout point is watched over by a 22-meter-high (72-ft.) statue of the **Virgen de la Inmaculada Concepción,** which can be seen from all over the city. Below the statue is the *teleférico* (cable car) that connects the two sections of the park, open Monday to Friday 11am to 6pm, Saturday and Sunday 10:30am to 7:30pm. Tickets cost $2.25 adults, $1 children; ticket combinations with the funicular cost $3 adults, $1.50 children. The gondola offers great views while suspended high above the park before arriving at Tupahue, which is the Mapuche name for this hill, meaning "place of God." Here you'll find the **Piscina Tupahue,** an attractive, rock-lined swimming pool (no phone). The pool is open Tuesday to Friday 10am to 6pm, Saturday and Sunday 10am to 7pm; admission for adults is $8 Monday to Friday, $9 Saturday to Sunday; children $6 Monday to Friday, $6.50 Saturday to Sunday. A walk down the road will take you to the **Camino Real** and its wine museum **Museo Enoteca** (☎ 2/232-1758). The museum is disappointing, but the restaurant is worth the visit for the marvelous views from the dining area and patio (see "Where to Dine," above). The museum offers a basic wine tasting at a bar that's relatively inexpensive. Nearby is the **Botanical Garden Mapulemu** (no phone). It's open daily 9am to 6pm; admission is 25¢ Saturday to Sunday. From Tupahue you can either head back on the gondola to Cumbre and the funicular, or take the Valdivia *teleférico* down, which will drop you off at the end of Avenida Pedro de Valdivia. It's also possible to head back down by foot following a road that ends at Avenida Valdivia, passing first by the Plaza Gabriela Mistral. Of course, this trip can be done in the reverse direction, which might be more convenient if you're starting from Providencia or Las Condes.

If you're driving up to the park, you can drive via the Valdivia entrance road that continues at the end of Pío Nono, winding around first to Tupahue, then to Cumbre, or via the road that climbs up from Avenida Pedro de Valdivia. The admission fee for cars is $2 per vehicle. It's also possible to take a taxi up, but you'll need to pay the park entrance fee as well as the fare. This is the only return option for late diners at the Camino Real. The Parque Metropolitano's hours are daily 8:30am to 9pm, cars until 10pm. There are also buses that go up Pío Nono and down Avenida Pedro de Valdivia.

PARQUE QUINTA NORMAL

If you still can't get enough of museums, take a taxi to the **Parque Quinta Normal,** located at 502 Matucana. This 39-hectare (96-acre) park was first used as an animal breeding site and acclimatization park for imported trees; today it's home to lawns, a wide variety of non-native trees, and a lagoon with boats. It's also home to the **Museo Nacional de Historia Natural** (☎ 2/680-4600), open Tuesday to Saturday 10am to 5:30pm, Sunday noon to 5:30pm; admission is 75¢ adults, 35¢ children under 18. The museum has a fairly interesting collection of stuffed animals and birds, mounted insects, plants, and anthropological exhibits. More worthwhile is the **Artequín Museum** at Av. Portales 3530 (☎ 2/681-8656), open Tuesday to Sunday 10am to 5pm; admission is $1.25 adults, 50¢ students. The museum is housed in a cast-iron building that was first used as the Chilean exhibition hall at the 1889 Parisian centenary of the French Revolution. The building was taken apart, shipped to Santiago, and reassembled here. The museum strives to introduce visitors to the art world through 120 reproductions of well-known works by artists from Picasso to Monet. Kids love the **Museo de Ciencia y Tecnología** (☎ 2/681-6022) for its interactive displays. It is open Tuesday to Friday 10am to 5:30pm, Saturday and Sunday 11am to 6pm; admission is $1 adults, 50¢ students. Last, there's the **Museo Ferroviario** (☎ 2/681-4627),with railway exhibits that include 14 steam engines and railway carriages. It is open Tuesday to Friday 10am to 5:30pm, Saturday and Sunday 11am to 5:30pm; admission is $1 adults, 50¢ students.

ESPECIALLY FOR KIDS

The Parque Metropolitano Zoo, Museum of Science and Technology, and Railway Museum described above all appeal to kids. Another place is **Parque Bernardo O'Higgins,** reached by taxi or Metro to Estación Parque O'Higgins. On weekends hundreds of families come here for the park's several kid-friendly attractions, such as Fantasilandia (☎ **2/689-3035**); admission is $7.50 adults, $6.50 children. It's open winter Saturday, Sunday, and holidays only, 11am to 8:30pm; summer Tuesday to Friday 2 to 8pm, Saturday and Sunday 11am to 8pm. It's the largest amusement park in Chile, complete with a roller coaster, toboggan ride, and haunted house. If your kids loves bugs, take them to the **Museo de Insectos y Caracoles** (☎ **2/556-1937**) for its collection of more than 1,500 mounted butterflies, beetles, and snails; admission is 25¢ adults, 10¢ children. It's open Monday to Sunday 10am to 8pm. There's also a **Museo del Huaso** (☎ **2/556-5680**), which highlights the culture and typical dress of the Chilean cowboy. Admission is free and it's open Tuesday to Friday 10am to 5pm, Saturday and Sunday 10am to 2pm.

ORGANIZED TOURS

Most hotels offer city tours and trips to Viña del Mar and the Andes for an additional price; if not, they'll at least know how to put you in touch with a tour operator. Also try **Turismo Cocha** at El Bosque Norte 0430 (☎ **2/230-1000;** fax 2/230-5110), **Sportstour** at Moneda 970, 14th floor (☎ **2/549-5200**), or **Ace Tourismo** at Av. O'Higgins 949 (☎ **2/696-0391**). These agencies offer a wide variety of day tours to ski resorts, coastal towns, wineries, and more. The information kiosk at Paseo Ahumada and Paseo Huérfanos in downtown Santiago organizes city tours.

SPECTATOR SPORTS & RECREATION

GYMS   For gyms, try **Fisic** at Tobalaba 607 in Providencia (☎ **2/232-6641;** $8 per visit) or **Bio Accion** at Av. Providencia 065 near the Baquedano Metro station (☎ **2/634-7282;** $6 for *each* apparatus used, such as sauna, weights, and so on).

HORSE RACING   Two racetracks hold events on either Saturday or Sunday throughout the year: the recommended **Club Hípico** at Blanco Encalada 2540 (☎ **2/683-9600**) and the **Hipódromo Chile** at Avenida Vivaceta in Independencia (☎ **2/270-9200**). The Hípico's classic event, El Ensayo, takes place the first Sunday in November; the Hipódromo's classic St. Leger, the second week in December.

POOLS   Your best bet is the public pool **Tupahue** atop Cerro San Cristóbal (no phone). Admission adults $8 Monday to Friday, $9 Saturday to Sunday; children $6 Monday to Friday, $6.50. Hours are Tuesday to Friday 10am to 6pm, Saturday and Sunday 10am to 7pm.

SKIING   For information about skiing in the area, see chapter 10, "Around Santiago & the Central Valley."

SOCCER (FOOTBALL)   Top games are held at three stadiums: **Estadio Monumental,** Avenida Grecia and Marathon; **Universidad de Chile,** Camp de Deportes 565 (both are in the Ñuñoa neighborhood); and **Universidad Católica,** Andrés Bello 2782, in Providencia. The most popular teams, Colo Colo, Universidad Católica, and Universidad play at these stadiums. Check the sports pages of any local newspaper for game scheduling.

TENNIS   Try one of the 22 courts at **Parque Tenis** at Cerro Colorado 4661, near the Parque Arauco mall in Las Condes (☎ **2/208-5689**); fees are $9 per hour weekdays, $14 evenings and weekends.

6 Shopping

SHOPPING CENTERS

Santiago is home to two American-style megamalls: **Parque Arauco** at Av. Kennedy 5413, open Monday to Saturday 10am to 9pm, Sunday and holidays 11am to 9pm, and **Alto Las Condes** at Av. Kennedy 9001, open Monday to Sunday 10am to 10pm. Both are nearly identical, offering hundreds of national brands and well-known international chains, junk-food courts, and multiscreen theaters (Parque Arauco has a slight edge with a few dozen more shops and three department stores). To get to Parque Arauco, take a cab or take the Metro to Escuela Militar and take a blue "Metro Bus" that will drop you off at the door. Note that weekends are hectic and jam-packed with shoppers.

Throughout Santiago, stores are typically clustered together in *gallerías,* labyrinthine mini-malls with dozens of independent shops; you'll find them virtually everywhere. In the city center, you'll find good shoe stores around Paseo Huérfanos and Estado and a variety of goods at Almacenes Paris department store on San Antonio and Alameda O'Higgins, or try the Santiago Centro on Matías Cousiño and Alameda O'Higgins. In Providencia, look for clothing and other goods at Avenida Ricardo Lyon and Avenida 11 de Septiembre in the **Mall Panoramico,** with 130 shops and live music on weekends. Several blocks away on General Holley, Suecia, and Bucarest streets you'll find more expensive, upscale clothing boutiques.

CRAFTS MARKETS

Crafts markets can be found around Santiago either as permanent installations or weekly events. **Las Condes Los Domínicos** at Av. Apoquindo 9085 (☎ 2/ 245-4513), open Tuesday to Sunday and holidays 10:30am to 7pm, is a permanent shopping area designed to resemble a colonial village; here you'll find everything from handknit sweaters to lapis lazuli to arts and crafts to live pheasants. Actually quite a pleasant place for a stroll, it sits next to the (usually closed) **San Vicente Ferrer de Los Domínicos Church,** built in the 18th century. To get here you can take any bus from Alameda O'Higgins marked APOQUINDO, but a taxi is the fastest, most direct way.

At Cerro Santa Lucía, on the other side of Alameda O'Higgins, sits the outdoor market **Fería Santa Lucía,** with a large amount of stalls hawking clothing, jewelry, and an assortment of arts and crafts. In **Bellavista** on weekends, a crafts fair runs along Pío Nono Street, where you'll find dozens of booths selling a variety of handsome and unusual items, such as jewelry, old records, and platform boots, and lots of do-it-yourselfers with trinkets displayed on fabric laid out on the sidewalk. For antiques fairs, see below.

SHOPPING FROM A TO Z

ANTIQUES

Antiques lovers should not miss the **Bío Bío Market,** also referred to as the Franklin Market and located at—where else but?—Bío Bío and Franklin streets, open Saturday and Sunday 9am to 7pm. Take the Metro to the Franklin station and walk up several blocks through a so-so selection of wares until you reach the antiques area. Here you'll find an intriguing selection of antique furniture, porcelain, glassware, old photos, and other antique odds and ends, especially at Bío Bío Street. You'll find an even higher quality selection at **Mapocho,** in the red warehouse near Parque de Los Reyes, at the corner of Brasil and Matucana streets, that houses dozens of small shops; it's open Saturday and Sunday 9am to 8pm. A superb spot in Providencia is at the corner of

Bucharest Street and Avenida Providencia, where dozens of galleries offer paintings, china, furniture, and nearly every knickknack imaginable. If you still haven't found what you want, and are looking for more economically priced goods, keep in mind that every Saturday and Sunday—and only in the morning—**Plazas Techadas** at Placer Street between San Diego and San Francisco opens its doors to antiques buyers. This sector was recently built to house antiques dealers who for 40 years sold their wares at the Bío Bío. This is not a particularly bad neighborhood, but keep an eye open.

ARTESANÍA

You'll find arts and crafts shops at Plaza Mulatto Gil de Castro, the Las Condes Los Domínicos market (see "Crafts Markets," above), and the Fería Santa Lucía (see "Crafts Markets," above); at the base of Cerro Santa Lucía on Alameda O'Higgins, inside the Indigenous Art Center (no phone), you'll also find a good, though pricey, selection of jewelry and arts and crafts. It's open Monday to Saturday 10am to 1pm and 3pm to 7pm. **Artesanías de Chile** at the Mapocho Station Cultural Cental, open Monday to Friday 10am to 8pm, Saturday 10:30am to 1:30pm, has a wide variety of artisan goods, including woodwork. **Chile Típico** at Moneda 1025, Local 149 (☎ 2/ 696-5504), open Monday to Friday 9:30am to 10:30pm and Saturday 10am to 2pm, is worth a stop. The **Artesanía Nehuen**, Dardignac 59, in Bellavista (☎ 2/ 777-7367), sells a variety of ceramics, textiles, and indigenous artworks, and will provide a free ride to your hotel for a purchase higher than $50; it's open Monday to Saturday 9:30am to 7pm. Many museums have small shops that sell a variety of photo books and arts and crafts, such as the Museo Chileno de Arte Precolombino (see "Seeing the Sights," above).

BOOKS

Libro's sells a plentiful and diverse array of English-language magazines and a smaller assortment of paperbacks at Av. Pedro de Valdivia 039 in Providencia (☎ 2/ 232-8839), open Monday to Friday 10am to 8pm, Saturday 10am to 2pm, or downtown at Paseo Huérfanos 1178 inside the Gran Palace Galería (☎ 2/699-0319), open Monday to Friday 9:30am to 7:30pm. **Librería Inglesa** with shops at Av. Pedro de Valdivia 47 (☎ 2/231-6270), Paseo Huérfanos 669, Local 11 (☎ 2/632-5153), Vitacura 5950 (☎ 2/219-2735), and Av. Providencia 2653, Local 10 (☎ 2/ 234-3619), sells English-language literature, nonfiction, and children's books. For the largest selection of books in Spanish, the **Fería Chilena del Libro** at Paseo Huérfanos 623 (☎ 2/639-6758) is your best bet, and it sells local and national maps. It has a smaller branch in Providencia at Santa Magdalena 50 (☎ 2/232-1422).

WINE

Don't miss the old-fashioned **Larbos** at Estado 26, downtown Santiago (☎ 2/ 639-3434), open Monday to Saturday 8am to 10pm, for gourmet foods, wines, and wonderful chocolates. There's a cluster of wine shops in Las Condes, such as the huge **El Mundo de Vino** at Av. Isidora Goyenechea 2931 (☎ 2/244-8888), open Monday to Saturday 10:30am to 8:30pm, Sunday 10:30am to 8pm, which has a wide selection and a knowledgeable staff. Also on Avenida Isidora Goyenechea at 3520 is **La Vinoteca** (☎ 2/334-1987), open Monday to Friday 9:30am to 8pm, Saturday 11am to 3pm. Around the corner at El Bosque Norte 038 is **Vinopolis** (☎ 2/232-3814), open Monday to Saturday 10am to 10pm, Sunday 10pm to 8pm, with a good selection; it also has a shop in Providencia at Av. Pedro de Valdivia 037 (☎ 2/333-0080). Most shops will ship wine for about $8 (to the United States). Note that most supermarkets offer a wide selection, and at cheaper prices too.

Lapis Lazuli, a Gem of a Gift

Looking for that special something to bring home to your loved ones? Try *lapis lazuli*, or simply "lapis" in the English-speaking world, a stone that can be found in only two places in the world: Afghanistan and Chile (although there are also spotty reserves in Russia). It's the only gem still referred to by its Latin name, *lapis* for stone and *lazuli* for blue. The color of lapis ranges from a bright royal blue to a violet-navy blue. It is formed when searing-hot, sulphur-rich geothermal vents pass through limestone: The higher the sulphur content, the bluer the stone. Lapis is used primarily for jewelry, but it's also commonly seen in sculptures and even counter tile.

Lapis has been used for 6,500 years, and was considered the most valuable gem until the Middle Ages. The Chinese used lapis for hair ornaments, the Romans carved it into beads, the Greeks recommended it for poisonous snake bites, and the Buddhists thought it encouraged peace of mind. Cleopatra used crushed lapis for eye makeup, and even King Tut's mask is inlaid with the stone. Indigenous peoples, especially the Incas, used lapis to create decorative pieces and jewelry, which have been excavated from sites in Chile, Bolivia, and Peru.

The best place to shop for lapis is in the **Bellavista** neighborhood, where a dozen stores are clustered along Bellavista Street between Pío Nono and Arzobispo Casanova. Here you'll find jewelry, chess sets, figurines, picture frames, and more, all fabricated from lapis. For truly outlandish works, try **PietArt,** which has jewelry and sculptures carved from lapis lazuli as well as copper and bronze art—all exquisite works, but expensive; it's at Los Conquistadores 2421, near the Providencia neighborhood (☎ **2/233-6404**), open daily 9:30am to 7pm.

7 Santiago After Dark

There are plenty of theaters, nightclubs, and bars to keep your evenings busy in Santiago. Like Buenos Aires, Santiago adheres to a vampire's schedule, dining as late as 11pm, arriving at a nightclub past 1am, and diving into bed before the sun rises. It can take a little getting used to, and there are many early-hour nighttime attractions if you can't bear late nights. Several newspapers publish daily movie listings and Friday weekend-guide supplements: *El Mercurio*'s "Wiken" or *La Tercera*'s "Guía Fin de Semana" are good examples. Both contain movie, theater, and live music listings and special events.

THE PERFORMING ARTS

Santiago is known for its theater, from large-scale productions to one-person monologues put on at a local cafe. However, it might be difficult to find a production that interests you because newspaper listings typically advertise the title, address, and telephone number, nothing else. Ask around for recommendations, either from the hotel staff or at a visitor's information center, such as the kiosk at Paseo Ahumada and Paseo Huérfanos, which typically have complete theater listings and can suggest particular acts.

The following are some of the more well-established theaters in Santiago. Four theaters in the neighborhood Bellavista offer contemporary productions and comedies in an intimate setting: **Teatro Bellavista** at Dardignac 0110 (☎ **2/735-6264**), **El Conventillo** at Bellavista 173 (☎ **2/777-4164**), **Tetro La Feria** at Crucero Exeter 0250 (☎ **2/737-7371**), and **Teatro San Ginés** at Mallinkrodt 76 (☎ **2/732-3035**), with adult-oriented acts and occasional plays for kids. As the name implies, the nearby

Teatro La Comedia at Merced 349 (☎ **2/639-1523**) hosts comedy, but it is better known for cutting-edge productions. In Las Condes, try the **Teatro Apoquindo** at Av. Apoquindo 3384 (☎ **2/231-3560**). The cultural center **Estación Mapocho** at the Plaza de la Cultura s/n (☎ **2/361-1761**), hosts a large variety of theater acts, often concurrently.

If symphony music, ballet, or opera is your thing, you won't want to miss a performance at the historic downtown **Teatro Municipal** at Agustinas 749 (☎ **2/639-0282**). The National Chilean Ballet performs here, with contemporary productions that might be danced to the tunes of tango, Chilean folklore, or Janis Joplin. Visiting orchestras and the Fundación Beethoven play at the **Teatro Oriente** at Avenida Pedro de Valdivia between Avenida Providencia and Avenida Andrés Bello (☎ **2/232-1306**), from May to late September; the ticket and information office can be found at Av. 11 de Septiembre 2214, #66. **Teatro Universidad de Chile** at Av. Providencia 043 (☎ **2/634-4746**) hosts ballet and symphony productions, both national and international, throughout the year.

THE CLUB, MUSIC & DANCE SCENE

Crowd-pulling national and international megabands typically play in the **Estado Nacional** or the **Teatro Monumental.** You'll find listings for these shows in the daily newspaper. If you're looking for something mellower, Bellavista is a good bet for jazz, bolero, and folk music that is often performed Thursday to Saturday in several restaurants/cafes. **La Tasca Mediterráneo**'s next-door cafe at Purísima 161 (☎ **20/735-3901**) hosts mostly jazz acts in a cozy atmosphere, but it can get crowded as the night wears on.

La Casa en el Aire at Antonia López de Bello 0125 (☎ **2/735-6680**) has a great ambience and interiors decorated with handicrafts and indigenous art, and is a relaxing place to enjoy a drink listening to soft live music. For funkier, modern music by local bands, try the small venue **Tomm Pub** at the corner of Bellavista and Constitución (no phone). This bar draws a 20- to 35-year-old crowd; there's also a small dance floor. For salsa dancing, try the **Habana Salsa** at Dominica 142 (☎ **2/737-1737**). Despite the hokey exterior of faux building facades, the spicy music will get your feet moving.

There are dozens of music venues spread across the city, but several are concentrated in the Ñuñoa neighborhood, about a 5- to 10-minute taxi ride from downtown and Providencia. **La Batuta** at Jorge Washington 52 (☎ **2/274-7096**) is a dance club on Saturdays, but the rest of the week it's a great spot to check out a wide variety of international and national contemporary and folk bands. The atmosphere is underground, but the crowd profile depends on who's playing.

The **Club de Jazz** at José Pedro Alessandri 85 (☎ **2/274-1937**) is one of the city's most traditional places (Louis Armstrong once played here), and every Thursday, Friday, and Saturday beginning at 11pm, several excellent bands get together and jam for the audience.

Santiago's club scene typically caters to an 18- to 35-year-old crowd, and it all gets going pretty late, from midnight to 6am, on the average. **Oz,** Chucre Manzur 5 (☎ **2/737-7066**), an enormously popular disco that plays mostly techno and rock, is quite fashionable. **Heaven,** Recoleta 345 (no phone), is another hip club with industrial decor, playing techno and pop music. Entering **Blondie** at Alameda 2879 (☎ **2/681-7793**) is like going back to 1985: hundreds of club-goers decked-out in new wave and Goth ensembles from that era, and music to match.

THE BAR SCENE

Bars that also feature live music can be found in "The Club, Music & Dance Scene," above.

DOWNTOWN

There are relatively few bars in downtown. **Scicosis** at José Miguel de la Barra 544 (☎ 2/634-4462), open daily until 3am, is sort of a one-stop Internet cafe and bar. It's casual and comfy, although there's not much atmosphere; the bar is near the Fine Arts Museum. For a more refined atmosphere, try the **Nueva York 27** at—where else?—Nueva York 27 (☎ 2/699-1555). It's open as a bar on Fridays only, until 4am, and usually hosts a live band to serenade drinkers. The best bar by far is the bohemian **El Biógrafo,** Lastarría 181 (☎ 2/633-4435), open daily until 11:30pm.

PROVIDENCIA

The **Bar Liguria** at Av. Providencia 1373 (☎ 2/235-7914), open to 2am on weeknights, until 5am on weekends, and closed Sunday, is Providencia's happening spot for a drink; it's a restaurant by day and bar by night, but serves snacks practically until closing time. The **Phone Box Pub** at Av. Providencia 1670 (☎ 2/235-9972), open Monday to Thursday until 1am, weekends until 3am, closed Sunday, "Chile's English pub since 1984," is good for a pint of brew and a snack. The pub is inside a small plaza off the main drag, and there's outside seating under a trellised roof. In the same plaza is the **Café del Patio** (☎ 2/236-1251), open Monday to Thursday until midnight, Friday and Saturday until 1:30am, a stylish vegetarian restaurant with a great bar, outside seating, and live jazz on weekends.

    Clavo Oxidado at Nueva de Lyon 113 (☎ 2/234-3673), open Monday to Saturday until 3am, is made entirely of recycled materials and features revolving art expositions; it has a long happy hour Monday to Friday 4 to 10pm. **Mister Ed** at Av. Suecia 152 (☎ 2/231-2624), open Monday to Saturday 6pm to 5am, transforms into a dancehall at 2am with live music, and is open on Sundays during the summer. Avenida Suecia literally overflows with revelers of all ages during the weekends. You could really just walk the neighborhood until something strikes your fancy, and it's all here: pubs, traditional and hip restaurants, loud clubs, and more. Happy hours are a standby in nearly every bar here.

LAS CONDES

Several restaurants convert into pubs or cocktail lounges in the evening. One of them is the **Geo Pub** at Encomenderos 83 (☎ 2/233-6675), open until midnight on weeknights, 2am on weekends, a cozy, contemporary Irish pub with the usual pints on draft that's very popular with an international crowd. **PubLicity** at El Bosque Norte 0155 (☎ 2/246-6414), open until 1am on weeknights and 3am on weekends, is almost too much of a sensory overload, combining English architecture with urban "publicity," or advertisements. It's very popular with upscale young adults and yuppies, and there is often live music. **Bohemia** at Av. El Bosque 0139 (☎ 2/333-1214), open Monday to Wednesday until 2am, Thursday to Sunday until 4am, caters to a more adult crowd, and has just about everything: a restaurant, bar, art gallery, live weekend music, and entertainment. **Branigan's Pub** at Las Condes 11271 (☎ 2/243-1108), open Monday to Sunday until 4am, has an intimate atmosphere for enjoying a quiet cocktail, and serves snacks.

CINEMAS

Megaplexes such as CineHoyts and Cinemark, with their multiscreened theaters, feature the widest variety of movies and a popular Monday to Wednesday discount price. More avant-garde and independent films can be found in "Cine Arte" theaters, such as **Cine Alameda,** Alameda O'Higgins 139 (☎ 2/639-2479), or **El Biógrafo,** Lastarria 181 (☎ 2/633-4435). The entertainment sections of *El Mercurio, La Tercera,* or *El Metropolitán* list titles, times, and locations.

Around Santiago & the Central Valley

Some of the most interesting attractions in Chile can be found right outside Santiago. Lush beaches, an eccentric port town, nature preserves, hot springs, wineries, and rolling countryside are a few examples of what's nearby. But there's more. There is a mind-boggling array of outdoor activities to be had, including skiing at one of four world-renowned resorts, hiking, rafting, biking, horseback riding, and more. These attractive destinations and excursions are all within several hours' drive from Santiago, which means it is possible to pack a lot of action into just a few days. If the smog begins to asphyxiate you in Santiago, these destinations will be even more attractive to you, as they are to the many *Santiaguinos* who flee the city on weekends.

There are several great destinations south of Santiago in the Central Valley, including the splendid, 400-year-old Hacienda Los Lingues hotel, thermal spas, and a full-service ski and summer resort.

EXPLORING THE REGION

Wineries, ski resorts, and coastal communities around Santiago can all be explored on day trips. You might find an overnight stay in Viña del Mar or Valparaíso an attractive option; it will allow for more time for exploring the area. If you use Santiago as a base, rental cars are obviously handy, especially if visiting area wineries or taking a drive down the coast to destinations such as Isla Negra. But rental cars are not entirely necessary. Public transportation—minivan shuttles to Santiago's ski resorts, for example—is almost preferred: you won't have to worry about getting chains for your rental-car tires and besides, you won't be using the vehicle during the day anyway. Public transportation aboard frequent, clean coaches from Santiago's downtown bus terminals is a great option for coastal destinations.

1 Viña del Mar

74 miles (120km) NW of Santiago; 5 miles (8km) N of Valparaíso

Viña del Mar is Chile's most fashionable beach resort, a city whose waterfront is lined with towering apartment buildings, boulevards, restaurants, hotels, nightclubs, and a casino. The town was founded in 1874 as a weekend retreat and garden residence for the wealthy elite from Valparaíso and Santiago, and it has remained the preferred beach destination for *Santiaguinos* ever since. Some refer to it as Chile's Riviera, but most simply call it "Viña"—you'll call it chaos if you come any time between December and late February, when thousands of Chileans and Argentines swarm the city.

Viña's attractive homes, lush gardens, manicured lawns, and beach culture—including surfers—are something of a contrast to the ramshackle streets of Valparaíso; indeed, it is difficult to believe the two cities are just 15 minutes from one another. There are plenty of fine beaches here, but it must be noted that the Humboldt Current that runs the length of Chile to Antofagasta makes for cold swimming conditions, even during the summer. Nevertheless, Viña is a wonderfully relaxing place to spend a day or two.

The city is divided into two sectors: the downtown and the beachfront. Several downtown locations are desirable for their proximity to the lush Quinta Vergara Park and shops, but it's about a 15-minute walk to the beach from here. The beach is better suited for tourists, with plenty of hotels and restaurants.

ESSENTIALS

GETTING THERE   Frequent, comfortable buses leave the Terminal Alameda in Santiago at Alameda O'Higgins 3712 (1 block from Terminal Santiago; Metro: University de Santiago), about every 15 minutes. Tur Bus and Pullman both offer service to and from Viña del Mar, for about $4 each way. In Viña you'll disembark at the terminal located at Avenida Valparaíso and Quilpué; it's close to the main plaza, and taxis are available.

VISITOR INFORMATION   The **Oficina de Turismo de Viña** is located on Plaza Vergara, next to the post office near Avenida Libertad and Avenida Arlegui (☎ 32/ 883154; toll-free in Chile, 800/800-830). Summer hours are Monday to Saturday 9am to 9pm, closed 2 to 3pm; off-season hours are Monday to Friday 10am to 7pm, closed 2 to 3pm, and Saturday 10am to 2pm. A helpful staff (including a few who speak basic English) can provide visitors with accommodations information, but without ratings. It's also a good place for information about where to go to rent a temporary apartment.

GETTING AROUND   Viña has a beachfront promenade that makes for a pleasant place to stroll and breathe in the sea air, as well as the lush Quinta Vergara Park. Driving is easier here than in Valparaíso, although during the summertime parking spaces are frustratingly scarce. To get to Valparaíso, take the commuter **train** "Merval" at Francisco Vergara between Bohn and Alvarez streets. The train runs every 20 minutes from about 6am to 10pm and costs 35¢. In Valparaíso, get off at the final stop, Estación Puerto (next to the visitor's center). The Merval is really the best way to get to and from both cities. **Taxis** can be hailed in the street, or your hotel can call one.

SPECIAL EVENTS   During the second or third week of February, Viña plays host to the **Festival de la Canción,** a weeklong event that draws national and international music artists to perform in the outdoor amphitheater in Quinta Vergara Park. It is without a doubt the largest music festival in Chile, drawing almost 30,000 spectators nightly to concerts and competitions that carry on until the crack of dawn. As you might expect, the city bursts at the seams during this event, and hotel reservations are imperative. For more information and exact dates, call the visitor's center. Viña also hosts a **Film Festival** between October 17 and 25 at the Teatro Municipal. Inquire at the visitor's center for any possible scheduling changes.

FAST FACTS: VIÑA DEL MAR

Banks   Most major banks can be found on Avenida Arlegui, and although they're open Monday to Friday 9am to 2pm only, nearly all have ATMs (RedBancs).

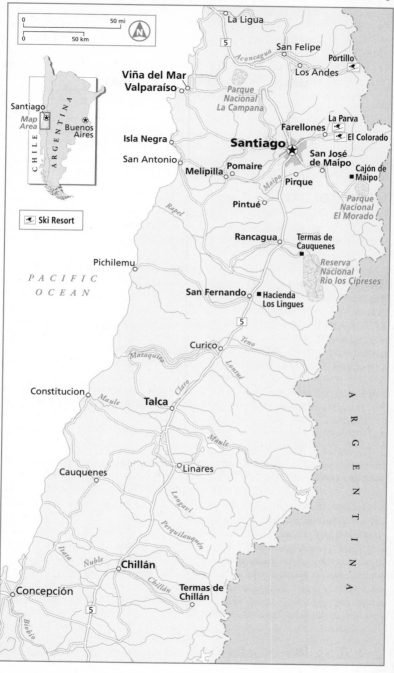

0   50 mi
0   50 km

N

La Ligua

5

Aconcagua

San Felipe

Portillo

Los Andes

Viña del Mar
Valparaíso

*Parque
Nacional
La Campana*

La Parva

Farellones

El Colorado

Santiago

Isla Negra

San José
de Maipo

San Antonio

Melipilla

Pomaire

Maipo

Pirque

Cajón de
■ Maipo

*Parque
Nacional
El Morado*

Pintué

Rapel

Santiago

Map
Area

Buenos
Aires

CHILE

ARGENTINA

✈ Ski Resort

Rancagua

Termas de
Cauquenes

*Reserva
Nacional
Rio los Cipreses*

Pichilemu

*PACIFIC
OCEAN*

San Fernando

■ Hacienda
Los Lingues

5

Curico

Teno

Mataquito

Lontué

Claro

Constitucion

Talca

Maule

Maule

Cauquenes

Linares

Longaví

A
R
G
E
N
T
I
N
A

Perquilauquen

Itata

Ñuble

Chillán

Concepción

Chillán

Termas de
Chillán

5

Biobío

Bookstores   For English-language books, try **Eurotex.** Valparaíso 554 (inside the Galería Paseo del Mar). **Contactolibros** at Vonn Schroeders 181 sells used paperbacks. The **Fería Chilena del Libro,** Av. Valparaíso 595, #7 (☎ **32/694583**), has Spanish books.

Car Rentals   Hertz Rent-A-Car, Av. 14 Norte 541 (☎ **32/689118**); **Flota Verschae,** Av. Libertad 1030 (☎ **32/971184**); **Bert,** Av. Libertad 892 (☎ **32/681151**).

Currency Exchange   *Cambios* (exchange houses) are open in the summer Monday to Friday 9am to 2pm and 3 to 8pm, Saturday 9am to 2pm; in the winter, Monday to Saturday 9am to 2pm and 4 to 7pm, Saturday 9am to 2pm. Several *cambios* can be found along Avenida Arlegui.

Emergencies   For police, dial **133,** for fire **132,** and for an ambulance, dial **131.**

Hospital   For medical attention, go to **Hospital Gustavo Fricke** on Alvarez and Símon Bolivar streets (☎ **32/675067,** or for emergencies 32/675267).

WHERE TO STAY
EXPENSIVE

Gala Hotel. Av. Arlegui 273, Viña del Mar. ☎ **32/686688.** Fax 32/689568. E-mail: galahotel@webhost.cl. 64 units. A/C MINIBAR TV TEL. $147 double; $184 junior suite. AE, DC, MC, V. Free parking.

Although not exactly "gala," this hotel's upscale accommodations feature panoramic windows and sensational views—but part of that view is of the dirty river directly below. This is where traveling executives stay while in Viña, principally for its proximity to Viña's commercial and financial center and for the hotel's large capacity. Room interiors are designed with contemporary wood headboards, floral bedspreads, and watercolor paintings; try to book a corner room for maximum views and sunshine. The marble and brass reception area is filled with sculptures and paintings, and is reached by walking to the back of the building. At the front of the building is a small *galleria* with a variety of shops.

Dining/Diversions: A restaurant serves international cuisine with lots of sunshine provided by panoramic windows. In the same area is a poolside bar—a great place for a drink even if you're not staying here.

Amenities: 24-hour room service, business center, pool, sauna, massage, gym, car rental, baby-sitting, laundry, convention center.

✪ **Hotel Monterilla.** Dos Norte 65, Plaza Mexico, Viña del Mar. ☎ **32/976950.** Fax 32/683576. www.monterilla.cl. E-mail: monterilla@entelchile.net. 20 units. $90 double; $100 apartment. AE, DC, MC, V. Free parking.

This appealing boutique hotel is one of the best in Chile. Warm, personal service and a central location are definite draws, but the chic, contemporary design is what really makes the Monterilla special. The interiors feature white Berber carpet, metal lamps, cushy orange chairs, and walls adorned with colorful postmodern art. The rooms are not huge, but they are elegant and the beds are supremely comfortable. Several of the rooms come with attractive metal-and-wood kitchenettes, a real bonus if you hate to eat out every night. There's also a cafe/restaurant that serves snacks and an excellent daily breakfast buffet. A small common area has glass walls that give it an open, airy feel, and there are several sofas for reading or relaxing. The Monterilla is a family-run hotel, and it derives its good taste from the fact that father and son are architects. A family daughter and her husband run the business, and service is friendly and personal. All in all, this is a great value, especially considering the convenient location near the beach and the casino.

⭘ **Hotel Oceanic.** Av. Borgoño 12925, Viña del Mar. ☎ **32/830006.** Fax 32/830390. www. hoteloceanic.cl. 28 units. TV TEL. $114–$130 seaview double. AE, DC, MC, V. Free parking.

The Oceanic enjoys a spectacular location on a rocky promontory with dramatic views of Valparaíso and the ocean crashing against the shore. The hotel is warm and friendly and full of places to sit and relax to the soothing sound of the sea. During the summer, the pebbled terrace with its oceanside pool and lounge chairs is the best around. The cozy rooms come with comfortable beds, wooden beams, and rose-colored drapes. (Some have sea views, and some look out to the busy road to Reñaca.) A few "attic" rooms are especially spacious and come with a breakfast nook and great views. A plant-filled restaurant looks out over the ocean, and is as popular with guests as it is with diners not lodging in the hotel. Due to the Oceanic's location between Viña and Reñaca, it is not within walking distance to most restaurants and points of interest, which are only a short taxi ride away. A set of booths selling a variety of arts and crafts is across the road.

Dining: The popular seafront **Rendezvous Restaurant** serves Chilean and international cuisine.

Amenities: Laundry, room service, outdoor pool, sauna, conference rooms.

Hotel O'Higgins. Plaza Vergara, Viña del Mar. ☎ **32/882016.** Fax 32/883537. www. panamericanahoteles.cl. E-mail: creservas@panamericanahoteles.cl. 265 units. TV TEL. $90–$100 double; $170 suite. AE, DC, MC, V. Free parking.

This traditional hotel, a stone landmark constructed in the heart of Viña in 1934, has sadly begun to show its age. Minor recent renovations, including new hallway carpet and fresh drapes and bedspreads, have improved its image somewhat, but a stale lobby, dark hallways, and worn furniture reveal that the glory days of the O'Higgins are over. Nevertheless, the hotel is still frequented by dignitaries. It's an interesting place to spend the night, if not for its historical appeal then for its downtown location (close to shops but on a noisy plaza), outdoor pool, and complete services, including two restaurants and the legendary Harry's Bar. Ask to see the accommodations if at all possible as the quality varies from room to room, and those facing the main plaza are nicer than side rooms. The O'Higgins often stages conventions and weddings in one of its 10 salons. Ask for price specials when booking.

Dining/Diversions: The hotel has a formal and a casual restaurant, and both serve international fare.

Amenities: Laundry, 24-hour room service, baby-sitting, kid's recreation center, conference rooms, Hertz rental car agency.

Hotel San Martín. Av. San Martín 667, Viña del Mar. ☎ **32/689191.** Fax 32/689195. www. ceac.cl/Hotelsanmartin. E-mail: Hotel-sanmartin@entelchile.net. 172 units. MINIBAR TV TEL. Seaview $90 double, $130 suite; street view $75 double, $120 suite. AE, DC, MC, V.

The San Martín began with a bang in 1958, opening as the only hotel with an ideal beachfront location and later lobbying to bring the casino to town. But it ran out of steam, and the tired interiors are visual proof that this hotel has passed its heyday. However, this hotel is still a good option for travelers who want to have an up-close view of the crashing waves and still be close to town, but don't book a room without a view—it's not worth it. Some seaview rooms come with sliding doors and a balcony, and they are not necessarily bad, but they do have dated wallpaper and furniture and a slightly musty smell. Also, the lobby's plastic plants and thin carpet are tacky. Service is very professional and there is a large restaurant and piano bar. "Apartment" guest rooms are aimed at families, with two bedrooms; suites have a small seating area separated by a curtain from the bedroom.

MODERATE

Hotel Albamar. Av. San Martín 419, Viña del Mar. ☎ **32/975274.** Fax 32/970720. 30 units. A/C MINIBAR TV TEL. $50 double; $70 suite. AC, DC, MC, V. Free parking.

The Hotel Albamar offers good value for the price due to its location—near restaurants and a block from the casino and the beach—and its comfortable rooms. The owners have completely renovated a separate building in the back, which I recommend for its ample suites and brand-new furnishings; however, the rooms in the main building are also decent, apart from a few that are quite dark. If you have a large enough group, you could practically rent out the entire separate building. The "double special" has extra space for a table and chairs and a freestanding shelving unit. The rooms feature a romantic design that is slightly frilly. There's also a basic restaurant and bar in the lobby area, and the hotel offers baby-sitting services.

Hotel Andalúe. Av. 6 Poniente 124, Viña del Mar. ☎/fax **32/684147.** E-mail: andalue@ ctcinternet.cl. 42 units. TV TEL. $50 double. AE, DC, MC, V. Free parking.

Another mid-range hotel with standard accommodations, the Andalúe sets itself apart in this price range with its high-quality beds. The hotel is actually divided into two different sections across the street from each other, both about the same in terms of design. Although the furnishings and decoration in the lobby lean a wee bit toward the 1970s (maybe it's the funny folkloric dance paintings), the restaurant fills with sunshine in the afternoon. There is also a proper bar, not just something tucked into a corner as an afterthought. The location is nice, too, just 2 blocks from the casino and beach.

Hotel Hispano. Plaza Parroquía 391, Viña del Mar. ☎ **32/685860.** Fax 32/680981. 30 units. TV TEL. $50 double. AE, DC, MC, V. Free parking.

Crisp and clean, the Hotel Hispano has pleasant rooms with large windows looking out onto an atrium patio. The Hispano is a good value in this price range, especially when you factor in its central location close to the Quinta Vergara Park (but not the beach). This is an older, well-kept hotel that has been family-run for 50 years. Rooms come with tiled or carpeted floors and average, but not uncomfortable, beds. There's a lounge and dining area for breakfast. Note that during the Song Festival the Hispano books early, and the surrounding area is very busy. The same goes for the Quinta Vergara Hotel (see below).

✪ **Offenbacker-hof Residencia.** Balmaceda 102, Cerro Castillo, Viña del Mar. ☎ **32/ 621483.** Fax 32/662432. E-mail: residoff@chilesat.net. 15 units. TEL. $38–$54 double. AE, DC, MC, V. Free parking.

Housed in a lovely Victorian building perched high atop Cerro Castillo, the Offenbacker has sweeping views of Viña del Mar and an exquisite patio cafe. Still, it is the friendly German-Chilean owners of the Offenbacker (named for the German town where they lived for 10 years) that make this bed-and-breakfast really special. The interiors are older, and in some rooms you might find the furnishings a tad worn. But most rooms are spacious and each features a different style characteristic of a B&B, from romantic to masculine. The attic rooms are well lit, but slightly smaller. Breakfast is served in the antique dining room downstairs or underneath an umbrella at a patio table outside. Without a doubt, you'll be wowed by the view, so be sure to get a room that has one. There's also a sauna, solarium, and hydromassage whirlpool.

Quinta Vergara. Errázuriz 690, Viña del Mar. ☎ **32/691978.** Fax 32/691978. 15 units. $50 double. MC, V. Free parking.

This little bubblegum-pink hotel, built around 1910 as a private home, sits at the entrance to the Quinta Vergara Park; several upper rooms look out onto its lush grounds. Some rooms have French windows and ample bathrooms. The Quinta Vergara has the feel of an older bed-and-breakfast, with shirred chiffon curtains and faded floral bedspreads. Service is exceptionally friendly and the location is ideal, although it's a long walk to the beach. A common area has that lived-in look, but the hotel is casual and guests are made to feel like they're in their own home. Internet access is available for an additional price.

WHERE TO DINE

Café Santa Fe. Ocho Norte 303. ☎ **32/691719.** Main courses $8–$11; fajitas $10–$18. AE. Mon–Sat 1–4pm and 7:30pm–1:30am; Sun 1–4pm. TEX-MEX.

Margaritas, shooters, fajitas, guacamole, colorful walls, and faux cacti—all of this will be familiar to Americans and probably explains why you always see some ex-pats here wolfing down a basket of chips and salsa. This restaurant is extremely popular with locals, too, principally because the food is so good, especially the Santa Fe fish. The chicken, steak, and shrimp fajitas come with every ingredient imaginable and are so large you might consider splitting an order. On weekends, especially in the summer, the music cranks and an outdoor patio overflows with diners and revelers.

Diego's Pizzas. Av. San Martín 636. ☎ **32/689512.** Individual pizzas $5–$9; salads $6. AE, DC, MC, V. Sun–Thurs 10am–midnight; Fri–Sat 10am–1:30am. PIZZA.

Diego's creative, artistic pizzas stand out from Domino's and Pizza Hut down the road for their dozens and dozens of far-out toppings, more than 50 kinds of empanadas, and wonderful, fresh salads. Every pizza has a name; the biggest seller at Diego's is the "Four-Season Pizza," with shrimp, mussels, smoked salmon, razor clams, onion, mozzarella, and tomato. A few are a little over the top, such as the "Jalapeño" that comes with guacamole and a blob of corn dough, but the majority of pizzas are very good. Large salads come "single" or "married" with chicken, ham, or tuna. The service is very friendly, and the owners have just remodeled the wood-and-tile dining room.

El Gaucho. Av. San Martín 435. ☎ **32/693502.** Main courses $6–$14. AE, DC, MC, V. Daily 12:30–3:30pm and 7:30–11pm. STEAKHOUSE.

Carnivores need only head to El Gaucho for ample servings of just about any kind of meat, served sizzling off the *parrilla,* or grill. This restaurant leans toward the Argentine style of barbecue, with their "interiors" appetizers, including blood sausage, sweetbreads, and crispy intestines. If that doesn't make your mouth water, try starting with grilled provolone cheese with oregano. El Gaucho serves beef loin, ribs, chicken, sausages, and other grilled items, as well as salads and side dishes. The atmosphere is warm, with lemon-yellow tablecloths, wood floors, and brick walls offset by wine racks featuring Chilean and French varieties.

✪ **Fellini.** Av. 3 Norte 88. ☎/fax **32/975742.** Main courses $7.50–$11. AE, DC, MC, V. Daily 1–4pm and 7:30pm–midnight. ITALIAN/INTERNATIONAL.

The extensive menu offered at Fellini is simply incredible—virtually everything and anything is offered, making this a great place for a group that can't agree on what to eat. The offerings include dozens of rich, homemade pastas, fresh seafood, grilled meats served draped in sauces such as Roquefort and cognac, stuffed crêpes, vegetarian and low-fat plates, the list goes on. Is it any good? You bet—just ask any of the locals who frequently drop in and greet the owner, who is usually at the door to greet customers by name. Everything is made fresh here, including the bread and the ice cream. The dining area is semi-elegant and warm, and the tables are well appointed. You can't miss Fellini: The pea-green exterior is visible a block away.

✪ **Las Delicias del Mar.** Av. San Martín 459. ☎ **32/901837.** Main courses $10–$12. AE, DC, MC, V. Daily 12:30–4pm and 7:30pm–midnight. SEAFOOD.

This Basque-influenced restaurant serves wonderfully sumptuous seafood dishes that are matched by sharp, attentive service. According to the menu, Las Delicias is known for its paella (which can be ordered for one or two people). Although the paella is decent, the fish dishes are really the most savory. This is one of the few Chilean restaurants to actually put time and thought into preparing a dish, and the results are mouth-watering: sea bass, salmon, or conger eel under a rich cream, mushroom, and shrimp sauce and topped with freshly grated Parmesan baked golden brown, or sole stuffed with cheese and prawns. Tangerine-colored walls, leafy plants, and cherrywood chairs and tables draped with colorful linens make for a warm, comfortable atmosphere.

✪ **Ristorante San Marco.** Av. San Martín 597. ☎ **32/975304.** Fax 32/884872. Main courses $6–$10. AE, DC, MC, V. Daily noon–4pm and 8pm–midnight. ITALIAN.

If you're in the mood for pasta, this is the place to come. San Marco is one of the best restaurants in the area, and has been since it opened its doors in 1957. Everything is made fresh daily here, from the pasta to the tiramisu. Most of the pastas are traditional and served with typical sauces, such as bolognese or alfredo, but you can have your fettuccine or tortellini with seafood or creamy basil sauce. San Marco offers an extensive list of rich, homemade desserts and a reasonably priced wine list. The simple dining area has wraparound windows festooned with hanging vines and tables draped with white linen tablecloths.

WHAT TO SEE & DO
BEACHES

The **Playa Caleta Abarca** beach is located in a protected bay near the entrance to Viña del Mar, next to the oft-photographed "flower clock" and the Cerro Castillo. Northeast and fronting the rows of terraced high-rise apartment buildings you'll find **Playa Acapulco, Playa Mirasol,** and **Playa Las Salinas** (the latter is near the naval base). These beaches all see throngs of vacationers and families in the summer. Beach-lovers might consider heading just north of Viña to **Reñaca**—it's close enough to take a taxi, or grab a bus numbered 1, 10, or 111 at Avenida Libertad and Avenida 15 Norte. Reñaca is the *in* spot that sees a slightly younger, and sometimes larger, crowd than Viña.

THE TOP ATTRACTIONS

Casino Municipal. Plaza Colombia between Av. San Martín and Av. Peru. ☎ **32/689200.** Admission $6 (charged only to enter game room). Hours vary, but generally: gaming room daily 6pm–4am (Sun–Thurs hours during winter are 6pm–2am); slot machines daily noon–4am; bingo daily 4pm–4am.

Built in 1930, the Casino Municipal was the most luxurious building in its day and is worth a visit even if you're not a gambler. The interior has been remodeled over time, but the facade has withstood the caprices of many a developer and is still as handsome as the day it opened. Semiformal attire (that is, no T-shirts, jeans, or sneakers) is required to enter the gaming room. The casino also holds temporary art exhibits on the second floor.

✪ **Quinta Vergara Park/Museum of Fine Art.** Near Plaza Parroquía. Museum ☎ **32/680618.** Park: Free admission; open daily 7am–6pm (until 7pm in summer). Museum: Admission 60¢ adults, 30¢ children; open Tues–Sun 10am–2pm and 3–6pm.

One of the loveliest parks in central Chile, the Quinta Vergara is also home to a large amphitheater that holds Viña's yearly Song Festival as well as the Museum of Fine Art. The Quinta, whose area is naturally fenced in by several steep hills, was once the residence of Portuguese shipping magnate Francisco Alvarez and his wife, Dolores, whose fondness for flora led her to create the park, planting a multitude of native and other exotic species. The museum is housed in the ornate **Palacio Vergara,** which was built by Francisco's great-granddaughter, and the collection includes art from the family collection and other works from collectors in Viña.

✪ **Museo de Arqueologia e Historia Francisco Fonck.** Av. 4 Norte 784. ☎ **32/686753.** Admission $1.60 adults, 30¢ children. Tues–Fri 9:30am–6pm; Sat–Sun 9:30am–2pm.

This museum boasts a large collection of indigenous art and archeological items from Easter Island, with more than 1,400 pieces and one of the six Moai sculptures outside Easter Island (the others are in England, the United States, Paris, Brussels, and La Serena in Chile). There is also a decent archeological exhibition of Mapuche pieces and other items from the north and central zones of Chile. Worth a look is the Museum of Natural History on the second floor, featuring birds, mammals, insects, and fossils.

✪ **Museo Palacio Rioja.** Quillota 214. ☎ **32/689665.** Admission 60¢ adults, 20¢ children. Tues–Sun 10am–1pm and 3–5:30pm.

This enormous 1906 belle époque stone mansion is worth a visit for a peek into the lives of the early-century elite in Viña del Mar. Built by Spaniard Fernando Rioja, a banker, and originally spanning 4 blocks, the palace took opulence to a new level, with a stone facade featuring Corinthian columns and a split double staircase, and interiors made of oak and stone with enough salons to fit a family of 20. Although a fraction of what it once was, the palm-fringed garden surrounding the house is idyllic.

2 Valparaíso

71 miles (115km) NW of Santiago; 5 miles (8km) S of Viña del Mar

Valparaíso is Viña del Mar's next-door neighbor, but the two couldn't be more different. This port town is Viña's blue-collar sister, with a history and vibrant culture that speaks strongly of the golden days before the Panama Canal, when every ship on its way around the Cape stopped here for supplies. The features of Valparaíso, with its multicolored jumble of clapboard homes and weathered Victorian mansions, sinuous streets, steep hills, and rollicking seafront bars, is enchanting, fascinating even—although it might not capture you at first. Valparaíso can be a little scary to first-time visitors, but give it a chance and allow the city to work its magic on you.

Valparaíso has spawned a generation of international poets, writers, and artists who have found inspiration in the city, including the Nobel prize–winning poet Pablo Neruda, who owned a home here. The bohemian flavor is still going strong, and the city is known for its eccentric and antiquated bars that stay open into the wee hours of the morning. The city is also known for its restaurants, some of which have the most dramatic sea views found anywhere in Chile.

But the real attractions here are wandering the city's streets, viewing the angular architecture of homes and mansions that cling to the hillsides, and especially riding the century-old, clickety-clack *ascensores,* or funiculars, that lift riders to the tops of hills. If you're the type who craves character and culturally unique surroundings, this is your place. Otherwise, you might want to make Valparaíso a day trip, and choose Viña for its more familiar surroundings.

ESSENTIALS

GETTING THERE   By Bus   Frequent, comfortable buses leave the Terminal Alameda in Santiago at Alameda O'Higgins 3712 (1 block from Terminal Santiago;

Metro: University de Santiago), about every 15 minutes. Tur Bus and Pullman offer service to and from Valparaíso, with fares running about $4 one-way. In Valparaíso you'll disembark at the terminal at Avenida Pedro Montt; taxis are available and a good idea at night. Consider buying a round-trip ticket if you plan to travel on weekends or holidays.

By Car   To get to Valparaíso from Santiago, take Alameda O'Higgins west until it changes into Ruta Nacional 68, 6 miles (10km) from the coast, and follow the signs to Valparaíso. There is one tollbooth ($2.50) along the way. Valparaíso is 71 miles (115km) northwest of Santiago. Parking can be arranged at most hotels and there's a parking garage on Errázuriz Street, across from the Plaza Sotomayor.

VISITOR INFORMATION/CITY TOURS   There are several **tourist offices** in Valparaíso; the best is at Muelle Prat (☎ **32/236322**), open Monday to Sunday 10am to 6pm. There's also an information kiosk at the bus station open Monday to Sunday 8:30am to 5:30pm. Panoramic **city tours** in minivans are offered by Meneses y Díaz, which leave from the visitor's center daily at 11am (☎ **32/594677**). The cost is $5; drivers do not speak English, but the twisting streets and dramatic views seen along the way say it all.

GETTING AROUND   Walking is really the only way to see Valparaíso, as parking is limited and most attractions lie within a compact area. To get to and from Viña del Mar, take a taxi or, better yet, ride the Merval, a commuter train that runs every 20 minutes from the Estación Puerto (next to Valparaíso's visitor's center) and costs 35¢.

SPECIAL EVENTS   Valparaíso's famed **New Year's Pyrotechnic Festival** takes place every December 31, lighting the sky with a spectacular fireworks display that can be seen throughout the city. A memorable way to see the show is atop one of the hills, such as Cerro Alegre or Cerro Concepción, or from one of the several boats that offer special excursions around the harbor. Ask at the visitor's center at Muelle Prat about making arrangements; reservations need to be made 1 to 2 weeks in advance, and you need to set sail before the port closes at 9pm. Plan where you'd like to be, arrive early, and expect to stay late, as heavy crowds make movement difficult. Another highlight during October is **Regatta Off Valparaíso,** a traditional Chilean regatta organized by the Arturo Prat Naval Academy, featuring more than 50 competing yachts. At the time this book went to press, the exact weekend was not known, so call the visitor's center.

WHERE TO STAY

The bulk of lodgings in Valparaíso take the form of scrappy *residenciales* with shared bathrooms, lumpy beds, and dingy lighting—the reason most travelers choose to lodge in Viña del Mar and visit Valparaíso by day instead. However, there are a few decent choices to be had in Valparaíso, and some travelers prefer the rough-and-tumble charm of the city as opposed to the predictable resort ambience of Viña.

✪ **Brighton Bed & Breakfast.** Paseo Atkinson 151–153, Cerro Concepción, Valparaíso. ☎/fax **32/22-3513.** E-mail: brighton-valpo@entelchile.net. 6 units. $45 double without bathroom; $50 double with bathroom; $60 suite. DC, MC, V. No parking.

This is one of the prettiest places to spend the night in Valparaíso. A big yellow Victorian perched high atop Cerro Concepción, this B&B offers stunning, sweeping views of the harbor and the city center below. Thin floral bedspreads, framed prints, and so-so furniture make for simple, unremarkable rooms, but the charming location more than makes up for it. Because this is a converted home, room sizes vary; try booking the "suite" with a balcony and sea view. There's also a cafe on the first floor

Valparaíso

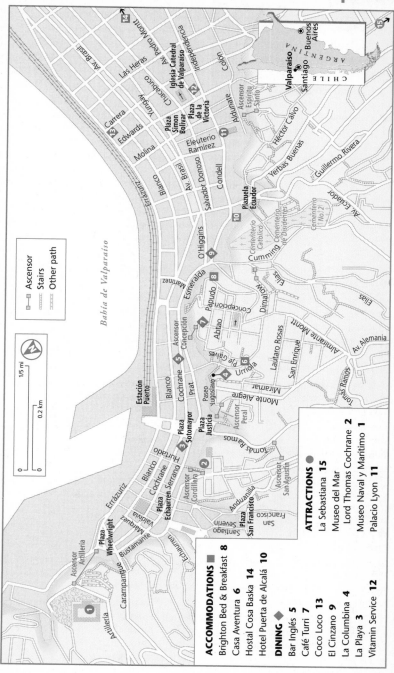

ATTRACTIONS ●
La Sebastiana **15**
Museo del Mar
Lord Thomas Cochrane **2**
Museo Naval y Marítimo **1**
Palacio Lyon **11**

ACCOMMODATIONS ■
Brighton Bed & Breakfast **8**
Casa Aventura **6**
Hostal Cosa Baska **14**
Hotel Puerta de Alcalá **10**

DINING ◆
Bar Inglés **5**
Café Turri **7**
Coco Loco **13**
El Cinzano **9**
La Columbina **4**
La Playa **3**
Vitamin Service **12**

with checkered black-and-white floors and two terrace patios. On weekends, the cafe has live bolero and tango music, and it stays open until 4am. To get here, take the Concepción ascensor and go left.

✪ **Casa Aventura.** Pasaje Gálvez 11, Cerro Alegre, Valparaíso. ☎/fax **32/75-5963.** E-mail: casatur@ctcinternet.cl. 3 units. TEL. $10 single; $20 double. No credit cards. No parking.

This tiny gem of a hostal has a central location, clean, attractive interiors, Spanish courses, and Internet access. With just three rooms (two with twin beds, one a double), the atmosphere is quiet and intimate, with a sunny living area and couches for just hanging out. The German-Chilean couple who own Casa Aventura opened the hostal a year ago, and they typically cater to budget travelers and students who take part in their 1- to 2-week on-site Spanish courses. The renovated Victorian building has wood floors and high ceilings and is sparsely decorated with contemporary art. Beds have fluffy down comforters, and two rooms are dark, one very sunny and bright. Guests have use of the kitchen and can wash clothes for $4. Casa Aventura also arranges private excursions in and around the city to places such as La Campana. The small Spanish courses should be reserved in advance by e-mail; beginning, intermediate, and advanced courses are held privately or in groups, and cost $200 for 2 weeks and 20 hours of instruction.

Hostal Cosa Baska. Victoria 2249, Valparaíso. ☎ **32/234036.** Fax 32/219915. 12 units. TEL. $40 double. DC, MC, V. No parking.

Somewhat cheerless, but full of old charm gleaned from the early 1900s architecture and soaring ceilings, this *residencial* is neat and clean, with older beds and burgundy carpets. Some rooms have large French doors that open onto Victoria Street, and some come with antique furnishings. The location between the National Congress building and Parque Italia in Victoria is convenient for sightseeing, and the small staff is helpful and friendly. There's also a small dining area for breakfast.

Hotel Puerta de Alcalá. Piramide 524 (off Av. Condell), Valparaíso. ☎ **32/22-7478.** Fax 32/74-5642. www.chileinfo.cl/puertadealcalahotel. E-mail: puertadealcalahotel@entelchile.net. 21 units. MINIBAR TV TEL. $35 double. AE, DC, MC, V. Parking.

This brand-new hotel just off busy Avenida Condell is a tad frumpy, but it is comfortable and without a doubt one of the better hotels in the city. Rooms come with soundproof windows and are somewhat dark; however, an on-site restaurant is light and pleasant, due in part to a five-floor atrium that allows sunshine to cascade in. Style isn't a high point here, as boxes of tacky plastic flowers attest; however, friendly service is, and they'll even arrange tours in Valparaíso and to locations as far away as Portillo Ski Resort.

WHERE TO DINE
EXPENSIVE

✪ **Café Turri.** Calle Templeman 147 (Cerro Concepción; take the Concepción lift). ☎ **32/259198.** Reservations recommended for outdoor seating for dinner. Main courses $10–$15. AE, DC, MC, V. Daily 10:30am–2am. INTERNATIONAL/CHILEAN.

A classic, and worthy of its regional fame, Café Turri is one of the best restaurants in Chile. Outstanding food, gorgeous views, and a good-natured, attentive waitstaff make this truly a gastronomic experience. Housed in a converted home built a century ago by an English immigrant, the restaurant sits high atop the Cerro Concepción and occupies three floors, two with outdoor seating for dining or just having a coffee and soaking up the view. Café Turri's specialty is seafood, but they also serve a variety of meat and chicken dishes. The remarkably extensive, and somewhat traditional, menu includes sea bass, salmon, congrio, albacore tuna, and more, each cooked 24 different ways, as well as exquisite appetizers and desserts.

✪ **La Columbina.** Pasaje Apolo 91–77. ☎ **32/236254.** Main courses $10–$15. No credit cards. Daily noon–midnight (Fri–Sat until 2am). INTERNATIONAL/CHILEAN.

This terrific restaurant occupies three floors of a beautiful Victorian building and includes a tearoom with stained-glass windows and a panoramic view; a restaurant/pub with wood floors, oriental rugs, and a pretty terrace shaded by striped awnings; and a more formal dining area with linen tablecloths, antiques, and smartly dressed waiters. In the evening, the pub offers an additional menu of appetizers, including Mexican and Thai platters, as well as excellent, artfully prepared entrees, such as filet mignon marinated in dark beer and herbs freshly picked from their garden. Wood-burning stoves, sumptuous views, a colorful, amicable staff (especially the barman), and live jazz, tango, and bolero music on Fridays and Saturdays make for a great atmosphere. I always have a difficult time choosing between this restaurant and the Café Turri.

MODERATE

Bar Inglés. Entrance on Cochrane 851 or Blanco 870. ☎ **32/214625.** Main courses $7–$11. No credit cards. Mon–Fri 9am–11pm. CHILEAN.

So-so food and a slightly overpriced menu do not make the Bar Inglés a great value, but the old-world atmosphere merits a visit, especially to sidle up to the long oak bar for a coffee or beer. The ambience is early 1900s, with antique tile floors, wooden pillars and walls, and tables draped with white linen. Smaller items such as sandwiches are usually fairly good, but main courses are too simple for the asking price. Still, the Bar Inglés remains a local favorite among businessmen, who spend long lunches pounding out deals.

Coco Loco. Blanco 1781, 22nd floor. ☎ **32/227614.** Main courses $11–$16. AE, DC, MC, V. Daily noon–4pm and 7:30–11pm (until midnight Fri–Sat). SEAFOOD.

This port version of the popular Santiago restaurant features two floors—one of which is a *giratorio,* a revolving dining area underneath a glass dome that allows diners to appreciate all the splendor of Valparaíso. The restaurant is more upscale than its companions along the port, and it doesn't have that old-world Valparaíso ambience either. Nevertheless, the Coco Loco offers an excellent menu of grilled, poached, and fried fish served with tasty sauces, and a range of hot appetizers that typically feature shellfish. There are also beef and chicken dishes if you're not in the mood for seafood.

✪ **El Cinzano.** Aníbal Pinto 1182. ☎ **32/213043.** Main courses $6.50–$10. AE, DC, MC, V. Sun–Wed noon–1am; Thurs noon–2:30am; Fri–Sat noon–4:30am. CHILEAN.

Since 1896 this classic restaurant has been the popular hangout for poets, intellectuals, musicians, and the like who come for late-night *chorrillanas,* a Valparaíso specialty of steak, eggs, onions, and french fries tossed together and heaped on a platter. During lunch and dinner, waiters in smart black jackets and bow ties serve typical Chilean seafood fare and grilled meats, as well as their other specialty: *vino arreglado,* or "fixed" wine with strawberry, peach, or *chirimoya* (custard apple). The Cinzano frequently hosts dinner dances on the second floor, and the weekend really heats up with one of the most lively ambiences around, with customers serenaded to the sounds of live tango singers.

INEXPENSIVE

La Playa. Serrano 568. ☎ **32/59-4262.** Main courses $3–$7. No credit cards. Mon–Wed noon–2am; Thurs–Sat noon–5:30am. CHILEAN.

Founded in 1903, this traditional bar serves up cheap Chilean lunches and even cheaper *picoteos* (appetizer platters) and beer in the evening, when it converts into a pub after 10pm, serving a mostly younger crowd. The long oak bar, wooden floors, marine memorabilia, and gigantic mirrors rescued from the Seven Mirrors brothel offer old Valparaíso charm. The food is standard Chilean fare, such as crab soup and filet mignon *a la pobre,* and on Thursdays, Fridays, and Saturdays there's live jazz, rock, and blues music starting at 1:30am. On Monday evenings La Playa holds live poetry readings. This is the epicenter of late-night life, and can get packed after midnight.

Vitamin Service. Pedro Montt 1746. ☎/fax **32/212689.** Sandwiches $2–$5. No credit cards. Daily 9am–10pm. CAFETERIA.

Vitamin Service looks a bit like an ice cream parlor, which it really is; however, it serves excellent fresh juices that can be "vitaminized" for a slightly higher price, as well as espresso, sandwiches, and *onces* (afternoon tea). This is a good place to start the day with breakfast or to take a break for an *once*. The *once completo* for $5 includes coffee, juice, toast, half a ham-and-cheese sandwich, and cake. Of course, there's also ice cream. The Vitamin Service is located close to Plaza Victoria.

WHAT TO SEE & DO

✪ **Museo Naval y Marítimo.** Paseo 21 de Mayo, Cerro Artillería. ☎ **32/283749.** Admission 90¢ adults, 35¢ kids under 12. Tues–Sun 10am–5:30pm.

This fascinating museum merits a visit even if you do not particularly fancy naval and maritime-related artifacts and memorabilia. The museum is smartly designed and divided into four salons: the War of Independence, the War against the Peru-Bolivia Confederation, the War against Spain, and the War of the Pacific. Each salon holds interesting artifacts, such as antique documents, medals, uniforms, and war trophies. Of special note is the Arturo Prat room with artifacts salvaged from the *Esmeralda,* including a barnacle-covered clock registering the moment the ship was sunk during the War of the Pacific.

Palacio Lyon. Av. Condell 1546. ☎ **32/257441.** Natural history museum: Admission $1.25 adults, 50¢ students and seniors; Wed and Sun free. Tues–Sat 10am–6pm; Sun 10am–2pm. Municipal gallery of art: Free admission. Mon–Sat 10am–7pm.

This grand, 50-room palace was built as a residence in 1881, but today houses both the **Museo de Historia Natural** and the **Galería Municipal de Arte de Valparaíso.** The natural history museum is a dusty, oddball collection of stuffed and mounted birds and animals mixed in with odd artifacts that include a two-headed baby marinating in a bottle of formaldehyde. Visitors will get the feeling that the museum means well, but it obviously suffers from a lack of funds. The art gallery holds changing exhibits inside the palace's wonderfully spacious basement.

Museo del Mar Lord Thomas Cochrane. Calle Merlet 195 (via the Ascensor Cordillera). ☎ **32/213124.** Free admission. Tues–Sun 10am–6pm.

High atop Cerro Cordillera sits Lord Cochrane's Museum of the Sea inside the old residence of Juan Mouat, who built the house in 1841 in colonial style with all the trimmings, including its own observatory. Now it houses a display of model ships once owned by Lord Cochrane. If the theme doesn't interest you, the dramatic view will.

✪ **La Sebastiana.** Calle Ferrari 692. ☎ **32/256606.** Admission $2.75 adults, $1.30 students. Mon–Fri 10:30am–2pm and 3:30–6pm; Sat–Sun 10:30am–6pm.

La Sebastiana is one of poet Pablo Neruda's three charming homes that have since been converted into museums honoring the distinguished Nobel Laureate's work and life. Neruda usually spent New Year's here for the spectacular firework display he was able to view from the home. La Sebastiana is exceptionally enjoyable because the staff allow visitors to wander about freely without an accompanying guide.

There are self-guiding information sheets in a variety of languages that explain the significance of important documents and items on display, as well as Neruda's whimsical collection of eccentric knickknacks culled from his journeys through the Americas and abroad. Neruda called himself an "estuary sailor"—although terrified of sailing, he nevertheless was fascinated by the sea, and he fashioned his homes to resemble boats, complete with porthole windows. A cultural center has been built below the house, with a gallery and a gift shop. Don't miss this fascinating attraction.

The walk from Plaza Victoria is a hike, and you might want to take a taxi. From Plaza Ecuador there's a bus, Verde "D." Or you might opt to take *La Cintura,* or "The Belt," a bus route that takes riders up and down and around the snaking streets of Valparaíso and eventually stops a block or so from Neruda's house (be sure to tell the driver that's your final destination because the bus continues on). The bus leaves from Plaza Echaurren near the Customs House (La Aduana), and is called Bus Verde "O."

Walking Tour: From the Port to the Heights of Valparaíso

Start: Muelle Prat, Visitor's Center
Finish: Ascensor Concepción or Calle Esmerelda.
Time: 1 to 3 hours.
Best Times: Saturday and Sunday are less hectic, but begin after 10am when everything opens.

This splendid walk should not be missed. Visitors are treated to rides aboard the city's famed *ascensores,* followed by a stroll through the narrow, picturesque streets that wind erratically through Valparaíso's most charming neighborhoods, Cerro Alegre and Cerro Concepción. Along the way are chances to visit museums and fine restaurants, as well as relax and soak up the dramatic view of the city and port from park benches at several lookout points. There are several variations to this route, one of which is to walk it the reverse direction by beginning at Ascensor Concepción on Calle Prat, across from the Turri Clock Tower.

1. **Muelle Prat/Visitor's Center.** Begin at the visitor's center at Muelle Prat. You might consider taking a 90¢ "cruise" aboard one of the many launches that ferry visitors around the Valparaíso harbor for 20 minutes. Just head toward the dock—an eager skipper will find you. One company, **Maite,** offers a harbor tour aboard a yacht on weekends and holidays for $2 (☎/fax **32/838172;** www.chileweb.net/maite). You might want to pick up a few souvenirs from the many booths at the pier.

   Head away from the **pier** and cross Errázuriz to reach:
2. **Plaza Sotomayor.** This plaza acted as the civic center of Valparaíso until 1980. At the plaza's entrance you'll encounter the **Monument to the Heroes of Iquique,** under which the remains of Prat, Condell, and Serrano, heroes of the War of the Pacific, are buried. To the right of the plaza sits the Navy Command

Headquarters, built in 1910 and once used as the seat of the provincial government, as well as the presidential summer residence until 1930.

To the left of the plaza, next to the Palacio de Justicia, ride the Ascensor Peral (ca. 1902) for 10¢ to the top of Cerro Alegre and there you'll find:

3. **Paseo Yugoslavo.** This pleasant terrace walkway was built by Pascual Baburizza in 1929 and named in honor of his heritage. Continue along the terrace until you pass:

4. **Palacio Baburizza.** This 1916 home was built for the nitrate magnate Ottorino Zanelli, and later became the home of Baburizza until his death in 1941. It now houses the city's Fine Arts Museum, which is unfortunately closed for a slow renovation. You can go inside the house, however, to see a computerized virtual display of the works, including those by local artists such as Juan Francisco González and Juan Mauricio Rugendas, among a small collection of European paintings.

Continue along Paseo Yugoslavia, past the La Columbina restaurant. The road curves to the right around a tiny plaza; follow it until you reach Calle Alvaro Besa. Take Alvaro Besa as it winds down the hill, or take the shortcut down **Pasaje Bavestrello,** a cement stairway at the left. Continue until you reach Calle Urriola, which you'll cross, then walk up 20 meters (22 yds.) and turn left into another stairway, Pasaje Gálvez. The narrow walkway twists and turns, passing the colorful facades of some of the most striking homes in Valparaíso. At Calle Papudo, climb the stairway and turn left into:

5. **Paseo Gervasoni.** This pleasant walkway, lined with stately, 19th-century mansions, looks out onto the port of Valparaíso. At the end of the walkway, you'll find Café Turri, an idyllic place for lunch or coffee. First you might want to check out:

6. **Casa Mirador de Lukas.** The museum displays a permanent exhibition of hundreds of illustrations made by Renzo Pecchenino, a wonderful cartoonist and satirist for the newspaper *El Mercurio,* ☎ **32/221344;** open Tuesday to Sunday 10:30am to 2pm and 3:30 to 6:30pm; admission is 90¢. It is possible to end the walking tour here and descend via Ascensor Concepción. I recommend that you keep walking. Continue around Gervasoni until you reach Papudo.

You take a detour here 2 blocks up Calle Templeman to visit the:

7. **Anglican Church of St. Paul.** Built in 1858, this unadorned church was not officially recognized until 1869, when the Chilean government repealed a law banning religions other than Catholicism. The church houses a grand organ donated by the British in 1901 in honor of Queen Victoria. You can hear this magnificent instrument at work at 12:30pm every Sunday.

Double back to Calle Papudo, head southeast (turning right if returning from the church) until reaching:

8. **Paseo Atkinson.** At the entrance to Paseo Atkinson, you'll pass a Lutheran church, built in 1897 and housing the antique organ (ca. 1855) that was once played in the Anglican Church. Paseo Atkinson is another breathtaking pedestrian walkway, bordered by antique homes featuring the zinc facades and guillotine windows popular with the British in the early 20th century. Continue down the pedestrian stairway until you reach Calle Esmerelda, and the end of the walk. You can also descend by doubling back and riding the Ascensor Concepción to Calle Prat.

OTHER SHORT WALKS

THE PORT NEIGHBORHOOD   Begin at the **Customs House** (Aduana), the grand, colonial American–style building built in 1854 and located at the north of town at Plaza Wheelwright at the end of Cochrane and Calle Carampangue. It is possible to

Walking Tour: The Port to the Heights of Valparaíso

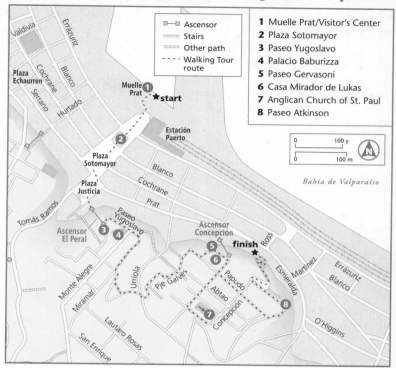

visit this customs house, if it intrigues you. To the right you'll find the **Ascensor Artillería,** built in 1893 (and it shows); it costs 10¢. The wobbly contraption is a delight, and it takes visitors to the most panoramic pedestrian walkway in Valparaíso, **Paseo 21 de Mayo.** This lovely promenade has a lookout gazebo from which it is possible to take in the town's bustling port activity. There's also a tiny cafe. Follow the walkway until reaching the **Museo Naval y Marítimo** (described under "What to See & Do," above). To return, double back and descend via the *ascensor,* or head down the walkway that begins at the cafe, and take a left at Calle Carampangue.

PLAZA VICTORIA/MUSEO A CIELO ABIERTO/LA SEBASTIANA (PABLO NERUDA'S HOUSE)

Plaza Victoria is the prettiest plaza in Valparaíso, which is why cityfolk come here to stroll, sit, and socialize. In the late 1880s this plaza was the elegant center of society, as is evident by the grand trees, trickling fountain, and sculptures imported from Lima that recall that era's heyday.

From the plaza, head south on Calle Molina to Alduante for the **Open Air Museum,** which features more than 20 murals painted on cement retainer and building walls along winding streets. The project, inaugurated in 1992, features murals conceived by well-known Chilean painters and carried out by students. Begin at the steep stairway at Alduante Street and turn left at Pasaje Guimera, and left again at the balcony walkway that leads to **Ascensor Espíritu Santo** (you can ride the funicular up and backtrack this route, walking down). Continue along Calle Rudolph until reaching Calle Ferrari. It's possible to walk up Ferrari to number 692 and **La Sebastiana,** Pablo Neruda's old house (described in "What to See & Do," above), although it's a bit of a hike. Head down Ferrari all the way to Edwards and Colón. Note that the Open Air Museum runs through an interesting but grubby, somewhat rough neighborhood, and for that reason might not appeal to everyone.

VALPARAÍSO AFTER DARK

Valparaíso is famous for its nightlife, especially its bohemian pubs and bars where poets, writers, tango aficionados, sailors, university students, and just about everyone else spend hours drinking, dancing, and socializing well into the early morning hours. In fact, most restaurants and bars do not adhere to a set closing hour, but instead close "when the candles burn down."

Most places serve snacks, especially bars and pubs that operate as restaurants by day. **Cinzano,** facing Plaza Aníbal Pinto on Calle Esmerelda (☎ 32/213043), hosts dinner dances and spotlights tango music and singers in a wonderful, early 20th century ambience. **La Columbina** (☎ 32/236254) is frequented by the 30-and-up crowd for its comfortable ambience, live jazz and bolero music, and view of the glittering lights of Valparaíso that spread out below; take a cab or the funicular Ascensor Peral and walk down Paseo Yugoslavo.

A few hip spots run along Errázuriz and include **Barlovento,** Errázuriz 1156 (☎ 32/595723), one of the few modern bars in town, designed with halogen lights and metallic tables; **La Piedra Feliz,** Errázuriz 1054 (☎ 32/256788), has wooden floors and a tranquil atmosphere—until they fire up live music in the evening from Tuesday to Sunday; and the more traditional **Roland Bar,** Errázuriz 1152 (☎ 32/235123).

Ecuador Street is packed with discos and bars, and although its rank as the in spot has waned, it's still a popular area, especially among the 20- to 40-year-old crowd. Try **Bar Azul,** Ecuador 167 (no phone), which has candlelit tables, jazz on weekends, and, as the name states, a blue interior; there's also **Bar Emile Dubois,** Ecuador 144 (☎ 32/213486), an offbeat bar/disco whose name is an homage to the first person to die under capital punishment in Chile, and where drinks come with names like *strangulation.*

3 Excursions Outside Valparaíso & Viña del Mar

ISLA NEGRA

78 mi (125km) W of Santiago

The coast south of Valparaíso is dotted with small towns, none of which hold much interest to the traveler apart from Isla Negra, a tiny village and home to Pablo Neruda's third, and most interesting, home. Isla Negra, which means Black Island, is not an island but a promontory. There are several good cafes and restaurants here, such as the **Café del Poeta** (located within the museum) and the **Hostería La Candela,** making for a pleasant half-day trip. The coastal strip has been declared a Zona Típica (Heritage Zone) to preserve the area from becoming overrun by multistoried apartment buildings. You can get here from Valparaíso **by bus** with the company Pullman (☎ 32/224025), which leaves every half hour from the bus terminal. To get here **by car,** you'll need to drive back out toward Santiago on Ruta 68 until you see the sign for Algarrobo and the road back toward the coast. Isla Negra is south of Algarrobo.

✪ **Casa Pablo Neruda.** Costanera of Isla Negra. ☎ 35/461284. Admission $4. Summer Tues–Sun 10am–8pm; winter Tues–Fri 10am–2pm and 3–6pm; Sat, Sun, and holidays 10am–8pm.

This was Neruda's favorite home, and the best preserved of his three houses. It's packed full of books by his favorite authors and the whimsical curios, trinkets, and toys he collected during his travels around the world, including African masks, ships in bottles, butterflies, and more. You can see the home by guided (bilingual) tour only, which lasts about 40 minutes.

PARQUE NACIONAL LA CAMPANA

Chile is home to the southernmost palm tree in the world, the Palma Chilena (*Jubaea chilensis*). This particular palm has the thickest trunk of any of the hundreds of known species of palm. It was almost harvested to extinction for its sap that was used to make *miel de palma,* which is much like pancake syrup. The Chilean Palm has been planted in parks in London and California, but you can see thousands of them here at the La Campana National Park, about 27 miles (43km) from Viña del Mar. These palms grow very slowly and do not produce their first fruit until after 40 years, and can live as long as 800 years.

The park also offers surprisingly beautiful views, such as from the lookout point on Cerro La Campana that allows hikers to view the Andes on one side and the Pacific on the other. Charles Darwin stood at this very spot and admired the view in 1834. There are three sectors in the park, each with separate entrances: Palmar de Ocoa, Granizo, and Cajón Grande. There is an easy walk in the Cajón Grande sector, and a longer, 3-hour climb in the Granizo sector. The Granizo sector is the park's main entrance, and here you'll find a park ranger station with information (☎ **33/441342**).

Palmar de Ocoa is where you really get to view the sea of thick palms. This section of the park can be reached by road or by foot from the Sector Granizo (which is really a full-day trip that is best done as a backpack trip). There is a 3.5-mile (6km) trail here to a waterfall. To get here by car, take Ruta 5 north through Llaillay and take the turn-off to Los Maitenes and Palmar de Ocoa. You'll need to drive or arrange a tour to come to this sector because there is no bus service.

The park is open daily 8:45am to 5:30pm (☎ **33/441342**; www.procorp.cl/web/index2.html). Admission is $3 adults, $1 children under 12. **Buses Golondrina** leaves from Santiago's San Borja Terminal every 30 minutes (☎ **2/778-7082**) and arrives at San Francisco de Limache—from here you take a *colectivo* (shared taxi). Due to changing service, ask at the visitor's centers in Valparaíso or Viña del Mar for information about tours and transportation to La Campana. By car from Santiago, take Ruta 68 through Casablanca, then head right toward Villa Alemana and then Limache.

4 Cajón de Maipo

San Alfonso is 41mi (65km) E of Santiago

Cajón de Maipo is part *huaso* (a kind of Chilean cowboy), part artist's colony, part small-town charm tucked into a valley in the foothills of the Andes. From Santiago it's less than 1 hour to the heart of the valley, the reason so many city denizens come to exchange the city smog and cement for Cajón de Maipo's rugged, pastoral setting of towering peaks, freshly scented forest slopes, and the roar of the Maipo River as it descends along its route to the sea.

The highlight of this area is **El Morado National Park** (see "Attractions & Activities," below), but it is certainly not a requisite destination. Cajón de Maipo offers a wide array of outdoor activities, such as rafting, horseback riding, hiking, climbing, and more, but it also offers a chance to linger over a good lunch or picnic, stroll around the area, and maybe even lay your head down for the night in one of the charming little cabañas that line the valley.

The well-paved road through this valley follows the trajectory of the Maipo River. Along the way you'll pass dozens of stalls set up by locals who sell fresh bread, honey, *kuchen* (a dense cake), empanadas, and chocolate to passers-by.

Then you'll pass the tiny hamlets of Vertientes and San José de Maipo, the principal city of the area founded in 1792 when silver was discovered in the foothills. The colonial adobe homes and 18th-century church still surround the traditional plaza in the center of town. Continuing southeast the road curves past San Alfonso and eventually reaches a police checkpoint where drivers register before continuing on the dirt road to El Morado. It is about a 2-hour drive to El Morado, due to the potholed condition of the dirt portion of the road past San Gabriel.

ESSENTIALS

GETTING THERE   By Bus   Blue and white buses leave from the Metro station at Parque O'Higgins (line 2) to San José de Maipo about every 15 minutes from 6am to 11:30pm, and every half hour for San Alfonso. If you're going to El Morado, you need to catch a local bus in the Cajón de Maipo. Your hotel should be able to arrange a private minivan tour to Cajón de Maipo.

By Car   The route to Cajón de Maipo is fairly straightforward, but it's possible to miss the turn-off if you're not paying attention. Head south on Avenida Los Leones in Providencia. The road will change its name to España, then Macul. Continue through the neighborhood of La Florida, and take a left at the fork at Puente Alto. If you plan to go to El Morado, note that there is a police checkpoint where drivers must show their documents, including a passport.

WHERE TO STAY

✪ **Cascada de las Animas.** San Alfonso s/n, San Alfonso. ☎ **2/861-1303.** www.cascadalasanimas.cl. E-mail: cascadaa@ctcinternet.cl. 9 units. $52 cabaña for 2. No credit cards. Free parking.

This tourism center is run by the bohemian Astorga-Moreno family, long-time residents who own a tremendous amount of acreage outside San Alfonso, part of which is used for excursions and 80 campground and picnic sites scattered about a lovely, wooded hillside. What is really special here, however, are their enchanting log cabins, set amid sylvan, leafy surroundings and uniquely built with carved wood details. The cabins are rustic, but snug and comfortable, with fully equipped kitchens and wood-burning stoves. Many have second-floor bedrooms, so the living and dining area is left for relaxing and not sleeping, as is the case with many cabañas. A bonus at Cascada is they've got an ideally situated outdoor swimming pool. They offer kayaking, rafting, and horseback riding excursions and there is a full-service restaurant. The ambience is a cross between outdoorsy and new age, as the owners also offer meditation, healing programs, and a women's spiritual retreat.

✪ **La Bella Durmiente.** Calle Los Maitenes 115, San Alfonso. ☎ **2/861-1525.** www.labelladurmiente.com. E-mail: labelladurmiente@mail.com. 5 units. TV. $55 double. No credit cards. Free parking.

Located at the end of a steep dirt road, these fairy-tale cabañas seem as if they've jumped out of the tale *Sleeping Beauty,* which is what the name means—but the word *durmiente* also refers to the thick wooden railroad planks used to build these quaint cabins. Each cabaña is distinct, and all are handcrafted from wood and stucco and nestled among a grove of trees that surround a small restaurant and pool. The style is rustic but refined; three are set among thick woods, so are slightly darker, although two, including the cozy honeymoon cabin, have sunny patios. There are cabins for two to six guests; the latter is especially nice with a large dining area. If you don't want to cook, you can opt for full pension. Maid service comes only with the full pension price.

Piedra Luna. Calle Los Maitenes 100, San Alfonso. ☎/fax **2/861-1542**. E-mail: mastorga@rdc.cl. 5 units. Cabañas $75 for 6; $37–$52 for 2. No credit cards. Free parking.

Piedra Luna is a set of cabañas within one large building, somewhat like a rustic, wood-and-stone condominium unit. It's just across the road from La Bella, and although it's not as charming, the couple who own and run the establishment strive to make you feel like part of the family. The cabañas are decent, with comfy beds and large windows from which to gaze at the stars at night; two have mountain views. The simple kitchens are okay, but they don't exactly inspire you to cook. Cabañas meant for four are ridiculously tight; go for a six-person cabaña instead. There are two doubles prices, as one comes with a separate bedroom. In the main building is a large living area with tables, a couch, and large-screen TV. The English- and German-speaking owners can often be found here, and they are always up for a good chat.

WHERE TO DINE

Casa Bosque. Camino el Volcán 16829. ☎ **2/871-1570**. Main courses $10–$16. AE, DC, MC, V. Sun, Wed, Thur 1pm–9:30pm; Fri–Sat 1pm–1am. STEAKHOUSE.

If you don't eat at Casa Bosque, stop here anyway to admire the fabulously outlandish architecture. The local artist who designed Casa Bosque has left his mark on many buildings in Cajón de Maipo, but none as dramatically as here: polished, raw tree trunks are kept in their natural shape, forming madcap doorframes, ceiling beams, and pillars; oddly shaped windows and amorphous stucco fill in the gaps. It's pure fantasy, and adults will love it as much as kids. If you're wondering about the food, Casa Bosque is a *parrilla,* and it serves delicious grilled beef, chicken, and sausages from a giant indoor barbecue, which you can pair with fresh salads, creamy potatoes, or a grilled provolone cheese, along with a few vegetarian dishes, all served by waiters in tunics.

However, there's a major drawback at the Casa Bosque: During the weekend lunch hour, this large restaurant is absolutely packed, mostly with families with screaming kids. It must also be said that service on weekends is atrocious, and waiters are so overwhelmed that they tend to ignore several of their tables completely. Better to come on a weekday.

Cascada de las Ánimas. Just past San Alfonso, turn right at sign. ☎ **2/861-1303**. Main courses $5.50–$11; sandwiches $3–$5. No credit cards. Dec–Mar daily 8am–midnight; Nov–Apr open Sat, Sun, and holidays only. CHILEAN/VEGETARIAN.

Cascada serves a delightful menu of Chilean and vegetarian dishes, but what's really special here is this woodsy restaurant's idyllic location vertiginously high above the Maipo River. For the best view, grab a table outside on the sunny deck. The menu offers a plentiful variety of dishes, including pastas, meats, and seafood. The fish is especially good, particularly the sole marinated in herbs and served with rosemary-flavored rice. For lunch you might be interested in something lighter, such as a sandwich or bowl of hearty *cazuela,* the popular Chilean chicken stew. Vegetarian dishes include tofu sautéed with vegetables and soy sauce and served on a bed of rice. The food is prepared simply, but with heart, and there's music and dancing in the evenings.

✪ **La Petite France.** Camino el Volcán 16096. ☎ **2/861-1967**. Main courses $7.50–$10. No credit cards. Tues–Sun noon–midnight. FRENCH BISTRO.

The walls of La Petite France, with its Edith Piaf posters and ads for French products, are pure French kitsch, which might make this little restaurant seem like an anomaly given its location in rural Chile. But the locals love it, and you will too. Since opening 2 years ago, La Petite's cuisine has consistently drawn in diners with a menu that successfully blends French bistro classics with flavorful Chilean and international dishes. Menu highlights include filet mignon in a puff pastry with Roquefort sauce and turkey breast stuffed with almonds, plums, and apples in a cactus sauce. Of course, there's also pâté, escargot, and Croque Monsieur. The outstanding desserts are laid out enticingly across a long table: tarte tatin, crème brûlée, and chocolate layer cake are just a few of the mouth-watering choices.

✪ **Trattoria Italiana.** Camino el Volcán 9831. ☎ **2/871-1498.** Main courses $7.50–$9. No credit cards. Thurs–Sun 1–11:30pm. ITALIAN.

Owned and operated by a Genovese family who immigrated to this region several years ago, Trattoria Italiana serves wonderful homemade pastas and stone oven–baked pizzas (pizzas are served Saturday and Sunday only). Everything is made using organic and local farm ingredients, such as the delicious mozzarella bought from a family in Cajón de Maipo and smoked here at the restaurant. Pastas include raviolis, cannelloni, fungi fettuccine, and pesto lasagna, but you might want to nibble an antipasti platter with fresh focaccia bread. The cozy restaurant has indoor and outdoor seating at wooden tables; the staff gives a warm welcome to all who pass through the doors. It's open Thursday to Sunday only, but if you're in the area during one of these days, don't miss a stop here.

ATTRACTIONS & ACTIVITIES

EL MORADO NATIONAL PARK　This 3,000-hectare (7,410-acre) park is 56 miles (90km) from Santiago. It takes its name from the sooty-colored rock of the Morado mountain (*morado* means "dark" or "bruised"). The views at El Morado are impressive; the pretty alpine landscape never ceases to awe its visitors. And there's a great spot to take in all this beauty at the attractive mountain lodge **Refugio Alemán at Lo Valdés.** The *refugio* serves a tasty fixed-price lunch and dinner, and you can eat out on the deck while gazing out at the snowcapped peaks. Refugio Alemán has clean, bunk-bed–style accommodations should you decide to spend the night. Reserve at ☎ **2/232-0476** (note that their telephone isn't always working). Per-person rates are $39; full-board rates are $59.

　　The somewhat ragged complex at **Baños Morales** features several hot spring pools open 8:30am to 8pm during the summer and 10am to 4pm April to September (☎ **2/226-9826**). It can get a little packed during the peak of summer. It is possible to camp here, and there are a few basic, and not very cheery, *hosterías.* There are more hot springs at **Termas de Colina,** located in a gorgeous mountain setting. To get there by car, continue past Lo Valdés up an increasingly poor road, climbing past a mine to where the road ends. If you don't have a car, there are transport services to Termas de Colina at Baño Morales.

RAFTING　Rafting the Maipo River is extremely popular among *Santiaguinos* and foreigners alike. Although the season runs from September until April, the river really gets going from November to February, when rafters can expect to ride Class III and IV rapids. Two reliable companies offer half-day rafting excursions: **Cascada de las Animas** (☎ **2/861-1303** in Maipo) arranges rafting trips from its tourism complex (see "Where to Stay," above) just past San Alfonso, but it's best to reserve beforehand from the office in Santiago at Orrego Luco 40 (☎ **2/234-2274;** www.cascada-expediciones.com/ch). Another highly respected outfitter is **Altué Expediciones,** in Santiago, Encomenderos 83 (☎ **2/232-1103;** www.altue.com).

HORSEBACK RIDING　Visitors to El Morado can rent horses with a guide at Baños Morales or Termas de Colina (see "El Morado National Park," above) for about $6 to $15 per person, depending on group size and duration. The best horseback ride, however, is a half day with Cascada Expediciones through its own private chunk of the Andes (see above). This ride is suitable for families. Cascada offers multiple-day horse-back trips, including a 12-day Andes cross.

5 Pomaire

40mi (65km) W of Santiago

If you love ceramic pottery, Pomaire is your place. Pomaire is a small, dusty village that has dedicated itself to producing clay pottery by the ton, and its main street (almost the only street here) overflows with shops selling vases, funny little figurines, decorative pieces and pots, plates, and other kitchen crockery—all at low, low prices.

The village is an old *pueblo de indios,* something like an Indian reservation confined to one town, created in the late 1700s southwest of Santiago. A journey here also gives visitors an opportunity to sample *comida campestre,* home-style regional foods such as *cazuela* (a chicken stew), *pastel de choclo* (a meat and corn casserole), *chancho* (pork) served stewed, fried, or mixed in with doughy bread, and the area's famous empanadas that weigh 1.5 kilos (3.3 pounds), which can be found at **El Parrón de Pomaire** restaurant. The two best restaurants here are **Los Naranjos** and **San Antonio.** The town itself is tiny, and all of these restaurants are but a few short blocks apart. Note that Pomaire is pretty much shut down on Mondays, and weekends are crowded.

To get to Pomaire, you can rent a car or take **Buses Melipilla,** which has several daily trips from the San Borja Terminal in Santiago at Alameda O'Higgins 3250. The bus will leave you at the end of the road to Pomaire, where you'll have to take a *colectivo,* or shared taxi, into town. To get here by car, take Ruta 78 toward San Antonio until you see the sign for Pomaire 2 miles (3km) before Melipilla. You can check at the Santiago visitor's center to see if any tours are being offered here. The Undurraga Winery (see "The Wineries of the Central Valley," below) is on the way to Pomaire, and feasibly you could visit both.

6 The Wineries of the Central Valley

The international popularity of Chilean wine has soared over the past decade, as Chilean winemakers increasingly export quality vintages that are sold at lower prices than American and European counterparts. Chileans often brag about their industry, claiming a wine tradition that stretches back to the days of the Spanish conquest.

But modern wine production didn't really take off until the late '70s, when Spaniard Miguel Torres introduced modern techniques that revolutionized the industry. Chileans love their wine, but they haven't caught on to some of the finer varieties currently being produced—instead, most wineries export the bulk of their wine to Europe and the United States. In fact, Chile is now the third-largest exporter of wine to the United States, behind France and Italy. Even French and American companies such as Châteaux Lafite and Robert Mondavi are jumping on the bandwagon, forming partnerships with several large wine houses.

The majority of wineries can be found within 20 miles (35km) outside Santiago, south toward the Central Valley. This Mediterranean-like region provides fertile ground for grape production, and is close enough for a half-day trip. The easiest way to get to these wineries is by rental car. If you don't have your own transportation, go to the tourism kiosk at Ahumeda and Húerfanos and inquire whether there are any tours available. Also, all the travel agencies listed in chapter 9, "Santiago," offer day trips. Apart from wine tasting, several wineries are historic monuments and worth the visit for the architecture alone. Concha y Toro is a prime example.

Concha y Toro. Av. Virginia Subercaseaux 210, Pirque. ☎ **2/853-0042.** Tours in English Mon–Fri 10am, noon, and 3:30pm; Sat 10am and noon. Tours in Spanish Mon–Fri 11am, 2:30pm, and 4:30pm; Sat 11am. Reservations recommended. Tour free; wine-tasting 75¢ a glass.

Located at the southeastern edge of Santiago, this winery is the largest and best known, sort of the Gallo winery of Chile. It was founded by mining magnate Francisco Subercaseaux and expanded in 1883 by his nephew Don Melchor Concha y Toro, who imported European vines and built grand wine cellars. Today, the winery counts nine vineyards around the Central Valley. Don Melchor also enlisted the help of Gustave Renner to design a magnificent 24-hectare (59-acre) garden to surround the winery and his beautiful, stately manor house (illustrated on the labels of Santa Emiliana, a popular table red).

Today the grounds, including tranquil ponds, grand old trees, roses, and a riot of colorful flowers, are maintained by eight full-time gardeners. A visit to Concha y Toro includes a tour of the garden and the original *bodega,* ending in a well-designed tasting room where you can taste and purchase wine. Note that this is a very popular winery. Don't miss the Don Melchor Cabernet Sauvignon or the Almaviva Cabernet Sauvignon (although at more than $60 a bottle, it's possibly Chile's most expensive wine). To get here by car, at the Puente Alto cross the Maipo River toward Pirque until you're at Av. Virginia Subercaseaux 210, or you can take a taxi.

Cousiño-Macul. Av. Quilín 7100, Peñalolen, Santiago. ☎ **2/284-1011.** Bilingual tours Mon–Sat 11am; reservations required. Free admission. Wine-tasting $1 per glass.

If you visit just one of Chile's traditional wineries, make it this one. Cousiño-Macul's vineyard not only produces some of the finest wines in Chile, but is also an extraordinarily beautiful estate that affords a glimpse into the opulence that defined Chile's elite families during the late 19th century. The vineyard's history stretches back to 1546, when Juan Jufré planted Chile's first grapevines here at the site of an old Incan village called Macul. The property changed hands over the centuries until it was bought by coal magnate Matías Cousiño in 1856. His only son, Luís, along with his wife, Isabel Goyenechea, founded the present winery in 1871, importing European grapevines and inviting French designer Gustave Renner to create a spectacular garden. The Cousiños also erected a home in Santiago, the magnificent **Palacio Cousiño** (see "Seeing the Sights," in chapter 9). The winery is still owned by the Cousiño family today, and wine-tasting tours include a visit to a small museum that charts the property's history as well as a viewing of the tremendous collection of red wines.

Tours include a visit to the antique *bodegas* and a demonstration of wine-bottling. Visitors can purchase wine at a 15% discount. Don't miss the Antiguas Reservas or Finis Terrae cabernet sauvignons. To get here by car from Santiago, take Avenida Américo Vespucio Sur and at the Quilín turnabout, take Avenida Quilín toward the Andes; the winery is behind the park. By bus, take bus no. 390 or 391 at Alameda O'Higgins in Santiago and get off at Tobalaba and Quillín streets. You could also take a cab.

Undurraga. Old road to Melipilla, Km34. ☎ **2/817-2346.** Tours Mon–Fri 10am–4pm; call ahead for a reserved time. Free admission. No wine-tasting.

This is another century-old winery steeped in tradition. There are actually two facilities—the original site 10 minutes from Santiago, and a new full-service facility several hours south of Santiago in the Colchagua Valley. Founded by Don Francisco Undurraga Vicuña in 1885, this was the first winery to import grape varieties from Europe, such as Germany's Riesling and France's Sauvignon Blanc, Cabernet Franc, Merlot, and Pinot Noir. This venerable winery, the Fundo Santa Ana, does not offer wine tastings or sales, but the whitewashed colonial buildings set among wonderful palm-lined gardens and the in-depth description of the history and means of wine production can be enlightening.

The modern facility in the Colchagua Valley does, however, offer wine tastings and tours, and they'll take you on a tour of the vineyards by horseback or horse-drawn carriage, if you so choose. Call the winery for more information. You can't go wrong with one of Undurraga's Chardonnays or Cabernet Sauvignons. You can get here only by private vehicle: Take Ruta 78 toward San Antonio; at Km34 take the old road to Melipilla past Molloco.

Viña Santa Rita. Hendaya 60, #202, Las Condes, Santiago. ☎ **2/362-2100** or 2/ 362-2520. Fax 2/228-6335. http://santarita.com. Guided tours, reservations required, Tues–Fri at 10:30, 11:30am, 12:15, 3, and 4pm; Sat and Sun 12:30 and 3:30pm. Tours $6 per person, includes wine-tasting.

Located about an hour from downtown Santiago, Santa Rita offers wine-tasting tours and beautiful, lush garden surroundings that make for an extremely pleasant afternoon excursion. Founded in 1880 by Domingo Fernández Concha near his hacienda Alto Jahuel, which once gave refuge to Bernardo O'Higgins after his failed bid for independence in 1814, the winery offers tours through its *bodega* and wine-tasting in its Casa de Paula Jaraquemada, both national monuments. There's also a restaurant. Santa Rita produces a wide selection of varieties and prices, including the "120" line that is wildly popular in Chile. Don't miss the Casa Real Cabernet. To get here by car, head south on the Panamericana for 26 miles (42km) until Buin, where you'll see signs for Santa Rita.

7 The Nearby Ski Resorts

Every year, thousands of Americans and Europeans head south during the austral (southern hemisphere) winter to hit the slopes of the Andes at one of Chile's famed **ski resorts.** If you're in Chile from mid-June to late September, you might consider joining the ranks—it's easy to arrange, and you can go for just the day. Resorts centered on the Farallones area, such as Valle Nevado, La Parva, and El Colorado, can be reached in a 1- to 1½-hour drive from Santiago, although there's first-class and economical lodging in the area should you decide to spend the night. At 2½ hours from Santiago, the venerable, world-renowned Portillo is a very viable option, too, and anyone thinking of skiing for several days or a week might consider bunking in its all-inclusive hotel.

Skiing in Chile is becoming so popular worldwide that a sizeable percentage of ski patrols and instructors at these resorts are foreigners from countries such as the United States and France. All resorts are high above the treeline, so you'll have to trade forests for views of rugged Andean peaks and, at Farallones, that ever-present, nefarious sea of smog that settles over Santiago.

GETTING TO THE RESORTS   If you don't have your own transportation, **Ski Total** (☎ 2/246-6881) offers minivan transfers to all resorts for around $10 per person. You must come to their offices at Av. Apoquindo 4900, #40 (in the Omnium shopping mall in Las Condes—the best way to get there is by taxi) no later than 8am. If your hotel is reasonably close, they'll pick you up. Call for more information.

PORTILLO

Centro de Ski Portillo. Renato Sanchez 4270, Santiago. ☎ **800/829-5325** in the U.S., or 2/263-0606. Fax 2/263-0595. www.skiportillo.com. E-mail: info@skiportillo.com. Lift tickets $30 adults, $22 kids 12 and under. AE, DC, MC, V.

For 50 years, the world-renowned Portillo Ski Resort has hosted everyone from the U.S. Ski Team to Fidel Castro, and it continues to entertain a veritable Who's Who in skiing and snowboarding. Portillo is set high in the Andes on the shore of beautiful Lake Inca, about a 2½-hour drive from Santiago, near the Argentine border. Although open to the public for day skiing, Portillo really operates as a weeklong, package-driven resort that includes lodging, ski tickets, all meals, and use of their plentiful amenities. There are no other hotels in the area, ensuring short lift lines and lots of untracked powder.

Portillo's greatest asset is the heavy snowfall it receives each year (although there's snowmaking equipment just in case), which also means that the road to the resort can close for days and tire chains are frequently required. Argentines and Brazilians constitute 50% of the guests here; in July, the resort is popular with families (with day care, activity programs, and a superb ski school, it's easy to see why); August and September see a more adult crowd.

The grand yet rustic hotel, with its sumptuous leather-paneled dining room and bar, forgoes glitz for a more relaxed atmosphere encouraged by its American owners. Rooms are average-size and bathrooms are somewhat cramped, but hot, powerful showers make up for it. The suites are modern and come with a living area, and families can rent an apartment with connecting rooms. There's cheaper lodging at the Octagonal Lodge, which has smaller rooms fitted with two bunk beds. The rooms are comfortable and they come with balconies and the same amenities as the hotel. The Inca Lodge is another bunkhouse, popular with 20-somethings.

Portillo really pushes the Saturday to Saturday ski packages, and although there are a wealth of activities, a week might be too long for some—check for availability of a weekend or 4-night stay.

The ski resort has 12 lifts, including five chairs, eight T-bars, and a unique Va et Vient "slingshot" lift that leaves skiers at the top of short but vertiginous chutes. The terrain is 70% intermediate/advanced, 20% moderate, and 10% easier. Portillo puts on special events for guests, such as races and a nighttime torchlight parade.

WHERE TO STAY   Hotel Portillo's 7-day packages include lodging, lift tickets, four meals per day in the dining room, and use of all facilities. Rates shown are per person; the range reflects the low to high season: double with lake view $940 to $2,045, suites $1,505 to $3,275, family apartments (min. four people) $735 to $1,595. Children under 4 are free, kids 4 to 11 pay half price, and kids 12 to 17 pay about 25% less than adults. In July, check out the "Kids Ski Free" week. The **Octagonal Lodge** features four bunks to a room, and includes the same amenities as above for $610 to $1,185. The **Inca Lodge** charges $520 to $815.

Guests of the hotel and the Octagonal Lodge take their meals in the hotel's dining room, which serves a superb international menu, from gourmet to hamburgers, including a kid's menu. Guests of the Inca Lodge take their meals in a cafeteria on the first floor. There's also a bar that hosts nightly live music, and there's a disco with bar.

Amenities at the hotel include room service, cybercafe, laundry, gift/sport shop, fitness center, outdoor heated pool, sauna, massage, beauty salon, ski tuning and repair, ski rental, full-court gymnasium, game room, theater, child-care center.

Valle Nevado. Office at Gertrudis Echeñique 441. ☎ **2/206-0027.** Fax 2/208-0695. www. vallenevado.com. E-mail: info@vallenevado.com. Lift tickets $30 adults, $20 kids 12 and under. AE, DC, MC, V.

Valle Nevado is a 9,000-hectare (22,230-acre), full-service ski resort featuring three hotels, seven restaurants, a condominium complex, and dozens of shops squeezed into one compact village straddling a ridge overlooking a plunging canyon. It is

French-designed, somewhat like the St. Moritz of Chile. European chefs and instructors from North America, France, Switzerland, and elsewhere give the place an international feel. The terrain at Valle Nevado is not as steep as Portillo, but it offers more variety and longer runs.

Many *Santiaguinos,* especially families with kids, head to Valle Nevado for the day because of its close proximity to the city; that also means it can get very busy on weekends even though the parking lot closes after 200 cars. The resort went through an expansion last year with the completion of new condominium units. If management ever makes good on its long-promised ski lift to the base of El Plomo (17,815 ft. high), it will be the highest ski resort in the world. Valle Nevado offers lodging in three comfortable hotels with singles, doubles, and suites; there are no double beds, however. Prices include lodging, ski tickets, breakfast, après-ski, and dinner, which can be taken in any one of the resort's restaurants.

The ski resort has 27 runs serviced by three chair lifts and six T-bars, as well as a helicopter service for those who want to ski steep powder. There's also hang gliding, paragliding, and organized ski safaris. The terrain is 15% expert, 30% advanced, 40% intermediate, and 15% beginner.

WHERE TO STAY   All-inclusive prices are per person, double occupancy, and the range reflects low to high season (prices drop as length of stay increases). The five-star **Hotel Valle Nevado** features full amenities and a ski-in, ski-out location for $160 to $376 per night. There's also a piano bar, glass-enclosed gym, sauna, cozy lounge, and more.

The four-star **Hotel Puerta del Sol** consists mostly of suites that go for $145 to $375 a night, which isn't that much more than a double. North-facing rooms with balconies and views of the mountain are $130 to $328 per night; south-facing rooms that overlook the parking lot and do not have balconies are $116 to $296 per night. Amenities at the Puerta del Sol include cable TV, a sauna, a game room, a piano bar, and a gym.

Hotel Tres Puntas has many bunk-bed rooms; each features a minibar, cable TV, and a full bathroom. This hotel is frequented by a younger crowd, which is why you'll find the liveliest bar here; room prices range from $97 to $215 per night.

Valle Nevado has many good, even excellent restaurants that serve international, French, Italian, and Chilean cuisine—and there is sushi in the lounge bar. There is a second bar in the Hotel Tres Puntas.

Amenities: In addition to the above, the following amenities are available for all hotels at no additional charge with some packages (inquire first whether they are included in your hotel's package): room service, laundry, outdoor heated pool, whirlpool, sauna, fitness gym, cinema, child-care center, game room. There's also a bank, high-end boutiques, and a minimarket, and the bars feature changing nightly music and themed parties.

LA PARVA

La Parva Centro Esquí. La Concepción 266, #301. ☎ **2/264-1466** (in Santiago), or 2/220-9530 (direct). Fax 2/264-1575. www.laparva.cl. Lift tickets low to high season: $25–$30 adults, $17–$22 kids 5–12 and seniors, $6.50–$9 kids 4 and under. Interconnect tickets with Valle Nevado are $35–$40 adults, $22–$27 kids 12 and under. A 20% discount is offered to women on Wed and students on Thurs.

This resort is the smallest and most exclusive of the group. The name *La Parva* means "The Haystack," which is the name of the peak that overlooks the resort. La Parva is a great place to ski, with decent terrain that doesn't see the crowds that flock to Valle Nevado. For a few bucks more, you can ski the two with an interconnecting ticket.

La Parva is somewhat like a private club for well-heeled families from Santiago, many of whom own a condo or chalet here. There are few lodging options for the outside visitor, apart from a few apartments, but if you're coming up for the day only, it's not an issue.

The view from La Parva is spectacular, but it is of often-smoggy Santiago. The resort's terrain breaks down into 10% expert, 30% advanced, 45% intermediate, and 15% beginner. There are four chairs and 10 surface lift runs, such as T-bars. There are a few very good restaurants at the base and slopeside, including **La Marmita de Pericles** (no phone), an Alpine, fondue-style restaurant.

The **Apartments at La Parva** (☎ 2/264-1574 in Santiago; fax 2/264-1575, 2/211-4400 at La Parva) are weeklong, Friday-to-Friday rentals. Apartments range from luxury to standard, and they also feature a kitchen; rates include use of a swimming pool and daily maid service. Prices shown reflect low and high season: luxury $3,400 to $4,400, superior $2,600 to $3,400, and standard $2,000 to $2,600. Luxury ranges from four to five bedrooms for a maximum of 10 people; superior ranges from three to four bedrooms, maximum eight people; and standard, includes two bedrooms, maximum six people.

EL COLORADO/FARELLONES

El Colorado. Apoquindo 4900, #47–48 (Edificio Omnium). ☎ **2/246-3344.** Fax 2/206-4078. www.elcolorado.cl. E-mail: ski-colorado@ctcinternet.cl. Lift tickets low to high season: $25–$32 adults, $16–$20 kids 5–12, $6 seniors and kids 4 and under. Prices $18–$24 on Wed for women, Mon for students. AE, DC, MC, V. Ski rental available.

El Colorado is a very popular resort for its versatility, both because of its location just 24 miles (39km) from Santiago and its large size. It's a great resort—one of my favorites, really—because the snow conditions always seem better and there are fewer people than Valle Nevado. The resort is actually made of up of two villages, Villa Farellones and Villa Colorado, that are connected by two ski lifts.

Farellones is the older, more economical option located just slightly downhill from Colorado, and is popular with beginning skiers, tobogganists, snowman builders, and the like. El Colorado's modern center is really the hub of the resort, and skiers generally come directly here. The resort features plenty of terrain for beginners, but it includes several steep powder runs.

There are several cafeterias, as well as **El Alambique,** a restaurant serving Swiss Alpine fare. The 1,000-hectare (2,470-acre) resort has five chair lifts and 17 surface lifts, such as T-bars. There's a bit of off-piste skiing, and there are 22 runs: 4 for experts, 3 advanced, 4 intermediate, and 11 beginner. El Colorado has snowmaking equipment.

For lodging, try the **El Colorado Apart-Hotel** (☎ 2/246-0660). Per person, average weekly lodging rates are, low to high season, $493 to $869 for two, $428 to $737 for four, one bathroom; larger guest rooms with two bathrooms and a capacity of up to seven guests are $505 to $875 for four, $395 to $651 for seven-guest occupancy.

8 The Central Valley

The minute you drive out of Santiago, the scenery changes dramatically to wide fields of grapevines, a testament to the nation's thriving wine industry. As you head farther south, the smog begins to thin and more fields unfold until you enter what's known as the Central Valley. Less than one tenth of Chile's land is arable, and a good chunk of it can be found here. The region has both rich soil and a Mediterranean climate conducive to agriculture, and the fresh fruits and vegetables grown here can be bought from one of the many food stands that dot the Panamericana Highway. The region is

The "Wild West" of South America

During the colonial period, the Central Valley was fundamentally agrarian and largely dependent on cattle production. Land was disproportionately divided among its citizens, and wealthy families, who owned the bulk of land, developed their property into ranches called *haciendas* or *estancias*. To tend their giant herds of cattle, hacienda owners hired Chilean "cowboys" called *huasos*. The term *huaso* is believed to have come from the Mapuche term for "shoulders" (the Mapuche, unaccustomed to the sight of horses, assumed that the rider was attached to his horse by its shoulders).

The *huaso* tradition is as much mystery as it is reality, and folks define a "huaso" in a number of different ways, even though the style remains constant. You'll recognize a *huaso* by his wide-brimmed hat, a poncho that is either colorful and short-waisted or long and earth-toned (these longer ponchos are woven so tightly that they're water-resistant), and metal spurs the size of a pinwheel. The *huaso* saddle is fitted with stirrups made of intricately carved wood. Often, especially when attending a special event, the *huaso* wears black leather chaps that cover the leg from ankle to knee and are adorned with tassels.

The *huaso* struts his stuff in one of the occasional **rodeos** that are popular in the Central Valley. The Chilean rodeo is very different from its American counterpart, although some rodeos feature riders attempting to dominate a bucking bronco. Rodeos got their start in Chile in the days when haciendas would round up stray cattle to divide and brand them. Today's rodeo takes place in a half-moon arena called a *medialuna*. Here *huasos* begin the match by demonstrating their agility atop their mounts, followed by the main event in which a *huaso* attempts to pin a young bull against a wall while on horseback, aiming for the rear, which will earn him the most points, and not for the head, which will earn him nothing.

Rodeos are held from September to May, especially during the Independence holiday on September 18 and 19. The city of Rancagua hosts the rodeo championships in September. For more information, call the Federación del Rodeo Chileno at ☎ **2/699-0115.**

---

indeed a food-lover's delight, with so many savory country restaurants along the Panamericana just outside Santiago that many call it the gastronomic axis.

The Central Valley is both urban and rural: Semi-trucks and cars race along the Panamericana from Santiago to flourishing cities such as Rancagua and Talca, but outside those cities, a quick detour off the interstate puts you between poplar-lined, patchwork fields on a dirt road that sees more hooves than wheels. There are several fascinating destinations in this region, but cities such as Rancagua and Talca are not among them. Below are a few of this region's highlights, all the way down to Chillán.

A THERMAL SPA

Termas de Cauquenes. Road to Cauquenes, near Rancagua. ☎/fax **72/899010.** 50 units. MINIBAR TV TEL. Per person $37 riverview double; $48 patio view double. Add $25 per person for full pension. AE, DC, MC, V.

This out-of-the-way thermal spa (about 71 miles/115km from Santiago) is worth the journey from Santiago if you have the time, for its beautiful spa facilities inspired by Vichy in France, its historical appeal, and its lovely, oak-lined park. Termas de

Cauquenes was founded by Spaniards in 1646, although Indians in the area had already enjoyed the curative waters for some time. General San Martín soaked here, and so did Bernardo O'Higgins, who came to Cauquenes to nurse his wounds after the disastrous Battle of Rancagua. Charles Darwin even paid a visit in 1834.

In 1876, a millionaire by the name of Apolinario Soto bought the property and renovated the grounds with a hacienda-style hotel centered on a well-manicured garden and bubbling fountain. There is a tiny chapel and a beautiful, Gothic-style thermal pavilion fitted with colorful stained glass, marble floors, and two facing rows of cubicles with marble bathtubs. The building is known as the "cathedral" for its resemblance to one, and its original design has been thankfully maintained over time. The marble baths are of course more than a century old, but they've added modern whirlpools.

Termas de Cauquenes is now owned by a Swiss chef and his daughter, both of whom are expert at whipping up fine cuisine. The superb menu changes weekly, offering fresh seafood and meats that embrace regional recipes. The dining area is sunny and spacious, with the old-world charm of leather chairs and a long oak bar.

After a good soak in the mineralized water, which is said to alleviate rheumatism and arthritis-related ailments, and a leisurely lunch, you can walk over to the garden park for a stroll or a seat under the rustling, towering oak and eucalyptus trees. The hotel-spa sits above the rushing River Cachapoal and is close to several natural attractions. There is also an outdoor swimming pool.

The hotel's age means some creaky floors and old-fashioned bathrooms. The rooms are best called unpretentious. Some have ceramic floors and open onto the garden patio; others face the river and are soaked in afternoon sun. It is possible to visit for the day, and the cost is $6 for use of the baths only; the swimming pool is for hotel guests only. There are also massages, manicures, and pedicures offered.

En Route to the Spa

If you're driving to the hotel, head south toward Rancagua, and take the road left marked EL TENIENTE or COYA. **El Teniente** is the world's largest underground copper mine, and full-day tours are available for visitors 18 years and older; call Turismo Vigía at ☎ **2/633-7567.**

The road branches off to El Teniente, but continue ahead until you see the sign for the branch-off to Cauquenes. There is another posted access road from the Panamericana south of Rancagua, but don't take it—it's long and bumpy. To get to the spa by bus, you need to take a bus to the Rancagua terminal, and from there a bus to the hotel. Buses leave from Rancagua twice daily, once in the morning and once in the late afternoon. Call the hotel for a current time schedule.

While in the area, you'll want to pay a visit to the **Reserva Nacional Rio Los Cipreses,** a relatively unknown gem of a nature reserve 9 miles (14km) from Cauquenes; it's open daily 8:30am to 6pm; admission is $3. There is a Conaf administration center with park information, including trails and a guide to the flora and fauna of the reserve. Here it is possible to watch wild parrots swoop from trees and tiny caves high on cliffs; there are also rabbitlike *vizcachas* and red foxes, and of course a blanket of cypress trees.

This reserve is highly recommended, but you'll need your own car to get here. If you plan to stay in the hotel, inquire as to whether they can take you there.

A LOVELY RANCH, FOR A DAY TRIP OR OVERNIGHT

✪ **Hacienda Los Lingues.** Reservations in Santiago: Av. Providencia 1100, #205. ☎ **2/235-5446.** Fax 2/235-7604. www.travelvision.com. E-mail: loslingues@entelchile.net.

19 units, 2 suites. TEL. $224 double with breakfast; $440 double with full board. Day tours $46. AE, DC, MC, V.

About 77.5 miles (125km) south of Santiago nestled among poplar-lined country fields and rolling hills is the Hacienda Los Lingues. The Hacienda is one of the oldest and best-preserved haciendas in Chile, and is now run as a splendid, full-service hotel as a member of the exclusive Relais & Châteaux group. If the hotel is a bit pricey for your budget, or if you lack the time for an overnight stay, the Hacienda offers day tours that include a welcome cocktail, tour of the hacienda, lunch in the cavernous wine *bodega,* a horse demonstration, and optional use of a swimming pool. There's also horseback riding at an additional cost.

King Phillip III bestowed this beautiful estate to the first mayor of Santiago in 1599, and it has remained in the same family for 400 years. The center of the estate features portions of the structures that were built here in the early 17th century, but most of the buildings were built around 250 years ago. The thick stone and adobe walls, terra-cotta tile roofs, *cal y canto* (a kind of stone and mortar) wine cellar, and hand-carved doors have been superbly maintained, as have the interiors, which will truly enchant visitors.

From the French salon, with its ruby-red velvet wallpaper and matching furniture, to the classic, formal sitting room, every room is accented with crystal chandeliers, oriental rugs, and antique furniture, and literally brimming with decorative pieces, family photos, collector's items, and fascinating odds and ends that you could spend hours observing and admiring. The guest rooms are decorated individually with antique armoires and tables, iron bedframes and crocheted bedspreads, ancestral family photos, fresh flowers, and a bucket of champagne. A bountiful breakfast is served to you in bed.

Hacienda Los Lingues is actually a working ranch that grows fruit, such as pears and lemons, for export. The estate is also home to one of the most prestigious horsebreeding farms in Latin America. The hotel claims that their horses are purebred descendents of those brought over by the Spanish conquistadors, which were themselves descendents of African varieties. They are beautiful creatures, and have been trained to "corral"—that is, gallop sideways; ask for a demonstration or take one for a ride.

There is also a newer swimming pool complex, a 5-minute walk from the hotel, as well as two clay tennis courts, a game room with an antique snooker table, and a man-made lagoon stocked with trout for fly-fishing.

Now for the staff. It's hard to find a staff prouder of its establishment than the one here at the Hacienda. The hotel is currently run by the charismatic Don Germán, a family descendent who, if he has time, likes to keeps guests entertained at dinner—which, by the way, is excellent, and served family-style at a long, formal table. You'll want to join Germán for an after-dinner drink in the French salon so that he might explain where he got the chunk of Roman tile, what his letter from Queen Elizabeth means, or who the dour-looking woman is in the giant oil painting that hangs on the wall.

To get there, the Hacienda extorts $320 for a private van for a day trip for one to eight people, and $400 for the van if you spend the night. The cheaper alternative is to take a bus to San Fernando (in Santiago, ride to the Univ. de Santiago Metro stop for the bus terminal), then a taxi to the hotel. No matter how you get here, try to plan a trip here if you have the time.

Amenities: Horseback riding, tennis, fly-fishing, outdoor swimming pool, gift shop, game room.

9 Chillán & Termas de Chillán Resort

252 miles (407km) S of Santiago

Chillán is a midsize city known for three things. It's the birthplace of Chilean liberator Bernardo O'Higgins; the **Termas de Chillán** 50 miles (80km) from the city is one of South America's largest and most complete ski and summer resorts; and the **Feria de Chillán** is one of the largest and most colorful crafts and food markets in the country.

A tidy city of 145,000, with five attractive plazas and tree-lined streets, Chillán is a pleasant enough place to spend an afternoon, but it really offers little more of interest to the foreign visitor. If you're driving south to the Lake District, you might consider spending the night here.

Chillán is divided into two sectors: the downtown area and Chillán Viejo, or Old Chillán. The town's history is one of relocations and disasters. Founded as a fort in 1565, Chillán was attacked, abandoned, and rebuilt several times until the government moved the whole settlement to what is now Chillán Viejo.

Probably the worst tragedy to hit the town happened in 1939, when an earthquake destroyed 90% of the city and killed 15,000 of its residents. Fronting the city's central Plaza Bernardo O'Higgins, which is planted with a medley of tree species, including one lofty redwood, is the **Cathedral,** whose utilitarian design seems aimed more at seismic protection than style. Here you'll notice a monumental cross in remembrance of the many who died during the earthquake.

From the plaza, walk 1 block southeast on Constitución and right on Avenida 5 de Abril for 2 blocks until you reach the ✪ **Feria de Chillán.** Here you'll find baskets, *huaso* clothing and saddles, chaps and spurs, pottery, knitwear, and more. There's a colorful fish and vegetable market here, too. The market is not dangerous by any means, but occasionally pickpockets do strike, so keep an eye on your belongings. The market is open every day.

If you still have time, head to the **Mexican Murals** at the Escuela Mexico, Av. O'Higgins 250; it's open Tuesday to Friday 9:30am to 12:30pm and 3 to 6pm; Monday and Saturday 9:30am to 12:30pm. Admission is free. Two famous muralists from Mexico, David Siqueiros and Xavier Guerrero, painted the interior library and stairwell of this school in remembrance of Chillán's residents who were killed in the 1939 earthquake. The library's mural, *Death to the Invader,* is especially impressive.

ESSENTIALS

GETTING THERE   By Air   Chillán is served by the Aeropuerto Carriel Sur in Concepción, about an hour away. There are direct flights here from Santiago several times daily from **Lan Chile/Ladeco** and **Avant.** If you've made hotel reservations in town or in Termas de Chillán, their transfer service will pick you up. If not, you must take a taxi to the bus terminal where buses for Chillán leave every 20 minutes.

By Bus   Linea Sur and **Tur Bus** offer daily service from most major cities, including Santiago. The bus terminal in Chillán is located at Av. O'Higgins 010, and from there you can grab a bus for the Termas.

By Train   Ferrocarriles del Sur offers a 5-hour train trip from Santiago, leaving from the Estación Central and arriving in Chillán at the station at Brasil Street. The cost is $9 per person and there are three trips daily.

VISITOR INFORMATION   Sernatur can be found at 18 de Septiembre 455 (☎ 42/223272; it's open Monday to Saturday 8:30am to 6pm; from November to March, it's open on Sundays from 8:30am to 6pm. It has a large amount of published material.

WHERE TO STAY & DINE

If you're looking for local color and cheap prices, go to the **Municipal Market** across the street from the Fería de Chillán, where simple restaurants prepare seafood, local dishes such as *pastel de choclo,* and dishes with Chillán's famous sausages. Also, across the street from the Café París is the **Fuente Aleman** (☎ **42/21720**), with good sandwiches, quick meals, and food to go.

Café París. Arauco 666. ☎ **42/223881.** Main courses $3–$10. AE, DC, MC, V. Daily 8am–2am. CAFE/CHILEAN.

The París has a cafe on its bottom floor and a smaller restaurant upstairs, and although both serve from the same menu, diners usually order full meals upstairs and sandwiches below. The upstairs is a little tacky, but the dining room is comfortable and the staff is friendly. The menu is exhaustive, with sandwiches, soups (and a very good *cazuela*), quick dishes, meats, seafood, empanadas, even a mini ice-cream parlor. And it's open all day.

Centro Español. Arauco 555. ☎ **42/2240674.** Main courses $6-$10. MC, V. Hours vary; open for dinner 8–11pm, and occasionally for lunch noon–3pm. SPANISH.

Like most cities in Chile, Chillán has a Centro Español that tries to stay true to its name by offering several Spanish dishes in addition to typical Chilean fare like grilled meats and seafood. There have been complaints that quality has waned slightly, but it's still one of the best restaurants in Chillán.

Gran Hotel Isabel Riquelme. Arauco 600, Chillán. ☎ **42/213663.** Fax 42/211541. 75 units. TV TEL. $70 double. AE, DC, MC, V.

The Gran Hotel faces the main plaza and is a huge green building with a flat, unadorned facade. This was Chillán's first hotel, but others have since surpassed the hotel in quality. The rooms have good linens, but the design is somewhat old-fashioned and dowdy. Rooms are, however, very spacious, almost twice the size of the rooms at Las Terrazas. There is a large restaurant just past the lobby, which serves Chilean and international fare, and there's a bar, but both tend to be closed during the winter on weekdays. Call to inquire.

Hotel Las Terrazas. Constitución 664, Chillán. ☎ **42/227000.** Fax 42/227001. www.lasterrazas.cl. E-mail: lasterrazashotel@entelchile.net. 36 units, 2 suites. MINIBAR TV TEL. $44 double weekday; $67 double weekend. AE, DC, MC, V.

Las Terrazas is popular with business executives and is really the best hotel in Chillán. The hotel is in a commercial building; the lobby is on the fifth floor, guest rooms are on the sixth, and most have lofty views, some of the Chillán volcano in the distance. All rooms are first-rate, with classic design and matching floral curtains and bedspreads. The lounge has cushy couches to sink into and read, and there are tables and chairs for cafe service and breakfast.

Paso Nevado. Av. Libertad 219, Chillán. ☎ **42/221827.** Fax 42/237666. 15 units. TV TEL. $55 double. AE, DC, MC, V.

The Paso Nevado is a good value for its comfortable rooms and amicable service, and it always seems willing to drop the price by about 20%, if you ask. Rooms are average size, accented with wood furniture, and in good shape due to the relative newness of the establishment. There's a small interior patio with tables and a bar. The hotel is several blocks from the main plaza, across the street from a movie theater—considering there are very few cinemas in Chile, this is really saying something.

Termas de Chillán. Av. Libertad 1042, Chillán. ☎ **42/223887** (in Chillán), or 2/233-1313 (in Santiago). www.termaschillan.cl. E-mail: ventanac@termachillan.cl. Lift tickets $40 adults, $25 children (on average; prices fluctuate from high to low season). AE, DC, MC, V.

About 50 miles (80km) from the city is Termas de Chillán, a full-season resort that is principally known for skiing, but it also offers great hiking, biking, and horseback riding opportunities here in the summer. Most visitors to Chile head to Pucón, Puerto Varas, or even Patagonia for those kinds of summer-season activities because the locations are more uniquely beautiful than Chillán. However, you might find a hot springs spa and the 5-hour distance from Santiago to be more advantageous.

The resort is nestled in a forested valley under the shadow of the 10,535 foot-high (3,212m) Chillán Volcano. Skiers and snowboarders love this resort's ample size. The resort has 28 runs, 3 chair lifts, and 5 T-bars, as well as heli-skiing, dog-sledding, an international ski school, equipment rental, and restaurants.

But what really makes the Termas stand out from the pack are its spa facilities. There are nine thermal pools, steam baths in caves, and three state-of-the-art spa centers that offer hydrotherapy, aromatherapy, mud baths, and massages. Special treatments like Reiki (a healing treatment that seeks to channel and direct the body's natural life force), anti-inflammatory plant wraps, and a space-age "Sensory Capsule" pretty much put it in a class of its own. It is possible to visit the thermal pools and spa for the day. Admission to the thermal baths is $11 and the steam caves $18. Contact the hotels for spa prices.

There are two hotels here: the brand-new, luxury **Gran Hotel Termas de Chillán** with 120 rooms and the three-star **Hotel Pirigallo** with 48 rooms. The Gran Hotel is sumptuous, with a rich, warm lobby accented by contemporary wood art and a roaring fire. It has amenities such as a gym, squash court, game room, conference room, hair salon, and more.

Rooms are everything you'd expect in terms of comfort, but they are somewhat unremarkable for the price. Rates include breakfast and dinner, ski tickets, and spa facilities (low to high season: $815 to $1,605 per week, per person). The Pirigallo is the older unit, but it's comfortable and wraps around an outdoor thermal pool (rates include the same amenities as the Gran Hotel; low to high season: $595 to $1,095). The complex has several casual and fine restaurants.

A BRIEF STOP IN LAS TRANCAS
You'll pass through the tiny village of Las Trancas just before you get to Termas de Chillán.

Hotel Parador Jamón, Pan y Vino. 10km from Termas de Chillán. 15 units. ☎ **42/222682.** Fax 42/211054. $100 double, with breakfast and dinner; $110 cabin, no meals. No credit cards.

This is a good bet in Las Trancas, although the lobby and game room are cold and battered. Rooms are average and laid out motel-like around a summer-only pool. The A-framed cabins come with kitchenettes and are equally standard. The restaurant is one of the best in the area, however, especially with its cozy ambience of a medieval-style fireplace and beams festooned with hams, gourds, and corncobs. Great Serrano ham, but a pretty basic menu. Open Monday to Sunday 1 to 4pm and 7pm to midnight.

Hotel Pirineos. 5 miles (8km) from Termas de Chillán. ☎ **42/222889.** www.vallelastrancas.cl. 26 units. $80–$120 double; $100–$130 double with dinner. No credit cards.

One of the cheapest places in the area that isn't a student bunk-bed arrangement. It's still not a great value due to the tired rooms and poorly constructed bathrooms. The lounge is nice, however, and there is a giant fireplace. In the summer, there is an outdoor pool. Consult the hotel for discounts in the off-season.

Get Your Funds in Order Before You Arrive

Note that there are no ATMs anywhere in Termas de Chillán or Las Trancas, so do your banking beforehand.

✪ **Hotel Robledal.** 5 miles (8km) from Termas de Chillán. ☎/fax **42/214407.** www.hotelrobledal.cl. E-mail: hotelrobledal@hotmail.com. 22 units. MINIBAR TV TEL. $120–$180 double, with breakfast and dinner. AE, DC, MC, V.

This is a new hotel, surrounded by oak and beech trees and serenaded by a babbling creek. The entrance is flanked on one side by an airy, comfortable lobby with a copper fireplace and bar, and on the other by a restaurant. Guest rooms feel like condominiums, starkly decorated, but warm and brightly lit by an abundance of windows; some have sliding doors and terraces. Among the amenities are an outdoor pool, a sauna, a whirlpool, a game room, and child care.

The Desert North &
San Pedro de Atacama

Northern Chile is home to the driest desert in the world and the wonderful adobe village San Pedro de Atacama. Just 10 years ago, few besides copper miners thought to come to this region. And often, San Pedro never even made it onto maps of the country. What a difference a decade makes! Once-sleepy San Pedro is now home to several elegant hotels, good restaurants, lively bars, and more outfitters than grocery stores. The native Indian population and migrants from Santiago and Europe enchanted with the town's ethereal loveliness can't say they're exactly pleased with the world's new interest in this region, but it's undeniable that it will continue to grow. Why? It's just about one of the most fascinating spots on earth.

EXPLORING THE REGION

The town of **Calama** is not a destination in itself, but a gateway of sorts. It's the nearest airport to San Pedro, and the city is a convenient jumping-off point to the outdoor attractions and colonial villages that lie in the Atacama Desert region. Visitors plan for at least four days to visit this region's highlights, or six to seven days to really explore the region thoroughly. Unless you're a desert freak, most visitors find that more than a week is too much. The best—and really only—place to base yourself is San Pedro; from here you can take part in a multitude of day trips. You may consider spending a night in Calama, especially if you want to visit the Chuquicamata mine.

Keep in mind that travel through this region requires special considerations. Immense distances between sites of interest means the traveler would do best to focus on one area of Chile's northern desert rather than trying to pack in too many stops. We've covered Chile's "hot spot" in the northern desert, the Atacama Desert and the village of San Pedro, but many tour operators offer multiple-day excursions to a variety of locations in this beautiful environment, some of which may not be highlighted in this book. If you've rented a car or have signed on with a tour agency, it is imperative that you consider safety first. **Bring plenty of water**—up to a gallon per person per day—and **extra food,** as well as **sunscreen, a hat, warm clothing** and even a **blanket** (in the event you have to spend a chilly night on the road) and **sunglasses**. Ask your rental car agency (or your tour operator) about procedures for road emergencies and breakdowns, and *always* double check the state of any **spare tires.** Be certain to give at least one person your planned itinerary, even if it's the car rental agency. For obvious reasons, solo travel is *not* the ideal way to explore this region.

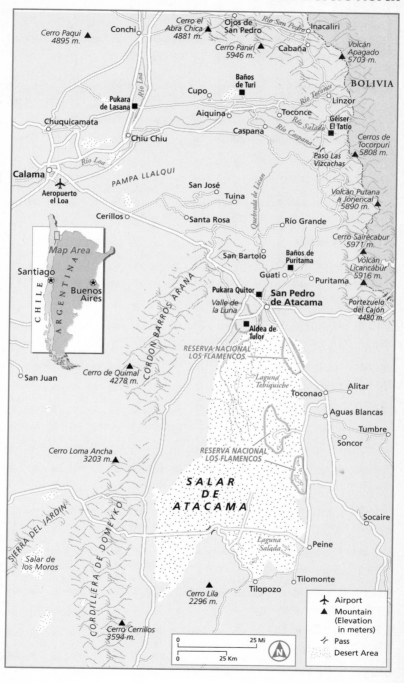

Cerro Paqui 4895 m.

Conchi

Cerro el Abra Chica 4881 m.

Ojos de San Pedro

Río San Pedro

Inacaliri

Cerro Paniri 5946 m.

Cabaña

Volcán Apagado 5703 m.

BOLIVIA

Baños de Turi

Cupo

Río Toconce

Pukara de Lasana

Aiquina

Toconce

Linzor

Chuquicamata

Chiu Chiu

Caspana

Río Salado

Río Caspana

Géiser El Tatio

Cerros de Tocorpuri 5808 m.

Río Loa

Paso Las Vizcachas

Calama

PAMPA LLALQUI

San José

Volcán Putana a Jorjencal 5890 m.

Aeropuerto el Loa

Tuina

Cerro Saïrécabur 5971 m.

Cerillos

Santa Rosa

Río Grande

Volcán Licancábur 5916 m.

CHILE   ARGENTINA

Map Area

Santiago

Buenos Aires

San Bartolo

Baños de Puritama

Puritama

Guati

Portezuelo del Cajón 4480 m.

Pukara Quitor

San Pedro de Atacama

Valle de la Luna

San Juan

Cerro de Quimal 4278 m.

Aldea de Tulor

RESERVA NACIONAL LOS FLAMENCOS

Laguna Tebiquiche

Toconao

Alitar

Aguas Blancas

Tumbre

Cerro Loma Ancha 3203 m.

RESERVA NACIONAL LOS FLAMENCOS

Soncor

SALAR DE ATACAMA

Socaire

SIERRA DEL JARDIN

CORDILLERA DE DOMEYKO

CORDÓN BARROS ARANA

Salar de los Moros

Laguna Salada

Peine

Cerro Lila 2296 m.

Tilopozo

Tilomonte

Cerro Cerrillos 3594 m.

0   25 Mi

0   25 Km

N

✈ Airport

▲ Mountain (Elevation in meters)

⤼ Pass

⋯ Desert Area

Another serious consideration is **flash floods.** Though the region receives only a few days of rainfall each year, it can come in a torrential downpour known as the "Bolivian Winter," which drowns the region in flash floods and causes substantial damage to roads and bridges. The Bolivian Winter can strike anywhere during the summer between December to early March.

1 Calama & the Chuquicamata Copper Mine

976 miles (1,574km) N of Santiago; 61 miles (98km) NW of San Pedro de Atacama

Calama was an important administrative center in what was once Bolivian territory, until Chilean troops seized the area in 1879. This city of 120,000 is alive due primarily to the mining interests in the area. Most travelers spend the night here only when they're stuck on their way in or out of the area, or if they're interested in visiting the Chuquicamata Copper Mine. The Indian ruins **Pukará de Lasana** and the colonial village **Chiu Chiu** are also close to Calama, although they can be visited on the way back to Calama from San Pedro via the Tatío Geysers, if you've rented your own vehicle.

GETTING THERE

BY PLANE   Calama's **Aeropuerto El Loa** (no phone) is served by both Lan Chile and Avant airlines; Avant typically includes two stopovers in Copiapó and Antofagasta. A taxi to Calama costs around $2. To get to San Pedro de Atacama, hire one of the transfer services outside for around $10 per person, or take a taxi for about $35—and be sure to fix a price before leaving the airport.

BY BUS   It takes around 22 hours to reach Calama by bus. Buses are an economical choice, but even a *cama salon* with reclining seats hardly mitigates a torturously long ride. **TurBus** leaves from Santiago's Terminal Alameda at O'Higgins 3750 (☎ 2/270-7500), and **Pullman Bus** leaves from the Terminal Norte at the Central Station (☎ 2/778-7086).

BY TRAIN   There is a train to Oruro across the Bolivian border that leaves every Wednesday at 11pm, crossing the Salar de Uyuni. To buy a ticket, go to **Buses Tramaca** at Balmaceda 1777 (☎ 55/342004); tickets are $20 per person. There is only one class and the ride takes about 30 hours. Some visitors to San Pedro make this side trip; contact a tour operator in San Pedro for tours and more information.

BY CAR   Considering a total driving time of 20 to 22 hours (without stops), few actually drive to Calama, but many find it convenient to rent a car in Calama to explore at their own pace. A word of caution, however, if you choose to rent. This is a vast desert and most areas are fairly isolated; roadside service is not unheard of, but it's not very common either. Travel prepared for the worst, and bring extra water and food and warm clothes in case you must spend the night on the road. Also, consider renting a 4×4 if you plan to really explore along poorly maintained roads. Rental car companies in Calama include: **Avis** at Chacabuco 180 (☎ 55/232210); **Budget** at 21 de Mayo 650 (☎ 55/252978); **Hertz** at Hotel El Paso, Velásquez 1109 (☎ 55/231487); or **American** at General Lagos 559 (☎ 55/252234). There are also rental agency kiosks at the airport.

WHAT TO SEE & DO

TOUR OPERATORS   The following tour operators offer excursions around the north of Calama and trips to the Tatío Geysers and San Pedro de Atacama: **Ecología Andina** at Quemazón 2231 (☎ 55/318561), **Moon Valley Tourist Service** at Calle

Sotomayor 1814 (☎ **55/317456**), and **Atacama Desert,** Latorre 1760 (☎ **55/312055**). **Nativa Expediciones** at Abaroa 1796 (☎ **55/319834**) offers adventurous day trips and multiple-day trips.

CHUQUICAMATA COPPER MINE

The northern desert is full of ghost towns left over from Chile's nitrate-mining days, but the copper mining industry is alive and well, as is evident by Calama's Chuquicamata mine, the largest open-pit mine in the world. Few wonders generate the visual awe a visitor experiences when gazing into this gigantic hole in the ground. The mine is so big that it can be seen from space. The principal pit measures 2½ miles (4km) across and more than half a kilometer deep—everything at its bottom looks Lilliputian, which is especially shocking when you see that what appears to be a kid's toy is actually a colossal dumptruck with wheels that measure 10 feet (3m) in diameter. The Guggenheim brothers initiated construction of the mine in 1911, but did not produce a bar of copper until 1915. Today, the mine yields more than 600,000 tons of copper per year and is owned by the government-controlled company Codelco. There is a planned company town at the edge of the mine, with about 13,000 residents.

Tours run Monday to Friday, except holidays, and start at 9:45am, but as there's just one tour daily and limited space, it is recommended that you arrive at least by 9am, even 8am during January and February. To get there, take a regular taxi or an inexpensive collective taxi from the main plaza in Calama on Calle Abaroa to the company mining town, and sign up for the tour at the Sede de Chuqui Ayuda a la Infancia Desvalida at José Miguel Carrera and Tocopilla streets. The tour is conducted from a bus, with several stops to get out and peer into the pit. There is no admission price; however, they do accept donations. For safety reasons, it is recommended that visitors do not wear shorts or sandals.

OTHER ATTRACTIONS

Museo Arqueológico y Etnográfico. Parque El Loa. No phone. Admission $1, free for seniors. Tues–Sun 10am–1pm and 3–7:30pm.

This museum sits in the El Loa park, about 2km (1 mile) from the city center, so you'll need to grab a taxi to get there. The Museo Arqueológico was remodeled and expanded last year, and it holds an interesting collection of artifacts from the Atacama region and displays interpreting pre-Columbian history and civilization.

WHERE TO STAY

Be advised if you are renting a car to explore the region, that parking in Calama is plentiful and either free or a nominal charge.

Hotel El Loa. Abaroa 1617. ☎ **55/341963.** 30 units. TV TEL. $12 per person. No credit cards.

Budget travelers will find the El Loa a very simple but decent option in Calama. It's a little low on style, but it's very clean, and there's a kitchen that can be used by guests. The hotel has a fair number of singles, so if you're traveling alone and looking for cheap digs, this is your place. It can get crowded in the summer at the Hotel El Loa, so you might consider making a reservation at least a few days ahead during that time.

Hotel El Mirador. Calle Sotomayor 2064. ☎/fax **55/340329.** 15 units. TV. $60 double. No credit cards.

This is one of the more interesting hotels in Calama. The El Mirador is a pretty, old-fashioned hotel furnished with antiques and featuring hardwood floors, a plant-filled patio, and a pleasant sitting area decorated with old photos of the region. Most of the rooms are ample in size, and the largest room has a neat bathroom with a clawfoot bathtub. The hotel offers several tours around the area.

Park Hotel Calama. Camino Aeropuerto 1392. ☎ **55/319900.** Fax 55/319901. www. parkplaza.cl. E-mail: parkcalama@parkplaza.cl. 102 units. MINIBAR TV TEL. $165 double standard; $190 double superior. AE, DC, MC, V.

The Park Hotel is one of Calama's best hotels, and it is a good bet for travelers seeking dependable, high-quality accommodations near the airport. Okay, so the airport is only 2 miles (3km) from Calama anyway, but they're ½ mile (1km) away, and they'll pick you up and drop you off there for free. The hotel's interiors are painted in desert pastels, and the uncomplicated design features off-white couches and iron and wood furniture. The hotel sees a fair number of traveling executives. The rooms are average-sized and very comfortable. The large, circular, outdoor pool makes for a refreshing desert respite.

Dining/Diversions: There's also a restaurant that serves fine international cuisine and a piano bar.

Amenities: 24-hour room service, laundry, sauna gym, outdoor swimming pool, tennis court, car rental, excursions.

WHERE TO DINE
Apart from a couple of chains, there are only a few decent places to eat in Calama. **Tavola Caldo,** Vicuña Mackenna 2033 (no phone), serves good Italian fare, including pasta, and it has outdoor seating. If you're looking for hearty Chilean cuisine, try **Bavaria** at Calle Sotomayor and Abaroa (☎ **55/341496**); it serves barbecued meats, seafood, and sandwiches. Calama locals' favorite for Chinese is **Tong Fong,** Calle Vivar 1951 (no phone). For fine dining, head to the **Park Hotel**'s restaurant, which serves international cuisine; it's at Camino Aeropuerto 1392 (☎ **55/319990**).

NEARBY EXCURSIONS TO COLONIAL VILLAGES & PUKARÁS
A memorable excursion near Calama is a visit to the several colonial-era villages that still function as agricultural centers, and the Atacama Indian ruins built in the 12th century. Most tour companies in Calama offer trips to this region for around $15 per person.

Chiu Chiu is a colonial village founded by the Spanish in the early 17th century, and it boasts the most picturesque church in the north, the **Iglesia San Francisco,** open Tuesday to Sunday 9am to 1pm and 3 to 7pm. The whitewashed adobe walls of this weather-beaten beauty are 120cm (47 in.) thick, and its doors are made of cedar and bordered with cactus, displaying a singular, Atacamanian style. Inside are interesting items such as a crucifix built for carrying during a procession and a painting on both sides of a canvas of the Passion of Christ. Chiu Chiu was first occupied by Indians around 1000 B.C. and was part of an extensive trading route that included Brazil; it continued as such until its demise brought about by the railway that began service in 1890.

Another fascinating attraction is the **Pukará de Lasana,** a 12th-century Indian fort abandoned after the Spanish occupation and restored in 1951 when it was declared a national monument. You'll want to spend some time wandering the labyrinthine streets that wind around 110 two- to five-story ancient building remains.

North of Chiu Chiu is the engaging village of **Caspana** that appears sunken into the earth and is surrounded by a fertile valley interestingly cultivated in a formation much like steps. The flowers and vegetables grown here are sold to markets in Calama. In the center, visitors will find a tiny museum dedicated to the culture of the area and an artisan shop selling textiles made from alpaca. Visitors are typically warned not to buy any item made of cactus, as the species is closing in on extinction. Also in Caspana is the charming **Iglesia de San Lucas,** built in 1641 of stone, cactus, and mortar and covered in adobe. The church is not officially open, but if you find the caretaker, he will unlock the door for you.

Near Caspana is the **Pukará de Turi,** which was the largest fortified city of the Atacama culture, built in the 12th century, and widely believed to be an Incan administrative center. The size of these ruins is impressive, with wide streets, circular towers, and buildings made of volcanic stone and adobe. The Pukará is well worth a visit.

2 San Pedro de Atacama

61 miles (98km) SE of Calama; 1,040 miles (1,674km) N of Santiago

Quaint, unhurried, and built of adobe brick, San Pedro de Atacama sits in the driest desert in the world, a region replete with bizarre land formations, giant sand dunes, jagged canyons, salt pillars, boiling geysers, and one smoking volcano. Better to call it a moonscape than a landscape. For adventure seekers there is a wealth of activities to participate in, including hiking, mountain biking, and horseback riding—or you can just sightsee with a tour van. This region was the principal center of the Atacamañian Indian culture, and relics such as Tulor, an ancient village estimated to have been built in 800 B.C., still survive. There's also a superb archeology museum that boasts hundreds of artifacts that have been well preserved by the desert's arid climate.

But it is perhaps San Pedro's intangible magic that captivates its visitors in the end. Many will tell you it is as much of a place for one's "inside" as it is for one's "outside." One well-known Chilean architect has been noted to say, "The first day you begin to discover things; the third day you throw away your agenda; and by the seventh day you don't even know who you are, and that is the most fabulous moment, one that many associate with God." This spiritual penchant has fomented somewhat of an artistic, bohemian atmosphere in San Pedro, but really it appeals to just about everyone.

Unfortunately, as with any uniquely beautiful place, San Pedro has been discovered, and today it is a thriving tourism center that is so popular from October to March that visitors might feel overwhelmed by the presence of so many *gringos.* Somehow, however, San Pedro maintains its mellow charm. This is one of my favorite places in Chile for its one-of-a-kind, breathtaking beauty.

ESSENTIALS

GETTING THERE   By Car   From Calama, head southeast on the route marked "San Pedro de Atacama" and continue for 61 mi (98km).

By Bus   Several bus companies provide service to San Pedro from Calama: **Buses Frontera,** Antofagasta 2041 (☎ 55/318543), offers the most daily trips; **Tramacá,** Granaderos 3048 (☎ 55/340404) and **Buses Atacama** (Abaroa 2105-B ☎ 55/314757) also offer daily service to San Pedro.

VISITOR INFORMATION   Sernatur operates a small visitor's center at the plaza on the corner of Antofagasta and Toconao (☎ 55/85-1240). Hours are Saturday to Thursday 9:30am to 1:30pm and 3 to 7pm.

ORIENTATION   San Pedro de Atacama is divided into several *ayllus,* or neighborhoods; however, the principal area of the town can be walked in about 10 minutes or less. Most businesses do not list street numbers (marked "s/n" for *sin numero,* or without number). Many sights are within walking or biking distance, such as Quitor and Tulor, and it is possible to bike to the Valley of the Moon and through the Devil's Canyon. You'll need a tour to get to the Tatio Geysers.

| **Important Info to Know Before Arriving in San Pedro** |

Although San Pedro boasts several luxury hotels, there are no banks or pharmacies in town, and medical service is limited to a small clinic. San Pedro is at 2,438m (7,997 ft.) above sea level, and a small percentage of visitors may be affected by the high altitude; see "Health" in chapter 8, "Planning Your Trip to Chile," for remedies. The electricity in town is cut off after midnight, although a few hotels and businesses are now using solar panels and generators for 24-hour electricity.

WHAT TO SEE AND DO

TOUR OPERATORS The boom in tourism has consequentially given birth to dozens of tour operations, offering everything from sightseeing to active travel at pretty much comparative prices. The following are a few reliable operators. Two tour companies who arrange custom tours, specifically ones that require equipment or cultural tours, are **Atacama Desert Expeditions,** Tocopilla 19, an upscale operation that works in conjunction with the Lodge Terrantai (☎ **55/85-1140;** www.adex.cl), and **Nativa Expeditions,** Tocopilla s/n, which can arrange 1-day and multiple-day trips that lean more toward adventure travel (☎ **55/85-1095;** e-mail: nativaexp@ yahoo.com). All-inclusive trips cost a bit more, anywhere from $80 to $100 a day per person. For trips to any of the destinations listed below, try **Desert Adventure** at the corner of Tocopilla and Caracoles (☎/fax **55/85-1067;** e-mail: deserts@ctcinternet. cl); **Pangea Expediciones,** Tocopilla s/n, which offers all the tours around Atacama and specializes in tours over the border of Bolivia, including a 3-day trip to the Salar de Uyuni (☎ **55/85-1111;** e-mail: pangeaexp@yahoo.com); or **Cosmo Andino Expediciones** at Caracoles s/n (☎ **55/85-1069**).

The average price for tours to the Valle de la Luna is $6; the Tatio Geysers tour costs about $20, which includes the entrance fee at the thermal baths.

A CAN'T-MISS ATTRACTION IN TOWN

✪ **Museo Arqueológico Padre le Paige.** Toconao and Padre le Paige. No phone. Jan–Feb daily 10am–1pm and 3–7pm; rest of the year Mon–Fri 9am–noon and 2–6pm, Sat and Sun 10am–noon and 2–6pm. Admission $2.

This tiny museum near the plaza is one of Chile's best, offering a superb collection of pre-Columbian artifacts gathered by Padre le Paige, a Belgian missionary who had a fondness for archeology. What makes this museum especially unique is the well-preserved state of the artifacts, due to the arid conditions of the region. You'll find thousands of ceramics, textiles, tablets used for the inhalation of hallucinogens, tools and more displayed according to time period. However, the unquestionable highlights here are the well-preserved mummies, including "Miss Chile," a female mummy that still has bits of skin and hair intact, and the creepy display of skulls that shows how the elite once used cranial deformation as a show of wealth. Don't miss a visit here.

VALLE DE LA LUNA

The ✪ **Valle de la Luna** (Valley of the Moon) is a popular destination for its eerie, freeze-dried land formations encrusted with veins of pure salt, and a giant sand dune that sits like a saddle between two viewpoint ridges. The best time to come is when the sun sets, to watch the colors of the desert melt from pink to gold, but you'll often have to share the view with a dozen or more tourists. This valley is also at its best on the eve of a full moon, when ghostly light makes the land formations appear even stranger. The Valley of the Moon sits 9 miles (14.5km) from San Pedro and can be reached by bicycle or vehicle. To get here, head west out town on Caracoles and turn left on the signed, dirt road (the old road to Calama). All tour companies offer this excursion.

SALAR DE ATACAMA & THE FLAMINGO NATIONAL RESERVE

San Pedro sits on the edge of a gigantic mineralized lake that is covered in many parts by a weird, putty-colored crust. This *salar*, or salt flat, is a basin that collects water but has no outlet, leaving behind an accumulation of minerals, including a sizeable percentage of the world's lithium reserves. Visitors will notice that the aridity of this region permits unbelievable long-distance visibility. A highlight is a stop at the Flamingo Reserve near Solcor, which allows a chance to glimpse a few of the birds who come here to nest. There's also an interpretive center (no phone); open September to May 8:30am to 8pm, and June to August 8:30am to 7pm. To get here, head south toward Toconao, 20 miles (33km) from San Pedro. Once you've passed through Toconao, keep your eyes open for the entrance to the flamingo reserve signed "Laguna Chaxa."

GEYSERS DEL TATIO/BAÑOS DE PURITAMA

Without a doubt a highlight in the Atacama Desert, the ✪ **Geysers del Tatio** (Tatio Geysers) are nonetheless not the easiest excursion—there's not a lot of physical activity required, but tours leave at the crack of dawn (the geysers are most active around 6 to 8am). At 4,321m (14,173 ft.), these are the highest geysers in the world. It's an unforgettable sight watching big fumaroles spew violently from blowholes in the ground and various odd, bubbling, and sputtering mud pits. Exercise extreme caution when walking near thin crust; careless visitors burn themselves here frequently. Herds of *vicuñas*, the llama's wild cousin, are known to graze in this area, so keep your eyes open for these delicate creatures. The geysers are 59 miles (95km) north of San Pedro. Those driving their own vehicle will want to pay sharp attention to the road and signs, especially because visitors set out in darkness to reach Tatio. Ask for a detailed map and directions at your rental car agency to verify that you know where you're going. Head north out of San Pedro toward the Azufrera Polán. At the 45km mark you'll turn right at a signed intersection until, at the 54km mark you reach the camp Volcán Apagado. Continue straight ahead until the next intersection at 68km and head right to Campamento Apagado. Another intersection at 73km will point you toward the airstrip Tocopuri, where, at 79km you'll head left until 84km, where you'll turn right and continue until passing Campamento Corfo and arriving at the geyser field.

There's a hot spring pool near the geyser field, but the best hot springs are on the road to the geysers at **Baños de Puritama,** an oasis composed of well-built rock pools that descend down a gorge, about 37 miles (60km) from the geysers. They are run by the luxury Hotel Explora (see "Where to Stay," below), and cost $10 to enter; there are changing rooms and bathrooms here. Most tour companies leave around 4 to 5am for the 2½-hour journey to Tatio, and they usually include a stop at Puritama. For travelers with a rental car, it is possible to continue on to Calama from here, so you may want to save this excursion for your last day. Note that some visitors have experienced difficulty driving here due to unfamiliarity with the road and vague turn-off points. Anyone doing the San Pedro–Tatio–Calama route should have a reliable local resident clearly map out the route for them, or leave it to tour companies to take them.

PUKARÁ DE QUITOR

This 12th-century, pre-Inca defensive fort clings to a steep hillside some 2 miles (3km) outside San Pedro. Although formidable, the fort was no match for the Spanish with their horses and arms made of metal, and it was conquered in 1540 by Francisco de

Aguirre and 30 men. To get there, walk, bike, or drive west up Tocopilla Street and continue along the river until you see Quitor at your left.

ALDEA DE TULOR

This fascinating attraction is the Atacama's oldest pueblo, estimated to have been built around 800 B.C. Tulor remained intact in part because it had been covered with sand for hundreds of years, and today it is possible to see the walls that once formed the structures of this town. There are a few reconstructed homes on view as well. It's 5½ miles (9km) southwest of San Pedro, so you'll need to bike or drive.

OUTDOOR ACTIVITIES

BIKING   The Atacama region offers superb terrain for mountain bike riding, including the Quebrada del Diablo (Devil's Gorge) and Valle de la Muerte (Death Valley); however, it is also enjoyable to ride across the flat desert to visit sites such as Tulor. For bikes, try **Pangea Expediciones,** Tocopilla s/n, which not only rents high-quality mountain bikes for $12 per day (☎ **55/85-1111**), but also plans excursions such as a descent from the *altiplano*. It also has detailed maps for riders.

HORSEBACK RIDING   Horseback riding is a fun way to experience the Atacama, especially if you're adept at galloping. **Rancho Cactus,** Toconao 568 (☎ **55/85-1506;** e-mail: rancho_cactus@uol.cl), owned by friendly couple Farolo and Valérie, rents horses by the hour for about $10 an hour. They also plan multiple-day, full-service excursions. A 2-day trip, including food and camping equipment, costs $150 per person, eight-person maximum.

VOLCANO ASCENTS   Climbing one of the four volcanoes in the area requires total altitude acclimatization and a good physical state—previous mountaineering experience wouldn't hurt either. The most popular volcanic ascent is up Volcano Láscar to 5,400m (17,712 ft.). Many tour companies offer this excursion; try **Nativa Expediciones,** Tocopilla s/n (☎ **55/85-1095;** e-mail: nativaexp@yahoo.com).

WHERE TO STAY
VERY EXPENSIVE

✪ **Hotel Explora.** Domingo Atienza s/n (main office: Americo Vespucio Sur 80, Piso 5, Santiago). ☎ **55/85-1110** (local), 2/206-6060 in Santiago (reservations). Fax 2/228-4655. Toll-free fax 800/858-0855 (U.S.), 800/275-1129 (Canada). www.explora-chile.com. E-mail: explora@entelchile.net. 52 units. TEL. Double occupancy, per person: 3 nights, $1,296; 4 nights, $1,706; 7 nights, $2,441. Rates include accommodations, meals, open bar, excursions, and airport transfers. Reduced tariffs available for children under 12 and young adults 13 to 20 years old. AE, DC, MC, V.

With the boom in tourism in San Pedro, a luxury hotel was inevitable, and residents should be thankful it was Explora. Although the hotel encompasses a considerable chunk of desert, it manages to keep a low profile with its location tucked away at the end of a dusty street. Most visitors to San Pedro don't even know it's there. Like its counterpart in Patagonia, the Explora in Atacama is elegant yet unpretentious. The hotel is somewhat cubist in design, with a freestanding lobby, bar, and restaurant and 52 linked one-story rooms that extend in an angular ring from the main unit. The minimalist exterior is painted entirely white, with splashes of pale blue and yellow. Inside, the lounge and guest rooms are tastefully decorated with local art and painted in quiet, primary tones. Cut-out window displays hold Atacama Indian artifacts found when the hotel broke ground, and in many ways the collection rivals San Pedro's museum. The lounge, with soaring ceilings, is enormous, stretching the length of the building and scattered with plush, multicolored couches and wicker chairs draped in sheepskin. Ceiling fans and cool ceramic floors make this a soothing respite from the searing heat, but when it's chilly, they throw a few logs in one of the many fireplaces around the lounge. The rooms have ultra-comfortable beds made with crisp linens and fluffy down comforters; each bathroom comes with a Jacuzzi tub and a hanging shower head that's about a quarter meter (10 in.) in diameter. Each room has a blue-trimmed window that stretches the length of the building—if you can, try to get a room facing the Volcano Licancabúr to really appreciate your location. Above the main building is an open deck with an outstanding view of the desert. A slatted walkway takes guests to the oasislike swimming pools (there are four of them), designed to resemble irrigation ditches and each with its own sauna.

Explora operates as an all-inclusive hotel, offering 3-night, 4-night, and 7-night packages that include transfers, meals, an open bar, and all excursions. Every evening one of their full-time bilingual guides meets with guests to plan daily excursions.

Dining: Meals are included in the price, and the international gourmet cuisine served is as outstanding as the view from the dining room; therefore, guests normally take their meals in the hotel's restaurant. Explora offers four meals per day: a buffet breakfast, lunch, and dinner (with a daily set menu offering two choices of appetizers and main courses) and an afternoon tea. Beverages, including cocktails and wine, are also included in the price. They also have a weekly barbecue in their on-site *quincho*.

Amenities: Four outdoor pools, sauna, mountain bikes, horseback riding, daily excursions with bilingual guides, conference room, laundry, gift shop selling outdoor apparel and local crafts, TV room, library, massage, baby-sitting.

EXPENSIVE

Hostería San Pedro de Atacama. Solcor 370. ☎ **55/85-1011.** Fax 55/85-1048. E-mail: hspedro@chilesat.net. 25 units. TEL. $80 double; $120 cabaña for 4. AE, DC, MC, V.

Hostería San Pedro is housed within a renovated and expanded antique *casco*, something akin to an hacienda, and was the first hotel in the area. The motel-like establishment has comfortable rooms spread across a large property that includes San Pedro's only gas pump—the reason you'll see a fair amount of traffic drive in and out throughout the day. Across from the main building are seven cabañas, each with two bedrooms, spacious bathrooms, but no living area, that sleep a total of four to five people; these units are the loudest, especially when a tour bus or two starts its engine. For a quieter respite, choose one of the detached, sunny double rooms in back that look out onto a very nice pool/Jacuzzi/patio area. More rooms can be found in the hotel's main building, with stone walls, larger bathrooms, but less light. All are carpeted and clean, and they have 24-hour electricity. The pool area, with its patio filled with tables for relaxing or eating, is a strong point, as is the hostería's restaurant, which serves an ample selection of international/Chilean dishes.

Hotel Tulor. Domingo Atienza s/n. ☎/fax **55/85-1027.** E-mail: tulor@chilesat.net. 9 units. TEL. $86 double. AE, DC, MC, V.

This hotel is owned by the person who discovered the Tulor ruin site, hence the name. The Tulor is on a quiet street just down from the Hotel Kimal (see below) and behind an adobe wall. The circular buildings are made of adobe and thatched roofs. The rooms are unremarkable, with nondescript beige walls, thin carpet, and a tiny table and chair; some seem crammed with too many beds. For the price, you'd do better at the Kimal; however, the Tulor does come with a patio and kidney-shaped swimming pool, and its standalone restaurant is very appealing. If you're an archeology buff, the owner will gladly share information about the Tulor site and arrange excursions there and to other attractions in the area.

✪ **La Aldea.** Solcor s/n. ☎/fax **55/85-1149** or 55/85-1333. 9 units, 3 cabañas. TEL. $90 double; $117 3-person cabaña. No credit cards.

This chic adobe hotel is owned by two architects, who have bestowed great taste to its interiors. The principal drawback here is the 10-minute dusty walk to the center of town, and although that doesn't seem like much, it can be a bother. The welcoming lobby, lounge, and restaurant are built of stone, adobe walls, cinnamon-colored wood, ironwork, and thatched roofs, all very smart—sort of New York meets Santa Fe. A curving stairwell leads to a game room and lounge; downstairs are a few couches and a black leather recliner. Several rooms branch off from the main unit, and although they are slightly dark, they have a cooling effect on a hot day. They are also spacious enough to give some breathing room. Perhaps the best rooms are in the separate cabañas for three, which are cylindrical two-stories with banister-less, circular stairwells, fresh white walls, and lots and lots of light; two of them are brand-new. Outside is a turquoise pool, surrounded by a funny AstroTurf and a nicer pebbled courtyard—it's one of the few in San Pedro. Service is just slightly aloof, but nothing that would make your stay less enjoyable.

Amenities: Laundry, room service, TV room, swimming pool, bicycles, horseback riding.

✪ **Lodge Terrantai.** Tocopilla s/n. ☎ **55/85-1140.** Fax 55/85-1037. www.terrantai.cl. E-mail: atacamadesert@adex.cl. 14 units. TEL. $137 double; all-inclusive package doubles, per person: 2-night $542, 3-night $733, 4-night $870, 5-night $1,018. Special Fri–Mon weekend package for 3 nights is $547. Rates include accommodations, meals, airport transfers, and excursions. MC, V.

If the prices at the Explora are a little beyond your budget, but you're looking for something of comparable quality, you might try this appealing little hotel near the main street. The Terrantai is in a 100-year-old home that was renovated by two well-known Chilean architects, who preserved the building's flat-fronted facade, adobe walls, and thatched roof. The style is pure minimalism, and every inch of the interior hallways and the rooms are made of stacked river rock. The rooms are very comfortable, with down comforters, linen curtains, soft reading lights, and local art. Most rooms have large floor-to-ceiling windows that look out onto a pleasant garden patio. The Terrantai has a small restaurant with wooden tables and a white-tiled, mosaic floor; dinner is served here only during the summer, which means that prices are slightly cheaper during the off-season.

Dining: Guests opting for the package normally take their meals in the hotel's restaurant. During the slow season, the restaurant is open for breakfast only for guests paying a nightly rate.

Amenities: Outdoor pool (more like a soak tub), daily excursions with bilingual guides, laundry.

MODERATE

✪ **Hotel Kimal.** Domingo Atienza 452 (at Caracoles). ☎ **55/85-1152.** Fax 55/85-1030. E-mail: kimal@entelchile.net. 10 units. TEL. $68 double. AE, DC, MC, V.

This appealing little hotel is tucked behind an adobe wall, with tiled walkways that lead to the 10 rooms, each with its own small outdoor seating area. The hotel feels more intimate than most in San Pedro. The rooms are fringed outside by pimiento trees and are fairly straightforward: adobe walls, thick foam beds, a bathroom, and a freestanding closet, but they're softly lit by skylights and are very soothing. Of all the hotels in this price range, I enjoy the Kimal the most, especially for its good, on-site restaurant **Paacha.** The hotel is run by an amiable English woman, and is on a quiet side street.

La Casa de Don Tomás. Tocopilla s/n. ☎ **55/85-1055.** Fax 55/851175. www.rdc.cl/dontomas. E-mail: dontomas@rdc.cl. 38 units. $72 double; $192 cabin for 8. AE, DC, MC, V.

The Don Tomás was, for a while, a solid moderate-price option, but several other hotels have since surpassed it, and now it seems a bit expensive for what it has to offer. The hotel is made of adobe brick centered on a gravel courtyard/parking lot, and there are a few large cabañas behind the main unit. The main building has a dining area and a minilounge; a dozen rooms branch off from this central area, but the majority have separate entrances, much like a motel. The rooms are average-size, with white ceramic floors and surprisingly so-so beds. The service is perhaps better than the accommodations. On the average it's a decent place, but you might want to check out other hotels before booking here.

INEXPENSIVE

✪ **Hotel Tambillo.** Antofagasta s/n. ☎/fax **55/85-1078.** 12 units. TEL. $38 double. No credit cards.

The Tambillo is the best option in this price range. The 12 rooms are lined along both sides of a narrow, attractive pathway inlaid with stone; rooms have arched windows and doors. Rooms come with no decoration other than two boldly striped bedspreads, but it's not unappealing—on the contrary, the atmosphere is fresh and clean. There's a large restaurant that serves breakfast, lunch, and dinner, and a tiny sheltered patio. It's a 4-block walk to the main street.

Residencial Casa Corvatsch. Antofagasta s/n. ☎/fax **55/85-1101.** 28 units. $35 double, private bathroom; $17 double, shared bathroom. MC, V.

The Casa Corvatsch is a popular place with budget travelers, and there are two options. The main building has the low-budget, attic rooms, which are very unremarkable and have shared bathrooms—they're literally a room with a bed, nothing else. A walkway out back leads to the other option, which is four carpeted rooms with private bathrooms, brick walls, and better beds. The Casa Corvatsch is owned by a Swiss-Chilean couple, and they run excursions, offer airport transfers, and have Internet access on site. It's about a 5-block walk to the main street.

WHERE TO DINE
MODERATE

✪ **Adobe.** Caracoles s/n. ☎ **55/85-1089.** Reservations not accepted. Main courses $6.50–$10. AE. Daily 8am–12:30am. CONTEMPORARY CHILEAN.

This is one of the best choices in San Pedro, both for the good food and even better ambience. The Adobe is a popular place for eating, drinking, or just hanging out in front of the bonfire that blazes every evening in the semi-enclosed outdoor area. There are a few tables with molded banquettes inside, near the entrance, but the best spot is at one of the wooden tables under a thatched roof that wraps around the fire area. The Adobe is known for its set breakfasts, which can include pancakes, eggs, a fruit salad, and espresso, but really any meal is delicious here. The menu offers typical Chilean treats such as empanadas, but there's also pasta, salads, grilled meats, and a set menu for $7 to $9 that includes a soup, main dish, and dessert.

La Casona. Caracoles 195. ☎ **55/85-1004.** Reservations not accepted. Main courses $5–$9; sandwiches $1.50–$4. AE, DC, MC, V. Daily 9am–11pm. CHILEAN.

La Casona is housed in an old colonial building with soaring ceilings and whitewashed walls. Candelit, wooden tables adorned with a few sprigs of flowers and a crackling fireplace set a quieter ambience—although there's a pool table and bar in the rear room that can get fairly lively. The owner is from Finland, but the menu is typically Chilean, with appetizers such as a *palta reina or york* (an avocado half filled with tuna or chicken salad) and main dishes such as grilled tenderloin in a creamy pepper sauce.

They also serve pastas and *picadillos,* those appetizer plates that are a great snack during the cocktail hour. The service here is usually very friendly.

La Estaka. Caracoles 259. ☎ **55/85-1201.** Reservations not accepted. Main courses $5–$10; sandwiches $2–$4.50. AE, DC, MC, V. Daily 8:30am–1:30am. INTERNATIONAL/CHILEAN.

La Estaka is part hip, part hippie, and one of the most popular restaurants in San Pedro, especially in the evening when the music is turned up and the *vino caliente* starts to flow. The plentiful, yet simple, menu offers both meat and vegetarian dishes, omelets, pasta, salads, and sandwiches in a funky ambience that features semi-outdoor seating with a netlike roof, dirt floor, and molded banquettes, and a spacious indoor eating area with lofty ceilings and large wood tables. The lunch hour is quite mellow, and there's a bar at the entrance that gets pretty loud.

Restaurant Hostería San Pedro. Solcor 370. ☎ **55/85-1011.** Reservations not accepted. Main courses $8–$13. AE, DC, MC, V. Daily 7am–11pm. CHILEAN.

The Hotel San Pedro's in-house restaurant serves a wider variety of dishes than most eateries in San Pedro, as well as classic Chilean fare such as *lomo a la pobre,* steak with onions, fries, and an egg plopped on top. The best deal is the set menu that costs $7 for lunch or dinner, and they serve a variety of soups, pastas, and breakfast of pancakes and eggs. The nondescript interior is not necessarily bad, but definitely not the reason to come here—although if you tire of the adobe/dusty-floor restaurants in town, the squeaky clean interiors here might be appealing. This is one of the few restaurants not in the pueblo's active downtown area, so it is, therefore, a quieter option.

✪ **Restaurant Paacha.** Caracoles (corner of Domingo Atienza). ☎ **55/85-1030.** Reservations not necessary. Main courses $4–$9. AE, DC, MC, V. Daily 8am–midnight. INTERNATIONAL/CHILEAN.

This restaurant has a little more class than its competitors. A thatched roof, tables draped with white tablecloths centered on a chimney with a softly crackling fire, and tasty cuisine make the Paacha a good bet for dining in San Pedro. Paacha, owned by the neighboring Kimal Hotel, serves a more creative blend of international and Chilean cuisine, with an ample offering of meat dishes such as steak fillet with Roquefort sauce and walnuts and curry chicken with chopped fruit. There's also a small, pleasant bar, occasional live folk music, and an ice cream stand. I've eaten here twice and the service was sluggish both times, but the ambience is so nice that it didn't seem much of an issue.

INEXPENSIVE

Café Buena Tierra. Caracoles s/n. No phone. Reservations not necessary. Empanadas and sandwiches $2.50–$4. No credit cards. Daily 9am–10:30pm. CAFE.

This tiny cafe is known for its vegetarian, whole-meal empanadas made from scratch while you wait. Of course, the wait can be long, but it's worth it. Café Buena Tierra makes every pizza and bread item the same way, and there's nothing quite like fresh toast for breakfast, especially when you pair it with an espresso and one of their fresh fruit juices; they also serve pancakes. Although they've semi-expanded, seating is still limited, but they'll make a sandwich or empanada to go if you can't get a seat.

Café Etnico. Tocopilla s/n. No phone. Reservations not necessary. Snacks $1.50–$5. No credit cards. Daily 7am–9:30pm. CAFE.

This is a good all-in-one spot: coffee, fresh baked pies and cakes, sandwiches, a good book exchange, and four Internet terminals. What Café Etnico has on offer changes daily according to the mood of the bar guys behind the counter. They also give tourist information about excursions around San Pedro, including little-known areas.

The Chilean Lake District

The region south of the Biobío River to Puerto Montt is collectively known as the Lake District, a fairy-tale land of emerald forests, white-capped volcanoes, frothing waterfalls, and plump, rolling hills dotted with hundreds of lakes and lagoons that give the region its name. It is one of the most popular destinations in Chile, not only for its beauty, but for the diverse outdoor and city-themed activities available and a well-organized tourism structure that allows travelers to pack in a lot of action and yet rest comfortably and well fed in the evening.

The Lake District is home to the Mapuche Indians, who fiercely defended this land against the Spanish for 300 years. German settlers came next, clearing land and felling timber for their characteristic shingled homes. Both ethnic groups have left their mark on the region through architecture, art, and food—the Mapuche near Temuco and the German around Puerto Varas and Valdivia.

The region is dependent on fishing, tourism, and, unfortunately, the timber industry, which has done much to destroy the Lake District's once nearly impenetrable forests. Along the Panamericana, trucks roar by with the day's fresh haul of giant trunks, destined for the wood-chip mill and an export ship. However, the many national parks and reserves give visitors a chance to surround themselves in virgin forest that is unique for its stands of umbrella-shaped *araucaria* and 1,000-year-old *alerce* trees (see the box "The *Alerce* and the *Araucaria:* Living National Monuments," later in this chapter).

The weather here during summer is usually balmy, but winter is a different story. This region sees a *heavy* amount of rainfall, much like the Pacific Northwest of the United States. If you plan to visit the Lake District, it's a good idea to bring clothing that will keep you dry.

EXPLORING THE REGION

The Lake District is composed of the **Región de la Araucanía,** which includes the city **Temuco** and the resort area **Pucón,** and the **Región de los Lagos,** where you'll find the port cities **Valdivia** and **Puerto Montt,** charming villages such as **Puerto Varas** and **Frutillar,** and the island **Chiloé** (see chapter 13, "Chiloé," for information on Chiloé). There's plenty more to see and do outside these principal destinations, including hot springs, boat rides, adventure sports, beaches, and kilometer after kilometer of bumpy dirt roads that make for picturesque drives through magical landscapes. Towns such as Puerto Varas and Pucón make for excellent bases to take part in all of these activities.

Another great attraction here is Chile's proximity to the **Argentine Lake District** (see chapter 6, "The Argentine Lake District"), where you'll find the equally beautiful cities **Bariloche** and **San Martín de los Andes.** If you're planning on visiting both countries, it makes sense to cross the border in the Lake District because Chile and Argentina are separated by a 1- to 2-day boat ride or several hours by road. It is entirely feasible to do somewhat of a loop through both country's Lake Districts, first heading into Argentina from Puerto Varas via the lake crossing, then heading north and either passing through Villa La Angostura and back into Chile in the Puyehue region, or heading from Bariloche to San Martín de los Andes and entering through Chile toward Pucón. Of course, this trip can be done the reverse way. Most visitors find they need just 2 to 4 full days to explore each destination.

1 Temuco

420 miles (677km) S of Santiago; 69 miles (112km) NW from Pucón

Outside magazine called Temuco one of "The World's Great Towns," and although that claim might seem dubious to the average visitor, Temuco offers enough attractions to warrant a half day getting to know Chile's third-largest city.

Historically known as *La Frontera* (The Frontier), this is where the Mapuche Indians kept Spanish conquistadors at bay for 300 years until Chile's Frontier Army founded a fort on the shore of the River Cautín in 1881. The city grew like a boomtown as Spanish, German, French, Swiss, and English immigrants poured into the region, and in less than 15 years the city counted 7,000 residents and train service that connected it with the north and south. Temuco is still one the country's fastest-growing cities, as is evident by the thundering buses, bustling downtown crowds, and increasingly poor air quality that threaten to absorb whatever charm remains in this historic town.

Temuco serves as a jumping-off point to a handful of national parks, such as **Conguillío, Villarrica,** and **Huerquehue.** It is also the gateway to the wildly popular **Pucón.** If you plan to use Temuco solely as a transfer point for outlying regions, try to at least stop at the Mercado Municipal (Municipal Market), described in "What to See & Do," below.

ESSENTIALS
GETTING THERE
BY PLANE   Manquehue Airport (no phone) is about 5 miles (8km) from the city center. To get to Temuco, hire a cab outside or arrange transportation with Transfer & Turismo de la Araucania, a minivan service at the airport that charges $5 for door-to-door service (☎ **45/339900**). This transfer service will also take a maximum of six people directly to Pucón for $45. Both Avant and Lan Chile/Ladeco serve Temuco.

BY BUS   To get to Temuco from Santiago by bus, try **TurBus** (☎ **2/270-7500**), which leaves from the Terminal Alameda at Avenida Bernardo O'Higgins 3750; or **Cruz del Sur** (☎ **2/770-0607**), which leaves from the Terminal Santiago at Avenida Bernardo O'Higgins 3848. A one-way economical ticket costs about $10; a seat in executive class costs about $21. Most buses arrive at Temuco's new **Terminal Rodoviario** (no phone). From here you can take a taxi to your hotel.

BY TRAIN   EFE (☎ **2/632-2802** in Santiago, or 45/233416 in Temuco; www.efe.cl) offers one of the few train services in Chile, with economy, salon, and sleeper coaches. Opinions about the service are varied; however, most say that quality and comfort are decent, but the clackety-clack of the rails keeps more than a few riders up all night. EFE's "La Frontera" has daily service to Santiago, leaving at 8pm

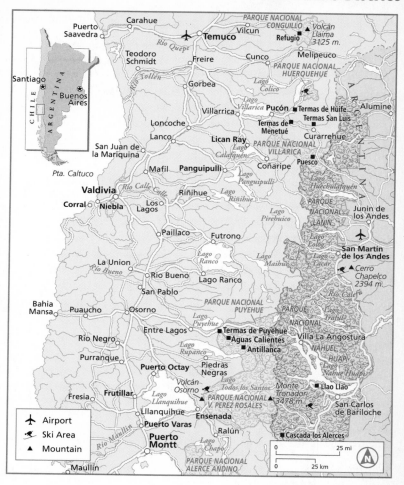

Airport
Ski Area
Mountain

and arriving at 8am; hours are the same for Santiago to Temuco. The train station in Temuco is at Barros Arana and Lautaro; in Santiago, the station is at Bulnes 582. Tickets are $16 sleeper, $12 economy.

BY CAR   It is impossible to miss Temuco when arriving by car, as the Panamericana drives right through town. Follow the signs to downtown to the left.

VISITOR INFORMATION

Sernatur operates a well-stocked tourism office at the corner of Claro Solar and Bulnes streets at Plaza Aníbal Pinto (☎ **45/211969**). Hours from December to March are Monday to Saturday 8:30am to 7:30pm; the rest of the year, Monday to Friday 9:30am to 1pm and 3 to 7pm.

NEARBY GUIDED TOURS

MultiTour, Bulnes 307, #202 (☎ **45/237913;** fax 45/233536; www.chile-travel. com/multitour.html; e-mail: cinopa@entelchile.net), offers a wide variety of bilingual excursions, including city tours, day trips to Conguillío National Park, and 3-hour, 8-hour, and overnight cultural trips through Mapuche communities. These cultural trips include visits to a *ruca*, a typical Mapuche Indian home and the opportunity to visit with Mapuches; the "working" overnight requires participation in tasks such as chopping wood and taking animals out to pasture.

GETTING AROUND

Getting around Temuco is easy by foot. To get to outlying areas such as national parks, it's best to rent a car or go with a tour. To get to Pucón (see "Villarrica & Pucón," below), try **Buses JAC,** corner of Balmaceda and Aldunate (☎ **45/231340**), which operates from its own terminal, leaving every half hour on weekdays and every hour on weekends and holidays.

If you want to rent a car to see the outlying sights, Hertz, Avis, and First all have kiosks at the airport. In downtown Temuco, **Hertz** can be found at Las Heras 999 (☎ **45/235385**); **Avis** at Vicuña Mackenna 448 (☎ **45/238013**); **First** at Antonio Varas 1036 (☎ **45/233890**); or **Dacsa** at A. Bello 770 (☎ **45/211515**).

FAST FACTS: TEMUCO

Currency Exchange   There are a few *casas de cambio* and banks with 24-hour cash machines along Bulnes Street at the main plaza.
Hospital   Clíníca Alemana, Senador Estenbanez 645 (☎ **45/244244**).
Laundry   Marva Laundromat has two locations at 415 and 1099 Manuel Montt.
Travel Agency   Agencia de Viajes y Cambios Christopher, Bulnes 667, #202 (☎ **45/211680**).

WHAT TO SEE & DO

For a sweeping view of Temuco, take a taxi or hike up the heavily forested **Cerro Ñielol,** which also features four trails and a restaurant near the summit. It's open Monday to Sunday 8am to 10pm; admission is $1 adults, 30¢ children. At the site marked LA PATAGUA, you'll find a plaque commemorating the agreement signed here in 1881 between the Mapuche Indians and the Chilean Army for peaceful settlement of Temuco. If you're there between March and May, the Cerro Ñielol is also an ideal spot to catch Chile's national flower in bloom, the crimson, trumpet-shaped *copihue.*

The manicured grounds of **Plaza Aníbal Pinto** in the city center are a relaxing break from the commercial bustle surrounding it. Within the plaza you'll find the sizeable *La Araucanía* monument depicting the clash between the Mapuche and the Spanish. There's also a gallery with temporary exhibits.

Walk up Bulnes Street to Portales and enter one of Chile's finest markets, the ✪ **Mercado Municipal,** open Monday to Saturday 8am to 8pm, Sunday and holidays 8:30am to 3pm; from April to September the market closes at 6pm Monday to Saturday. Rows of stalls sell everything from high-quality woven ponchos, knitwear, textiles, woodwork, hats, silver Mapuche jewelry, *mate* gourds, and assorted arts and crafts. Around the perimeter, fishermen and food stalls aggressively vie for business while butchers in white aprons hawk their meats from behind dangling sausages and fluorescent-lit displays of every cut imaginable. Another market, the **Fería Libre** at Aníbal Pinto, offers a colorful chaos of fruit and vegetable stands as well—not much for the tourist, but then the highlight here is the traditional Mapuche Indian vendors who come in from *reducciónes* to sell their goods. The market is open Monday to Sunday 8:30am to 5pm; from March to December, it closes at 4pm.

Temuco also has the **Museo Regional La Araucana** at Alemania 084 (☎ **45/211108**), open Tuesday to Friday 10am to 5:30pm, Saturday 11am to 5:30pm,

Sunday 11am to 2pm; admission is $1. The museum features exhibits charting Indian migration and history, along with displays of Mapuche jewelry and weapons. There's really not a lot to see, so you should consider visiting this museum only if you've run out of things to do.

WHERE TO STAY

Private parking or ample street parking is available and free for all hotels.

✪ **Don Eduardo.** A. Bello 755, Temuco. ☎ **45/214133.** Fax 45/215554. www.chile-hotels. com/doneduar.htm. E-mail: deduardo@ctcinternet.cl. 29 units w/ kitchenette, 5 standard. MINIBAR TV TEL. $60 standard; $78 suite with kitchenette. AE, DC, MC, V.

Impeccable, cozy, well-designed rooms with comfortable beds make the Don Eduardo a standout in Temuco. Most rooms come with a kitchenette and are worth booking for their ample size that includes a separate living area. Some of the gleaming bathrooms come with whirlpool tubs for the same price, so be certain to ask for one. Standards are on the ninth floor and are fitted with large windows with city views; these rooms are designed so that they can be converted into "apartments" for large parties. Try bargaining for a price, as the manager is usually eager to make a deal, especially in the winter. Friendly staff, free airport pickup, and an ever-so-slight edge in quality make this better than the Aitué (see below) around the corner.

Holiday Inn Express. Ortega 1800, Temuco. ☎ **800/36666** or 45/223300. Fax 45/224100. 40 units. $88 double. AE, DC, MC, V.

Predictable the way a Holiday Inn always is, this hotel is best used as an overnighter for those on their way out of Temuco. With clean rooms, comfortable beds, cable TV, and a location ½ block from an American-style shopping mall with the usual fast food joints, you might feel like you never left the States. The principal drawback of this hotel is its distance from downtown; however, it is close to the locally renowned La Estancia barbecue restaurant (see "Where to Dine," below). Also, kids under 18 can room with their parents for free, and there's a pool, whirlpool, and restaurant.

Hotel Aitué. Antonio Varas 1048, Temuco. ☎ **45/211917.** Fax 45/212608. www. hotelschile.com/hotels/aitue.html. 38 units. MINIBAR TV TEL. $53 double; $71 junior suite. AE, DC, MC, V.

This family-owned and operated hotel offers good value for the price, including a business center with an Internet connection and free airport pickup. Double rooms are about average size while junior suites are substantially larger, but most of the space is in a useless foyer without a seating area. Each well-lit room comes with mahogany furniture and fairly comfortable beds. The staff is knowledgeable and friendly and strives to make guests feel at home. The hotel has a popular convention salon downstairs, and it also offers a small bar and lounge, as well as a fireside dining area serving breakfast and snacks.

✪ **Hotel Continental.** Antonio Varas 708, Temuco. ☎ **45/238973.** Fax 45/233830. E-mail: hcontine@ctc-mundo.net. 40 units. TEL. $45 double with bathroom; $27 with shared bathroom. AE, DC, MC, V.

Inaugurated in 1889, the Continental is the oldest hotel in Chile, with a rich local history and a guestbook that has registered names such as Gabriela Mistral and Pablo Neruda (who preferred room 9). Virtually nothing has changed at the Continental, certainly not the wooden bar where locals still meet for the dice game *cacho,* nor the elegant dining room with period bronze chandeliers and mounted deer antlers, nor the lobby's imported Viennese leather chairs. The stark rooms come with high ceilings, antique furniture, and a sink; most have tiny windows. The major drawbacks at the

Continental are squeaky floors, thin walls, and the beds (all singles)—the springy, wobbly contraptions seemingly haven't been changed since 1889. You'll have to give up a little comfort for a chance to spend the night the way they did at the turn of the century, but the hotel does exude a certain romantic charm. Where else can you spend the night in the same room as ex-presidents Aguirre and Salvador Allende (room 11)? Recommended for a visit even if you choose not to stay. The old-world dining room serves good, traditional fare (for restaurant information, see "Where to Dine," below).

Tierra del Sur. Bulnes 1196, Temuco. ☎/fax **45/232439.** 15 units. MINIBAR TV TEL. $50 double. AE, DC, MC, V.

This small, modern hotel seems out of place in its modest neighborhood, just across a set of railroad tracks where the paved road turns to dirt. Designed and built by a local architect (including simple, handcrafted furniture), the Tierra del Sur has bold blue- and mustard-colored stucco walls, a compact, motel-like layout and saunas, indoor and outdoor pools, a Turkish steam bath, and tiny kitchenettes in every room. The rooms are average-size, with a tiny bar-and-stool setup for eating. The 10-minute, unattractive walk to the downtown plaza is really the only negative point of the Tierra del Sur. Service is friendly, and inside the lobby there's a bright cafe serving breakfast and lunch, if you choose not to cook. A nice touch is the *quincho,* a covered barbecue house near the pool for grilling dinner.

WHERE TO DINE

Don't miss the **Mercado Municipal,** open Monday to Saturday 8am to 8pm, and Sunday 8:30am to 3pm, for a quick, inexpensive lunch at one of the market's dozen or so restaurants. To get there, enter at Portales at Bulnes or Adulante streets. Waiters will harangue you until you feel suckered enough to choose their establishment, but the best bets are at **The Turista, El Chilote,** or **La Caleta.** For sandwiches and other quick meals, try **Dino's** at Bulnes 360 (☎ **45/213660**), **ñam ñam** at the corner of Portales and Prat (no phone), or **Bierstube** at Vicuña Mackenna 530, if you like your sandwich with sauerkraut (no phone). In general, reservations are not needed for the restaurants listed here.

Centro Español. Bulnes 483. ☎ **45/210343.** Main courses $8–$11. AE, MC, V. Daily 8:30am–2am. CHILEAN.

This huge, two-story restaurant features a dining room that opens onto a pretty interior patio, along with a classic motif and menu. Chilean staples such as grilled and fried meats and fish fill the largest percentage of the menu, but the restaurant does try to live up to its name with a few Spanish dishes. On Fridays the Centro holds a *Meson de Sancho* dinner dance; Sundays the atmosphere is family-oriented, with lots and lots of kids.

The Continental Hotel. Antonio Varas 708. ☎ **45/238973.** Main courses $5–$11. AE, DC, MC, V. Daily noon–3pm and 8–11:30pm. CHILEAN.

Located in an antique hotel of the same name (see above), the Continental is still the traditional favorite in town. The food is prepared simply, with many dishes following the standard fried entree with mashed potatoes format. Several highlights are cheese soufflé, crab stew, and Parmesan scallops. One of the real reasons to dine at the Continental is for the old-world ambience. Inside the century-old, barn-size dining area, giant bronze chandeliers hang from a soaring ceiling; the room is so spacious, in fact, that conversation echoes when there are but a few diners. Also, if you hate the soft music droning in the background, just ask them to turn it down. The restaurant offers a set menu for lunch and dinner for $4.50 and $6.50, respectively.

✪ **La Estancia.** Ortega 2340. ☎ **45/221385.** Main courses $6–$11. AE, DC, MC, V. Mon–Sat noon–4pm and 7pm–midnight; Sun noon–4pm. STEAKHOUSE.

This restaurant is regionally known as one of the best Chilean *parrillas* in the south of Chile, although La Pampa (see below) is nipping at its heels. Sizzling cuts of beef can be ordered individually or as part of a mixed *parrillada,* and there are also chicken, fish, salads, and a range of appetizers, including excellent Serrano ham. The entire restaurant is decorated with cowhide chairs, menus, and hanging hams. The surrounding grounds are quite pleasant and include an expansive garden.

✪ **La Pampa.** Caupolicán 155. ☎ **45/882116.** Main courses $6.50–$15. AE, DC, MC, V. Mon–Sat noon–4pm and 7:30pm–midnight; Sun noon–4pm. STEAKHOUSE/ARGENTINE.

Excellent grilled meats, fresh salads, seafood, and an extensive wine list that includes export-only varieties make La Pampa a great place to dine. It was opened 3 years ago by two Argentine transplants who came for a visit and never went home. Temucans are no doubt thankful, as evidenced by a dining room that usually fills after 8pm. Try the trout with Roquefort sauce, or one of the Argentine specialties such as *matambre,* thin meat rolled with spinach and egg. Don't miss the weekend-only *asado criollo,* thick ribs slowly grilled for 3 hours.

Quick Biss. Antonio Varas 755. ☎ **45/211219.** Main courses $2.50–$5. AE, DC, MC, V. Daily 10am–11pm. CAFETERIA.

Modern, with wooden booths and zebra-striped walls, this cafeteria is very popular with downtown workers for its reasonable prices. Diners fill their trays with an assortment of items such as salads, hot dishes, sandwiches, soups, and desserts, or a simple empanada. Solo diners often sit at a large bar near the entrance where they watch the news or a soccer game while eating. The *autoservicio,* or self-service, lunch runs from 12:30 to 4pm, dinner from 6 to 9pm, and there is also a simple menu offered all day.

EXCURSIONS FROM TEMUCO
PARQUE NACIONAL TOLGUACA

This compact, 6,400ha (15,808-acre) national park offers several enjoyable hiking trails and the **Hotel Termas de Tolguaca** (☎ **45/881211;** www.termasdetolhuaca. co.cl; e-mail: tolhuaca@ctcreuna.cl), a hot springs complex and hotel. Tolguaca's highlights are its valley surrounded by glacier-scoured peaks and Volcán Tolguaca. Two of the park's popular trails, **Mesacura** and **Lagunillas,** both 7½ miles (12km) long, are full-day hikes that wind through a virgin forest of laurel, *araucaria,* and evergreen beech, some of which tower more than 30m (98 ft.) tall. The Lagunillas trail ends at a panoramic vista point that looks directly out at Volcán Tolguaca. To get to these trails, hikers must first take the **Salto Malleco** trail, which passes the **Río Malleco** and its namesake lagoon until it comes upon a thundering, 50m (164 ft.) waterfall; this trail is 5 miles (8km) long and relatively moderate (it is possible to fish here in the lagoon). From here the trail forks; the left trail is Mesacura and the right Lagunillas. The park is open from November to April only, 8am to 8pm. Admission is $3 adults, $1 children under 12, and there are several campsites and picnic areas (for more information, call ☎ **45/236312**). During the summer, park rangers give daily talks. Apart from the beauty of this park, one of its principal draws is its hot springs, the **Termas de Tolguaca,** with a pleasant hotel, a restaurant, and two large thermal pools with hydromassage lounge seats. Pool day-use costs $11 adults, $5.50 kids. The hotel has rooms and cabañas; guests have free use of the facilities. You'll need your own vehicle to get here, or you can arrange a trip with a tour company. Bring rain gear regardless of the season.

The *Alerce* & the *Araucaria:*
Living National Monuments

The Lake District and its neighboring forests in Argentina are home to two of the oldest trees on the planet: the *alerce* and the *araucaria,* otherwise known as larch and monkeypuzzle trees, respectively. The *alerce* is frequently likened to the North American sequoia for its longevity and massive height and trunk circumference. These venerable giants grow less than a millimeter each year, and can live for more than 3,000 years, which makes the *alerce* the world's second-oldest tree after the California bristlecone pine. They are best viewed in the Alerce Andino National Park and Pumalín Park. The wood is prized for its water resistance; its bark makes for excellent caulking, which led to heavy overexploitation during the past decade.

But perhaps the most fascinating of the two is the *araucaria,* called *pehuén* by the Mapuche. The *araucaria* tree is unmistakable for its gangly branches and thick, thorny leaves that feel waxy to the touch. Mature trees can grow as high as 50m (164 ft.), and take on the appearance of an umbrella, which is why they're often called *Las Paraguas* (The Umbrellas). The *araucaria* thrives in cold environments with loose soil of volcanic origin, at an altitude between 800m and 2,000m (2,624 ft. to 6,560 ft.). They do not reach reproductive maturity until they are about 200 years old and can live as long as 1,250 years. They are best seen in Tolguaca, Villarrica, and Conguillío national parks, but they're virtually everywhere around the Lake District, and many people even plant them in their yards. The *araucaria* seed, an edible nut, was the principal source of food for the Mapuche Indians; later the tree was coveted for its quality wood and, as with the case of the *alerce,* overexploitation destroyed the majority of its forests. Today, both the *alerce* and the *araucaria* have been declared protected national monuments.

CONGUILLÍO NATIONAL PARK

Ranked as one of Chile's finest national parks, Parque Nacional Conguillío surrounds the spectacular smoking cone of Volcán Llaima and features a dense forest of spindly *araucaria* trees. Conguillío, in fact, was created to protect this concentration of *araucaria.* It's a lovely park and a great attraction year-round due to several splendid hiking trails, a ski resort, and an outstanding park information center. Volcán Llaima is one of the most active volcanoes on earth and has registered 40 eruptions since 1640, most recently in 1994. In the southern section of the park it is possible to witness the tremendous destruction lava has wreaked on the surrounding forest. Conguillío is divided into three separate sectors with as many access points. The western side of the park is commonly known as **Las Paraguas** (The Umbrellas); the eastern side is accessed from the north in sector Laguna Captren, and the south at Sector Truful-Truful. Visitors will find the park's administration center, campgrounds, and most hiking trails here in the eastern sector.

The eastern access point is at the village **Cherquenco;** from here a 13-mile (21km) rutted road ends at the **Centro Esquí Las Araucarias** (☎ **45/562313**) in Las Paraguas. This ski center has two T-bars, a ski school, equipment rental, and a restaurant and bar. Ticket prices are $13 Monday to Friday and $18 on weekends. The center offers dormitory-style lodging with two single-sex rooms and about 10 bunk beds without bedding for $10 per person. There's also a condominium with units for six that go for $85 a night. It's a fun little resort, and the views are simply breathtaking, as is its location nestled in a forest of *araucaria*.

An unpaved and poorly maintained road connects a Conaf **visitor center**, which is open daily 9am to 1pm and 3 to 7pm (☎ **45/212121**), with the towns **Curacautín** in the north and **Melipeuco** in the south. Because Conaf is at an equal distance from both entrances, many visitors like to enter at one point and exit at the other. The information center has interpretive displays highlighting the park's flora, fauna, and physical geology, including an interesting section devoted to volcanism. During the summer, park rangers offer informative talks and walks and a host of educational activities, which they post in the visitor center.

There's an easy, hour-long, self-guided trail that leaves from the Conaf center, but if you really want to get out and walk, you'll want to take the **Sierra Nevada trail**. This moderate, 5-hour hike is the best in the park, taking visitors through thick forest and rising to two lookout points that offer sensational volcano and lake views, before dropping back down to the Captrén Lagoon near the Conaf center. The trailhead is on the western shore of Lake Conguillío at the Conaf center. A second, 5-hour hike along moderate terrain, **Los Carpinteros,** weaves its way through stands of *araucaria* trees that are several hundred, some more than 1,000, years old. This trail leaves from Laguna Captrén at the Conaf center. Keep your eyes peeled for woodpeckers.

GETTING THERE & BASICS   If you plan to rent a vehicle, try to get one with a high clearance—it's not essential, but it helps. Most tour companies in Temuco plan excursions to this park. Bus service from Temuco's main terminal is available only to Curacautín and Melipeuco; from here you'll need to take a taxi or hitch a ride. The road is paved only to the park entrance, so during the winter you'll need a 4×4 or tire chains during or just after a snowstorm to get to the ski center.

The park is open April to November 8am to 11pm and May to Oct 8:30am to 5pm. The park entrance fee is $5 for adults and $1.25 for children. There is a cafeteria and a store at Conaf's park information center in the Sector Truful-Truful.

WHERE TO STAY   If you're looking to camp, you'll have to do it here in one of the seven campsites along the shore of Lago Conguillío because backcountry camping is not permitted. It's not cheap, either: about $22 per campsite. From October to April the park service has cabins that go for an average of $50 per night; information about rentals can be found inside the store next to the visitor's center in Sector Truful-Truful (☎ **45/213299**). A great option is one of the wooden cabins at **La Baita** (☎ **45/ 581075**), for $85 per night, located midway between Conaf and the town Melipeuco. La Baita is an attractive ecotourism complex, complete with a restaurant, a store, park information, and guided excursions such as hiking, skiing, and snowshoeing.

A REMOTE LODGE OUTSIDE TEMUCO

Trailanqui. Los Laureles a Colico Km5. ☎ **45/578218,** or for reservations in Temuco 45/ 234119. Fax 45/214915. www.trailanqui.cl. E-mail: info@trailanqui.cl. 22 units, 9 cabañas. TEL. $34–$87 double; $60–$147 suite; $50–$127 cabaña. AE, DC, MC, V.

This out-of-the-way, woodsy resort should appeal to anyone looking to get away from it all for a night. Families especially love this resort for its wealth of activities, including fishing, horseback riding, and swimming—there's even a minigolf course—that keep everyone busy. For this reason the Trailanqui can take on the feel of an upscale summer camp. The resort is spread out along the shore of a crystal-clear river, and it offers hotel rooms, apartments, cabins, and campsites. Its spacious lounge has a huge fireplace made of volcanic rock and floors made of cypress trunks. The Trailanqui is made entirely of cypress, in fact, offset with large picture windows, burlaplike wallpaper, sheepskin rugs, and deer antler chandeliers. Double "full" rooms are substantially larger than double standard rooms and are the same price. Apartments have two bedrooms and a wood-burning stove, but no kitchen. Cabañas come fully stocked and have decks overlooking the river.

There's a brand-new heated pool with mineralized water and hydromassage, as well as a beach and swimming platform on the river. It can get a little crazy here in January and February with the amount of people who flock here for their summer vacation, but off-season promises tranquility. The hotel will arrange excursions to Conguillío National Park.

Dining: Guests typically take meals in the hotel's restaurant (guests in cabañas can cook their own), which is also open year-round to the public. The restaurant serves a fixed-price menu of home-style Chilean dishes during the high season in a dining area down by the river; they serve from a regular menu (chicken and meat dishes, seafood) during the low season in the restaurant within the hotel. There's also a bar near the lounge.

Amenities: Room service, laundry, conference rooms, tennis courts, volleyball, soccer field, nine-hole golf course, horseback riding, mountain bike rental, rafting, outdoor heated pool, sauna, baby-sitting, billiard room, Ping-Pong, minimarket.

2 Villarrica & Pucón

Villarrica is a quiet town that never really took off as a vacation resort, despite owning a lovely view of Volcán Villarrica. Cheaper accommodations can be found here, and the town is decidedly less touristy, but it sits a half-hour ride away from the more popular Pucón and attractions such as Villarrica and Huerquehue national parks and the ski resort.

Nationally and internationally known as the **"Adventure Capital of Chile,"** Pucón offers every outdoor activity imaginable: fly-fishing, rafting the Trancura River, hiking Huerquehue and Conguillío national parks, skiing the slopes of Volcán Villarrica— even climbing to its bubbling crater. Yet what makes Pucón a great destination is its flexibility. There's also an abundance of low-key activities, such as hot spring spas and scenic drives through spectacular landscapes. You could just hang out on the beach and sun yourself, as hundreds do during the summer.

VILLARRICA
15.5 miles (25km) W of Pucón; 474 miles (764km) S of Santiago

Decidedly less popular than neighboring Pucón, Villarrica does have a charm of its own. It's a more authentic Lake District *pueblo;* the compact downtown area hums with activity as regular townsfolk go about their daily business. The town is also closer to Temuco and attractions such as Lican Ray on Lake Calafquén, Panguipulli, and the Coñaripe hot springs.

GETTING THERE   Buses JAC (☎ **45/442069**) leaves every half hour for Pucón from its location at Bilbao 610, near Pedro de Valdivia. In Pucón, JAC's location is O'Higgins 492. The fare is under a dollar. A taxi to or from Pucón costs about $8. To get to Villarrica by air, you'll need to fly into Temuco or Pucón (see "Getting There" for Temuco or Pucón, above and below).

VISITOR INFORMATION   A good **tourism office** can be found at Av. Pedro de Valdivia 1070 (☎ **45/411162**). It's open daily 8:30am to 11pm December 15 to March 15 and daily 8:30am to 6:30pm the rest of the year; it often closes on winter afternoons when the weather is rotten.

WHAT TO SEE & DO

You might consider a day trip to Villarrica to stroll the streets, have lunch, and drop in to visit the **Museo Histórico y Arqueológico**, Pedro de Valdivia 1050 (no phone), with displays of Mapuche items, such as masks, and trademark silver pieces and jewelry. Outside you'll find an authentically thatched *ruca,* a traditional Mapuche home. The museum is open Monday to Friday 9am to 1pm and 3 to 7:30pm. The festival **Muestra Cultural Mapuche** takes place here in Villarrica from January to late February, with music, *artensanía* (handcrafts), dancing, and other activities (for more information, call the visitor's center at ☎ 45/411162).

WHERE TO STAY & DINE

Hostería Kiel, General Korner 153 (☎ **45/411631;** fax 45/410925; www.villarricanet. com/yachting), has comfortable rooms ($50 to $65 double) and a direct view of Volcán and Lake Villarrica that you can enjoy from your very own porch. Or try **Cabañas Monte Negro** at Pratt and Montt streets (☎ **45/411371**); it charges $112 for two to six people (no credit cards), and has eight newer cabins near the lake that sport a direct view of the volcano. Private parking or ample street parking is available and free.

For excellent seafood dishes, try **El Rey de Marisco,** on the coast at Valentín Letelier 1030 (☎ **45/412093**), or **Hostería Kiel,** General Korner 153 (☎ **45/411631**), for simple Chilean fare and a superb view of Volcán Villarrica. **The Travellers,** Valentín Letelier 753 (☎ **45/412830**), has that international traveler's hostel vibe, and a menu to match with Chinese, Indian, Mexican, Thai, and Chilean dishes and the ever-popular happy hour from 6 to 9:30pm.

PUCÓN

69 miles (112km) E of Temuco; 15.5 miles (25km) E of Villarrica; 489 miles (789km) S of Santiago

Pucón is a picturesque little town almost entirely dependent on tourism, but thankfully it has not embellished its streets with gaudy tourist traps. Instead, a creative use of timber creates the architectural tone. During the early 1900s, Pucón's economy centered on the timber industry, but the town's fate as a travel destination was sealed when the first hotel went up in 1923, attracting hordes of fishermen. Ten years later, the government built the stately Hotel Pucón, drawing hundreds more visitors each year, who at that time had to travel here by boat from Villarrica. Today, there are many lodging options, from comfortable hostels to grand hotels to intimate lodges, and there are even more adventure outfitters ready to fill your days.

It is important to note that the summer season, particularly December 15 to the end of February, as well as Easter week, is jam-packed with tourists. Hotel and business owners gleefully take advantage of this and jack up their prices, sometimes doubling their rates.

GETTING THERE   By Plane   Visitors normally fly into Temuco's **Manquehue Airport** and then arrange transportation for the 1- to 1½-hour ride into Villarrica or Pucón. Most hotels will arrange transportation for you, although it's usually at an additional cost. Transfer & Turismo de la Araucania (☎ **45/339900**), a minivan service at the airport, will take a maximum of six guests to Pucón for $45. However, Pucón has been furiously working away at its own airport and hopes to have regular flights directly from Santiago on Lan Chile/Ladeco sometime in early 2001. Consult Lan Chile for the status of flights directly into Pucón (☎ **600/600-4000**).

By Car   From the Panamericana Highway south of Temuco, follow the signs for Villarrica onto Ruta 199. The road is well marked and easy to follow. If coming from

Valdivia, take 205 to the Panamericana Norte (Highway 5). Just past Loncoche, continue east, following signs for Villarrica and Pucón.

By Bus   TurBus (☎ 2/270-7500) offers service to Pucón from destinations such as Santiago, stopping first in Temuco and Villarrica. The trip is about 11 hours and generally a night journey; the cost is about $13 for an economy seat and $28 for an executive seat. Buses JAC has service from Temuco every half hour from its terminal at Bustamante and Aldunate.

VISITOR INFORMATION   Sernatur (☎ 45/443338) operates a helpful tourism office at the corner of Brasil and Caupolicán streets; it's open daily 8:30am to 10pm December to March and 8:30am to 8pm the rest of the year. The city of Pucón has an excellent Web site crammed with information at **www.pucon.com**.

GETTING AROUND   There are dozens of tour companies providing transportation and tours to all points of interest around Pucón; they generally advertise everything in their front windows. However, this is another place where renting a car is a great option if you want to get out and leisurely see the sights. In Temuco, **Hertz** has an office at Las Heras 999 (☎ 45/441664). In Pucón, try **Christopher** in front of the supermarket (☎ 45/449013) or **Pucón Rent A Car** on the Camino Internacional 1395-1510 (☎ 45/441992).

OUTDOOR ACTIVITES

With so many outdoor adventures available here, it's no wonder there's a surplus of outfitters eager to meet the demand. When choosing an outfitter in Pucón, remember that you get what you pay for. Be wary of seemingly fly-by-night operations or those that treat you like just another nameless tourist. You want a memorable experience for the fun you've had, not for the mishaps and accidents. Most outfitters include insurance in the cost of a trip, but first verify what their policy covers.

For more things to see and do in this area, see "Hot Springs Outside Pucón" and "Natural Attractions Outside Pucón," below.

TOUR OPERATORS   Politour, O'Higgins 635 (☎ 45/441373; http://politur. com; e-mail: turismo@politur.com), is a well-respected tour company that offers fishing expeditions, Mapuche-themed tours, and sightseeing trips around the Seven Lakes area, in addition to volcano ascents. They're slightly more expensive than other agencies, but are worth it. **Aguaventura,** Palguín 336 (☎ 45/444246), is run by a competent, dynamic French trio and specializes in snowboarding in the winter with a shop that sells and rents boards, boots, and clothing. In the summer the focus is rafting and kayaking, and they offer a great half-day canyoneering and rappelling excursion; they also plan horseback rides. **Trancura,** O'Higgins 211-c (☎ 45/441189; www. trancura.com), operates a variety of excursions, but it's known for rafting and volcano climbs. Trancura seems to offer just about everything, including ski rental at several locations along the main strip. It's a large company with the lowest prices around, but there have been complaints about lackluster service. Still, they're the only tour agency that offers wild-boar hunting. **Sol y Nieve,** O'Higgins and Lincoyán (☎ 45/441070; www.chile-travel.com/solnieve.htm; e-mail: solnieve@entelchile.net), has been on the scene for quite a while, offering rafting and volcano ascents, as well as fishing, airport transfers, and excursions in other destinations around Chile. **¡ecole!,** General Urrutia 592 (☎ 45/441675; e-mail: trek@ecole.mic.cl), offers a unique trip to a private *araucaria* forest, **Cañi.** If you can't get to Conguillío, you'll want to see the *araucaria* trees here. It's a good excursion, especially if it's raining and you're unsure what to do.

BIKING   Several outfitters on the main street, O'Higgins, rent bicycles by the hour and provide trail information and guided tours. Bicycle rentals run an average of $10 for a half day. You can also just tootle around town, or take a pleasant, easy ride around the wooded peninsula.

CLIMBING THE VOLCANO   An ascent of Volcán Villarrica is perhaps the most thrilling excursion available here—but you've got to be in decent shape to tackle it. The excursion begins early in the morning for the long climb, which requires crampons and ice-axes. There's nothing like peering into this percolating, fuming crater. The descent is a combination of walking and sliding on the way down on your behind in the snow. Volcán Villarrica is perpetually on the verge of exploding, and last year trips were called off for some time until the rumbling quieted down. Tour companies that offer this climb are **Trancura, Politour, Aguaventura,** and **Sol y Nieve** (see "Tour Operators," above). The average cost is $50, and does not include lunch.

FISHING   You can pick up your fishing license at the visitor's center at Caupolicán and Brasil. Guided fishing expeditions typically go to the Trancura River or the Liucura River. See a list of outfitters above for information, or try **Off Limits,** Fresia 273 (☎ 45/441210).

GOLFING   Pucón's private, 18-hole Peninsula de Pucón golf course is open to the playing public. For information, call ☎ 45/441021, ext 409. The cost is $45 for 18 holes.

HIKING   The two national parks, Villarrica and Huerquehue, offer outstanding hiking trails that run from easy to difficult. An average excursion with an outfitter to Huerquehue, including transportation and a guided hike, costs about $25 per person.

HORSEBACK RIDING   Half-day and full-day horseback rides are offered throughout the area, including in the Villarrica National Park and the Liucura Valley. The **Centro de Turismo Huepil** (☎ 09/643-2673) offers day and multiple-day horseback rides, including camping or a stay at the Termas de Huife, from a small ranch about a half hour from Pucón (head east out of Pucón and then north toward Caburgua; take the eastern road toward Huife and keep your eyes open for the signs to Centro de Turismo Huepil). You'll need to make a reservation beforehand. All-inclusive multiple-day trips cost about $100 per person, per day. A wonderful couple, Rodolfo and Carolina, run this outfit. Rodolfo is a superb equestrian professor who used to train the Spanish Olympic team. Beginning riders are given an introductory course in the corral before setting out. Contact a tour agency for day rides in Villarrica Park, which go for about $65 for a full day. Tour agencies will also organize rides that leave from the **Rancho de Caballos** (☎ 45/441575) near the Palguín thermal baths. If you're driving, the Rancho is at 30km on the Ruta International toward Argentina.

RAFTING   Rafting season runs from September to April, although some areas might be safe to descend only from December to March. The two classic descents in the area are the 8½-mile (14km) Trancura Alto, rated at Class III to IV, and the somewhat gentler Trancura Bajo, rated at Class II to III. Both trips are very popular and can get crowded in the summer. The rafting outfitter **Trancura** (see "Tour Operators," above) also offers an excursion rafting the more technical Maichin River, which includes a barbecue lunch. The 3-hour rafting trip on the Trancura Alto costs an average of $22; the 3-hour Trancura Bajo costs an average of $13.

SKIING   The **Centro Esquí Villarrica** gives skiers the opportunity to schuss down a smoking volcano—not something you can do every day. There's a sizeable amount of terrain here, and it's all open-field skiing, but regrettably the owners (**The Grand Hotel Pucón**) rarely open more than two of the five chairs. Sometimes they offer a lame excuse, but it's slacker city here and laziness is closer to the truth. You'll need to take a chair lift to the main lodge, which means that non-skiers too can enjoy the lovely views from the lodge's outdoor deck. There's a restaurant, child-care center, and store. The Centro has a ski school and ski equipment rental; there are slightly cheaper rentals from Aguaventura, Sol y Nieve, and Trancura, among other businesses along O'Higgins. Lift tickets vary according to season and day of the week; the average price is $25. Most tour companies offer transport to and from the resort.

WHERE TO STAY

Pucón is chock-full of lodging options, nearly all of them good to excellent. If you're planning to spend more than several days in the region, you might consider renting one of the abundant cabañas, two- to three-bedroom cabins that are normally less expensive and come with living areas and kitchens. Keep in mind that Pucón is very busy during the summer, and accommodations need to be reserved for visits between December 15 and the end of February. Prices listed below show the range from low to high season; high season is November to February, but verify each hotel's specific dates. You might consider visiting during off-season as lodging prices drop almost 50%. Private parking or ample street parking is available and free for all hotels.

Expensive

Gran Hotel Pucón. Clemente Holzapfel 190, Pucón. ☎/fax **45/441001**, or for reservations (in Santiago) 2/353-0000. Fax 2/207-4586. E-mail: ghp-sk@entelchile.net. 145 units. MINIBAR TV TEL. $118–$140 double. Kids under 10 stay free in parents' room. AE, DC, MC, V.

The Gran Hotel is a landmark built by the state government in 1936 when fishing tourism began to take off in Pucón. It is an excellent choice for families, but otherwise I have mixed opinions about it. The owners renovated the premises somewhat recently, but one has the feeling they still have a ways to go, especially if they want to keep the "Grand" in its name. The hotel's palatial hallways, stately dining areas, and lovely checkerboard patio seem to belie the ugly teal they saw fit to paint the hotel last year. Indeed, the old-world beauty of these common areas, with their marble and parquet floors, lofty ceilings, and flowing curtains, still look a tad scruffy. The rooms are not exactly noteworthy, but they are not bad either: spacious, with comfortable beds and views of the volcano or the lake. The superior room has an alcove with one or two additional beds for kids. The hotel is run somewhat like a cruise ship, with nightly dinner dances, stage shows, music and comedy, as well as a team of activity directors who run a kids' "miniclub" and host classes for adults, such as cooking or tango. The hotel sits on the most popular beach in Pucón. It's a hectic, active place, but kids love it.

Dining/Diversions: The hotel's bar hosts a nightly show that can include comedy, magic, dancing, and a live band, followed by a contest. Note that in the summer the bar is open for guests only. Every Tuesday and Friday the hotel hosts dinner dances in the main salon preceded by a Vegas-style musical act.

Amenities: Concierge, room service, laundry, gift shop, conference rooms, gym, outdoor and indoor pools, sauna, game rooms, child-care center, squash court, full-size gym court, bingo.

✪ **Hotel Antumalal.** Camino Pucón–Villarrica, Km2. ☎ **45/441011.** Fax 45/441013. www.antumalal.com. E-mail: antumalal@entelchile.net. 16 units. TEL. $145 double. AE, DC, MC, V.

The minute you arrive here you know you've come upon something special. Perhaps it is the Antumalal's unique Bauhaus design and its lush, beautiful gardens, or perhaps it's the sumptuous view of sunset on Lake Villarrica seen nightly through the hotel's picture windows or from its wisteria-roofed deck. Either way, this is simply one of the best hotels in Chile. Low-slung and literally built into a rocky slope, the Antumalal was designed to blend with its natural environment. The lounge is a standout, with walls made of glass and slabs of *araucaria* wood, goat skin rugs, tree-trunk lamps, and couches built of iron and white rope. It's retro-chic and exceptionally cozy, and the friendly, personal attention provided by the staff heightens a sense of intimacy with one's surroundings. You won't be issued a room key here: The staff wants you to feel as though you're in your own home—that is, with unlocked doors. The rooms are all the same size, and they are wonderful, with panoramic windows that look out onto the same gorgeous view, as well as honeyed-wood walls, a fireplace, and a big, comfortable bed. Guests don't just walk into a room; they *sink* into it. The bar is especially interesting, with high-backed leather chairs and a stone fireplace. Lovely, terraced gardens zigzag down the lake shore, where guests have use of a private beach. A kidney-shaped pool is half-hidden under a lawn-covered roof, and the tennis courts are a short walk away. All fit for a queen—indeed, Queen Elizabeth graced the hotel with her presence several decades ago, as has Jimmy Stewart and Barry Goldwater. The bathrooms could use an update, but it seems such an unimportant issue when there is so much else offered. And by the way, the bright, handsome dining area not only serves up a spectacular view, it also serves some of the best food in Pucón. Right next door is a small cottage alongside the Antumalal, now rented as the "Royal Cottage," with three bedrooms and a kitchen.

Dining/Diversions: The hotel's restaurant serves international cuisine and is one of the best in the region both for the food and the view (see "Where to Dine," below). The leather-and-wood bar has a fireplace.

Amenities: Room service, laundry, mini gift shop, informal conference room, outdoor pool, tennis court, private dock, boat tours, massage, evening turndown.

✪ **Hotel del Lago.** Miguel Ansorena 23, Pucón. ☎ **45/291000.** Fax 45/291200. www. hoteldellago.cl. E-mail: hodelago@casino.cl. 122 units. MINIBAR TV TEL. $156–$210 double; $176–$232 suite. AE, DC, MC, V.

Pucón's sole five-star luxury hotel boasts a casino, the only cinema in town, and so many amenities that on lazy days you might not feel like leaving the hotel. Attractively designed and recently built, the Hotel del Lago is airy and bright, with a lobby covered by a lofty glass ceiling. There's a certain amount of excitement here in the lobby as a result of the constant hustle and bustle; the front doors seem almost perpetually in motion. Once inside your elegant, comfortable room, however, you won't notice. All the hotel's furnishings were imported from the United States, and rooms are tastefully decorated with furniture and wood trim made of faux-weathered pine, accented with iron headboards, crisp linen, and heavy curtains colored a variety of creamy pastels, all very light and bright. The bathrooms are made of Italian marble and are decently sized, as are double-size rooms—note that a double standard comes with two twins. The suites feature a separate living area. The Suite Volcán has the volcano view, but rooms facing west enjoy the late afternoon sun. There's an indoor pool, decorated to resemble a Grecian bath, and a full-service, state-of-the-art gym, arguably one of the best of any hotel in Chile. A concierge can plan a variety of excursions for guests, as well as transport to the ski center. The Hotel del Lago offers many promotions and package deals from March to December, often dropping the double price to $130; a 3-day, 2-night stay costs $342 and includes dinner.

Dining: The hotel counts two restaurants and a spacious bar: The **Rincón Café** serves breakfast and simpler fare and the upscale restaurant **El Almendro** serves Mediterranean cuisine.

Amenities: Concierge, valet service, 24-hour room service, laundry, gift shop, conference room, gym, outdoor and indoor pools, sauna, solarium, massage, beauty salon, game rooms, baby-sitting, casino, bingo hall, cinema.

Moderate

Hotel Munich. Geronimo de Alderete 275, Pucón. ☎/fax **45/442293.** 10 units. TV TEL. $68–$85 double. AE, DC, MC, V.

The Hotel Munich is a nice, moderately priced hotel with a touch of charm here and there. The rooms have enough elbow room, and each comes with its own terrace; they are also clean and well lit. The lobby is filled with oil paintings that the owner displays as part of a makeshift gallery; the lounge feels like a living room. There is a small dining area for buffet breakfast or afternoon tea and snacks; you can also order breakfast in your room. The service is friendly, but a little lax.

Hotel & Spa Araucarias. Caupolicán 243, Pucón. ☎ **45/441286.** Fax 45/441963. www.cepri.cl/araucarias. E-mail: araucari@cepri.cl. 25 units. TV TEL. $70–$90 double. AE, DC, MC, V.

The rooms could use a lick of paint, but otherwise the Hotel & Spa Araucarias is a good bet for its well-manicured grounds, attractive indoor pool, outdoor deck, and extras such as an on-site gift shop. The size of the rooms is a little tight—not too much space to walk around in, but enough to open your suitcase. If you're looking for something a little more independent and spacious, try one of the four connected cabins in the back. The hotel has a "spa" room with a sauna and a great, heated indoor pool fitted with hydromassage lounges. The name comes from the *araucaria* trees that flank the entrance; there's also an *araucaria* sprouting from a grassy courtyard in the back. An attractive restaurant serves lunch and dinner.

La Posada. Av. Pedro de Valdivia 191, Pucón. ☎ **45/441088.** Fax 45/441762. E-mail: laposada@unete.com. 17 units. TV TEL. $45–$89 double. AE, DC, MC, V.

This traditional hotel is housed in a 75-year-old home built by German immigrants, located on the main square 2 blocks from the beach. Everything about this old-fashioned hotel, from its exterior to its dining area to its backyard swimming pool, is very attractive—except the rooms, that is, which are plain and inexplicably do not keep up the charm of the hotel's common areas. These old buildings always seem to come with fun-house floors that creak and slant in every direction. All in all, it's a comfortable enough place to hang your hat for the evening.

Malahue Hotel. Camino International 1615, Pucón. ☎ **45/443130.** Fax 45/443132. www.pucon.com/malalhue. E-mail: malalhue@entelchile.net. 24 units, 3 cabañas. TV TEL. $59–$73 double; $76–$102 cabaña. AE, DC, MC, V.

This attractive new hotel is about a 15-minute walk from town, but offers excellent value in handsome accommodations. It was designed to feel like a modern mountain lodge, made of volcanic rock and native wood, and is set on an open space in a residential area. The interiors are impeccably clean, and rooms are decorated with country furnishings. There's a restaurant and a cozy lounge with a fireplace and couches. Cabañas have two bedrooms, a trundle bed in the living area, and a fully stocked kitchen. The location isn't ideal, but the accommodations are fine.

Inexpensive

¡ecole! General Urrutia 592, Pucón. ☎/fax **45/441675.** 16 units. $10–$12 per person. DC, MC, V.

Nearly 40 partners own this pleasant hostel, which offers small but clean and comfortable rooms with beds that come with goosedown comforters. ¡ecole! sees a predominantly international crowd, from backpackers to families traveling on a budget. It has a very good vibe throughout, and a nice outdoor patio with picnic tables. In the small lounge there is great reading material, from travel guides to environment-oriented literature to logging protest rosters. The hostel is part restaurant/part lodging/part ecology center, offering day trips to various areas, but especially to the private park Cañi, an *araucaria* reserve. It's very popular in the summer, when it's wise to book at least a week or two in advance.

La Tetera. General Urrutia 580, Pucón. ☎/fax **45/441462.** www.tetera.cl. E-mail: info@ tetera.cl. 6 units. $24–30 double; $34–$42 double with shared bathroom. No credit cards.

Rooms at La Tetera are simple but meticulously clean, and shared bathrooms are not much of an issue as they are just outside your door. It's all squeezed in pretty tight, but guests have use of a private, sunny common area with chairs and a picnic table, and a short walkway connects to an elevated wooden deck. A Swiss-Chilean couple own La Tetera, and they offer a book exchange and good tourism information, and will arrange excursions and help with trip planning. La Tetera (the teakettle) lives up to its name with two menu pages of teas, along with sandwiches, daily specials, and pastries. A common area next to the cafe has the only TV in the place.

Cabañas

✪ **Almoni del Lago Resort.** Camino Villarrica a Pucón, Km19. ☎ **45/262252.** Fax 45/ 442304. www.pucon.com/almoni. E-mail: almoni@pucon.com. 8 cabañas. TV. $218 cabaña for four. MC, V.

Location is everything at the Almoni, with its lush, gorgeous grounds leading down to the lapping shores of Lake Villarrica just a few feet from the deck of your cabin. The tennis courts on the shore, the pool, everything is here. Cabins for two, four, and eight guests are available; ask for specials for multiple-day stays. Cabins are fully equipped, access is controlled, and guests are given their own remote gate opener. A kiosk sells basic food items and other sundries. Each cabaña has its own deck right on the water, although a few are fairly close together, so you might end up getting to know your neighbor. Prices drop a whopping 50% in off-season.

Cabañas Ruca Malal. O'Higgins 770, Pucón. ☎/fax **45/442297.** www.cepri.cl/rucamalal. E-mail: avalle@cepri.cl. 9 units. TV. $36–$98 cabin for 4; $70–$118 cabin for 6. MC, V.

These custom-made, cozy wooden cabins are tucked away in a tiny forested lot at the bend where busy O'Higgins becomes the road to Caburga. The grounds, however, are peaceful, and they burst with bamboo, beech, magnolias, and rhododendron. The design of each cabin features log stairwells, carved headboards, and walls made of slabs of evergreen beech trunks cut lengthwise. They are well lit and have full-size kitchens and daily maid service. A wood-burning stove keeps the rooms toasty warm on cold days. In the center of the property is a kidney-shaped swimming pool; there's also a whirlpool and sauna, but unfortunately you'll have to pay extra to use them. As with most cabins, those designed for four people means one bedroom with a double bed and a trundle bed in the living area; book a cabin for six if you prefer two bedrooms. Those with a sweet tooth will delight in Ruca Malal's on-site chocolate shop.

✪ **Las Cabañas Metreñehue.** Camino Pucón a Caburga, Km10. ☎/fax **45/441322.** www.pucon.com/metrenehue. E-mail: kublank@ctcinternet.cl. 7 units. TV TEL. $50–$130 for 2; $100–$130for 6. AE, DC, MC, V.

These pastoral cabañas are surrounded by dense forest and bordered by the thundering Trancura River, about a 10-minute drive from downtown Pucón, and are for those seeking a country ambience away from town. There are cabins built for seven guests; a few two-storied cabins can fit eight. All are spacious and very comfortable, with wood-burning stoves, decks, and ample kitchens. Some come with bathtubs, and a few have giant picture windows; all have daily maid service. The two cabañas in the back have a great view of the volcano. Around the 3ha (7-acre) property are walking trails, a swimming pool, a volleyball court, a soccer field, and a river where guests can fish for trout. The cabins are popular with families in the summer, and sometimes large groups take advantage of the *quincho,* the poolside barbecue site. There's also mountain bike rental. The German owners are gracious and multilingual, and live in the main house (and reception area), near the cabins. Parties of two to five will have to pay a $130, six-guest rate during the summer.

Puerta Pucón Cabañas. Camino Pucón–Villarrica, Km4.5. ☎ /fax **45/442496.** www. puertapucon.com. E-mail: consultas@puertapucon.com. 9 cabañas (14 units). TV TEL. $34–$50 for 2; $51–$60 for 4. No credit cards.

These brand-new wooden cabins are spread out over a large grassy lot overlooking Lake Villarrica (a road separates the cabins from the beach). They are comfortable and relatively inexpensive, and a good bet for families with kids, especially for the pool, play area, "kids' clubhouse," and baby-sitting service; daily maid service is also included. All cabins have tiny kitchens, living areas, wood-burning stoves, small decks with table and chairs, and sweeping views of the lake. However, five of the cabins (*cabañas chicas*) are large cabins split into two units, and are somewhat cramped. Solitary cabins for four are larger, but the view shrinks. One cabin built for seven guests could really be called a house. The spacious property features walking trails, and there's also a private beach and docking area a 5-minute walk down the hill and across the road. Puerta Pucón is a 3-minute drive from downtown.

WHERE TO DINE

Pucón has a good selection of cafes that serve *onces,* the popular coffee-and-cakes, late-afternoon snack, in addition to a lunch menu. **Holzapfel** at Holzapfel 524 (☎ **45/443546**) offers promotional lunches that usually include a free beer, but Holzapfel is really known for its desserts and out-of-this-world chocolates. **Café de la "P,"** Licoyán 395 (☎ **45/442018**), has a menu with sandwiches, cakes, coffee drinks, and cocktails. It's a warm cafe, and a nice place to unwind with a drink in the evening. It's open until 4am in the summer. If none of the restaurants below whet your appetite, you might try the **Hotel del Lago**'s two restaurants, El Rincón Café or El Almendro, the latter of which serves Mediterranean food. (see "Where to Stay," above). In general, reservations are not required for the restaurants listed here.

Alta Mar. Fresia 301. ☎ **45/442294.** Main courses $5–$9. No credit cards. Daily noon–4pm and 7:30pm–midnight. SEAFOOD.

Seafood is the specialty here, as you can tell by the marine decor. It's the best spot for seafood in Pucón, offering a wide range of fish usually served grilled, fried, or sautéed in butter and bathed in a sauce. Their ceviche is tasty, and so are the razor clams broiled with Parmesan cheese. Sometimes the waiter gets decked out in full sailor fashion, complete with a captain's cap. Outdoor seating is available on the front deck during warm months.

✪ **Antumalal.** Camino Pucón–Villarrica, Km2. ☎ **45/441011.** Fax 45/441013. Reservations recommended. Main courses $9–$14. AE, DC, MC, V. Daily noon–4pm and 8–10pm. INTERNATIONAL.

The Hotel Antumalal's restaurant serves some of the most flavorful cuisine in Pucón, with creative dishes that are well prepared and seasoned with herbs from an extensive garden. Try a thinly sliced beef carpaccio followed by chicken stuffed with smoked salmon, or any one of the pastas. There's a good selection of wine and an ultra-cool cocktail lounge for an after-dinner drink. It's worth a visit for the view of Lake Villarrica alone, and you can soak it in from inside the attractive dining area or, better yet, from a terrace patio.

Buonatesta Pizzeria. Fresia 243. ☎ **45/441434.** $5–$8 pizzas. AE, DC, MC, V. Daily 11am–4pm and 6:30–11:30pm. PIZZERIA.

Buonatesta has great pizzas, but they're not the saucy versions most are typically used to. The tiny restaurant, located behind the Puerto Pucón, has a cozy dining area with framed photos of Mapuches. The menu features more than a dozen combinations of pizzas, from sausage and onions to vegetarian, as well as fresh pastas and salads.

¡ecole! General Urrutia 592. ☎/fax **45/441675.** Main courses $5.50–$8. DC, MC, V. Daily 8am–11pm. VEGETARIAN.

This vegetarian restaurant includes one salmon dish among heaps of creative dishes like calzones, quiche, pizza, burritos, chop suey, and more. Sandwiches come on homemade bread, and breakfast is good, featuring American breakfast as well as Mexican and Chilean. ¡ecole! uses locally and organically grown products and buys whole wheat flour and honey from a local farm. There are also fresh salads. The service is slightly disorganized, and during the slow, slow winter months they usually offer an abbreviated daily menu.

Il Fiore. Holzapfel 83. ☎ **45/441393.** Main courses $5.50–$12. MC, V. Daily 12:30–3:30pm and 8pm–1:30am (until midnight Apr–Nov). ITALIAN.

Rich, homemade pastas are the specialty at Il Fiore. The menu lists about eight versions, including *sorrentinos* and fettuccine, each with a choice of three or four sauces. Highlights include the *tallarin relleno Il Fiore,* fresh *tallarines* stuffed with chicken and spinach and bathed in a béchamel and walnut sauce. If you can't decide, the *triptíco La Nona* comes with three different pastas. There are also salads and appetizers. The restaurant sits about ½ block from the plaza, with a cozy ambience with a wood-burning stove as the centerpiece. Service can be a little inattentive here.

✪ **La Marmita de Pericles.** Fresia 300. ☎ **45/441114.** Fondue for 2 $25 average. AE, DC, MC, V. Daily 7:30–11pm. FONDUE.

Cozy and candlelit, La Marmita specializes in warm crocks of fondue, as well as the other Swiss favorite, *raclette.* Both involve a diner's participation, which usually makes for an amusing dinner. Fondue can be ordered with a variety of ways, with standard bread cubes, squares of breaded meat, or vegetables. A *raclette* runs along the same lines, heating cheese to eat with cured meats and potatoes; it's not as fun as fondue, but enjoyable nevertheless. Unfortunately, this restaurant closes during the winter, which is the perfect season for this kind of food.

Puerto Pucón. Fresia 246. ☎ **45/441592.** Main courses $7.50–$10.50. AE. Daily 11am–3:30pm and 7–11:30pm (until 2am during summer). SPANISH.

Puerto Pucón pays homage to its owner's Spanish heritage through its design and well-made classics such as paella. Seafood is the focus here, and it is served in a multitude of ways: Have your razor clams, shrimp, and calamari sautéed in garlic or wrapped in a crêpe and smothered in crab sauce. The atmosphere is typical Spanish, with white stucco walls, bullfight posters, flamenco-dancer fans, and racks of wine bottles; the fireplace is especially nice, and there's a small bar. During warmer months there is a front deck, which can get packed.

Restaurant Cambalache. O'Higgins 524. ☎ **45/442734.** Main courses $8–$15. AE, DC, MC, V. Daily noon–4pm and 6:30pm–midnight. Closed Tues Mar–Nov. STEAKHOUSE.

This *parrilla* has a nicer atmosphere than other steakhouses on the main drag, with pine walls, wood floors, a chimney, and a live tree shooting through the dining area. It offers a better selection, too, and an all-you-can-eat barbecue with samplings of sausage, chicken, pork, beef, or lamb that comes with salad and dessert for $15 adults,

$7 kids. The multilingual staff is amicable, and there is an outdoor seating area, but it's open only during the warm months. Cambalache also serves grilled fish and, during high season, wild boar and venison.

Pucón After Dark

Pucón's **casino** can be found inside the five-star Hotel del Lago (see "Where to Stay," above), with three gaming rooms and a bingo hall. There's a good bar here that appeals to all ages, and the place is open very late. The Hotel del Lago also has the town's only **cinema;** contact them for playlists (☎ **45/291000**), or check the newspaper. For bars, **Mamas and Tapas,** O'Higgins 597 (no phone), has a hip design and attracts a 25- to 40-year-old crowd. **Bar Bazul,** Lincoyán 361 (no phone), has food and outdoor seating, and **El Living,** at the corner of Colo Colo and O'Higgins (no phone), has sushi by day and techno music by night; it's open very late.

HOT SPRINGS OUTSIDE PUCÓN

All the volcanic activity in the region means there's plenty of *baños termales,* or hot springs, that range from rustic rock pools to full-service spas with massage and saunas. Nothing beats a soothing soak after a long day packed with adventure. Also, like the Cañi Reserve, the hot springs make for a good rainy-day excursion.

✪ **Termas de Coñaripe.** Camino Coñaripe to Liquiñe at Km15. ☎ **45/431407;** ☎/fax 2/558-9738 (in Santiago). 14 units, 3 cabañas, 1 apartment. TV TEL. $91–$114 double standard; $125–$156 double standard, full board. Day-use fee $9.50 adults, $4.50 children for use of outdoor pools, and an additional $3.50 for indoor pool. DC, MC, V. Thermal baths open daily 9am–11pm, year-round.

These *termas* boast a magnificent location in a narrow valley hemmed in by lush, sheer mountains and Lago Pellaifa. Location aside, Coñaripe is handsomely built with touches of Japanese design. There are four outdoor pools, one with a slide, and one indoor pool with whirlpool lounges and a waterfall. They're so neat you'll want to dive in immediately once you get a look. A babbling creek meanders through the property. The thermal spa's on-site trout fishery means there's fresh fish for dinner every evening, and kids love to feed the teeming schools of trout. Inside the lobby and the hallways, the floors are made of a mosaic of cypress trunks. Rooms are carpeted and spacious, and suites come with a queen bed. If you require quiet, you might not want a room near the busy pool. The cabañas come with two rooms with double beds and one with two twins.

Along with all this beauty and the deluxe amenities comes the inevitable crush during the summer months, and it's not unusual for these hot springs to see almost *1,000* visitors per day at peak high season from January 1 to February 15. There are so many people that guests who have booked for a week often leave, shell-shocked, after only a few days. During this time the hotel opens a special fast-service cafeteria to alleviate the packed dining room at lunch. Off-season crowds drop dramatically, and during the winter you might have the place to yourself. A restaurant serves Chilean fare, and there is transfer service from Villarrica that costs $8 for adults, $4 for children.

Amenities: Room service, laundry, conference room, gym, tennis courts, outdoor pools, massage, mountain bikes, horseback riding, heliport, billiard table.

✪ **Termas de Huife.** Road to Huife, 33km east from Pucón. ☎/fax **45/441222.** www.chilehoteles.cl/termashuife. E-mail: huife@ceprinet.cl. 10 units. MINIBAR TV TEL. $118 double. Day-use fee $9 adults, $4.50 children 12 and under. AE, DC, MC, V. Thermal baths open daily 9am–8pm, year-round.

Termas de Huife, a relaxing escape for the body and mind, is popular with tourists and locals alike for its idyllic thermal baths and setting. Nestled in a narrow valley on the shore of the transparent River Liucura, Huife operates as a full-service health spa for day visitors and guests who opt to spend the night in one of their cabañas or suites. This is one of my favorite *termas,* both for its cozy accommodations and gorgeous landscaping, complete with narrow canals that wind through the property and river-rock hot springs flanked by bamboo and palm fronds. The complex features two large outdoor thermal pools kept at 96° to 98° degrees and a cold-water pool, as well as private thermal bathtubs, individual whirlpools, and massage salons arranged around an airy atrium. The four-person cabañas and double suites are housed in shingled, rust-colored buildings along the river, about a 2-minute walk from the main building. All come with wood-burning stoves, and the cabañas have a living area. The bathrooms deserve special mention for their Japanese-style, sunken showers and baths that run thermal water.

Nearby, a swinging bridge takes guests to a nature trail that winds through a forest of beech and laurel. The service is first-rate, and the gracious owner strives to see that every visitor leaves rested and feeling physically in top shape. The only complaint I have is that the food is too heavy and without much variety. The resort has a transfer from the airport and Pucón for an additional cost, and can plan excursions throughout the area. To get here, take the road east out of Pucón toward Lago Caburgua until you see a sign for Huife, which turns off at the right onto an unnamed dirt road. Follow the road until you see the well-marked entrance for Termas de Huife.

Dining: There is a cafeteria for dining in swimsuits and a more formal restaurant upstairs.

Amenities: Restaurant, cafeteria, massage, minigym, sauna, two hot springs pools, one cold-water pool, private individual whirlpool baths, game room with a pool table, conference rooms.

Termas de Menetúe. Camino Internacional, Km30. ☎/fax **45/441877.** E-mail: kublank@ctcinternet.cl. 6 cabañas. TV TEL. $65 cabaña for 2. Day-use fee $8.50 Apr–Nov, $9.50 Dec–Mar. No credit cards. Thermal baths open Dec–Mar 9am–9pm; Apr–Nov 9am–6pm.

These thermal baths are better for a day visit than an overnighter because the cabins sit so far away from the complex. There are two pools here. The reception area and restaurant look out onto a giant, grass-encircled swimming pool, and a short path takes visitors around to a woodsier setting, with one average-size pool serenaded by a gurgling waterfall. It's a relaxing, bucolic place with giant ferns and a gently flowing stream. The spa house has individual baths, but they're rather creepy and dark; better to join the floating masses in one of the outdoor pools. The pine cabins are for two to six people. They come with a fully stocked kitchen and wood-burning stove, and are a 5-minute walk from the baths. Menetúe rents out bicycles and can point out a few trails for walking. A restaurant serves decent Chilean cuisine, and there's a snack bar near the second pool.

Termas Los Pozones. Road to Huife, 34km from Pucón, just past Termas de Huife. No phone. $50–$60 cabañas for 4. Day-use fee $5.50 before 9pm; $8.50 after. No credit cards. Thermal baths open 9am–3am winter; 9am–6am summer.

Los Pozones is Huife's rustic neighbor, well known in the region for its cheaper prices, natural setting, and late hours—they stay open until 3am in the winter and 6am in the summer for the (mostly) young adults who want to keep the party going after leaving the discos in Pucón. The hot springs are reached by walking down a long, steep path that means a long, steep climb after your soak, although plans are in store for a cable-operated people mover. One other drawback is the unsightly iron pipe that cuts through the property, bringing thermal water to its neighbor Huife. Los Pozones expanded last year from two to six rock pools, and has built three cabañas high above the springs across from the road. The simple but pleasant cabañas come with kitchens and have lovely views, although it's a walk to get to the springs.

Termas San Luis. Ruta Internacional Pucón, Km27. ☎ **45/412880.** $60 double. Day-use fee $8 adults, $5 children, and $7 for a private bathtub. No credit cards. Thermal baths open 9am–midnight summer; 10am–6pm winter.

Located high in the saddle of the Curarrehue Valley, the attractive Termas San Luis is popular for its well-built thermal pools and view of Volcán Villarrica, but mostly for the rare paved access road that gets you there. It's also close enough to the border to draw a large amount of Argentine visitors. The compact resort is centered on two swimming pools built with stone tiles, one outdoor and the other covered by a fiber-glass shell much like a greenhouse; both are surrounded by plastic lounge chairs for reclining after a long soak. If you'd like to spend the night, San Luis has six wooden cabins perched on a slope overlooking, unfortunately, the parking lot, although a few are hidden behind trees. The cabins sleep four to six guests, meaning one double bed, three singles, and a living-room trundle bed. They are bright and pleasant, but can get very cold in the winter unless the wood-burning stove is continually stoked. The spa house features a tiny sauna and a massage salon at an additional cost.

Dining: A large, shingled restaurant stretches the length of the pool area, with a separate dining room for nonsmokers.

Amenities: Massage, sauna, indoor and outdoor pools, children's play area, a tiny chapel, nature trails, three lagoons (one of which has boat rental for fishing).

NATURAL ATTRACTIONS OUTSIDE PUCÓN
PARQUE NACIONAL HUERQUEHUE
Smaller though no less attractive than its rivals Conguillío and Villarrica, Parque Nacional Huerquehue boasts the best short-haul hike in the area, the **Sendero Los Lagos.** This 12,500ha (30,875-acre) park opens as a steeply walled amphitheater draped in matted greenery and crowned by a forest of lanky *araucaria* trees. There are a handful of lakes here; the first you come upon is Lago Tinquilco, which is hemmed in by steep forested slopes. At the shore you'll find a tiny, ramshackle village with homes built by German colonists in the early 1900s. A few residents offer cheap accommodations, but the best place to spend the night is in a campground near the entrance or at the Refugio Tinquilco (see "Where to Stay," below).

There's a self-guided trail called **Ñirrico** that is a quick 400m (436-yd.) walk, but if you're up for a vigorous hike, don't miss the spectacular **Tres Lagos** trail that begins at the northern tip of Lake Tinquilco. The path first passes the **Salto Nido de Aguila** waterfall, then winds through a forest of towering beech, climbing to a lookout point with a beautiful view of Lago Tinquilco and the Villarrica volcano. From here the trail begins zigzagging up and up through groves of billowy ferns and more tall trees until finally (2 to 3 hours later) arriving at the beautiful, *araucaria*-ringed **Lago Chico,** where you can take a cool dip. A relatively flat trail from here continues on to the nearby Lakes **Verde** and **Toro.** Bring plenty of food and water, and come prepared with rain gear if the weather looks dubious.

On your way to or from the park you can make a detour to the **Ojos de Caburga,** where two aqua-colored waterfalls crash into the tiny Laguna Azul. There are a few picnic tables here, and you can take a dip if the weather's nice. The turn-off point is about 9 miles (15km) from Pucón.

GETTING THERE & BASICS   The park is 22 miles (35km) from Pucón. There is no direct bus service to the park, but most tour companies offer minivan trans-portation and will arrange to pick you up later should you decide to spend the night.

If you're driving your own car, head out of Pucón on O'Higgins toward Lago Caburga, until you see the sign for Huerquehue that branches off to the right. From here it's a rutted, dirt road that can be difficult to manage when muddy. Conaf charges $5 for adults and $1 for kids to enter, and is open daily 8:30am to 6pm.

WHERE TO STAY   Conaf has a campground near Lago Tinquilco and charges $15 per site, maximum six people. The best option for a roof over your head is the attractive **Refugio Tinquilco** (☎ 2/777-7673; fax 2/735-1187), a spacious lodge with bunks for $7.50 per person (you'll need your own sleeping bag), and regular rooms with complete bedding for $50 double. They also have a good restaurant and offer full pension for an additional $10.

PARQUE NACIONAL VILLARRICA

This gem of a park is home to three volcanoes: the show-stealer Villarrica, Quetrupillán, and Lanín. It's quite a large park, stretching 61,000ha (150,670 acres) to the Argentine border and that country's Parque Nacional Lanín, and is blanketed with a thick, virgin forest of *araucaria* and evergreen and deciduous beech. A bounty of activities are available year-round, including skiing and climbing to the crater of the volcano (see "Outdoor Activities" under "Pucón," above), hiking, horseback riding, bird watching, and more.

The park has three sectors. Most visitors to the park head to **Sector Rucapillán** (the Mapuche's name for Volcán Villarrica, meaning House of the Devil). Volcán Villarrica is one of the most active volcanoes in the world, having erupted 59 times from the 16th century until now. Every day, Villarrica belches out several dozen minor explosions; last year the explosions were so earth-rattling that all activity in the area had to be shut down. There are two trails here, the 9-mile (15km) **Sendero Challupén** that winds through lava fields and *araucaria,* and the 3-mile (5km) **Sendero El Glaciar Pichilancahue,** which takes visitors through native forest to a glacier. The park ranger booth at the entrance can point out how to get to the trailheads. You'll also find the interesting **Cuevas Volcánicas** in this sector. Ancient, viscous lava that flowed from the volcano created underground tunnels, 400m (1,312 ft.) of which have been strung with lights and fitted with walkways that allow you to tour their dark, dripping interiors.

Visitors are provided with a hard hat; the cave's humid, cold air requires that you bring warm clothing regardless of the season. There are also exhibits describing volcanism and bilingual tours. It's open daily 10am to 8:30pm during the summer and 10am to 6:30pm during the winter; admission is a steep $11 for adults and $5 for children (☎ 45/442002).

The second sector, **Quetrupillán,** is home to wilder, thicker vegetation and a multiple-day backpacking trail that wanders through virgin forest and past the **Termas de Palguín** (which is also accessible by road), a rustic hot springs. Here you'll also find several waterfalls, including the crashing **Salto el León.** There's a horse stable here (see "Horseback Riding" under "Pucón," above) that offers trips around the area. The dirt road to Palguín that branches off from the road to Curarrehue to Palguín is rough but passable; however, the road from Palguín to Coñaripe is nearly impossible to pass, even with four-wheel drive.

Finally, the third sector, **Puesco,** is accessed by Ruta 119 south of Curarrehue. There's a Conaf post and several hikes through the park's wildest terrain, including pine forests, lakes, and rugged mountains.

3 Siete Lagos: Panguipulli & Lican Ray

Panguipulli is 33mi (54km) south of Villarrica; Lican Ray is 19mi (31km) S of Villarrica

Few day-long sightseeing drives surpass the beauty of the Siete Lagos (Seven Lakes) region south of Pucón, where you can follow a half-paved, half-dirt loop around Lago Calafquén, with stops in the picturesque resort towns Panguipulli and Lican Ray. As its name implies, the region is home to seven lakes, one of which is across the border in Argentina, and all are set among rugged, verdant mountains that offer photo opportunities at every turn. (For more on the Argentina side of the Lake District, see chapter 6.)

DRIVING THE SIETE LAGOS ROUTE

Renting a car is obviously the best option here, but several tour companies offer this excursion. Driving south from Villarrica, you drive first to Lican Ray and then through Coñaripe, circling the lake until reaching Panguipulli. From here you take the paved road toward Lanco (although signs might say LICAN RAY as well), until you see the sign for Lican Ray and Villarrica. This rough dirt road continues to Villarrica (there's a good lookout point along the way), or forks to the right to Lican Ray, where you can again catch the paved road to Villarrica. Take a good look at the map before making any decisions; note that none of these roads are numbered or have names. Of course, the trip can be done in the reverse direction, which might be more desirable for an afternoon soak at the hot springs just south of Coñaripe (see "Hot Springs Outside Pucón," above).

LICAN RAY

This tiny resort town hugs the shore of Lago Calafquén, offering toasty beaches made of black volcanic sand and a forested peninsula for a leisurely drive or stroll. The lake is warmer than others in the region, and is therefore better suited for swimming; you can also rent a boat here. The name comes from Lican Rayén, a young Mapuche woman from the area who is said to have fallen in love with a Spanish soldier. The town was founded as a trading post, and today there are about 2,000 permanent residents, except for the period from December 15 to February 28 when the population doubles with the arrival of summer vacationers.

The first weekend in January is the busiest time of year—the town hosts its **Monumental Barbecue of Lican Ray,** when residents line up 100 barbecues along the main street, General Urrutia, to roast lamb and throw an enormous outdoor party. There's also the **Noche Lacustre** the second week in February, when the bay fills with boats for a variety of contests and activities, followed by an evening fireworks display. Lican Ray is less crowded and less expensive than Pucón, and during the off-season you'll practically have the place to yourself.

There are a few places to stay here: **Hotel Becker,** Manquel 105 (☎ **45/431021**), has modest but comfortable rooms, a restaurant, and a deck from which you can enjoy the lakefront view, and charges $35 double in off-season, $55 double in high season. **Hostería Inaltulafquén,** Cacique Punulef 510 (☎/fax **45/431115**), has good rooms and an even better dining area and deck, and it is ideally located across from the Playa Grande beach; it charges $30 to $45 double). The hostería is run by two helpful Canadians, who also offer excursions. For dining, try the restaurant at Hostería Inaltulafquén or **Noñas,** General Urrutia 105 (☎ **45/431021**), with an extensive menu that offers everything from barbecue meats to clay oven–baked pizzas. It also has outdoor seating during the summer.

A Note on Camping

If you're looking to pitch a tent, the road between Lican Ray and Coñaripe is full of campsites, some of which are quite nice, with showers and barbecue pits. Try **Cabañas and Camping Foresta** (☎ **45/211954**) at 1¼ miles (2km) from Lican Ray, which has well-built sites and comfortable cabins for four guests (about $80 to $100 during the summer, $40 to $60 during winter). Also, keep your eyes open during this stretch for lava formations from the 1971 eruption of Volcán Villarrica.

PANGUIPULLI

This little town with the impossible-to-pronounce name (try "pan-gee-*poo*-yee") occupies a cove on the shore of Lago Calafquén. During the summer, Panguipulli's streets bloom a riot of colorful roses, which the town celebrates in January during the **Semana de las Rosas** (Rose Week) festival. Panguipulli was founded as a timber-shipping port and today has nearly 8,300 residents. The town's primary attraction is its charming **Iglesia Parroquial**, Diego Portales and Bernardo O'Higgins (in front of the gas station). Mass is held from November to February Thursdays and Saturdays at 8pm; Sundays and holidays 8:30am and 11am; the church is open all day (no phone). The Swiss priest who initiated the building of this church in 1947 modeled its architecture after churches he had seen in Switzerland, with two latticed towers painted in creamy beige and red and topped off with black shingled steeples.

If you decide you'd like to stay in this region, you might want to check out the **Hotel Riñimapu,** Casilla 512, Lake Riñihue, Panguipulli (☎ **63/311388,** ☎/fax in Santiago 2/696-1786), south of Panguipulli and on the shore of Lago Riñihue. The Riñimapu is a wonderful remote lodge that draws guests from around the world for its fly-fishing, horseback riding, and hiking—but it is the tranquility here that encourages guests to really lose themselves in the beauty of the surroundings. The woodsy lodge has 16 attractive rooms, a restaurant, and a bar, and charges $60 double, about $50 more for meals. To get here, head south out of Panguipulli on the paved then dirt road toward Lago Riñihue, and continue for 12½ miles (20km) until reaching the hotel.

4 Valdivia

520 miles (839km) S of Santiago; 90 miles (145km) SW of Pucón

Chileans often say that Valdivia is one of the most beautiful cities in Chile; I think that's an overstatement. The city unquestionably exudes charm through its colonial homes and vibrant waterfront, but it is as though every building from every decade from every architectural style were thrown in a bag, shaken up, and randomly scattered about the city.

One thing is for certain: The city is tenacious. Valdivia has suffered attacks, floods, fires, and the disastrous earthquake of 1960 that nearly drowned the city under 3m (10 ft.) of water. During World War II, Valdivia's German colonists were blacklisted, ruining the economy. So if Valdivia looks a little weary—well, it's understandable. If you're in Pucón or Temuco, Valdivia makes for an interesting day or 2-day diversion, especially to visit the tiny towns and ancient forts at the mouth of the bay that protected the city from seafaring intruders. Some of the best museums and galleries in Chile can be found here, too.

Valdivia, with about 115,000 residents, is divided by a series of narrow rivers, notably the Río Valdivia and the Río Calle Calle that wrap around the city's downtown area. Along the Río Valdivia is the city's bustling waterfront, where fishmongers peddle their fresh catches of the day and pleasure boats disembark for a variety of journeys around the region's twisting waterways. These rivers have produced some of the world's top rowing athletes, and many mornings you can see spidery figures plying the glassy water. Across the Río Valdivia is the Isla Teja, a residential area that's home to the Universidad Austral de Chile, the reason you see so many students riding bikes around town.

ESSENTIALS
GETTING THERE
BY AIR Valdivia's Aeropuerto Pichoy (☎ **63/272294**) is about 19 miles (30km) northeast of the city; Lan Chile/Ladeco and Avant have daily flights from Santiago and weekday flights from cities such as Temuco. A taxi to town costs about $12, or you can catch a ride on one of Transfer Valdivia's minibuses for $3.

BY BUS The bus terminal can be found at Anwandter and Muñoz, and nearly every bus company passes through here; there are multiple daily trips from Pucón and Santiago (the average cost for a ticket from Santiago to Valdivia is $11, from Pucón to Valdivia it is $3.75).

BY CAR From the Panamericana Highway, take Ruta 205 and follow the signs for Valdivia. A car is not really necessary in Valdivia, as most attractions can be reached by boat, foot, or taxi. It's about a 2-hour drive from Pucón to Valdivia.

VISITOR INFORMATION
Sernatur's helpful **Oficina de Turismo,** near Muelle Schuster at Arturo Prat 555 (☎ **63/215739**), has a well-stocked supply of brochures. The office hours from March to November are Monday to Friday 8:30am to 1pm and 2:30 to 6:30pm; from December to February, hours are Monday to Saturday 9am to 7pm and Sunday 10am to 7pm. There's also an information kiosk at the bus terminal open daily 8am to 9pm.

SPECIAL EVENTS
The city hosts a grand yearly event, the **Semana Valdiviana,** with a week of festivities that culminates with the **Noche Valdiviana** on the third Saturday in February. On this evening, hundreds of floating candles and festively decorated boats fill the Rio Valdivia; in the evening the city puts on a fireworks display. Note that Valdivia is crowded during this time, so hotel reservations are essential.

FAST FACTS: VALDIVIA
Car Rental **Assef Y Mendez Rent A Car** can be found at General Lagos 1335 (☎ **63/213205**), and **Hertz** at Rámon Picarte 640 (☎ **63/218316**); both have airport kiosks.

Currency Exchange *Casas de cambio* can be found at **La Reconquista** at Carampangue 325 (☎ **63/213305**), and **Turismo Cochrane,** Arauco 435 (☎ **63/212214**), but banks **Banco Santander** at Pérez Rosales 585 and **Banco Corpbanca** at Rámon Picarte 370 have ATM machines in addition to money exchange.

Hospital The hospital can be found at Simpson 850 (☎ **63/214066**).

Laundry Self-service Laundromats are **Lavamatic** at Walter Schmidt 305, #6 (☎ **63/211015**), or **Lavazul** at Chacabuco 270, #12 (☎ **63/211122**).

Valdivia

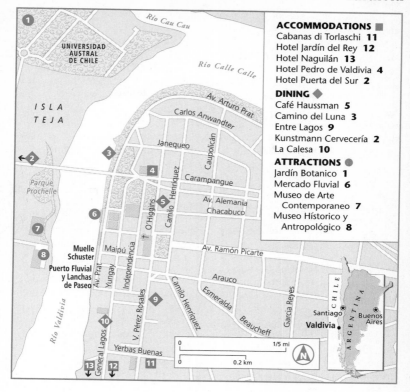

ACCOMMODATIONS ■
Cabanas di Torlaschi **11**
Hotel Jardín del Rey **12**
Hotel Naguilán **13**
Hotel Pedro de Valdivia **4**
Hotel Puerta del Sur **2**

DINING ◆
Café Haussman **5**
Camino del Luna **3**
Entre Lagos **9**
Kunstmann Cervecería **2**
La Calesa **10**

ATTRACTIONS ●
Jardín Botanico **1**
Mercado Fluvial **6**
Museo de Arte
    Contemporaneo **7**
Museo Hístorico y
    Antropológico **8**

WHAT TO SEE & DO

Several tour companies offer trips to Niebla (see "Niebla, Corral & Isla Mancera," below) and other surrounding areas, including city tours. Try **Turismo Kohler,** José Martí 83 (☎ **63/255335**), **Agencia Cochrane,** Arauco 4351, (☎ **63/212213**), and **Turismo Cristopher,** Independencia and Arauco streets (☎ **63/225144**). All offer travel agency services and can book plane tickets.

BOAT TRIPS

An enjoyable way to explore the Valdivia region is with one of the many boat tours that depart from the pier Muelle Schuster at the waterfront, including yachts, catamarans, and an antique steamer. Tours are in full swing during the summer, and although there's limited service during the off-season, it is possible for a group to hire a launch for a private trip. The most interesting journeys sail through the **Carlos Andwanter Nature Sanctuary** to the **San Luis de Alba de Cruces Fort** and to **Isla Mancera** and **Corral** to visit other 17-century historic forts; both tours run about 5 to 6 hours round-trip and usually include meals. The Nature Sanctuary was created after the 1960 earthquake sank the banks of the Río Cruces, thereby spawning aquatic flora that, with the surrounding evergreen forest, is now home to more than 80 species of birds, including black-neck swans, red gartered coots, and buff-necked ibis.

Tour Fluvial Bahía (no phone) operates throughout the year with quick trips around Isla Teja ($5 per person), and tours to Isla Mancera and Corral (see "Niebla, Corral & Isla Mancera," below) can be arranged during the off-season with a negotiated price or when there are enough passengers; children under 10 ride free. Other trips to Isla Mancera and Corral are offered by **Orión III** (☎ **63/210533;** e-mail: hetours@telsur.cl), which also includes a stop at the Isla Huapi Natural Park; the price is $30 per person, including lunch and snacks, and there are discounts for children under 10. By far the most luxurious is the **Catamarán Extasis** (☎ **63/295674**), which offers Isla Mancera and Corral tours with lunch and snacks included, and evening dinner cruises; both cost about $30 per person. The cheapest is the *Tatiana* (no phone), which leaves at 1pm and returns at 6pm; cost is $2 per person.

An interesting journey is aboard the *Collico* (☎ **09/319-3284**), a completely restored 1907 German steamer, with tours to the Nature Sanctuary and historical sightseeing journeys along the Río Calle Calle and the Collico area. There's a required minimum of 10 guests (or a negotiated fee), and reservations must be made at least 48 hours in advance ($22 per person, includes lunch). **Isla del Río** (☎ **63/225244**) also offers full-day tours of the Nature Sanctuary from 1:30 to 7:30pm for $30 per person, including lunch.

OTHER ATTRACTIONS

The bustling **Mercado Fluvial** at Muelle Schuster (Avenida Prat at Maipú) is the principal attraction in Valdivia, and is worth a visit for the dozens of fishermen who hawk fresh conger eel, hake, and spindly king crabs in front of colorful fruit and vegetable stands. Take a peek behind the fish stands to view the lanky pelicans and enormous sea lions barking for handouts. Across the street, the **Mercado Municipal** holds few attractions apart from a couple of souvenir shops and decent, inexpensive restaurants. Hours for the various shops here are erratic, but generally Monday to Sunday 9am to 6pm, with some restaurants open later.

A block up from the waterfront, turn right on Yungay and head south until the street changes into **General Lagos** at San Carlos. A pleasant stroll for several blocks along General Lagos offers picturesque evidence of German immigration to the area through the stately, historic homes that dot the street. The houses, built between 1840 and 1930, belonged to affluent families and many have been restored and maintained, despite the various earthquakes and other natural disasters that have beset them since construction.

An interesting stop along the way is the **Centro Cultural El Austral,** General Lagos 733 (no phone), commonly known as the Casa Hoffman for the Thater-Hoffman family, who occupied the home from 1870 until 1980. It's open Tuesday to Sunday 10am to 1pm and 4 to 7pm; admission is free. The first floor of this handsome building has been furnished to re-create the interior as it would have looked during the 19th century, complete with period antiques, paintings, and a few very garish chandeliers. Upstairs, the Center holds temporary art exhibitions and painting classes. At the junction of General Lagos and Yerbas Buenas, you'll find the **Torreón Los Canelos,** a 1781 defensive tower built to protect the southern end of the city.

ISLA TEJA

Isla Teja is a tranquil residential area that is also home to the Universidad Austral de Chile and a splendid history museum, the ✪ **Museo Hístorico y Antropológico Mauricio van de Maele** (☎ **63/212872**). It's open Monday to Sunday 10am to 1pm and 2 to 8pm December 15 to March 15, and Tuesday to Sunday 10am to 1pm and 2 to 6pm the rest of the year; admission is $1.75 adults, 25¢ children 12 and under.

To get there, cross the Pedro de Valdivia bridge, walk up a block, turn left, and continue for half a block. The museum is housed in the grand family home of Karl Anwandter, brewery owner and vociferous supporter and leader of German immigrants. Outside, two 19th-century carriages flank the entrance. Inside on the first floor is a varied collection of antiques culled from local well-to-do families and notable figures such as Lord Cochrane, including furniture (even a double piano), photos, letters, medals, and everyday objects. There are also a few conquest-era artifacts, such as a Spanish helmet, as well as an excellent display of Mapuche Indian silverwork, textiles, and tools. An interesting collection of sepia-toned photos depicts settlers' images of Mapuches.

Leaving the museum, turn right and continue north on Los Laureles until you reach the **Universidad Austral de Chile.** Once inside the campus, the road veers right; follow it and the signs to the **Jardín Botánico,** a lovely botanical garden created in 1957 that features a labeled collection of native trees and vegetation from every region in Chile and around the world. It's open December to March daily 8am to 8pm; April to November daily 8am to 7pm. Cut west through the campus to Los Lingues Street and turn right until you reach the gated entrance to **Parque Saval,** a sizeable park with rodeo stands, a children's playground, a picnic area, and the pretty Laguna Los Lotos. Admission is 30¢, and it's open daily 8am to 8pm.

NIEBLA, CORRAL & ISLA MANCERA

These three villages offer a chance to view Valdivia's historic defense system through its weathered 17th-century forts strategically situated near the estuary's door to the Pacific, their rusty cannons still pointed at enemies long past. **Niebla** lies 11 miles (18km) from Valdivia and is home to the **Castillo de la Pura y Limpia Concepción de Monfort de Lemus** (no phone), an interesting defensive fort founded in 1671 and renovated in 1767. It's open December to February daily 10am to 7pm, and March to November 10am to 5:30pm, closed Monday; admission is $1, free for kids under 8. The fort is carved partially out of rock and features details such as cannons and a powder room, as well as a small museum. The town itself is mostly a hodgepodge of seafood restaurants and cabañas popular with students for the cheap rent, but it's not unattractive, and there are a few beaches for walking.

To get there, take a private taxi for about $6, or grab a *colectivo* taxi for 35¢ at the waterfront. In the summer it is possible to take a tour boat to Niebla; in the off-season, you'll need to take the road. To get to Corral from Niebla's fort, take a taxi to the dock at the town's entrance.

Across the bay sits **Corral** and the area's first and most powerful fort, the **Castillo San Sebastian de la Cruz,** built in 1645 and reinforced in 1764. From December 15 until the end of February, mock soldiers in 1777 uniforms perform a reenactment that includes firing cannons and muskets twice daily at 3 and 5pm. The city itself is a picturesque jumble of brightly painted wooden homes and fishing boats, an old German colony that never really recovered from the tidal wave that wiped out a significant chunk of the town after the 1960 earthquake. Before-and-after pictures can be seen inside the tiny **Museo de Corral** (no phone) at the dock, which is open December 15 to March 15 daily 9am to 1pm and 2 to 6:30pm, and the rest of the year daily except Wednesday 2 to 6pm. To get to Corral, take a tour boat from Valdivia during high season, or take a ferry from the fishing dock just before entering Niebla.

Either on the way to Corral or on the way back, ask to be dropped off at idyllic **Isla Mancera** (and ask to be picked up!) for a pleasant stroll and a visit to the fort **Castillo de San Pedro de Alcántara** (no phone). Admission is $1, and it's open November 15 to March 15 daily 10am to 1pm and 4 to 8pm, and Tuesday to Sunday 10am to 1pm and 2 to 6pm the rest of the year. It was built in 1645 and restored in 1680 and again in 1762 to house the Military Government of Valdivia. Inside the grounds are the crumbling ruins of the San Francisco Convent and an underground supply room. It is possible to walk the circumference of the island in 20 to 30 minutes, and there is a site for picnics with great views.

WHERE TO STAY

Private parking or ample street parking is available and free for all hotels.

Cabañas Di Torlaschi. Yerbas Buenas 283, Valdivia. ☎ **63/224103.** Fax 63/224003. 16 cabañas. TV TEL. $51–$60 double. No credit cards.

These fully equipped cabañas feature charming exteriors, pleasant, well-lit kitchens, and a decent location on a residential street near downtown; they're also quiet due to the grammar schools at the front and side that empty at the end of the day. The friendly owners and staff strive to make guests feel at home, and offer a wealth of tourism information so that guests can plan excursions in and around Valdivia. The 16 wood cabañas are situated around a courtyard walkway planted with climbing ivy. Guests park just outside their door, and there is a security gate that shuts during the evening. Each cabaña is identical, with two bedrooms upstairs (one comes with a double bed and the other, two twins) and a sofa that unfolds into a bed downstairs, with a maximum of six guests allowed. Unfortunately, the bathroom is also downstairs, but this is really the only drawback. These cabañas are popular with foreigners, especially Europeans and Argentines.

Hotel Jardín del Rey. General Lagos 1190, Valdivia. ☎/fax **63/218562.** 19 units. TV TEL. $34–$45 double. AE, DC, MC, V.

Set back from the street and fronting a well-manicured garden, the Hotel Jardín del Rey is housed in a magnificent 1922 stone mansion whose exterior will enchant any visitor. Unfortunately, one step inside is where the appeal ends. It's not that the hotel is necessarily disagreeable, but the framed prints, faded carpet, and unremarkable rooms make one wonder why the owners seem reluctant to capitalize on this building's charm. Nevertheless, the hotel is comfortable, and has a small sunroom in the back. It's also popular enough to require 3 weeks' notice when making a reservation in the summer. The second-story balcony winds around the lobby, which is furnished with a few chairs and couches. Ask for a room upstairs as these are brighter and quieter. Breakfast is served in the wooden downstairs dining room. The staff is friendly.

✪ **Hotel Naguilán.** General Lagos 1927, Valdivia. ☎ **63/212851.** Fax 63/219130. www. chilehoteles.cl/bwhotelnaguilan. E-mail: naguilan@telsur.cl. 32 units. MINIBAR TV TEL. $55–$64 standard double (older units); $89–$109 double (newer units). AE, DC, MC, V.

Although it sits about a 10-minute walk from the edge of downtown, the Hotel Naguilán boasts a pretty riverfront location and solid, attractive accommodations. The hotel's elegant lobby, with its softly lit, polished-brass-and-wood bar and jazz music quietly playing in the background, as well as the hotel's restaurant and convention room are all housed in an interesting structure (ca. 1890) that once held a shipbuilding business. All rooms face the Río Valdivia and the evening sunset; from here it's possible to watch waterfowl and colorful tugs and fishing skiffs motor by. The rooms are divided into 15 newer ones in a detached building and 17 in an older wing. The newer "Terrace" units sit directly on the riverbank and feature contemporary floral design in rich colors, classic furniture, ample bathrooms, and comfy beds, as well as a terrace patio. The older wing is more economical and features a few dated items, such as 1960s lime-green carpet, but each room, and the entire hotel, is impeccably clean.

A lawn and a swimming pool separate the older wing from the riverfront. The staff offers professional and attentive service, and the hotel has a private dock from which guests board excursion boats. More than anything, though, the handsome design and great view make this hotel a winner. Note that breakfast is not included in the price.

Dining: The Naguilán's restaurant is one of the most attractive features of the property, with beige tablecloths, fresh-cut flowers, and the river passing just outside the window. It serves a good selection of international cuisine.

Amenities: Room service, laundry, outdoor pool, game room, children's play area, conference salon, outdoor snack bar.

Hotel Pedro de Valdivia. Carampangue 190, Valdivia. ☎ **63/212931.** Fax 63/203888. www.hotelpedrodevaldivia.telsur.cl. E-mail: pedroval@telsur.cl. 77 units. MINIBAR TV TEL. $65 double; $87 suite. AE, DC, MC, V.

The Pedro de Valdivia is located in the heart of the city in front of a plaza, and it is popular with foreign travelers for its proximity to the waterfront, Isla Teja, and shops and restaurants. The oldest hotel in Valdivia, it could use a fresh roll of carpet and a few repairs here and there, but is comfortable and fairly clean nonetheless. All double rooms with queen-size beds have terraces and face north toward the river, and are better than doubles with two twins that face the busier plaza. The bright suites come with an extra space for a few chairs, but are not significantly bigger than the decent size doubles; all rooms have spacious bathrooms. There are also four two-bedroom guest rooms with one bathroom. Perhaps the nicest part of the hotel is its airy, well-lit lobby with a giant mural painted by two well-known artist brothers depicting the arrival of Pedro de Valdivia to this area, as well as its cozy bar and the outdoor patio and pool. The Valdivia also has a well-equipped business center with Internet access and a large-screen TV.

Dining/Diversions: The **Don Pedro** restaurant serves an international menu with fish, meats, and pasta and has a daily set menu for dinner and lunch for $10. In the winter, the restaurant is upstairs near a giant fireplace; in the summer it can be found downstairs. The **Doña Inés** bar is open until 12:30am.

Amenities: Pool, Internet access, business center.

Puerta del Sur. Los Lingues 950, Isla Teja , Valdivia. ☎ **63/224500,** or for reservations (in Santiago) 2/633-5101. Fax 63/211046. www.alarton.cl/puerta. E-mail: pdelsur@ctcinternet.cl. 40 units. $98–$144 double; $173–$206 suite. AE, DC, MC, V.

This quiet resort just across the bridge on Isla Teja offers all the amenities and comfort a guest would expect from a five-star hotel, and it boasts a gem of a location on the shore of the Nature Sanctuary. It's about a 7-minute walk to downtown, but you'll feel miles away. All rooms come with views of the river and are very comfortable; double superiors are roomy, as are the sparkling, marbled bathrooms. This is one of the few hotels in Chile to offer doubles with either a queen or two full-size beds instead of singles. The suites come with giant, triangular picture windows, but are not much larger than a double superior.

Outside, a path winds past the pool and whirlpool to a private dock where guests can be picked up for boat tours or launch one of the hotel's canoes for a tranquil paddle. For kids, there's a play area and a game room with Ping-Pong. The wood-and-brick hotel has an airy lobby set off by a second-story U-shaped balcony and pastel brocade couches next to two fireplaces. It's an elegant hotel, but it lacks the zing a five-star normally features due to the bland decoration that looks like it was meant for an office building. Also, breakfast is not included with the price. The hotel features a medley of packages, some full pension, at lower rates for stays of 3 to 7 days; ask about discounts.

Dining/Diversions: The hotel has a semiformal restaurant serving excellent international cuisine. A set menu for lunch or dinner costs $14. There's also a bar.

Amenities: Laundry, room service, outdoor pool, whirlpool, sauna, massage, workout machine, volleyball courts, canoeing, tennis court, kid's playground, game room, baby-sitting.

WHERE TO DINE

For an inexpensive meal, try the **Municipal Market** near the waterfront at Yungay and Libertad, where you'll find several basic restaurants with fresh seafood and Chilean specialties. In general, reservations are not required for the restaurants listed here.

Café Haussman. O'Higgins 394. ☎ **63/202219.** Sandwiches $2–$4. No credit cards. Mon–Sat 8am–9pm. CAFE.

The Haussman is known for its *crudos,* steak tartare and raw onion spread on thin bread, which it has served since opening its doors in 1959. The tiny, old-fashioned cafe has just four booths and a counter, and is frequently packed with downtown workers who drop in for a quick meal or a slice of homemade *kuchen.* There are no frills, but good sandwiches, local color, and Kunstmann beer on tap.

✪ **Camino del Luna.** Costanera at Arturo Prat. ☎ **63/213788.** Main courses $6.50–$10. AE, DC, MC, V. Daily 12:30–11:30pm; bar open until 2am. SEAFOOD.

The Camino del Luna serves excellent seafood and other dishes aboard a floating restaurant moored at the waterfront. The menu includes delicious fare such as seafood crêpes, abalone stew, and *congrio* steamed in wine, bacon, asparagus, and herbs, as well as Greek and chef salads and a long list of terrific appetizers. Inside, the well-appointed, candlelit tables and light nautical theme are much nicer than the pea-green facade and red Coca-Cola neon outside would indicate. A changing daily set menu goes for $7.50, and kids under 12 eat free on Saturday and Sunday when they order from a special kids' menu. And yes, the restaurant does sway when vessels speed by, but not too much.

Entre Lagos. Pérez Rosales 622. ☎ **63/212047.** Main courses $5–$8. AE, DC, MC, V. Daily 9am–1:30pm and 3:30–8pm. CAFE.

Entre Lagos is one of the best-known shops in the region for its mouth-watering chocolates and colorful marzipan, and its neighboring cafe is equally good. Nothing on the menu is short of delicious, from the juicy sandwiches and french fries down to the heavenly cakes and frothy cappuccinos. The restaurant serves a dozen varieties of crêpes, such as ham and cheese, and abalone and shrimp in a creamy crab sauce. Entre Lagos is a great spot for lunch or to relax for an afternoon *once* or coffee. It also offers a set menu for $6.50 that includes a main dish, soup, and coffee. Don't miss the sweet shop to sample a few truffles or to buy a jar of homemade marmalade.

Kunstmann Cervecería. 950 Ruta T-350. ☎/fax **63/292969.** Main courses $6–$10. DC, MC, V. Mon–Sat noon–midnight; Sun noon–7:30pm. GERMAN PUB.

The popular Kunstmann brewery serves four varieties of beer on tap (they'll let you sample all before ordering), in a newer, microbrew-styled restaurant with wooden tables and soft, yellow light. The hearty fare includes appetizer platters of grilled meats and sausages for snacking, German-influenced dishes such as smoked pork loin with cabbage, and sandwiches, salads, and spaetzle. Kunstmann also has an on-site brewery museum as a diversion, and sells Kunstmann-logo T-shirts, mugs, and the like. This is a nice place to stop on the way back from Niebla (see "Niebla, Corral & Isla Mancera," above).

✪ **La Calesa.** Yungay 735. ☎ **63/225437.** Dinner reservations recommended. Main courses $9–$12. Daily 1–3:30pm and 8–12pm. PERUVIAN.

Owned and operated by a Peruvian family, the cozy La Calesa features spicy cuisine served in the old Casa Kaheni, a gorgeous, 19th-century home with high ceilings, wood floors, and antique furnishings. The menu features Peruvian fare along with several international dishes. Standouts include grilled beef tenderloin and sea bass in a cilantro sauce; *ají de gallina,* a spicy chicken and garlic stew with rice; or any of the nightly specials. The *pisco* sours are very good, as is the wine selection. There's a lounge/waiting area and a great wooden bar lit by giant windows looking out onto a backyard garden and the river. Unfortunately, even though there are only 10 tables, the service at La Calesa can be slow and inattentive, especially for groups of four or more.

5 Puyehue

Termas de Puyehue is 45 miles (73km) E of Osorno; 59 miles (95km) W of Antillanca; 58 miles (93km) W of the Argentine border

This region is chiefly known for the **Termas de Puyehue** hot springs and the **Antillanca** ski and summer resort at the base of the Casablanca Volcano in Puyehue National Park. The region, including its namesake lake and national park, is remarkably beautiful, with thick groves of junglelike forest, emerald lakes, picture-perfect volcano backdrops, waterfalls that tumble hundreds of feet into crystalline lakes and rivers, and roads narrowed by overgrown, enormous ferns. You won't find a tourist-oriented town here, such as Pucón or Puerto Varas, but there are several good lodging options in the area. You'll also find a fair amount of outdoor activities, scenic drives, and one of the best lookout points in Chile that can even be reached by car during the summer.

Puyehue is a worthwhile diversion from Osorno or Puerto Montt, and is an even better destination when used as a stopover point on the road to or from Argentina. Some travelers opt to loop through the Lake Districts of Argentina and Chile by booking a one-way ticket to Bariloche via the popular "lake crossing" (see "Parque Nacional Vicente Pérez Rosales & the Lake Crossing to Argentina," below ") and later hopping on a bus headed for Puyehue, passing first through Villa Angostura at the Argentina-Chile border and crossing at the international pass Cardenal Antonio Samore.

The road from Osorno to Puyehue is rather flat and banal, but the scenery viewed when crossing from Villa Angostura to Puyehue is stunning. Note that during the winter, chains might be required when crossing the border (if you are driving a rented vehicle). If you're here during the winter months, you can even ski at Antillanca resort. The city of Osorno holds few attractions for the visitor, and is used as a transportation hub only.

GETTING THERE

BY PLANE   Lan Chile, Ladeco, and Avant all serve Puerto Montt Osorno's **Carlos Hott Siebert Airport** (no phone); from there you'll need other transportation. Many tour companies in Puerto Montt offer day trips to Puyehue.

BY BUS   Bus service from Osorno is provided by **Bus Norte**, with daily service to and from Puyehue: From Bariloche, Argentina, the following companies head to Osorno and stop along the highway near Puyehue or directly at the Hotel Termas de Puyehue: **Andes Mar** and **Río de la Plata.** If you're trying to get to Puyehue from Pedro Montt, you'll need to take a bus to Osorno's bus terminal and then transfer onto a bus to Puyehue.

BY CAR   Termas de Puyehue is about 46½ miles (75km) east from Osorno via Route 215. The border with Argentina, Control Fronterizo Cardenal Antonio Samore, is open November to March 8am to 9pm, and April to October 8am to 7pm. The road is in poor shape on the Chilean side, so plan on driving slowly.

EXPLORING PUYEHUE NATIONAL PARK

Puyehue National Park is one of Chile's best-organized national parks, offering a variety of trails to suit all levels, well-placed park information centers, and concessions that provide lodging, camping, restaurants, and hot springs. The 107,000ha (264,290-acre) park sits between the Caulle mountain range and the Puyehue Volcano, and is divided into three sectors: **Anticura, Aguas Calientes,** and **Antillanca.** Visitors head east toward Argentina to access Anticura, where they'll encounter a park ranger information station just before the border, as well as trailheads for day hikes and the 10-mile (16km) backpacker's trail up and around the Puyehue Volcano. There's a self-guided, short hike to the Salto del Indio waterfall where you'll see 800-year-old evergreen beech trees, known locally as *coigue.*

To get to Antillanca, visitors pass first through the Agua Calientes sector, where there are hot springs, cabins, and campgrounds, as well as a park information center. The most popular excursion in this region is the absolutely spectacular ascent to a lookout point atop the Raihuén crater, reached by foot or vehicle about 2½ miles (4km) past the Antillanca hotel and ski resort. This *mirador* can be reached only during temperate months, and is not worthwhile on a heavily overcast day. The park ranger information stations are open daily 9am to noon and 2:30 to 6pm, or contact Conaf (☎ **64/374572**). They sell an information packet about the region's flora and fauna and issue fishing licenses. For information about day visits to the hot springs at Termas de Puyehue or Aguas Calientes, see "Where to Stay & Dine," below. To get here, you need to catch a bus in Osorno, or book a tour with an operator out of Temuco or Pucón.

OTHER ATTRACTIONS

Along the road to Puyehue, at about Km25 on Ruta 215, just before the ramshackle town of Entre Lagos, is Chile's first car museum, the well-designed **Auto Museum Moncopulli** (☎ **64/204200;** www.moncopulli.cl). Admission is $3 adults, $2 students, and $1 kids; it's open April to October, Tuesday to Sunday 10am to 7pm, and November to March, Tuesday to Sunday 10am to 8:30pm. Owner Bernardo Eggers has assembled a collection of 40 Studebakers from the years 1930 to 1961, as well as antique vehicles, such as a 1929 Model A fire engine. There's also a collection of antique radios, cameras, photos, and various knickknacks. The museum is lovingly cared for by Eggers, and is interesting for its unexpected location in rural Chile as much as for anything inside.

WHERE TO STAY & DINE

Private parking or ample street parking is available and free for all hotels.

Aguas Calientes Turismo y Cabañas. Camino a Antillanca Km4. ☎/fax **64/236988.** www.puyehue.cl. E-mail: hotel@puyehue.cl. 23 cabañas. TV. $50–$85 cabin, 2 guests; $65–$85 cabin, 4 guests. AE, DC, MC, V.

These A-frame cabins are a cheaper alternative to Termas de Puyehue, and are in fact owned by the same company. There's a hot spring/spa facility here included in the price of the cabañas, and it can be used for the day for a fee. The cabañas sleep four to eight guests, and are simple affairs with fully stocked, plain, but decent kitchenettes. The drawback here is that the beds are really crammed into small spaces. A cabin for five, for example, has one bedroom with a double bed, and three twins in the living room that take up so much space there's hardly any left for the dining table. Ask for a cabin with two floors, as those come with separate living/eating areas. All cabins come with decks and a barbecue. There are also two nicely developed campgrounds called Chanleufu and Los Derrumbes, with barbecue pits, free firewood, and hot showers ($12 to $15 for one to four campers, $20 to $28 for five to eight campers).

The hot springs facility features indoor and outdoor pools (the outdoor is by far the nicest pool; the indoor is akin to a high school Olympic pool). There are also a sauna and picnic area. Day-use fees are $7 adults, $3 kids for the indoor pool; $2 adults, $1 kids for the outdoor pool. A private herbal bath costs $9. There is also massage for $20 an hour.

Antillanca Hotel and Tourism Center. Road to Antillanca, at about 10km past Ñilque, or (in Osorno) O'Higgins 1073. ☎/fax **64/235114.** E-mail: antillanca@telsur.cl. 73 units. TEL. $83–$115 double superior; $61–$77 double standard. MC, V.

Antillanca (the name means "the jewel of the sun") is really nothing to write home about, but the lovely surroundings and the ski/summer resort is really one of Chile's gems—if you can hit it on a good weather day. The resort is open year-round, offering trekking, fishing, mountain biking, canoeing, and ascents of Volcán Antillanca in addition to skiing. The ski resort is a local favorite, tiny but steep, with three T-bar lifts and one chair lift. Heavy, powdery snowfall makes for great skiing, but often a storm or *huelche* (a freezing western wind) blows in, essentially ruining the day; also note that car chains are often required during the winter, but they can be rented from a guard's post before driving up the winding road. Depending on the season, visitors can walk, drive, or take a lift up to a lookout point with one of the most magnificent views in Chile.

The hotel could really stand to renovate its rooms, especially considering the price. Couples would do well to view the options, as the only room that comes with a double bed also comes with two twins and is considered a quadruple with a higher price (although the hotel might be willing to charge the double price outside high season). The rooms are fairly spacious, but many are nothing more than dormitory style, with four bunks to a room and early '80s furniture to boot.

If you're looking for something cheaper, you might consider the *refugio,* the slightly shabby, older wing of the hotel popular with students and young adults for its rooms costing about a third less. The split-level lobby/restaurant/bar/lounge area is a delight, however, cozy and with character derived from pillars made of tree trunks that still have branches and a giant fireplace. There's also a deck for sunbathing. Up to two kids under 12 per family stay free.

Dining/Diversions: There's a restaurant and a small self-service cafeteria. There's also a bar and a disco.

Amenities: Laundry, room service, sauna, gym, game room, video room, conference room, free mountain bikes, store.

Ski Resort: Lift tickets Monday to Friday cost $28 adults, $16 students; Saturday to Sunday and holidays cost $31 adults, $24 students. Ski and snowboard equipment rental is available and sold in packages that include a lift ticket for $42 adults and $24 students. If you're not skiing but want to ride a chair lift to the top, the cost is $7. The ski resort operates roughly from June through September.

✪ **Termas de Puyehue.** Ruta 215, Km76. ☎ **2/293-6000.** Fax 2/283-1010. www. puyehue.cl. E-mail: ventas@puyehue.cl. 132 units. MINIBAR TV. $86–$124 double. AE, DC, MC, V.

The first thing you'll notice is the sheer size of this classic, grand hotel. The entrance's stone facade alone nearly dwarfs guests when they enter through its revolving doors. Termas de Puyehue is more aptly called a lodge, for its lofty ceilings and giant stone fireplaces, wood walls and floors, and country setting. The compound opens out onto a giant circular lawn and view of Lake Puyehue, and features two attractively designed, enormous thermal pools, as well as massage rooms, mud baths, herbal baths, saunas, game rooms, and more. Termas de Puyehue was built between 1939 and 1942, and has undergone recent, substantial renovations as well as the addition of 52 brand-new, "five-star" suites. This is a good thing, because Puyehue had been coasting on its reputation for some time.

Standard double rooms here are nicely appointed with thick cotton bedding and drapes in soft colors, but are not extraordinary, which is surprising for such an esteemed hotel. Rooms come with a forest view or, for about $15 more, a lake and sunset view, and all are fairly spacious with very comfortable beds. The new suites will be elegant and roomy, but at press time were just reaching completion and a full description was unavailable. Standard rooms on the first floor are cheaper because they are supposedly of lower quality, but the difference is negligible.

What makes Puyehue really special are the activities and excursions offered, including horseback riding (no galloping), trekking, mountain biking, windsurfing, fishing, tennis, and farm tours through organic gardens (all for an extra cost).

If you don't choose to stay at the hotel, you can still use the thermal spa facilities for a fee. The facilities here are more upscale than those at Agua Calientes, including an attractive, "tropical" indoor pool under a glass roof so high it feels like a gymnasium. The costs charged to day visitors are indoor pool, $13 adults, $8.50 kids; outdoor pool, $7.50 adults, $3.50 kids. Hours are Monday to Thursday 9am to 8pm, and Friday to Sunday and holidays 9am to 9pm. Herbal, mud, sulfur, and marine salt baths run $9 to $15.

Dining: Guests take their meals in the hotel's restaurant, which serves outstanding international and Chilean cuisine. There's also a cozy bar with a giant stone fireplace. Guests can order from a menu, or pay $17 for half-pension, which includes dinner.

Amenities: Room service, laundry, conference room, tennis courts, outdoor and indoor thermal pools, massage, sauna, full-service spa, mountain bikes, horseback riding, game room, child-care center, windsurfing, outdoor tours, excursions.

6 Lake Llanquihue, Frutillar & Puerto Varas

Lago Llanquihue is the second largest lake in Chile, a body of clear, shimmering water whose beauty is superseded only by the 2,015m-high (6,609 ft.), perfectly conical, snowcapped Volcán Osorno that rises from its shore. The peaks of Calbuco, Tronador, and Puntiagudo add rugged beauty to the panorama, as do the rolling, lush hills that peek out from forested thickets along the perimeter of the lake. But the jewel of this area is without a doubt the 253,780ha (626,837-acre) Vicente Pérez Rosales National Park, the oldest park in Chile and home to Volcán Osorno and the strangely hued emerald waters of Lago Todos los Santos.

This splendid countryside and the picturesque, German-influenced architecture of the homes and villages that ring Lago Llanquihue draw thousands of foreign visitors each year, many of whom come to take part in the famous lake crossing to Bariloche, Argentina. But just as many adventure-seekers come to take part in the vast array of outdoor sports and excursions to be had here, including fly-fishing, rafting, volcano ascents, trekking, or just sightseeing. Puerto Varas is similar to Pucón in that it offers a solid tourism infrastructure, with quality lodging and restaurants, nightlife, and

A "Health" Warning

Every January, this otherwise lovely region is beset by horrid biting flies called *tábanos,* and their swarmlike presence and painful nips can ruin an outing. One way to deter them is to avoid wearing dark clothing and any shiny object, which seem to attract them; they are also usually more prevalent on sunny days.

several reliable outfitters and tour operators. Visitors are advised to consider lodging in Frutillar, Puerto Varas, or Ensenada instead of Puerto Montt, as these three towns are nicer and closer to natural attractions than Puerto Montt.

FRUTILLAR & PUERTO OCTAY
Frutillar is 36mi (58km) S of Osorno, 29mi (46km) N of Puerto Montt

Frutillar and Puerto Octay offer a rich example of the lovely architecture popular with German immigrants to the Lago Llanquihue area, and both are situated to take advantage of the dynamite view of the Osorno and Calbuco volcanoes. The towns are smaller than, though as charming as, their neighbor Puerto Varas. They make a great day trip, and the coastal dirt road that connects the two is especially beautiful, with clapboard homes dotting an idyllic countryside. In other words, bring your camera. Apart from all this scenic beauty, there are a few museums documenting German immigration in the area. You might even consider staying in Frutillar, which has a good supply of attractive lakeside hotels and bed-and-breakfasts.

Frutillar was founded in 1856 as an embarkation point with four piers. Later, the introduction of the railway created a spin-off town that sits high and back from the coast, effectively splitting the town in two: Frutillar "Alto" and "Bajo," meaning high and low, respectively. You won't find much worth seeing in the Alto section, a semi-ratty collection of wood homes and shops.

Puerto Octay was founded in the second half of the 19th century by German immigrants; folks in the region know it for a well-stocked general goods store run by Cristino Ochs. In fact, the name *Octay* comes from "donde Ochs hay," roughly translated as "you'll find it where Ochs is." Today there are about 2,000 residents in this sleepy town, which can be reached by renting a car or with a tour. If you'd like to spend the night here, stay at **La Suizandina,** Camino Internacional Km28 (☎ **09/ 884-9541;** www.suizandina.com), which has cabañas that sleep two to four people for $10.50 per person and dormitory-style lodging in a charming, grass-roofed hostel. It's owned by a Swiss-Chilean couple, and offers canoes and bikes for rent, serves great breakfasts, and has kitchen facilities.

VISITOR INFORMATION   The **Oficina de Información Turística** is located along the coast at Constanera Philippi (☎ **65/421080**); it's open January to March daily 8:30am to 1pm and 2 to 9pm; April to December Monday to Friday 8:30am to 1pm and 2 to 5:45pm.

WHAT TO SEE & DO

Excursions to **Parque Nacional Vicente Pérez Rosales** from Frutillar can be arranged by your hotel with a company such as AlSur or Aguamotion out of Puerto Varas (see "Outdoor Activities" under "Puerto Varas," below). In Frutillar, spend an afternoon strolling the streets and enjoying the town's striking architecture. The town really gets hopping during the last week of January when it hosts, for 9 days, the **Semanas Musicales,** when hundreds of Chilean and foreign musicians come to participate in various classical music concerts. Call the visitor center at ☎ **65/421080;** tickets are never hard to come by.

The two most-visited attractions in town are **the Museo de la Colonización Alemana de Frutillar** and the **Reserva Forestal Edmundo Winkler.** The museum (☎ 65/421142) is located where Arturo Prat dead-ends at Calle Vicente Pérez Rosales. Admission is $2.50 adults, $1 kids 12 and under; it's open April to November, Monday to Sunday 10am to 1:30pm and 3 to 6pm, and December to March, 9:30am to 1:30pm and 3 to 7pm. It features a collection of 19th-century antiques, clothing, and artifacts gathered from various immigrant German families around the area.

The Reserva is run by the University of Chile, and features a trail winding through native forest, giving visitors an idea of what the region looked like before immigrants went timber crazy and chopped down a sizeable percentage of trees in this region. It's open year-round, daily from 10am to 7pm; admission costs 75¢ for adults and 35¢ for kids. To get there, you'll have to walk a kilometer up to the park from the entrance at Caupolicán Street at the northern end of Avenida Philippi. If you've got time to spare, you might consider paying a visit to the town **cemetery,** which affords visitors a panoramic view of the lake. To get there, continue farther north up Avenida Phillipi.

WHERE TO STAY

Private parking or ample street parking is available and free for all hotels.

✪ **Hotel Ayacara.** Av. Philippi 1215, Frutillar. ☎/fax **65/421550.** 8 units. TEL. $74–$93 double; $99–$123 Capitan double. AE, DC, MC, V.

The Ayacara is a top choice in Frutillar, housed in a superbly renovated, antique home on the coast of Lago Llanquihue. The interior of the hotel is made of light wood and this, coupled with large, plentiful windows, translates into bright accommodations. The rooms come with comfy beds, crisp linens, wood headboards, country furnishings, and antiques brought from Santiago and Chiloé; they're decorated in a tasteful beach/nautical theme. The Capitan room is the largest and has the best view. An attractive dining area serves dinner during the summer, and there's a small, ground-level outdoor deck and a TV/video lounge. The staff can arrange excursions around the area; fly-fishing excursions are their specialty. They can also arrange baby-sitting services.

Hotel Elun Lihue. 200m (218 yds.) from start of Camino Punta Larga, at the southern end of Costanera Phillipi, Frutillar. ☎ **65/420055.** www.hotelelun.cl. E-mail: elun@ctcinternet.cl. 14 units. TV TEL. $68–$86 double standard; $73–$96 double superior. DC, MC, V.

This four-star, azure-colored hotel is a good bet for anyone seeking modern accommodations, a room with a view, and a quiet, forested location. The hotel, opened in 1999, is made almost entirely of light, polished wood, and was designed to take full advantage of the panorama at its footsteps. The lounge, bar, and lobby sit under a slanted roof that ends with picture windows; there's also a deck should you decide to lounge outside. Double standard rooms are decent size and feature Berber carpet and spic-and-span white bathrooms. The superiors are very large and come with a comfy easy chair and a table and chairs. One particular room, number 24, has a corner window and a side window that looks out over Frutillar (it goes for $83 in the winter and $118 in the summer). The hotel is attended personally by its owners. A restaurant serves dinner only during the summer, and breakfast can be ordered in your room. The owners will arrange excursions around the area.

Amenities: Laundry, room service, conference room, minibusiness center, sauna, Avis car rental, mountain bikes, boat and fishing excursions, cafe, library.

Hotel Klein Salzburg. Av. Philippi 663, Frutillar. ☎ **65/421201.** Fax 65/421750. E-mail: frutillar@frutillarsur.cl. 8 units. TV TEL. $40–$89 double. AE, DC, MC, V.

The Hotel Klein Salzburg is housed in a large wooden home built in 1911 and painted blue and white. It sits on the lakefront, but only one room has a view—the "VIP" room, which is larger than the rest and has a small balcony (rates for this room are $104 during high season December 15 to March 15, and about $50 the rest of the year). The hotel has a lot of antique charm, complete with creaky wooden floors, but the decoration is as sugary sweet as the delicious cakes and tortes it serves in its regionally renowned tearoom: flowered wallpaper, duck motifs, and pink trim, all a tad cutesy, but not too overbearing. There's a room with a separate kids' room with two twins in a claustrophobic attic alcove, but kids like it.

Hotel Residenz Am See. Av. Philippi 539, Frutillar. ☎ **65/421539.** Fax 65/421858. 12 units. TV. $36–$72 double, including breakfast. AE, DC, MC, V.

This pleasant wooden hotel is a steal in the low season when you factor in the lakefront view and its clean, comfortable accommodations. Run by an elderly German couple, the Residenz has rooms that range in size, and a few of the doubles are large enough to fit an extra twin. The rooms that look out onto the lake are slightly more expensive than those facing the back, but the rooms in the back receive glorious afternoon sun. Suites have an additional room for relaxing. The owners have a shop selling arts and crafts and have decorated the place with woven wall hangings that are for sale. Downstairs there's a tea salon where guests are served German breakfast (included in the room price); in the afternoon, folks drop by for tea.

Hotel Villa San Francisco. Av. Philippi 1503, Frutillar. ☎/fax **65/421531.** www.aeroplan.cl. E-mail: iberchile@telsur.cl. 15 units. TV TEL. $40–$60 double. AE, MC, V.

The Villa San Francisco sits high on a cliff and features a layout similar to the Elun Lihue (see above), with rooms that all face the lake, some with a view of the volcano. All of the peach- and lemon-colored rooms are identical, decorated with simple but attractive furnishings that include comfortable beds and wicker headboards. Some guests might find the rooms a little on the small side, although most come with a terrace and four have corner windows. The new owners of this hotel are ecology minded, and they've invested a great deal in idyllic gardens that surround the property. There's also a great barbecue area that sits on a grassy perch looking straight out toward the volcano, as does a glass-enclosed dining area. The staff will arrange excursions around the area for guests.

✪ **Hotel Volcán Puntiagudo.** Camino Fundo Las Piedras s/n. ☎ **65/421646.** Fax 65/421640. www.hotelvolcanpuntiagudo.com. E-mail: puntiagudo@surnet.cl. 10 units. TEL. $56–$71 double per night, 1–2 nights; $56–$71 double per night, 3–4 nights. Open Dec 15–Apr 30 only. AE, DC, MC, V.

This chic, Bauhaus-designed hotel is another excellent option, especially if you're looking for a pastoral setting without compromising a great view. Owned by a German family who located to the area 7 years ago, the Puntiagudo is set upon a field of rolling green countryside about a 5-minute drive from downtown Frutillar. Within its perimeters are a swimming pool, a tennis court, and plenty of room for kids to run around—one of the reasons this hotel appeals to families. Another family-friendly feature are the five rooms that come with a loft that has two twins; parents pay $8 to $10 for kids ages 2 to 10.

The design of the hotel, however, is what really makes the Puntiagudo unique. Metal and cement interiors, bold colors varying from blue to mauve to yellow (including a ruby-red hallway), surprisingly spacious rooms, each with a king-size bed, ambient lighting, and a picture window that runs the length of the room, and all with the same gorgeous view, make this place a standout. The lobby area has books and magazines for sale and for lending out, as well as postcards; next to the lobby is a fashionable cafe serving excellent meals made with organic ingredients. Unfortunately, dinner is served only during January and February, and the hotel is completely closed from May to December 15. You'll need a car or a taxi to get into town.

WHERE TO DINE

In general, reservations are not required for the restaurants listed here.

Club Alemán. San Martín 22. ☎ **65/421249.** Main courses $5–$12. AE, DC, MC, V. Daily noon–4pm and 8pm–midnight. GERMAN/CHILEAN.

Nearly every city in the Lake District has a Club Alemán, and Frutillar is no exception. You'll find a few German dishes here, such as pork chops with sauerkraut, but the menu leans heavily toward traditional Chilean fare. Periodically, game specials such as duck and goose are on the menu, and there are set lunch menus for $6.50 on weekdays and $11 on Sundays that include a choice of fish or meat. The atmosphere is congenial, and the service is very good.

El Ciervo. San Martín 64. ☎ **65/420185.** Main courses $5.50–$10. AE, DC, MC, V. Daily noon–10pm. CHILEAN.

This newer restaurant specializes in smoked meats and game, and lives up to its name (which means "deer" in Spanish) by offering grilled venison in pepper sauce, tasty but at $15 the most expensive item offered here. There are other delights, such as smoked pork chops "Kassler" with mashed potatoes and sauerkraut, filet mignon in a mushroom sauce, and pork leg pressure-cooked to tenderness and served with applesauce. The dining area is not particularly bad, but mounted deer antlers don't do much to add to the cold atmosphere. It's a good spot for lunch, as it serves lighter fare such as sandwiches.

✪ **Selva Negra.** Antonio Varas 24. ☎ **65/421164.** Main courses $5.50–$8.50. AE, DC, MC, V. Daily noon–midnight. INTERNATIONAL/GERMAN.

Delicious food and creative dishes are to be expected when dining at this semi-casual restaurant housed in a hutlike replica of a German dry-goods *bodega*. German-influenced dishes abound, such as white sausage and sauerkraut, and smoked pork chops with red cabbage. There is also a host of other interesting options, such as half a pineapple filled with sautéed shellfish, chicken with orange sauce, pork steeped in port, and cuts of meat from a barbecue grill. Top it all off with hot bananas bathed in caramel sauce. The owners speak English, German, and French, and service is friendly.

PUERTO VARAS

12 miles (20km) N of Puerto Montt; 617½ miles (996km) S of Santiago

Puerto Varas is on the shore of Lago Llanquihue, and is also an adventure travel hub and gateway to the **Parque Nacional Vicente Pérez Rosales** (see "Parque Nacional Vicente Pérez Rosales & the Lake Crossing to Argentina," below, for more information). It is a tidy little town, with lovely architecture and a bustling center. Puerto Varas extends more services to its visitors than Frutillar, including a spanking-new casino, tour operators, and more, but it's busier too, and can get crowded during the summer months, but not as much as Pucón. The city was founded by German immigrants and later became an important exit port for goods being shipped from the Lago Llanquihue area to Puerto Montt. Today, Puerto Varas relies heavily on tourism, but it is also a residential community for many who work in Puerto Montt. Puerto Varas has many good hotels and several excellent restaurants.

VISITOR INFORMATION   The **Oficina de Turismo Municipal** at San Francisco 441 is open from December 15 to March 15 Monday to Sunday 8am to 9pm, and the rest of the year Monday to Friday 8am to 4:45pm (☎ **65/232437**).

GETTING THERE

BY PLANE   **El Tepaul** airport lies an almost equal distance from Puerto Montt and Puerto Varas; it's about 15½ miles (25km) from the airport to Puerto Varas (☎ **65/252019**). A taxi from the airport costs $16 to $22, or you can arrange a transfer with **Andina del Sud** (☎ **65/257797;** e-mail: adsmontt@chilesat.net) for about $6.50 per person. Lan Chile, Ladeco, and Avant all serve the El Tepaul airport. Ask your hotel about transfers.

BY BUS   The following buses offer service to and from major cities in southern Chile, including Santiago: **Buses Cruz del Sur,** San Pedro 210 (☎ **65/233008**); **Buses Tas Choapa,** Walker Martínez 230 (☎ **65/233831**), and **Buses Lit,** Walker Martínez 227-B (☎ **65/233838**). Buses **Tas Choapa** and **Andesmar** (☎ **65/252926**) both offer daily service to Bariloche, Argentina.

BY CAR   Puerto Varas is just 12 miles (20km) north of Puerto Montt and 55 miles (88km) south of Osorno via the Panamericana. There are two exits leading to Puerto Varas, and both deposit you downtown. To get to Frutillar, you need to get back on the Panamericana, go north, and take the exit for that town.

GETTING AROUND

BY BUS   **Buses Cruz del Sur** offers transportation to Chiloé and nearly 15 daily trips to Puerto Montt, leaving from an office in Puerto Varas, at San Pedro 210 (☎ **65/233008**). There are also cheap minibuses that leave frequently from the corner of San Bernardo and Walker Martínez, across from the pet shop, leaving you at the bus terminal in Puerto Montt. You'll also find minibuses at San Bernardo and Martínez that go to Ensenada, Petrohué, and Lago Todos los Santos every day at 9:15am, 11am, 2pm, and 4pm, and **Andina del Sud,** Antonio Varas 437 (☎ **65/257797**), has daily trips to this area as well.

BY CAR   Renting a car is perhaps the most enjoyable way (but also the most expensive) to see the surrounding area. You might consider renting one especially if you plan to spend most of your time sightseeing: **Llanchahue Rent a Car,** San José 301 (☎ **65/233745**); **Turismo Nieve,** San Bernardo 406 (☎ **65/232299**); **Adriazola Turismo,** Santa Rosa 340 (☎ **65/233477**); or **Travi Viajes,** Camino Ensenada, Km1 (☎ **65/233491**).

WHERE TO STAY

Private parking or ample street parking is available and free for all hotels.

Expensive

Colonos del Sur. Del Salvador 24, Puerto Varas. ☎ **65/233369,** or for reservations 65/233039. Fax 65/233394. www.colonosdelsur.cl. E-mail: colonosdelsur@entelchile.net. 54 units. MINIBAR TV TEL. $80–$100 double; $140–$160 suite. AE, DC, MC, V.

Boasting a waterfront location next door to the new casino and a charming German colonial architecture, the Colonos del Sur is a standard favorite among travelers to Puerto Varas and one of the nicer hotels in town. It was built with a tremendous amount of wood, all of it native species such as *alerce* and beech. The common areas are large and plentiful, including a tea salon and lounge, and feature a quaint yet handsome decor sprinkled with various antique furnishings and objects such as foot-operated sewing machines. The tea salon is one of the best in Puerto Varas, both for its rich cakes and waterfront location. The rooms are not especially noteworthy but do offer solid quality. Doubles with a lake view are slightly larger, for the same price; others face the casino. The large suites, however, stand out with wraparound windows, sparkling bathrooms, and attractive decorations such as crocheted bedspreads. There's a small indoor pool wedged into a downstairs corner and a subterranean sauna.

Dining/Diversions: A scenic restaurant serves international and German food. There's also a bar and a cafe/tea salon.

Amenities: Laundry, room service, indoor pool, sauna, whirlpool, conference salon, business center, baby-sitting.

✪ **Hotel Cabañas del Lago.** Klenner 195, Puerto Varas. ☎ **65/232291.** Fax 65/232707. E-mail: calago@entelchile.net. 65 units, 21 cabañas. TV TEL. $99–$114 double; $120–$136 junior suite; $92–$130 cabañas. AE, DC, MC, V.

Recent renovations and sweeping views of Puerto Varas and Volcán Osorno make Hotel Cabañas del Lago the highest quality lodging available in town. The lakeview and park suites, if you can afford one, are luxuriously appointed and colossal in size; one could get lost in the bathroom alone. A junior suite is a slightly larger double, and might be worth booking for the larger windows and better decoration. Doubles are not overly spacious, with cramped bathrooms, but have been updated with curtains and bedding. Doubles with a lake view are the same price as rooms that overlook the cabañas.

The hotel takes advantage of its location with lots of glass in its attractive lounge and restaurant, which, like all the rooms, sports a country decor. The common areas have the feel of a mountain lodge, complete with deer antler chandeliers. There's also a large sun deck. The hotel began 20 years ago with its small, two- to five-person cabañas, which I do not entirely recommend due to their outdated interiors. The kitchens are very basic and the living area uses a twin bed and trundle bed as couches. It's too close for comfort, and really suitable for families only.

Dining/Diversions: The **El Ciervo** restaurant serves wild game and other daily specials from an extensive, excellent menu. There's also a bar, **El Tronador.**

Amenities: Laundry, room service, indoor heated pool, sauna, conference rooms, game room, billiard room, gift shop, baby-sitter, car rental.

Moderate

Cabañas Altué. Av. Vicente Pérez Rosales 1679, Puerto Varas. ☎ /fax **65/232294.** 9 units. TV TEL. $34–$66 cabañas for 2–3; $59–$107 cabañas for 4–6. No credit cards.

Located at the quiet end of the beach in Puerto Chico, about a 10-minute drive from downtown Puerto Varas, these cabañas do not have a view of the volcanoes, but they do have views and are situated among one of the most impressive arboreal gardens in the region. Guests arrive to a circular driveway ringed with roses and fronted by a huge magnolia tree; the cabañas themselves are surrounded by *araucaria,* pine, *alerce,* and more. The nine cabins are perched above the beach behind a row of eucalyptus trees, with a vista of Puerto Varas and the beach. The cabins were freshly painted this year and are decent and comfortable, with a separate kitchen/dining room and a deck. Nearly every plant or tree in the surrounding garden is unique, often from other regions in Chile. This is a place for those who want direct beach access, fragrant surroundings, and an address outside town.

Hotel & Cabañas Los Alerces. Av. Vicente Pérez Rosales 1281, Puerto Varas. ☎ **65/235984.** Fax 65/23621. E-mail: cabanaslosalerces@entelchile.net. 44 units, 10 cabañas. TV TEL. $65–$85 double; $50 cabaña for 2–3. AE, DC, MC, V.

This hotel/cabaña complex is for travelers who want beach access and/or an independent cabaña with cooking facilities (it's about a 2-minute drive out of Puerto Varas).

Los Alerces has undergone substantial renovations as a result of new ownership and the results are wonderful. Each of the rooms is decorated differently, but with a common country decor accentuated with framed antique photos and other period pieces culled over the years by the owners. The rooms are arranged around a bright atrium, and all are designed so that they take advantage of the view of the lake—but the hotel's neighboring lots are cluttered and not particularly eye-catching. All rooms have floral wallpaper and cotton or crochet bedspreads; some lean toward the romantic, some are decidedly more masculine. But it's the cabañas that are really special at Los Alerces. Each identical cabaña comes with three bedrooms and a large living area with real couches that are not considered an extra bed. They come with a fully stocked, open kitchen, giant corner windows, leafy surroundings, wood walls, and a cozy wood-burning stove. During the low season, two to three guests pay $50, four to five pay $75, six pay $100; however, during the high season, two to three guests can expect to pay the full six-person rate of $140.

Hotel Bellavista. Av. Vicente Pérez Rosales 60, Puerto Varas. ☎ **65/232011.** Fax 65/232013. www.hotelbellavistachile.com. E-mail: hotelbellavista@entelchile.net. 38 units. TV TEL. $63–$90 double; $81–$116 suite. AE, DC, MC, V.

Another waterfront hotel with gorgeous views, the Bellavista also has four larger guest rooms that face a forested cliff for those seeking quieter accommodations, and duplex units with three to four upstairs beds that are great for families with kids. It also has one of the best suites in town, a two-story apartment with giant windows and a thoroughly contemporary, country design. A lounge and bar also face the back, and are lit by wall and ceiling windows, whereas the separate restaurant/coffee shop looks directly out over the lake. The Bellavista is painted the same color as a Key lime pie, and while it's not highly noticeable, the walls of the rooms could use a lick of paint. Doubles are just slightly worn, with unremarkable furnishings. This hotel is considered the closest competition to the Licarayén (see below); the Bellavista is larger but the Licarayén has the slight edge with its renovations and friendlier service (service here can be absent-minded). The Bellavista's casual restaurant offers fixed-price lunch menus for $7 along with a range of international dishes.

Hotel El Greco. Mirador 134, Puerto Varas. ☎ **65/233388.** Fax 65/233380. E-mail: elgreco@ctcinternet.cl. 12 units. TV TEL. $28–$57 double. AE, DC, MC, V.

This is usually where I spend the night in Puerto Varas, both for its low price and delightful interiors. A block's walk up from downtown, the hotel is an antique, shingled home painted lemon and lilac. The most distinguishing characteristics of the El Greco are hundreds of paintings and drawings rendered by local artists. A comfortable living area is packed with antiques, magazines, and photo books, and there's a small dining area and a separate common area lit by skylights, with tables, a classic jukebox, and more artwork. The rooms are small, but they're as comfortable as your own bedroom. The amiable owner is a painter himself; his gallery here was set up to give local artists a much-needed space to hang their pieces.

Hotel Licarayén. San José 114, Puerto Varas. ☎ **65/232305.** Fax 65/232955. 23 units. TV TEL. $47–$70 double standard. AE, DC, MC, V.

This is one of Puerto Varas's best values, for its comfortable accommodations, waterfront views, and central location. The lobby and rooms are cheery and well lit, and the double standard rooms are average-size. You might consider spending the extra $20 for a double superior because these rooms come with lake views, balconies, and whirlpool tubs. Superiors are also substantially larger than standards and come with big, bright bathrooms. Only a few standards have lake views, so ask for one; L-shaped suites are ample, and come with a couch. The hotel may not have the antique character of Colonos del Sur (see above), but the rooms are just as good, if not better. There's a principal lounge/lobby and another seating area for relaxing, as well as a pleasant dining area for breakfast, again with lake views. The hotel sits on the main plaza and is close to everything. The service is cordial and professional.

Hotel Los Tilos. Av. Costanera 1057, Puerto Varas. ☎ **65/232814.** Fax 65/233126. E-mail: lostilos@ctcinternet.cl. 12 units. $40–$65 double. No credit cards.

Hotel Los Tilos is much like a bed-and-breakfast, situated in a renovated old home, with a lounge and cafe occupying the old living and dining areas, and rooms that feel like you're truly in a bedroom. The home is a pretty structure made of wood painted blue, yellow, and white, and sits on the shore with direct access to the beach. The rooms are decent, but fairly average in terms of style and quality; half have a full view, the other half a side view. The downstairs interiors are decorated in a colonial style with antiques and tapestries. It's about a 2-minute drive and 20-minute walk to the center.

Inexpensive

✪ **Casa Azul.** Mirador 18, Puerto Varas. ☎ **65/232904.** E-mail: casaazul@telsur.cl. 5 units. $11–$13 per person. No credit cards.

You can't beat Casa Azul for price, access to a fully stocked kitchen, and stylish, comfortable accommodations. This tiny home was recently converted into a hostel, and offers small rooms furnished with beds, tables, and chairs made entirely of tree trunks and branches. There's a back bedroom for three with a garden/lake view, three bedrooms for two, and the "cave," a tiny attic room with a double bed on the floor and not much headroom. The German-Chilean couple who runs Casa Azul is very friendly, and will help you arrange excursions and car rentals. Bathrooms are shared here. An enormous dog, Butch, guards the front door. The kitchen is really a bonus for those tired of eating out, and it's set up so you have your own storage area. Breakfast is not included.

Colores del Sur. Santa Rosa 318, Puerto Varas. ☎ **65/338588.** Fax 65/311311. 5 units. $10–$13 per person. No credit cards.

Centrally located on the second floor above a gift shop, the Colores del Sur offers the same character as Casa Azul, with inexpensive lodging and a central living area with large tables and couches. It's a comfortable place where you can use the kitchen, but it is not organized as well as Casa Azul. There are a couple of bright bedrooms that face the street. This hostel is frequented by a younger backpacker and budget traveler crowd, and is often confused with the more upscale hotel Colonos del Sur. Bathrooms are shared, and breakfast is not included.

WHERE TO DINE

Unless otherwise indicated, reservations are not required for the restaurants listed here.

✪ **Café Mamusia.** San José 316. ☎ **65/237971.** Main courses $4–$9; sandwiches $2–$7. MC, V. Summer daily 8:30am–2am; winter Mon–Fri 9am–11pm, Sat–Sun 10am–11pm. CHILEAN CAFE/BAKERY.

The Mamusia is locally renowned for its delicious desserts and pastries, especially the cake and *kuchen* it sells from its bakery at the entrance to the cafe. The atmosphere is somewhat like a tearoom or ice cream parlor, but there are delicious sandwiches and full meals throughout the day as well. Café Mamusia is also a great place for breakfast, and serves the full "American" version for $6. Typical Chilean favorites such as *pastel de choclo,* empanadas, or *escalopas* are served here, as well as lasagna, pizza, and grilled meats and fish; sandwiches come on homemade bread. There is also a set menu with several options for about $5.

Club Alemán. San José 415. ☎ **65/232246.** Main courses $8.50–$14.50. DC, MC, V. Daily 11am–midnight. GERMAN/CHILEAN.

This Club Alemán seems to offer more German specialties than its fellow clubs, with goose, duck, and bratwurst served with onions, potatoes, and applesauce; pork chops with caramelized onions and sauerkraut; goulash with spaetzle; steak tartare; and other dishes, in addition to Chilean favorites. Sandwiches are much cheaper than main dishes ($2 to $5.50) and are substantial. There are also appetizing desserts, such as crêpes *diplomatico,* with bananas, ice cream, and chocolate sauce. The dining area is on the second floor and is divided into two small, separate sections, one with booths.

✪ **Color Café.** Los Colonos 1005. ☎ **65/234311.** Main courses $6.50–$10. AE, DC, MC, V. Dec–Mar daily noon–1am; Apr–Nov daily 8pm–1am. INTERNATIONAL.

The Color Café recently opened to great success, chiefly for its stylish decor, good wine list, and diverse menu. Clean, crisp interiors offset by contemporary oil paintings, a long bar, and a couple of futon couches near a blazing, wood-burning stove set the ambience. The periodically changing menu features delicious bistro-style cuisine, including Caesar salads, soups, quiches, pastas, sandwiches, and main courses such as Roquefort fillet and chicken stuffed with ham and cheese in a mustard-chive sauce. It's a good place for a cocktail and an appetizer of regional smoked salmon. The Color Café is about a 5-minute drive from downtown Puerto Varas.

Dane's. Del Salvador 441. ☎ **65/232371.** Main courses $4–$8; sandwiches $2–$6. MC, V. Daily 8am–11pm. CHILEAN CAFE.

It's often hard to get a table during the lunch hour in this extremely popular restaurant, and it's easy to see why. Dane's serves inexpensive, hearty food in good-size portions and mouth-watering desserts, including ice cream and cakes. The interior is simple and unassuming, and much of the food is standard Chilean fare, all of it good or very good. The fried empanadas, especially shellfish, deserve special mention. Dane's serves a daily set menu for $6 Monday to Saturday, and $9 on Sunday, as well as a special dish, or *plato del día,* for $4. It's less busy before 1pm or after 3pm. You can also buy food to go from the front counter.

Donde La Chamaca. Del Salvador s/n (corner of San Bernardo). ☎ **65/232876.** Main courses $5–$10. No credit cards. Daily 11am–midnight. SEAFOOD.

This restaurant is short on ambience, but more than makes up for it with delicious seafood and huge portions. It sits on the second story of the market, and serves ultra-fresh trout, salmon, and conger eel paired with a multitude of sauces such as crab, butter, and caper; creamy mixed shellfish; *cordon bleu;* and more. Many of their *entradas,* or appetizers, make good lunch dishes, such as the *chupe de jaiva* or *chupe de pulpo,* crab and octopus stew, respectively. The service is friendly.

✪ **Ibis.** Av. Vicente Pérez Rosales 1117. ☎ **65/232017.** Main courses $7–$14. AE, DC, MC, V. Mon–Sat 12:30–3pm and 8pm–midnight. INTERNATIONAL/CHILEAN.

This popular restaurant is one of the best in Puerto Varas, namely for its creative cuisine and vast menu featuring everything from meat to pasta to sushi. Menu highlights include the flambéed Ecuadorian shrimp in cognac, pistachio salmon, beef fillet in a sauce of tomato, garlic, and chipotle pepper, and lamb chops with mint sauce. Crêpes come stuffed with items such as mushrooms and shrimp and then bathed in a sea urchin sauce. To begin, you might try a salad such as endive and Roquefort, and end the meal with crêpes suzette. The eating area is small but warm, and is decorated with crafts-oriented art; there's also a bar. The wine list also merits mention for its variety.

✪ **Merlin.** Imperial 0605. ☎ **65/233105.** Reservations recommended. Main courses $13–$16. AE, DC, MC, V. Daily 7pm–midnight. CHILEAN.

Merlin is arguably the finest restaurant in Puerto Varas. It is also one of the only restaurants in Chile that has managed to take Chilean cooking to a new level by exchanging the same tired recipes for creative dishes while still using only local ingredients. Simply put, the food is superb. The German chef who has been running this restaurant for 8 years changes the menu seasonally. A few examples from the spring menu include crawfish bisque, smoked salmon–and–chive ravioli, rabbit with asparagus and olive risotto, and curried abalone, shrimp, and vegetables served with almond rice. The wine list also deserves mention for its selection of fine varietals not usually seen in this region.

At press time, Merlin was busy relocating to a renovated antique, shingled home near the coast, where it intends to expand the dining room and add a wine-tasting room in the cellar, as well as a bistro/bar serving lighter fare. The restaurant plans to keep its old location running as a backpacker's hostal and pub. Call to inquire if it's open for lunch.

WHAT TO SEE & DO: A WALK AROUND TOWN

Puerto Varas is compact enough to explore by foot, which is really the best way to view the wooden colonial homes built by German immigrants from 1910 until the 1940s. Eight of these homes have been declared national monuments, yet there are at least a dozen more constructed during the period of expansion that began with the installation of the railroad that connected Puerto Varas with Puerto Montt.

Walk up San Francisco from Del Salvador until reaching María Brunn, where you turn right to view the stately **Iglesia del Sagrado Corazon de Jesus,** built between 1915 and 1918. The neo-Romantic design of the church, made entirely of oak, was modeled after the Marienkirche in the Black Forest. Continue along María Brunn and turn right on Purísima, where you'll encounter the first group of the simple yet intriguing colonial homes. The first is **Casa Gasthof Haus** (1930), now run as a hotel, then **Casa Yunge** (1932), just past San Luis on the left, and on the right, **Casa Horn** (1925), and finally **Casa Kaschel** at Del Salvador, where you turn left. If you'd like to see more, walk to Dr. Giesseler Street and turn right, following the train tracks for several blocks, passing the **Casa Opitz** on the right (1913, and now a hotel) until you see **Casa Maldonado** (1915) on the left.

Turn left on Nuestra Señora del Carmen to view the five homes left and right, including the **Casa Juptner** (1910). Double back and continue along Dr. Giesseler, turn left on Estación and right on Decher, passing the **Casa Emhart** (1920) and several other homes on the left. Continue until reaching **Parque Philippi,** where you'll find a lookout point. Double back, turn left on Bellavista, right on Klenner, and left on Turismo, at whose corner sits the eclectic **Casa Kuschel** (1910), with its Bavarian baroque tower. At the end of Turismo is the Avenida Costanera; turn right and take a stroll down the boardwalk.

OUTDOOR ACTIVITIES

TOUR OPERATORS & OUTFITTERS Puerto Varas has a few reliable, competent outfitters and tour operators offering excursions around the region, and even as far away as the Aisén region along the Carretera Austral. Perhaps the most difficult excursion in this region is an ascent up Volcán Osorno, which requires adequate physical fitness and a guided tour company that can provide necessary gear such as ropes and crampons. **Tranco Expediciones,** Santa Rosa 580 (☎ 65/311311; www.geocities.com/trancoexpediciones), **AlSur Expediciones,** Del Salvador 100 (☎ /fax **65/232300;** www.puertovaras/alsur.cl; e-mail: alsur@telsur.cl), and **Aquamotion Expediciones,** San Pedro 422 (☎ **65/232747;** fax 65/235938; www.aquamotion.cl; e-mail: turismo@aquamotion.cl), offer ascents to the top of Volcán Osorno, as well as trekking, rafting, sea kayaking, horseback riding, canyoneering, rock climbing, horseback riding, photo safaris, and more. They also custom-plan excursions and offer packages that include accommodations. AlSur also offers kayaking trips to Pumalín Park and sells Patagonia outdoor gear; Aquamotion has a good gift shop, including music; Tranco sells outdoor clothing. All are competent, solid bets with excellent guides.

For city tours and sightseeing tours around the Lake District, including trips to Frutillar, Puyehue, Chiloé, and Parque Nacional Alerce Andino, try **Andina del Sud,** at Del Salvador 72 (☎ **65/232811;** e-mail: adsvaras@chilesat.net). Andina del Sud is the company that provides boat excursions on Lago Todos los Santos and the Chilean leg of the lake crossing to Argentina (for information, see "Parque Nacional Vicente Pérez Rosales & the Lake Crossing to Argentina," below).

BOATING   During the summer it is possible to rent kayaks and canoes at the pier, located near the main plaza. For a sailing cruise around Lago Llanquihue, try **Motovelero Capitán Haase** (☎ **65/235120;** fax 65/235166; e-mail: captain@chilesat.net). Mr. Haase, the amicable owner and captain, offers four daily cruises aboard his yacht, built in 1998 in an attractive, antique design. The "Sunrise" cruise from 7:30 to 10:30am, including breakfast, is geared primarily toward fishermen. An early afternoon cruise from 11:30am to 1:30pm, with snacks, is for families with kids. "Sunset with the Captain" from 6 to 9:30pm is a quiet, romantic trip using sails and no motor. A "Party Cruise" goes from 10pm to 2am, and ships out only when there's a minimum of 20 passengers.

FISHING   This region is noted for its excellent fly-fishing opportunities, namely along the shores of Río Puelo, Río Maullín, and Río Petrohue. Many hotels will set up tours with guides, but the central hub for information, gear, and fishing licenses is at **Gray's Fly-Fishing Supplies,** which has two shops at San José 192 and San Francisco 447 (☎ **65/310734;** www.grayfly.com; e-mail: fishing@grayfly.com). Gray's has a roster of fly-fishing guides who will arrange outings to all outlying areas, for river and lake fishing.

The excellent, but very exclusive, full-service **Río Puelo Lodge** (☎ **2/960-1001** in Santiago; www.rio-puelo-lodge.cl; www.troutandducks.com), caters to fly-fishermen but also offers horseback riding, boat rides, water-skiing, and more. The stately wood-and-stone lodge is tucked well into the backcountry on the shore of Lago Tagua Tagua, and is reached by vehicle and boat. Packages run $320 per person, per day, including meals, open bar, guide, boats, horseback riding, trekking, and heated pool. Ask about discounts for non-anglers.

HORSEBACK RIDING   **Campo Aventura,** San Bernardo 318, Puerto Varas (☎ **65/232910;** e-mail: outsider@telsur.cl), offers horseback riding October 15 to April 15, leaving from a camp in Valle Cochamó, south of the national park, with day and multiple-day trips. The 9-day horseback journey follows the trail of Butch Cassidy and the Sundance Kid. Gear and bilingual guides are provided, and guests can lodge in their mountain bunkhouses. Other tour companies, such as **AlSur** or **Aquamotion** (see "Tour Operators & Outfitters," above), offer day horseback-riding trips in Vicente Pérez Rosales National Park.

RAFTING   Few rivers in the world provide rafters with such stunning scenery as the Río Petrohue, whose frothy green waters begin at Lago Todos los Santos and end at the Reloncavi Estuary. Along the way, rafters are treated to towering views of the volcanoes Osorno and Puntiagudo. The river is Class III and suitable for nearly everyone, but it is not a slow float, so timid travelers might consult with their tour agency before signing up. The tour operators listed above offer rafting.

A SIDE TRIP FROM PUERTO VARAS TO ENSENADA

Ensenada is a tiny settlement at the base of Volcán Osorno. Its proximity to Petrohué and Lago Todos los Santos makes it a convenient point for lodging if you plan to spend a lot of time around the Vicente Pérez Rosales National Park. When driving from east from Puerto Varas to Ensenada along the road that winds around Lake Llanquihue, you might consider stopping at the following points of interest. Two-and-a-half miles (4km) outside Puerto Varas is a Chilean rodeo *medialuna* ("half moon"), where events are held during February and on Independence days September 18 to 19. Still on the same road, at Km34 is one of the best teahouses in the region, ✪ **Café Bellavista** (☎ 65/212040), which serves out-of-this-world cakes and pastries, but is unfortunately open only Saturday, Sunday, and holidays after 4pm. They have a flock of llamas running around the property.

GETTING THERE   If you have your own vehicle, take the coastal road east out of Puerto Varas and continue for 29 miles (46km) until you reach Ensenada. In Puerto Varas, you'll find minibuses at the intersection of San Bernardo and Martínez that go to Ensenada, Petrohué, and Lago Todos los Santos every day at 9:15am, 11am, 2pm, and 4pm. **Andina del Sud,** Del Salvador 72 (☎ 65/232811), has daily trips to this area as well.

Where to Stay & Dine

Private parking or ample street parking is available and free for all hotels

✪ **Hotel Ensenada.** Ruta Internacional 225, Km45. ☎ **65/21207.** Fax 65/212028. 25 units. $60 double; $80 double with volcano view. AE, DC, MC, V. Open Oct–Apr.

The Hotel Ensenada is not just a hotel; it is a veritable museum whose lobby is so jam-packed with colonial German antiques, you'll need an afternoon just to see it all. The hotel itself is a living antique, built more than 100 years ago for travelers on their way to Argentina, and it's important to keep this in mind, because although it offers an acceptable level of comfort, the rooms do reflect the hotel's age. It's such a fun place, though, that most visitors, 90% of them foreigners, don't seem to mind. All rooms on the second floor have private bathrooms, and for the most part the rest share with one other room. Apart from lace curtains, freshly cut flowers, and a framed print, rooms are sparsely decorated. If they're not too full, ask to see several rooms as each one is differently sized. The hotel is situated on a 500ha (1,235-acre) private forest that's perfect for taking a stroll or riding a bike—which comes free with the room—and there's a tennis court, canoes, and motorboats. The old-fashioned kitchen serves simple, Chilean cuisine with vegetables straight from the garden. Unfortunately, the hotel closes seasonally from May to September.

✪ **Yankee Way.** Road to Ensenada east of Puerto Varas, Km42. ☎ **65/212030.** Fax 65/212031. wwwsouthernchilexp.com. E-mail: reserve@southernchilexp.com. 17 units, 2 chalets. $100 average per person. No credit cards.

The name "Yankee Way" is a play on words, a gringo's pronunciation of Llanquihue, and coincidentally owned by the American who began Digital Systems. The lodge is luxury at its finest; in fact, it would be impossible to list every service and fine detail in this review alone. From the minute you arrive at the circular driveway, you know that no expense has been spared to make this lodge stand apart from any other in Chile, the reason it is patronized by wealthy entrepreneurs, Chilean military generals, actors, sports stars, and more. The setting is ideal: nestled in a thick forest of cinnamon-colored *arrayán* trees on the shore of Lago Llanquihue, and offering up an astounding view of the volcano directly in front of the lodge.

The complex is made entirely of wood painted terra-cotta and forest green. Lodging options come in a variety of shapes and sizes: There are two chalets, eight bungalows, five two-bedroom suites, and four standard hotel rooms. Prices for each vary and can often be negotiated, especially when it comes to high and low season. It's best to contact the hotel or its Web page for an up-to-date price list and to inquire about full-service packages, which typically run about $300 per person, per day. Each lodging type has the same first-class decor: dark green walls, ebony leather couches, sunken bathtubs, and copper-detailed showers, and furniture and art imported from Mexico and Argentina are standard appointments.

The hotel's main bar and dining area has to be seen to be believed: marble and brass chandeliers, fireplaces made of volcanic rock, orangey leather chairs, a basement "cave" for wine tasting, and a cigar bar that sells Havanas. The hotel began as a fishing lodge—there are five on-staff guides—but now offers a wide variety of activities, including the region's only sailcraft for floating on the lake. The owner invited several artists to provide the finishing touches, such as an enormous beech tree carved and painted into a mural of Chilean culture. Even if you don't stay here, try to make a stop for lunch or coffee to view this gorgeous lodge with your own eyes.

Dining/Diversions: An outstanding restaurant serves a variety of international dishes, and there's a cafe, bar, wine-tasting cellar, and cigar bar.

Amenities: Laundry, luxury spa with a gym, sauna and hot tubs, massage, business center, conference rooms, room service, kayaks, sailcraft, fly-fishing excursions.

PARQUE NACIONAL VICENTE PÉREZ ROSALES & THE LAKE CROSSING TO ARGENTINA

About 40 miles (65km) from Puerto Varas sits Chile's oldest national park, Vicente Pérez Rosales, founded in 1926. It covers an area of 250,000ha (617,500 acres), incorporating the park's centerpiece, Lago Todos los Santos, and the Saltos de Petrohué and three volcanoes: Osorno, Tronador, and Puntiagudo. The park is open during the summer 9am to 8pm, and during the winter 9am to 6pm; admission to the Saltos de Petrohué is $2. Conaf's **information center** (no phone) can be found near the Hotel Petrohue; the center adheres loosely to these hours: December to February 8:30am to 8pm, March to November 8:30am to 6:30pm.

By far the most popular excursions here are boat rides across the unbelievably emerald waters of **Lago Todos los Santos,** and there are several options. **Andina del Sud** offers a 2-hour sail around Isla Margarita and a 3-hour sail to Peulla, where visitors are given the option to lodge in the Peulla Hotel, then return or continue on to Bariloche with the Argentine company Cruce de Lagos. Andina del Sud has a ticket office at the pier and an office in Puerto Varas, at Del Salvador 72 (☎ **65/232811**). The boat ride to Bariloche is spectacular, offering rugged, panoramic views; however, some travelers have complained that 1-day trips to Bariloche are not worth the money on stormy days, and that the companies shuttle passengers in and out too quickly. The ferry portions of this journey are broken up by short bus rides from one body of water to the other.

There are relatively few hiking trails here. The shortest and most popular trail leads to the **Saltos de Petrohué,** located just before the lake (admission $3). Here you'll find a wooden walkway that has been built above the start of the Río Petrohué; from here it is possible to watch the inky-green waters crash through lava channels formed after the 1850 eruption of Volcán Osorno. If you're serious about backpacking, pick up a copy of the JLM map *Ruta de los Jesuitas* for a description of longer trails in the park, one of which takes you as far as Lago Rupanco and Puerto Rico (the town, not the Caribbean island!), where you can catch a bus to Osorno. Day hikes take visitors around the back of Volcán Osorno. A trail to a rustic hot springs called **Termas de Callao** can be completed in a day, but it is accessed solely by boat, which you'll need to hire at the Petrohué dock (six-person maximum, $50). The round-trip hiking time is 5 to 6 hours, and you must arrange with the boat's captain to pick you up later.

✪ **Hotel Petrohue.** Lago Todos los Santos. ☎/fax **65/258042.** www.petrohue.com. 21 units. $67–$94 double. AE, DC, MC, V.

This woodsy lodge sits at the departure point for the famous boat crossing to Bariloche, on the shore of the emerald Lago Todos los Santos. The location makes it an obvious choice if you have plans to make this journey and do not want to hassle with early-morning transfers to the boat, but even if you do not plan to take that trip, it is such a pleasing lodge that you might consider staying here anyway. The building is entirely made of timber, save the stone entrance steps and a generous supply of windows. The rooms are comfortable and furnished simply, and there's a fantastic attic honeymoon suite with a wood-burning stove and skylights. The common areas feature a large dining room and one of the coziest fireside bars around, both appointed with a scattering of antiques and old photos.

The highlight of this lodge is its friendly service, and the administrator works overtime to see that guests feel at home. The only downsides of the Petrohue are the throngs of people who arrive daily to visit Lago Todos los Santos, and the hotel's noisy generator. The lodge offers mountain bike rental and excursions around Vicente Pérez Rosales National Park.

✪ **Hotel Peulla.** Lago Todos los Santos. ☎/fax **2/889-1031** in Santiago. 83 units. $125 double. AE, DC, MC, V

Passengers on the 2-day journey to Bariloche stop for the night at this giant lodge, which sits on the shore of Lago Todos los Santos. It's possible to spend several days here if you'd like, to take part in trekking, fishing, and kayaking in the area. The lodge's remoteness is perhaps its biggest draw, surrounded as it is by thick forest and not much else. The Peulla is a mountain lodge, with enormous dining rooms, roaring fireplaces, and lots of wood. It's an exceptionally agreeable place, with a large patio and sprawling lawn, although the price is high. You can reserve rooms at a lower rate through a travel agency.

7 Puerto Montt

12 miles (20km) N of Puerto Varas; 630 miles (1,016km) S of Santiago

This port town of roughly 110,000 residents is the central hub for travelers headed to Lagos Llanquihue and Todos los Santos, Chiloé, and the national parks Alerce Andino and Pumalín. It is also a major docking zone for dozens of large cruise companies circumnavigating the southern cone of South America and several ferry companies with southern destinations to Laguna San Rafael National Park and Puerto Natales in Patagonia.

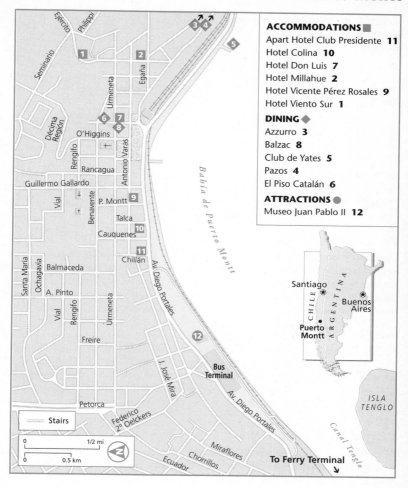

ACCOMMODATIONS ■
Apart Hotel Club Presidente **11**
Hotel Colina **10**
Hotel Don Luis **7**
Hotel Millahue **2**
Hotel Vicente Pérez Rosales **9**
Hotel Viento Sur **1**

DINING ◆
Azzurro **3**
Balzac **8**
Club de Yates **5**
Pazos **4**
El Piso Catalán **6**

ATTRACTIONS ●
Museo Juan Pablo II **12**

    The town presents a convenient stopover point for travelers, but is not a particularly attractive destination in itself due to its mishmash of modern office buildings, run-down wooden homes, and scrappy industrial port. However, Puerto Montt's small downtown can be a pleasant place to take a stroll on a sunny day, and the city offers great restaurants and an extensive outdoor market that sells almost every Chilean handicraft brought in from various areas around the Lake District.

    Puerto Montt was founded in 1853 by German immigrants and their stalwart promoter Vicente Pérez Rosales, who named the town after another promoter of immigration, President Manual Montt. The waterfront here was rebuilt after the devastating earthquake of 1960, which had destroyed the city's port, church, and neighborhood of Angelmó. Today, it is the capital of Chile's Región X, a thriving city that invests heavily in salmon farming, shipping, and tourism.

ESSENTIALS
GETTING THERE
BY PLANE   El Tepaul airport (☎ **65/252019**) is served by all national airlines, including **Lan Chile/Ladeco,** San Martín 200 (☎ **65/253141**), with six daily flights to Santiago, and **Avant,** Benavente 305 (☎ **65/278317**); the Peruvian airline **Aero Continente,** O'Higgins 167 (☎ **65/347777**), has four daily flights from Santiago. **Aero Sur,** Urmeneta 149 (☎ **65/252523**), has flights from Chaitén. A bus from the airport to the city's downtown bus terminal costs $1.50; a taxi costs between $11 and $15. Note that you should agree on a fare first. There are several car rental agencies at the airport, including Hertz and Avis.

BY BUS   Puerto Montt's main terminal is at the waterfront, about a 10-minute walk from downtown, and there are taxis. Regular bus service to and from most major cities, including Santiago, is provided by **Cruz del Sur** (☎ **65/254731**), **TurBus** (☎ **65/253329**), **Tas Choapa** (☎ **65/254828**), and **Bus Norte** (☎ **65/252783**).

BY CAR   The Panamericana highway ends at Puerto Montt.

VISITOR INFORMATION
The municipality has a small **tourist office** in the plaza at the corner of Antonio Varas and O'Higgins (☎ **65/261700**); it's open December to March daily 9am to 9pm, and April to November Monday to Friday 9am to 1pm and 2:30 to 6:30pm, Saturday to Sunday 9am to 1pm. There is also an office in the bus terminal on the second floor, and two new kiosks on the pedestrian street Calle Talca near Calle Urmeneta.

ORIENTATION
Puerto Montt is divided into *poblaciónes,* or neighborhoods, scattered around the city's hilltops. From the city center to the east is the **Pelluco** district, where many of the city's good restaurants can be found, and to the west is the district **Angelmó,** with the city's fish market, port departures, and Fería Artesanal with great shopping; the two districts are connected by the coastal road Diego Portales. The city center is laid out on a grid system that abuts a steep cliff.

GETTING AROUND
BY FOOT   The city center is small enough to be seen on foot. The crafts market and fish market in Angelmó is a 20-minute walk from the center, but you can take a cab. You'll need a taxi to reach the Pelluco district.

BY BUS   Buses Cruz del Sur (☎ **65/252783**) leaves for Puerto Varas 15 times daily from the bus terminal, and so do the independent white shuttle buses to the left of the coaches; look for the sign in the window that says PUERTO VARAS. Cruz del Sur also serves Chiloé, including Castro and Ancud, with seven trips per day. **TransChiloé** (☎ **65/254934**) goes to Chiloé 11 times per day from the terminal.

SPECIAL EVENTS
The second week in January Puerto Montt hosts a **Día del Curanto,** preparing this popular Chilote dish the traditional way—in earthen holes—in public places around the city. In February the city holds its annual **Semana Puertomontina,** with week-long festivities that culminate with a fireworks display over the bay. The festival usually takes place the first or second week in February, and is held to celebrate Puerto Montt's anniversary.

Renting a Car for Local Trips & for the Carretera Austral

This is one of those places where renting a car can come in handy, given the ample sightseeing opportunities and pleasant drives. Local car rental agencies in Puerto Montt include **Hertz** at Antonio Varas 126 (☎ 65/259585; www.hertz.com), **Avis** at Urmeneta 1037 (☎ 65/253307; www.avis.com), **First** at Av. G. Gallardo 211 (☎ 65/252036), **Econo Rent** at Av. G. Gallardo 450 (☎ 65/254888), **Hunter Rent A Car** at Antonio Varas 449 (☎ 65/251524), and **Ace Turismo** at Antonio Varas 445 (☎ 65/254988; www.geocities.com/lagosandinos). Hertz, Avis, and Ace Turismo rent cars for the Carretera Austral, leaving the vehicle in Coyhaique or Punta Arenas. A typical rental runs $600 to $800 per week, with a $450 to $550 drop-off fee—this includes everything but gas. Some companies insist that you rent a truck with 4×4 (the importance of this during the summer is debatable; during the winter it could help if the road turns muddy). Others rent mid-range vehicles. Call or visit the Web sites to see if you can work out a deal, especially in the low season.

FAST FACTS: PUERTO MONTT

Currency Exchange   **Turismo Los Lagos,** Talca 84; **Trans Afex,** Av. Diego Portales 516; **Inter/Cam,** O'Higgins 167, 1st floor; **La Moneda de Oro,** in the bus terminal, Office #37; and **Eureka Tour,** Antonio Varas 445. Exchange houses are generally open Monday to Friday 9am to 1pm and 2 to 6pm, Sat 9am to 1pm. For ATMs, try Banco de A. Edwards at Pedro Montt 55 (☎ 65/264520) or Banco Santander at Antonio Varas 501 (☎ 65/252412). Banks are open Monday to Friday 9am to 2pm.

Hospital   Hospital Base Seminario s/n (☎ 65/261100) and the Hospital de la Seguridad at Panamericana 400 (☎ 65/257333).

Internet Cafe   **Mundo Sur Cibercafe,** San Martín 232; **Tetris Entel,** Antonio Varas 529; and **Travellers Center,** Av. Angelmó 2456 (☎ 65/262099). Internet service cost averages $4 per hour.

Laundry   **Narly** at San Martín 167 (no phone), or **Lavandería Center** at Antonio Varas 700 (☎ 65/252338).

WHAT TO SEE & DO

TOUR OPERATORS & TRAVEL AGENCIES   The Patagonia clothing store at Antonio Varas 445 is Puerto Montt's contact for **AlSur** in Puerto Varas, which offers rafting the Río Petrohue, ascents of Volcán Osorno, horseback riding, photo safaris, and other great trips (☎ 65/287628). **Ace Turismo** at Antonio Varas 445 (☎ 65/254988) is in the same office, and offers just about everything, including tours to Vicente Pérez National Park, the Termas de Puyehue, Chiloé, sightseeing tours around the circumference of Lago Llanquihue, 2-night treks around Volcán Osorno with an overnight in a family home, and more.

Petrel Tours at Benavente 327 (☎ 65/251780) is a full-service travel agency and offers city tours and sightseeing excursions around the area and to the Vicente Pérez Rosales National Park. **Andina del Sud** at Antonio Varas 447 (☎ 65/257797) is another agency offering classic trips such as city tours and sightseeing journeys, and has a transportation service to attractions, as well as the monopoly on Lago Todos los Santos for the lake crossing to Bariloche. **Travellers** at Av. Angelmó 2456 (☎ 65/262099; e-mail: travlers@chilesat.net) is somewhat like a one-stop travel shop, with information and booking arrangements with nearly every outfitter, hotel, and program around Chile. If you're looking for information, especially outside this area, this is your place.

Museo Juan Pablo II. Av. Diego Portales 991. No phone. Admission $1. Mar–Dec daily 9am–noon and 2–6pm; Jan–Feb daily 9am–7pm.

This museum contains a medley of artifacts culled from this region. There's an interesting interpretive exhibit of the Monte Verde archeological dig that found bones estimated to be 12,000 years old. There's also an open-air railway exhibit next to the museum. Truthfully, the museum really holds little of interest, but if you're in the area it's worth a quick stop.

SHOPPING   Puerto Montt is a great place to pick up souvenirs. On Avenida Angelmó, from the bus terminal to the fish market, is the ✪ **Fería Artesenal de Angelmó** (open daily 9am–7pm), with dozens of stalls and specialty shops that peddle knitwear, ponchos, handicrafts, jewelry, regional foods, and more from areas around the Lake District, including Chiloé. It's about a 15-minute walk from the plaza, or you can take a taxi.

WHERE TO STAY

Private parking or ample street parking is available and free for all hotels.

EXPENSIVE

✪ **Apart Hotel Club Presidente.** Av. Diego Portales 664, Puerto Montt. ☎ **65/251666.** Fax 65/251669. E-mail: infocp@presidente.cl. 26 units. TV TEL. $75–$95 double. AE, DC, MC, V.

This well-tailored, handsomely designed hotel is a terrific option in Puerto Montt. The hotel's classic, nautical-themed design appeals equally to executives and tourists, and handy kitchenettes give guests an extra ounce of freedom. Located on the waterfront in a central location close to shops, the Presidente is on busy Portales Avenue, but double-paned windows keep noise to a minimum. All rooms were designed to give guests maximum space, and all have either queen- or king-size beds. The doubles are spacious, but the superiors are much larger and worth the extra $15. Most come with a small loveseat to sink into and a table and chairs. The rooms are decorated with creams and navy blue, striped curtains, and nubby bedspreads. A breakfast buffet is served daily in the comfortable restaurant/bar next to the lobby; there's an additional sitting area on the second floor.

Hotel Don Luis. Calle Urmeneta and Quillota, Puerto Montt. ☎ **65/259001.** Fax 65/259005. E-mail: hdluis@entelchile.net. 60 units. TV TEL. $90 standard; $105 superior. AE, DC, MC, V.

The Don Luis is part of the Best Western chain, and offers pleasant, comfortable accommodations with traditional decor. For the price, you'd do better staying at the Club Presidente (see above), but occasional discounts might make this hotel more attractive. The lobby has glass walls, shiny white floors, and English-style furniture; the rooms run along a slightly similar design. The hotel renovated its rooms and sparkling white bathrooms last year, but not the carpet, which could stand to be replaced. Also, several rooms had a light musty odor during my last visit, but this problem is often temporary and it wasn't present throughout the whole building. Corner rooms and those on the 7th and 8th floors have the best views. Junior suites have a terrace, and superiors come with a queen. Double-paned windows ensure tranquil evenings. The hotel often caters to executives and conventioneers, who enjoy its central location and business services.

Dining: There's a snack bar/lounge/restaurant on the second floor with angled walls made entirely of glass.

Amenities: Laundry, business center, conference rooms, sauna, room service.

Hotel Vicente Pérez Rosales. Antonio Varas 447, Puerto Montt. ☎ **65/252571.** Fax 65/ 255473. www.hotelperezrosales.cl. E-mail: hotelvpr@telsur.cl. 82 units. TV TEL. $99–$112 double. AE, DC, MC, V.

The Vicente Pérez Rosales is for those who prefer to stay in a large hotel with all the trimmings, for example, revolving doors, uniformed bellhops, a boundless lobby, and semiformal dining room. The hotel was built in 1962 using traditional German architectural designs common in the Puerto Montt area. For years it was the most important hotel in the city, and its attention to cleanliness and maintenance has kept it top-ranked. The restaurant, with its honey-wood floors, creamy tablecloths, and delicate light, is especially lovely. In the lobby, the mast of a ship crashes through a stone fireplace's mantel, which is surrounded by dozens of sofas where guests plop down for an afternoon read. Wood and brass elevators lift guests to their rooms, which are all sized differently. Those with a view of the water do not cost extra, so try to book one. Also, try to get a room on the third floor or up because these rooms have recently been remodeled, and always ask for special rates during the low season because suites can drop in price to $108.

Dining/Diversions: A semiformal restaurant serves international cuisine. There is also a bar tucked away on the second floor and a tea salon.

Amenities: Laundry, conference center, gift shop, minibusiness center, room service.

✪ **Hotel Viento Sur.** Ejército 200, Puerto Montt. ☎ **65/258701.** Fax 65/258700. E-mail: m.spondelli@entelchile.net. 27 units. TV TEL. $90–$110 double standard; $140–$180 suite. AE, DC, MC, V. Parking.

This appealing bed-and-breakfast–style hotel is my favorite in Puerto Montt. The main body of the hotel is within an 80-year-old home clinging to a cliff, with a decade-old, added-on wing below that keeps with the architectural uniformity of the establishment. The hotel has luminous, blonde-wood floors and is brightly lit by a generous supply of windows that look out over Puerto Montt's bay. The rooms are unique, each with a folk-art and nautical theme. Each door has a stained-glass cutout; inside walls of the rooms are washed with muted colors. The upstairs rooms in the old house have tall ceilings, the rooms in the lower wing have the cozy feel of a ship's cabin, and rooms on the fourth floor have terraces or balconies. Doubles come in standard, superior, and suite sizes, and nearly all have a view of the bay. Suites come with whirlpool tubs. A large patio juts out from the front of the hotel.

One of the perks at the Viento Sur is the delicious breakfast buffet served in the restaurant, which is locally considered one of the best in Puerto Montt (see "Where to Dine," below). There's also a sauna and a conference room.

MODERATE

Hotel Colina. Calle Talca 81, Puerto Montt. ☎ **65/253501.** Fax 65/23857. 40 units. TV TEL. $30–$40 double; $44–$60 suite. No credit cards.

This sparsely decorated, large hotel is a good option in this price category, and it has a downtown location facing the coast. Many of the rooms come with a sea view, and are clean and neat, with wood-paneled walls, okay beds, and spacious bathrooms. Long, airy hallways decorated with an occasional blown-up photo of a Chilean landscape are about the only decoration in this no-frills hotel, but if sleeping is all you plan to do here, the lack of style shouldn't matter. Although the hotel features an open lobby, its blandness and constant blare from a corner TV doesn't encourage guests to linger. The two darker suites are strange: There's so much room you almost don't know what to do with it. There's a restaurant on the basement-level floor for breakfast, but chances are you'll be eating dinner out.

Hotel Millahue. Copiapó 64, Puerto Montt. ☎ **65/253829.** Fax 65/256317. E-mail: jacortes@entelchile.net. 25 units. TV TEL. $30–$47 double. No credit cards.

This older hotel is not particularly fancy, but it does offer clean, large double rooms and friendly service, and it's one of the best lodging choices in this price category. All double rooms are sized differently but priced the same, and rooms on the fourth and fifth floors are the nicest, especially those whose numbers end in 06 and 07. There isn't a lobby per se, but there is a dining area for breakfast and hearty, set-menu Chilean meals should you decide to eat in. Beds are average but offer standard comfort. The hotel is run by its owner, a friendly woman who strives to make guests feel as though they were in their own home.

WHERE TO DINE

Puerto Montt is Chile's **seafood capital,** offering the widest variety of shellfish and fish found anywhere in the country. It'd be a crime if you left here without sampling at least a few delicacies, such as sea bass or conger eel. If you're feeling adventurous, try a Chilean favorite, such as abalone, sea urchin, or the regional barnacle. And where better to see, smell, and taste these fruits of the sea than the **Fish Market of Angelmó,** located at the end of Avenida Angelmó where the artisan market terminates; it's open Monday to Sunday 10am to 8pm. Like most fish markets, it's a little grungy, but it's a colorful stop nevertheless and there are several restaurant stalls offering the freshest local specialties around. A word of caution: There have been reports that a few food stalls like to overcharge tourists, so double-check your bill with the menu.

Apart from the restaurants below, there are a handful of inexpensive cafes in Puerto Montt, including **Central** at Rancagua 117 (☎ **65/254721**), **Dino's** at Antonio Varas 550 (☎ **65/252785**), and **Super Yoco** at Quillota 259 (☎ **65/252123**), which has lunches, empanadas, and appetizer platters. If you're in the mood for pizza, try **Di Napoli** at Av. General Gallardo 119 (☎ **65254174**). With the exception of Azzurro, these restaurants in general do not require reservations.

Azzurro. Av. General Gallardo at Av. España, Pelluco. ☎ **65/318989.** Reservations recommended on weekends. Main courses $4.50–$8. No credit cards. Mon–Sat 1–3:30pm and 8pm–midnight. ITALIAN.

Fresh pasta served in rich sauces is this Italian eatery's mainstay, but that's not all they serve—the stuffed Roquefort chicken and pizzas are also good, and they can even whip up a sushi dinner if you call 24 hours in advance. The folk-artsy blue dining area has hand-painted stenciling and is decorated with craftwork; it's a fun, pleasant atmosphere. The pastas are to die for, such as lasagna, fettuccine, or cannelloni stuffed with crab and spinach, or with ricotta, walnuts, eggplant, and fresh basil, and bathed in a choice of 11 sauces. The specialty is smoked trout ravioli, for which the restaurant won a regional culinary award. There are also salads and an extensive wine list.

✪ **Balzac.** Calle Urmeneta 305. ☎ **65/313251.** Main courses $7–$9. No credit cards. Mon–Fri noon–3:30pm and 8–11:30pm; Sat–Sun 8–11:30pm. CHILEAN/FRENCH.

Balzac is one of the best restaurants in Puerto Montt, and is accordingly popular with local residents and tourists alike. The idea behind Balzac is to create innovative dishes with a French flavor, using only fresh, regional products and ingredients. Plenty of Chilean specialties abound, such as garlic shrimp *píl píl* or conger eel with a caper or Chardonnay sauce. You'll see a few French classics here, such as *boeuf bourguignon,* but the emphasis is seafood, of which there's a large variety, including albacore tuna or a *curanto* stew for two. The brightly painted interior is an attractive surrounding for enjoying your meal. The wine list features fine Chilean varieties.

Club de Yates. Av. Juan Soler Manfredini 1. ☎ **65/263606.** Main courses $6–$14. AE, DC, MC, V. Daily noon–3pm and 8–11pm. SEAFOOD.

The light-blue Yacht Club looks like a traditional seafood restaurant that sits out over the water like a pier. Inside, though, the atmosphere is white tablecloths, candlesticks, and sharp waiters in bow ties; in other words, it's one of the more elegant dining areas in town. This is a good place to come if you're looking for typical Chilean seafood dishes, such as razor clams broiled with Parmesan, sea bass *Margarita*, a creamy shellfish sauce, boiled abalone, avocado halves filled with shrimp salad, and the like. It has a great waterfront view, and is located about ½ mile (1km) from the plaza toward Pelluco.

El Piso Catalán. Quillota 185, 2nd floor. ☎ **65/313900.** Main courses $5–$13. No credit cards. Daily 12:30–4:30pm and 8pm–2am. SPANISH.

The Piso Catalán is a great choice for a good, inexpensive lunch, which is why this tiny second-story restaurant is usually packed with downtown workers. The basic fixed-price lunch is an incredible $1.75, and there are three more fixed-price lunches that rise to $6. The atmosphere is as enjoyable as the menu; the dining areas are in two rooms of an old wooden home, artistically decorated and well lit. The regular menu offers a bounty of tapas, those little Spanish appetizers that range from garlic shrimp to an egg tortilla—all cost between $3 and $8.50 each. There are just seven main dishes here, so you might consider ordering several tapas instead and sharing with your dining partner.

✪ **Hotel Viento Sur.** Ejército 200. ☎ **65/258701.** Main courses $7–$9. AE, DC, MC, V. Daily 12:30–3:30pm and 7:30–10:30pm. CONTEMPORARY CHILEAN.

Like Balzac (see above), the Viento Sur takes regional ingredients and really puts them to work, creating flavorful, well-prepared dishes. Another reason to come here is for the intimate dining area with its expansive view of the bay—if you get a table near the window, that is. The restaurant is built of polished blond wood, with linen tablecloths and a nautical theme. Mouth-watering dishes include beef tenderloin in a cilantro sauce, saffron conger eel, and chicken marinated in port with almonds. Although there are set hours for dining, the restaurant serves cocktails, tea, and cakes all day, should you be looking for a good place to take a break. There's also a tiny bar.

Pazos. Liboro Guerrero 1, Pelluco. ☎ **65/252552.** Main courses $4.50–$10. No credit cards. Mon–Sat 12:15–3pm and 8:15–10pm; Sun 12:15–3pm only. CHILEAN.

This is the place to come if you're interested in sampling *curanto* but don't have time to make it to Chiloé. *Curanto* is that island's specialty, a mixture of mussels, clams, sausage, chicken, pork, beef, and a gooey pancake steamed in a large pot and served with a cup of broth. Although Pazos is locally known for this dish, it also serves a variety of seafood items, such as sea urchin omelets and the shellfish cornucopia, *sopa marinera*. The restaurant is on the waterfront in Pelluco, in a 90-year-old home painted mint green; the tables have red-and-white checkered tablecloths. It's very popular with summer visitors to Puerto Montt.

8 Ferry Crossings to the Carretera Austral & Sailing to Patagonia Through the Fjords

Few fjordlands in the world surpass the elegant beauty of Chile's southern region. The entire coast of Chile is composed of thousands of little-explored islands, canals, and sounds that are difficult to reach—that is, until several cargo ferries caught on to the idea to market the area as a sailing destination. **Navimag** offers a popular sailing trip through the southern fjords to Puerto Natales in Patagonia. The company also offers journeys to the Laguna San Rafael Glacier, as does the freight ferry **Transmarchilay** and the luxury liners *Skorpios* and *Patagonian Express* (which leaves from Puerto Chacabuco). Both cruises are unforgettable.

For information about the journey to the Laguna San Rafael Glacier, see chapter 14, "The Carretera Austral."

Navimag. Offices in Puerto Montt at Av. Angelmó 2187 in the Terminal de Transbordadores (☎ **65/432300**) and Santiago at El Bosque Norte 0440 (☎ 2/442-3120); in Chaitén, call ☎ 65/731570. www.navimag.com. Prices given below. AE, DC, MC, V.

Navimag offers a sensational 4-day/3-night journey through the southern fjords to **Puerto Natales,** near Torres del Paine National Park (the trip can also be done in the reverse direction—see the section on Puerto Natales in chapter 15, "Patagonia & Tierra del Fuego," for departure dates and times). This is a great option for anyone thinking about visiting Patagonia, but it is not recommended for travelers with a limited amount of time in Chile and a desire to see a multitude of sites. Navimag's ship, M/N *Puerto Edén,* is a passenger and freight ferry with a variety of cabins, none of them, however, the height of luxury. The cruise is not only unforgettable for the spectacular views it offers, but also for the camaraderie that occurs among the passengers. The journey goes through fjords, channels, and past coves, and one unfortunate, several-hour crossing of the Golfo de Penas, or "Gulf of Grief," where, depending on climatic conditions, passengers may experience seasickness (if you are prone to this, consider taking anti-seasickness medication).

The *Puerto Edén* leaves Puerto Montt every Monday and arrives at Puerto Natales on Thursday. Cabin prices include all meals. Check to see if your cabin has a private bathroom and interior or exterior windows (which might not be an issue if you're out of the room all day). You may have to share with strangers unless you fork over the entire price of a Cabina Armador (about $1,745 for two). The most deluxe accommodations go for about $550 per person, triple occupancy, then $350 per person, quadruple occupancy. Prices drop from here, but be forewarned that the very cheapest bunks are booked by young travelers and are separated by curtains, and many are close to the engine room and get stuffy and incredibly noisy. Also note that the low-season (April to August) prices drop substantially; a cabin, for example, is $350 per person, double occupancy.

FERRY SERVICES Puerto Montt is the hub for all ferry companies. If you are planning a trip down the Carretera Austral, you'll need to travel to or from Puerto Montt by ferry (unless you enter through Argentina). During the summer, passengers and autos can cross into Pumalín Park and Caleta Gonzalo by ferry. This route is preferred, but available only from December to March. For information about ferry crossings to Caleta Gonzalo, see the section on Pumalín Park in chapter 14.

Throughout the year, Transmarchilay and Navimag offer service to Chaitén from Puerto Montt, and Transmarchilay also goes to Chaitén from Quellón, Chiloé.

Rumors have circulated that a new company called **Detroit** is planning to introduce speedy service from Puerto Montt to Chaitén aboard a catamaran. At press time, there was no information available, but you might want to check with the visitor's center.

Navimag's (see above) ferries to **Chaitén** leave once a week (usually Fridays) from March 15 to November, and three times per week during the summer; call for days because they tend to vary. The trip takes 10 hours, and costs $15 per person for the right to stay in the salon with tables and chairs, or $20 per person for a semi-reclining seat.

Transmarchilay, in Puerto Montt at Av. Angelmó 2187, Terminal de Transbordadores (☎ **65/270416**), offers ferry crossings to **Chaitén** aboard the ship *Pincoya* leaving Mondays at noon and Tuesdays, Thursdays, and Fridays at 9pm for $17 per passenger and an additional $75 for autos (prices are set to increase slightly for the high season January to February); the trip takes 10 hours and passengers sleep in reclining seats. Shorter ferry rides also leave from Quellón, Chiloé to Chaitén in January and February only on Monday, Wednesday, and Friday at 3pm; fares are about $20 per person and $100 per vehicle.

13 Chiloé

The "Grand Island of Chiloé" is a land of myths and magic—of emerald, rolling hills shrouded in mist and picturesque bays lined with brightly painted fishing boats. Residents here live in *palafitos,* rickety and charming shingled houses with corrugated roofs that rise above the water on stilts. Throughout the region, lovely wooden churches modeled after a Bavarian, neoclassic style appear like a beacon in every cove.

Visually appealing as it is, Chiloé is truly defined by its people, the hardy, colorful Chilotes who can still be seen plowing their fields with oxen or pulling in their catch of the day the same way they have done for centuries. Spanish conquistadors occupied Chiloé as early as 1567, followed by Jesuit missionaries and Spanish refugees pushed off the mainland by Mapuche Indian attacks. For 3 centuries Chiloé was the only Spanish stronghold south of the Bío Bío River, and its isolation produced a singular culture among its residents who, after so much time, are now a *mestizo* blend of Indian and Spanish blood. The Chilotes' rapid and closed speech, local slang, , mythical folklore, and style of food, tools, and architecture was and still is uniquely different from their counterparts on the mainland. The downside of Chiloé's extremely limited contact with the outside world is a dire poverty that has affected (and continues to affect) many of the island's residents. Most residents live in pastoral settings, and each family typically has its own small farm and basic livestock, most of the animals of which can usually be seen pecking and grazing along the side of the road. Here it is as common to see residents traveling on horseback or by fishing skiff as it is by vehicle.

The rectangular body of Chiloé and the tiny islands on the eastern shore that complete the archipelago render it South America's second-largest island, bordered by the Pacific Ocean on the west and the Gulf of Ancud on the east. Chiloé's principal cities are **Ancud** in the north, **Castro** on the island's eastern shore, and **Quellón** at the southern tip, and visitors can take a recommended short ferry ride to **Isla Quinchao.** Chiloé also boasts the **Parque Nacional de Chiloé** on the western shore. The island's tourism infrastructure is improving, but as of yet visitors should expect to find modest accommodations, usually within old homes or in simple hotels.

Chiloé

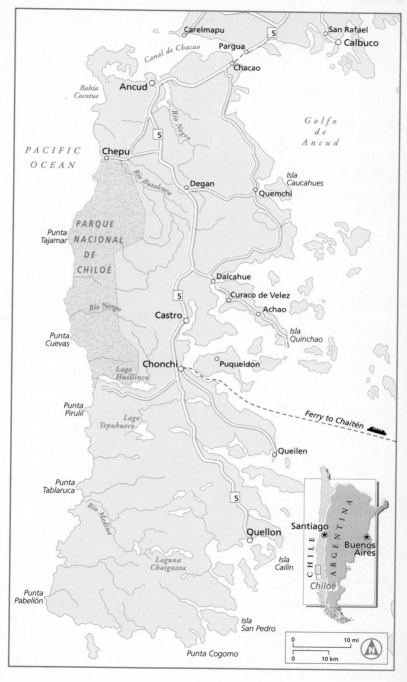

Carelmapu

Canal de Chacao

Pargua

5

San Rafael

Calbuco

Chacao

Bahía
Cocotue

Ancud

Golfo
de
Ancud

Río Negro

5

PACIFIC
OCEAN

Chepu

Río Butalcura

Degan

Isla
Caucahues

Quemchi

Punta
Tajamar

PARQUE
NACIONAL
DE
CHILOÉ

Río Nango

Dalcahue

Curaco de Velez

Achao

5

Castro

Isla
Quinchao

Punta
Cuevas

Lago
Huillinco

Chonchi

Puqueldon

Punta
Pirulil

Lago
Tepuhueco

Ferry to Chaitén

Punta
Tablaruca

Río Medina

5

Queilen

Punta
Pabellón

Laguna
Chaiguata

Quellon

Santiago

CHILE

ARGENTINA

Buenos
Aires

Isla
Cailin

Chiloé

Isla
San Pedro

Punta Cogomo

0   10 mi

0   10 km

323

EXPLORING THE ISLAND

Most visitors use Castro as a central base for exploring the island, although the appealing town of Ancud (the island's largest city) warrants an overnight stay. Quellón is considered primarily a ferry departure point for Chaitén on the Carretera Austral (see chapter 14). On a clear day—not very often—one can see Volcán Osorno and the towering, snowcapped Andes in the distance.

You'll need a day to explore Castro, Dalcahue, and Achao, a day to see the national park, and a half-day to tour Ancud, with a stop in Chacao. If you're planning on doing a lot of hiking or camping at the national park, obviously you'll want to plan for more days.

1 Chiloé Essentials

GETTING TO THE ISLAND

BY BOAT   There's been talk of building a bridge between the mainland and Chiloé, but until then, two ferry companies operate continuously between Pargua (on the mainland) and Chacao (on the island), shuttling passengers and vehicles. If you are taking a bus to Chiloé, you won't need to worry about paying the fare because it's included in the price of the bus ticket, but if you've rented a car the cost is $12 one-way. The ride lasts about 40 minutes.

BY BUS   Several companies provide service to Ancud, Castro, and Quellón from Puerto Montt and even Santiago. In Puerto Montt, daily departures for Ancud and Castro leave from the bus terminal: **Cruz del Sur** (☎ **65/254731**), has 16 trips per day; **TransChiloé** (☎ **65/254934**) has 11 trips per day, as does **Queilen Bus** (☎ **65/621140**). From Puerto Varas, try **Cruz del Sur** at San Pedro 210, with 5 trips per day. **Cruz del Sur** (☎ **2/779-0607**) offers service from Santiago to Chiloé; the trip takes about 17 hours. Buses rides across the strait on the ferry; you can remain in your seat or step out and walk around.

GETTING AROUND THE ISLAND

Chiloé's beauty is best revealed by sightseeing with a car in order to stop along the way at historic churches and the many well-built lookout points throughout the archipelago. If it fits into your budget, consider joining a tour or renting a car in Puerto Montt or in Chiloé. In Ancud, car rental can be found at **Eben Ezer,** Copec Pudeto Bajo s/n (☎ **65/623793**). In Castro, car rental is at **ADS Rent A Car** at Esmeralda 260 (☎ **65/637373**). Local bus service from town to town is frequent and inexpensive. More information about bus service can be found in the sections for each specific town below.

Living off the Land: A Lodging Alternative

An interesting option for travelers is Chiloé's growing *agroturismo* (agricultural tourism) **industry,** which allows guests to lodge with a rural family and take part in daily activities such as farming and dairy production. The program is inexpensive, and it is an excellent way to learn about Chilote culture in depth, but understand that these are not luxury facilities, and most programs expect their guests to offer a hand with daily chores. Many travelers who have taken part in this program have remarked that it was one of the most fulfilling experiences of their trip. Of course, most families speak little or no English, so a basic knowledge of Spanish will help guests communicate more effectively with their hosts. For more information, contact **Fundación con Todos** in Ancud (☎ **65/622604;** fax 65/624062; e-mail: contodos@chilesat.net).

2 Ancud

59 miles (95km) SE of Puerto Montt; 91 miles (146km) N of Castro

Ancud is Chiloé's largest city, founded in 1767 as a defensive fort to monitor passing sea traffic to and from Cape Horn. It was for many years the capital of Chiloé until the provincial government pulled up stakes and moved to Castro in 1982. Ancud is a charming, rambling port town with about 23,000 residents, and it makes for a pleasant night's stay. Ancud is convenient for its proximity to Puerto Montt (but keep in mind that Castro is a more convenient base if you want to reach the island's outlying areas). This was the last Spanish outpost in Chile, and visitors can view the fort ruins here; there's also a good museum depicting Chilote history and culture.

GETTING THERE & DEPARTING   By Bus   For regular bus service from Puerto Montt to Ancud, see "Chiloé Essentials," above. Ancud has a central bus station, the **Terminal Municipal,** at the intersection of Avenida Aníbal Pinto and Marcos Vera; from here, you'll need to grab a taxi to get to the center of town, or a local bus headed toward the plaza. Frequent buses leave from this station for destinations such as Castro, Dalcahue, and Quellón; try **Cruz del Sur** (☎ 65/622265), **Transchiloé** (☎ 65/622876), or **Queilen Bus** (☎ 65/621140).

By Car   Ruta 5 is a well-paved road that links Ancud with nearly every city on the island.

ORIENTATION   Ancud is spread across a tiny peninsula, with the Canal de Chacao to the east and the Golfo de Quetalmahue to the west, and it is 17 miles (27km) from the Chacao ferry dock. The city is not laid out on a regular grid pattern, and its crooked streets might easily confuse anyone driving into the city. **Avenida Aníbal Pinto** is the main entrance road that funnels drivers into the center of town. Most visitors will find that all attractions are located within several blocks of the plaza.

VISITOR INFORMATION   Sernatur's office is on the plaza, at Libertad 655 (☎ 65/622800). It's open 8:30am to 8pm, Monday to Sunday during January and February; the rest of the year it's open Monday to Thursday 8:30am to 5:30pm and Friday 8:30am to 4:30pm, and closed on weekends.

SPECIAL EVENTS   From the second week in January to the last week of February, the city hosts the **"Different and Magical Summer of Ancud."** The event kicks off with classical music concerts and a 3-day food and folklore festival at the Arena Gruesa (third week in January) and a shore-fishing contest the second week of February, and culminates with a fireworks display, again in Arena Gruesa, the third week of February. For more information, call ☎ 65/622800.

FAST FACTS: ANCUD

Currency Exchange   There are no places to exchange money here, but there are a couple of ATMs on Ramírez near the plaza.
Ferry   Offices for the ferry company, Transmarchilay, for the Quellón-Chaitén connection, are next to the Sernatur office on the plaza at Libertad 669 (☎ 65/622317).
Hospital   The **hospital** is at A. Latorre 301 (☎ 65/622356).
Internet Access   On the Costanera, Salvador Allende 740 (no phone).
Laundry   Clean Center, Pudeto 45, half a block from the plaza.

WHAT TO SEE & DO

For boating excursions around Chiloé, try **Britt Austral Adventure** (☎ 65/625977 or 09/642-8936; e-mail: tours@austral-adventures.com). These North American and

British outfitters offer excursions by boat around Chiloé, as well as Pumalín Park. They also have excursions on land around the island.

○ Museo Regional de Ancud Audelio Bórquez Canobra. Libertad 370. ☎ **65/ 622413.** Admission $1 adults, 50¢ children. Jan–Feb Mon–Fri 11am–7:30pm, Sat–Sun 10am–7pm; Mar–Dec Mon–Fri 10am–6pm, Sat–Sun 10am–2pm.

This handsome, well-designed museum features a wide variety of exhibits related to the history and culture of Chiloé. The museum includes a large courtyard with sculptures depicting the mythological characters that form part of Chilote folklore, as well as a replica of the ship *Ancud* that claimed possession of the Strait of Magellan in 1843, and a replica of a thatched Chilote house. Inside, two salons offer interactive displays and a variety of archeological items, such as Indian arrowheads and nautical pieces, as well as displays explaining the farming and wool production techniques used by Chilotes. Temporary exhibits feature such themes as "Centuries of Textile Art in Chiloé."

Fuerte San Antonio. San Antonio and Cochrane (below Hostería Ancud). No phone. Free admission.

Built in 1770 and fortified with cannons aimed at the port entrance, Fort San Antonio was Spain's last stronghold in Chile after the War of Independence. The Spanish flag last flew here on January 19, 1826, and just 6 days later Peru's El Callao surrendered, ending Spanish rule in South America forever. If anything, Fort San Antonio is interesting for this fact, and for the sweeping ocean view the site affords.

SHOPPING

For a selection of regional handicrafts, including knitwear, baskets, and carved wooden utensils and crafts, try the **Centro Artesanal** in the Municipal Market (irregular hours, open late during the summer and to around 4pm during the winter). For superb smoked salmon and other local foodstuffs, stop on your way in or out of Chiloé at **Die Raucherkate,** a German-owned smokery located about 1 mile (2km) before the Chacao ferry dock (☎ **65/622990**).

WHERE TO STAY

Street parking is plentiful and free in Ancud.

Cabañas Las Golondrinas. Baquedano s/n, Balneareo Arena Gruesa, Ancud. ☎/fax **65/ 622823.** 5 cabañas, 2 bungalows, 7 apartments. TV TEL. $35 cabaña for 2, low season; $75 bungalow for 2, high season. AE, MC, V.

This is a great choice for travelers seeking a little independence as well as crashing views of the ocean. Las Golondrinas offers pleasant accommodations complete with kitchens. They include cabins with two bedrooms that sleep up to six (two sleep in the living area on *very* basic foam settees); bungalows with three bedrooms for up to six guests; and apartments that sleep four. All guest rooms sit precariously high on a cliff, about 30 feet up from the beach, and the complex is just 4 blocks from Ancud's plaza. The interiors are made of wood, with giant windows and decks.

Hospedaje Alto Bellavista. Calle Bellavista 449, Ancud. ☎ **65/622384.** 10 units. $19–$28 double. No credit cards.

The green-and-red Hotel Bellavista sits on a winding street a block up from downtown, in an old home with one of the kitschiest living rooms around, crammed with photos, wood carvings, and other fun knickknacks. The friendly owner offers clean but very modest accommodations. A steep stairwell leads to most of the rooms on the second floor, with a variety of double- and triple-bed arrangements, but the two rooms on the first floor are the perhaps the best of the lot, with crisper furnishings. There's a small eating area for breakfast.

Hostal Lluhay. Lord Cochrane 458, Ancud. ☎/fax **65/622656.** E-mail: lluhay@entelchile. net. 10 units. $18–$26 double. No credit cards.

This hostal is on a dirt road 1 block up from the pier, and it caters to a predominately international crowd; in fact, a giant sign in front welcomes guests in a dozen languages. Rooms are slightly dark and very humble, but many bathrooms have been newly tiled. The open lounge has a fireplace and a picture window that looks out onto the sea, which should make you overlook an occasional hole in the burgundy carpet. The couple who own the Lluhay couldn't be nicer, and they're eager to show off their 200-year-old piano and antique Victrola.

Hostería Ahui. Costanera 906, Ancud. ☎ **65/622415.** 18 units. $30 double. Kids stay free in parents' room. No credit cards.

The weatherbeaten, shingled facade of the Ahui would be appealing in a rustic sort of way if it weren't for the FOR SALE sign posted out front—which indicates a somewhat uncertain future for this barn of a hotel. The owner doesn't seem to be having much luck selling, so it's worth a shot to score one of the five sunny rooms that face the ocean. The simple rooms are what you'd expect for this price range, with average furnishings and beds. The hotel's size gives guests some breathing room, unlike many hostals in town. The staff is open to negotiating a lower price, especially in low season. There's a spacious, bright restaurant downstairs that tends to cater to large groups.

✪ **Hostería Ancud.** San Antonio 30, Ancud. ☎ **65/622340.** Fax 65/622350. www. panamericanhoteles.cl. E-mail: creservas@panamericanahoteles.cl. 24 units. TV TEL. $69–$97 double. AE, DC, MC, V.

Part of the Panamerican Hotel chain, the Hostería Ancud is the best option in this price range, especially for its location fronting the Gulf of Quetalmahue and next to the ruins of the old Fort San Antonio. All rooms come with a view of the ocean, as does the airy, split-level lounge and restaurant and the large outdoor deck. Rooms are somewhat tight, but offer quality comfort. The interior bedroom walls are made of polished alerce logs, and the lobby is adorned with wood carvings from the region. The hostería also has one of the better restaurants in town (see "Where to Dine," below) as well as a cozy bar with a giant fireplace.

✪ **Hotel Caulín.** Road to Caulín, 5.5 miles (9km) from port of Chacao. ☎ **65/267150.** Fax in Santiago 2/225-8697. 4 units, 13 cabañas. $40–$65 cabin. No credit cards.

This is the spot for anyone looking for a waterfront location outside town. The Hotel Caulín has a dining area and four comfortable rooms in a pretty, antique home, but what's really nice are the cabins, eight of which sit 100 feet from the shore and five that sit high on a bluff. This lodging option is really better for those with a private vehicle because the hamlet of Caulín is about 15.5 miles (25km) from Ancud, although taxi service is available for a moderate cost. All cabins look out over a splendid estuary, and they are backed by forest. Each cabin is named after a local tree, and all feature two bedrooms, one with a full-size bed and the other with a twin and bunkbed. The spacious living area has wood floors and is warmed by a *cancahua,* a ceramic fireplace typical of the region. The interiors are attractive with tweedy bedspreads and curtains, and there's a fully stocked kitchen. The Hotel Caulín also has a restaurant (and there's another down the beach), summer swimming pool, tennis court, sauna, and pool table, and offers horseback riding.

I "Sea-food" Everywhere: What to Eat on Chiloé

Part of Chiloé's appeal is the wide variety of seafood available around the island's shores and the typical dishes found only here on the island. Below are a few regional specialties to keep an eye out for:

Cancato   Salmon stuffed with sausage, tomatoes, and cheese and steamed in tinfoil.

Carapacho   A rich crab "casserole" with a breaded crust.

Curanto   Perhaps the most famous dish here in Chiloé, traditionally prepared in a hole in the ground (similar to a New England clambake). First, hot rocks are placed in the hole and then layered with mussels, clams, beef, pork, chicken, sausage, and potatoes and topped off with chewy pancakes called ***milcaos.*** Of course, most restaurants cook this dish in a pot, and often call it ***pulmay;*** it is then served with a cup of broth.

Hotel Galeón Azul. Av. Pedro Montt 228, Ancud. ☎ **65/632359.** Fax 65/632808. 16 units. $77–$96 double. No credit cards.

Like the Hostería Ancud, this hotel's strength is its location—perched high on a cliff above the sea—and although the rooms are not as nice, some travelers prefer the character of this bed-and-breakfast more than the Ancud. With porthole windows, a nautical motif, and curved walls, the big, sunflower-yellow hotel feels somewhat like a ship; upstairs an intriguing, narrow hallway has a high ceiling that peaks into skylights. The hotel is next to the regional museum; large windows look out onto the museum's sculpture garden. The rooms are so-so, with dated furnishings and walls that look suspiciously as though made of plywood; the small bathrooms could also use a face-lift. The most attractive part of the hotel is its sunny restaurant, with glass walls that look out onto the ocean.

WHERE TO DINE

For good, inexpensive seafood meals, including Chilote dishes such as *curanto, carapacho,* and *cancato*, try **La Pincoya** at Av. Prat 61 (☎ **65/622613**), which also offers great views of fishermen at the pier engaging in hectic business from their colorful fishing skiffs. One restaurant popular with tourists and locals alike is **Sacho** (no phone), which can be found inside the market. Across from the market is **El Cangrejo** (no phone), which specializes in crab *carapacho* and features walls covered in graffiti and business cards. Another good bet is **Kurantón** at Prat 94 (☎ **65/622216**), which, as the name implies, specializes in *curanto.* None of the restaurants here get busy enough to warrant making reservations.

Galeón Azul. Av. Pedro Montt 228. ☎ **65/632359.** Main courses $5–$10. No credit cards. Daily 11am–3pm and 7–11pm. CHILEAN.

The Galeón's dining area is painted as yellow as its exterior, and it offers great views, so be sure to get a table that sits up against the front windows. The menu here features several Chilote specials such as *curanto,* as well as the standard Chilean fish and meat grilled and served with a choice of sauces. Try the salmon stuffed with ham and mushrooms or the garlicky *locos* (abalone).

Hostería Ancud. San Antonio 30. ☎ **65/622340.** Main courses $7–$10. AE, DC, MC, V. Daily noon–11pm. INTERNATIONAL/CHILEAN.

The semi-elegant dining area here commands a superb view of the ocean, and there's a good offering from the menu that mixes Chilean specialties with international dishes. Seafood such as oysters on the half shell and king crab are offered as appetizers, as well as king crab casserole and conger eel with sea urchin sauce. Meat dishes include pork loin with mustard sauce and risotto. There's also a bar for a quiet evening drink. If weather permits, you can watch the sunset from the deck.

✪ **Ostras Caulín.** On the shore in Caulín. ☎/fax **09-643-7005**. Main courses $8–$15. AE, DC, MC, V. Daily noon–10pm (until midnight Jan–Feb). CHILEAN.

Oyster lovers should not miss this tiny restaurant on the shore of Caulín, about 5.5 miles (9km) from Chacao and 15.5 miles (25km) from Ancud (follow the signs and turn right onto a gravel road). The restaurant sits on an estuary, where they farm their own oysters, and they offer three sizes: *especial, extra,* and *exportación,* all on the half shell and all exceptionally fresh. The menu is limited, offering just oysters or a fixed-price meal that serves 15 oysters, followed by a bowl of oyster chowder, a plate of roast beef and potatoes, and dessert for about $15. It's a lot of food, so you might consider splitting a fixed meal. The service here is attentive, and the dining area has a nice view. This is a pleasant place to stop off on your way in or out of Chiloé, but you'll need your own car or a taxi to get here.

3 Castro

91 miles (146km) S of Ancud; 61 miles (99km) N of Quellón

Castro is spread across a promontory on the western shore of Chiloé, midway from Ancud and Quellón. It is the capital of Chiloé and Chile's third-oldest city, boasting a population of about 20,600 inhabitants. Visitors to the island often choose Castro as a base for its central proximity to a host of attractions. But the town has a charm all its own, with its city church brightly painted like an Easter egg, and the city's colorful homes on stilts, known as *palafitos.*

ESSENTIALS
GETTING AROUND   By Bus   You'll find the bus terminal at the corner of Esmerelda and Sotomayor. For buses to Dalcahue and Isla Quinchao, take **Buses Arriagada** at San Martín 681; for Dalcahue and Chonchi, take **Colectivos** from the Terminal Municipal; for Isla Lemuy, take **Buses Gallardo** from its office at San Martín 681; and for transportation to the national park, take **Buses Arroyo** or **Buses Ojeda** from the Terminal Municipal. The majority of these bus companies are independently owned and operated, so it's difficult to obtain reliable information about schedules and fares in advance. I recommend showing up at the terminal or checking at the tourist information kiosk (see "Visitor Information," below) to ask questions or book a tour.

By Car   To get to Castro from Ancud, head south on the island's only highway for 146km (88 miles), and from Quellon, north on the highway for 59 miles (99km).

VISITOR INFORMATION   A tiny, privately run **tourism kiosk** on the main plaza offers a fairly poor selection of information. During the summer, the kiosk is open all day, but during the winter it can close unexpectedly.

SPECIAL EVENTS   Every February, for 1 week, Castro hosts one of the more interesting events in Chile, the **Festival Costumbrista Chilote,** a celebration of the unique Chilote culture, history, and mythical folklore that make up Chiloé. The festival highlights the island's gastronomy, played out through expositions and booth after booth selling mouth-watering samples of *curanto, yoco, licor de oro,* and more. There are also demonstrations of the giant wooden press used to make *chicha,* an alcohol usually made from fermented apples. For more information, call ☎ **65/632289.**

FAST FACTS: CASTRO

Currency Exchange   **Julio Barrientos,** Chacabuco 286 (☎ **65/635079**), is open Monday to Friday 9am to 12pm and 3 to 7pm; Saturday 9am to 12pm; from December to March they do not close for lunch.

Hospital   **Hospital Agusta Rifat,** Freie 852 (☎ **65/632444**).

Internet Access   Café de la Brújula, O'Higgins 308 (☎ **65/633229**); open daily 10am to midnight.

Laundry   **Clean Center,** Serrano 490 (☎ **65/633132**).

Travel Agency   Lan Chile's representative is **Pehuén Expediciones,** Blanco 229 (☎ **65/635254**); open Monday to Friday 9am to 1:30pm and 3 to 7pm, Saturday 10am to 1pm, closed Sunday.

WHAT TO SEE & DO IN CASTRO

You might begin a tour of Castro at the plaza and the neo-Gothic **Iglesia de San Francisco** church, painted brightly in peach, lilac, and white. It's impossible to miss, and that's really the point; this 1912 national monument always stands out, especially on dreary, gray Chiloé days (which is pretty much three quarters of the year).

From there, head down Esmerelda toward the waterfront and drop by the town's small **Museo Regional de Castro,** half a block from the plaza (☎ **65/635967**). It's open January to February Monday to Saturday 9:30am to 8pm and Sunday 10:30am to 1pm; March to December, Monday to Friday 9:30am to 1pm and 3 to 6:30pm, Saturday 9:30am to 1pm, and closed on Sunday. The museum features displays of Chilote farming and household wooden implements, such as plows and weaving looms; religious icons; Indian artifacts such as arrowheads, bones, and *boleadores;* as well as an interesting photographic exhibit of the damage done to Castro after the 1960 earthquake and flood.

Castro's main attraction would have to be its *palafitos,* colorful houses built near the shore but atop stilts over water. There are four main spots to view these architectural oddities. The first two sites are at the town entrance, the third site is on the coast at the end of San Martín, and the fourth is at the cove of the Castro Fjord, on the way out of town on Ruta 5. Residents are often baffled as to why tourists find these dwellings so fascinating because locally they are considered Castro's "ghetto," occupied by poor folk with questionable sanitary conditions.

A short taxi ride will take you to the **Parque Municipal,** home to the Costumbrista Festival in February and the surprisingly well-designed **Museo de Arte Moderno** (MAM) (☎ **65/635454**). Admission is free, and it's open January and February, Daily 10am to 6pm; December and March 11am to 2pm; April to October closed, although they might open for a private viewing if you call ahead. If the weather is clear, visitors to the park are treated to superb views of Castro and the Andes. The Museum of Modern Art, housed in several renovated shingled buildings, is one of the only contemporary art museums in the country, and it often hosts exhibitions by some of Chile's most prominent artists.

SHOPPING

The **Fería Artesanal,** on Lillo at the port, brings together dozens of artisans who offer a superb selection of handknitted woolen goods and handicrafts. Here you'll find the island's typical tightly woven ponchos; the raw wool used makes them water resistant. Vendors open their booths independently, and hours are roughly from 10am to 5pm from April to November, and 10am to 9pm from December to March.

WHERE TO STAY

Hotel parking is provided, with the possible exception of a few of the most expensive hotels on Chiloé. In any case, street parking is plentiful and also free.

Hostal Casablanca. Los Carrera 308, Castro. ☎ /fax **65/632726.** 10 units, 3 cabañas. TV. $28–$45 cabaña. No credit cards. Parking available.

This hostal has characterless rooms that are too confined, but the cabañas in the back are worth checking out. The three colorful, attached rooms sit on stilts on a lot behind the hostal, and they are surrounded by homes built of bright metal siding, but it's not unattractive and the lot is very quiet. The cabins are for three to four guests, and they come with fully equipped kitchens. Guests park under the cabañas on a gravel lot. The owner often rents out one or all three of the cabañas to long-term executives working in the salmon fisheries during the winter, so they might not be available during that time.

✪ **Hostal Kolping.** Chacabuco 217, Castro. ☎ /fax **65/633263.** 11 units. TV TEL. $23–$37 double. No credit cards.

This hostal is a great value in this price range, and really the best place to stay if you're looking for inexpensive lodging. The rooms are sunny and immaculately clean, and they come with beds with thick foam mattresses that are adequately comfortable. There's not much to report on the style of the rooms, as they are all nondescript, but they are reasonably spacious and so are the bathrooms. The exteriors are attractive, with a newly replaced shingled facade; they also covered the deck, thereby creating a bright dining area and wide foyer. A German company owns this and other Kolping hostals around the Lake District, including the Termas de San Luis, and they can be relied on for economical, quality lodging.

✪ **Hostería Castro.** Chacabuco 202, Castro. ☎ **65/632301.** Fax 65/635688. 29 units. TV TEL. $60–$75 double. AE, DC, MC, V. Parking available.

This hostería is about as upscale as hotels get in Castro. Built in 1970, the hotel has done a decent job of maintaining the place, but a slight renovation wouldn't hurt, as evidenced by the dated leather sofas and end tables with faded glass rings. The bar and its giant cast-iron fireplace contributes to the warm atmosphere. The hotel overlooks the ocean, and all rooms on the eastern side (rooms ending in odd numbers) have views of the water; rooms on the western side have a leafy view of a stand of trees. It's important to note that rooms are very cramped, so much so that it is hard to walk around the bed. A few are slightly more spacious for the same price, so be sure to ask for one. The white-tiled bathrooms are ample. The A-frame, shingled roof has a skylight in the form of a glass band that runs through the roof's middle, letting in a cascade of light that brightens the interior hallways even on overcast days. Service is exceptionally friendly, and the hotel administrator is also a fishing guide willing to share angling information.

Dining/Diversions: Revelers may enter through the hotel's basement door to the small bar/disco **Public,** which is actually fairly entertaining and appeals to a wide, 25- to 50-year-old age group. The **Las Araucarias** restaurant is reviewed separately (see "Where to Dine," below).

Amenities: Laundry, room service, conference center, gift shop selling Patagonia-brand outdoor clothing, post office.

Hotel Casita Española. Los Carrera 359, Castro. ☎ /fax **65/635186.** 13 units. TV TEL. $27–$44 double. AE, MC, V. Parking available.

All 13 rooms are exactly the same here, set up motel-like with two stories. The lobby faces the street, but the rooms are reached via a pretty walkway sandwiched between a tall residential building and the hotel. You won't be wowed when you walk into your room, but the quality is about par for the price: average, thick foam mattresses, drab but decent decor, a tiny desk used primarily as a TV stand, and okay bathrooms with tubs. There's an eating area next to the reception area for breakfast.

Unicornio Azul. Pedro Montt 228, Castro. ☎ **65/632359.** Fax 65/632808. 17 units. TV TEL. $45–$75 double. No credit cards.

Many people say this is the best place to stay in Castro—but I'll let you be the judge. It's a fun place to stay, but don't expect regal comfort. Certainly the hotel has character, housed as it is in a pretty Victorian on the waterfront and with funky interiors decorated with framed prints of unicorns. But the quality the Unicornio Azul seems to promise from the lobby falls short once you step into the rooms. The best rooms sit high above the main building facing out toward the water, and they come with tiny balconies and wooden floors. But they're unremarkable, and no elevators and a long flight of stairs means it's a hike to get to them. Downstairs rooms are darker but carpeted, and a few come with bathtubs. The hotel was built in 1910 and renovated in 1986—both "Years of the Comet," as the staff likes to say. The exterior is painted as pink as a Mary Kay Cadillac, and much of the wooden beams and floor-runner carpets are sugary shades of pink too. The owners of this hotel also own Ancud's Galeón Azul.

Dining: A bar/restaurant housed in the living and dining area of this old Victorian home serves everything from hamburgers to filet mignon, as well as seafood, and they have a kid's menu.

WHERE TO DINE

Café La Brújula del Cuerpo. O'Higgins 308. ☎ **65/633229.** Main courses $5–$7; sandwiches $2.50–$5. MC, V. Daily 10am–midnight. CAFE.

This sizeable cafe on the plaza (the name translates as "the Body's Compass") is the social center for residents of Castro. It's perennially active for its friendly service and extensive menu that offers sandwiches, salads, main dishes, ice cream, desserts, espresso, and delicious fresh juices. The cafe/restaurant is open all day, and you'll often find travelers writing out postcards here. There's one computer for Internet use, just about the only public site in town.

Del Mirador. Blanco 388. ☎ **65/633958.** Main courses $4–$10. AE, DC, MC, V. Daily 10am–midnight. CHILEAN.

This restaurant has probably the longest and most creative menu in Castro, offering dishes such as chicken in cherry sauce. You can order just about any kind of meat or fish and bathe it in a choice of 15 sauces, including nut, crab, or sea urchin sauce. The atmosphere is family-style, and there's a TV blaring in one of the dining areas. Del Mirador also serves pizza, sandwiches, pasta, and afternoon teas. Not much here in terms of traditional Chilote food.

Las Araucarias. Chacabuco 202. ☎ **65/632301.** Fax 65/635688. Main courses $5.50–$11. AE, DC, MC, V. Mon–Sat noon–midnight; Sun Dec 15–Mar 15 only, noon–11pm. INTERNATIONAL/CHILEAN.

Las Araucarias is Hostería Castro's restaurant, and is one of the top places to dine in town. The atmosphere is better during lunchtime, with the view and the airy interiors brought on by the two-story-high ceilings and a wall of windows; at night the dining room's size seems to encourage echoes, but it is comfortable nevertheless. The menu is steak and seafood, and it features Chilean classics and Chiloé specialties such as *carapacho* and *curanto*. Other delicious seafood dishes offered are crab casserole, sea-urchin omelets, and garlicky squid. There's also a wide selection of meat dishes, such as filet mignon wrapped in bacon and served with sautéed vegetables. You might want to call ahead, as the hotel often has a buffet special (usually on weekends) that is usually themed (German food, for example), and although it is quite good, it might not be what you're in the mood for.

✪ **Octavio.** Pedro Montt 261. ☎ **65/632855.** Main courses $6–$7. No credit cards. Daily 10am–midnight. CHILEAN.

Octavio has the best atmosphere in Castro, with an idyllic, airy dining area that sits directly over the water, and a panorama of windows to enjoy the view. It also has a woodsy, shingled exterior and interior. Octavio is a great place to come for Chilote specials—it's known around town for its *curanto*. It also serves seafood specials such as *mariscal,* a shellfish stew made with onion and cilantro, and other typical Chilean dishes, such as breaded cutlets and filet mignon. Simple menu and simple food, but all very good, and a few sandwiches and soups. Octavio is typically more popular with visitors to Castro, while Sacho (see below) is more popular with locals.

Restaurant Palafito. Lillo 30. ☎/fax **65/635476.** Main courses $5–$8. No credit cards. Daily noon–11pm. SEAFOOD/CHILEAN.

Another restaurant with a waterfront view—but this restaurant is a *palafito,* perched over the water on stilts. Although not as stylish as the Octavio, it does offer more seafood dishes. It's pretty standard fare, though, such as conger eel and salmon grilled or fried with an assortment of side dishes and salads.

✪ **Sacho.** Thompson 213. ☎ **65/632079.** Main courses $4.50–$8. No credit cards. Daily noon–4pm and 8pm–midnight. SEAFOOD/CHILEAN.

Sacho serves the best cuisine in Castro, a fact clearly evident by the throngs of locals who patronize the restaurant daily. There are two seating areas, neither of which is particularly eye-catching, but the upstairs dining room at least has large windows and a view. The specialty here is seafood, and they serve the cheapest abalone *locos* I've seen anywhere in Chile. Try starting off with a plate of clams Sacho raw, steamed, or broiled and served with onion, lemon, whisky, and Parmesan, then follow it up with a *cancato*. The Monday through Friday basic fixed lunch is $6, and the executive fixed lunch is $9.50, which includes wine. Typically the only fish served here is conger eel and salmon, but they do have hake and sea bass from December to March.

4 Excursions Outside Castro

Few Chilean towns supersede the charming beauty of **Dalcahue, Achao,** and **Curaco de Vélez,** the latter two located on the **Isla Quinchao.** The towns and the country-side separating them are Chiloé highlights, offering gorgeous scenery and a glimpse into the Chilote's culture and day-to-day life.

DALCAHUE & ISLA QUINCHAO

Just off of Route 5, the island's only major highway, **Dalcahue** is a little town whose prosperity is best illustrated by the hustle and bustle of salmon industry workers at the pier, unloading and loading crates of fish byproducts to be processed. Dalcahue's other thriving industry (although to a smaller scale) is its **Fería Artesenal,** located at the waterfront about 2 blocks southwest of the plaza. Every Thursday and, especially, Sunday, artisans come to Dalcahue from the surrounding area to hawk their knitwear, baskets, hand-carved wood items, clothing, and more. During the summer, increased tourism usually draws Chilote musicians who play in front of the Port Municipal building. At the plaza you'll have a chance to view another of the island's famous parochial churches. This particular attractive church features a scalloped portico and is one of the largest in Chiloé. Across the plaza, on the corner, you'll find the **Museo Histórico Arqueológico Etnográfico** (no phone); it's open daily 10am to 6pm, with a cluttered array of stuffed birds, Indian and colonial-era artifacts.

For directions to Dalcahue, see "Essentials" under Castro, above. All transportation stops in Dalcahue first, before crossing over to Quinchao.

Several blocks away at Dalcahue's pier, you'll find the ferry to **Isla Quinchao,** a 5-minute ride, which crosses every day and almost continuously from 7am to 10:30pm ($3 for cars, $3.50 for pickup trucks). This is one of Chiloé's most-populated and loveliest islands, a magical landscape of plump, rolling hills where smoke slowly wafts from picturesque, wooden homes, and Chilote farmers can be seen tilling their land with oxen and a plow. The island also affords the visitor with spectacular views of the Gulf of Ancud and the scattered, pint-sized islands that sit between the Isla Quinchao and the mainland.

The first town you'll encounter upon exiting the ferry is **Curaco de Vélez,** a historic village whose former prosperity brought about by wool production and whaling can be witnessed through the grand, weatherbeaten homes that line the streets. The homes are characterized by a great variety of shingle styles, from concave to convex, circular to triangular. The town's antique church unfortunately burned to the ground in 1971.

Continue southeast along the island's single, unnamed main road to **Achao,** a former Jesuit colony founded in 1743 that features the oldest church in Chiloé. Made entirely of cypress, alerce, and mañío, this church appears as plain as a brown paper bag from the outside, but one step inside and all impressions change due to its multi-colored interiors and whimsical decorations. Throughout the Island of Quinchao, you'll find wooden gazebos atop well-designed lookout points. Here's hoping the weather allows you to take full advantage of them.

PARQUE NACIONAL CHILOÉ

Chiloé National Park, on the western coast of Chiloé, covers 43,000 hectares (106,210 acres) and is divided into three sectors: **Chepu, Islote Metalqui,** and **Anay,** the latter of which is connected by a dirt road that branches off Ruta 5, about 15 miles (24km) south of Castro. For transportation to the national park, take **Buses Arroyo** or **Buses Ojeda** (no phone) from the Terminal Municipal. The park is wild and wet—very, very wet. Many backpackers come in the summer to hike through the park's primordial forest and along vast stretches of sandy beach that often peak into sand dunes

Visitors first arrive at the tiny village of **Cucao,** the gateway to the national park, which was devastated by a 1960 tidal wave; today it is a collection of rickety homes. **Posada Darwin** (☎ **65/633040**), closed June and July, is a restaurant that serves pizzas and seafood and offers inexpensive cabañas. Across the suspension bridge visitors will find the park interpretation center run by Conaf (Chile's national park service), which has environmental displays and information about hiking trails. From here hikers have an option of three trails. The short, 839-yard (770m) **Sendero el Tepual** winds through thick, humid tepú forest. The **Sendero Dunas de Cucao** is about ½ mile (1km), and it passes alternately through dense vegetation and open stretches of sand dunes. The most beautiful hike is a 20km (12-mile) backpacking route via a long trail on the coast, which weaves in and out of evergreen forest and sandy beach until arriving at Conaf's backcountry refuge, **Cole.** From here it's another 2 hours to

Conaf's other refuge, **Anay.** Parque Nacional Chiloé has a variety of campsites, and it is open every day 9am to 7pm; admission is $1 adults, children free. While here, keep your eyes open for the miniature deer (*pudú*).

GUIDED TOURS AND OTHER ACTIVITIES

Pehuén Turismo at Thompson 229 (☎ **65/635254;** e-mail: pehuentr@entelchile. net) offers a huge variety of tours in the area, including hiking in the national park, guided visits to Dalcahue and Achao, horseback riding, boat tours, and overflight tours that give passengers an aerial view of the island. It's really the most complete tour agency; however, **Queilén Travels** at Gamboa 502 (☎ **65/632594**) also offers guided tours around the area.

14 The Carretera Austral

South of Puerto Montt the population thins and the vegetation thickens. This is La Carretera Austral, or the Southern Highway, Chile's wettest and wildest region—a region that has only recently opened itself up to the traveling public. The Carretera Austral is a 620-mile (1,000km) dirt and gravel road that bends and twists through scenery so primeval, you often feel as though you are the first explorer to pass through here: thick, virgin rainforest; glacial-fed rivers and aquamarine lakes; jagged, white-capped peaks that rise above open valleys; and precipitous cliffs with cascading ribbons of waterfalls at every turn. If you like your scenery remote and rugged, this is your place.

The Carretera Austral runs from **Puerto Montt** in the north to **Puerto Yungay** in the south, and passes through two regions: the southern portion of the **Región Los Lagos** and the **Región Aisén**, whose capital city **Coyhaique** is home to more than half the population in the area. Apart from Coyhaique, the region was previously accessible from other locations only by ferry or plane, and vehicles servicing the tiny villages and fishing hamlets that make up the area's civilization had to enter from Argentina. It's no wonder they call it the "last frontier."

The road exists thanks to ex-dictator Augusto Pinochet, whose paranoia of Argentine encroachment convinced him that a road would fortify Chile's presence in this isolated region. Construction of the Carretera Austral began in 1976, with the first leg completed in 1983. The second leg, which connected the Aysén region to Puerto Montt, was completed in 1988. The third leg, from Coyhaique to Puerto Yungay in the south, was only completed in 1996. Considering the scant population this road serves, critics have likened Pinochet's Carretera to a white elephant, for the road's staggering cost both in price ($300 million dollars and counting) and in the lives of more than two dozen men. Either way, the dictator unwittingly created one of the most appealing travel destinations in Chile.

1 Driving the Carretera Austral

Although it is possible to reach most destinations in this region by ferry, bus, or plane, road improvements and an expansion of services mean an increasing number of travelers are choosing to drive the Carretera Austral. If you're a fan of road trips or a photo buff, you'll relish the opportunity to explore and shoot this magnificent region at your own pace—something you can't do from a bus. It's not as enormous an undertaking as it sounds, but it can be costly, especially when you factor in the cost of ferry rides, drop-off fees, and gas.

Several agencies in Puerto Montt and Coyhaique offer one-way car rentals, and some allow you to cross into Argentina or leave the car as far away as Punta Arenas, Chile. (See the box "Renting a Car for Local Trips & for the Carretera Austral" in chapter 12, "The Chilean Lake District," for details on renting a car in Puerto Montt.) Alternatively, you could rent a car in Coyhaique and drive north, stopping in Puyuhuapi and on to Futaleufú. Although you'd have to backtrack to Coyhaique to return the car, this is a less expensive option. (See the section "Coyhaique," below, for information on renting a car.)

The most troublesome considerations are flat tires, gas shortages, and foul weather, any of which can strike at any time. With advance preparation, however, these obstacles can be overcome.

FERRY CROSSINGS   The trip from Puerto Montt to Caleta Gonzalo or Chaitén requires a ferry crossing (in operation from December to March only). For crossings to Caleta Gonzalo, see "Ferry Crossings to Caleta Gonzalo" below under "Parque Nacional Alerce Andino." See "Ferry Crossings to the Carretera Austral & Sailing to Patagonia Through the Fjords" in chapter 12 for information on ferries to Chaitén.

GAS   Service stations can be found at reasonable intervals, and some smaller towns such as Futaleufú sell gas in jugs from stores or private residences, but most travelers take precautions by carrying a backup canister of fuel. Canisters can be purchased from any service station.

CROSSING INTO ARGENTINA   Drivers who head into Argentina must prove that they are the owner of their car, or have their rental agency set up the proper paperwork to show they are driving a rental car. Make sure to ask your rental agency about this. Drivers must fill out a detailed form and are then given a copy to carry with them until crossing back into Chile.

ROAD CONDITIONS   The Carretera Austral is made entirely of dirt and gravel, which can get slippery during a storm. A 4×4 vehicle is not entirely necessary, but it can be of help, especially if you plan to travel during the time of year when snowfall is a possibility. Giant potholes are the exception, not the norm, but they can cause a car to spin out or even flip if driving too fast. For this reason, drivers are cautioned to keep speed between 40kmph (25 m.p.h.) and 60kmph (37 m.p.h.). When it's wet or the road curves, you need to slow down even more.

HITCHHIKERS   Road courtesy dictates that you might have to pick up a hitchhiker or two along the way. Most hitchhikers are humble, local folk who simply do not have the means to get from place to place (during the summer many foreign backpackers try to get a lift, too). Use your own judgment. You should always lend a hand to anyone whose car has broken down.

GETTING AROUND BY BUS

There's inexpensive, frequent summer service and intermittent winter service to and from destinations along the Carretera Austral for those who choose not to drive. It takes longer, and you won't have the opportunity to stop at points of interest along the way; however, every town has a tour operator that can usually get you to outlying sites for day trips. Also, the breathtaking scenery never fails to dazzle, even if you can't get off the bus.

For the 5-hour journey from Puerto Montt to Hornopirén (for the summer-only ferry to Caleta Gonzalo), take **Buses Fierro** (☎ 65/253600), which leaves from the main bus terminal three times daily. The bus makes one 30-minute ferry crossing before landing in Hornopirén (cost is $5). From there you take another ferry to Caleta Gonzalo, where buses meet ferry arrivals for the journey to Chaitén. Buses from Chaitén leave for Futaleufú an average of five to six times per week during the summer, and about three times per week during the winter.

Buses from Chaitén to Coyhaique, stopping first in Puyuhuapi, leave up to four times per week during the summer and twice per week during the winter. For information about buses from Chaitén, see "Getting There" under "Chaitén," below. Note that bus schedules are subject to change without notice.

2 Parque Nacional Alerce Andino

20mi (32km) SE of Puerto Montt

The Carretera Austral begins as Ruta 7, just outside the city limits of Puerto Montt, and follows the coast of Reloncaví Sound until it reaches **Parque Nacional Alerce Andino,** one of Chile's little-known national parks. This 39,255ha (96,960-acre) park is home to the *alerce,* which is often compared to the sequoia for its thick diameter and height. These venerable giants can live more than 3,000 years, making them the second-oldest tree, after the American bristlecone pine. The *alerce* was designated a national monument in 1976, and heavy fines are levied against anyone caught harming or cutting one down. Other species in the park include evergreen beech, *mañío, canelo, ulmo,* and thick crops of ferns. It can get pretty wet here year-round, so bring rain gear just in case.

The park itself is serviced by a rough dirt road that leads to a **Conaf guard station** in what's known as the **Chaica sector,** where there is a campground and the trailhead for the ½-hour round-trip walk to a waterfall and a fenced-off 3,000-year-old *alerce* tree. The walk to Lago Triángulo is about 6 miles (10km) from the campground. Roads, trails, and campgrounds are often washed out or impeded by falling trees.

Be sure to check the park's condition before heading out. For more information, contact the Conaf office in Puerto Montt at Ochagavía 464 (☎ **65/290712**).

The park's second sector at **Lago Chapo** also has campgrounds and two muddy trails for day hikes through the park's rainforest, a section of which has a thick stand of alerce trees. Though this sector sees fewer visitors, it is more difficult to get to if you do not have your own vehicle because buses go as far as the pueblo Correntoso, a two-hour walk from the park entrance (although it is possible to arrange a tour; see "Getting There," below). At the park ranger station here it is possible to rent canoes for a paddle across Lago Chapo.

GETTING THERE   If you're driving, head south on Ruta 7, winding past tiny villages on a gravel road until you reach Chaica, about 22 miles (35km) from Puerto Montt, where a sign indicates the road to the park entrance at the left. The park ranger station is open 9am to 5pm, so leave your car outside the gate if you plan to return later than 5pm. Travelers without a vehicle can take **Buses Fierro** (☎ 65/253600) headed in the direction of Hornopirén from the main terminal in Puerto Montt (ask to be dropped off at Chaica); however, the bus, which costs $1.10, leaves visitors at an entrance road 2½ miles (4km) from the park ranger station. You might consider hiring a tour operator to take a day trip or possibly to organize an advance pickup date if you plan to camp. To get to the Lago Chapo sector, head south on Ruta 7 for about 5½ miles (9km) to Chamiza where, just before the bridge, take a left toward the town

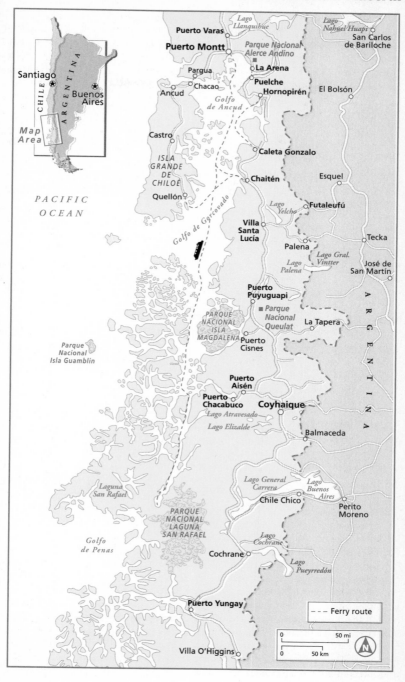

Correntoso and drive 12 miles (19km) to the park entrance. Buses Fierro (☎ **65/ 253600**) has several daily trips, costing $1, to Correntoso that leave from the main terminal in Puerto Montt, from here it's a two-hour walk to the park entrance. For tours to either of the park's sectors, try **Andina del Sud,** in Puerto Varas at Antonio Varas 437 (☎ **65/257797;** e-mail: crucedelagos@chilesat.net); the company also has an office in Puerto Montt, at del Salvador 72 (☎ **65/232811**).

WHERE TO STAY

✪ **Alerce Mountain Lodge.** Carretera Austral, Km36. ☎ /fax **65/286969.** www. mountainlodge.cl. E-mail: smontt@telsur.cl. 11 units, 3 cabañas. All-inclusive packages run per person, double occupancy: 2 nights/3 days $460; 3 nights/4 days $680; 4 nights/5 days $880. AE, DC, MC, V. Free parking.

If you're a forest lover looking for a quiet, remote lodge in the middle of the woods, this place is for you. The Alerce Mountain Lodge sits on the shore of a small lake—which must be crossed by a hand-drawn ferry—at the edge of the national park, and is surrounded by dense stands of stately, 1,000-year-old *alerce* trees. The company who built the Alerce initially bought the land to harvest dead trunks, but quickly saw the potential of building a lodge where people could trek, horseback ride, or just relax under a canopy of these towering trees.

The lodge is about an hour's drive from Puerto Montt (they provide transportation from there), and is built almost entirely of handcrafted *alerce* logs, with giant trunks acting as pillars in the spacious, two-story lobby. The woodsy effect continues in the cozy rooms, which are decorated with local crafts and feature windows looking out into the forest. The cabins have a view of the lake and come with a living room and two bedrooms, and accommodate a maximum of five guests. One of the highlights at this lodge is the virtual guarantee that you won't see anyone else, because the surrounding trails are not open to the general public. Bilingual guides lead horseback rides and day hikes that can last as long as 7 hours or ½ hour. The Alerce Mountain Lodge typically sees American and European visitors; many who come here enjoy the lodge's location so much that they end up staying an extra day or two.

FERRY CROSSINGS TO CALETA GONZALO

The portion of the Carretera Austral from Puerto Montt to Caleta Gonzalo crosses two bodies of water—meaning you'll have to make two ferry crossings, or get to Caleta Gonzalo by driving up from the south. The first ferry crossing from La Arena to Puelche runs year-round; unfortunately the second, from Hornopirén to Caleta Gonzalo, is available January and February only. This means that the rest of the year the only ways to get from Puerto Montt to Caleta Gonzalo are: to travel through Argentina, reenter Chile at Futaleufú and then drive north; or to take the year-round ferry from Puerto Montt to Chaitén (see chapter 12)—or the ferry from Quellón, in Chiloé (see chapter 13), to Chaitén—and then drive from Chaitén to Caleta Gonzalo.

Leaving from Chaica, south of Puerto Montt, the road continues for 8 miles (13km) to Caleta La Arena, departure and arrival point for the 30-minute ferry ride that connects with Caleta Puelche. **Transmarchilay** ferries, Av. Angelmó 2187, Puerto Montt (☎ **65/270416**), make about nine runs a day, from 8am to 9pm or so, depending on the season and any unforeseen changes. From Puelche it's a 33½-mile (54km) drive to Hornopirén, a pretty village that is the **summer ferry terminal** for trips to Caleta Gonzalo, in Pumalín Park. Transmarchilay offers service between Hornopirén and Caleta Gonzalo every day except Mondays and Fridays, leaving Hornopirén at 3pm and Caleta Gonzalo at 9am; the fare is $15 per person, $80 per car, and $100 per pickup truck.

3 Pumalín Park

The Pumalín Park Project, the world's largest private nature reserve, spans 750,000 acres (an almost contiguous 1,000 square miles) and incorporates a breathtaking landscape that includes temperate rainforest, glaciers, fjords, thundering waterfalls and rivers, and stands of ancient *alerce* trees. It's a marvelous place that exists thanks to American millionaire and philanthropist Douglas Thompkins, who made his fortune in fashion retailing before cashing in his stake and buying his first chunk of land here in 1991.

It was a controversial move. Although any nature-lover would think Thompkins did Chileans and the world a favor by spending his money on this ecological cause, the move did not sit well with the Chilean government. Understandably, the government was uneasy with the foreign ownership of so much land, especially because it stretched from the Pacific Ocean to the Argentine border. The controversy grew to almost absurd proportions while Thompkins and his wife Kristine fought to make their vision understood by the Chilean public.

Years have passed, the public and the government have slowly grown to accept the project, and today Pumalín boasts a growing number of visitors. Thompkins plans to eventually donate this park to the Fundación Pumalín, who will run it as a national park under a private initiative. The facilities are superb, and they clearly bear the stamp of contemporary American design, with exceptionally attractive cabins, well-groomed campgrounds, and a cafe selling tasty meals.

A soggy walk through this jungle, with its tall moss-draped trees choked by sinuous vines and its enormous, billowy ferns, is worth the journey, and makes for an excellent introduction to the Carretera Austral. But remember this is a rainforest, and torrential downpours can go on for days, even in the middle of summer.

WHAT TO SEE & DO

The park's **main information center** is at **Caleta Gonzalo,** reached by ferry from Hornopirén in the summer and by Chaitén in the winter (visitors must first take a ferry to Chaitén from Puerto Montt, or from Quellón in Chiloé). The northern section of the park is accessible by road from Hornopirén, which has an information center (☎ 65/217256), but the park is cut in two, and visitors will need to take a ferry to Caleta Gonzalo regardless to reach the southern section. In the Caleta Gonzalo center, visitors will find photos, brochures, and locally produced crafts. There's also a new information center in Chaitén, at O'Higgins 62 (☎ 65/731341), and in Puerto Montt (☎ 65/250079). For advance information, request brochures in the United States (☎ 415/229-9339; e-mail: pumalín@earthlink.org). For general information, try www.pumalinpark.org.

HIKING   At Caleta Gonzalo, trails include the 3-hour round-trip **Sendero Cascada,** which meanders along a footpath and elevated walkways through dense vegetation before terminating at a crashing waterfall. The **Sendero Tronador,** 7½ miles (12km) south of Caleta Gonzalo, takes visitors across a suspension bridge and up, up, up a steep path and wooden stepladder to a lookout point, with views of Volcán Michinmáhuida, then down to a lake with a campground, round-trip about 3 ½ hours. The **Sendero los Alerces** is an easy, 40-minute walk through old stands of *alerce.* There is also a tough-going, 3-day backpacking trip, the **Sendero Inexplorado,** for experienced hikers only.

OTHER ACTIVITIES   Pumalín offers **horse pack trips** and trips to the remote **Cahuelmo Hot Springs,** all with advance reservation only. You can also tour an **organic farm** or sign up for **boat trips** around the fjord and to the sea lion rookery.

ORGANIZED TOURS AlSur (☎/fax **65/232300;** www.puertovaras/alsur.cl; e-mail: alsur@telsur.cl) offers hiking, sightseeing, and kayak tours through the park, including a visit by boat to the remote Cahuelmo Hot Springs. Also, **Altué Sea Kayaking,** based out of Santiago at Encomenderos 83, Las Condes (☎ **2/232-1103;** www.altueseakayak.co.cl; e-mail: altue@entelchile.net), offers kayak trips in Pumalín that it often combines with kayaking in Chiloé.

WHERE TO STAY & DINE

Cabañas and Camping Pumalín. Caleta Gonzalo s/n. ☎ **65/250079,** or in the U.S. 415/229-9339. Fax 65/255145; in the U.S., 415/229-9340. www.pumalinpark.org. E-mail: pumalin@earthlink.org. 7 units. $65 double; $10 each additional guest. AE, DC, MC, V. Free parking.

These rustic yet luxurious cabins are built for two to six guests and feature details like nubby bedspreads, gingham curtains, carved wood cabinets, and other fine features. Only one comes with a kitchen, the "family" cabin at Reñihué, a more remote cabin with fishing access that goes for $90 for four. The cabins are small but cozy, with a double bed and twin on the bottom floor and two twins above in a loft. Each shingled cabin was designed differently, and all offer lots of light.

The cabins sit next to the **Café Caleta Gonzalo,** which serves delicious organic food with main courses ranging from $7 to $10, as well as hearty breakfasts, sandwiches, and soups. The cafe is open Monday to Sunday 7:30am to 11:30pm.

The sites at **Camping Pumalín,** on the beautiful Fiordo Reñihué, are well-kept rooms offering a firepit (firewood costs extra), a sheltered area for cooking, bathrooms with cold-water showers, and an area for washing clothing; the cost is $2 per person. About 8½ miles (14km) south of Caleta Gonzalo is the **Cascadas Escondidas Campground,** with sheltered tent platforms, picnic tables, cold-water showers, bathrooms, and the trailhead to three waterfalls. The cost to camp here is $8 per group. There are more than 20 campsites throughout the park, many of them accessible by boat or by backpacking trail; consult the park for more information.

4 Chaitén

260 miles (420km) N of Coyhaique

Chaitén is a sleepy hamlet that serves as a jumping-off point for exploring Pumalín, Futaleufú, and the Carretera Austral. There's not much to see or do here, but visitors often find that it makes a convenient stopover point, especially during the winter when ferry service is limited. The town's main attraction is really the view of **Volcán Michinmáhuida** in the distance, although perennial wet weather often impedes visibility of anything except the puddled, potholed streets.

GETTING THERE

BY BOAT For information about ferries to Chaitén, see chapter 12 under "Ferry Crossings to the Carretera Austral & Sailing to Patagonia Through the Fjords."

BY AIR Daily flights from Puerto Montt are offered by **Aeromet** at Todesco 55 (☎ **65/731275**), and air-taxi **Aerosur** at Carrera Pinto and Almirante Riveros (☎ **65/731228**). It is not recommended that travelers fly in stormy weather.

BY BUS Bus schedules in this region are always subject to change, and both **Chaitur,** Diego Portales 350 (☎ **65/731429**) and **B&V Tours,** Libertad 432 (☎ **65/731390**), have information about service to destinations such as Caleta Gonzalo, Futaleufú, Puyuhuapi, and Coyhaique. Buses to all destinations leave daily from

December to March; from April to November, buses to Futaleufú leave three times weekly, as do buses to Caleta Gonzalo, and two times weekly to Coyhaique, with a stop at Puyuhuapi.

VISITOR INFORMATION & TOUR OPERATORS

Several tour operators offer set trips and custom-built trips to outlying areas. Try **Chaitur,** Diego Portales 350 (☎ **65/731429;** e-mail: nchaitur@hotmail.com), or **Ñuke Mapu** in the Galería Genisis (☎ **65/731578**)—both agencies often work together, offering trips to the Yelcho Glacier and Pumalín Park, horseback riding, rock climbing, kayaking, and even mountain biking to destinations as far as Coyhaique. Pumalín Park has an office in Chaitén at O'Higgins 52 (☎ **65/731341**), and it is the best place to pick up information about the area.

WHERE TO STAY

Private parking or ample street parking is available for all hotels.

✪ **Hostal El Verde Puma.** O'Higgins 52, Chaitén. ☎ **65/731184.** www.pumalinpark. com. 2 units, 1 apartment. $18–$36 per person; $36–$75 apartment. No credit cards.

Owned and operated by the Pumalín Park Project, this brand-new, fine hostal offers the most attractive and modern accommodations in Chaitén, designed with the same rustic-chic details as its counterparts in the park. The cream and forest green hostal is in an old but newly renovated shingled building, and sits above the park's information center and gift shop. The rooms are quite small, but the interiors are almost luxurious, with contemporary decorations and linens. There's one bedroom for two with a full-size bed, and another with three beds that singles must share with other travelers; the latter room has a sliding scale from $18 to $36 depending on the number of guests occupying the room. The wooden gourmet kitchen has a large, copper-hooded stove and a cozy eating area where guests can take meals. Out back is a wonderful apartment consisting of one large room with a double bed and a long counter and kitchenette.

✪ **Hostería Los Coihues.** Pedro A. Cerda 398, Chaitén. ☎/fax **65/731461.** http:// members.xoom.com/loscoihues. E-mail: coihues@telsur.cl. 8 units. $15–$20 per person. AE, DC, MC, V.

This is one of the nicer hotels in Chaitén, and it's downright cheap. The unassuming, log-cabin building sits several blocks back from the waterfront, and has a comfortable dining area/lounge with windows facing Volcán Michinmáhuida. The rooms have wood floors and are somewhat plain, but are warm, and the bathrooms sparkle. Doubles have a full-size bed or two twins, and triples have a twin and bunk bed. The friendly Argentine family who own and run the hotel came to Chaitén and were so smitten they never left; one family member is a mountaineer enthusiast who organizes outdoor adventures. Daily excursions are available for an additional cost, and a typical 3-day/3-night package can include a walk on the Yelcho Glacier, trekking, and hot springs, with meals, lodging, and transportation for $294 per person. Fly-fishing packages are $662 for two. They arrange these packages under the assumption you'll be flying into Chaitén, so ask for other arrangements if you plan to arrive by ferry.

Hotel Mi Casa. Av. Norte 206, Chaitén. ☎/fax **65/731285.** www.gochile.cl/hotel/micasa. E-mail: hmicasa@telsur.cl. 20 units. $55–$75 double. No credit cards.

The Hotel Mi Casa is located on a hill just above town, offering a direct view of Volcán Michinmáhuida and the colorful rooftops below, all taken in from a winding deck. The unadorned rooms are nothing to go wild about, but the warm, friendly service, decent restaurant, and extra amenities give it a slight edge above several of its competitors. Two rooms have a double bed and an extra twin for parents traveling with a child. Although many have thin carpet, the rooms are large enough and kept toasty warm. A winding path out back leads to a gym with weights and a Ping-Pong table and continues to a sauna and massage cabin. Several sitting areas in the hotel include a TV room with a VCR. A fun extra is the hotel's *quincho,* where they often host lamb, beef, and pork barbecues grilled the Chilean way on a spit over a roaring fire. The hotel will arrange excursions and has package deals, including excursions for 3 and 5 days, for $550 and $890 per person, respectively.

Hotel Schilling. Av. Corcovado 230, Chaitén. ☎ **65/731295.** Fax 65/731298. $18–$27 per person. No credit cards.

The Hotel Schilling has a bright, cheery lobby and a waterfront location, but the rooms are dowdy and not a great value. Nevertheless, it's still one of the better hotels in Chaitén, and it's possible to negotiate the price, especially in the off-season or for multiple-day stays. Some rooms come with private bathrooms, although rooms with shared bathrooms are slightly cheaper. The decor consists of colorful velveteen bedspreads and frilly lamps, and rooms are heated only by a wood-burning stove in the hall; a few come with a TV. There's a nice dining area and bar on the bottom level.

Residencial Astoria. Av. Corcovado 442, Chaitén. ☎ **65/731263.** 8 units. $13–$19 private bathroom; $9–$13 shared bathroom. No credit cards.

If you can get past the dark, musty bottom floor, this *residencial* is a good bet for inexpensive accommodations. There are two bedrooms on the first level, but better accommodations are on the sunny second floor, which has a giant living room with windows that face out over the ocean (and a Copec gas station). Low ceilings, especially in the shower, are inconvenient for anyone over 6 feet, and it can get fairly cold in the rooms. The walls are thin, but the *residencial* is very clean and the beds are comfortable.

WHERE TO DINE

There aren't a lot of options here in Chaitén for dining, especially during the off-season when many eateries close or limit their menus. Reservations are not necessary, unless otherwise noted.

Hotel Mi Casa. Av. Norte 206. ☎/fax **65/731285.** Main dishes $3–$7. No credit cards. Daily 6am–midnight. CHILEAN.

This restaurant has a sweeping view of Chaitén and the waterfront and its dining room is nicer in the day than the evening, when fluorescent lights go on. The menu features simply prepared, average dishes, such as filet mignon with mashed potatoes. All the food is organic, however, and the staff will arrange a special lamb barbecue for couples and groups, if you call ahead.

Restaurant Brisas del Mar. Av. Corcovado 278. ☎ **65/731266.** Main courses $4–$10. MC, V. Dec–Mar daily 8:30pm–midnight. CHILEAN.

This is one of Chaitén's better restaurants, but it's open only during the summer. Brisas del Mar sits on the waterfront and has a sunny, semi-casual dining area. The menu offers a typically Chilean selection of seafood and meats.

Restaurant Flamengo. Av. Corcovado 218. No phone. Main courses $5.50–$10. No credit cards. Daily 8:30am–2am high season; daily 10am–midnight low season. CHILEAN.

The best thing that can be said about the Flamengo is that it is open all day, year-round. However, it's somewhat expensive given the simple dishes it serves and its casual atmosphere. Flamengo offers grilled meats, fish, and chicken with a choice of a dozen sauces and often has shellfish specials during the summer.

5 South from Chaitén: Futaleufú

96 mi (155km) SE of Chaitén

The road south between Chaitén and Villa Santa Lucía, where drivers turn for Futaleufú, passes through mountain scenery that affords spectacular views of Volcán Michinmáhuida, the Yelcho Glacier, and Lago Yelcho. At 15½ miles (25km), you'll arrive at Amarillo, a tiny village and the turn-off point for the 3-mile (5km) drive to Termas de Amarillo.

Termas de Amarillo. No phone. $4 adults, $2 children 12 and under; $4 for camping. Nov–Apr daily 9am–8pm; Mar–Oct daily 9am–6pm.

This seemingly half-built hot springs site is a good place for a soak. There's a large temperate pool along with several outdoor and private indoor pools (private meaning a cement pool inside a shack). There are several sites to camp here, or you can lodge at the modest, family-run **Cabañas y Hospedaje Los Mañios** about 100m (109 yds.) from the hot springs, for $10 per person, or $40 for a cabin for six (☎ **65/731210**).

CONTINUING ON TO FUTALEUFÚ

Farther south the road curves past the northern shore of Lago Yelcho and the Yelcho en la Patagonia Lodge (see below), and at 37 miles (60km) crosses the Puente Ventisquero, which bridges a milky green river; this is where you'll find the trailhead to the **Yelcho Glacier.** To get there, take the short road before the bridge and then walk right at the almost imperceptible sign indicating the trail. A 1½-hour muddy hike takes visitors through dense forest to the Yelcho Glacier.

At Villa Santa Lucía, the Carretera Austral continues south to Puyuhuapi, but visitors should consider a trip to Futaleufú, an idyllic mountain town with adventure activities and one of the most challenging rivers to raft in the world. The road to Futaleufú is worth the trip itself for its majestic views at every turn, first winding around the southern end of Lago Yelcho before passing the Futaleufú River and Lakes Lonconao and Espolón and on to the emerald valley surrounding the town of Futaleufú.

AN ADVENTURE LODGE

✪ **Yelcho en la Patagonia Lodge.** Lago Yelcho, Km54, Carretera Austral, Región X. ☎ **65/731337**, or for reservations, 2/334-1309 in Santiago. www.chilecom.com/yelcho/. E-mail: yelcho@chilecom.com. 8 suites; 6 cabañas; 15 camp sites. $65 double; $95 cabaña for four. MC, V.

The Yelcho Lodge enjoys a privileged location on the shore of Lago Yelcho, and is this general region's only complete resort, with elegant, attractive accommodations and a full range of excursions, especially fly-fishing. Yelcho offers three options: suites, cabañas for two to six guests, and 15 well-equipped camp sites complete with barbecues. The white, shingled cabañas come with spacious kitchens, but there's also a restaurant that serves gourmet cuisine, as well as barbecue roasts. The cabins have a deck and barbecue and a view of the lake seen through a stand of *arrayán* trees; note that cabins for six mean two sleep in the living area. The lodge and the indoor accommodations are made entirely of native woods, including handsome two-tone floors made of *mañío* and *alerce*. The lodge offers excursions with bilingual guides for fly-fishing the Yelcho River and Lago Yelcho, locally renowned for its plentiful salmon and trout, and treks to the Yelcho Glacier, mountain biking, horseback riding, and visits to the Amarillo hot springs and Futaleufú. The lodge will pick you up from nearly any nearby location.

FUTALEUFÚ

132 miles (213km) SE of Chaitén; 121½ miles (196km) NE of Puyuhuapi

Futaleufú is one of the prettiest villages in Chile, a town of 1,000 residents who live in colorful clapboard homes nestled in an awe-inspiring amphitheater of rugged, snowcapped mountains. Futaleufú sits at the junction of two rivers, the turquoise Río Espolón and its world-renowned cousin the Río Futaleufú, whose whitewater rapids are considered some of the most challenging on the globe. Every November to April, this quaint little town becomes the base for hundreds of rafters and kayakers who come to test their mettle on the "Fu," as it's colloquially known, although just as many come to fish, hike, mountain bike, paddle a canoe, or raft the gentler Río Espolón. Futaleufú is just kilometers from the Argentine border, meaning it is possible to get here by road from Puerto Montt by crossing into Argentina, a route sometimes preferred for its paved roads.

Note that there are no banks or gas stations here in Futaleufú. Residents do, however, sell gas out of wine jugs and other unwieldy containers; just look for signs advertising BENCINA.

GETTING THERE & AWAY

BY PLANE   **Aerosur** offers air-taxi charter flights from Puerto Montt and even Chaitén, weather permitting (☎ **65/252523** in Puerto Montt, or 65/731268 in Futaleufú). It's entirely feasible to fly into Esquel in Argentina from Buenos Aires and then travel by road 40 miles (65km) to Futaleufú.

BY BUS   There isn't a bus terminal here, so ask at your hotel or call each company for schedules, locations and prices. Winter service is sketchy; try calling **B&V Tours** in Chaitén to see if they have an upcoming trip (☎ **65/731390**). **Skorpios Turismo,** which operates out of the Hospedaje Emita at Miraflores 1281 (☎ **65/250725**), offers service to Puerto Montt via Argentina, leaving Futaleufú on Tuesdays and Puerto Montt on Thursdays. The bus leaves at 8am and arrives 12 hours later.

BY CAR   From Chaitén, take Ruta 7 south and go left to Ruta 235 at Villa Santa Lucía. The road winds around the shore of Lago Yelcho until Puerto Ramírez, where you head northeast on Ruta 231 until you reach Futaleufú.

WHAT TO SEE & DO

Futaleufú was put on the map by travelers with one goal in mind: to raft or kayak the internationally famous, Class V waters of the village's namesake river. This is one of the most challenging rivers to descend in the world. You've got to be good—or at least be experienced—to tackle frothing whitewater so wild that certain sections have been dubbed "Hell" and "The Finisher." But rafting and kayaking companies will accommodate more prudent guests with shorter sections of the river. If you just can't handle the Futaleufú, the Río Espolón offers a gentler ride.

American Olympic kayaker Chris Spelius now runs the Futaleufú-based **Expediciones Chile,** a rafting and kayaking excursion center. It's headquartered at the Hostería Río Grande, O'Higgins 397 (☎ **65/721320,** or in the U.S. 888/488-9082; www.raftingchile.com). He also offers a kayak skills course from a remote tent camp with lodge support. Day trips can be organized on the spot, but it's best to reserve ahead of time. Two excellent, U.S.-based companies offer rafting on the Río Futaleufú, as well as other destinations in Chile: **Bío Bío Expeditions** (☎ **800/2-GO-RAFT** in the U.S.; www.bbxrafting.com) and **Earth River Expeditions** (☎ **800/643-2784;** www.earthriver.com). Both offer all-inclusive, multiple-day packages.

For **fishing licenses,** go to the municipal building at O'Higgins 596 (☎ 65/721241); it's open Monday to Friday 8am to 1:30pm and 2:30 to 5pm. For more information on fishing, see "Fly-Fishing Lodges in the Futaleufú Area," below.

WHERE TO STAY IN THE AREA

It's slim pickings here, and you'll be charged a lot for what you get. Outside Futaleufú there are several options for lodging, including campsites that dot the road between here and Villa Santa Lucía. If you'd like to do a little fishing, but are looking for something more economical, check out the **Hostal Alexis** (☎ 65/731505), located just before Puerto Ramírez and situated on the grassy bank of Lago Yelcho. There's a hotel in an old, converted farmhouse, and a dozen campsites with wooden half-walls that protect sites from the wind. You can fish directly from the shore here, but the owners also offer fishing excursions. Open November to April only, $35 double.

Hospedaje Familiar Ely. Balmaceda 409, Futaleufú. ☎ **65/721205.** 5 units. $15–$18 per person. No credit cards.

The friendly woman who owns and runs this *hospedaje* offers decent but no-frills accommodations in an old, shingled building. The rooms are somewhat cramped and the floors squeak, but that's pretty common for lodging in this price range for this town. Two of the rooms share a bathroom. Guests take breakfast in a downstairs living room that also acts as a lobby. There's also a backyard cement patio.

✪ **Hostería Río Grande.** O'Higgins 397, Futaleufú. ☎ **888/488-9082** in the U.S., or 65/721320. www.raftingchile.com. E-mail: office@raftingchile.com. 10 units, 1 apartment for 6. $75 double. MC, V. Hotel and restaurant closed June–Sept.

This wooden, two-story hostería is popular with foreign tourists for its outdoorsy design and especially its restaurant and pub. An outdoor tour office that organizes excursions is next door as well, so there's usually a fair amount of people around. It's one of the better hotels in town, with walls painted boldly in tangerine and blue, although the rooms seem slightly expensive for their dull, standard furnishings and office-building carpet. However, the atmosphere is relaxed and guests can expect a standard level of comfort. There's also an apartment (but no kitchen) for six guests.

The Río Grande's **restaurant** is the unofficial hangout spot in town, and it has a nice atmosphere for relaxing with a beer. One of the owners is an American who has tailored the menu to satisfy the tastes of gringo clientele, so there's a lot on offer. There's seafood throughout the week, but try to make it on Wednesday and Saturday when the restaurant receives its fresh fish delivery by air.

✪ **Posada La Gringa.** Sargento Aldea s/n, corner of Aldea, Futaleufú. ☎ **65/258633.** 8 units. $70 double. No credit cards. Hotel closed May–Oct.

This attractive white-and-green clapboard hotel sits on a large, grassy property with excellent views of the countryside stretched out before it. With well-maintained, clean, pleasant rooms, the hotel is open from November to April only.

WHERE TO DINE

Apart from the Hostería Rio Grande's restaurant (see above), there's **Restaurant Skorpios,** Gabriela Mistral 255 (☎ 65/731228), which doesn't usually serve from a menu; instead, it offers about four choices per day of simple meat and seafood dishes (no credit cards accepted). **Café Restaurant Futaleufú,** Pedro Aguirre Cerda 407 (☎ 65/721295), is really simple, with metal chairs and a short menu with 10 or so simple dishes that all cost the same ($6; no credit cards accepted). Sample items include homemade spaghetti and chicken stewed with peas; there's also a range of sandwiches.

FLY-FISHING LODGES IN THE FUTALEUFÚ AREA

Futaleufú Lodge. 8km from Futaleufú, Route 231, Futaleufú, Región X. ☎/fax **32/ 812659.** www.marksport.com/sponsors/futaleufu/. E-mail: soniad@entelchile.net (e-mail answered Apr–Dec only). All-inclusive, 7-day packages $3,800 per person.

The Futaleufú is an intimate little lodge nestled in the Las Escalas Valley in the mountains 5 miles (8km) from town, on the shore of the Futaleufú River. Like the Isla Monita Lodge, the Futaleufú is rustic yet luxurious, but unlike the Isla Monita, which has a more masculine aesthetic, this lodge is aimed at couples (the capacity here is six people). The owners, American Jim Repine and his wife Sonia, are very amiable, and the setting is ideal. They offer trekking and horseback riding, and can arrange a kayak or rafting trip down the Futaleufú River (at an additional cost).

Isla Monita Lodge. Lago Yelcho, Futaleufú, Región X. Tours are arranged through Frontier Tours in the U.S.; call ☎ **800/245-1950.** Fax 412/935-5388 in the U.S. Information also available in Santiago at ☎ 2/273-2198. Average, all-inclusive packages run $3,275 per person, not including transportation.

This exclusive, newly renovated lodge can be found on a private island in Lago Yelcho, and its location affords anglers the most diverse fly-fishing conditions found in Chile. Fly-fishers have their choice of the Palena, Futaleufú, or Yelcho rivers, all within a short drive from the lodge, and there are wading and floating excursions. The lodge has room for just eight guests. You can't beat the location, encircled by a ring of rugged peaks. Guests typically reach the lodge by plane from Chaitén. The season runs November to April.

Río Palena Lodge. Km14 outside Palena, Route 235. ☎ **888/891-3474** in the U.S. Fax 860/434-8605 in the U.S. www.flyfishingchile.com. E-mail: riopalenalodge@erols.com. 7-night/8-day packages average $3,600 per person, including lodging, meals, guides, and transportation from Puerto Montt or Palena.

Situated on the shore of the Río Palena and offering front-door fishing, this handsome lodge, owned by an American, is made entirely of native wood. It backs up against a leafy slope, and there's a long deck for kicking back and telling fish tales. The lodge has space for just eight guests, who normally spend their days pulling in brown and rainbow trout. There's also hiking, horseback riding, and bird watching for non-anglers. The season here is from November to May.

6 Puyuhuapi

123 miles (198km) S of Chaitén; 138 miles (222km) N of Coyhaique

Just south of Villa Santa Lucía is the end of Chile's Región X Lake District (also called Región Los Lagos) and the beginning of Región XI, better known as Región Aisén. South of here you enter a flat valley and the utilitarian town La Junta. The only thing of any interest there is a gas pump and well-stocked store. The view begins to pick up farther along, until the scenery goes wild as the valley narrows and thick green rainforest rises steeply from the sides of the road, just outside the entrance of Parque Nacional Queulat. When the valley opens, the Seno Ventisquero (Glacier Sound) unfolds dramatically, revealing the charming town of Puerto Puyuhuapi on its shore.

Puerto Puyuhuapi was founded by four young immigrant German brothers and their families who set up camp here in 1935 and eked out a prosperous living in the thick jungle. Part of their earnings came from a surprisingly successful **carpet factory,** whose humble, shingled building you can still visit Monday to Friday at 10:30, 11, 11:30am, 4, 4:30, and 5pm; Saturday to Sunday and holidays the tour is offered just once at 11:30am. Admission is $2 adults and $1 kids.

The most popular attractions in this region are **Parque Nacional Queulat** and the five-star, sumptuous **Termas de Puyuhuapi Spa & Hotel** (see "Outside Puerto Puyuhuapi," below) just south and on the other side of the sound a 5-minute boat ride away. If the Termas de Puyuhuapi's prices are beyond your limit, you might opt to stay at a more economical hotel in Puerto Puyuhuapi or, during the off-season, at El Pangue cabañas, and take a soak in the hot springs for the day. You can then spend the following day exploring Parque Nacional Queulat.

EXPLORING PARQUE NACIONAL QUEULAT

Parque Nacional Queulat's scenery will make your jaw drop. Every national park has a unique characteristic and Queulat's is its emerald, virgin rainforest, some of it so thick and impenetrable that it has yet to be explored. What makes this park special is that you can drive through the heart of it, and there are several spectacular lookout points reached by car or a brief walk. Be sure to keep your eyes open for the *pudú*, a miniature Chilean deer that is timid but can often be seen poking its head out of the forest near the road.

The 154,093ha (380,610-acre) park has several access points but few trails and no backpacking trails. If entering from the north, you first pass a turn-off that heads to the shore of **Lago Risopatrón** and a very attractive camping spot that charges $13 per site. There's an 8½-mile (14km) round-trip (5 to 6 hours) trail here that leads trekkers through rainforest and past Lago los Pumos. Continuing south of Puerto Puyuhuapi, visitors arrive at the park's star attraction, the **Ventisquero Colgante,** a tremendous, U-shaped river of ice suspended hundreds of feet above a sheer granite wall. From the glacier, two powerful cascades fall into Lago los Témpanos below. To enter this part of the park, Conaf charges $3 per adult and 50¢ per child 12 and under; visitors can drive straight to a short trail that takes them to the glacier's lookout point. To get closer, cross the hanging bridge that's before the campground and take the **Sendero Mirador Ventisquero Colgante,** a moderate, 3- to 4-hour hike that takes you to the lake below the glacier. As of this writing, a concession has made plans to offer a 45-minute boat ride around this lake for $3.50 per person; check at the Conaf station, which is open December to March 8:30am to 9:30pm and April to November 8:30am to 9:30pm. To camp in this area, the park charges $13 per site. For more information, contact Conaf's offices in Coyhaique at ☎ **67/212125.**

Traveling farther south, the scenery becomes more rugged as the road takes visitors through 17 sharp curves up the Cuesta de Queulat and to views of glacier-capped peaks, and then down again where the road passes the trailhead to the **Sendero Río Cascada.** Even if you don't feel like walking the entire 1-mile (1.7km) trail, at least stop for a quick stroll through the enchanted forest of this area, with giant trunks covered with shaggy lichen and spongy moss. The trail leads to a granite amphitheater draped with braided waterfalls that fall into an ice-capped lake. Note that Conaf is slow-moving when it comes to clearing trails of fallen trees, especially on the Río Cascada trail. If you're able, you can scramble over the trees, but it takes some maneuvering that will tack extra time onto your journey. Check with Conaf at the Ventisquero Colgante entrance for the status of a trail, or factor obstacles into your trip time. The station is open December to March 8:30am to 9:30pm and April to November 8:30am to 9:30pm; ☎ **67/212125.**

WHERE TO STAY & DINE

Private parking or ample street parking is available for all hotels. Also, restaurant reservations are not necessary, unless otherwise noted.

IN PUERTO PUYUHUAPI

Try **Café Rossbach,** Aysé s/n (☎ 67/325202), if you're looking for something to eat—cakes are the specialty. The Rossbach is next to the carpet factory, across from the gas station. **El Pangue** has a restaurant, but it's 11 miles (18km) away. Call beforehand to see if you can get a table (see "Outside Puerto Puyuhuapi," below).

✪ **Hostería Alemana.** Av. Otto Uevel 450, Puerto Puyuhaupi. ☎ **67/325118.** 6 units. $40–$45 double. No credit cards.

The German woman who runs this hotel emigrated to Puerto Puyuhuapi more than 30 years ago, and her roots are reflected in the style of the establishment, including delicious breakfasts with sliced meats and *kuchen.* The hotel is in a well-maintained, flower-bordered antique home that just got a fresh coat of paint this year. Only one room comes with a private bathroom, and one triple comes with a wood-burning stove. All are spacious and scrubbed.

Residencial Marily. Av. Otto Uevel s/n, Puerto Puyuhuapi. ☎ **67/325201.** Fax 67/325102. 7 units. Per person, $25 private bathroom; $10 shared bathroom. No credit cards.

Just across the street from the Hostería Alemana is this inexpensive *residencial.* The place doesn't have much style, but it is clean and the beds are surprisingly comfortable for a *residencial.* The floors are wood, the walls mauve and light blue, and some rooms share a bathroom; there is a TV in the lounge. Without a doubt the best thing about this place has to be the stuffed puma in the living room.

OUTSIDE PUERTO PUYUHUAPI

✪ **El Pangue.** Carretera Austral Norte, Km240, Región XI. ☎ /fax **67/325128.** E-mail: cpangue@entelchile.net. 13 cabañas. $50–$100 per person (prices vary; contact the hotel for information). No credit cards.

El Pangue is located at a breathtakingly beautiful site just kilometers from the edge of Parque Nacional Queulat, 100 feet (30m) from the dark waters of Lago Risopatrón, and 11 miles (18km) from Puerto Puyuhuapi. Dense rainforest, including huge *nalca* plants, encircle the complex; a winding stream provides a fairy-tale spot for a quiet walk or a quick dip. The staff and facilities are commendable, and although the lodge focuses heavily on fly-fishing from November to May, the excursions and amenities are diverse enough to keep everyone happy, including mountain biking, hiking, canoeing, and boat rides. Guided fly-fishing is offered here and around the region with motorboats, floating tubes, Mackenzie boats, and rafts.

Lodging consists of cozy, attractive wood cabins that fit two to three guests. There are also two "houses" with kitchens for seven guests each; only four of the cabins have kitchens. The open-room, split-level cabins have a small table and chairs and an extra bed/couch; bathrooms have sunken tubs. The main building houses an excellent restaurant, game room, and lounge; outside is a *quincho* where there are frequent lamb barbecues. El Pangue has just installed a partially roofed, heated swimming pool, two whirlpools, and a sauna. There is an interesting aviary of sorts with ducks, geese, pheasants, and chickens. Off-season rates drop dramatically, from April to October.

Dining/Diversions: El Pangue's well-lit restaurant serves international cuisine; there's also a bar/lounge.

Amenities: Laundry, room service, travel information, outdoor heated pool, whirlpool, sauna, fly-fishing expeditions and boats, mountain bikes, horseback riding, canoes, business center.

✪ **Termas de Puyuhuapi Spa & Hotel.** Puerto Puyuhuapi, Región XI. ☎ /fax in Santiago **2/225-6489,** or in Puyuhuapi 67/325103. E-mail: info@patagoniaconnex.cl. 25 units. TEL. $145–$160 double, meals not included. 3-night packages including the cruise to Laguna San Rafael cost about $1,000 per person. half-price for kids. AE, DC, MC, V.

This region's top attraction is an extraordinary place to spend the night or visit for the day. Termas de Puyuhuapi Spa & Hotel is perhaps the best hotel/thermal spa complex in Chile, and its deserved reputation draws visitors from all over the world for its remote, magnificent location, elegant design, and multitude of indoor and outdoor thermal pools and full-service spa. The hotel is nestled in thick rainforest on the shore of the Seno Ventisquero; to get here, guests must cross the sound via a 5-minute motorboat ride. There, visitors find an indoor complex with a giant pool, whirlpools, steam baths, spa, and three open-air pools, one a rock pool framed by ferns. Even when it's raining, Termas de Puyuhuapi shines—in fact, the wet weather seems to just go with the place, especially when low clouds cling to the peaks of the mountains in the forefront.

The Termas was just a handful of ramshackle cabins until German Eberhard Kossmann bought the property and built his handsome complex of shingles and glass; the only remaining original building is one of the cabañas, which is probably the least appealing lodging option. Nine large suites are on the shore, and they come with a deck that hangs out over the water during high tide. There are six newer, and smaller, no smoking suites that come with a more stylish decor (especially the "Captain's Suite") featuring contemporary art and flecked Berber carpet. Other options include a duplex with a fireman's ladder that leads to a loft with three twins for kids, and two cabins that sleep four to six people, but they do not come with a kitchen stove or a view. Of special note is the superb cuisine served here at the hotel; really some of the best I've had in Chile.

Outside, a winding path takes guests to two short hikes through the rainforest, and there's a pier for dropping a kayak in for a paddle in the sound. But the big outdoor attractions here are Puyuhuapi's fly-fishing expeditions and the connection with *Patagonia Express,* a boat that takes visitors to the Laguna San Rafael Glacier (see "Puerto Aisén, Puerto Chacabuco & Laguna San Rafael National Park," below, for more information on the Patagonia Express). Both are sold as packages. Guests typically fly into Coyhaique and transfer to the Termas by vehicle. On the return trip they board the *Express* for a visit to the glacier, and get dropped off in Puerto Chacabuco for the night, then back to the airport.

Amenities: Room service, thermal pools, whirlpools, sauna, massage, herbal wraps, mud baths, conference salon.

Day Use: Call for scheduled boat-crossing times. The cost to use the pools is $25, more if you decide to take a sauna or have a massage.

7 Coyhaique

138 miles (222km) S of Puyuhuapi; 480 miles (774km) N of Cochrane

The province Aisén includes the capital city Coyhaique and a handful of natural reserves whose rivers and lakes draw thousands every year for superb fly-fishing opportunities. Visitors who are not traveling the Carretera Austral can fly into Coyhaique from Santiago or Puerto Montt; travel to southern Patagonia from here requires that you fly again to Punta Arenas, unless you have your own car and plan to take the long and gravelly road through flat Argentine *pampa.*

Driving south out of Parque Nacional Queulat, the scenery doesn't fail to continue provoking oohs and ahhs at every turn. The pinnacle of Cerro Picacho comes into view before entering Villa Amengual, a service village for farmers who seem oblivious to the sensational landscape surrounding them. This scenery is marred at times, unfortunately, by the terrible destruction caused by settlers who burned much of the area for pastureland. Tall, slender, evergreen beech tree trunks bleached silver from fire can still be seen poking out from regrowth forest or littered across grassy pastures in a messy testament to these fires, many of which raged out of control.

The road passes through rinky-dink towns such as Villa Mañihuales before arriving at a paved road that appears like a heaven-sent miracle after hundreds of kilometers of jarring washboard. At a junction south of Mañihuales, drivers can head to Puerto Aisén and Puerto Chacabuco, the departure point for boat trips to Laguna San Rafael and Puerto Montt, and then southeast toward Coyhaique, passing first through the Reserva Nacional Río Simpson.

Coyhaique is a compact, urban city that is home to more than half the population of the entire Aisén region—about 40,000 residents. It's really the only city in the region with a full range of services—most important, banks. The city boasts a beautiful location at the base of a basalt cliff called Cerro MacKay and is surrounded by green rolling hills and pastures. The city also sits at the confluence of the Simpson and Coyhaique rivers, both renowned for trout and salmon fishing and the reason so many flock to this region. The other prime attraction here is the Laguna San Rafael Glacier, an enormous glacier that can be visited on a modest ship or a luxury liner from Puerto Chacabuco. Beyond fishing, visitors can choose from a wealth of activities within a short drive of the city.

ESSENTIALS
GETTING THERE & AROUND

BY PLANE   Coyhaique's **Aeropuerto de Balmaceda** (no phone) is a 50-minute drive from downtown; this is where larger, long-distance planes land. A variety of minibus shuttles await each arriving flight, offering transportation to Coyhaique for about $6 to $7. Flights to closer destinations such as Chile Chico or Cochrane leave from the Teniente Vidal airport just outside town. **Avant** has one daily flight to Santiago via Puerto Montt; its office is at General Parra 202 (☎ **67/237570**). **Lan Chile** has two to three flights daily; its office is at General Parra 211 (☎ **67/231188**). Both **Aerohein,** Baquedano 500 (☎ **67/232772**), and **San Rafael,** Av. 18 de Septiembre 469 (☎ **67/233408**), offer charter flights; **Transporte Don Carlos,** Subteniente Cruz 63 (☎ **67/231981**), offers regional flights.

BY BOAT   It is possible to arrive by boat at Puerto Chacabuco near Puerto Aisén (from Puerto Montt), then travel by road for the 41½ miles (67km) to Coyhaique. For schedule information, see "Puerto Aisén, Puerto Chacabuco & Laguna San Rafael National Park," below. Ferry company offices in Coyhaique are at **Transmarchilay,** Av. 21 de Mayo 417 (☎ **67/231971**), and **Navimag,** Ibáñez 347 (☎ **67/233306**).

BY BUS   Coyhaique has a bus terminal at Lautaro and Magallanes streets, but many companies use their own office for departures and arrivals. For buses with a final destination in **Chaitén,** try Buses Norte at General Parra 337 (☎ **67/232167**), which leaves on Tuesdays and Saturdays. For **Puerto Aisén** and **Chacabuco,** try Buses Don Carlos at Subteniente Cruz 63 (☎ **67/232981**) with five trips per day, or Buses Suray at Eusebio Ibar 630 (☎ **67/238287**). For **Puerto Ibáñez,** try Minibus Don Tito at Pasaje Curico 619 (☎ **67/250280**).

BY CAR   If heading south on Ruta 7, the highway comes to a fork—one paved road and one dirt. The choice here is clear, especially if you've been driving on gravel all day. The well-signed, paved route heads first toward Puerto Aisén, and then switches, heading southeast for a beautiful drive through the Río Simpson National Reserve before hitting town. At the city entrance, a sign points left for the center of town.

Coyhaique

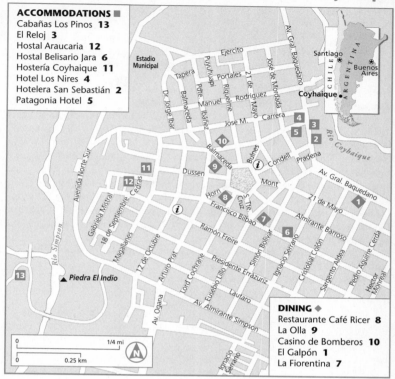

ACCOMMODATIONS ■
Cabañas Los Pinos **13**
El Reloj **3**
Hostal Araucaria **12**
Hostal Belisario Jara **6**
Hostería Coyhaique **11**
Hotel Los Nires **4**
Hotelera San Sebastián **2**
Patagonia Hotel **5**

DINING ◆
Restaurante Café Ricer **8**
La Olla **9**
Casino de Bomberos **10**
El Galpón **1**
La Fiorentina **7**

VISITOR INFORMATION

A helpful **Sernatur** office can be found at Bulnes 35 (☎ **67/231752;** www.
patagoniachile.cl; e-mail: sernatur_coyhai@entelchile.net); it's open December to
February daily 8:30am to 8:30pm, and March to November Monday to Friday
8:30am to 5:30pm. Sernatur produces a glossy magazine packed with information
about the region and full listings of services. For information about the surrounding
natural parks and reserves, you can try **Conaf**'s office at Av. 12 de Octubre 382
(☎ **67/212125**).

Car Rental for Local Trips & the Carretera Austral

Among the companies to try: **AGS Rent a Car,** Av. Ogana 1298, and at the airport
(☎ **67/235354;** fax 67/231511); **Rent a Car Aisén,** Francisco Bilbao 926 (☎ **67/
231532;** fax 67/233555); **Turismo Prado,** Av. 21 de Mayo 417 (☎/fax **67/
231271**); **Ricer Rent a Car,** Horn 48 (☎/fax **67/232920**); and **Automundo AVR,**
Francisco Bilbao 510 (☎ **67/231621;** fax 231794). If you can't find what you want
with these companies, request a list from the visitor's center, as there are many
independent offices that rent cars here in Coyhaique.

ORIENTATION

Coyhaique claims possibly the most unusual city layout in Chile due to its pentagon-shaped plaza and one-way streets that can be totally confusing to the visitor, especially when driving. Most services and hotels are near the plaza, and you'll find it convenient to stick to walking when in the city. The rest of the city is on a regular grid pattern.

FAST FACTS: COYHAIQUE

Currency Exchange   Turismo Prado at Av. 21 de Mayo (☎ **67/231271**), **Emperador** at Francisco Bilbao 222 (☎ **67/233727**), and **Lucia Saldivia** at Condell 140 (☎ **67/231125**). Exchange houses are open Monday to Friday 9:30am to 7:30pm and Sat 8:30am to 1pm.

Hospital   The city's Regional Hospital is at Calle Hospital 68, near Carrera. For emergencies, dial **131.**

Internet Access   Entel has Internet access and a calling center at Prat 340 (☎ **67/231223**).

Laundry   There's a **Lavanderia Q.L.** at Francisco Bilbao (tel **67/232266**) and a **Lavaseco Universal** at General Parra 55, #2 (☎ **67/231769**). Both are open Monday to Saturday 9am to 1pm and 3 to 7pm.

Outdoor & Fishing Gear   Patagonia Outdoors, Horn 47 (no phone), has a wide selection.

Post Office   Correos de Chile is at Cochrane 202 (no phone).

WHAT TO SEE & DO IN COYHAIQUE

Museo Regional de la Patagonia Central. Av. Baquedano 310. ☎ **67/213176.** Admission 75¢ adults; free for students. Open Dec–Feb daily 8:30am–8pm; Mar–Nov Mon–Fri 8:30am–1:30pm and 2:15–5:30pm.

This museum has two compact rooms, one a natural history exhibit packed with stuffed birds, armadillos and turtles, and rock and petrified wood samples, the other an ethnographic exhibit featuring photographs, colonial machinery, and other antique items. There is also one interesting photo exhibit of workmen building the Carretera Austral. As of this writing, the museum's future location is uncertain, and you might consider calling to verify its status beforehand.

Reserva Nacional Coyhaique. 4km from Coyhaique on the road to Puerto Aisén. ☎ **67/212125.** Admission $1, camping $6.50. Open daily 8:30am–6pm.

You don't need to go far in Coyhaique to surround yourself in wilderness. This little reserve is just under 2 miles (3km) from town on the road to Puerto Aisén, and is a great place to go for a walk through native forest, have a picnic, pitch a tent, or hike to the spectacular lookout point that affords views of the entire region. A ranger station at the entrance has complete trail information. From here, a short trail leads to a campground and then continues to Laguna Verde, with picnic areas. The longest (and most rewarding) trail is the Sendero Las Piedras, which rewards hikers with wide-open views of the surrounding area and city below. The reserve's proximity to the city means it's entirely feasible to walk there. **Aventura Turismo** and **Tour Australis** (see "Outdoor Activities in the Area," information below) can both arrange a trip there.

Reserva Nacional Río Simpson. Road to Puerto Aisén. ☎ **67/212125.** Museum open daily 8:30am–1:30pm and 2:15–6:30pm.

The only way to see this reserve, really, is by car—which you'll do anyway if you take the road from Coyhaique to Puerto Aisén. The road winds along the shore of the Río Simpson, passing through impressive scenery and offering two crashing waterfalls, the Bridal Veil and the Virgin, which are signposted and located on the side of the road.

If you've been anywhere in the Aisén region and have seen dozens of waterfalls already, you might want to just slow down for a quick glimpse. There's also a museum here without anything of much interest and an information center. Unfortunately, trails in this reserve are not regularly maintained and therefore tough to hike; inquire at the information center as to their status.

OUTDOOR ACTIVITIES IN THE AREA

TOUR OPERATORS   In addition to horseback riding, **Aventura Turismo** at General Parra 222 (☎ **67/234748;** e-mail: aventuraturismo@entelchile.net) also offers rafting on the Río Simpson (depending on river conditions) or trips south to Lago Elizalde and the Marble Cathedrals of Lago Carrera. **Expediciones Coyhaique** at Portales 195 (☎ **67/232300;** www.expecoy.es.vg; e-mail: juliomeier@patagoniachile.cl) is the best bet for fly-fishing, and their guide Julio Meier is the man who knows where to find the choice spots. For sightseeing trips along the Carretera Austral and to Puerto Aisén, and trips to view Telhuelche Indian rock, call **Tour Australis,** Moraleda 589 (☎ **67/ 239696**). They typically offer trips from November to May only, but can put together a trip for a small group any time of the year. This company also acts as a full-service travel agency.

FISHING   Since their introduction in the late 1800s, trout and salmon have thrived in the crystalline waters in southern Chile, but nowhere in the country has fly-fishing taken off as it has here in the Aisén region. The burgeoning amount of fly-fishing guides alone bears testament to the truth of this region's claim as one of the premier fishing destinations on the globe, drawing thousands of anglers from around the world to reel in 3-, 5-, and even 10-pounders. Even if you've never fished before, this might be your opportunity to give it a go. **Sernatur** (see "Visitor Information," above) issues a complete listing of all fly-fishing guides in the Aisén region, some of whom work independently, some with a tour operator. If you're coming here mainly to fly-fish, there are several full-service luxury lodges in the region. All have on-site guides, both Chilean and foreign, especially American. Most offer activities for non-angling spouses and friends (see "Fly-Fishing Lodges Around Coyhaique," below).

Tour operators organize day, multiple-day, and weeklong excursions to fly-fishing spots such as Rivers Simpson, Baker, and Nirehuao and Lakes Bertrand and General Carrera. Some combine excursions with other activities such as horseback riding or hiking.

HORSEBACK RIDING   Trips often head to the Coyhaique Reserve and Lago Margaritas, but tour companies offer a variety of destinations. Some arrange all-inclusive, multiple-day trips. Aventura Turismo (see "Tour Operators," above) offers a full-day horseback riding trip for $50 per person to Coyhaique Alto, including a hike and a barbecue.

SKIING   The **Centro Esquí El Fraile** (☎ 67/250023) is located 15½ miles (25km) from Coyhaique, offering five ski runs serviced by two T-bars. It's a tiny resort, but can make for a fun day in the snow, and it's one of the few resorts in Chile that has tree skiing. There are also cross-country skiing opportunities here. Tickets cost $23 per day, and it's possible to rent equipment for an average of $18. Again, Aventura Turismo is the one to call for transfer service here.

WHERE TO STAY

For decent, but very, very basic accommodations that usually come with a shared bath-room, try the following hostels. **Hospedaje María Esther,** Lautaro 544 (☎ **67/ 233023**), has six rooms and kitchen facilities for $10 to $14 per person. **Hospedaje**

Lautaro, Lautaro 269 (☎ 67/238116), charges about the same rate, and although it's a little nicer than María Esther, it's usually closed during the winter.

Private parking or ample street parking is available for all hotels.

EXPENSIVE

✪ **Cabañas La Pasarela.** Km1.5, road to Puerto Aisén, Coyhaique. ☎ **67/234520.** E-mail: lapasarela@patagoniachile.cl. 11 units, 4 cabañas, 2 apartments. TV TEL. $90 double; $145 cabin for 5. AE, DC, MC, V.

These attached rooms and cabins nestled on the shore of Río Simpson are good for those who'd like a more rural surrounding not too far from town. The complex is on the other side of the river, away from the main road, and to get there guests must first cross a wooden suspension bridge. Cabañas La Pasarela is geared toward fly-fishermen, with private guides from Chile and the United States who lead guests on expeditions to great fly-fishing sites. But guests also like this lodge because you can fish right at the bank of the Río Simpson outside your door. The cozy restaurant is one of the best in town, and the fireside bar is a great place to unwind with a drink. All of the structures are made of cypress logs and have black, shingled roofs. For all its charm, it must be said that the place could do with a little more sprucing up in the rooms; they're a little on the dark side. A pebbled walkway goes up to four A-frame cabañas. Note that you've got to be family or really good friends to rent one of the cabins, because three twins are in the bottom living area next to the kitchen.

✪ **Hostal Belisario Jara.** Francisco Bilbao 662, Coyhaique. ☎ **67/234150.** www.belisariojara.itgo.com. E-mail: belisariojaralodge@entelchile.net. TV TEL. 9 units, 1 apartment. $70–$90 double. No credit cards.

This boutique hotel is Coyhaique's best lodging in this price range. The charming architectural design of the Belisario Jara features honey-colored wood frames nailed together in varying angles, giving every room and sitting area a unique size and shape. A twisting, split-level hallway winds around the rooms, and the roof is a cupola topped off with a steeple and weathervane. The hotel is made of army-green stucco and windows aplenty, so it's bright and airy, and the crisp, white walls are accented here and there with local arts and crafts. Rooms are average size, some brighter than others, and all have ceramic floors. The softly lit, cozy dining area/bar is really the highlight of the hotel, with a wooden table and chairs for relaxing fireside. French doors open out onto the front garden; the hotel sits on a busy street but is set back far enough so that you do not notice. The hotel has an apartment on the second floor of an old home on the main road, separate from the main building, that comes with a kitchen and can fit up to six guests.

✪ **Hostería Coyhaique.** Magallanes 131, Coyhaique. ☎ **67/231137.** Fax 67/233274. www.hotelsa.cl. E-mail: hotelsa@ctcinternet.cl. 40 units. MINIBAR TV TEL. $90–$110 double. MC, V.

This hostería is Coyhaique's largest, and it sits in a quiet part of town surrounded by a well-trimmed lawn and garden. It is a more traditional hotel with loads of services, including its own boat service to the Laguna San Rafael Glacier. A leafy hallway leads guests to their rooms, which come with gleaming bathrooms and a classic decoration colored in rich green and maroon. The doubles come in two sizes; the matrimonial double with a full bed is larger than the double with two twins, but they're the same price. A dark-wood lobby leads into the bar, and around the corner is a semiformal restaurant; there's a more casual restaurant downstairs with great views of the countryside. Outside, there's a kidney-shaped pool and lots of grass for kids to romp around. The hotel offers a "Flash San Rafael" package that includes lodging, most meals, and two day-long excursions, one to the glacier and the other to a sister hotel on Lake Elizalde for a Chilean barbecue, for $546 to $599 per person, double occupancy.

Dining/Diversions: There is a bar and a restaurant (see "Where to Dine," below).

Amenities: Laundry, room service, outdoor pool, conference rooms, excursions.

Patagonia Hotel. General Parra 551, Coyhaique. ☎ /fax **67/236505.** www.patagoniahotel. cl. E-mail: patagoniah@patagoniachile.cl. 12 units. MINIBAR TV TEL. $75–$90 double. AE, DC, MC, V.

The Patagonia Hotel is another good option in this price range. This unassuming hotel sits on a quiet residential street and offers average-size rooms with mahogany furniture and comfortable beds. Six of the rooms are in a row just off the lobby and the others are reached by stairs. The hotel's main interior is dominated by an airy restaurant and bar, which has an towering, slanted ceiling with prominent wood beams, blond wood, and peach walls offset by stone. Although the Patagonia offers high quality, the style is a little sterile.

MODERATE

✪ **Cabañas Los Pinos.** Camino Teniente Vidal, Parcela 5, Coyhaique. ☎ **67/234898.** 3 cabañas. $32–$47 per person. No credit cards.

These neat, handcrafted log cabins are nestled in a pine forest on the shore of Río Simpson, about a 5-minute drive from downtown. There are cabins for three, four, or six people with a wood-burning stove; the cabin for six has one bedroom with a full-size bed and one with two bunks. The cabin for four is a little tight, but the charm of the place makes up for it. The cabin for six comes with a kitchen; the other two cabins must share a separate eating area, which guests usually don't mind considering the eating area is an idyllic little cabin with a beautiful view, great cooking facilities, and two tables for four. The couple who own and run the property are very friendly, and they have a vehicle for excursions.

El Reloj. Av. Baquedano 444. ☎ /fax **67/231108.** 6 units. TV TEL. $45 double. No credit cards.

This bed-and-breakfast–style hotel is housed in a forest green–and–lemon old home flanked by two *araucaria* trees. The hotel is surrounded by an abundance of greenery, which is pleasant, but it shades the windows, so the rooms are fairly dark. The rooms are a little on the small side, but are appealing; some have stone walls, and all have old wood floors. It's a cozy enough place and very clean. There's a common living area, and a small restaurant serving local fare, such as wild hare, sheep cheese, and fresh salmon. The restaurant is open to the public, but limited seating keeps the numbers low. The hotel also has a tiny shop that sells various souvenirs.

✪ **Hotelera San Sebastián.** Av. Baquedano 496, Coyhaique. ☎ **67/233427.** 7 units. TV TEL. $55 double. No credit cards.

This hotel's mustard exterior is so nondescript you might miss it the first time you pass by. But don't let the outside fool you: Inside, each room offers high-quality interiors and lovely views of the Coyhaique River meandering through grassy countryside. Huge bedrooms are tastefully painted in rose and cream, with matching linens and curtains, and are impeccably clean, as are the bathrooms. The eating area is a bit cold, resembling an ice cream parlor with linoleum floors and metal chairs. The hotel is on a busy street, but it sits back, tucked away between two buildings and therefore is very quiet. Note that all rooms except one have views.

Hotel Los Nires. Av. Baquedano 315, Coyhaique. ☎ **67/232261.** Fax 67/233372. E-mail: hotel_losnires@entelchile.net. 21 units. TV TEL. $51–$55 double. AE, DC, MC, V.

The Hotel Los Nires is a good mid-range choice, offering clean, bright rooms with decent, average furnishings. The rooms are average size, but if you want extra space the staff can put a full-size bed in a room built for a triple, charging guests the triple rate at $61 to $69. The hotel has a large restaurant on the bottom floor that is open to the public, but guests take their breakfast in a sunny dining area off the lobby. The hotel's wood facade repeats itself indoors, with wood slat paneling.

INEXPENSIVE

Hostal Araucaria. Cesar Gerardo Vielmo 71, Coyhaique. ☎ **67/232707.** 6 units. TV. $37–$42 double. No credit cards.

The Hostal Araucaria sits on a quiet street across from the Hostería Coyhaique's large garden park. This slightly weathered hostel could use a touch of paint here and there, and possibly a new roll of carpet, but overall it is a pretty decent option. There's an upstairs sitting area, and a downstairs dining area that feels a bit like someone's own living room. The woman who owns and runs this hostel is very welcoming.

WHERE TO DINE

There are several cafes downtown that are good for a quick bite, such as **Café Oriente** (☎ **67/231622**), Condell 201, with pizzas and sandwiches. The **Café Alemana** (☎ **67/231731**) is a very nice cafe almost next door at Condell 119—and despite its name and the waitresses' uniforms, does not serve German food. You'll find quick meals and sandwiches here, including a towering club sandwich.

For the listings below, reservations are not necessary, unless otherwise noted.

Casino de Bomberos. General Parra 365. ☎ **67/231437.** Main courses $6–$8. No credit cards. Daily 11am–4pm and 7:30pm–midnight. CHILEAN.

Chile's unpaid firemen need some way to make a buck, and here's their solution: Open a cafe in the fire station. The atmosphere is plain but fun, and the menu features every classic dish known in Chile. The food is tasty; the fixed-price lunch is $7, with an appetizer, drink, and main dish. On Sundays there are baked and fried fresh empanadas.

✪ **El Galpón.** Aldea 31. ☎ **67/232230.** Main courses $6–$9. AE, DC, MC, V. Daily 5pm–midnight. CHILEAN.

The Galpón's dining room sits above the surrounding buildings, offering good views of Coyhaique and beyond. The menu is quite long, with good appetizers featuring boiled abalone and shredded king crab with a lemon sauce. If you're in the mood for seafood, this is your place, although there are just as many meat items, such as grilled filet mignon or pork, on the menu.

✪ **Hostería Coyhaique.** Magallanes 131. ☎ **67/231137.** Main courses $6–$12. MC, V. Daily 1–11pm. INTERNATIONAL/CHILEAN.

Decent cuisine and ambience put the Hostería above most restaurants in Coyhaique. The spacious, semiformal restaurant features an extensive menu serving international and Chilean fare, including pastas, salads, grilled meats, and pan-fried seafood, with a choice of sauces such as garlic or peppercorn. There's another restaurant downstairs, which is really more enjoyable for its cozier ambience and valley view. If you're waiting for a table, the Hostería has a bar and small lounge; if you just feel like a cocktail and an appetizer platter of cheeses and meat or shellfish, this is your spot.

La Fiorentina. Francisco Bilbao 574. ☎ **67/238899.** Individual pizzas $3–$6. MC, V. Daily 9am–midnight. PIZZA/CHILEAN.

La Fiorentina serves a long list of pizzas and hearty, home-style dishes that can even be ordered to go—and stays open all day. The fixed-price lunch offers two selections and costs $4.50; it's very popular with the locals, who usually sit alone at lunchtime with their eyes glued to the TV blaring in one eating area. The atmosphere is very, very casual, but the service friendly and attentive.

La Olla. Prat 176. ☎ **67/234700.** Main courses $6.50–$12. MC, V. Daily noon–3:30pm and 8pm–midnight. CHILEAN.

This tiny restaurant offers a brightly lit, semi-casual dining area with floral tablecloths, and attentive service. The Olla looks as though it promises more, but the menu is surprisingly brief. The fare is typical Chilean, with classics such as beef tenderloin and fried conger eel paired with the usual french fries or mashed potatoes. The food is hearty and good, but too simple. There is, however, a decent paella on Sundays. The owner is usually on hand and likes to chat with customers.

✪ **La Pasarela.** Road to Puerto Aisén, Km1.5. ☎ **67/234520.** Reservations required. Main courses $7–$9. AE, DC, MC, V. Daily 1–3pm and 7:30–10:30pm. CHILEAN.

La Pasarela is about the best thing going in town. To get here, you need to take a taxi ride just outside town and across a wooden suspension bridge. The atmosphere is great: stone walls, wood beams, a roaring fireplace, and a comfortable bar for relaxing with a *pisco* sour. Through the windows, diners watch the Río Simpson rush by. The Pasarela is part of a cabaña/hotel complex, and usually whips up specials according to the guests' whims. Standbys include grilled meats and pastas. There is usually a fixed-price meal for lunch and dinner, including appetizer, main dish, dessert, and coffee for about $8 for lunch and $10 for dinner. Diners who are not lodging at La Pasarela must always call ahead for a reservation for dinner.

Restaurante Café Ricer. Horn 48. ☎ **67/232920.** Main courses $6–$10. AE, DC, MC, V. Daily 8:30am–1am. CHILEAN/INTERNATIONAL.

This restaurant is a favorite with traveling gringos, and just about everyone else in town, too. The large, pub-style restaurant is fashioned of logs, and a handcrafted wood staircase leads to a mellower, slightly more formal dining area upstairs. The food is fairly good, although slightly overpriced; a salmon with sausage and onions means one bite of sausage and a few slivers of onion only. The waitresses' frumpy diner uniforms and distracted service don't seem to reflect the style of the restaurant. The atmosphere is lively, though, and it's a good place for a casual meal and a beer.

SOUTH FROM COYHAIQUE
A SIGHTSEEING EXCURSION AROUND LAGO ELIZALDE

The Seis Lagunas (Six Lagoons) and Lago Elizalde region just south of Coyhaique offers a sightseeing loop that passes through fertile, rolling farmland and forest and past several picturesque lakes, all of which are known for outstanding fly-fishing. This area is little visited and is a great place to escape the crowds. If you're tempted to stay and fish for a few days here, there are lodges that cater to this sport, described in "Fly-Fishing Lodges Around Coyhaique," below. If you rent your own car, pick up a good map because many of these roads have no signs. Aventura Turismo (see "Tour Operators," above) offers an excursion here.

Leaving Coyhaique via the bridge near the Piedra del Indio (a rock outcrop that resembles the profile of an Indian), head first to Lago Atravesado, about 12 miles (20km) outside town. The road continues around the shore and across a bridge and enters the Valley Lagunas. From here, you'll want to turn back and drive the way you came until you spy a road to the right that heads through country fields, eventually passing the "six lagoons." Take the next right turn toward Lago Elizalde. This pretty, narrow lake set amid a thick forest of deciduous and evergreen beech is a great spot for picnicking and fishing. There is often a boat-rental concession here in the summer. There's a lodge here, but it's open only occasionally, usually when it books a large group. From here you'll need to turn back to return to Coyhaique; follow the sign for Villa Frei, which will lead you onto the paved road to Coyhaique instead of back-tracking the entire route. Keep an eye open for El Salto, a crashing waterfall that freezes solid in the winter.

Lago General Carrera & the Marble Cathedrals

The Lago General Carrera straddles the border of Argentina (where it is known as Lago Buenos Aires) and is Chile's largest lake. There are two reasons to pay a visit here: the robin's-egg blue hue of the water and the "Marble Cathedral," a series of limestone caves polished and sculpted by centuries of wind and water whose black and white swirls are a magnificent contrast to the blue water below. It's entirely feasible to make an entire circuit around Lago Carrera, crossing by ferry between Chile Chico and Puerto Ibáñez (reservations are a good idea for travelers with a vehicle; ☎ 67/ 237932), but it's not recommended for anyone with a short amount of time in Chile as you will need to spend the night somewhere along the way, most likely in Chile Chico. Try the charming **Hostería de la Patagonia,** just outside town on the Camino Internacional (☎ 67/411337), with an in-house restaurant. It charges $30 double; no credit cards accepted.

If you're looking for a day trip, however, a boating excursion to the Marble Cathedrals is a very interesting option—but at 138 miles (223km) from Coyhaique along a paved, then dirt road, it's a long round-trip drive to get to the dock in Puerto Tranquilo. A charter boat service takes visitors around and inside the marble caves for a half-day journey. You could plan a picnic and kick back along the shore. And (as if you haven't already guessed), the lake is great for fishing.

Fly-Fishing Lodges Around Coyhaique

El Saltamontes Lodge. Casilla 565, Coyhaique. ☎ /fax **67/232779.** Reservations arranged by The Fly Shop in the U.S. (☎ 800/669-3474). 2 cabañas, 1 suite. All-inclusive packages average $3,450 per angler, $2,250 for non-anglers per week. AE, DC, MC, V.

This rustic, charming lodge can be found on the shore of the Nireguao River, about 62 miles (100km) from Coyhaique. This river is one of the highest rated in South America for the big, fat trout who gorge on the area's abundance of grasshoppers. Two anglers are paired with a guide, who leads them to various spots accessible by foot, horse, or vehicle. Beginners usually have a lot of luck here. The lodge has four bedrooms, each with a view.

Heart of Patagonia Lodge. Casilla 324, Coyhaique. ☎ /fax **67/233701.** E-mail: mjenkins@ netline.cl. 5 units. Average 7-day, full-service packages cost $3,800 per person, less for non-anglers. No credit cards.

This lodge is closest to Coyhaique, if convenience is a big issue for you. The seven-bedroom, well-appointed lodge on the shore of Río Simpson is owned by an American and his Chilean wife, who offer good-natured service. Lunches are prepared stream-side so as not to interrupt your fishing. They'll take you to other rivers and lagoons for shore and drift fishing. There are plenty of activities for guests who do not fish, including hiking and horseback riding, and the owners charge less for non-angling guests. They also charge a 1- to 2-night fee if you're not interested in a package.

Paloma Lodge. Freire 436, Coyhaique. ☎ /fax **67/215848.** 4 units. All-inclusive 7-night packages average $2,850 per person, double occupancy. MC, V.

The Paloma is about 22 miles (35km) from Coyhaique, and is good for its proximity to the city, a wide variety of excursions, and a remote location near Lago Elizalde. Beyond fly-fishing, in which two to three guests are paired with a guide, there are hiking and boat excursions. Fishing here is along the Paloma and Simpson rivers and Lakes Azul and Desierto. The lodge offers comfortable accommodations and a fly-tying room.

The Terra Luna Lodge. Km1.5, Camino Chile Chico, Puerto Guadal. In Santiago, Arzobispo Casanova 3, Providencia. ☎ **2/737-3048.** www.terra-luna.cl. 8 units. $120–$190 double; $35 more per person, per day, for meals. All-inclusive packages run an average of 4 days/ 3 nights at $850 per person. AE, MC, V accepted only when paying at main office in Santiago.

This is a good lodge for anglers with non-fishing spouses. The Terra Luna Lodge is owned by the French-Chilean outfitter company Azimut, which offers excursions all over Chile. The location here on the shore of blue Lago Carrera is ideal. There are quite a few things on offer here: Laguna San Rafael, hiking, horseback riding, and of course fishing. The lodge is close to the Río Baker. All-inclusive packages include transportation from Coyhaique. Several classes of rooms here are a bit less expensive than those of the lodge's competitors.

8 Puerto Aisén, Puerto Chacabuco & Laguna San Rafael National Park

Puerto Aisén is 42 mi (68km) W of Coyhaique

Puerto Aisén was a vigorous port town until the 1960s, when silt filled the harbor and ships were forced to move 10 miles (16km) away to Puerto Chacabuco. Puerto Aisén still bustles, but it really offers few attractions to the visitor. The same could be said for Puerto Chacabuco; however, the majority of visitors to this region pass through here at some point to catch a ship or ferry to the spectacular Laguna San Rafael Glacier or to Puerto Montt. Most travelers arriving by ferry from Puerto Montt head straight to Coyhaique, and vice versa, but the full-day ferry ride to Laguna San Rafael leaves early and returns late, so many travelers find it convenient to spend a night here in Puerto Chacabuco.

It's recommended that you at least take a day trip to Puerto Aisén and Puerto Chacabuco, more than anything for the beautiful drive through the Reserva Nacional Río Simpson and the equally beautiful view of Aisén Sound at the journey's end. Both towns have pleasant squares for a quick stroll, and you can have lunch perched above the pier at the Hotel Loberías de Aysen (see "Where to Stay & Dine," below). If you don't have your own transportation, you can try **Buses Suray** at Eusebio Ibar 630 (☎ **67/238287**). The best bet is to call **Tour Australis** at Moraleda 589 (☎ **67/ 239696**), which offers day trips around this area. The tours operate November 15 to March 15 only, but the agency will arrange trips any time of the year for small groups.

Another excursion that is growing in popularity is a 2-hour boat trip to **Termas del Chilconal** in the middle of the dramatic Aisén Sound. The fare is about $30 per person and is arranged through the travel agency **Turismo Rucarary** in Puerto Aisén at Teniente Merino 668 (☎ **67/332862;** e-mail: turismorucaray@entelchile.net). This travel agency offers other excursions around the area and sells ferry tickets.

PARQUE NACIONAL LAGUNA SAN RAFAEL

If you're not planning a trip to Patagonia, the Laguna San Rafael National Park and its namesake glacier is a must-see. It's the foremost attraction in the Aisén region, drawing thousands of visitors each year to be dazzled by the tremendous vertical walls of blue ice that flow 28 miles (45km) from the Northern Ice Field and stretch 2½ miles (4km) across the Laguna San Rafael. Around these walls, thousands of pint-size and ship-size aquamarine icebergs float in soupy water, forming jagged sculptures. If you're lucky enough, you'll see a few come crashing off the iceberg in a mammoth kerplunk.

The glacier is actually receding, and quite quickly. The first explorers here in 1800 described the glacier as having filled three-quarters of the Laguna; when you're here you can appreciate how much has disappeared.

The Laguna San Rafael National Park is a staggering 1.7 million ha (4 million acres) large, incorporating the ice field and the glaciers that drain from it. Most of the park is inaccessible except by ship, from which visitors slowly cruise through narrow canals choked with thick vegetation. Like Torres del Paine, the park's singular beauty prompted UNESCO to declare Laguna San Rafael a World Biosphere Reserve. Visitors set sail in Puerto Chacabuco or Puerto Montt aboard an all-inclusive luxury liner or modest ferry for day and multiple-day trips. The ship anchors near the glacier and passengers board zodiacs (inflatable motorized boats) for a closer look at the icebergs and to appreciate the tremendous size of the face of the glacier, which in some places rises as high as 70m (230 ft.). A smaller fraction of visitors book an overflight excursion for a bird's-eye view of the glacier's entirety, which includes a touchdown at the park's center near the glacier for an hour-long visit.

It rains endlessly in this national park, but it is not a reason to cancel a trip to the glacier. Although this region sees heavy rainfall throughout the year, your best bet for clear skies is from November to March. Even on foul-weather days, the glacier is usually visible as the clouds tend to hover just above it. Bring protective rain gear just in case, or inquire when booking a ticket, as many companies provide guests with impermeable jackets and pants.

FERRY JOURNEYS THROUGH THE FJORDS TO LAGUNA SAN RAFAEL

This extraordinary journey is about a 124-mile (200km) sail from Puerto Chacabuco, but many visitors leave from Puerto Montt for a round-trip journey or to disembark in Puerto Chacabuco. Some visitors, especially on the high-end cruises, plan a multiple-day journey to Laguna San Rafael as the focal point of a trip to Chile. There are many options here. When booking a trip, consider the journey's length and whether you will be traveling at night and therefore missing any portions of scenery. If you're doing a loop, you should be able to see everything.

Navimag. Offices in Puerto Montt at Av. Angelmó 2187 in the Terminal de Transbordadores (☎ **65/432300**) and Santiago at El Bosque Norte 0440 (☎ 2/442-3120). In Chaitén, call ☎ 65/731570. In Coyhaique, Ibáñez 347 (☎ 67/233306). www.navimag.com. Prices vary, but average $400–$600 per person for the 4-night, round-trip journey from Puerto Montt. The 2-night, round-trip journey from Puerto Chacabuco costs about $280–$400 per person. AE, DC, MC, V.

Both Navimag and Transmarchilay offer modest passenger and cargo ferry service to Laguna San Rafael, but Navimag has the slight edge in quality and sleeping arrangements. There are several embarkation options here. Navimag's ship M/N *Evangelistas* leaves from Puerto Montt, arrives in Puerto Chacabuco the next day, the Laguna San Rafael the following day, and then returns to Chacabuco and back to Puerto Montt. You can get on or off at Puerto Chacabuco for a cheaper, shorter trip. Like the rest of the companies, guests are taken close to the icebergs aboard a dinghy. There are cabins for four with a private or shared bathroom, and with an exterior or interior view. If you're a couple or alone, you might have to share with strangers, unless you're willing to fork out the entire price for a four-person cabin. Like Navimag's ship to Puerto Natales, the cheapest bunks are for the adventurous or very young only. Prices include meals, your bunk, and excursions. Vehicles cost $80 to $120 one-way from Puerto Montt to Chacabuco.

Patagonia Expedition. In Santiago, Av. Providencia 2331, #602. ☎ **2/335-5951.** Fax 2/335-0581. In Coyhaique, Magallanes 131 (in the Hotel Coyhaique). ☎ 67/231137. Fax 67/233274. www.hotelsa.cl. E-mail: hotelsa@ctcinternet.cl. The day excursion from Puerto Chacabuco is $263 per person. The Flash San Rafael 3-day program costs $550 per person; the 5-day program costs $800 per person, double occupancy. Kids under 12 receive a 30% discount. Includes lodging, meals, and excursions. AE, DC, MC, V.

Not to be confused with Patagonia Express, the Expedition is another high-quality boat service offering day trips from Puerto Chacabuco and package tours that include a stay in the Hostería Coyhaique, which owns this company. The Flash San Rafael 3-day tours include lodging, a 1-day trip to the glacier, and a day excursion south of Coyhaique to the beautiful Lago Elizalde region, where there is yet another company hotel where guests are treated to a lamb barbecue. The Flash Plus 5-day package offers the same activities, but guests spend the fourth night at the hotel in Lago Elizalde (this 5-day trip requires a minimum of six guests). The Expedition is of the same general quality as the Patagonia Express. Kids here are given less of a discount than the Express, but the Expedition operates from December to March and the Express from January to February only.

Patagonia Express. In Santiago, Fidel Oteíza 1921, #1006. ☎ **2/225-6489.** Fax 2/274-8111. www.patagoniaconnex.cl. Prices average $1,000 per person for the 3-night package, including 1 night in Puerto Chacabuco and 2 nights at Termas de Puyuhuapi; half-price for kids under 16. The day excursion from Puerto Chacabuco (Jan–Feb only) is $260 per person, half-price for kids under 16. Includes all meals and excursions. AE, DC, MC, V.

Patagonia Express works in conjunction with the Termas de Puyuhuapi (see "Where to Stay & Dine" under "Puyuhuapi," above), leaving from Puerto Montt and including a 2-night stay at the luxury hotel and 1 night in Puerto Chacabuco. This is another premium excursion with sharp service and wonderful accommodations, but unlike Skorpios, you do not spend the night on board the ship. If the package price is beyond your reach, Patagonia Express operates a day trip leaving from Puerto Chacabuco on Fridays, from January to February.

Skorpios. In Santiago, Agusto Leguia Norte 118, Las Condes. ☎ **2/231-1030.** Fax 2/232-2269. In Puerto Montt, Av. Angelmó 1660. ☎ 65/256619. Fax 65/258315. www.skorpios.cl. E-mail: skorpios@tmm.cl. Cost for the 6-day/6-night journey is $850–$3,700 per person; the 4-day/4-night journey is $450–$1,500 per person. Prices include all meals, drinks, and excursions, and vary from high season to low season. Half-price for kids when they room with their parents. AE, DC, MC, V.

Skorpios is the upscale cruise service to Laguna San Rafael, offering deluxe on-board accommodations, great food, and all-around high quality. The wood-hewn cabins come with berths or full-size beds (or both, for families), in standard rooms or suites. There are three ships: the *Skorpios I, II,* and *III,* for 70, 160, and 110 people, respectively, although the trips are not usually heavily booked. Skorpios offers 6-day cruises leaving from Puerto Montt and 4-day cruises from Puerto Chacabuco. The 6-day takes visitors first along the coast of Chiloé near Ancud, then down to the glacier. On the return trip, the ship detours up the Fjord Quitralco to visit the remote hot springs there. Heading back to Puerto Montt, the ship cruises along the southern coast of Chiloé, stopping in Castro for an afternoon excursion. The 4-day journey also includes a stop at the hot springs. Skorpios offers service from September to May.

Transmarchilay. In Santiago, Agustinas 715, #403. ☎/fax **2/633-5959.** In Puerto Montt, Av. Angelmó 2187, Terminal de Transbordadores (☎ 65/270416; fax 65/270415). In Coyhaique, Av. 21 de Mayo 417 (☎ 67/231971). www.elcolono.cl. Prices vary, but average $575 cabin and $275 reclining seat, round-trip, per person. Round-trip from Chacabuco costs $475 cabin, $225 reclining seat. AE, DC, MC, V.

Transmarchilay mirrors Navimag's service, with a passenger and freight ferry that stops first in Puerto Chacabuco, and again on the return trip. This is without a doubt the cheapest option here, but there are only eight cabins, and lots and lots of reclining seats: a *cama* folds out into a bed, a pullman reclines about halfway, and a *turista* tilts back just a little. If you're doing the entire 4-night trip, these reclining seats can be murder, but if it's just 2 nights from Chacabuco, you might be willing to give up a little comfort for the low price. Transmarchilay includes all meals and excursions in the price.

OVERFLIGHT TRIPS TO THE LAGUNA SAN RAFAEL

Three companies arrange overflight trips to the Laguna San Rafael, which include a few hours near the glacier. It is a spectacular experience to view the glacier in its entirety (which means you won't want to do this trip on a cloudy day). These are charter flights, so you'll have to get a group together or fork over the entire price. Prices range from $600 for a five-seater plane to $1,000 for an eight-person twin engine. Try **Transportes Don Carlos** at Subteniente Cruz 63 (☎ **67/231981**), **Aerohein** at Av. Baquedano 500 (☎ **67/232772**), or **Transportes San Rafael** at Av. 18 de Septiembre 469 (☎ **67/233408**).

WHERE TO STAY & DINE

Hotel Loberías de Aysen. Carrera 50, Puerto Chacabuco, Región XI. ☎ **67/351115.** Fax 67/351188. 27 units. TEL. $55–$60 double. DC, MC, V. Free parking.

Puerto Chacabuco's slight shabbiness belies its lovely location on the shore of Aisén Sound, and thankfully this hotel does it justice with wraparound windows in a large dining area and lounge. The Loberías de Aysen is really the obvious choice for its location right above the pier, and because it is the only decent hotel in Puerto Chacabuco. This is where most travelers with ferry connections spend the night when they don't want to make the early-morning journey from Coyhaique. It's a large complex with a garden, a kid's play area, 27 bedrooms, and 12 cabins with two and three bedrooms for four to six guests. Only the cabins for four come with kitchens, and unfortunately none come with views. The rooms have been recently renovated with new wallpaper, paint, and linens. Even if you're not planning on staying here, stop by for a coffee or *pisco* sour before heading back to Coyhaique.

Patagonia & Tierra del Fuego

15

Few places in the world have captivated the imagination of explorers and travelers like Patagonia and Tierra del Fuego. It has been 4 centuries since the first Europeans sailed through on a boat captained by Ferdinand Magellan. And yet this vast, remote region is still for the most part unexplored. Sailors from around the world continue to test their luck and courage in these harrowing straits and fjords. Mountaineers stage elaborate excursions through rugged territories only to be beaten back, like their predecessors, by unrelenting storms. A traveler can drive for days without seeing another soul on the vast Patagonian *pampa,* his perception of time and distance so warped that he believes he is the only human left on planet. What seduces so many people to Patagonia is the idea of the "remote"—indeed, the very notion of traveling to The End of the World. It is a seduction, but also an illusion. After all, people do live here—very few people, in relation to the populations of both Chile and Argentina, but those who do are hardy survivors.

A harsh, wind-whipped climate and Patagonia's geological curiosities have produced some of the most beautiful natural attractions in the world: the granite towers of Torres del Paine and Los Glaciares national parks, the Southern and Northern Ice Fields with their colossal glaciers, the flat *pampa* broken by multicolored sedimentary bluffs, the emerald fjords and lakes that glow an impossible sea-foam blue. In the end, this is what compels most travelers to plan a trip down here. Beyond landscapes, the region's "cowboys" (called *gauchos* in Argentina or *baquedanos* in Chile), with their trademark berets and sheepskin saddles, lend a certain air of romanticism.

EXPLORING THE REGION

For its tremendous size, Patagonia and Tierra del Fuego are surprisingly easy to travel, especially now that most destinations have opened airports. It's entirely feasible to plan a circuit that loops through, for example, Ushuaia, Punta Arenas, Torres del Paine, and then El Calafate and El Chaltén. If you're planning a trip to Chile or Argentina, you'll really want to include a visit to this region if possible—there's so much to see and do here, you'd be missing out if you went home without having put foot in this magical territory. How much time you plan on spending in Patagonia is entirely up to you. If you're planning a backpacking trip in Torres del Paine, for example, you'll want to spend between 5 and 10 days there—however, those with plans for a few

Calling Between Chile & Argentina

One would think that two neighboring countries would offer low telephone rates for calls made from one to the other, but not so with Chile and Argentina. Visitors can expect to pay the same or higher rates as a call to the U.S., often around $1 per minute. When calling from Argentina to Chile, first dial **00-56,** then the area code and number. The prefix for Chilean cell phones is **09,** but callers from Argentina will drop the 0; so to call a Chilean cell phone from Argentina dial **00-56-9** and then the number.

When calling from Chile to Argentina, you must first call whichever carrier you're using (ask your host, your hotel or at a calling center for the carrier prefix, usually either **123, 181 or 120**), followed by **0-54,** then the area code and number. Argentine area codes always begin with a "0" prefix, which you'll drop when dialing. For example, if dialing from Punta Arenas, Chile, to Ushuaia, Argentina, you'll dial 123 (or whichever carrier you're using), then 0-54-2901 and the number. When dialing Argentine cell phone numbers (which begin in 15), drop the 15 and replace it with the region's area code.

light walks and sightseeing drives in that national park might find that four days are a good enough dose. If Patagonia is your focus destination in Chile and/or Argentina, two to three weeks is sufficient for visits to the region's highlights, less if you plan to remain in one country only. A quick trip to Patagonia might include two days in El Calafate, three in Torres del Paine, and two days in Punta Arenas. A longer journey could begin with several days in El Chaltén, two in El Calafate, five in Torres del Paine, two in Punta Arenas, and a flight or cruise to Ushuaia for three to four days.

Prices jump and crowds swell from early November to late March, and some businesses open during this time frame only. The busiest months are January and February, but these summer months are not necessarily the best months to visit Patagonia, as calmer weather prevails from mid-October to late November, and mid-March to late April.

1 Punta Arenas, Chile

157½ miles (254km) SE of Puerto Natales; 1,916 miles (3,090km) S of Santiago

Punta Arenas is the capital of the Magellanic and Antarctic Region XII, and it is Patagonia's most important city. Upon arrival it seems unbelievable that Punta Arenas is able to prosper as well as it does in such a forsaken location on the gusty shore of the Strait of Magellan, but its streets hum with activity and its airport and seaports bustle with traffic passing through the strait or in transit to Antarctica. The town has made a flourishing living from carbon mines, wool production, petroleum, the fishing industry, and as a service center for cargo ships; really, it seems there is nothing this outpost of 110,000 can't produce.

Punta Arenas's earliest wealth is reflected in the grand stone mansions that encircle the main plaza, which were built with earnings from the sheep *estancias,* or ranches, of the late 1800s. Gold fever followed, and then flight from the First World War, and hundreds poured into the region from Yugoslavia, Russia, Spain, and Italy. Today, Punta Arenas's streets are lined with residential homes with colorful, corrugated rooftops, business offices and hotels downtown, and an industrial port—all a bit weather-whipped but attractive in its own way. The city considers itself somewhat of an independent republic due to its isolation from the rest of Chile, and this in turn

Patagonia

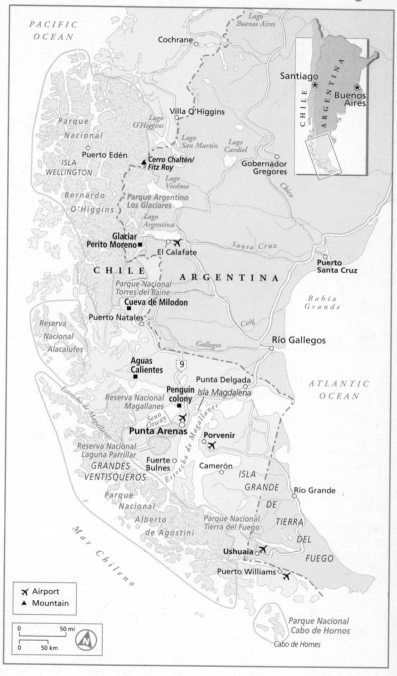

PACIFIC
OCEAN

Cochrane

Lago
Buenos Aires

Santiago

CHILE
ARGENTINA

Buenos
Aires

Villa O'Higgins

Parque
Nacional

Lago
O'Higgins

Lago
San Martín

Lago
Cardiel

Puerto Edén

Cerro Chaltén/
Fitz Roy

Gobernador
Gregores

Chico

ISLA
WELLINGTON

Lago
Viedma

Bernardo

O'Higgins

Parque Argentino
Los Glaciares

Lago
Argentina

Glaciar
Perito Moreno

El Calafate

CHILE

ARGENTINA

Santa Cruz

Puerto
Santa Cruz

Parque Nacional
Torres del Paine

Cueva de Milodon

Bahía
Grande

Reserva
Nacional
Alacalufes

Puerto Natales

Coig

Gallegos

Río Gallegos

Aguas
Calientes

9

Punta Delgada

ATLANTIC
OCEAN

Penguin
colony

Isla Magdalena

Reserva Nacional
Magallanes

Seno
Otway

Punta Arenas

Porvenir

Estrecho de Magallanes

Reserva Nacional
Laguna Parrillar

Fuerte
Bulnes

Camerón

ISLA

Río Grande

GRANDES
VENTISQUEROS

GRANDE

Parque
Nacional

DE

TIERRA

Alberto
de Agostini

Parque Nacional
Tierra del Fuego

DEL

FUEGO

Mar Chileno

Ushuaia

Puerto Williams

✈ Airport
▲ Mountain

Parque Nacional
Cabo de Hornos

Cabo de Hornos

0   50 mi

0   50 km

367

Cruising from Punta Arenas to Ushuaia, Argentina

Cruceros Australis operates an unforgettable journey from Punta Arenas to Ushuaia and Ushuaia to Punta Arenas aboard its ship, the M/V *Terra Australis*. This cruise takes passengers through remote coves and spectacular channels and fjords in Tierra del Fuego and then heads into the Beagle Channel, stopping in Puerto Williams on Isla Navarino and later Ushuaia, Argentina. The trip can be done as a 7-night, 8-day round-trip journey, a 4-night one-way from Punta Arenas, or a 3-night, one-way journey from Ushuaia. Many guests aboard the *Terra Australis* plan their entire trip to South America around this cruise.

The beauty of this cruise is that you are taken to places in Tierra del Fuego that few have a chance to see. Passengers are shuttled via zodiacs (motorized inflatable boats) to shore for two daily excursions that can include visits to glaciers or a sea elephant rookery, walks to view elaborate beaver dams, horseback rides, and a chance to fly over the Cordillera Darwin (for an additional price). There are several excellent bilingual guides who give daily talks about the region's flora, fauna, history, and geology. Service aboard the *Terra Australis* is impeccable, and the food is quite good. The accommodations are comfortable, ranging from suites to simple cabins. All-inclusive, per person prices (excluding cocktails) for a mid-range cabin range from $1,046 to $1,679 one-way from Punta Arenas and $1,535 to $2,239 round-trip. This cruise operates from late September to April. For reservations or information, contact their offices in Santiago at Av. El Bosque Norte 0440 (☎ **2/442-3110;** fax 2/203-5025) or in Punta Arenas at Av. Independencia 840 (☎ **61/224256**), or check out their Web site at www.australis.com.

has affected the personality of its people, an indefatigable bunch who brace themselves every summer against the gales that blow through this town like a hurricane. The wind, in fact, is so fierce at times that ropes are strung up in and near the plaza for people to hold onto. If that weren't enough, residents here now have to contend with the ozone layer, which opened completely for the first time last year.

All of this history and the extremity of Punta Arenas's climate, as well as its position overlooking the renowned Magellan Strait, make for a fascinating place to explore. There's enough to do here to fill a day or two, and you'll want to at least spend the night here, even if your plans are to head directly to Torres del Paine.

GETTING THERE

BY PLANE   Punta Arenas's **Aeropuerto Presidente Ibañez** is 12 miles (20km) north of town, and it's serviced with daily flights from Santiago and Puerto Montt by **LanChile/Ladeco,** Lautaro Navarro 999 (☎ **600/661-3000** or 61/241100); Avant, Roca 924 (☎ **61/228312**); and the Peruvian airline **Aero Continente,** corner of O'Higgins and Roca (☎ **61/220392**). The airline **Aerovias DAP,** O'Higgins 891 (☎ **61/223340**), has flights to and from Ushuaia every Wednesday and Friday from October to March, and Wednesdays only April to September; it also has daily service to Porvenir and the only air service to Puerto Williams. To get to Punta Arenas, hire a taxi for about $9 or take one of the transfer services there (which can also arrange to take you back to the airport): **Ecotour** (☎ **61/223670**) and **Buses Transfer** (☎ **61/229613**) have door-to-door service for $5 per person; Buses Transfer has bus service to and from its office for $3 per person.

BY BUS   From Puerto Natales: **Bus Sur** at José Menéndez 565 (☎ **61/244464**) has four daily trips; **Buses Fernandez** at Armando Sanhueza 745 (☎ **61/242313**) has seven daily trips; **Buses Transfer** at Pedro Montt 414 (☎ **61/229613**) has two daily trips; and **Buses Pacheco** at Av. Colón 414 (☎ **61/242174**) has three daily trips.

To and from Ushuaia, Argentina: **Buses Tecni Austral** and **Buses Ghisoni** at Lautaro Navarro 975 (☎ **61/222078**) leave Punta Arenas Tuesday, Thursday, Saturday, and Sunday and return from Ushuaia on Monday, Wednesday, and Saturday. **Buses Pacheco** at Av. Colón 900 (☎ **61/242174**) has service to Ushuaia on Monday, Wednesday, and Friday and returns on Tuesday, Thursday, and Saturday. Buses cross through Porvenir or Punta Delgada.

BY CAR   Ruta 9 is a paved road between Punta Arenas and Puerto Natales. Strong winds often require that you exercise extreme caution when driving this route. To get to Tierra del Fuego, there are two options: Cross by ferry from Punta Arenas to Porvenir, or drive east on Ruta 255 to Ruta 277 and Punta Delgada for the ferry crossing there (for more information, see "The Far South: Puerto Williams, Chile," below).

CAR RENTAL   **Hertz** at O'Higgins 987 (☎ 61/248742), **Lubac** at Magallanes 970 (☎ 61/242023), **Budget** at O'Higgins 964 (☎ 61/241696), **Emsa** at Roca 1044 (☎ 61/241182), **First** at O'Higgins 949 (☎ 61/220780), and **Rus** at Av. Colón 614 (☎ 61/221529).

VISITOR INFORMATION

There's an excellent **Oficina de Turismo** (☎ **61/200610**) inside a glass gazebo in the Plaza de Armas. The staff are not only helpful, they also sell a wide range of fascinating historical and anthropological literature and postcards. The office is open from October to March, Monday to Friday 8am to 8pm, Saturday 9am to 6pm, and Sunday 9am to 2pm. From April to September, it's open Monday to Friday 8am to 7pm, and closed Saturday and Sunday. **Sernatur**'s office at Waldo Seguel 689 (☎ **61/225385**), on the other hand, is harried and inattentive; it's open Monday to Friday 8:15am to 8pm.

FAST FACTS: PUNTA ARENAS

Currency Exchange   **La Hermandad,** Lautaro Navarro 1099 (☎ **61/248090**); **Cambios Gasic,** Roca 915, #8 (☎ **61/242396**); **Cambio de Moneda Stop,** José Nogueira 1168 (☎ **61/223334**); or **Scott Cambios,** corner of Av. Colón and Magallanes (☎ **61/245811**). Casas de cambio are open Monday to Friday from 9am to 1pm and 3 to 7pm and Saturday from 9am to 1pm. For banks with 24-hour ATM machines, go to Banco Santander at Magallanes 997 (☎ **61/247145**), Banco de Chile at Roca 864 (☎ **61/206033**), and Banco de A. Edwards at Plaza Muñoz Gamero 1055 (☎ **61/241175**). Banks are open Monday to Friday 9am to 2pm.

Hospital   **Hospital de las FF.AA Cirujano Guzman,** Avenida Manuel Bulnes and Guillermos (☎ **61/207500**), or the **Clínica Magallanes,** Av. Manuel Bulnes 1448 (☎ **61/211527**).

Internet Access   **Telefoníca,** Bories 798 (☎ **61/248230**); **Austro Internet,** Croacia 690 (☎ **61/229297**) Internet service costs an average of $4 per hour.

Laundry   **Lavandería Antarctica,** Jorge Montt 664; **Autoservicio Lavasol,** O'Higgins 969; or **Lavandería Lavasuper,** José Nogueira 1595.

Pharmacy   **Farmacias Cruz del Sur,** Bories 658 (☎ **61/227018**) and José Nogueira 1120 (☎ **61/244871**); **Farmacia Marisol,** Fagnano 681 (☎ **61/224650**); and **Farmacias Salco** at Bories 683 (☎ **61/229241**) and Bories 970 (☎ **61/229227**).

Post Office   The central post office is at José Menéndez and Bories (☎ **61/222210**); hours are Mon–Fri 9am–6pm and Sat 9am–1pm.

WHAT TO SEE & DO IN PUNTA ARENAS

You might begin your tour of Punta Arenas in the Plaza Muñoz Gamero, in whose center you'll find a bronze sculpture of Ferdinand Magellan, donated by José Menéndez on the 400-year anniversary of Magellan's discovery of the Strait of Magellan. The leafy plaza is a beautiful place to take a seat, and several vendors here have set up stands selling crafts and souvenirs. From the plaza on Avenida 21 de Mayo, head north toward Avenida Colón for a look at the Teatro Municipal, designed by the French architect Numa Mayer and modeled after the magnificent Teatro Colón in Buenos Aires. Head down to the waterfront and turn south toward the pier to watch the shipping action. At the pier is a 1913 clock imported from Germany that has a complete meteorological instrumentation and hands showing the moon's phases and a zodiac calendar.

City Cemetery. Av. Manuel Bulnes and Angamos. No phone. Free admission. Daily 7:30am–8pm.

They say you can't really understand a culture until you see where they bury their dead, and in the case of the cemetery of Punta Arenas, this edict certainly rings true. The City Cemetery was opened by the Governor Señoret in 1894 and features a giant stone portico donated by Sara Braun in 1919. Inside this necropolis lies a veritable miniature city, with avenues that connect the magnificent tombs of the region's founding families, settlers, and civic workers and a rather solemn tomb where lie the remains of the last Selk'nam Indians of Tierra del Fuego. As interesting are the cypress trees that line the walkways, which have been trimmed into tall, bell-shaped spheres. You can walk here, but it's a good 20 minutes or more from the plaza.

✪ **Instituto de Patagonia/Museo del Recuerdo.** Av. Manuel Bulnes 01890. ☎ **61/ 217173.** Admission 75¢. Mon–Fri 8:30–11am and 2:15–6pm; Sat 8:30–12:30pm.

The Instituto de Patagonia is run by the University of Magallanes and directed by the region's chief historian Dr. Mateo Martinic. Here you'll find an engaging exhibit of colonial artifacts called the Museum of Remembrances. Antique machinery and horse-drawn carts are displayed around the lawn and encircled by several colonial buildings that have been lifted and transported here from ranches around the area. One cabin shows visitors what home life was like for a ranch hand, another has been set up to resemble a typical dry goods store, another is a garage with a 1908 Peugeot, and another, a carpenter's workshop. There's a library on the premises with a collection of books and maps on display and for sale. To get into the colonial buildings, you'll need to ask someone in the museum's office to unlock them for you. The museum is about 2½ miles (4km) out of town, so you'll need to take a taxi. The Zona Franca (a duty-free shopping center) is just down the street, so you could tie in a visit to the two.

✪ **Museo Salesiano Maggiorino Borgatello.** Av. Manuel Bulnes and Maipú. ☎ **61/ 221001.** Admission $2.50. Tues–Sun 10am–12:30pm and 3–6pm.

This fascinating museum is well worth a visit, offering insight into the Magellanic region's history, anthropology, ecology, and industrial history. The first room you enter is a dusty collection of stuffed and mounted birds and mammals that at turns feels almost macabre. It's an old collection, and some specimens such as the pygmy owl are in such desperate shape that it nearly provokes a laugh; nevertheless, it allows you to fully appreciate the tremendous size of the condor and the puma. In the adjoining room is a reproduction of the Milodon cave near Puerto Natales, where remains of a prehistoric giant sloth were found. Several rooms in the museum hold displays of Indian hunting tools, ritual garments, jewelry, an Alacalufe bark canoe, and colonial and ranching implements. The beautiful black-and-white photos of the early

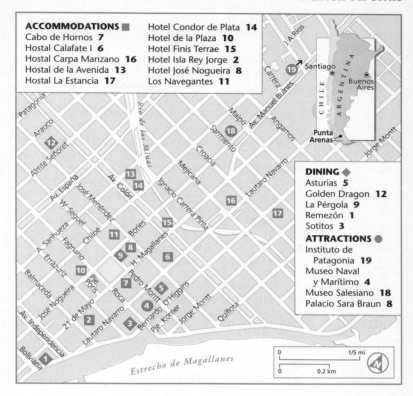

ACCOMMODATIONS ■
Cabo de Hornos **7**
Hostal Calafate I **6**
Hostal Carpa Manzano **16**
Hostal de la Avenida **13**
Hostal La Estancia **17**
Hotel Condor de Plata **14**
Hotel de la Plaza **10**
Hotel Finis Terrae **15**
Hotel Isla Rey Jorge **2**
Hotel José Nogueira **8**
Los Navegantes **11**

DINING ◆
Asturias **5**
Golden Dragon **12**
La Pérgola **9**
Remezón **1**
Sotitos **3**

ATTRACTIONS ●
Instituto de
  Patagonia **19**
Museo Naval
  y Marítimo **4**
Museo Salesiano **18**
Palacio Sara Braun **8**

missionary Alberto d'Agostini are well displayed, and there's a sizable exhibit charting the region's petroleum production. Plan to spend at least an hour here.

Museo Naval y Marítimo. Pedro Montt 981. No phone. Admission $1.25. Tues–Sat 9:30am–12:30pm and 3–6pm.

Punta Arenas's tribute to its seafaring history is this Naval and Maritime Museum. Here you'll find photos depicting the various ships and the port activity over the past century, as well as small ship replicas and other artifacts. This museum is really recommended only for those with a strong interest in nautical-related items.

✪ **Palacio Sara Braun.** Plaza Muñoz Gamero 716. ☎ **61/248840.** Admission $1 adults; free for under 16. Tues–Sun 10am–1pm and 6–8:30pm.

✪ **Museo Regional Braun Menéndez.** Magallanes 949. ☎ **61/244216.** Admission $1.50; Sun and holidays free. Mon–Sat 10:30am–5pm; Sun 10:30am–2pm.

These two attractions are testament to the staggering wealth produced by the region's large-scale, colonial-era sheep and cattle *estancias*. The museums are the former residences of several members of the families Braun, Nogueira, and Menéndez, who believed that any far-flung, isolated locale could be tolerated if one were to "live splendidly and remain in constant contact with the outside world." Splendid is an understatement when one gets a glimpse of these veritable palaces. The Palacio Sara Braun is now partially occupied by the Hotel José Nogueira and the Club de la Unión, a meeting area for the city's commercial and political leaders. Sara Braun, who emigrated from Russia with her brother Mauricio Braun, was the widow of the shipping, wool, and cattle magnet José Nogueira. The Museo Regional Braun Menéndez is the former residence of Mauricio Braun and Josefina Menéndez, a marriage that united the two largest fortunes in the Magellanic region. With the falling price of wool and the nationalization of *estancias* during the 1960s, the families lost a large percentage of their holdings, and their descendants have since moved out, settling in places such as Buenos Aires.

The homes are national monuments and both have been preserved in their original state. French architects planned the neoclassical exteriors, and European craftsmen were imported to craft marble fireplaces and hand-paint walls to resemble marble and leather. The interior fixtures and furniture were also imported from Europe, including gold and crystal chandeliers, tapestries from Belgium, Arabian tables inset with abalone, stained-glass cupolas, English and French furniture, hand-carved desks, and more. Although one is awed by the grandeur of these palaces, the knowledge that these families single-handedly exterminated the Native Indians in the region on their quest for wealth leaves the visitor with a sad sense of ambivalence. The Museo Menéndez also has a salon devoted to the ranching and maritime history of the region. Tours are conducted in Spanish; however, the museums offer literature in English.

SHOPPING

Punta Arenas is home to a duty-free shopping center called the **Zona Franca,** with several blocks of shops hawking supposedly cheaper electronics, home appliances, imported foodstuffs, sporting goods, perfumes, clothing, toys, booze, and cigarettes. The savings here are negligible, except for alcohol, and the selection isn't what you'd hope for, although there certainly is a lot on offer, including a few supermarkets. Really, this is a good place to stock up on supplies if you're planning a backpack trip to Torres del Paine—otherwise, forget it. The Zona Franca is located on Av. Manuel Bulnes, just outside town. Because of its proximity to the Museo del Recuerdo (see "What to See & Do in Punta Arenas," above), you might want to tie a visit in here with that attraction; take a taxi or grab any *colectivo* that says ZONA FRANCA on its sign. It's open Monday to Saturday 10am to 12:30pm and 3 to 8pm, and closed Sundays and holidays.

For regional crafts, try the great selection available at **Chile Típico,** Carrera Pinto 1015 (☎ **61/225827**), or **Artesanía Yoyi,** Av. 21 de Mayo 1393 (☎ **61/229156**). Both have knitwear, carved wood items, lapis lazuli, postcards, and more.

EXCURSIONS OUTSIDE PUNTA ARENAS

TOUR OPERATORS

Many tour operators run conventional city tours, trips to the Seno Otway colony and Fuerte Bulnes, as well as short visits and multiday, all-inclusive trekking excursions to Torres del Paine National Park. However, more and more adventure-travel outfitters are popping up around town, offering day and week-long trips to Tierra del Fuego, including all-inclusive kayaking, mountaineering, hiking, fly-fishing, and horseback combination trips.

Turismo Yamana, Av. Colón 568 (☎ **61/240056;** www.chileaustral.com/yamana; e-mail: yamana@chileaustral.com), offers kayak trips on the Strait of Magellan for a half day ($35 per person) or full day ($70), minimum two persons. The company also offers multiple-day trips to Lago Blanco in Tierra del Fuego for trekking, horseback riding, and fishing. If you're a bird watcher, Turismo Yamana can put you in touch with an English-speaking ornithologist guide. Newcomer **Inhospita Patagonia,** Lautaro Navarro 1013 (☎ **61/224510;** e-mail: inhospita@chileanpatagonia.com), leans heavily on the adventure side, including climbing and trekking in Torres del Paine, kayaking the Strait of Magellan, and multiple-day trekking and horseback riding trips to Tierra del Fuego. The tour company **VientoSur,** Fagano 585 (☎ **61/ 226930;** e-mail: vientosur@chileaustral.com), offers all conventional tours, as well as tours to Torres del Paine; overnight tours with this company include lodging in a hotel in Torres del Paine. They also arrange tours to Porvenir.

FUERTE BULNES

In 1843, Captain Juan Williams, the naturalist Bernardo Philippi, 16 sailors and soldiers, and two women set sail from Ancud in Chiloé to the Strait of Magellan to plant the Chilean flag in this region before European colonists could beat them to it. They chose a rocky promontory that dominated the strait and named it **Fuerte Bulnes.** Although this promontory was strategically appropriate for monitoring seafaring traffic, the location proved undesirable, and they pulled up stakes and moved 15½ miles (25km) north, founding what is today Punta Arenas. In recognition of the historical value of Fuerte Bulnes, the Chilean government reconstructed the site in 1943, its centenary anniversary, and made it a national monument. Here you'll find reproductions of the log cabins that housed the settlers, a chapel, and several cannons. There are no set hours, and admission is free.

Just before Fuerte Bulnes is a short road leading to **Puerto Hambre.** The site was founded as Rey Felipe by Pedro Sarmiento de Gamboa in 1584, and settled by 103 colonists who were tragically stranded after tremendous storms prevented their ships from returning to shore. The name Puerto Hambre (Port Hunger) was given by the British captain Thomas Cavendish who found only one survivor when he docked here in 1587 (the rest had died of starvation and exposure). In 1993, the Chilean ambassador José Miguel Barros found the plan for Rey Felipe in the library of the Institute of France in Paris, and it is the oldest known document of urban history in Chile. The only thing you'll find here is a plaque and the remains of a chapel, but imagining yourself in the place of these settlers on this forsaken plot is worth the visit. Admission for both Fuerte Bulnes and Puerto Hambre is free, with unspecified hours. To get here, drive south from Punta Arenas to the road's end, or take a tour with **Buses Transfer,** Pedro Montt 966 (☎ **61/229613**), or **Eco Tour Patagonia,** Lautaro Navarro 1091 (☎ **61/223670**). Buses Transfer leaves at 9am, Eco Tour at 9:30am; the cost is $13 per person.

PENGUIN COLONIES AT SENO OTWAY & ISLA MAGDALENA

One of the highlights of a visit to Punta Arenas is a trip to the penguin colonies at Seno Otway or Isla Magdalena. At both colonies visitors are allowed to watch the amusing Magellanic penguins (also called Jackass penguins for their characteristic bray) at their nesting sites, whisking out sprays of sand or poking their heads out of their burrows. These penguins form lifelong partnerships and divide their chores equally: Every morning around 10am and in the afternoon around 5pm, the penguin couples change shifts—one heads out to fish, the other returns from fishing to take care of their young. When this changing of the guard begins, the penguins politely line up and waddle to and from the sea. Viewing takes place from September to late March, but they're best viewed from November to February.

Seno Otway is a smaller colony, with an estimated 3,000 penguins, and it's accessible by road about 40 miles (65km) from Punta Arenas. A volunteer study group has developed the sight with roped walkways and lookout posts, including a peek-a-boo wall where you can watch the penguins diving into the ocean. Tours are offered in four languages, and there is a tiny cafe here, too. Admission is $3.50; hours are September to April 8am to 8:30pm. Both **Buses Transfer,** Pedro Montt 966 (☎ **61/229613**) and O'Higgins 1055 (☎ **61/243984**), and **Eco Tour Patagonia,** Lautaro Navarro 1091 (☎ **61/223670**), offer transportation to Seno Otway, leaving at 4pm daily (most tour companies also have similar trips). The cost, not including the entrance fee, is $13. Your hotel can probably arrange a tour here as well. If you drive here in your own vehicle, come for the morning shift-change, when the crowds are thinner. Take Ruta 9 toward Puerto Natales, then turn left on the dirt road that branches out near the police checkpoint.

   Isla Magdalena is much larger than Seno Otway, with an estimated 150,000 penguins sharing nesting space with cormorants. These penguins are more timid than those at Seno Otway, but the sight of so many of these birds bustling to and fro is decidedly more impressive. To get here, you need to take a ferry, which makes for a pleasant half-day afternoon excursion. **Turismo Comapa,** Av. Independencia 830, 2nd floor (☎ **61/225804**), puts this tour together. Its boat, the *Barcaza Melinka,* leaves from the pier at 3:30pm, returning at 8:30pm on Tuesdays, Thursdays, and Saturdays from December to February ($30 for adults, $15 children under 12).

SKIING IN THE AREA

Punta Arenas has a ski resort that operates from mid-June to mid-September: the **Centro de Esquí Cerro Mirador,** situated at the border of the Reserva Nacional Magallanes. If you're here during the season, this little resort is a fun place to spend the afternoon, notable more than anything for its view of the Strait of Magellan, Tierra del Fuego, and—on a clear day—Dawson Island. During the summer they often run their only chair lift to carry you to the top of the peak, or you can hike the hill yourself. The resort has 10 runs, ski rental, and a cafeteria. Ski lift tickets cost about $20. The resort (☎ **61/241479**) is very close to town; to get here, take a taxi.

WHERE TO STAY

In general, lodging in Punta Arenas is somewhat expensive for the caliber of accommodations available. Note that price ranges reflect the low to high season—high season being from October 15 to April 15—and that each hotel is willing to negotiate a price, especially if you book the more expensive hotels with a travel agent. For all hotels, parking is either free, or street parking is plentiful.

EXPENSIVE

Cabo de Hornos. Plaza Muñoz Gamero 1025, Punta Arenas. ☎ **61/242134.** Fax 61/229473. www.panamericanahoteles.cl. E-mail: rescabo@panamericanahoteles.cl. 91 units. TV TEL. $166 double. AE, DC, MC, V.

In 1962, the Cabo de Hornos was built as the first grand hotel in Punta Arenas. The style of the lobby, especially the Hornos's retro-chic bar, is reminiscent of this era, and not in an unattractive way. But then there are the rooms, which seem carelessly mismatched with clashing fabrics and outmoded furniture (especially the funny headboards fashioned with padded sections about 3 feet above the mattresses). The bathrooms here are circa 1962, with clunky toilets and bidets, but they've been well maintained. The best things this hotel has to offer are its direct view of the Strait of Magellan (try to get a corner room), the location directly overlooking the main plaza, and a tremendous breakfast buffet. Even so, the price is much higher than you'd expect for what's offered. The Cabo de Hornos is part of the Panamericana Hotel chain.

   Dining/Diversions: The hotel's **Navarino** restaurant serves regional and international food as well as a daily breakfast buffet. There's also an adjoining bar.

   Amenities: Laundry, 24-hour room service, conference room.

Hotel Finis Terrae. Av. Colón 766, Punta Arenas. ☎ **61/228200.** Fax 61/248124. www.hotelfinisterrae.com. E-mail: finister@ctcreuna.cl. 70 units, 2 suites. TV TEL. $140–$160 double. AE, DC, MC, V.

This hotel is very popular with foreigners, especially Americans, and it's part of the Best Western chain. The well-lit accommodations here are exceptionally comfortable, with king beds in double rooms and a softly hued decor in peach and beige, with wood trim and wooden headboards. The decor is not as brand-new as that of the Los Navegantes (its closest competitor, see below), but it's slightly warmer. The singles here are tiny, so be sure to ask for a larger double for the single price, which they will likely agree to, especially during slower months. There are quite a few places to relax within the confines of the hotel, including a front lobby, a fireside lounge with a sundry of couches, a snack restaurant, and a top-floor lounge and restaurant with an enormous A-framed ceiling fronted with windows on both ends that look out over the city and the Strait of Magellan. The view from these two salons is undoubtedly the best in Punta Arenas.

Dining/Diversions: The **Finis Terrae** has a full-service, penthouse restaurant with good international food and an even better panoramic view. There's also a bar/lounge on the top floor, and a coffee shop on the lobby floor.

Amenities: Laundry, room service.

Hotel Isla Rey Jorge. Av. 21 de Mayo 1243, Punta Arenas. ☎/fax **61/248220.** E-mail: islareyjorge@ctcinternet.cl. 25 units, 4 junior suites. TV TEL. $143 double. AE, DC, MC, V.

This smaller hotel is housed in an antique English-style mansion, 2 blocks from the plaza. There's a compact lounge lit by a pergola-like glass ceiling, decorated with a blue country-style theme. Altogether it's a lovable little hotel, although a few scratches and scrapes in the paint need to be taken care of. The snug rooms with angled eaves are just slightly dark, but kept toasty warm. Rooms have a classic, executive-style decor, in navy blue and burgundy offset with brass details. The friendly staff let it be known that they rarely charge the advertised price, so ask for a discount. Downstairs, in what was the brick-walled cellar, is an intimate restaurant and a popular pub (with a separate entrance), where they serve, among more standard fare, regional dishes such as Calafate (a wild berry) mousse and grilled beaver.

Dining/Diversions: The hotel's restaurant and pub, El Galeón, serves international and regional cuisine.

Amenities: Laundry, room service.

✪ **Hotel José Nogueira.** Bories 959, Punta Arenas. ☎ **61/248840.** Fax 61/248832. www.hotelnogueira.com. E-mail: nogueira@chileaustral.com. 25 units, 3 suites. MINIBAR TV TEL. $118–$198 double. AE, DC, MC, V.

I strongly recommend this hotel if it's within your budget. The Hotel José Nogueira is in the partially converted neoclassical mansion once owned by the widow of one of Punta Arenas's wealthiest entrepreneurs, and half of the building is still run as a museum. The mansion was built between 1894 and 1905 on a prominent corner across from the plaza, with materials imported entirely from Europe. The José Nogueira is not only appealing for its historical value, but also offers classic luxury. The rooms here are not as large as you would expect, but high ceilings accented by floor-to-ceiling curtains compensate for that. All are tastefully decorated, either in rich burgundy and navy blue–striped wallpaper or rose and cream combinations, Oriental rugs, and lithographs of local fauna; the bathrooms are sparkling white. In Chile, "singles" are normally tight rooms without enough space to even think; the Nogueira's is the largest I've seen yet, but it does come with a single bed. The suites have ample bathrooms with Jacuzzi tubs and a living area in the open bedroom. The maids here dress in old-fashioned long smocks. There isn't a lounge per se, as the brief lobby with two leather couches leads into the popular restaurant La Pérgola, which is housed under the Nogueira's glass-enclosed terrace that once served as a "winter garden." The parlor and conference center that are connected to the lobby can be used for special meetings, but they are typically toured as part of the museum. Downstairs is a popular pub in what once was the wine cellar.

Dining/Diversions: The Nogueira's excellent restaurant, La Pérgola, is located in the hotel's glass-enclosed "winter garden," and serves a variety of international and regional dishes (see "Where to Dine," below).

Amenities: Laundry, room service, conference room.

Los Navegantes. José Menéndez 647, Punta Arenas. ☎ **61/244677.** Fax 61/247545. www.hotel-losnavegantes.com. E-mail: hotelnav@chilesat.net. 50 units. MINIBAR TV TEL. $110–$139 double. AE, DC, MC, V.

Los Navegantes is another recommended hotel, and it's a bit cheaper than the Hotel Finis Terrae (see above). The hotel went through an entire face-lift this year, renovating all of its rooms with handsome linens and curtains, fresh paint, and wallpaper. Even the restaurant was revitalized in a Tuscan motif with mustard-colored walls and spiraling iron chandeliers. The bathrooms are a bit cramped, but they've been kept sparkling clean. The hotel is located downtown, and rooms come with a view of the city or a bland interior view, but they are the same price. The Los Navegantes isn't as cozy as the Finis Terrae, due to its stark hallways and fluorescent-lit lobby, but the rooms are fine, and the old-fashioned, low-lit bar with leather banquettes provides a comfortable place to sink into with an evening drink. Professional service and airport transfers from Monday to Sunday round out this hotel.

Dining/Diversions: The hotel's restaurant, popular with locals, is backlit by an interior garden; the menu offers international and Chilean cuisine, and there's a separate bar and lounge.

Amenities: Laundry, room service, conference room, travel agency.

MODERATE

Hostal Carpa Manzano. Lautaro Navarro 336, Punta Arenas. ☎ /fax **61/248864.** 10 units. TV TEL. $46–$54 double. No credit cards.

If you're looking for a moderate lodging option, this is the best deal going. This comfortable little hostel is located in a residential area about a 7-block walk from the main plaza, so it's not exactly centrally located, but it is quiet. There's a front common area that looks like the dining area of a home and a long hallway that leads to tidy, sunny rooms that face a plot of flowers. The beds are comfortable, and each room has a private bathroom and cable TV.

Hostal de la Avenida. Av. Colón 534, Punta Arenas. ☎ /fax **61/247532.** 7 units. TV. $50 double. AE, DC, MC, V.

This olive-colored, homey hostel looks as though it were run by a little old lady, judging by the sugary dining area decorated in floral prints and porcelain figurines. A plant-filled walkway is half-covered with a fiberglass ceiling, and the three rooms that face the covered portion are dungeon-like dark; ask for one of the four rooms upstairs that receive more light. Rooms are simple, with brick walls. The hostel is located on Avenida Colón, just a block or 2 from services and restaurants.

Hotel Condor de Plata. Av. Colón 556, Punta Arenas. ☎ **61/247987.** Fax 61/241149. 13 units. MINIBAR TV TEL. $35–$60 double. AE, DC, MC, V.

This hotel, a half block from the Hostal de la Avenida, is recommended only in a pinch. The rooms are outdated and a little dismal, with tired furnishings and coffee-colored carpet that looks grungy no matter how clean they keep it. The breakfast and bar area is like a cave, making you want to eat in a hurry and get out of there.

Hotel de la Plaza. José Nogueira 1116, Punta Arenas. ☎ **61/241300.** Fax 61/248613. E-mail: hplaza@chileaustral.com. 17 units. TV TEL. $68–$83 double. AE, DC, MC, V.

The Hotel de la Plaza's lobby feels like a hangout in a college dorm, but the antique rooms with high ceilings, crisp linens, and antique furnishings make up for it. As the name states, this hotel is on a corner across from the plaza, in an old home built 90 years ago for men who worked for the sheep rancher José Menéndez. The rooms are bright, with white walls and tall windows that look out onto the plaza or neighboring buildings; each room still has its original wood molding. The bathrooms are dark and tiny. The halls are adorned with historic black-and-white photos from the region, and the lobby displays posters celebrating climbing achievements by mountaineers who have stayed here in the past. There are several couches in this lobby, but it's unattractive and doesn't encourage you to linger.

INEXPENSIVE

Hostal Calafate I. Lautaro Navarro 850, Punta Arenas. ☎ **61/248415.** 5 units. TV TEL. $32 double with shared bathroom. No credit cards.

Hostal Calafate II. Magallanes 22, Punta Arenas. ☎ **61/241281.** 18 units. TV TEL. $45 double with private bathroom; $32 double with shared bathoom. No credit cards.

The Hostal Calafate I and II are joint-owned hostels. Calafate I is in an old white–and–mint green wooden home and is perhaps the best inexpensive lodging option in town—the reason it tends to book up days in advance. It's nothing special, but the owners are gracious and each room is clean and comes with cable TV. It is ideal for anyone looking for three or four individual twin beds, as there is just one room with a double bed. The best deal here is the sole apartment out back, which has a fully stocked kitchen, three twin beds, and a separate entrance. The Calafate II is more like a standard hotel, and it's located around the corner from the plaza. Rooms come with a private or shared bathroom, but both the rooms and the bathrooms are pretty tight.

Hostal La Estancia. O'Higgins 765, Punta Arenas. ☎ **61/249130.** E-mail: estancia@ ctcinternet.cl. 8 units, all with shared bathroom. TEL. $30 double. AE, DC, MC, V.

If you're trying to keep expenses down, the Hostal La Estancia offers low-cost rooms and a kitchen that guests may use to cook meals. The hostel, located in a residential area that is a 10-minute walk from downtown, is an old home with creaky wooden floors, humble rooms, and a sunny, pleasant dining area with a TV.

WHERE TO DINE

There are plenty of excellent restaurants in Punta Arenas, most of which serve local fare such as lamb, king crab, and shellfish. All major hotels have good restaurants if you feel like dining in. For a quick bite, try the casual cafes **El Quijote,** Lautaro Navarro 1087 (☎ **61/241225**), open 10am to 11pm, or **Patiperros,** Av. Colón 782 (☎ **61/245298**), open 11am to 1am. Another local favorite, although slightly overpriced, is the diner-style **El Mercado,** Mejicana 617 (☎ **61/247415**). If you're not planning a trip to Chiloé, you might want to try El Mercado's version of that island's specialty: *curanto,* a heaping surf-and-turf platter with tomato broth. For all restaurants listed, reservations are not necessary except where noted.

Asturias. Lautaro Navarro 967. ☎ **61/243763.** Main courses $7–$13. AE, DC, MC, V. Daily noon–3pm and 8–11:30pm. SPANISH/CHILEAN.

Locals rave about Asturias, but I find that other restaurants have slowly usurped it, especially in terms of ambience. The dining room features Spanish white stucco and ironwork, but is too plain and over-lit to encourage intimacy. Asturias specializes in Spanish cuisine, such as paella, and seafood. You'll find standard salmon, sea bass, and shellfish dishes here, and great abalone loco appetizers when in season. Asturias is best known for its mouth-watering salmon dish prepared with cheese and sausage and steamed in a tinfoil pouch with garlic and wine.

Golden Dragon. Señoret 908. ☎ **61/241119.** Main courses $6–$10. AE, DC, MC, V. Daily 11:30am–3pm and 8–11:30pm. CHINESE.

Housed in a lovely old home high above the city, this Chinese restaurant has great views of the Strait of Magellan—if you get a table near the window. The exterior is a contrast to the standard Oriental interior decor, with lemon-yellow and red walls and ceilings, Chinese lamp screens, and other trinkets that don't let you forget what kind of food is on offer. Typical Chinese dishes, such as sweet and sour pork, chop suey, and chow mein, are on the menu, and it's all fairly good, although not entirely in line with the Chinese food you've had before. I'd recommend the *congrio* (conger eel) sweet and sour, but I'd stay away from anything battered and fried as it comes out a little too floury.

✪ **La Pérgola.** Bories 959. ☎ **61/248840.** Main courses $7.50–$12. AE, DC, MC, V. Daily noon–3:30pm and 7:30pm–midnight. REGIONAL.

La Pérgola is just that: a restaurant located inside the glass-enclosed, vine-draped "winter garden" that once was part of the stately mansion owned by Sara Braun, now part of the Hotel José Nogueira. The ambience is as lovely as the cuisine. You won't have any trouble identifying dishes here, as the menu provides photos of each dish, including king crab quiche, curried lamb with glazed carrots, filet mignon in three sauces, and pork loin in a cherry sauce. There's even salmon sashimi. An ample wine list and desserts such as tiramisu round out the menu. Small tables do not make this restaurant a suitable place for large groups.

✪ **Remezón.** Av. 21 de Mayo 1469. ☎ **61/241029.** Main courses $8–$10. AE, DC, MC, V. Daily noon–3pm and 7:15pm–midnight. Closed Mon Apr–Sept. CONTEMPORARY REGIONAL.

This is my favorite restaurant in all of Chilean Patagonia. Remezón breaks from the traditional mold with a warm, intimate dining area decorated with a jumble of art and slightly kitsch items that are as personal as the chef's daily changing menu. The food is, in a word, divine: not too pretentious but always prepared with fresh, regional vegetables, seafood, and meats seasoned to delicious perfection. It's difficult to find a restaurant in Chile that serves well-prepared dishes, but Remezón is the exception. The menu features five appetizers and as many main dishes handwritten on a chalkboard; usually the chef approaches your table and explains each item to diners before ordering. Sample dishes include broiled Parmesan scallops; calamari, zucchini and avocado salad; goose marinated in *pisco* and lemon; and crêpes stuffed with king crab and cream. There's always a vegetarian dish on offer, such as vegetable *pastel de choclo*, a casserole topped with a corn crust. The gracious owners love good cooking, and it shows. Remezón is located on the edge of town; you can either taxi here or enjoy an after-dinner stroll back to downtown. Prices are not listed on the menu, so you have to inquire when ordering.

Restaurant Hotel Finis Terrae. Av. Colón 766. ☎ **61/228200.** Main courses $6–$15. AE, DC, MC, V. Daily 6:30am–11pm. CHILEAN/INTERNATIONAL.

This restaurant is located on the top floor of the Hotel Finis Terrae. Although the food is not as good as what you'll find at the other restaurants mentioned in this section, it's decent, but what makes this restaurant unique are the incredible views seen through enormous arched windows that wrap around the dining area. This is a great place for breakfast, and it opens early at 6:30am. The ambience leans toward the casual, and the menu has enough options to satisfy anyone, from beef stuffed with king crab in an herb sauce to sea bass with mussels and spinach; there are also soups and sandwiches for a light lunch. On Fridays and Saturdays the restaurant has a buffet for $15 adults and $11 kids.

✪ **Sotitos.** O'Higgins 1138. ☎ **61/221061.** Main courses $6–$14. AE, DC, MC, V. Daily 11:30am–3pm and 7–11:45pm. CHILEAN.

Sotitos is the local favorite in Punta Arenas. Don't be fooled by the plain green front with the weathered sign: Sotitos has handsomely renovated its semiformal interiors with brick walls and white linen tablecloths. If you're looking for traditional Chilean cuisine, this is your restaurant. Sotitos offers everything and more than most Chilean restaurants, including steak and seafood, local baked lamb, Valencia shellfish rice (which must be ordered ahead of time), pastas, and fresh salads. The key is that everything is of high quality, regardless of how simple the dish. The service here is superb, attentive but not overbearing. On Fridays, Saturdays, and Sundays they fire up their *parrilla* for barbecued meats. There's a no-smoking section up front, but it's usually empty.

PUNTA ARENAS AFTER DARK

The city has a fair amount of bars and pubs plus a few discos, although you wouldn't want to go to a disco unless you like to hang out with teenagers and listen to bad techno music. One of the most popular pubs for all ages is in the **La Taberna** (☎ 61/248840) cellar bar, below the Hotel José Nogueira at the corner of Bories and Sequel across from the plaza; it serves a long list of appetizers. Another popular spot is the **Pub 1900** (☎ 61/242759), at the corner of Avenida Colón and Bories; yet another pub is the **El Galeón** at Av. 21 de Mayo 1243, below the Hotel Isla Rey Jorge (☎ 61/248220). If you just can't get enough karaoke, head to **El Coral,** Bories 817 (☎ 61/243851), which also serves food. The **Cabo de Hornos Hotel** (☎ 61/242134), on the plaza, has a 1960s-chic bar with abstract paintings and pinhole lights. The cinema **Commercial Cine Magallanes,** at Plaza Muñoz Gamero 765 across from the tourism kiosk at the plaza (☎ 61/223225), has one screen; call or check newspaper listings for what's playing.

2 Puerto Natales, Chile

157½ miles (254km) NW of Punta Arenas; 71 miles (115km) S of Torres del Paine

Puerto Natales is a rambling town of 15,000, spread along the sloping coast of the Señoret Canal between the Ultima Esperanza Sound and the Almirante Montt Gulf. This is the jump-off point for trips to Torres del Paine, and nearly every visitor to this park will find himself spending at least one night here. The town itself is nothing more than a small center and rows and rows of weather-beaten tin and wooden houses, but it has a certain appeal, and it boasts a stunning location with grand views out onto a grassy peninsula and the glacier-capped peaks of the national parks Bernardo O'Higgins and Torres del Paine in the distance. Along the Costanera, elegant black-necked swans drift along the rocky shore. From May to September, the town virtually goes into hibernation, but come October, the town's streets begin to fill with travelers decked out in parkas and hiking boots on their way to the park.

Puerto Natales is the capital of the Ultima Esperanza Sound, founded in 1911 as a residential center and export port for local sheep ranches. Tourism has now replaced wool as a dominant economic force, evident by the plethora of hostels, restaurants, and tour companies found here.

ESSENTIALS

GETTING THERE & GETTING AROUND

BY BUS Puerto Natales is the hub for bus service to Torres del Paine National Park and El Calafate, Argentina. For information about bus service to and from Torres del Paine, see "Getting There & Away" under "Parque Nacional Torres del Paine," below. There are frequent daily trips between Punta Arenas and Puerto Natales. In Puerto Natales each bus company leaves from its own office.

To & from Punta Arenas **Buses Fernandez,** Eberhard 555 (☎ 61/411111), has seven daily trips; **Bus Sur,** Baquedano 558 (☎ 61/411325), has six daily trips; **Buses Pacheco,** Baquedano 244 (☎ 61/414513), has six daily trips (and the most comfortable buses); and **Transfer Austral,** Baquedano 414 (☎ 61/412616), has three daily trips. The cost is around $5 one-way.

To Get to El Calafate, Argentina **Buses Zaahj,** Arturo Prat 236 (☎ 61/412260), leaves at 9am; **Bus Sur,** Baquedano 534 (☎ 61/411325), leaves at 9am; and **Cootra,** Baquedano 244 (☎ 61/412785), leaves at 6:30am. The cost is $20 one-way.

BY CAR Ruta 9 is a paved road that heads north from Punta Arenas. The drive is 157½ miles (254km) and takes about 2½ to 3 hours. If you're heading in from El Calafate, Argentina, you have your choice of two international borders: Cerro Castillo (otherwise known as Control Fronterizo Río Don Guillermo) and Río Turbio (otherwise known as Controles Fronterizos Dorotea y Laurita Casas Viejas). Cerro Castillo is the preferred entry point for its easier access. Both are open 24 hours from September to May, and 8am to 11pm the rest of the year.

Car rentals in Puerto Natales are offered by **Motorcars** at Baquedano 380, #3 (☎ 61/413593), **EMSA** (an Avis representative) at Av. Manuel Bulnes 632 (☎ 61/410775), and **Bien al Sur** at Av. Manuel Bulnes 433 (☎ 61/414025). Bien al Sur also rents bicycles, but the wind will probably dissuade you from pedaling.

BY BOAT **Navimag** runs a popular 3-night ferry trip between Puerto Natales and Puerto Montt, passing through the southern fjords of Chile. This journey passes through breath-taking scenery, and it makes for an interesting way to leave from or head to Chile's Lake District. The trip is described in chapter 12, "The Chilean Lake District," under "Ferry Crossings to the Carretera Austral & Sailing to Patagonia Through the Fjords." Navimag leaves once a week on Thursday evenings; its offices can be found next to the Hotel Costa Australis at Pedro Montt 262 (☎ 61/414300; www.navimag.com).

ORIENTATION

Puerto Natales is built on a grid pattern, and you'll find you spend most of your time within a 5-block radius. There is the main plaza, Plaza de Armas, along which runs Calle Eberhard, the street where you'll find the post office and the town's yellow cathedral. Calle Eberhard dead-ends a block away at Blanco Encalada; this street, Avenida Manuel Bulnes (1 block to the right), and Baquedano (1 block up from Blanco Encalada) are the principal streets with most of the supermarkets, banks, and tourism-oriented businesses. Along the shore of Puerto Natales runs Pedro Montt, also called the Costanera. The Costanera is an excellent place for a stroll.

Tips for Renting Camping Equipment

If you don't feel like lugging your own gear down here, there are several agencies that rent equipment. Typical daily rental prices are two-man tents $6, sleeping bags $3, stoves $1.50, sleeping mats $1, and backpacks $3. During the high season, it's best to reserve these items. The following companies rent equipment: **Casa Cecilia,** Tomás Roger 60 (☎ **61/411797;** e-mail: redcecilia@entelchile.net); **Onas,** Eberhard and Blanco Encalada (☎ **61/412707;** e-mail: onas@chileaustral.com); and **Agencia Fortleza,** Arturo Prat 234 (☎ **61/ 410595;** e-mail: monoforteleza@hotmail.com).

VISITOR INFORMATION

Sernatur operates a well-stocked and informed office on the Costanera at Pedro Montt and Philippi (☎ **61/412125**); it's open October to March, Monday to Friday 8:30am to 8pm, Saturday and Sunday 9:30am to 1pm and 2:30 to 6:30pm; April to September, it's open Monday to Friday 8:30am to 1pm and 2:30 to 6:30pm, closed Sundays and holidays. **Conaf** has its park headquarters at O'Higgins 584 (☎ **61/ 411438**). Sadly, it's not the best source of information, even though it manages the park. Instead, head to a tour operator for information (see "Tour Operators & Adventure Travel Outfitters," below).

FAST FACTS: PUERTO NATALES

Currency Exchange   There are several exchange houses on Blanco Encalada; try Mily, Blanco Encalada 183, and their other office on the same street, at 266 (☎ **61/ 411262;** open Monday to Saturday 10amto 8pm). The only ATM in town is at the Banco de Santiago, located at the corner of Blanco Encalada and Manuel Bulnes (the ATM is open 24 hours).

Hospital   Frankly, the town's public hospital is horrible. It's on the corner of Pinto and O'Higgins (☎ **61/411583**). For major medical emergencies, it's best to get yourself to Punta Arenas.

Internet Access   Turismo Mily, Blanco Encalada 183 (☎ **61/411262**), and **Turismo María José,** Av. Manuel Bulnes 386 (☎ **61/414312**), have Internet services. Connections in Puerto Natales are excruciatingly slow.

Laundry   ServiLaundry, Av. Manuel Bulnes 513 (no phone) Hours vary, but it's open more or less Monday to Saturday 9am to 1pm and 2 to 8pm.

Pharmacy   Farmacias Marisol is at Baquedano 331 (☎ **61/411591**).

Post Office   The post office is on the Plaza de Armas next to the cathedral (no phone; open Monday to Friday 9am to 6pm, Saturday 9am to 1pm).

EXCURSIONS OUTSIDE PUERTO NATALLES

CUEVA DE MILODON

In 1896, Capitan Eberhard found a scrap of hairy skin and a few bones in a large cave near his property that was later determined to be a *Milodon,* a prehistoric ground sloth. The story of the *Milodon* was popularized by Bruce Chatwin's travelogue *In Patagonia,* and this is a principal reason most come to view this national monument. Although the *Milodon* is depicted in a full-size replica at the cave's entrance, most of the *Milodon*'s remains were shipped off to London, which means the real attraction is the 30m (98 ft.) high, 200m (656 ft.) deep cave itself, which has a weird shaggy roof and is surrounded by interesting conglomerate rock formations. There's an interpretative center with a few *Milodon* bones and a display showing the geological formation of the cave, as well as a historical display of the Indians who inhabited this and nearby caves as far back as 12,000 years ago. This attraction is really recommended only if you happen to be passing by, or if you've run out of things to do in Puerto Natales. The cave is located 15 miles (24km) north of Puerto Natales, so you'll need your own car or a tour to get here. To get here, take the road to Torres del Paine; at 12½ miles (20km) turn left, and then drive for 2½ miles (4km) to the cave's turn-off. The site managed by Conaf and open 8:30am to 7pm; admission is $4 adults, $2 children (☎ 61/411438 in Puerto Natales).

SAILING TO PARQUE NACIONAL BERNARDO O'HIGGINS

This national park encompasses a tremendous amount of terrain, but it's unreachable except for boat tours to the glaciers Balmaceda and Serrano. There are several boat excursions that leave from Puerto Natales, sailing first through the Ultima Esperanza Sound past the Antonio Varas Peninsula, stopping for a walk up to the narrow Serrano Glacier that plunges into a small bay choked with icebergs. The boat then sails past the Balmaceda Glacier. This journey is highly recommended, although it's a full-day excursion and might bore some travelers because it doubles back along the same route. The best way to do it is to leave Torres del Paine via one of the zodiac services that drops riders off at the Serrano Glacier, where they take the boat back to Puerto Natales, or vice versa (see "Getting There & Away" under "Parque Nacional Torres del Paine," below).

There are two companies that offer the excursion. The cutter *21 de Mayo* with offices at Eberhard 560 (☎ 61/411978; www.chileaustral.com/21demayo; e-mail: 21demayo@chileaustral.com), leaves at 8am and arrives at the Serrano Glacier at 11:30am, where it stays for 1½ hours, returning at 5pm. The cost is $33 per person, not including lunch (box lunches are provided for $10 more). A new service offered by **Aventour** at Av. Manuel Bulnes 689 (☎ 61/410253; www.aventouraventuras. com; e-mail: *sargoma@directo.cl*), takes visitors along a similar route aboard its wooden yacht *Nueva Galicia,* leaving at 7:30am and arriving at the Serrano Glacier at 11am for a half hour, then across the adjoining river to its lodge, the Hostería Monte Balmaceda (see below). There visitors can take a walk around the self-guided nature trail, have lunch in the restaurant, and reboard, arriving at Puerto Natales at 5:30pm. The cost for this trip is $60 per person.

Hostería Monte Balmaceda. Aventour's office in Puerto Natales, Av. Manuel Bulnes 689. ☎ **61/410253.** Fax 61/410825. www.aventouraventuras.com. E-mail: sargoma@directo.cl. 16 units. $50 May–Sept; $108 Oct and Apr; $145 Nov–Mar. AE, DC, MC, V.

This *hostería* sits along the Río Serrano and across from the glacier of the same name— a remote, stunning location that can be visited only by boat. Although the site provides a direct view of the glacier as it tumbles down the mountain, it unfortunately cannot be viewed from any of the rooms. Why the owner decided to design the rooms in three rows like army barracks that face each other can only be explained by the fact that he is an ex-military man. Nevertheless, the circular, separate restaurant is lovely (and comes with views), and the self-guided trail they've built around the property is really a delight, giving visitors lots of space to quietly walk and enjoy nature; there are fishing opportunities here as well. The rooms are not noteworthy, but brand-new and spacious enough. If you plan to stay here and visit Torres del Paine, it's possible to take the spectacular ride up the Río Serrano to a drop-off point near Conaf's administration and visitor's center.

TOUR OPERATORS & ADVENTURE TRAVEL OUTFITTERS

The glut of tour operators in Puerto Natales can be divided into two groups: conventional sightseeing day tours to Torres del Paine, the Perito Moreno Glacier in Argentina's Los Glaciares National Park, and the Cueva de Milodon; and adventure travel outfitters that arrange multiday, all-inclusive excursions, including trekking the "W" or the Circuit (see "Trails in Torres del Paine," below) and climbing in Torres del Paine, kayaking the Río Serrano in Parque Nacional Bernardo O'Higgins, and horseback trips. Keep in mind that it's very easy to arrange your own trekking journey in Torres del Paine; the bonus with these outfitters is that they carry the tents (which they'll set up) and food (which they'll cook). They also will pick you up from the airport and provide guided information about the flora and fauna of the park. Conventional day tours include stops at the Nordenskjold Trail and the icebergs at Lago Grey.

CONVENTIONAL DAY TOURS These tours are for people with a limited amount of time in the area. Tours typically leave at 7:30am and return around 7:30pm, and cost about $28 per person, not including lunch or park entrance fees. Try **Turismo Mily,** Blanco Encalada 183 (☎ **61/411262**), **Turismo María Jose,** Av. Manuel Bulnes 386 (☎ **61/414312**), and **Turismo Zaahj,** Arturo Prat 236 (☎ **61/412260**); Zaahj includes a stop at the Cueva de Milodon.

ADVENTURE TRAVEL Apart from the local guiding outfitters here in Puerto Natales, several American and Chilean companies offer well-planned trekking excursions in Torres del Paine, specifically Mountain-Travel Sobek and Cascada Expediciones (both have bases here and in Punta Arenas; see "The Active Vacation Planner" in chapter 8, "Planning a Trip to Chile," for more information). **Bigfoot Expeditions,** Blanco Encalada 226 (☎ **61/414611;** www.bigfootpatagonia.com; e-mail: explore@bigfootpatagonia.com), is the leader of the pack here in Puerto Natales; in Santiago, its office is at Helvecia 210 (☎ **2/335-1796;** fax 2/335-1798). Bigfoot offers a variety of multiday trekking journeys through the park: a 2-night/3-day kayaking trip down the Río Serrano; horseback trips through the park; a 5-day trek through the Sarmiento Mountain Range; and sailing through the Canal of the Mountains (which can be extended to include area kayaking, fishing, and trekking). Bigfoot also owns the concession for the ice walk across Glacier Grey (described in "Parque Nacional Torres del Paine," below), and they are the ones to call for climbing and mountaineering in the park. Bigfoot can arrange custom tours, and all-inclusive tours include all lodging (including hotels in Santiago and Puerto Natales), transfers, meals, and equipment. **Onas,** Blanco Encalada and Eberhard (☎/fax **61/412707;** www.onaspatagonia.com; e-mail: onas@chileaustral.com), is another adventure travel company that offers trekking excursions in Torres del Paine. The company offers a 2-day kayak trip down the Río Serrano (Onas has a half-day zodiac trip down the Río Serrano; see "Getting There & Away" under "Parque Nacional Torres del Paine," below). Onas works in conjunction with **Andescape** next door, visible by the giant PATH@GONE sign at the top of the corner building (☎ **61/412592;** www.chileaustral.com/andescape; e-mail: andescape@chileaustral.com). Andescape has the concession for several *refugios* in the park, but it really acts as a clearinghouse for regional travel-related matters. If you're looking for a one-stop shop and *refugio* reservations, this is it. **Aventour,** Av. Manuel Bulnes 689 (☎ **61/410253;** www.aventouraventuras.com; e-mail: sargoma@directo.cl), works mainly out of Parque Nacional Bernardo O'Higgins, and has a variety of excursions, transfers, and boat journeys that can get you to the park through the back route up the Río Serrano. **Turismo Yamana** and **Inhospita Patagonia,** both out of Punta Arenas, are two other very reliable companies that offer all-inclusive trekking trips to Torres del Paine; for more information, see "Tour Operators" under "Excursions Outside Punta Arenas," above.

WHERE TO STAY

It seems that anyone and everyone who owns a home large enough to rent out a few rooms has decided to hang a HOSPEDAJE sign above their door. These simple, inexpensive accommodations can be found everywhere, but other higher-end options are to be had, even though they're not cheap. The high season in Puerto Natales is longer than in any other city in Chile, generally considered to run from October to April, and the price range shown reflects this. For all hotels, parking is either free, or street parking is plentiful.

EXPENSIVE

✪ **Hotel Costa Australis.** Pedro Montt 262, Puerto Natales. ☎ **61/412000.** Fax 61/411881. www.australis.com. E-mail: costaus@ctcreuna.cl. 50 units. TV TEL. $90–$181 double. AE, DC, MC, V.

This hard-to-miss, sunflower-yellow hotel on the coast offers the highest caliber lodging in Puerto Natales, and it's your best bet if you're looking for optimum comfort. The hotel was designed by a local architect, who planned the entire facade with floor-to-ceiling windows that face out onto the sound, which means that whether you're in the bar, the restaurant, or the lounge, you always have sweeping views and a splendid evening sunset. The Costa Australis is the town's largest hotel, but it retains a certain coziness with its grasscloth wallpaper offset by wooden trim and ceilings, stiff potted palms, and soft light. The Dickson Bar is a great place to unwind with one of its well-prepared *pisco* sours. Spacious doubles come with a sea view or a view of the buildings in the back (which go for $75 to $147), and all feature glossy wood paneling and attractive furnishings. The price is nevertheless fairly high, even by U.S. standards, and therefore might not be appealing to anyone who plans to arrive late and leave early.

Dining: The hotel has two restaurants, one for snacks and breakfast, and a semi-formal dining area for dinner (see "Where to Dine," below).

Amenities: Laundry, room service, gift shop, travel planning.

Hotel Martín Guisinde. Bories 278, Puerto Natales. ☎ **61/412770.** Fax 61/412820. E-mail: hgrey@ctcreuna.cl. 20 units. TV TEL. $60–$140 double. AE, DC, MC, V.

This hotel sits on a residential street near the casino, and its boxy, brown exterior is an odd match for its classically designed rooms. Every room is a little tight but immensely comfortable, with crisp linens, rich floral-and-stripe wallpaper with matching bedspreads, and wood furniture. Nothing is out of place here. The hallways are a little cold, but the restaurant in front is a comfortable place for a meal or a drink, and they serve a hearty breakfast. The Martín Guisinde is owned by the same people who run the Hostería Lago Grey (see "Where to Stay in Torres del Paine," below), and they will arrange excursions around the region.

Dining/Diversions: The hotel's restaurant offers a basic menu of predominately Chilean cuisine.

MODERATE

Hostal Francis Drake. Philippi 383, Puerto Natales. ☎/fax **61/411553.** 12 units. TEL. $34–$69 double. DC, MC, V.

The Hostal Francis Drake is nearly identical to the Los Pinos (see below)—the only difference is about $30, but you might want to give negotiating a try (credit card users get a discount as well). Both are located on the same block, and like the Los Pinos, this small inn has just 12 rooms, all very clean. The exterior is appealing, with latticed wood trim; inside there's a plant-filled eating area for breakfast. There's also a salon with a TV. The friendly owner who runs the hotel can help with transfers and travel information and provide box lunches for excursions.

Hostal Los Pinos. Philippi 449, Puerto Natales. ☎ **61/411735.** Fax 61/411326. 12 units. $40 double. No credit cards.

The Hostal Los Pinos is a great value for the price. This unassuming hotel is tucked behind two cypress trees, across from the local high school and 3 blocks from the plaza. I really like this small hotel because it makes you feel at home, especially while relaxing in the ample living area, with its low ceilings and glass walls that let the outside world in without making you feel too exposed. Oriental rug runners lead to squeaky clean rooms with enough details here and there that bring them a step above most moderate accommodations found in town. The bathrooms aren't huge, but they'll do.

Hotel Capitán Eberhard. Pedro Montt (the Costanera) 58, Puerto Natales. ☎ **61/411208.** Fax 61/411209. www.busesfernandez.com. E-mail: hoteleberhard@busesfernandez.com. 24 units. TV TEL. $44–$99 double. AE, DC, MC, V.

The Capitán Eberhard was the first hotel in Puerto Natales, built 30 years ago on the Costanera and featuring a commanding view of the sound and the peaks behind it. The rooms could use an update, with low-to-the-floor beds and drab furnishings, but the bar and restaurant are still as handsome as ever. Try to get a room with a view of the sound (this is one of the few hotels that has one); otherwise, look for lodging elsewhere, because the price is too high for what you get. The hotel is offset with various ornaments, such as a stuffed eagle, fox pelts, antique photos, and the like. The black and wood bar is the best in Puerto Natales, but the lounge upstairs is a pinch tacky and it reeks of smoke. The hotel's tiny, handsome restaurant serves Chilean fare.

Hotel Cisne Cuello Negro. Road to Torres del Paine, northeast of Puerto Natales, Km3. In Punta Arenas, José Menéndez 918. ☎ **61/411498,** or reservations 61/244506. Fax 61/248052. www.pehoe.com. E-mail: gerencia@pehoe.com. 41 units. TV TEL. $80 double. AE, DC, MC, V.

This hotel sits a 2-mile (3km) taxi ride outside town, and it's ideal for those who want to be surrounded by a bit of greenery and history. The Hotel Cisne is in the old mutton-canning and wool plant that once operated as a collection and export site for various sheep ranches. The old wooden buildings provide great places to walk and explore, especially if you have kids. The hotel itself is a three-story white building with red tin awnings, and it fronts a grassy slope that leads into the sound. After a fire burned part of the building, they rebuilt an airy restaurant lit by a plant-filled atrium. Rooms are spacious and comfortable, with good beds and sunny views. There are two large suites surrounded by floor to ceiling windows. Much of the time the hotel sells packages to guests with a limited amount of time in the area, including transportation from Punta Arenas, 3 nights' accommodation, a 1-day tour through Torres del Paine, and a catamaran journey to Parque Nacional Bernardo O'Higgins and the Serrano Glacier.

Hotel Glaciares. Eberhard 104, Puerto Natales. ☎ **61/412189.** Fax 61/411452. 18 units. MINIBAR TV TEL. $41–$86 double. DC, MC, V.

The Hotel Glaciares's best deal going is the fleet of transfer vehicles they use to shuttle guests in and out of the park for day trips or to locations as far away as Ushuaia. Guests here are usually satisfied with their accommodations, but I feel the quality is not up to par with the price. The rooms are modest, but have cushiony beds and powerful showers. Upstairs there's a bright lounge area, but the grenadine-colored carpet will make your teeth hurt. The front-desk service suffices, but could be a little more energetic.

Hotel Lady Florence Dixie. Av. Manuel Bulnes 659, Puerto Natales. ☎ **61/411158.** Fax 61/411943. E-mail: florence@chileanpatagonia.com. 18 units. TV TEL. $75 double Oct–Apr; $35 double May–Sept. AE, DC, MC, V.

This hotel is about as downtown as downtown gets in Puerto Natales, located on bustling Avenida Manuel Bulnes. The owners have recently gone through a substantial renovation, tearing down the old home that fronted the establishment (the rooms are set far back from the street), and rebuilding a new unit that includes four brand-new superior rooms and a restaurant for guests only. Guests enter the wooden gate and find a courtyard and a motel-like setup that's nicely designed with wooden banisters and trim. The rooms are comfortable, and it's one of the few hotels in this price range that have cable TV, if that's important to you. You might consider one of the front rooms because they are spanking new, with gleaming bathrooms, and they have soundproof windows. The two women who run the place are very accommodating.

Kotenk Aike Cabañas. Costanera (Pedro Montt), northeast of Puerto Natales, Km2. ☎ **61/412581.** Fax 61/225935 (in Punta Arenas). 5 cabañas. TV. $70 cabaña for 5. MC, V.

These cabins are about 1¼ miles (2km) out of town on an exposed grassy slope, and they're a good bet if you're looking for your own room with a kitchen. The German-style, A-frame cabañas sit apart from each other, and each has two upstairs bedrooms, one with a full-size bed and one with three twins; all are brightly lit. There's a tidy kitchen with a burner, a microwave, and a table. The distance from town means you'll have to walk or taxi, but the all-embracing views are worth it.

INEXPENSIVE

Casa Cecilia. Tomás Roger 60, Puerto Natales. ☎/fax **61/411797.** E-mail: redcecilia@ entelchile.net. 13 units. Nov 15–Feb, $32 double, $21 double with shared bathroom; Mar–Nov 14, $20 double, $11 double with shared bathroom. AE, DC, MC, V.

Casa Cecilia is a budget favorite in Puerto Natales, consistently garnering rave reviews from guests for its full range of services, pleasant rooms, and delicious breakfasts. The front lobby acts as a travel agency of sorts, providing information, arranging excursions, and renting equipment; beyond that is a common area and a kitchen that guests can use—and they do. Rooms are stacked on two floors and encircle an atrium; some come with private bathrooms, some shared, and they are a good value for the price. However, rooms are lit by the interior atrium, not from the outside. The Swiss-Chilean couple (she's Cecilia) speak several languages and are very friendly. This hostel is popular with a wide range of ages and types.

Concepto Indigo. Ladrilleros 105, Puerto Natales. ☎ **61/413609.** Fax 61/410169. www. conceptoindigo. E-mail: indigo@entelchile.net. 7 units. $35 double; $30 double with shared bathroom. AE, DC, MC, V. Closed May–Aug.

The Concepto Indigo is a hip, outdoorsy hostel/restaurant located along the Costanera. It's a purple barn of a building with a rock-climbing wall, so you won't have any trouble spotting it. The rooms are inexpensive, but remarkable only for the tremendous view of the sound seen through giant windows—especially the corner room, which has a full-size bed and a twin. Only one room comes with a private bathroom, but there are several bathrooms, so you most likely won't find that sharing is a problem. The best thing about Concepto Indigo is its restaurant downstairs, with wraparound views, stacks of magazines, and a few couches to kick back in. When the wind picks up (which it usually does), the place really whistles and shakes.

WHERE TO DINE

Along with the following restaurants, there are several that serve inexpensive fare, such as **RePizza,** Blanco Encalada 294 (☎ **61/410361**), a popular place for pizzas, and **El Cristal,** Av. Manuel Bulnes 439 (☎ **61/411850**), which has a very basic menu of sandwiches, grilled or breaded meats, french fries, and the like, as well as a daily set lunch for about $5. For all restaurants listed, reservations are not necessary except where noted.

Concepto Indigo. Ladrilleros 105. ☎ **61/413609.** Main courses $6–$11. AE, DC, MC, V. Daily 11am–11pm; bar closes at 1am. Closed May–Aug. VEGETARIAN.

This is Puerto Natales's sole vegetarian restaurant; the only meat item here is a ham sandwich. The menu is simple, with grilled or sautéed salmon, scallops, king crab, pastas, and spongy pizzas. The sandwiches are served on wagon-wheel bread, and are hefty enough for a dinner. There's also a good wine selection. Concepto Indigo is another restaurant with a great atmosphere, with hip decor and candlelit tables, good music, and an evening slide-slow presentation of Torres del Paine. The restaurant is a cozy place for an evening drink.

El Rincón de la Tata. Arturo Prat 238. No phone. Main courses $5–$8. MC, V. Daily 10:30am–midnight. CHILEAN.

This little cafe doesn't have the best cuisine in town, but it undoubtedly has one of the best atmospheres, candlelit and warm. It's kind of like a pub, casual and friendly. The walls are adorned with old Chilean kitsch, and they always have a band like Santana playing in background. Better to stick with one of the huge sandwiches or a pizza and a beer than any of the main courses.

Hotel Capitán Eberhard. Pedro Montt 58. ☎ **61/411208.** Main courses $7–$10. AE, DC, MC, V. Daily 7am–10am, noon–2:30pm, and 8–11:30pm. CHILEAN.

Like the Costa Australis (see below), this restaurant features a lovely view of the sound, but the difference is the Eberhard is cozier and full of old-fashioned Puerto Natales charm. Nothing has changed in this dining room since the hotel's inception 30 years ago, including the unique notched wooden ceiling. The menu features typical Chilean fare and very good salmon dishes, such as salmon with a creamy seafood sauce. Try the abalone in salsa verde appetizer. There's also a kid's menu. The bar is handsomely designed, with a black bar and tables offset by cinnamon-colored wood.

✪ **Hotel Costa Australis.** Pedro Montt 262. ☎ **61/412000.** Main courses $8–$16. AE, DC, MC, V. Daily 8–10am, noon–3pm, and 7:30–11pm. INTERNATIONAL.

If you're looking for tasty cuisine and a wonderful ambience, dine at the Costa Australis. The sunset views from the picture windows in combination with your candlelit table make for a sumptuous environment. There are really two restaurants here: one that serves sandwiches, cakes, and coffees all day, and a more formal restaurant that offers a menu with more interesting fare than most restaurants in Puerto Natales. There are several complete dishes and a mix-and-match menu, but the restaurant serves regional meats and seafood in more creative ways than the other restaurants in Puerto Natales: wild hare marinated in red wine and herbs, lamb stew with potatoes, pork loin with mustard and whiskey. Even the side dishes have a little more flair. Top off your dinner with a white chocolate mousse or minty pears poached in wine with chocolate ice cream. The restaurant also serves breakfast.

✪ **La Caleta.** Eberhard 169. ☎ **61/413969.** Main courses $4–$9. No credit cards. Daily 11am–3am. CHILEAN.

La Caleta is a simple restaurant that belies the quality of its food. Neither the dining room nor the presentation is worth writing home about, but the food is consistently good, and the portions are hearty, whether meat or seafood. Try the abalone in a creamy salsa verde or "Congrio (conger eel) Caleta" with seafood sauce; it's very rich, but satisfying, as is the steak with pepper sauce. La Caleta has begun serving lamb roasted on a revolving spit in the typical Patagonian style. They also have a parsley *ceviche* and mussels in garlic. The cantina-style homemade borgoña won't win any wine awards, but it goes along with the atmosphere.

✪ **Restaurante Edén.** Blanco Encalada 345. ☎ **61/414120.** Main courses $8–$13. AE, DC, MC, V. Daily 11am–3pm and 7–11:30pm. CHILEAN/STEAKHOUSE.

Puerto Natales has long needed a solid restaurant, and the brand-new Restaurante Edén has complied, offering great cuisine and an attractive dining area. It's a pity about the run-of-the-mill sign they've festooned above the entrance, but that's the only negative thing here. Near the entrance, two men are busy at work in front of the sizzling grill and a typical Patagonian fire pit that slowly roasts spits of the region's famous lamb. But the Edén also specializes in seafood, with dishes like king crab soufflé, abalone stew, or salmon in an avocado sauce. The best thing here is the meat or seafood *parrillas* ($8.50 and $12, respectively), which offer a variety of lamb, sausage, beef, chicken, and pork or a medley of fish and shellfish in a lemon sauce; both come sizzling on minibarbecues.

Restaurant Marítimo. Pedro Montt 214-A. ☎ **61/414467.** Main courses $4–$8. No credit cards. Daily 11am–11pm. SEAFOOD.

Locals and tourists flock to this restaurant, but I have a hard time understanding what the excitement is about. Certainly the seafood is fresh, and the location is ideal on the Costanera, but the food is bland, the service is absent-minded, and the nighttime fluorescent lights are blinding. I've had good appetizers here—abalone salad and lemony king crab among them—but the fish dishes are fried to a crisp and served three ways: with butter, with butter and garlic, and without. The prices are reasonable, however.

3 Parque Nacional Torres del Paine, Chile

70mi (113km) N of Puerto Natales, 223mi (360km) NW of Punta Arenas

This is Chile's prized jewel, a national park so magnificent that few in the world can claim a rank in its class. I have lived in the park for 2 years, and rain or shine I have not approached a single day without stopping to marvel at its grand and diverse beauty. Granite peaks and towers soar from sea level to upward of 2,800m (9,184 ft.). Golden *pampas* and the rolling steppes are home to grazing guanacos and more than 100 species of colorful birds, such as parakeets and flamingos, that come to nest each spring. Antarctic beech emits a strong cinnamon aroma. Chilean firebush blooms a riotous red; delicate porcelain orchids and ladyslippers seem unfit for such inhospitable terrain. Electric-blue icebergs cleave from Glacier Grey. Resident gauchos ride by atop sheepskin saddles. Condors float effortlessly even on the windiest day. The park is not something you visit; it is something you experience.

Although it sits next to the Andes, ✪ **Parque Nacional Torres del Paine** is a separate geologic formation created roughly 3 million years ago when bubbling magma began growing and pushing its way up, taking a thick sedimentary layer with it. Glaciation and severe climate weathered away the softer rock, leaving the spectacular

Paine Massif whose prominent features are the *Cuernos* (which means "horns") and the one-of-a-kind Torres—three salmon-colored, spherical granite towers. The black sedimentary rock can still be seen atop the elegant Cuernos, named for the two spires that rise from the outer sides of its amphitheater. *Paine* is the Tehuelche Indian word for "blue," and it brings to mind the varying shades found in the lakes that surround this massif—among them the milky, turquoise waters of Lagos Nordenskjold and Pehoe. Backing the Paine Massif are several glaciers that descend from the Southern Ice Field.

Torres del Paine was once a collection of *estancias* and small-time ranches; many were forced out with the creation of the park in 1959. The park has since grown to its present size of 242,242ha (598,338 acres), and in 1978 was declared a World Biosphere Reserve by UNESCO for its singular beauty and ecology. This park is a backpacker's dream, but just as many visitors find pleasure staying in lodges here and taking day hikes and horseback rides—even those with a short amount of time here are blown away by a 1-day visit. There are options for everyone, part of the reason the number of visitors to this park is growing by nearly 10,000 per year.

WHEN TO COME, CLIMATE CONSIDERATIONS & WHAT TO BRING

This is not the easiest of national parks to visit. The climate in the park can be abominable, with wind speeds that can peak at 100 m.p.h. and rain and snow even in the middle of summer. The period in which your chances are highest of avoiding wind and rain are early October to early November and mid-March to late April, but keep in mind that the only thing predictable here is the unpredictability of the weather. Spring is a beautiful time for budding flowers and birds; during the fall the beech forests turn striking shades of crimson, orange, and yellow. The winter is surprisingly temperate, with relatively few snowstorms and no wind—but short days. You'll need to stay in a hotel during the winter, but you'll practically have the park to yourself. Summer is ironically the worst time to come, especially late December to mid-February, when the wind blows at full fury and crowds descend upon the park. When the wind blows it can make even a short walk a rather scary experience—just try to go with it, not fight it, and revel in the excitement of the extreme environment that makes Patagonia what it is (though sometimes, admittedly, it'll just drive you nuts).

Equip yourself with decent gear, especially hiking boots (if you plan to do any trekking), weatherproof outerwear, and warm layers, even in the summer. The ozone problem is acute here, so you'll need sunscreen, sunglasses, and probably a hat. Don't ever leave indoors without slathering on sunscreen.

VISITOR INFORMATION   The park's administration and visitor's center can be reached at ☎ **61/691931.**

GETTING THERE & AWAY

Many travelers are unaware of the enormous amount of time it takes to get to Torres del Paine. There are no direct transportation services from the airport in Punta Arenas to the park, except with package tours and hotels that have their own vehicles. The earliest flight from Santiago to Punta Arenas arrives at around noon; from there it's a 3-hour drive to Puerto Natales. The last bus to the park leaves at 2:30pm for the 2-hour journey to the park. If you're relying on bus transportation (as most do), it's only logical that you will need to spend the night in Punta Arenas or Puerto Natales. If you've arranged a package tour or hotel stay that picks you up at the airport, remember that the trip can be very tiring if you factor in a 4-hour flight from Santiago and 5 hours in a vehicle.

BY BUS   Several companies offer daily service from October to April. During the low season, only two companies, Bus Sur and JB, offer service to the park. Buses to Torres del Paine enter through the Laguna Amarga ranger station, stop at the Pudeto catamaran dock, and terminate at the park administration center. If you're going directly to the Torres trailhead at Hostería Las Torres, there are minivan transfers waiting at the Laguna Amarga station that charge $3 one-way. The return times given below are when the bus leaves from the park administration center; the bus will pass through the Laguna Amarga station about 45 minutes later.

   JB at Arturo Prat 258 (☎ **61/412824**) leaves at 7am, 8am, and 2:30pm and returns at 1, 2:30, and 6:30pm; **Fortaleza Aventura** at Arturo Prat 234 (☎ **61/410595**) leaves at 7am and 2pm, returning at 2 and 6pm; **Buses Paori** at Eberhard 577 (☎ **61/411229**) leaves at 7:30am, returning at 2pm; **Turismo María Jose** at Av. Manuel Bulnes 386 (☎ **61/414312**) leaves at 7:30am, returning at 2pm; and **Andescape** at Eberhard 599 (☎ **61/412592**) leaves at 7am, returning at 12:15pm. The cost is around $8 one-way.

BY TOUR VAN   If you have just a little time to spend in the park, or would like to get there at your own pace, check into the minivan tour services that plan stops at the Salto Grande waterfall and carry on to Lago Grey for a walk along the beach to view giant icebergs (see "Tour Operators," under Puerto Natales, Chile).

BY CAR   Heading north on Pedro Montt out of town, follow the dirt road for (32 miles (51km) until you reach Cerro Castillo. From here the road turns left and heads 29 miles (47km) toward the park (keep your eyes open for another left turn that is signed TORRES DEL PAINE). You'll come to a fork in the road; one road leads to the Lago Sarmiento Conaf station, another to the Laguna Amarga station. If you are planning to head to the Torres trailhead and Hostería Las Torres hotel complex on your way out, then take the Lago Sarmiento entrance; it's faster, and you'll get to view the blue, blue waters of Lago Sarmiento. You can park your car at the Hostería Las Torres, the park administration center, the Pudeto catamaran dock, or the Lago Grey ranger station.

CROSSING LAGO PEHOE BY CATAMARAN   At some point you'll likely cross Lago Pehoe either at the beginning or end of your trip. The catamaran *Our Lady of the Snows* has several crossings per day and is timed to meet all buses; the cost is a steep $15 one-way. Times vary according to demand and season; they are posted outside the refugio Pehoe, and every *refugio* in the park has a time schedule.

GETTING TO THE PARK BY BOAT   Relatively few people are aware that they can arrive by a zodiac-catamaran combination that takes visitors from Puerto Natales through the Ultima Esperanza Sound and up the Río Serrano, or vice versa. This is a highly recommended way to do one leg of the trip rather than ride both ways in a vehicle, but it's an all-day affair. Along the winding turquoise river, visitors are taken through territory that rivals Alaska, past the glaciers Tyndall and Geike, and eventually to the Serrano Glacier. Here they disembark for a walk up to the ice, then board another boat for a 3½-hour ride to Puerto Natales. It's not cheap—the cost runs about $60 to $85 per person, depending on the season. You can also do a round-trip journey leaving from and returning to the park for $60. Two companies also offer a 2-night/3-day kayak descent down the Río Serrano, meeting the boat for the ride to Puerto Natales. For address and telephone numbers, see "Tour Operators & Adventure Travel Outfitters" under "Puerto Natales," above. **Onas** is the oldest-running company with zodiac service, leaving at 8:30am from the administration office (they'll pick you up from longer distances for an extra charge). Two companies,

Aventour and **21 de Mayo,** have just started business taking guests down the Río Serrano. Aventour includes an additional stop at its lodge and offers round-trips up and down the river that start from its lodge near the Serrano Glacier. Although the companies will throw a tarp over your suitcase, their zodiacs are not roofed.

WHERE TO STAY & DINE IN TORRES DEL PAINE

For all hotels, parking is either free, or street parking is plentiful.

HOTELS AND HOSTERÍAS

Hostería Lago Grey. Office in Punta Arenas, Lautaro Navarro 1061. ☎ **61/410220** (direct). ☎/fax 61/225986 (reservations). www.chileaustral.com/grey. E-mail: hgrey@ ctcreuna.cl. 20 units. Oct–Apr $195 double; May–Sept $95 double. AE, DC, MC, V.

This spruce little white *hostería* is tucked within a beech forest, looking out onto the beach at Lago Grey and the astounding blue icebergs that drift to its shore. It's well on the other side of the park, but they have a transfer van and guides for excursions to all reaches of the park. The 20 rooms are spread out from the main common area, with a restaurant and lounge area. The rooms are comfortable, but the walls are a tad thin. Also, when the wind whips up, this side of the park is colder, but the location is more tranquil than that of Las Torres, with plenty of trails that branch out from its location including the stroll along the beach out to the Pingo Valley and the strenuous hike up to Mirador Ferrier. The transfer van will pick you up from anywhere in the park.

Hostería Las Torres. Office in Punta Arenas, Magallanes 960. ☎ **61/226054.** Fax 61/ 4111572. www.chileaustral.com/lastorres. E-mail: lastorres@chileaustral.com. 20 units. $197 double superior; $149 standard. AE, DC, MC, V.

This *hostería* sits at the trailhead to the Torres on an *estancia* that still operates as a working cattle ranch. The complex includes a ranch-style hotel, a large campground, and a hostel, meaning there's a fair amount of traffic coming in and out daily. The main building has a restaurant, a bar, and half the guest rooms; the other half of the rooms are located in a brand-new separate unit, but the newer rooms are identical to the old. The superior rooms are slightly larger than the standard, and they come with central heating; other than this, the difference is slight. The rooms are not especially noteworthy, but they are comfortable, and there's a relaxing lounge with couches and game tables for guests only. The entire building is made of terra-cotta–colored logs, situated on an idyllic grassy expanse that is backed by the Paine Massif. The *hostería* offers guided excursions and horseback rides; more often than not, you'll find a horse grazing just outside your door.

Dining: The *hostería's* restaurant deserves special note for its delicious evening buffet dinner, which costs $25 per person. They serve from a menu throughout the day.

Amenities: Laundry, room service, horseback riding, park transportation, guided excursions.

Hostería Mirador del Payne. Office in Punta Arenas, Fagnano 585. ☎ **61/228712.** www. mundosur.com/mirpayne. E-mail: payne@mundosur.com. 20 units. TEL. Oct–Mar $128 double; Apr–Sept $90 double. AE, DC, MC, V.

This *hostería* is an old *estancia* outside the park, and it boasts a commanding view of the Cuernos that rise behind a beautiful grassy field and Lake Verde. If you really want to get away from crowds, this is your hotel, although it doesn't put you directly near the Paine Massif. The rooms are in a unit separate from the main lodge, which has a restaurant, bar, and fireside lounge. The *hostería* offers great horseback-riding opportunities for an additional cost of $20 for 3 hours. Access to the *hostería* is via one of two ways: by a road that branches off before arriving at the park or by a moderate

2-hour trail that leads to the park administration center. Guests arrive by road, but more than a few opt to end their stay here with a horseback ride to the park administration center to continue on to another hotel within the park's boundaries.

Hostería Pehoe. Office in Punta Arenas, José Menéndez 918. ☎ **61/244506.** Fax 61/244052. www.pehoe.com. E-mail: gerencia@pehoe.com. 25 units. $160 double. AE, DC, MC, V.

The Hostería Pehoe was built before Torres del Paine was declared a national park, and it's the oldest hotel here. It's located on an island in Lago Pehoe, accessible via a long walkway that connects it with the shore. The view of the Cuernos from here is really impressive, but unfortunately none of the rooms comes with that view because they are situated behind the main building in a grove of beech trees. It's an awesome location nevertheless, but the rooms are run-of-the-mill and overpriced at $160 for their outdated decorations and construction. Still, it's the cheapest hotel within the park limits. Guests normally take their meals in the hotel's restaurant, which offers so-so fare at above-average prices.

✪ Hotel Explora Salto Chico. In Santiago, Américo Vespucio Sur 80, 5th floor. ☎ **2/206-6060.** Fax 2/228-4655. www.explora-chile.com. E-mail: reservexplora@explora-chile.cl. 31 units. TEL. Packages per person, double occupancy: 3 nights/2 days $1,296; 4 nights/3 days $1,706; 7 nights/6 days $2,441. AE, DC, MC, V.

Few hotels in Chile have garnered as much fame as the Hotel Explora, and deservedly so. The Explora's location is simply stunning, looking out over the blue waters of Lago Pehoe and directly at the dramatic Cuernos formation. At the left exterior, the raging Salto Chico cascades into the Río Paine. The hotel was designed by several renowned Chilean architects to take full advantage of its location, with a band of picture windows that wrap around the full front of the building and large windows in each room—even the bathrooms come with cut-outs in the wall so that while you're brushing your teeth, you'll still have your eyes on the gorgeous panorama. Explora's style is comfortable elegance. The softly curving, blonde-wood interiors were built entirely from native deciduous beech, as was the handcrafted furniture. Glowing lights and chintz sofas line the drawn-out lounge, with several comfortable nooks for curling up fireside. The rooms are superb, with checkered linens imported from Barcelona, wicker furniture, handsome slate-tiled bathrooms, powerful showers, and warming racks for drying gear. Explora operates as a full-service lodge with packages that include direct airport transfers, meals, open bar, and excursions. Every evening, 3 of the 10 full-time guides meet with guests to discuss the following day's excursions, which range from easy half-day walks to strenuous full-day hikes. There are about seven excursions to choose from, including horseback rides and photo safaris. In the morning, a fleet of vans whisks guests off to their destination and back again for lunch; guides carry picnic lunches for full-day hikes. The set menu is limited to two choices, generally a meat and vegetarian dish, and it must be said that the food quality has at times been uneven—never bad, but not as outstanding as one would expect from a hotel of this caliber. Americans make up a full 50% of the guests, who typically leave thrilled with their visit. Note that two of the days in the package are misleading: the first-day arrival to the hotel is around 6pm, time for a short hike to a lookout point only, and the last day isn't really a day at all, as guests leave after breakfast for the drive back to the airport.

Dining/Diversions: Guests take their meals at the hotel: Explora's all-inclusive packages include meals in their restaurant, with a breakfast buffet and a fixed menu at lunch and dinner, with a meat and vegetarian option.

Amenities: Explora has a house connected by 100 steps down from the main hotel that has an indoor pool, outdoor Jacuzzi, saunas, and two full-time massage therapists. The hotel's downstairs lounge has a satellite TV, videos of the park, and a small library. The hotel has its own boat for crossing Lago Pehoe, but it's used to drop off guests for hikes only, and on days with heavy wind, the boat cannot cross.

REFUGIOS & ALBERGUES

These cabinlike lodging units can be found at the base of trails or in the backcountry. They are moderately priced options for those who are not interested in pitching a tent, and although most have bedding or sleeping bags for rent, your best bet is to bring your own. All come with hot showers, a cafe, and a common area for hiding out from bad weather. Simple meals and sandwiches are sold; dinners average $10 per person, or you can bring your own food and cook in their kitchens. Each *refugio* has rooms with two to six bunks, which you'll have to share with strangers when they're full. Per-person rates average $15. Some of these *refugios* are very attractive, and all are situated in gorgeous locations. During the high season you'll need to book a bed at least 2 days in advance, but busier *refugios* can book up 4 to 5 days ahead. All agencies in Puerto Natales take reservations, or you can call or e-mail (shown below). There is a *refugio* near the park administration center, but it has a lousy sleeping arrangement, with an upper floor and two rows of sleeping berths, much like a camp-out. This *refugio* is on a first-come, first-serve basis.

The following *refugios* can be reserved by calling ☎ **61/226054** or by e-mailing lastorres@chileaustral.com.

- **Refugio Chileno.** Probably the least-frequented *refugio* for its position halfway up to the Towers (most do the trail as a day hike). Still, it's nicer to stay in this pretty valley than down below.
- **Albergue Las Torres.** This *albergue* sits near the Hostería Las Torres, with a full-service restaurant. Horseback rides can be taken from here.
- **Refugio Los Cuernos.** Possibly the park's loveliest *refugio,* at the base of the Cuernos and with two walls of windows that look out onto Lago Nordenskjold.

The following *refugios* can be reserved by calling or faxing **61/412592** or by e-mailing andescape@chileaustral.com. These three *refugios* are exactly the same in terms of their cabinlike design.

- **Refugio Grey.** Tucked in a forest on the shore of Lago Grey, this *refugio* is a 10-minute walk to the lookout point for the glacier. It's an ideal setting, and it has a cozy fireside seating area.
- **Refugio Dickson.** Another less-frequented *refugio* for its location well on the other side of the park. It has a fantastic location on a grassy glacial moraine, and looks directly at the Dickson Glacier.
- **Refugio Pehoé.** This *refugio* is the hub for several of the trailheads to the park administration center, Glacier Grey, and the French Valley, as well as the docking site for the catamaran. It is, therefore, constantly busy and service is notoriously bad here.

CAMPING IN TORRES DEL PAINE

Torres del Paine has a well-designed campground system with free and concession-run sites. All *refugios* have a campground, and all concession sites charge $4 per person, which includes showers (hot water is available at Los Cuernos, Chileno, and the site at Hostería Las Torres only), water, and bathrooms. The site at Las Torres provides barbecues and firewood. Free campgrounds are run by Conaf, and they can get a little dingy, with deplorable outhouses. Beginning in March, mice become a problem for campers, so always leave food well stored or hanging from a tree branch. The JLM hiking map (available at every bookstore, kiosk, and travel agency and at the park entrance) denotes which campgrounds are free and which cost a fee.

TRAILS IN TORRES DEL PAINE

There is a multitude of ways to hike or backpack in Torres del Paine. All are determined on how much time you have here and what kind of walking you're up for. The best way to plan a multiple-day hike here is to begin at the Hostería Las Torres, reached from the Laguna Amarga ranger station, although some prefer to begin by crossing Lago Pehoe by catamaran and start the trip up to the glacier or the French Valley. You'll want to pick up one of JLM's Torres del Paine maps (sold everywhere) to plan your itinerary. Walking times shown below are average. The minimum amount of days shown means walking 4 to 8 hours a day, and if you want to take it easy, plan for extra days and maybe a day or two for bad weather.

LONG-HAUL OVERNIGHT HIKES

The "W." Approximately 35mi (56km) total. Beginning at Hostería Las Torres or Refugio Pehoe. Terrain ranges from easy to difficult.

This segment of the Paine Massif is so called because hikers are taken along a trail that forms a *W*. This trail takes hikers to the park's major geological features—the Torres, the Cuernos, and Glacier Grey—and it's the preferred multiple-day hike for its relative short hauls and timeframe that requires 4 to 5 days. As well, those who prefer not to camp or carry more gear than a sleeping bag, food, and their personal goods can stay in the various *refugios* along the way. Most hikers begin at Hostería Las Torres and start with a day-walk up to the Torres. From here, hikers head to the Los Cuernos *refugio* and spend the night, or continue on to the Italiano campsite near the base of the valley; from here hikers walk up to the French Valley. The next stop is Pehoe refugio, where most spend the night before hiking up to Glacier Grey. It's best to spend a night at Refugio Grey, and return to the Pehoe refugio the next day. From here, you'll take the catamaran across Lago Pehoe to an awaiting bus back to Puerto Natales.

The Circuit. Approximately 37mi (60km) total. Beginning at Laguna Amarga or Hostería Las Torres. Terrain ranges from easy to difficult.

The Circuit is a spectacular, long-haul backpacking trip that takes hikers around the entire Paine Massif. It can be done in two ways: with the "W" included or without. Including the "W," you'll need 8 to 11 days; without it, from 4 (if you're a speed walker ready for 8- to 12-hour hiking days) to 7 days. The Circuit is less-traveled than the "W" because it's longer and requires that you camp out at least twice. I don't recommend doing this trail if you have only 4 or 5 days. This trail is for serious backpackers only because it involves several difficult hikes up and down steep, rough terrain and over fallen tree trunks. You'll be rewarded for your effort, however, with dazzling views of terrain that varies from grassy meadows and winding rivers to thick, virgin beech forest, snowcapped peaks and, best of all, the awe-inspiring view of Glacier Grey seen from atop the John Garner Pass. If you're a recreational hiker with a 4- to 6-hour hike tolerance level, you'll want to sleep in all the major campgrounds or *refugios*. Always do this trail counter-clockwise for easier ascents and with the scenery before you. If you're here during the high season and want to get away from crowds, you might contemplate walking the first portion of this trail beginning at Laguna Azul. This is the old trail, and it more or less parallels the Circuit but on the other side of the river, passing the gaucho post La Victorina, the only remaining building of an old *estancia*. At Refugio Dickson you'll have to cross the river in the *refugio*'s dinghy for $3. To get to Laguna Azul, you'll need to hitchhike or arrange private transportation.

DAY HIKES

These hikes run from easy to difficult, either within the "W" or from various trail-heads throughout the park. Again, the times given are estimates for the average walker.

Las Torres (The Towers). 3 hours one-way. Difficult.

The trail to view the soaring granite Towers is a classic hike in the park, but certainly not the easiest. It leaves from the Hostería Las Torres. The beginning is a steep, 45-minute ascent, followed by up-and-down terrain for 1½ hours to another 45-minute steep ascent up a granite moraine. It's all or nothing because the Torres do not come into full view until the very end.

Valle Francés (French Valley). Departing from Refugio Pehoe or Refugio Los Cuernos. 2½–4½ hours one-way. Moderate/difficult.

There are several ways to hike this trail. From Refugio Pehoe, you'll pass by the blue waters of Lake Skottsberg and through groves of Chilean firebush and open views of the granite spires behind Los Cuernos. From Refugio Los Cuernos, you won't see the French Valley until you're in it. You can walk a bit into the valley for direct views of the hanging glacier that descends from Paine Grande, or continue the steep climb up into the valley itself for a view of an enormous granite amphitheater.

Glacier Grey. 3½ hours one-way. Moderate.

This walk is certainly worth the effort for an up-close look at the face of Glacier Grey. The walk is not as steep as the Las Torres hike, but it's longer. The walk takes hikers through thick forest and open views of the Southern Ice Field and the icebergs slowly making their way down Lago Grey. A turn-off just before the lookout point takes you to Refugio Grey.

Lago Grey. Departing from the parking lot past the entrance to Hostería Lago Grey. 1–2 hours. Easy.

Not only is this the easiest walk in the park, it is one of the most dramatic for the gigantic blue icebergs that rest along the shore of Lago Grey. There's a peninsula with a fairly easy trail that takes walkers to a lookout point where you can see the glacier in the distance. This walk begins near the Hostería Lago Grey; they offer a hour-long zodiac trip around the icebergs and are currently attempting to bring back boat service to the glacier. Ask for more information at the *hostería* (see "Hotels and Hosterías," above).

Lago Pingo. Departing from the Lago Grey parking lot past the entrance to Hostería Lago Grey. 1–4 hours one-way. Easy/moderate.

Lago Pingo consistently sees fewer hikers, and is a great spot for bird watching. The trail begins as an easy walk through a beautiful valley, past an old gaucho post. From here the trail heads through forest and undulating terrain and past the Pingo Cascade until it eventually reaches another old gaucho post, the run-down but picturesque Zapata *refugio*. You can make this trail as long or as short as you'd like. The trail leaves from the same parking lot as the Lago Grey trail.

Mirador Nordenskjold. 1 hour one-way. Easy.

The trailhead begins near the Pudeto catamaran dock. This trail begins with an up-close visit to the crashing Salto Grande waterfall. Then the trail winds through

Antarctic beech and thorny bush to a lookout point with dramatic views into the French Valley and the Cuernos, looking over Lago Nordenskjold. This trail is a good place to see wildflowers.

OTHER OUTDOOR ACTIVITIES IN THE PARK
HORSEBACK RIDING

A horseback ride in Torres del Paine can be one of the most enjoyable ways to see the park, especially from the Serrano *pampa* for big, bold views of the Paine Massif. **Baquedano Zamora,** with a Puerto Natales office at Eberhard 566 (☎ **61/413953;** e-mail: baqueano@entelchile.net), operates the horse-riding concession in the park, with stables close to the park administration center. It offers a wide variety of trips across the Serrano *pampa* to Lago Grey and excursions around the Laguna Amarga and Laguna Azul sectors. It also offers multiple-day trips that include camping and stays in *refugios.* The cost depends on the number of riders (10 maximum): 1- to 3-hour rides, $30 to $47 per person; 3- to 5-hour rides, $35 to $53; and 5- to 8-hour rides, $45 to $70. Some trips require prior experience; other excursions can be taken by beginners. Hostería Las Torres has horseback riding to its Refugios Chileno and Los Cuernos; its Punta Arenas office is at Magallanes 960 (☎ **61/226054;** e-mail: lastorres@chileaustral.com). Both full-day trips cost $69 per person, and they leave from their premises at the hotel.

ICE CLIMBING

There is nothing as thrilling as a walk across Glacier Grey. Trips begin from the Refugio Grey at 9am and return at 5pm, with an hour walk to the entrance site and then back to the *refugio.* Guests are provided with full equipment, including crampons, ice axes, ropes, and harnesses, and are given basic ice-climbing instructions. Visitors who have taken this hike have consistently given rave reviews for the chance to peer into deep blue crevasses and explore the glacier's otherworldly contours up close. Bigfoot Expeditions runs this concession, and reservations are recommended, although there is often space for walk-ins. You need to spend the previous night at the Refugio Grey or in its campsite; the office in Puerto Natales is at Blanco Encalada 226 (☎ **61/414611;** www.bigfootpatagonia.com; e-mail: explore@bigfootpatagonia. com). The cost is $55 per person, which includes a box lunch; credit cards are accepted at their concession site at Refugio Grey.

4 El Calafate, Argentina

138 miles (222km) S of El Chaltén; 1,691 miles (2,727km) SW of Buenos Aires

El Calafate is a tourist-oriented village that hugs the shore of turquoise Lago Argentino, a location that combined with the town's leafy streets gives it the feel of an oasis in the desert *pampa* of this region. The town depends almost entirely on its neighboring natural wonder, the Perito Moreno Glacier, for tourism. Thousands of visitors come for the chance to stand face-to-face with this tremendous wall of ice, one of the few glaciers descending from the ice field that is not retreating.

The town was named for the calafate bush found throughout Patagonia that produces a sweet berry commonly used in syrups and jams. The saying here is "Once you try the calafate, you'll always come back"—a bit of an exaggeration, but then Argentines in Patagonia are known for such overstatements. (Commonly seen posters and stickers claim the right to the entire Southern Ice Field, although more than three quarters of it falls in Chile.) El Calafate has suffered from a tourist trap mentality for years, charging outlandish rates for horrible service and lining its streets with knick-knack shops and bookstores manned by the rudest clerks this side of the Andes. Thankfully this tendency is waning as more migrants head south to set up businesses that are meant to really serve visitors. The town itself is quite a pleasant little place, but you won't find many attractions here—they are all within the confines of Los Glaciares National Park.

ESSENTIALS
GETTING THERE
BY PLANE   El Calafate's brand-new **Aeropuerto Lago Argentino** (no phone) has dramatically changed transportation options here; before you would have to fly into Río Gallegos and then take a long bus ride across the flat *pampa*. Service is from Argentine destinations only: **Aerolíneas Argentinas** (☎ 11/4340-3777 in Buenos Aires), **Southern Winds** (☎ 02944/423704 in Bariloche), and **LADE** (☎ 02944/423562 in Bariloche), all have daily flights from Buenos Aires; Southern Winds and Aerolíneas Argentinas have four weekly flights from Ushuaia; and Southern Winds has a Sunday flight from Bariloche. At the time of this printing, these companies did not have an office in El Calafate, but any travel agency can book tickets for you.

BY BUS   El Calafate has a bus terminal located on Julio A. Roca, reached by taking the stairs up from the main street Av. del Libertador. To and from Puerto Natales, Chile: **Buses Sur** (☎ 02901/491631) and **Turismo Zaahj** (☎ 02902/411325) have five weekly trips leaving at 8am, as does **Cootra** (☎ 02902/491444). To get to El Chaltén, take **Chaltén Travel,** which leaves at 8am and returns from Chaltén at 6pm (☎ 02902/492212), **Caltur** (☎ 02902/491842), and **Interlagos Turismo** (☎ 02902/491179); the latter two leave at 7:30am and return from El Chaltén at 5pm.

BY CAR   Ruta 5, followed by Ruta 11, is paved entirely from Río Gallegos to El Calafate. From Puerto Natales, cross through the border at Cerro Castillo, which will lead you to the famous Ruta Nacional 40 and up to the paved portion of Ruta 11. The drive from Puerto Natales is roughly 5 hours, not including time spent at the border checkpoint.

GETTING AROUND
For information about transportation to and from the Perito Moreno Glacier, see "Getting There & Essentials" under "Parque Nacional Los Glaciares & the Perito Moreno Glacier," below. If you'd like to rent a car, you can do so at **Cristina,** Gobernador Gregores and Avenida 7 de Diciembre (☎ 02902/491674; e-mail: crisrent@infovia.com.ar), or **Freelander,** Gobernador Paradelo 253 (☎ 02902/491437; e-mail: freelander@cotecal.com.ar).

VISITOR INFORMATION
The city's **visitor information kiosk** can be found inside the bus terminal. They offer an ample amount of printed material and can assist in planning a trip to the Perito Moreno Glacier; open October to April 8am to 11pm daily and May to September 8am to 8pm daily (☎ 02902/491090).

WHAT TO SEE & DO IN EL CALAFATE
El Calafate is really nothing more than a service town for visitors on their way to visit the glaciers (see "Parque Nacional Los Glaciares & the Perito Moreno Glacier," below), but it does present a pleasant main avenue for a stroll, and as expected, there

are lots of souvenirs, bookstores and crafts shops to keep you occupied. Heading out of town on Av. del Libertador, you'll pass the **Museo Municipal** (no phone), open Monday to Friday 8am to 1pm and 3pm to 9pm, with a collection of farming and ranching implements, Indian artifacts, and historical and ethnographical displays. It's a fairly interesting exhibit that's worth a stop if you have the time. And that's about it here in El Calafate, although if you are interested in bird watching, you could take a short walk to the Bahía Redonda at the shore of Lago Argentino to view upland geese, black-necked swans, and flamingos.

ATTRACTIONS & EXCURSIONS AROUND EL CALAFATE

For information about visiting the glaciers and the national park, see "Parque Nacional Los Glaciares & the Perito Moreno Glacier," below.

HORSEBACK RIDING **Cabalgata en Patagonia,** Julio A. Roca 2063 (☎ **02902/493203;** e-mail: cabalgataenpatagonia@cotecal.com.ar), offers two horse-back riding options: a 2-hour ride to Bahía Redonda for a panoramic view of El Calafate ($30) and a full-day trip bordering Lago Argentino, with an optional stop at the Walicho Caves where one can supposedly view Indian "paintings," which are billed as real but are really reproductions. This tour costs $50 per person and includes lunch. Book directly or with a travel agency.

VISITING AN *ESTANCIA*   An interesting option worth looking into is one of the several *estancias,* or ranches, that have opened their doors to the public, offering day activities, restaurant services, and even lodging should you opt to spend the night. Perhaps the most exclusive and well known is the **Estancia Helsingfors,** open October to March and located on the shore of Lago Viedma about 93 miles (150km) from El Calafate. Helsingfors offers lodging, horseback riding, overflights, bird watching, boat trips, and high gastronomy. For more information, contact their offices in Río Gallegos at Av. del Libertador 516 (☎/fax **02966/420719**).

All of the following *estancias* offer lodging, a restaurant, horseback riding, trekking, vehicle excursions, and transportation from El Calafate. The closest to El Calafate is the **Estancia Huyliche,** about 2 miles (3km) from downtown, open October to April; they also offer boating excursions (☎ **02902/491025;** e-mail: teresanegro@cotecal. com.ar). **Estancia Alice El Galpón,** open October to April, is 12 miles (20km) from El Calafate on Ruta 11, and offers activities that lean more toward ranching, including sheep-shearing and wool-packing demonstrations, sheep round-ups, and maintenance of the animals, as well as bird watching (☎ **02902/492290;** e-mail: info@elgalpon.com.ar). **Estancia Alta Vista,** at 20 miles (33km) from El Calafate on the dirt road Ruta 15 near the beautiful area of Lago Roca, is open October to March and offers ranch activities and fishing (☎ **02902/491247;** e-mail: altavista@cotecal. com.ar). **Estancia Nibepo Aike** is picturesquely nestled on the southeast edge of the national park about 37 miles (60km) from El Calafate, and it's also near Lago Roca, offering fishing and ranch activities (☎ **02966/422626;** e-mail: nibepo@internet. siscotel.com.ar).

WHERE TO STAY

For all hotels, parking is either free, or street parking is plentiful.

EXPENSIVE

✪ **Hotel El Mirador del Lago**. Av. del Libertador 2047, El Calafate. ☎ **02902/493176.** Fax 02902/493213. www.wam.com.ar/tourism/hoteles/mirador. E-mail: miradordellago@ cotecal.com.ar. 20 units, 2 suites. TV TEL. $130–$170 double. MC, V.

At a 10-minute walk from downtown, the Mirador del Lago isn't as conveniently located as its competitors, but the exceptionally friendly, personal service and amenities galore more than make up for it. The brick hotel with its peaked green awnings faces Lago Argentino, an otherwise interesting landscape if it weren't for a yellow building that somewhat mars the view. Rooms aren't huge, but they're not cramped either; there are a few suites if you need more space, and they come with hydromassage baths. The carpeted rooms have comfortable beds with checkered bedspreads and small windows, but they do the job and cast a reasonable amount of light. The hotel's strong suit is that it really works to make certain your stay is above average. Room service, the bar, and the restaurant function 24 hours a day. Beyond the TV room with regional videos, there is a library chock-full of multilingual information about the area and a souvenir and crafts shop. The hotel frequently offers promotional discounts.

Dining/Diversions: The bright, plant-filled restaurant serves breakfast as well as a wide variety of regional and Argentine dishes, and they host a folkloric dance show and dinner two to four times weekly.

Amenities: Laundry, room service, library, gift shop, sauna.

✪ **Hotel Kosten Aike.** Gobernador Moyano 1243, El Calafate. ☎ **02902/492424,** or 11/4811-1314 (reservations). Fax 02902/491538. E-mail: kostenaike@cotecal.com.ar. 60 units. MINIBAR TV TEL. $141–$188 double. AE, DC, MC, V.

This brand-new hotel offers the most attractive accommodations in El Calafate paired with high-quality service. The Kosten Aike is priced exactly the same as its competitor, the Posada los Alamos (see below); the difference here is that the Posada's design is buttoned-up conservative and the Kosten Aike is fresh and stylish, with just enough decorative details to put it a step above minimalism. Both the architect's and designer's good taste saved the Kosten Aike from the cookie-cutter style usually seen in new hotels. Furnishings and artwork imported from Buenos Aires include matching drapes and bedspreads in rust and beige accented with black geometric squiggles, papiermâché lamps, iron and rosewood tables and chairs, and petal-soft carpets, and all rooms feature sumptuous bathrooms. Doubles come in two sizes: superior and standard, and there are suites and junior suites. Superiors have bay windows and are very large, and because it seems the hotel has yet to reach a policy on whether they'll charge more for these rooms, ask for one for the same price when booking. The airy lobby is inlaid completely with gray stone.

Dining/Diversions: The Kosten Aike has a chic, earthen-linen and blonde-wood restaurant off the lobby that is open for guests and the public. The restaurant serves contemporary regional and Argentine fare. There's also a wine bar, fireside lounge and bar, and game room in the lobby.

Amenities: Laundry, 24-hour room service, gift shop, game room.

✪ **Hotel Posada Los Alamos.** Gobernador Moyano and Bustillo, El Calafate. ☎ **02902/491144.** Fax 02902/491186. www.posadalosalamos.com. E-mail: posadalosalamos@cotecal.com.ar. 144 units. TV TEL. $141–$188 double. AE, MC, V.

The Posada Los Alamos is as conservative as a Brooks Brothers suit. Because of the low-key design of the "complex" and the slightly aloof service, you can't help shake the feeling that you're in a private country club. The style is classic: a red-brick exterior fringed with the hotel's namesake alamo trees, plaid carpet, old English furniture, and windows with wooden, triangular eaves. The downstairs lounge has plenty of cushiony couches to sink into, and the lobby's large, cross-hatched windows look out onto an expansive lawn. Upstairs there is a restaurant and another lobby dominated by Swiss-style, geranium-patterned ruby and black couches and drapes—it's very colorful and quite an eyeful, but the bar is a very comfortable place to relax. The hotel has provided ample space in its rooms to move about, and each has a slightly different color and style. Ask for a room that looks out onto the quiet, grassy backyard instead of the street. The Posada can plan excursions, and it has a tennis court.

Dining: Across the street, a winding stone walkway leads to the hotel's excellent restaurant, La Posta, reviewed under "Where to Dine," below. The hotel has a casual restaurant upstairs for breakfast and snacks.

Amenities: Laundry, 24-hour room service, gift shop, tennis courts, convention center.

MODERATE

Hotel Amado. Av. del Libertador 1072, El Calafate. ☎ **02902/491023.** Fax 02902/491134. E-mail: familiagomez@cotecal.com.ar. 20 units. TV TEL. $57-$72 double. AE, MC, V.

The Hotel Amado sits on the main street next to all shops and restaurants. The hotel is an okay choice, far from exceptional but not particularly bad either. The hallway and the rooms are on the dark side, and doubles always come with an extra single that cramps the room—ask if they can move the single for extra breathing space. The red cotton bedspreads are somewhat tired, but beds have regular mattresses and box springs instead of a foam mattress. All in all, very clean if a bit worn.

Hotel Kapenke. Av. 9 de Julio 112, El Calafate. ☎/fax **02902/491093.** 32 units. TV TEL. $67 double. MC, V.

This hotel is a slight step up from the Amado (see above), about a half block away on a side street, and a good option for moderately priced lodging in El Calafate. The Kapenke underwent a minor renovation last year, installing new wallpaper and, in the hallway, lemon-yellow paint. The bathrooms are cramped, but the rooms are decently sized and come with a large chest of drawers and comfortable beds—ask for a room on the second floor as they are brighter. Apart from a few corner sitting areas spread about each floor, there is a large lounge with lots of padded wooden chairs.

Kalken Hostería. Teniente Feilberg 119, El Calafate. ☎ **02902/491073.** Fax 02902/491036. E-mail: hotelkalken@cotecal.com.ar. 32 units. TV TEL. $95-$110 double. MC, V.

Located on a corner lot about a half block from the bus terminal, this *hostería* is a solid option in this price range, offering comfortable accommodations and a pleasant restaurant. The style is old Spanish, with white stucco walls, iron chandeliers, and chunky wood furniture. Rooms are average sized, decorated with a single wood-framed print and standard linens. The split-level lounge and restaurant is airy and inviting, with a slanted, wood-beam roof. If you can't get a room at the Michelangelo (see below), book one here.

Michelangelo Hotel. Gobernador Moyano 1020, El Calafate. ☎ **02902/491045.** Fax 02902/491058. www.patagonia-travel.com/michelangelo.html. E-mail: michelangelohotel@cotecal.com.ar. 20 units. TV TEL. $97-$121 double. MC, V.

The Michelangelo is very popular with traveling foreigners, especially Americans. The hotel sits about a 2-block walk from the main street and catty-corner from the phone center, a convenient yet quiet location, and is recognizable by its A-frame porticos. Probably the best thing about the Michelangelo is its excellent restaurant (reviewed under "Where to Dine," below) and its comfortable rooms, although they're not especially noteworthy. Rooms are average sized with white walls, dark beams, and little decoration. The common areas have low ceilings and are made of stone and mortar, brick, and white stucco; the softly lit lounge has a handful of chairs, a banquette, and potted plants.

INEXPENSIVE

Hostal Lago Argentino. Campaña de Desierto 1070, El Calafate. ☎ **02902/491423.** 8 units. $35 double. No credit cards. Closed July to mid-Aug.

Like Los Dos Pinos (see below), the Hostal Lago Argentino offers different options for budget travelers. There are $8 beds in two-bunk, shared rooms in one wing and, across the street in a pink and blue building, modest yet tidy doubles with private bathrooms that for $35 make for a decent value in El Calafate. The rooms aren't huge, but there's a small seating area should you need a little space. The hostal is about a block from the bus terminal.

Los Dos Pinos. Av. 9 de Julio 358, El Calafate. ☎/fax **02902/491271.** www.losglaciares. com/lospinos. E-mail: losdospinos@cotecal.com.ar. 25 units. TV. $40 double; $10 per person cabaña. MC, V.

The Los Dos Pinos has just about every and any combination for budget travelers. At the bottom of the rung is the grassy campground, which comes with barbecue pits and costs $4 per person; next up is the $8 option for a bed in a six-bunk room that you might or might not have to share with strangers during the high season. There are several cabins and a few rooms that come with a kitchen. One floor has three rooms and a hall that leads to a shared kitchen and bathroom. The cabañas have kelly-green cement interiors and two bedrooms with one single and one bunk bed and a shared eating area and kitchen. The "deluxe" rooms are simple doubles with a private bathroom but no kitchen, and are a good deal for the price. The hostal sits at the end of a gravely dirt road about a 4-block walk to the main street, not exactly a choice location. Also, the surrounding grounds are unattractive because the lot seems to be in a perpetual state of half-completed construction.

WHERE TO DINE

For all restaurants listed, reservations are not necessary except where noted.

EXPENSIVE

✪ **La Posta.** Gobernador Moyano and Bustillo. ☎ **02902/491144.** Main courses $15–$20. AE, DC, MC, V. Daily 7pm–midnight. ARGENTINE.

Although it's in a building separate from the Posada Los Alamos, the La Posta is considered to be part of that hotel. This is El Calafate's most upscale restaurant, serving great cuisine and choice wines in a cozy, candlelit environment. The menu, printed in four languages, offers well-prepared dishes that effectively blend Argentine and international-flavored fare such as filet mignon in a puff pastry with rosemary-roasted potatoes, pasta such as king crab ravioli, seafood such as almond trout or curried crayfish, and the ever-popular barbecue *parrilla*, which on Fridays and Saturdays is cooked by a fully costumed gaucho. La Posta offers a daily set menu that includes an appetizer, main course, and dessert.

Michelangelo. Gobernador Moyano 1020. ☎ **02902/492104.** Main courses $12–$20. MC, V. Daily noon–3pm and 8–11pm. ARGENTINE.

The Michelangelo Hotel's restaurant is as popular with the public as it is with its guests. The semi-elegant dining area is very pleasing, with low ceilings, stone-and-mortar walls, and candlelit tables. The Michelangelo has added more exotic fare to its menu than La Posta, such as wild hare and smoked venison. The well-seasoned lamb dishes are quite good, as are other meat dishes, such as filet mignon or chicken with a balsamic and tarragon vinaigrette. The fresh pastas and fish dishes are light and simple, as are the salads.

MODERATE

Casablanca. Av. 21 de Mayo and Av. del Libertador. ☎ **02902/491402.** Main courses $6–$10; sandwiches $2.50–$5. No credit cards. Daily 10am–3am. CAFE/BAR.

The Casablanca is the local hangout for a beer and quick meal. There's a wooden bar and a dining area with tile floors and metal chairs and tables, and an elevated TV that's usually on. The menu is mostly sandwiches and empanadas, with one special and a popular steak and fries plate for $8, but sandwiches are your best bet here. Good spot for writing out postcards.

✪ **El Hornito.** Buenos Aires 155. ☎ **02902/492429.** Main courses $6.50–$11. MC, V. Daily 10am–1am. PIZZA/PASTA.

El Hornito (the "Little Oven") is one of my favorites in El Calafate, serving consistently delicious pastas and stone oven–baked pizzas. The tiny restaurant is about a half block from the bus terminal, and might be hard to spot—leaving from the terminal's front door, walk a half block up the gravely road Buenos Aires and look to your left. The restaurant has its own greenhouse, so you know that the vegetables are as fresh as their homemade pastas. Examples include pumpkin raviolis with a Roquefort sauce and incredible spinach crêpes with a tomato and cream sauce. The crispy pizzas run $7 for an individual and $16 for a large, and there are about 15 different varieties as well as vegetable tarts and *vino patero,* or homemade wine. The walls of El Hornito have been decorated with ranching antiques and historical photos.

✪ **El Rancho.** Gobernador Moyano and Av. 9 de Julio. ☎ **02902/491644.** Pizzas $6–$18. MC, V. Tues–Sun 6:30pm–midnight. PIZZA.

El Rancho's brick interior, with its white lace curtains and old photos, is cozy and inviting, but the restaurant's tiny size means you might have to wait for a table on busy evenings. There are 32 varieties of pizza on offer here and 5 varieties of hefty empanadas, all baked in the restaurant's clay oven. Also on the menu are fresh salads and a couple of steaks, if you're not in the mood for pizza but are looking for a warm, intimate ambience.

La Cocina. Av. del Libertador 1245. ☎ **02902/491758.** Main courses $7–$15. MC, V. Tues–Sun noon–3pm and 7:30–11pm. BISTRO.

This little restaurant serves bistro-style food, including fresh pastas such as raviolis and fettuccine, fresh trout, and meats that are prepared simply but are quite good. The crêpes stuffed with vegetables or combinations such as ham and cheese, and meat items, such as steak with a pepper and mustard sauce, are all served in a pleasing dining area. Of all the restaurants on the main street with a similar appearance to this one, such as the Paso Verlika, La Cocina is without a doubt the best.

La Tablita. Coronel Rosales 24. ☎ **02902/491065.** Main courses $7–$10. AE, MC, V. Daily 11am–3pm and 7pm–midnight (Wed closed for lunch). STEAKHOUSE.

Carnivores need not look any further. La Tablita is all about meat, and it's one of the local favorites in town for its heaping platters and giant *parrilladas* that come sizzling to your table on its own mini-barbecue. The *parrilladas* for two cost $29, but they really serve three diners given the size and assortment of chicken, sausage, beef, lamb, and a few innards you may or may not recognize. The sunny, airy restaurant can be found on the other side of the bridge that spans the Arroyo Calafate, about a 2-minute walk from downtown.

Parrilla Mi Viejo. Av. del Libertador 1111. ☎ **02902/491691.** Main courses $7–$10. MC, V. Daily 11am–3pm and 7pm–midnight. STEAKHOUSE.

Mi Viejo is another local barbecue favorite, with enough variety on the menu to satisfy everyone. Mi Viejo ("My Old Man") seems to refer to the crusty character manning the lamb barbecue spit at the restaurant's front entrance; either way, he serves up weighty, delicious cuts of meat. Three to five diners could eat from a $25 *parrillada* meat assortment, depending on their hunger. The menu also offers trout and salmon dishes and a few interesting plates such as pickled hare. The restaurant is located on the main drag, and its dining room is warm and pleasant.

Tango Sur. Av. 9 de Julio 265. ☎ **02902/491550.** Main courses $9–$12. No credit cards. Tues–Sun 7pm–5am. DINNER/SHOW.

The *porteño* owner of this restaurant/nightclub has brought tango to the south of Argentina. The new Tango Sur, in a lovely raspberry-colored building made of old brick, serves light meals and a nightly tango show of crooning and dancing. The interiors are crammed with memorabilia and antiques such as a megaphone, records, microphones, and anything related to tango that the owner found combing shops in Buenos Aires over a period of a year. The menu is brief, serving grilled steak, breaded beef *milanesas,* and sandwiches—better to order a drink and an appetizer platter.

PARQUE NACIONAL LOS GLACIARES & THE PERITO MORENO GLACIER

The Los Glaciares National Park covers 600,000 hectares (1,482,000 acres) of rugged land that stretches vertically along the crest of the Andes and spills east into flat *pampa.* Most of Los Glaciares is inaccessible to visitors except for the park's two dramatic highlights: the granite needles, such as Fitz Roy near El Chaltén (covered in "El Chaltén & the Fitz Roy Area, Argentina," below), and this region's magnificent Perito Moreno Glacier. The park is also home to thundering rivers, blue lakes, and thick beech forest. Los Glaciares National Park was formed in 1937 as a means of protecting this unique wilderness, notable for its landscape carved and sculpted by Ice Age and present-day glaciation. It was declared a World Heritage region by UNESCO in 1981.

If you don't get a chance to visit Glacier Grey in Torres del Paine, the Perito Moreno is a must-see. Few natural wonders in South America are as spectacular or as easily accessed as this glacier, and unlike the hundreds of glaciers that drain from the Southern Ice Field, the Perito Moreno is one of the few that are not receding. At the turn of the century, the Perito Moreno was measured at 750m (2,460 ft.) from the Peninsula Magallanes; by 1920 it had advanced so far that it finally made contact with the peninsula. Each time the glacier reached the peninsula, which would occur every 3 to 4 years, the Perito Moreno created a dam in the channel and the built-up pressure would set off a calving explosion for 48 to 72 hours, breaking the face of the glacier in a crashing fury. The phenomenon has not occurred in many years, but the Perito Moreno is usually reliable for a sending a few huge chunks hurling into the channel throughout the day.

What impresses visitors most is the sheer size of the Perito Moreno Glacier, a wall of jagged blue ice measuring 4,500m (14,760 ft.) across and soaring 60m (197 ft.) above the channel. From the parking lot on the Peninsula Magellanes, a series of vista-point walkways descend, which take visitors directly to the glacier's face. It's truly an unforgettable, spellbinding experience. There are opportunities to join an organized group for a walk on the glacier as well as boat journeys that leave from Puerto Banderas for visits to the neighboring glaciers Upsala and Spegazzini.

GETTING THERE & ESSENTIALS

At Km49 (30 miles) from El Calafate, you'll pass through the park's entrance, where there's an information booth with erratic hours. If you're looking for information about the park and the glacier, better to pick up an interpretive guide or book from one of the bookstores or tourist shops along Av. del Libertador in El Calafate. There is a restaurant near the principal lookout platform near the glacier, and a good, though expensive, restaurant inside the Los Notros hotel (see "Lodging Near the Glacier," below).

To get to the park:

BY CAR   Following Avenida del Libertador west out of town, the route turns into a well-maintained dirt road. From here it's 50 miles (80km) to the glacier.

BY TAXI OR *REMISE*   If you want to see the glacier at your own pace, hire a taxi or *remise* (a private taxi). The cost averages $80 for two, $90 for three, and $100 for four, although many taxi companies will negotiate a price. Be sure to agree on an estimated amount of time spent at the glacier.

BY ORGANIZED TOUR   Several companies offer transportation to and from the glacier, such as **Interlagos,** Av. del Libertador 1175 (☎ **02902/491175;** e-mail: interlagos@cotecal.com.ar); **Mundo Austral,** Av. del Libertador 1114 (☎ **02902/492365;** e-mail: mundoaustral@cotecal.com.ar); **Caltur** at Av. del Libertador 1177 (☎ **02902/491368;** e-mail: caltur@cotecal.com.ar); and **TAQSA** in the bus terminal (☎ **02902/491843**). These minivan and bus services provide bilingual guides and leave around 9am, spending an average of 4 hours at the peninsula; the cost for is $25 to $30 per person, not including lunch.

OUTDOOR ACTIVITIES

There are several exciting activities in this region, including a "mini-trek" that takes guests for a walk upon the glacier. The trip begins with a 20-minute boat ride across the Brazo Rico, followed by a 30-minute walk to the glacier. From here guests are outfitted with crampons and other safety gear, then spend approximately 1½ hours atop the ice, complete with a stop for a whisky on the thousand-year-old "rocks." This great trip gives visitors the chance to peer into the electric-blue crevasses of the glacier and truly appreciate its size. You can book this trip through any travel agency.

Solo Patagonia, Av. del Libertador 963 (☎ **02902/491298;** www.solopatagonia.com.ar), offers visitors navigation through the Brazo Rico to the face of the Perito Moreno, including trekking to the base of the Cerro Negro with a view of the Glacier Negro. Both Solo Patagonia and **Upsala Explorer,** Av. 9 de Julio 69 (☎ **02902/491034;** e-mail: info@upsalaexplorer.com.ar), offer a variety of combinations from Puerto Banderas to Los Glaciares National Park's largest and tallest glaciers, respectively the Upsala and Spegazzini. Upsala Explorer makes a stop at the Estancia Cristina for lunch and optional trekking and 4×4 trips to the Upsala Lookout. Solo Patagonia offers similar journeys, including a stop at the Onelli area for trekking, as well as navigation-only journeys. Both companies charge $125 to $150 for this all-day excursion.

LODGING NEAR THE GLACIER

✪ **Los Notros.** Main office in Buenos Aires: Arenales 1457, 7th floor. ☎ **11/4814-3934.** Fax 11/4815-7645. www.losnotros.com. E-mail: info@losnotros.com. 32 units. $280 double standard; $390 junior suite. All-inclusive, 2-night packages average $674 per person. AE, DC, MC, V.

Few hotels in Argentina boast as spectacular a view as Los Notros—but it doesn't come cheap. This luxury lodge sits high on a slope looking out at the Perito Moreno Glacier, and all common areas and rooms have been fitted with picture windows to really soak up the marvelous sight. Although the wood-hewn exteriors give the hotel the feel of a mountain lodge, the interior decor is contemporary, a well-harmonized, craftsy jumble of bright colors and prints. Each room is slightly different and handcrafted with personal touches like antique lamps and regional photos; crocheted or gingham bedspreads; lilac, peach, or lemon-yellow walls; padded floral headboards or iron bed frames; and tweedy brown or raspberry corduroy chairs. The beds are so comfortable you'll find it difficult to get up in the morning. The gleaming white bathrooms have cut-out windows that look into the room, and premium rooms have whirlpool baths. Inside the main building is a large, chic restaurant with glossy black floors, floor-to-ceiling linen curtains, and lots of ironwork. Upstairs is an airy lounge area with chaise longues positioned in front of panoramic windows; here you'll find a TV room with a selection of nature videos. Guests at the Los Notros frequently opt for one of the multiple-day packages that includes airport transfers, meals, box lunches for expeditions, nightly discussions, guided trekking, boat excursions, and ice walks. Although Los Notros offers 4-night packages, you might find that length of time too long unless you're looking to get away from it all for a while. Note that prices jump substantially during Christmas, New Year's, and Easter week.

Dining: Guests take their meals at the hotel; those paying a nightly rate can expect to pay $35 for a fixed meal or $48 when ordering from the menu.

Amenities: Laundry, room service, book and video library, conference room.

5 El Chaltén & the Fitz Roy Area, Argentina

138 miles (222km) N of El Calafate

El Chaltén is a tiny village of about 200 residents whose lifeblood, like El Calafate's, depends entirely on the throng of visitors who come each summer to marvel over the stunning towers of Mounts Fitz Roy, Cerro Torre, and Puntiagudo. This is the second most-visited region of Argentina's Los Glaciares National Park and quite possibly its most exquisite, for the singular nature of the granite spires here that shoot up, torpedo-like, above massive tongues of ice that descend from the Southern Ice Field. In the world of mountaineering, these sheer and ice-encrusted peaks are considered to present one of the most formidable challenges in the world, which is the reason hundreds of climbers are drawn here year after year. Because of the capricious nature of Patagonian weather, climbers can be seen camping out for weeks, even a full month, until they are presented with an opportunity to ascend.

Little more than 5 years ago, El Chaltén counted just a dozen houses and a hostal or two, but the Fitz Roy's rugged beauty and great hiking opportunities have created somewhat of a boom town here. The town sits nestled in a circular rock outcrop at the base of the Fitz Roy and is fronted by the vast, dry *pampa*. Visitors use El Chaltén either as a base from which to take day hikes or as an overnighter before setting off for a multiple-day backpacking trip.

ESSENTIALS
GETTING THERE
BY PLANE   All transportation to El Chaltén originates from El Calafate, which has daily plane service from Ushuaia, Buenos Aires, and Bariloche. From El Calafate you need to take a bus or rent a car; the trip takes from 3 to 3½ hours.

BY CAR Take the Ruta Nacional 11 west for 19 miles (30km) and turn left on Ruta Nacional 40 north. Turn again, heading northwest, on Ruta Provincial 23 to El Chaltén. The road is unpaved.

BY BUS Buses from El Calafate leave from the terminal, and all cost $50 round-trip. **Chaltén Travel,** with offices in El Chaltén in the Albergue Rancho Grande on Avenida del Libertador (☎ **02962/493005;** e-mail: chaltentravel@cotecal.ar), leaves El Calafate daily at 8am and El Chaltén at 6pm. Chaltén Travel can arrange private tours and day trips to outlying destinations such as Patagonian ranches, as well as a summer-only transportation up Ruta Nacional 40 for those crossing into Chile. **Caltur,** which leaves from El Chaltén's Hostería Fitz Roy at Av. del Libertador 493 (☎ **02962/491842;** e-mail: caltur@cotecal.com.ar), leaves El Calafate daily at 7:30am and leaves El Chaltén at 5pm. **Los Glaciares,** Avenida Güemes and Lago del Desierto (☎ **02962/493063;** e-mail: losglaciares@cotecal.com.ar), leaves El Calafate at 8am and returns at 5:30pm.

VISITOR INFORMATION

There is no fee to enter the park. The Park Service has an **information center** (www.elchalten.com.ar; no phone) located at the entrance to town; here you'll find maps, pamphlets, and brief interpretive displays about the region's flora and fauna. It's open daily 8am to 8pm. El Chaltén also has a well-organized visitor's center at the town's entrance—the **Comisión de Fomento,** Perito Moreno and Avenida Güemes (☎ **02962/493011**), open 8am to 8pm. In El Calafate, the **APN Intendencia** (park service) has its offices at Av. del Libertador 1302, with a visitor's center that is open 9am to 3pm (☎ **02902/491005**).

OUTDOOR ACTIVITIES

TOUR OPERATORS **Fitz Roy Expediciones,** Lionel Terray 535 (☎/fax **02962/ 493017;** www.elchalten.com/fitzroy; e-mail: fitzroyexpediciones@infovia.com.ar), offers a full-day excursion trekking through the Valle de Río Fitz Roy combined with ice climbing at the Glacier Torre. No experience is necessary, but they do ask that you be in fit condition. They can also arrange for you to make the descent back to the base on horseback. Fitz Roy Expediciones offers a variety of trekking excursions, including a complete 10-day circuit around the backside of the Fitz Roy and Cerro Torre peaks, for $1,000 per person, all equipment and meals included, as well as 2 nights' lodging in an *albergue.* **Alta Montaña** at Lionel Terray 501 (☎ **02962/493018;** e-mail: altamont@infovia.com.ar) also offers summer-only, day-trekking excursions. There are several resident mountaineering and trekking guides who speak English and can be hired on a freelance basis: Alberto del Castillo (☎ **02962/493017**), Jorge Tarditti (☎ **02962/4993013**), and Oscar Pandolfi (☎ **02962/493016**).

HIKING & CAMPING If you're planning on doing any hiking in the park, you'll want to pick up a copy of Zagier & Urruty's trekking map, *Monte Fitz Roy & Cerro Torre,* available at most bookstores and tourist shops in El Calafate and El Chaltén. You'll also need to register at the park service office at the entrance to El Chaltén. You won't find a well-defined circuit here as you do in Torres del Paine, but there is a loop of sorts, and all stretches of this 3- to 4-day loop can be done one leg at a time on day hikes. Trails here run from easy to difficult and take anywhere from 4 to 10 hours to complete.

One of the most spectacular day hikes, which can also be done as an overnight, 2-day hike, is the 12-mile (19km) trail to the **Mirador D'Agostini,** also known as Maestri, that affords exhilarating views of the spire Cerro Torre. The hike takes 5½ to 6 hours to complete and is classified as easy, except for the last steep climb to the lookout point. It's possible to camp nearby at the D'Agostini campground (formerly Bridwell). Leaving from the Madsen campground, a more demanding, though beautiful, trail heads to several campsites and eventually the Laguna de los Tres, where there is a lookout point for views of Mount Fitz Roy. This walk is best done as a overnight trip, as it's too much to undertake in 1 day. There are more day hikes in the region, but they do not fall inside the park's boundaries, such as to visit the windswept Lago Eléctrico, the Lago del Desierto, and Lago Toro, where it's possible to fish. All campgrounds are free except for those outside the park's boundaries. Free campgrounds do not have services; paid campgrounds have water and some have showers.

HORSEBACK RIDING   There's nothing like horseback riding in Patagonia, and two outfitters offer several day excursions: **Rodolfo Guerra** at Las Loicas 773 (☎ **02962/493020**) has horseback rides and a horsepack service for carrying gear to campsites. Also try the **El Relincho** at Av. del Libertador s/n (☎ **02962/493007**).

WHERE TO STAY IN EL CHALTÉN

For all hotels, parking is either free, or street parking is plentiful.

✪ **El Puma.** Lionel Terray 512, El Chaltén. ☎/fax **02962/493017.** 8 units. $130 double. No credit cards. Open Nov–Mar.

El Puma offers the most stylish and comfortable accommodations in El Chaltén. The owners of this hotel work with the outfitter Fitz Roy Expediciones, who have an office next door. The hotel sits back from the main road, and faces out toward snowy peaks, although without a view of Fitz Roy. Inside, warm beige walls and wooden beams interplay with brick, and are offset with soft cotton curtains and ironwork. Although the common areas have terra-cotta ceramic floors, all rooms are carpeted. The rooms are well designed and bright; the lounge has a few chairs that face a roaring fire. There's also an eating area with wooden tables and a small bar. Very friendly service.

✪ **Hostería El Pilar.** Ruta Provincial 23, 9 miles (15km) from El Chaltén. ☎/fax **02962/493002.** 10 units. $100 double. MC, V. Open Oct–Apr; rest of the year with a reservation.

The Hostería El Pilar is undoubtedly the choice lodging option in the area, outshining its competitors in both design and idyllic location. True, the hotel's location 9 miles (15km) from El Chaltén toward Lago del Desierto does put guests far from restaurants and shops, but then lovely, peaceful surroundings are what many guests look for when they come to visit the national park. The yellow-walled and red-roofed El Pilar was once an *estancia;* now it's tastefully and artistically decorated with just enough detail to not distract you from the outdoors. The lounge offers a few couches and a fireplace and is a comfy spot to lounge and read a book. Rooms are simple but attractive, with peach walls, comfortable beds, and sunlight that streams through half-curtained windows. Guests normally take their meals at the hotel's restaurant, which serves great cuisine and offers a set dinner menu for $19 per person. The hotel offers guided excursions and is located next to several trailheads. If you're driving here, really keep an eye open for the sign to this hotel because it's easy to miss.

Hostería Fitz Roy. Av. del Libertador s/n, El Chaltén. ☎ **02962/493062,** or 02902/491368 (reservations). Fax 02902/492217. www.caltur.com.ar. E-mail: caltur@cotecal.com.ar. 24 units. $80–$104 double. MC, V. Open Sept–May.

This mint-green hotel is spread out somewhat ranch-style, with a popular restaurant and regular bus service to El Calafate. Although the advertised price is $104, they rarely charge that fee, and if you make an advance reservation, chances are they'll drop the price as much as 40%. The hallways are very dark, but the rooms receive decent light, and none have a view of much of anything. The rooms at the Fitz Roy are painted an unattractive mauve and decorated with simple furnishings, but the owner keeps the rooms clean. If by chance you're traveling with five people and you all want to sleep in the same room, they've got one to fit you. This hotel is a decent value, but the service could use a smile.

Hostería Los Ñires. Lago del Desierto s/n, El Chaltén. ☎ **02962/493009.** www.elchalten.com. 12 units. $65 double with private bathroom; $12 bunk with shared bathroom. MC, V.

This hotel sells itself better in its literature than it does with its rooms. In general, this *hostería* offers unremarkable but clean, comfortable accommodations. In one wing are rooms with a private bathroom, and in another, a hostal setup with shared bunks and bathrooms and a common area with a kitchen. The rooms have white walls and no decoration other than a view of the Fitz Roy peak, and a wide variety of combinations, including several quadruples. If it's fairly slow in the hostal, they'll make sure you don't have to share your three-bed room with a stranger. The main building has a roomy restaurant and lounge. Breakfast is not included for guests in the hostal.

Hotel Lago del Desierto. MacLeod and Lago del Desierto sts., El Chaltén. ☎/fax **02962/493010.** E-mail: alessandra@arnet.com.ar. 14 units. $90 double. No credit cards.

El Chaltén's only "hotel" is a funny affair. Certainly it's clean, tidy, and well located, but every room is frumpy, even though each has a totally different decor. The beds do not touch any walls as the headboard wall is a receding alcove. The entire hotel is floored with glossy white tile, which makes the place feel a little cold even though the rooms are kept heated. Crazy floral wallpaper adorns the rooms on the second story; the rooms on the bottom floor are a little easier on the eyes. The family that owns and manages this hotel is exceptionally amiable.

✪ Posada Poicenoit & Albergue Rancho Grande. Av. del Libertador s/n, El Chaltén. ☎ **09262/493005.** E-mail: chaltentravel@cotecal.com.ar. 3 units, 12 dormitory-style rooms. $45 double; $12 per person dormitory. AE, MC, V. Open Oct–Apr.

These two jointly-owned lodging options sit next to each other. The Posada Poicenoit is a tiny, attractive hotel built of wood with just three rooms: two doubles and a quadruple, all with private bathrooms. There's a small foyer with high ceilings, filled with several wooden tables for breakfast or snacks. The rooms are simple but comfortable and sunny. Next door, an equally attractive hostal caters to a predominantly backpacker crowd, and each room has two bunk beds, and rooms are shared if you don't have three friends to help you fill it. The restaurant and eating area is a great place to unwind, with long wooden tables, a lofty ceiling, and broad windows. The best deal here is the *albergue*'s kitchen, which guests may use, including guests from the Posada Poicenoit.

WHERE TO DINE

During the winter only one restaurant valiantly stays open: **La Casita,** Av. del Libertador at Lionel Terray, in the pink building (☎ **02966493042**). La Casita offers average, home-style fare, including sandwiches, meats, pastas, stuffed crêpes, and absent-minded service; it accepts American Express, MasterCard, and Visa. At other times of the year, the best restaurant in town for food and ambience is **Patagonicus,** Guemes at Andreas Madsen (☎ **02966/493025**). Patagonicus serves mostly pizza and enormous salads in a woodsy dining area; no credit cards accepted. Another good restaurant can be found inside the **Hostería Fitz Roy,** Av. del Libertador s/n (☎ **02966/493062**), which serves Argentine and international fare such as grilled meats and seafood, pastas, and more in a pleasant dining area with white linen-draped tables; it accepts MasterCard and Visa. For sandwiches, snacks, coffee, and cakes, try the **Albergue Rancho Grande,** Av. del Libertador s/n (☎ **02966/493005**); no credit cards accepted. For all restaurants, reservations are not necessary.

6 The Far South: Puerto Williams, Chile

Puerto Williams has a population of 2,500 and is a small naval base and town located on Isla Navarino on the southern shore of the Beagle Channel. As a destination, it's superseded by its Argentine neighbor Ushuaia, chiefly due to the town's isolation and the difficulty getting there—which for some is part of its draw. Apart from a few hiking trails and a museum, there's not a lot to do, but adventurers setting out for or returning from sailing and kayaking trips around Cape Horn use the town as a base. Several boat companies leaving from Ushuaia or Punta Arenas stop off here. It's worth a walk through town past the colorful jumble of tin houses picturesquely nestled below verdant peaks. Alternatively, visitors can fly here for a multiple-day sailing adventure.

GETTING THERE & SAILING EXCURSIONS

BY AIR   Aerovias DAP (☎ 61/223340 in Punta Arenas, 61/621051 in Puerto Williams) flies to Puerto Williams from Punta Arenas three times a week (see "Getting There," under "Punta Arenas, Chile," above).

BY BOAT   Several companies in Ushuaia, Argentina offer sailing excursions to Puerto Williams: **Turismo de Campo,** in Ushuaia, Av. 25 de Mayo 76 (☎ **02901/437351;** www.turismodecampo.com), offers 2-day/1-night trips for $250 per person, including lodging aboard its sailboat and meals. **All Patagonia Viajes y Turismo,** in Ushuaia, Juana Fadul 26 (☎ **02901/433622;** e-mail: allpat@satlink.com), also offers sailing excursions for about the same price. From Puerto Williams, **Karanka Expeditions,** Casilla 09, Puerto Williams, offers sailing cruises as far as the Cape Horn for $120 per person, per day, with gourmet meals included (☎ **61/621127;** e-mail: vademasi@ctc.internet.cl), and **Canales Australis,** on the plaza (☎ **61/621050;** e-mail: vcaselli@munitel.cl), has 10-hour trips on a motorized boat around remote locations in the Beagle Channel for $60 per person, including lunch. Newcomer **Tekenika Sea Ice Mountains** has sailboat adventures that can leave guests in Ushuaia; its office is on the tiny plaza (☎ **61/627750**). The cruise ship *Terra Australis* makes a stop here; for information, see "Cruising from Punta Arenas to Ushuaia, Argentina" under "Punta Arenas, Chile," above.

WHAT TO SEE & DO

The **Museo Maurice van de Maele,** at Aragay 01 (☎ **61/621043**) is open 10am to 1pm and 3 to 6pm, featuring a good collection of Yaghan and Yamana Indian artifacts, ethnographic exhibits, and stuffed birds and animals. The museum's docent is an excellent anthropologist and naturalist who can provide tours in the area. Just outside town, next to the waterfall that cascades down to the road is a **hiking trail** that eventually splits into two trails. For a 2-hour round-trip climb up to Cerro La Bandera, take the trail leading left; for an 8-hour round-trip hike to the peak Dientes de Navarino, head right when the trail splits. There is a longer backpacking trail called Los Dientes, but it's recommended only for those with ample backpacking experience and good map and compass skills. The best map is JLM's *Tierra del Fuego* map, sold in most tourist shops and bookstores. **Inhospita Patagonia** in Punta Arenas, Lautaro Navarro 1013 (☎ **61/224510;** e-mail: inhospita@chileanpatagonia.com), arranges guided, all-inclusive trekking tours through this region.

WHERE TO STAY & DINE

The pickings are slim ever since the Wala Hotel closed this year, but basic, clean accommodation can be found at the **Hostal Camblor,** Patricio Cap Deville Street

(☎ **61/621033**), which has six brand-new rooms for $20 per person. The Camblor also has a restaurant that serves as the local disco on Friday and Saturday nights, so noise could be a problem. Another comfortable place is the **Hostal Pusaki,** Piloto Pardo 222 (☎ **61/621116**), which has three rooms and charges $15 per person. The amiable owners of the Pusaki are also owners of Puerto Williams's pub and restaurant, **The Micalvi** (☎ **61/621020**), housed in an old supply ship that is docked at the pier, and the meeting spot for an international crowd of adventurers sailing around the Cape Horn. Another restaurant is **Los Dientes de Navarino** (no phone), on the plaza.

7 Tierra del Fuego: Ushuaia, Argentina

286 miles (461km) SW of Punta Arenas; 368 miles (594km) S of Río Gallegos

The name *Ushuaia* comes from the Yamana Indian language meaning "bay penetrating westward," a fairly simple appellation for a city situated in such a spectacular location. It's the southernmost city in the world (although the naval base and town Puerto Williams is farther south across the channel), a fact Ushuaia sells as a tourist attraction for itself. Ushuaia is encircled by a range of rugged peaks and fronted by the Beagle Channel. It was first inhabited by the Yamana Indians until the late 1800s, when it became a penal colony for Argentine criminals who toiled here until 1947. The region grew as a result of immigration from Croatia, Italy, and Spain and migration from the Argentine mainland, with government incentives such as tax-free duty on many goods being part of the draw. Today, the city has about 40,000 residents. Ushuaia is a great destination with plenty of activities, and many use the city as a jumping-off point for trips to Antarctica or sailing trips around the Cape Horn.

ESSENTIALS
GETTING THERE
BY PLANE   There is no bus service to town from the Ushuaia Airport, but cab fares are only $4; always ask for a quote before accepting a ride. Air service frequency increases from November to March; the inauguration of El Calafate's airport in late 2000 means there will be direct flights there to Ushuaia—consult LAPA and Aerolíneas Argentinas, both of whom plan to have service. **Aerolíneas Argentinas,** Roca 116 (☎ **02901/421218**), has one to three daily flights to Buenos Aires, stopping first in Río Gallegos. **LAPA,** Av. 25 de Mayo 64 (☎ **02901/432112**), has two daily flights to Buenos Aires, with a stopover in Río Gallegos. At press time, **LADE,** Av. del Libertador 542 (☎ **02901/421123**), announced upcoming service to El Calafate in addition to its one daily flight to Río Gallegos. **Southern Winds,** Maipú 237 (☎ **02901/437073**), flies to destinations such as Cordoba, Mendoza, and Neuquen. **Aerovías DAP** now has air service to and from Punta Arenas for $120 one-way (plus $20 airport tax), leaving Wednesdays only at 9am from Punta Arenas and 10:30am from Ushuaia; its offices are at Av. 25 de Mayo 62 (☎ **02901/431110**).

BY BUS   Service from Punta Arenas, Chile, costs $35 and is offered by **Tecni Austral** (☎ **02901/431407** in Ushuaia, or 61/222078 in Punta Arenas), leaving Monday, Wednesday, and Friday at 7am; tickets are sold in Ushuaia from the Tolkar office at Roca 157, and in Punta Arenas at Lautaro Navarro 975. **Tolkeyen,** Maipú 237 (☎ **02901/437073**), works in combination with the Chilean company Pacheco for trips to Punta Arenas, leaving Tuesday, Thursday, and Saturday at 8am; it also goes to Río Grande, with three daily trips. Both companies take the route to Punta Arenas via Bahía Azul. Techni Austral offers service to Punta Arenas via Porvenir for the same price, leaving Saturdays at 6am. **Lidded LTD,** Gobernador Paz 921 (☎ **02901/ 436421**), Techni Austral, and Tolkeyen all have multiple day trips to Río Grande.

Ushuaia

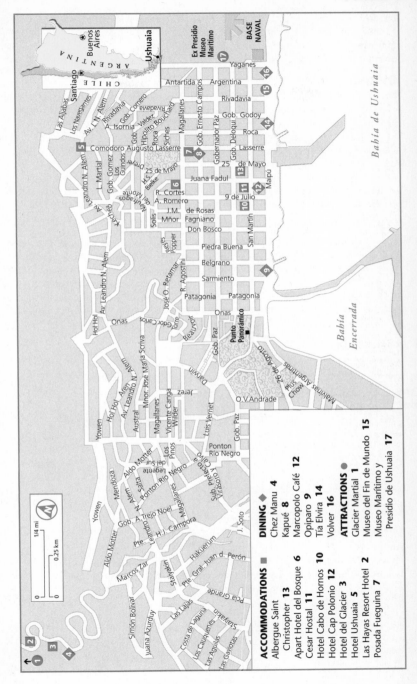

DINING ◆
Chez Manu **4**
Kapué **8**
Marcopolo Café **12**
Opíparo **9**
Tía Elvira **14**
Volver **16**

ATTRACTIONS ●
Glacier Martial **1**
Museo del Fin de Mundo **15**
Museo Marítimo y
Presidio de Ushuaia **17**

ACCOMMODATIONS ■
Albergue Saint
  Christopher **13**
Apart Hotel del Bosque **6**
Cesar Hostal **11**
Hotel Cabo de Hornos **10**
Hotel Cap Polonio **12**
Hotel del Glacier **3**
Hotel Ushuaia **5**
Las Hayas Resort Hotel **2**
Posada Fueguina **7**

BY BOAT　The company **Crucero Australis** operates a cruise to Ushuaia from Punta Arenas and vice versa aboard its ship the M/V *Terra Australis.* If you have the time, this is a recommended journey for any age, and it's covered in the box "Cruising from Punta Arenas to Ushuaia, Argentina," under "Punta Arenas, Chile," above.

GETTING AROUND

BY CAR　Everything in and around Ushuaia is easily accessible via bus or taxi or by using an inexpensive shuttle or tour service, so renting a car is really not necessary. Rentals, however, are very reasonable, from $50 to $80 per day. **Avis** at Avenida del Libertador and Belgrano drops its prices for multiple-day rentals (☎ 02901/422744); **Cardos Rent A Car** is at Av. del Libertador 845 (☎ 02901/436388); **Dollar Rent A Car** is at Maipú and Sarmiento (☎ 02901/432134); **Localiza Rent A Car** is at Av. del Libertador 1222 (☎ 02901/430739); **Seven Rent A Car** rents 4×4 Jeeps with unlimited mileage at Av. del Libertador 802 (☎ 02901/437604); and **Rastro Rent A Car,** Av. del Libertador 1547, offers unlimited mileage (☎ 02901/422021).

VISITOR INFORMATION

The **Subsecretaría de Turismo** has a helpful, well-stocked office at Av. del Libertador 674 (☎ **02901/432000;** fax 02901/424550; www.tierradelfuego.org.ar/ushuaia). They also have a counter at the airport that is open to assist passengers on all arriving flights. From November to March, the office is open every day 8am to 10pm; the rest of the year it's open Monday to Friday 8am to 9pm, weekends and holidays 9am to 8pm. The national park administration office can be found at Av. del Libertador 1395 (☎ **02901/421395;** open Mon–Fri 9am–3pm).

FAST FACTS: USHUAIA

Currency Exchange　**Banco Sud** at Avenida del Libertador and Godoy (☎ **02901/432080**); **Banco Nación** at Av. del Libertador 190 (☎ **02901/422086**). Both have 24-hour ATM machines.

Laundry　**Los Tres Ángeles,** Rosas 139, is open Monday to Saturday 9am to 8pm.

Pharmacy　**Andina** at Av. del Libertador 638 (☎ **02901/423431**) is open 24 hours a day.

Post Office　**Correo Argentino** is at Avenida del Libertador and Godoy (☎ **02901/421347**), open Monday to Friday 9am to 7pm, Saturday 9am to 1pm; the private postal company **OCA** is at Maipú and Avenida 9 de Julio (☎ **02901/424729**), open Monday to Saturday 9am to 6pm.

Travel Agency/Credit Cards　**American Express** travel and credit card services are provided by All Patagonia, Juana Fadul 26 (☎ **02901/433622**).

WHAT TO SEE & DO IN & AROUND TOWN

An in-town walk can be taken to the city park and **Punto Panorámico,** which takes visitors up to a lookout point with good views of the city and the channel. It can be reached at the southwest terminus of Avenida del Libertador, and is free.

✪ **Museo del Fin de Mundo.** Maipú 175. ☎ **02901/421863.** Admission $5 adults, $2 students; free for children under 14. Daily 10am–1pm and 3–7:30pm.

This museum's chief interest is its wealth of research materials. The main room has an assortment of Indian hunting tools and colonial maritime instruments. There's also a natural history display of stuffed birds and a "grandfather's room" set up to resemble an old general store, packed with antique products. But the strength of this museum is its 60 history and nature videos available for viewing and its reference library with more than 3,650 volumes, including a fascinating birth record. Its store has an excellent range of books about Patagonia for sale. The $5 admission price, however, seems a little steep.

✪ **Museo Marítimo y Presidio de Ushuaia.** Yaganes and Gobernador Paz. ☎ **02901/ 437481.** Admission $7 adults, $5 seniors, $1 children ages 5–12; free for children under 5. Daily 10am–1pm and 3–8pm.

Ushuaia was founded primarily thanks to the penal colony set up here in the late 1800s for hundreds of Argentina's most dangerous criminals. The rehabilitation system consisted of forced labor to build piers and buildings, and creative workshops for teaching carpentry, music, tailoring, and other trades—all of which coincidentally fueled the local economy. The museum is sort of Ushuaia's Alcatraz, offering a fascinating look into prisoners and prison workers' lives during that time through interpretive displays and artifacts, including the comical wool, striped prison uniforms they were forced to wear. There's a restaurant here, with "prison" meals and other theme items.

✪ **Glacier Martial/Aerosilla.** Av. Luis Fernando Martial, 4 miles (7km) from town. (No phone). Admission $5 adults, $3 children 8 and under. Daily 10:30am–5:30pm.

The Glacier Martial is a pleasant excursion that sits literally in the backyard of Ushuaia. Avenida Luis Fernando Martial winds 4 miles (7km) up from town to the base of a beautiful mountain amphitheater, where you'll find a chair lift that takes visitors to the small Glacier Martial. It's a long walk up the road, and there are no buses to take you there. Visitors usually hire a taxi for $5 and walk all the way back down, or arrange for the driver to pick them up later. At the base of the chair lift, don't miss a stop at ✪ **La Cabaña** (☎ **06/696-9511**), an excellent teahouse with a wraparound outdoor deck and mouth-watering cakes and pastries.

OUTDOOR ACTIVITIES

BOATING   Navigation excursions are very popular here, with several companies offering a variety of trips. The most popular excursion is a half-day trip cruising the Beagle Channel to view sea lions, penguins, and more. You'll find a cluster of kiosks near the pier offering a variety of excursions. **Motonave Barracuda** leaves twice daily for its 3-hour trip around the channel for $25 per person, visiting Isla de Lobos, Isla de Pájaros, and a lighthouse (☎ **02901/436453**). **Motovelero Tres Marías** also leaves twice daily and sails to the same location; however, they have a maximum of nine guests and add an hour's walk, crab fishing, cognac, and an underwater camera to the menu (☎ **02901/421897**). **Tierra del Sur** combines a bus/boat trip, visiting Estancia Harberton (see below) first, then embarking for a 1½-hour sail to a penguin colony during penguin season from November to April (☎ **02901/421897**). **Motovelero Patagonia Adventure** has an 18-passenger maximum and leaves daily; it visits the sea lion colony and includes a walk on the Isla Bridges for $35. This company also works with the Adventuras Isla Verde in the park for a full-day sail; inquire at their kiosk (☎ **1560-3181**).

FISHING   For a fishing license and information, go the Club de Pesca y Caza at Av. del Libertador 818 (no phone). The cost is about $25 for foreigners *per day.*

SKIING   Ushuaia's new ski resort, **Cerro Castor** (☎ **1560-5706**), is surprisingly good, with more than 400 skiable hectares, 15 runs, three quad chairs and one double, a lodge/restaurant, and a slopeside bar. Day tickets cost $22 to $34, depending on low or high season, and the resort is open from June 15 to October 15. To get there, take the shuttle buses **Pasarela** (☎ **02901/433712**) or **Bella Vista** (☎ **02901/443161**); the fare is $10.

TOUR OPERATORS

Several tour operators offer more unconventional tours, such as **Turismo de Campo,** Av. 25 de Mayo 70 (☎ **02901/437351;** www.turismodecampo.com; e-mail: info@ turismodecampo.com), which limits groups to eight people or less. Sample tours include day and multiple-day sailing trips around the Beagle Channel ($100 per person, lunch included) and to Puerto Williams, Chile (overnight in boat, $250 per person, meals included); it also offers trips to a typical Fuegian *estancia* and trekking in the national park. **All Patagonia Viajes y Turismo,** Juana Fadul 26 (☎ **02901/ 433622;** e-mail: allpat@satlink.com), is the local American Express travel representative, and acts as a clearinghouse for everything—if they don't offer it themselves, they'll arrange an excursion with other outfitters, and they can reserve excursions in other destinations in Argentina and Chile. All Patagonia offers three glacier walks for those in physically good shape, scenic flights over Tierra del Fuego ($35 per person for a half hour), and treks and drives in its Land Rover with nature guides. It also plans to offer flights to Antarctica. If you're not sure what you want, start here. **Canal Fun & Nature,** Rivadavía 82 (☎ **02901/437395;** www.canalfun.com; e-mail: canal@satlink.com), is a great company with excellent guides who provide 4×4 trips and walks culminating with a barbecue, as well as kayaking and nighttime beaver watching, and they'll custom-build a trip for you. **Rumbo Sur,** Av. del Libertador 350 (☎ **02901/430699;** www.rumbosur.com.ar; e-mail: informes@rumbosur.com.ar), and **Tolkeyen/PreTour,** Maipú 237 (☎ **02901/ 437073;** e-mail: pretour@tierradelfuego.org.ar), are two operators that deal with larger groups and arrange more classic excursions, such as a city tour and guided visits to the national park and Lagos Escondido and Fagnano.

EXCURSIONS AROUND USHUAIA

One of the most intriguing destinations around Ushuaia is the **Estancia Harberton,** the first ranch founded in Tierra del Fuego that is now run as a museum. The ranch is located on the shore of the Beagle Channel, and can be reached by road or boat. The entrance fee is $5 April to October and $7 November to March. Transportation to the *estancia,* 56 miles (90km) from Ushuaia, is provided by most travel agencies in town, for an average cost of $55 per person plus the entrance fee, provided you are a group of 4 or more. The *estancia* does not have a restaurant, but tour companies will, for an additional cost, include lunch at a restaurant on the way there. Roughly from October to April, several tour companies offer a catamaran ride to the *estancia,* a 6-hour excursion for $77 per person; try **All Patagonia,** Juana Fadul 26 (☎ **02901/ 433622**). Tour groups will also arrange an additional boat excursion to a **penguin colony** from the *estancia,* an add-on excursion that costs about $30 per person.

After the turnoff for Estancia Harberton, Ruta 3 begins to descend down to **Lago Escondido,** a beautiful lake about 37 miles (60km) north of Ushuaia that provides a quiet spot for relaxation or fishing the mammoth trout that call the lake home. The lake is home to a stately, gorgeous lodge, the **Hostería Petrel** (☎ **02901/433569;** www.hotelguia.com; e-mail: hpetrel@infovia.com.ar). The wood and stone lodge has nine rooms, and seven splendid wooden cabins have just been constructed on the shore. Each cabin has one bedroom and a trundle bed for two more in the living room, with folksy furniture made of thin tree trunks, and an ultra-peaceful front deck for kicking back and casting a line. The cabins cost $80 April to October and $100 November to March; double rooms in the lodge are $60 to $80 for the same dates. The cabins do not come with a kitchen, but the lodge has a restaurant; they also have a gift shop and Jacuzzi, and they hire a summer season fishing guide.

A Ride in the Park

If you don't feel like walking but would like to take in the sights at **Parque Nacional Tierra Del Fuego,** you can take a ride on **El Tren del Fin del Mundo,** a vapor locomotive that is a replica of the train used to shuttle prisoners to the forest to chop wood (☎ **02901/431600;** www.trendelfindelmundo.com.ar). The train departs from its well-built station (which houses a souvenir shop and cafe) near the park entrance four times daily; the journey is 1 hour and 10 minutes one-way, 2 hours 15 minutes round-trip. The cost is $25 adults, $10 kids, plus the $5 park entrance fee.

PARQUE NACIONAL TIERRA DEL FUEGO

Parque Nacional Tierra del Fuego was created in 1960 to protect a 63,000ha (155,610-acre) chunk of Patagonian wilderness that includes mighty peaks, crystalline rivers, black-water swamps, and forests of *lenga,* or deciduous beech. Only 2,000ha (4,940 acres) are designated as recreation areas, part of which offer a chance to view the prolific dam building carried out by beavers introduced to Tierra del Fuego in the 1950s.

The park's main claim to fame is that it's the only Argentine national park with a maritime coast. If you've been traveling around southern Argentina or Chile, chances are you won't be blown away by this park. Much of the landscape is identical to the thousands of kilometers of mountainous terrain in Patagonia, and there really isn't any special "thing" to see here. Instead, the park offers easy and medium day hikes to get out and stretch your legs, breath some fresh air, take a boat ride, or bird watch. Also, there are areas where the road runs through thick beech forest and then abruptly opens into wide views of mountains whose dramatic height can be viewed from sea level to more than 2,000m (6,560 ft.). Anglers can fish for trout here in the park, but must first pick up a license at the National Park Administration office at Av. del Libertador 1395 (☎ **02901/421395;** open Mon–Fri 9am–3pm), in Ushuaia. The park service issues maps at the park entrance showing the walking trails here, ranging from 980 feet (300m) to 5 miles (8km); admission into the park is $5. Parque Nacional Tierra del Fuego is located 7 miles (11km) west of Ushuaia on Ruta Nacional 3. Camping in the park is free, and although there are no services, potable water is available. At the end of the road to Lago Roca, there is a snack bar/restaurant. At Bahía Ensenada you'll find boats that take visitors to the Isla Redonda, where there are several walking trails. The cost is about $15, or $20 with a guide. All tour companies offer guided trips to the park, but if you just need transportation there, call these shuttle bus companies: **Pasarela** (☎ **02901/433712**) or **Bella Vista** (☎ **02901/443161**).

WHERE TO STAY

Accommodations are not cheap in Ushuaia, and quality is often not on a par with price. There's also a shortage of moderately priced hotels. Below are some of the best values that can be found here. For all hotels, parking is either free, or street parking is plentiful.

VERY EXPENSIVE

✪ **Hotel del Glaciar.** Av. Luis Fernando Martial 2355, Ushuaia. ☎ **02901/430640,** or 11/4393-4444 (reservations in Buenos Aires). Fax 11/4328-2575. E-mail: central@elsitio.net. 123 units. MINIBAR TV TEL. $145–$189 double; $235–$255 suite. AE, MC, V.

The Hotel del Glaciar is a wonderful hotel, especially if you're looking for a place above the hubbub of downtown. The grand hotel is approximately the same size as the

Las Hayas (see below), and it sits just above it, offering the same stunning views. The difference between the two is that this hotel leans more toward the ambience of a mountain lodge. The simple exterior and the tremendous lobby are built entirely of wood, and there's a partially sunken lounge centered on a freestanding fireplace, and yet another high-ceilinged lounge with massive windows that look out onto the Beagle Channel—a great place to sit back and contemplate the beauty of Ushuaia. The bright rooms are decent size, with a fresh, country decor; half come with a view of the glacier-topped mountain or, for 10 bucks more, a view of the Beagle Channel. One of the neat things about this hotel is its winter activity center that's housed in a "barn" out back, which functions as an excursion center where you can sign up for dog-sledding trips or rent gear such as snowshoes and snow boots. The hotel is a 40-minute walk up a winding road from town, but they operate a transfer shuttle if you don't feel like making the hike. Americans and Europeans typically lodge here.

Dining/Diversions: The hotel's restaurant, Temaukel, serves local specialities and international cuisine, and they also have a coffee shop and bar.

Amenities: Laundry, room service, gift shop, sauna, massage, excursions, conference centers, game room with video games, Ping-Pong and billiard tables.

✪ Las Hayas Resort Hotel. Av. Luis Fernando Martial 1650, Ushuaia. ☎ **02901/430710.** Fax 02901/430719. www.lashayas.com. E-mail: lashayas@overnet.com.ar. 90 units. TV TEL. $205–$225 double; $290–$350 junior suite superior. AE, DC, MC, V.

Ushuaia's sole five-star, luxury hotel has prices as sky-high as its location on the road to Glacier Martial, but if you're looking for elegant accommodations, this is for you. The hotel sits nestled in a forest of beech just below the Hotel del Glaciar (see above), a location that gives sweeping views of the town and the Beagle Channel. It's at least 2 miles (3km) from downtown, however, so you'll need to take a cab, hike, or use one of the hotel's summer-only transfer shuttles. The first floor holds a handful of conference centers; upstairs the sumptuous lounge stretches the length of the building; here you'll find a clubby bar, formal restaurant, and fireside sitting area. The rooms are lavishly decorated with rich tapestries, walls padded with fabric, and bathrooms that are big and bright. In fact, the rooms are quite fabric-heavy, and some have been doused with the same stripes-and-floral pattern that in some cases can be a veritable sensory overload. The ultra-comfortable beds with thick linens are dreamy. There are three suites: junior suites (which are hardly bigger than doubles); junior suite superiors with a couch and separate entryway; and gala suites with a separate living area and four-poster beds draped in still more fabric. A glass-enclosed walkway leads to one of Ushuaia's few swimming pools and an indoor squash court; the hotel also offers automatic membership at the region's golf club. The owner of Las Hayas promotes an air of genteel exclusivity, and therefore the hotel is not entirely suitable for children.

Dining: The hotel's gourmet restaurant has a menu that changes weekly, but always specializes in black hake and king crab dishes. The restaurant is open to the public. Downstairs, there's a more casual restaurant and an indoor garden dining area.

Amenities: Laundry, concierge, room service, gym, sauna, indoor heated swimming pool, Jacuzzi, conference centers.

EXPENSIVE

Hotel Cap Polonio. Av. del Libertador 746, Ushuaia. ☎ **02901/422140.** www.tierradelfuego.org.ar/cappolonio. E-mail: cappolonio@tierradelfuego.org.ar. 30 units. TV TEL. $85–$105 double. AE, MC, V.

This hotel is a good choice for its central location and chic, adjoining restaurant that essentially forms part of the hotel's entrance lobby. The hotel has a bright yellow and red exterior and sits on busy Avenida del Libertador; for this reason you'll want to request a room in the rear of the hotel as the noise outside can grow cacophonous on weekends. The rooms here at the Cap Polonio are some of the better rooms in town, but the shag carpet and frilly bedspreads are a little dowdy. Also, as with most hotels in town, a single bed is laughably narrower than a twin and might be uncomfortable for anyone over the age of 10; ask for a double instead.

Hotel Ushuaia. Lasserre 933, Ushuaia. ☎ **02901/423051.** Fax 02901/424217. 60 units. TV TEL. $80–$110 double. AE, MC, V.

This hotel is another that offers sweeping views; however, it is only an 8-block walk to downtown—convenient for anyone who wants to be closer to restaurants and services. The two-story hotel is shaped like a half moon and is anchored on a hill above a dusty residential area. The views are pleasant, but a little busy due to the jumble of wooden homes below and Ushuaia's ubiquitous, above-ground telephone wires. In this price range, the Hotel Ushuaia is one of the city's better values, offering very bright interiors and comfortable, spacious rooms. From the vine-draped reception area, long hallways stretch out on both sides; centered in the middle is a second-story restaurant with a lofty, V-shaped ceiling from which hang about 100 glass bubble lamps, a style that is somewhat 1970s, but attractive nevertheless. All doubles cost the same but range in three sizes; when making a reservation, ask for the largest double they have, which, incidentally, they'll also give to singles when they're not full.

✪ Posada Fueguina. Lasserre 438, Ushuaia. ☎ **02901/423467.** Fax 02901/424758. www.pfuegina.com.ar. E-mail: pfueguina@tierradelfuego.org.ar. 28 units, 5 cabañas. MINIBAR TV TEL. $90 double Apr–Dec; $130 double Jan–Mar. AE, MC, V.

This is one of my favorite hotels in Ushuaia, full of flavor and cozier than anything in town. The Fueguina has hotel rooms and a row of inviting, wooden cabañas (no kitchen) on a well-manicured lot, and their freshly painted cream and mauve exteriors stand out among the clapboard homes that surround it. Inside, oriental floor-runners, dark glossy wood, and tartan curtains set the tone. Most rooms are spacious; the second and third floors have views, and the three rooms on the bottom floor are brand-new. The cabins do not come with views, but they're so comfy you probably won't mind—anyway, you'll find yourself spending most of your time in the small sitting and dining area. The hotel is a convenient 3-block walk to downtown.

MODERATE

Apart Hotel del Bosque. Magallanes 709, Ushuaia. ☎/fax **02901/430777.** www.hostaldelbosque.com.ar. E-mail: aparth@iname.com. 40 units. MINIBAR TV TEL. $65 double Apr–Sept; $85 double Oct–Mar. AE, DC, MC, V.

The Apart Hotel del Bosque gives guests a huge amount of space, including a separate living/dining area and a kitchenette. However, the kitchenette is intended more than anything for heating water, not cooking—for that reason they include breakfast, which is not common with apart-hotels. The 40 guest rooms are spread out much like a condominium complex, each with a separate entrance and maid service. The exteriors and the decor are pretty bland (all have ceramic floors), but very clean. Inside the main building there's a cozy restaurant with wooden tables where they serve fixed meals. The hotel is located in a residential area about a 5-minute walk from downtown.

Cesar Hostal. Av. del Libertador 753, Ushuaia. ☎ **02901/421460.** E-mail: cesarhostal@ infovia.com.ar. 29 units. TV TEL. $65 double. AE, MC, V.

Hotel Cabo de Hornos. Av. del Libertador and Rosas, Ushuaia. ☎ **02901/422313.** 30 units. TV TEL. $50 double Apr–Aug; $75 double Sept–Mar. AE, MC, V.

I've put these two older hotels together because they are almost exactly the same, both a little lacking in style (read 1970s furniture and shag carpet), but the rooms are comfortable and generally acceptable for this price range. Both hotels are located on Avenida del Libertador, just steps away from most services, but again, it's a busy street, so ask for a room in the back if you need peace and quiet. Each has its own restaurant, although the Cabo de Hornos's is a larger *confitería* that is open to the public. The windows are small and the bedspreads a bit faded, but they're clean, and if you plan to spend the majority of your time outdoors, you probably won't mind. The two hotels have the same mini-twins that don't particularly allow you to stretch out, so ask for a *cama matrimonial,* or double bed.

INEXPENSIVE

Albergue Saint Christopher. Gobernador Deloqui 636, Ushuaia. ☎ **02901/430062.** www.saintchristopher.com.ar. E-mail: hostel_christopher@yahoo.com. 5 shared units. $10 per person. No credit cards.

This fun, inviting hostal is for those who are looking to spend a lot less, but you'll have to share a room with strangers if you don't have your own group. Rooms have two to three bunk beds, and are not always separated by sex, but they'll try to find you a same-sex room if you ask. The hostal attracts a vivacious crowd that ranges in age from 20 to 40 years of age. The staff are entertaining, and the common area is a great place to hang out and chat. Guests have use of the kitchen facilities, and the hostal is packed with information about excursions around the area.

WHERE TO DINE

A dozen *confiterías* and cafes can be found on Avenida del Libertador between Godoy and Rosas, all which offer inexpensive sandwiches and quick meals. In addition to the restaurants listed below, you might consider the Hotel del Glaciar's **Temaukel** (☎ **02901/430640**) or Las Hayas's **Luis Martial** (☎ **02901/430710**). Both offer great views and gourmet dining, as well as fixed meals and weekly changing menus. For all restaurants listed, reservations are not necessary except where noted.

✪ **Chez Manu.** Av. Fernando Luis Martial 2135. ☎ **02970/432253.** Main courses $8–$15. AE, MC, V. Mon–Sun noon–3pm and 8pm–midnight. FRENCH/INTERNATIONAL.

The Chez Manu offers great food and even better views seen through a generous supply of windows. The two transplants from France who run this restaurant, one of whom was once the chef at the five-star resort Las Hayas, stay true to their roots with a menu that offers French-style cooking using fresh local ingredients. A few sample dishes include black hake cooked with anise and herbs or Fueguian lamb. Thursday evenings they offer a special sushi menu, although sushi can be had any day of the week by making a reservation a full day ahead. The restaurant also serves an afternoon tea with cakes on Saturdays and Sundays from 5 to 8pm. The dining area has a fish tank in the center of the room with king crabs and other local mollusks.

✪ **Kapué Restaurant.** Roca 470. ☎ **02901/422704.** Reservations recommended on weekends. Main courses $15–$20. AE, MC, V. Nov 15–Apr 15, daily noon–2pm and 6–11pm; rest of the year, dinner only 7–11pm. ARGENTINE FINE DINING.

This is undoubtedly the best restaurant in Ushuaia, both for its superb cuisine, lovely view, and warm, attentive service. Kapué, which means "at home" in Selk'nam, is owned and operated by the friendly, gracious Vivian family—the husband is chef and his wife runs the dining area and even waits tables, and often one of their kids can be found behind the bar. The menu is brief, but the offerings are delicious. Don't start your meal without ordering a sumptuous appetizer of king crab wrapped in a crêpe and bathed in saffron sauce. Main courses include seafood, beef, and chicken; sample items include tenderloin beef in a plum sauce or a subtly flavored sea bass steamed in parchment paper. Kapué offers a special "sampler" with two king crab appetizers and a main dish, wine, dessert, and coffee for $50 per person. The chef is a wine connoisseur, and one of the highlights is the restaurant's wine bar and extensive gourmet wine list that ranges in price from $10 to $100; there's also wine by the glass. Finish it all off with a sorbet in a frothy champagne sauce. Kapué's dining area is cozy, and candlelit tables exude evening romance.

☺ Marcopolo Café Restaurant. Av. del Libertador 746. ☎ **02901/430001.** Main courses $6–$14. AE, MC, V. Daily 7:30–10:30am, noon–3pm, and 8pm–midnight. INTERNATIONAL.

This new, stylish restaurant is a wonderful place to dine, both for its varied menu and its atmosphere. The softly lit dining area has warm yellow walls and beige linen tablecloths, both of which are offset with artsy ironwork knickknacks, colorful candles, and watercolor paintings. The menu will satisfy most tastes, as it includes creative renditions and simple, familiar items such as chef salads and shrimp cocktails. Try a local specialty, such as trout stuffed with king crab or Fueguian lamb in a flaky potato pastry. There's also fresh, homemade pasta with a choice of six sauces. The Marcopolo is open early for breakfast and also has a cafe menu that offers sandwiches, soups, and pastries, which can be ordered all day.

Opiparo. Maipú 1255. ☎ **02901/434022.** Main courses $4–$8. MC, V. Daily noon–midnight. PIZZA/PASTA.

This diner-style restaurant can be found on the waterfront, and it serves pizza, pasta, and quick meals like chicken and beef *milanesas* with fries. There's two long pages of different kinds of pizza, which can be ordered individually or shared. The pastas are fresh, but very simple. This is where to go if you're looking for something casual.

Tía Elvira Restaurante. Maipú 349. ☎ **02901/424725.** Main courses $6–$19. AE, MC, V. Daily noon–2:30pm and 7–11:30pm. ARGENTINE BISTRO.

Tía Elvira is part restaurant, part minimuseum, with walls adorned with antique photos of the region and various artifacts its owners have collected during its 28 years in business. The menu features fairly straightforward Argentine dishes such as grilled meats, but the restaurant serves mostly simply prepared seafood, including king crab, trout, sea bass, and cod in a variety of sauces, such as Roquefort or Parmesan. There's also a list of homemade pastas, including lasagna and stuffed cannelloni. You'll want to pair your order with a side dish, so factor in another $1 to $4 to the price. The restaurant is on the waterfront, with up-close views of the canal and the pier.

Volver. Maipú 37. ☎ **02901/423977.** Main courses $7–$18. AE, MC, V. Daily noon–3pm and 7pm–midnight. Closed for lunch Mon. ARGENTINE.

Even if you don't eat here, don't fail to stop by just to see this crazy, kitschy restaurant on the waterfront. Volver is inside a century-old, yellow, tin-pan house that was once occupied by the first chief of police, a chauffeur, three prison escapees, and crab fishermen. Old newspapers and signs wallpaper the interiors, which are also packed with oddball memorabilia, photos, gadgets, trinkets, and antiques. The food is pretty good too, serving regional dishes such as trout, crab, lamb, and more, and homemade pastas. King crab is served in a dozen different ways, including soups, casseroles, or naturally with a side sauce. The desserts are primarily crêpes with local fruits like calafate. One complaint: Service can often be absent-minded or hurried, sort of "get-'em-in, get-'em-out."

Appendix A: Argentina & Chile in Depth

To understand how Argentina's European heritage impacts its South American identity, you must identify its distinct culture. Tango is the quintessential example—a sensual dance originated in the suspect corners of Buenos Aires's San Telmo neighborhood, legitimized in the ballrooms of France, and re-exported to Argentina to become this nation's great art form. (For more on the tango, see "Tango, a Dance of Seduction & Despair," in chapter 3, "Buenos Aires.") Each journey you take, whether into a tango salon, an Argentine cafe, or a meat-only *parrilla,* will bring you closer to the country's true character.

But beyond the borders of Argentina's capital and largest city, you will find a land of vibrant extremes—from the Northwest's desert plateau to the flat grasslands of the *pampas,* from the rainforest jungle of Iguazú to the towering blue-white glaciers of Patagonia. The land's geographic diversity is similarly reflected in its people; witness the contrast between the capital's largely immigrant population and the indigenous people of the Northwest. Read on and find out more.

On the other side of the Andes, Chile capitalizes on a stunning array of landscape and geology: the desert volcanoes of Atacama, the Mediterranean climes of the Central Valley, the snowcapped peaks of the Lake District, and the vast plains and granite cathedral peaks of Patagonia. But for all its natural wonder, Chile remains deliciously undiscovered. Some may have followed the news items about exiled dictator Augusto Pinochet, perhaps read the poetry of Pablo Neruda or the fiction of Isabel Allende. Chile is considered a "hot spot" for outdoor adventure, but much of the country still has regions that are little-visited or unexplored—both by foreigners *and* by Chileans.

Spectacular, untrammeled landscapes are just the beginning: Chileans themselves are warm and inviting, a proud people whose culture has been curiously defined by the geographical barriers that isolate them from the rest of South America. A staggeringly long coastline provides the country with what is arguably the richest variety of seafood in the world. A thriving capital city, a strong economy, and a modern infrastructure promise high-quality amenities and services. And, of course, activities from skiing to hiking to rafting to biking to some of the world's best fly-fishing abound. What follows is a historical and cultural introduction to a country where adventure, beauty, and hospitality await the willing traveler.

by Shane Christensen

By the time I first visited Argentina, I had already traveled fairly extensively in South America. I felt I had earned a strong sense of how sun, soccer, and Spanish colonialism had affected much of the continent, evidenced in both city and rural life. Across borders, I saw striking similarities between the family values, work ethics, and world views of Latin American societies. Had I tiptoed into Argentina from Chile, Bolivia, or Paraguay, I might have continued this comparison and, outside Buenos Aires, I did find that Argentina resembles its neighbors. But no one who lands in Buenos Aires fully believes they're in South America, at least not after witnessing Western Europe's remarkable influence throughout *Porteño* society. If you're suspicious, just head to an affluent neighborhood like Recoleta, where Parisian cafes, plazas, and buildings seem planted on the wrong continent.

Argentina is divided into distinct lands with very different people: the *pampas*—including Buenos Aires—the Northwest, Misiones, and Patagonia. Greater Buenos Aires, in which one third of Argentines live, is separated from the rest of Argentina both culturally and economically. Considerable suspicion exists between *Porteños,* as people of Buenos Aires are called, and the rest of the Argentines. Residents of the fast-paced metropolis who consider themselves more European than South American share little in common with the indigenous people of the Northwest, for example, who trace their roots to the Incas and take pride in a slower country life.

Argentines are predominantly descendants of European immigrants—Italians and Spanish at the forefront, followed by large numbers of French, Poles, Russians, and Germans—and they delight in telling you they are more European than South American. In fact, Argentina had a much smaller indigenous population than its Latin neighbors at the time of Spanish colonization, although a significant *mestizo* (half Indian, half white) community developed in the 19th century. Numerous *mestizos* worked with cattle, from which the legendary gaucho figure developed. Today, immigration continues but is mostly from the neighboring countries of Bolivia and Paraguay and is not favorably viewed by many Argentines.

2 Argentina's History 101

EARLY SETTLEMENT & COLONIZATION

Several distinct indigenous groups populated the area now called Argentina well before the arrival of the Europeans. The Incas had made inroads into the highlands of the Northwest. Most other groups were nomadic hunters and fishers, such as those in the Chaco, the Tehuelche of Patagonia, and the Querandí and Puelche (Guennakin) of the *pampas.* Others (the Diaguitas of the Northwest) developed stationary agriculture.

Many present-day Argentines feel they're really Europeans settled in South America, a perception fed by the country's immigrant heritage of Spanish, Italian, German, and French immigrants. Italian Américo Vespucio was the first European to arrive in 1502. Ferdinand Magellan arrived at the Río de la Plata in 1520, and Sebastian Cabot in 1526. Cabot discovered the Paraná and Paraguay rivers and established a fort at Sancti Spíritus. He also sent word back home of the presence of silver.

In 1535, Spain—having conquered Peru and aware of Portugal's presence in Brazil—sent an expedition headed by Pedro de Mendoza to settle the country. Mendoza was initially successful in founding Santa María del Buen Aire, or Buenos Aires (1536), but lack of food proved fatal. Mendoza, discouraged by Indian attacks and mortally ill, sailed for Spain in 1537; he died on the way.

Northern Argentina (including Buenos Aires) was settled mainly by people traveling from the neighboring Spanish colonies of Chile, Peru, and the settlement of Asunción in Paraguay. Little migration occurred directly from Spain; the area lacked the attractions of colonies like Mexico and Peru—rich mines, a large supply of Indian slave labor, and easy accessibility. Nevertheless, early communities forged a society dependent on cattle and horses imported from Spain, as well as such native crops as corn and potatoes. Pervasive Roman Catholic missions played a strong role in the colonizing process. The Spanish presence grew over the following centuries as Buenos Aires became a critical South American port.

INDEPENDENCE

The years 1806 and 1807 saw the first stirrings of independence. Buenos Aires fought off two British attacks, in battles known as the *Reconquista* and the *Defensa*. Around this time, a civil war had distracted Spain from its colonial holdings, and many Argentine-born Europeans began to debate the idea of self-government in the Buenos Aires *cabildo* (a municipal council with minimal powers established by colonial rulers). On July 9, 1816 (Nueve de Julio), Buenos Aires officially declared its independence from Spain, under the name United Provinces of the Río de la Plata. Several years of hard fighting followed before the Spanish were defeated in northern Argentina. But they remained a threat from their base in Peru until it was liberated by General José de San Martín (to this day a national hero) and Simón Bolívar from 1820 to 1824. Despite the drawing up of a national constitution, the territory that now constitutes modern Argentina was frequently disunited until 1860. The root cause of the trouble, the power struggle between Buenos Aires and the rest of the country, was not settled until 1880, and even after that it continued to cause dissatisfaction.

Conservative forces ruled for much of the late 19th and early 20th centuries, at one point deposing an elected opposition party president from power through military force. Despite the Conservatives' efforts to suppress new social and political groups—including a growing urban working class—their power began to erode.

THE PERÓN YEARS

In 1943, the military overthrew Argentina's constitutional government in a coup led by then army colonel Juan Domingo Perón. Perón became president in a 1946 election and was reelected 6 years later. He is famous (though by no means universally applauded) for his populist governing style, which empowered and economically aided the working class. His wife, Eva Duarte de Perón (popularly known as Evita), herself a controversial historical figure, worked alongside her husband to strengthen the voice of Argentina's women. (For more on Evita, see "Evita Perón: Woman, Wife, Icon," in chapter 3.) In 1955, the military deposed Perón, and the following years were marked by economic troubles (partly the result of Perón's expansive government spending) and social unrest, with a surge in terrorist activity by both the left and the right. While Perón was exiled in Spain, his power base in Argentina strengthened, allowing his return to the presidency in 1973. When he died in 1974, his third wife (and vice president), Isabel, replaced him.

THE DIRTY WAR & ITS AFTERMATH

The second Perónist era abruptly ended with a March 1976 coup that installed a military junta. The regime of Jorge Rafaél Videla carried out a campaign to weed out anybody suspected of having Communist sympathies. Congress was closed, censorship imposed, and unions banned. Over the next 7 years, during this "Process of National Reorganization"—a period known as the *Guerra Sucia* (Dirty War)—the country witnessed a level of political violence that affects the Argentine psyche today: Over 10,000 intellectuals, artists, activists, and others were tortured or executed by the Argentine government. The mothers of these *desaparecidos* (the disappeared ones) began holding Thursday afternoon vigils in front of the Presidential Palace, in Buenos Aires's Plaza de Mayo, as a way to call international attention to the plight of the missing. Although the junta was overturned in 1983, their weekly protests continue to this day.

Public outrage over the military's human rights abuses combined with Argentina's crushing defeat by the British in the 1982 Falkland Islands war undermined the dictatorship's control of the country. An election in 1983 restored constitutional rule and brought Raul Alfonsin of the Radical Civic Union to power. In 1989 political power shifted from the Radical Party to the Perónist Party (established by Juan Perón), the first democratic transition in 60 years. Carlos Saul Menem, a former governor from a province of little political significance, won the presidency by a surprising margin.

A strong leader, Menem pursued an ambitious but controversial agenda with the privatization of state-run institutions as its centerpiece. Privatization of inefficient state firms reduced government debt by billions of dollars and inflation was brought under control. After 10 years as president—and a constitutional amendment that allowed him to seek a second term—Menem left office. Meanwhile, an alternative to the traditional Perónist and Radical parties, the center-left FREPASO political alliance, had emerged on the scene. The Radicals and FREPASO formed an alliance for the October 1999 election, and their candidate defeated his Perónist competitor.

President Fernando de la Rua, not as charismatic as his predecessor, has been forced to reckon with the recession the Argentine economy has suffered since 1998. The country's commodity industries were hit hard by the Asian, Russian, and Brazilian financial crises, and Argentina's ability to borrow money from international lenders suffered. The economy is slowly improving, but unemployment remains stubbornly high, hovering at around 14%. De la Rua has worked to combat unemployment through labor law reforms and business-friendly policies. He has also followed a strict regimen of government spending cuts and revenue increases recommended by the International Monetary Fund. You will hear many Argentines complain about the state of their economy, although it's not as bad as many may think. The 1:1 dollar to peso exchange rate has helped stabilize prices, and the days of hyperinflation are over. There is considerable international investment in Argentina and a sense that Argentina is connecting to the new global economy. Argentina continues to enjoy one of the highest standards of living in South America. "Many of us are poor," explains one *Porteño,* "but no one here goes hungry."

3 A Taste of Argentina: Food & Drink

In Argentina meal times are, on average, later than English-speaking travelers may be used to. Dinner frequently does not begin until after 9pm, and restaurants stay open until well past midnight.

FOOD

Argentines can't get enough beef. While exporting some of the finest meat in the world, they still manage to keep enough of this national treasure at home to please natives and visitors alike. However, as this book went to press Argentina had reported an initial outbreak of **foot-and-mouth disease,** the virus that aggressively swept through Great Britain's cloven-hoofed livestock population. Several countries, including the United States, responded by banning the import of Argentinean beef. It is unclear what long-term effect the disease will have on Argentina's beef industry, but concerned travelers should consult the United States Department of Agriculture web site (www.usda.gov) to obtain the latest information on the outbreak.

The Argentine social venue of choice is the *asado* (barbecue). Families and friends gather at someone's home and barbecue prime ribs, pork, chicken, sausages, sweetbreads, kidneys . . . the list goes on. You can also enjoy this tradition while eating out; many restaurants are called *parrillas,* with open-air grills and, occasionally, large spits twirling animal carcasses over a roaring fire. For the full experience, ask for the *parrillada mixta* (mixed grill), which includes many of the items mentioned above. And don't forget the chimichurri sauce—an exotic blend of chili and garlic—to season your meat. A note on steaks: You can order them *bien cocida* (well done), *a punto* (medium rare), or *jugosa* (rare, literally "juicy").

But vegetarians exhale: Argentina offers some great alternatives to the strict red meat diet. One of the imprints Italians have left on Argentine culture is a plethora of pasta dishes, pizzas, and even *helado* (ice cream), reminiscent of Italian gelato. In addition, ethnic restaurants are springing up throughout Buenos Aires, stretching beyond traditional Spanish, Italian, and French venues to Japanese, Indian, Armenian, and Thai. Ethnic dishes come to life with fresh meats, seafood, and vegetables—the products of Argentina's diverse terrain. If you're just looking for a snack, try an empanada, a turnover pastry filled with minced meat, chicken, vegetables, or corn and varying a bit by region.

BEVERAGES

An immensely popular afternoon custom inherited from Paraguay is the sharing of *maté,* a tea made from the yerba maté herb. In the late afternoon, Argentines pass a gourd filled with the tea around the table, each person sipping through a metal straw. The drink is bitter, so you might opt to add some sugar. *Maté* is such an important part of daily life in Argentina that if people plan to be out of the house at teatime, they tote a thermos with them.

Argentina boasts a few excellent wine-growing regions; the best known is Mendoza, but Salta and La Rioja also produce impressive vintages. Malbec is the best Argentine red wine and functions as an engaging companion to any *parrillada.* The Torrontes grape, a dry white wine, has won various international competitions as well.

TYPICAL ARGENTINE DISHES

Look for some of these favorites on your menu:

- *Bife de chorizo:* Similar to a New York strip steak, but twice as big. Thick and tender, usually served medium rare.
- *Bife de lomo:* Filet mignon, 3 inches thick. Tender and lean.
- *Buseca:* Stew with sausages.

- *Locro criollo:* Beef stew with potatoes.
- *Milanesa:* Breaded meat fillet, sometimes in a sandwich.
- *Panqueques:* Either dessert crêpes filled with dulce de leche (caramel) and whipped cream, or salted crêpes with vegetables.
- *Provoletta:* Charbroiled slices of provolone cheese served at a *parrilla*.

4 Chile's People

by Kristina Schreck

One-third of Chile's 15 million people live in the Santiago metropolis alone. This disproportionate centralization in a country that stretches nearly 2,500 miles from north to south often leads to accusations that the government does more for the local populace than for residents in far-flung locales such as Punta Arenas. About 90% of the population is *mestizo,* a mix of indigenous and European blood that includes Spanish, German (in the Lake District), and Croatian (in southern Patagonia). Other nationalities, such as Italian, Russian, and English, have contributed a smaller influence. Indigenous groups such as the Aymara in the northern desert and the Mapuche in the Lake District still exist in large numbers, although nothing compared to their size before the Spanish conquest. It is estimated that there are more than a half-million Mapuches, many of whom live on poverty-stricken *reducciones,* literally "reductions," where they continue to use their language and carry on their customs. In southern Chile and Tierra del Fuego, indigenous groups such as Alacalufe and Yagan have been diminished to only a few remaining representatives, and some, such as the Patagonian Ona, have been completely extinguished.

Chileans are generous and usually welcoming, if not somewhat amused at the fact you've come so far to visit their country. They are self-effacing, and it is common to hear a Chilean point out a fellow countryman's limitations even though Chile is one of the most efficient, well-developed countries in Latin America. Their sense of humor is infectious, a drawn-out string of jokes that build on each other to keep the laugh going until it runs out of steam. They are a patriotic and proud people in all aspects, even in interpersonal relationships. It is common, for example, for a Chilean to give you the wrong answer rather than admit he or she doesn't know.

Although not inherently a racist country, Chile does suffer from an unhealthy dose of classism. A look at the voluminous society pages of the newspaper *El Mercurio* will give you an idea of Chile's conservative, elite families, many of whom place a ridiculous amount of value on a person's surname, place of education, and whether he or she has a fashionable address. Snobbish members of this class, especially those with affected accents, are referred to as *cuicos.* Chile does have a large (but shrinking) middle class, more so than most Latin American countries, yet 30% of the population lives under the poverty level.

Chileans place great value on the family unit. Unless they leave to study or marry, most children leave the household at a relatively late age, at least by North American standards. It is quite common to see a 25-year-old child living at home and without any pressure to leave. Many Chileans marry young and begin having children shortly thereafter, and consequently almost half the population is under the age of 25. Divorce is "illegal" in Chile, but couples are permitted to have their marriage annulled. Single Chileans have either a *pololo* (boyfriend) or a *polola* (girlfriend), a word that comes from a kind of insect that is known for ceaselessly buzzing around you. Chilean couples are very affectionate in public, and it seems every park or square is packed with young lovers kissing or strolling arm in arm.

5 Chile's History 101

EARLY HISTORY

Little is known of Chile's history before the arrival of the Spanish. Pre-Columbian cultures in Chile did not leave behind any written records, and archeologists have had to reconstruct Chile's indigenous history from artifacts found at burial sites, ancient villages, and forts. Because of this, much more is known about the northern cultures of Chile than their southern counterparts due to the north's extraordinarily arid climate and its ability to preserve, and preserve well, objects as fragile as 2,000-year-old mummies. Northern tribes such as the Atacama developed a culture that included the production of ceramic pottery, textiles, and objects made of gold and silver, but for the most part, early indigenous cultures in Chile were small, scattered bands that fished and cultivated simple crops. The primitive, nomadic tribes of Patagonia and Tierra del Fuego never developed beyond a society of hunters and gatherers, as severe weather and terrain prevented them from ever developing an agricultural system.

In the middle of the 15th century, the great Inca civilization pushed south in a tremendous period of expansion. Although the Incans were able to subjugate tribes in the north, they met their match with the Mapuche Indians in southern Chile. The Mapuche were fierce warriors who held fast to their territory, and the Inca civilization was forced to draw its boundary line there.

THE SPANISH INVADE

In 1535, and several years after Spaniards Diego de Almagro and Francisco Pizarro had successfully conquered the Inca empire in Peru, the conquistadors turned their attention south after hearing tales of riches that lay in what is today Chile. Already flushed with wealth garnered from Incan gold and silver, an inspired Diego de Almagro and more than 400 men set off on what would become a disastrous journey that left many dead from exposure and famine. De Almagro found nothing of the fabled riches, and he retreated to Peru.

Three years later, a distinguished officer of Pizarro's army, Pedro de Valdivia, secured permission to settle the land south of Peru in the name of the Spanish crown. The ambitious, Spanish-born Valdivia was more interested in the honor of conquering territory than in any riches it might yield. Valdivia left with just 10 soldiers and little ammunition, but his band grew to 150 by the time he reached the Aconcagua Valley, where he founded Santiago de la Nueva Extremadura on February 12, 1541. Santiago's early years were not auspicious: Fire, Indian attacks, and famine beset the colonists, but the town nonetheless held firm. Valdivia succeeded in founding several other outposts in Concepción, La Serena, and Valdivia, but, like the Incas before him, he was unable to overcome the Mapuche Indians south of the Bío Bío River. In a violent Mapuche rebellion, Valdivia was captured and suffered a gruesome death, sending frightened colonists north. The formidable strength of the Mapuche was not to be underestimated, and the tribe effectively defended their territory for the next 300 years.

Early Chile was a colonial backwater of no substantive interest to Spain, although Spain did see to the development of a feudal land-owning system called an *encomienda*. Prominent Spaniards were issued a large tract of land and an *encomienda,* or a group of Indian slaves, that the landowner was charged with caring for and converting to Christianity. Thus rose Chile's traditional and nearly self-supporting *hacienda* known as a *latifundo,* as well as a rigid class system that defined the population. At the top were the *peninsulares* (those born in Spain), followed by the *criollos* (creoles, or Spaniards born in the New World). Next down on the ladder were *mestizos* (a mix of Spanish and Indian blood), followed by Indians themselves. As the indigenous population succumbed to disease, the *latifundo* system replaced slaves with rootless *mestizos* willing, or forced, to work for a miserable wage. This form of land ownership would define Chile for centuries to come.

CHILE GAINS INDEPENDENCE

Chile was given its first taste of independence after Napoleon's invasion of Spain in 1808 and the subsequent sacking of King Ferdinand VII, who Napoleon replaced with his own brother. On September 18, 1810, leaders in Santiago agreed that the country would be self-governed until the king was reinstated as the rightful ruler of Spain. Although the self-rule was intended as a temporary measure, this date is now celebrated as Chile's independence day.

Semi-independence was not enough for many creoles, and soon thereafter Jose Miguel Carrera, the power-hungry son of a wealthy creole family, appointed himself leader and stated that the government would not answer to Spain or the viceroy of Peru. But Carrera was an ineffective and controversial leader, and it was soon determined that one of his generals, Bernardo O'Higgins, would prove to be a more adept leader. Carrera didn't take the competition lightly, and a power struggle ensued. Loyalist troops from Peru took advantage of the strife and crushed the fragile independence movement, sending Carrera, O'Higgins, and their troops fleeing to Argentina. This became known as the Spanish "reconquest," and it only served to intensify the creoles' desire to free themselves from Spanish ties. Across the border, in Mendoza, O'Higgins met Jose de San Martín, an Argentine general who had already been plotting the liberation of South America, which he believed could be accomplished only by conquering the ever-powerful viceroyalty seat in Peru. San Martín sought to liberate Chile first and then launch a sea attack on Peru from Chile's shore. In 1817, O'Higgins and San Martín crossed the Andes with their well-prepared troops and quickly defeated Spanish forces in Chacabuco, securing the capital. In April 1818, San Martín's army triumphed in the bloody battle of Maipú, and full independence from Spain was won. An assembly of prominent leaders elected O'Higgins as Supreme Director of Chile, but discontent within his ranks and with landowners led him to quit office and spend his remaining years in exile in Peru.

THE WAR OF THE PACIFIC

The robust growth of the nation during the mid- to late 1800s saw the development of railways and roads that connected previously remote regions with Santiago. The government began promoting European immigration to populate these regions, and it was primarily Germans who accepted, settling and clearing farms around the Lake District.

Increased international trading boosted the economy, but it was northern Chile's mines that held the greatest promise, specifically nitrate mines. Border disputes with Bolivia in this profitable region ensued, until a treaty was signed giving Antofagasta to Bolivia in exchange for not raising taxes on Chilean mines. Bolivia did an about face and hiked taxes, sparking the War of the Pacific that pitted allies Peru and Bolivia against Chile, all fighting for their share of the nitrate fields. The odds were against Chile, but the country's well-trained troops were a force to reckon with. The war was carried out both on land and in dramatic clashes at sea; the turning point came with the surrender of Peru's major warship, the *Huáscar*. Chilean troops then invaded Peru and didn't stop until they had captured Lima. With Chile as the final victor, both countries signed treaties that conceded Peru's Tarapacá region and Antofagasta to Chile. It was a breathtaking prize: Chile had increased its size by one-third with nitrate- and silver-rich land, and Bolivia had lost its contact with the coast.

THE MILITARY DICTATORSHIP

Chile has enjoyed a politically democratic past, but the road has not been smooth. However, no political event defines current-day Chile better than the country's former military dictatorship. In 1970, Dr. Salvador Allende, Chile's first socialist president, was narrowly voted into office. Allende avowed to improve the lives of Chile's poorer citizens by instituting a series of radical changes that might redistribute the nation's lopsided wealth. Although the first year showed promising signs, Allende's reforms ultimately sent the country spiraling into economic ruin. Large estates were seized by the government and by independent, organized groups of peasants to be divided among rural workers, many of them uneducated and unprepared. Major industries were nationalized but productivity lagged, and this, along with the falling price of copper, reduced the government's fiscal intake. Spending began outpacing income, and soon the country's deficit soared. Worst of all, uncontrollable inflation and price controls led to shortages, and Chileans were forced to wait in long lines to buy basic goods.

Meanwhile, the United States (led by Richard Nixon and Henry Kissinger) had been closely monitoring the situation in Chile. With anti-Communist sentiment running high in the U.S. government, the CIA allocated $8 million to undermine the Allende government by funding right-wing opposition and supporting a governmental takeover. Strikes were already being staged throughout Chile, the most damaging of which, a trucker's strike, nearly paralyzed the country.

On September 11, 1973, military forces led by General Augusto Pinochet toppled Allende's government with a dramatic coup d'etat. Military tanks rolled through the streets and jets dropped bombs on the Presidential Palace. Inside, Allende refused to surrender and accept an offer to be exiled. After delivering an emotional radio speech, Allende took his own life.

Many Chileans, especially wealthier citizens who had lost much under Allende, celebrated the coup as an economic and political salvation. But nobody was prepared for the brutal repression that would haunt Chile for the next 17 years. Congress was shut down, political parties and the news media were banned or censored, a strict curfew was imposed, and military officers took over previously nationalized industries and universities. Pinochet snuffed out his adversaries by rounding up nearly 7,000 political activists, journalists, professors, and any other "subversive" threats to the new status quo and subjecting them to horrifying torture. Many of these people were killed. Thousands more fled the country.

Pinochet set out to rebuild the economy using free-market policies that included selling off nationalized industries, curtailing government spending, reducing import tariffs, and eliminating price controls. From 1976 to 1981 the economy grew at such a pace that it was hailed as the "Chilean Miracle," but the miracle did nothing to address the country's high unemployment rate, worsening social conditions, and falling wages. More important, Chileans were unable to speak out against the government and those who did were often "disappeared," taken from their homes by Pinochet's secret police and never to be heard from again. Culture was filtered, and prohibitions were placed on artists, writers, and musicians with antigovernment messages or anything deemed "offensive."

The worldwide recession of 1982 put an end to Chile's economic run, but the economy bounced back again in the late 1980s. The Catholic Church began voicing opposition to Pinochet's brutal human rights abuses, and a strong desire for a return to democracy saw the beginning of nationwide protests and international pressure, especially from the United States. In a pivotal 1988 "yes or no" plebiscite, 55% of the voting public said no to military rule, and Patricio Alywin was democratically elected president of Chile. Pinochet agreed to hand over power, but not before he redesigned the constitution so that it would protect him and the military from future prosecution.

CHILE TODAY

Chile is on its third democratically elected president since the dictatorship, the left-leaning Ricardo Lagos. Even today the country remains divided over the legacy of Pinochet, and many wish the whole controversy would just go away. There are his fervent supporters who claim that deaths and torture were an inevitable evil required to put Chile back on track, and there are his adversaries, those who were exiled and many of whom lost relatives during the dictatorship and were never informed of their whereabouts. Pinochet appeared impossible to prosecute until 1998, when a visit to London to undergo surgery prompted a Spanish judge to level murder and torture charges against the former dictator and issue a request for his extradition. Lengthy legal wrangling ended with Pinochet's release and return to Chile; however, he is now under fire from Chilean prosecution and has been stripped of his immunity. At press time, the 85-year-old is undergoing medical examinations to determine if he is fit enough for trial, but Pinochet is already pointing the finger at officers within his ranks.

The early 1970s were a time of desperate economic hardship for Chileans. After the military coup, the Pinochet government hired a group of economic advisors who had been educated at the University of Chicago, earning them the nickname the "Chicago Boys." These economists instituted radical economic liberalization policies, such as privatization and reduced trade tariffs, and they sought to wean the country from its dependence on copper exports. It was a bumpy road, with many companies going bust when faced with international competition and a deep recession in the early 1980s. Workers' rights went ignored during the first decade, as the military government outlawed labor unions and workers' protests for better conditions and wages. Today, however, despite a somewhat sluggish past few years, the Chilean economy is the strongest in Latin America. The country is rich in natural resources; accordingly, its top industries are mining, forestry, fishing, agriculture, wine, and tourism. Chile's political stability and strong economy have boosted its credit rating, and many companies now look abroad for investment. Unfortunately, more than half the country's citizens still do not earn a decent living wage (the minimum wage is a scandalous $200 per month). Literacy is at an all-time high, but analysts claim that Chile could do much to increase education, especially with the onset of the electronic age.

Although Chileans are eager to help you, the *gringo,* as you fumble through a purchase, customer service in Chile lags well behind the booming tourism industry and an increasingly consumer-driven society. The tedious purchasing process at businesses such as pharmacies, where you order a remedy at one counter, pay for it at another counter, and then pick the purchase up at yet another, says it all. Chileans are reliable, but their attention to detail is often lacking. The good news is that punctuality in Chile is taken more seriously than it is in neighboring countries—still, don't expect Swiss precision.

6 A Taste of Chile: Food & Drink

Don't expect to come home raving about the food in Chile. Despite the amount of wonderful ingredients at hand, including fresh shellfish and fish, vegetables, and exotic fruits, Chilean restaurants rarely "prepare" food apart from a dozen classics such as *pastel de choclo* (corn and meat pie) and *chupe de jaiva* (crab casserole). Most restaurants rely on the same time-worn recipes; meat and fish are fried, grilled, or baked with little seasoning apart from salt and paired with rice or fries—not very memorable.

There are exceptions, however. Many restaurants, especially in Santiago, have stepped up over the past decade with superb, innovative cuisine. The capital's dining scene has also experienced an infusion of international cuisine with new offerings from French, Italian, Peruvian, Japanese, and other Asian-influenced restaurants, even Indian. Towns that attract tourists—Puerto Varas or Pucón, for example—usually feature a few good restaurants, and so do many hotels. Of course, there's nothing wrong with a basic meal here and there, and Chile's abundant fish markets are a typical place to find simply prepared but tasty and supremely fresh food.

A menu is called *la carta;* the term *menú* refers to a fixed lunch, which most restaurants offer, especially on weekdays. These fixed lunches go for about $4 to $10 and include an appetizer, main course, beverage or wine, coffee, and dessert, or a similar combination. Sometimes the menu is not advertised and you'll have to ask the waitstaff.

The best thing about eating in Chile is the cost. Sometimes you might feel you've paid too much for what you ordered, but generally main courses are moderately priced when compared to the United States. A few dining sections in this book have categorized restaurants as Expensive, more than $15; Moderate, $8 to $15; and Inexpensive, less than $8. The majority of restaurants in Chile serve entrees that range in price from $5 to $10. A 10% tip is customary.

MEALS & DINING CUSTOMS   It might take some adjusting to get used to the country's dining hours and size of meals. Breakfast is served anywhere from 7 to 10am, but Chileans rarely have more than coffee, juice, and toast; apart from *gringo*-oriented hotels and restaurants, it's difficult to find a place that serves a bigger morning meal. Typically your hotel will serve a continental breakfast (included in the room price) that might include cheese and ham. In Chile, lunch is still the main meal of the day (although this is changing somewhat), served from 1pm to as late as 3pm. In restaurants, Chileans normally order the daily fixed-price lunch, called the *menú del día, menú ejecutivo* or *colación.* It includes an appetizer, main dish, and sometimes dessert and wine—quite a meal if you plan on doing anything afterward, but always better, more varied, and less expensive than ordering directly from *la carta.*

Dinner is late—very late, with most restaurants opening no earlier than 8pm and closing at midnight. Even in private homes families eat dinner around 9:30 or 10pm. This giant hunger gap between lunch and dinner has given rise to the Chilean tradition of *onces*—literally "elevenses," or afternoon tea. At home, a Chilean might have a cup of tea with a roll and jam, but throughout the country you'll find *salones de té,* which serve complete *onces* that can include rich, sugary cakes, toasted cheese sandwiches, juice, ice cream, and more.

FOOD

APPETIZERS   Known as *entradas,* Chilean diners commonly order an appetizer before their meal, more often than not a shellfish appetizer, such as razor clams and Parmesan or an avocado half stuffed with crab. Bar appetizers are known as *picoteos,* hearty platters that often feature meats and cheeses, sometimes mixed with fries and usually enough for a light meal.

SANDWICHES & SNACKS   Chileans cling to the traditional heavy lunch, but many also lunch or snack on quick meals like sandwiches or empanadas, those tasty little fried or baked turnovers filled with shellfish, cheese, or a meat and onion mixture known as *pino.* Sandwiches are hefty and often require a knife and fork. A grilled ham and cheese is known as a *Barros Jarpa,* and a meat and melted cheese is known as a *Barros Luco.* Then there's the *completo,* a hot dog topped with thick globs of mayonnaise, mashed avocado, and chopped tomato, an impossibly messy Chilean favorite. Cheap cafes, commonly known as *fuentes de soda* (soda fountain) or *schoperías* (from the word *schop,* or draft beer), primarily serve fast snacks and sandwiches. One of the most common, inexpensive, and light dishes is *cazuela,* a very common chicken soup made with potatoes, corn, rice, and bell pepper.

MEAT   Although Chilean meat consumption is no match for the carnivores of Argentina, they do consume a lot of it. Chile also loves its lamb, especially in the Lake District and Patagonia region where the meat is butterflied or tied to a spit and slowly roasted over a wood fire. Beef is the focal point for the social Chilean *asado,* or barbecue, that commonly begins with an appetizer of savory grilled sausages. The most tender cuts of steak are *lomo* or *filet;* otherwise, you'll also find chicken and sometimes pork on all menus. Don't miss the traditional favorite, *pastel de choclo,* a casserole of ground beef and chicken, topped with a sweet, creamy corn mixture and baked until golden brown.

SEAFOOD   Fruits of the sea are this country's specialty, and the Chilean's love for the variety of weird and wonderful shellfish seems limitless. *Machas* (razor clams), the delicious but hard-to-get *loco* (abalone), *choros* or *choritos* (mussels), *ostras* (oysters), *ostiones* (scallops), or the outstanding *centolla* (king crab) are familiar. You might want to sample the popular but exotic *piure,* an iodine-rich, alien-looking "thing" that's usually served in soups, or the much-loved *erizo* (sea urchin). The most common fish types you'll see on menus are salmon, the delicious and buttery *congrio* (conger eel), *merluza* (hake), or *corvina* (sea bass), all of which are usually grilled, fried, or baked and served alone or with a sauce. Common, delicious dishes include *paila marina* (shellfish stew), *ceviche* (chopped fish and onion cooked in lemon juice), *chupes* (a casserole usually made with crab), or *caldillo* (a thick soup), usually made with *congrio.*

VEGETABLES   Chile's central valley is the breadbasket of this slender country, producing the majority of the country's fruits and vegetables. In the southern regions that are prone to cold weather and heavy rainfall, vegetables are grown in greenhouses—in fact, it seems that every rural household has one in their backyard. In Patagonia, vegetables and fruit are very difficult to come by, and what you get is of secondary quality and very expensive. Most restaurants do not serve vegetable dishes apart from salads or sometimes as appetizers, although you can order just about any vegetable in a salad, even beets, green beans, corn, and shredded carrots. The avocado is ubiquitous, well loved, and cheap, as are the tomato and onion, both of which are combined to form an *ensalada chilena*. Vegetarians might find themselves limited to a salad and fries, but there are a few good vegetarian restaurants in the country, especially in Santiago.

FRUITS   Chile harvests a rich, wonderful assortment of fruits in its central valley and in citrus groves in the desert north, producing known fruits such as apples, peaches, bananas, and oranges. But you'll want to sample one of the more wonderful, exotic fruits produced in this country, such as the delicious *chirimoya* (custard apple), *tuna* (cactus fruit), *pepino dulce* (a sweet pepper that tastes somewhat like a melon), or *membrillo* (quince).

DESSERTS   Chileans often order dessert after lunch and then again after dinner, even if it's just chopped fruit that's either fresh or from a can. Desserts to look out for include the gooey, sugary, lemon dessert *suspiro de límon.* Heavy German immigration has left its mark with dense, creamy cakes called *kuchen,* a specialty throughout the Lake District. A strange though tasty dessert popular throughout Chile is *mote con huesillo,* dried peaches soaked in a light syrup and served over barley grain. Flan is as popular here as everywhere in Latin America.

BEVERAGES

Chileans guzzle *bebidas* (soft drinks) such as Coca-Cola, Sprite, or the country's own Biltz and Pap, two sodas that resemble Fanta in color, if not in their unusual taste. Fruit juices are also popular, either sold in boxes at the supermarket or served fresh in restaurants, cafes, or roadway stalls. These fresh juices are a heavenly delight, and are usually made of *frambuesa* (raspberry), *naranja* (orange), *durazno* (peach), and more.

If you love coffee, you're in for a disappointment. Rarely will you stumble upon a restaurant that serves brewed coffee—even upscale restaurants often try to get away with serving a packet of Nescafe and a cup of boiling water. Ask if a restaurant serves real *café-café,* or if they have an espresso machine.

The water in Chile is safe to drink by anyone except those with exceptionally delicate stomachs. If you're still not sure, you'll find *agua mineral* served everywhere, either *sin gas* (plain) or *con gas* (carbonated).

BEER, WINE & LIQUOR   Start your meal with a tangy *pisco* sour, the Chilean national drink made of the grape brandy *pisco,* fresh-squeezed lemon, sugar, and sometimes an egg white. Chileans and Peruvians are divided over which country actually invented the *pisco* sour, but the drink was popularized in this country. Be careful—they're potent.

Chile is known for its excellent wine production, but the country unfortunately exports its very finest varieties to outside markets. However, you'll find that restaurants and shops offer a selection of good to excellent wine varieties at low prices compared to U.S. standards. A simple but decent red table wine like Santa Emiliana sells for $2.50 in the supermarket, for example. Apart from lager, you won't find a wide selection of beer in Chile. Escudo and Cristal are the major Budweiser-like brands, but there's also Austral, Becker, and the darker Morenita. If you're in the Lake District, order Kunstman, probably the best beer in Chile. A *schop* is a draft beer.

Appendix B:
Useful Terms & Phrases

Every Spanish-speaking country has its language idiosyncrasies. You'll find that the difference between Spanish spoken in Argentina and Chile is quite pronounced (no pun intended).

Argentine Spanish has a rich, almost Italian sound, with the double "ll" and "y" pronounced with a "J" sound. So *llave* (key) sounds like "*zha*-ve" and *desayuno* (breakfast) like "de-sa-*zhu*-no." *Usted* (the formal "you") is used extensively, and *vos* is used for the familiar "you" in place of *tú*.

Among the peculiarly Argentine terms you may come across are: *barbaro* (very cool); *Porteño* (a resident of Buenos Aires); *pasos* (steps in a tango); *bandoneon* (a cousin of the accordion, used in tango music); *colectivos* (local buses); and *subte* (the Buenos Aires subway).

Chilean Spanish has a singsong feel; sentences often end on a high-pitched note. Chileans habitually drop the "*s*" off the end of words, meaning words such as *gracias* (thank you) and *más* (more) sound more like "*gra*-cia" and "ma." Words that end in *-ido* or *-ado* frequently drop the "d;" for example, *pesado* (heavy) is pronounced "peh-*sao*."

When using the familiar *tú* verb tense, Chileans—especially younger Chileans—exchange the standard *-as* or *-es* ending for *-ai* or *-i*, so *como estas?* (how are you?) becomes *como estai?*

There are too many slang words to recount here, but several terms and tendencies are frequent enough to warrant mention. Chileans add emphasis to *sí* or *no* by tacking on the suffix *-pues*, which is then shortened to *-po*, as in "*¡Sí, po!*" *Ya* is commonly used for "yes" or "okay," and "*¡Ya, po!*" means "Enough!" *Cachai* (you know?) is peppered through conversations. Two very Chilean sayings are *al tiro* (right away) and *harto* (a lot or many).

1 Basic Words & Phrases

English	Spanish	Pronunciation
Good day	**Buenos días**	*bway*-nohss *dee*-ahss
How are you?	**¿Cómo está?**	*koh*-moh ess-*tah*?
Very well	**Muy bien**	mwee byen
Thank you	**Gracias**	*grah*-see-ahss
You're welcome	**De nada**	day *nah*-dah
Goodbye	**Adiós**	ah-*dyohss*
Please	**Por favor**	pohr fah-*vohr*
Yes	**Sí**	see

Useful Terms & Phrases

English	Spanish	Pronunciation
No	**No**	noh
Excuse me (to get by someone)	**Perdóneme**	pehr-*doh*-ney-may
Excuse me (to begin a question)	**Disculpe**	dees-*kool*-pay
Give me	**Déme**	*day*-may
Where is . . . ?	**¿Dónde está . . . ?**	*dohn*-day ess-*tah*?
the station	**la estación**	lah ess-tah-*seown*
a hotel	**un hotel**	oon oh-*tel*
a gas station	**una estación de servicio**	*oo*-nuh ess-tah-*seown* day sayr-*bee*-see-oh
a restaurant	**un restaurante**	oon res-tow-*rahn*-tay
the toilet	**el baño**	el *bahn*-yoh
a good doctor	**un buen médico**	oon bwayn *may*-thee-co
the road to . . .	**el camino a/hacia . . .**	el cah-*mee*-noh ah/*ah*-see-ah
To the right	**A la derecha**	ah lah day-*reh*-chuh
To the left	**A la izquierda**	ah lah ees-ky-*ehr*-dah
Straight ahead	**Derecho**	day-*reh*-cho
I would like	**Quisiera**	key-see-*ehr*-ah
I want	**Quiero**	*kyehr*-oh
to eat	**comer**	ko-*mayr*
a room	**una habitación**	*oon*-nuh ha-bee-tah-*seown*
Do you have . . . ?	**¿Tiene usted . . .?**	tyea-nay oos-*ted*?
a book	**un libro**	oon *lee*-bro
a dictionary	**un diccionario**	oon deek-seown-*ar*-eo
How much is it?	**¿Cuánto cuesta?**	*kwahn*-to *kwess*-tah?
When?	**¿Cuándo?**	*kwahn*-doh?
What?	**¿Qué?**	kay?
There is (Is there . . . ?)	**(¿)Hay (. . . ?)**	eye?
What is there?	**¿Qué hay?**	kay eye?
Yesterday	**Ayer**	ah-*yer*
Today	**Hoy**	oy
Tomorrow	**Mañana**	mahn-*yahn*-ah
Good	**Bueno**	*bway*-no
Bad	**Malo**	*mah*-lo
Better (best)	**(Lo) Mejor**	(loh) meh-*hor*
More	**Más**	mahs
Less	**Menos**	*may*-noss
No smoking	**Se prohíbe fumar**	say pro-*hee*-bay foo-*mahr*
Postcard	**Tarjeta postal**	tar-*hay*-ta pohs-*tahl*
Insect repellent	**Rapelente contra insectos**	rah-pey-*yahn*-te *cohn*-trah een-*sehk*-tos

2 More Useful Phrases

English	Spanish	Pronunciation
Do you speak English?	**¿Habla usted inglés?**	*ah*-blah oo-*sted* een-*glays*?
Is there anyone here who speaks English?	**¿Hay alguien aquí que hable inglés?**	eye *ahl*-ghee-en ah-*key* kay *ah*-blay een-*glays*?

English	Spanish	Pronunciation
I speak a little Spanish.	**Hablo un poco de español.**	*ah*-blow oon *poh*-koh day ess-pah-*nyol*
I don't understand Spanish very well.	**No (lo) entiendo muy bien el español.**	noh (loh) ehn-tee-*ehn*-do moo-ee bee-ayn el ess-pah-*nyol*
The meal is good.	**Me gusta la comida.**	may *goo*-sta lah koh-*mee*-dah
What time is it?	**¿Qué hora es?**	kay *oar*-ah ess?
May I see your menu?	**¿Puedo ver el menú (la carta)?**	*puay*-doe veyr el may-*noo* (lah *car*-tah)?
The check, please.	**La cuenta, por favor.**	lah *quayn*-tah, pohr fa-*vorh*
What do I owe you?	**¿Cuánto lo debo?**	*Kwahn*-toh loh *day*-boh?
What did you say?	**¿Cómo? (colloquial expression for American "Eh?")**	*Koh*-moh?
I want (to see)	**Quiero (ver)**	Key-*yehr*-oh (vehr)
a room	**un cuarto** or **una habitación**	on *kwar*-toh, *oon*-nuh ha-bee-tah-*seown*
for two persons	**para dos personas**	*pahr*-ah doss pehr-*sohn*-as
with (without) bathroom	**con (sin) baño**	kohn (seen) *bah*-nyoh
We are staying here only . . .	**Nos quedamos aquí solamente . . .**	nohs kay-*dahm*-ohss ah-*key* sohl-ah-*mayn*-tay
one night	**una noche**	oon-ah *noh*-chay
one week	**una semana**	oon-ah say-*mahn*-ah
We are leaving . . .	**Partimos (Salimos) . . .**	Pahr-*tee*-mohss; sah-*lee*-mohss
tomorrow	**mañana**	mahn-*nyan*-ah
Do you accept?	**¿Acepta usted?**	Ah-*sayp*-tah oo-*sted*
traveler's checks?	**cheques de viajero?**	*chay* kays day bee-ah-*hehr*-oh?
Is there a Laundromat?	**¿Hay una lavandería?**	Eye *oon*-ah lah-*vahn*-day-*ree*-ah
near here?	**cerca de aquí?**	*sehr*-ka day ah-*key*
Please send these clothes to the laundry.	**Hágame el favor de mandar esta ropa a la lavandería.**	Ah-ga-may el fah-*vhor* day mahn-*dahr* ays- tah *rho*-pah a lah lah- *vahn*-day-*ree*-ah

Useful Terms & Phrases

POSTAL GLOSSARY

Airmail **Correo Aéreo**
Customs **Aduana**
General Delivery **Lista de Correos**
Insurance (insured mail) **Seguro (correo asegurado)**
Mailbox **Buzón**
Money Order **Giro Postal**
Parcel **Paquete**
Post Office **Oficina de Correos**
Post Office Box (abbreviation) **Casilla**
Postal Service **Correos**
Registered Mail **Registrado**
Rubber Stamp **Sello**
Special Delivery, Express **Entrega Inmediata**
Stamp **Estampilla** or **Timbre**

TRANSPORTATION TERMS

English	Spanish	Pronunciation
Airport	**Aeropuerto**	Ah-ay-row-*pwer*-tow
Flight	**Vuelo**	Boo-*ay*-low
Rental car	**Arrendadora de Autos**	Ah-rain-da-*dow*-rah day autos

(*Note: In Chile, the English term "rent a car" is also common.*)

Bus	**Autobús**	ow-toh-*boos*
Bus or truck	**Camión**	ka-mee-*ohn*
Local bus	**Micro**	*mee*-kroh
Lane	**Carril**	kah-*rreal*
Baggage (claim area)	**Equipajes**	eh-key-*pah*-hays
Luggage storage area	**Custodia**	koo-*stow*-dee-ah
Arrival gates	**Llegadas**	yay-*gah*-dahs
Originates at this station	**Local**	loh-*kahl*
Originates elsewhere	**De Paso**	day *pah*-soh
Stops if seats available	**Para si hay lugares**	pah-rah see aye loo-*gahr*-ays
First class	**Primera**	pree-*mehr*-ah
Second class	**Segunda**	say-*goon*-dah
Nonstop	**Sin Escala**	seen ess-*kah*-lah
Baggage claim area	**Recibo de Equipajes**	ray-see-boh day eh-key-*pah*-hay
Waiting room	**Sala de Espera**	*Saw*-lah day ess-*pehr*-ah
Toilets	**Baños**	*bahn*-yos
Ticket window	**Boletería**	boh-leh-teh-*ree*-ah

3 Numbers

1	**uno** (*ooh*-noh)	17	**diecisiete** (de-*ess*-ee-*syeh*-tay)	
2	**dos** (dohs)	18	**dieciocho** (dee-*ess*-ee-oh-choh)	
3	**tres** (trayss)	19	**diecinueve** (dee-*ess*-ee-*nway*-bay)	
4	**cuatro** (*kwah*-troh)	20	**veinte** (*bayn*-tay)	
5	**cinco** (*seen*-koh)	30	**treinta** (*trayn*-tah)	
6	**seis** (sayss)	40	**cuarenta** (kwah-*ren*-tah)	
7	**siete** (*syeh*-tay)	50	**cincuenta** (seen-*kwen*-tah)	
8	**ocho** (*oh*-choh)	60	**sesenta** (say-*sen*-tah)	
9	**nueve** (*nway*-bay)	70	**setenta** (say-*ten*-tah)	
10	**diez** (dee-ess)	80	**ochenta** (oh-*chen*-tah)	
11	**once** (*ohn*-say)	90	**noventa** (noh-*ben*-tah)	
12	**doce** (*doh*-say)	100	**cien** (see-*en*)	
13	**trece** (*tray*-say)	200	**doscientos** (dos-see-*ehn*-tos)	
14	**catorce** (kah-*tor*-say)	500	**quinientos** (keen-ee-*ehn*-tos)	
15	**quince** (*keen*-say)	1,000	**mil** (meal)	
16	**dieciseis** (de-*ess*-ee-sayss)			

Index

Index

Index

Index

Index

Index

FROMMER'S® COMPLETE TRAVEL GUIDES

Alaska
Amsterdam
Argentina & Chile
Arizona
Atlanta
Australia
Austria
Bahamas
Barcelona, Madrid & Seville
Beijing
Belgium, Holland & Luxembourg
Bermuda
Boston
British Columbia & the Canadian Rockies
Budapest & the Best of Hungary
California
Canada
Cancún, Cozumel & the Yucatán
Cape Cod, Nantucket & Martha's Vineyard
Caribbean
Caribbean Cruises & Ports of Call
Caribbean Ports of Call
Carolinas & Georgia
Chicago
China
Colorado
Costa Rica
Denmark
Denver, Boulder & Colorado Springs
England
Europe

European Cruises & Ports of Call
Florida
France
Germany
Greece
Greek Islands
Hawaii
Hong Kong
Honolulu, Waikiki & Oahu
Ireland
Israel
Italy
Jamaica
Japan
Las Vegas
London
Los Angeles
Maryland & Delaware
Maui
Mexico
Montana & Wyoming
Montréal & Québec City
Munich & the Bavarian Alps
Nashville & Memphis
Nepal
New England
New Mexico
New Orleans
New York City
New Zealand
Nova Scotia, New Brunswick & Prince Edward Island
Oregon
Paris
Philadelphia & the Amish Country
Portugal

Prague & the Best of the Czech Republic
Provence & the Riviera
Puerto Rico
Rome
San Antonio & Austin
San Diego
San Francisco
Santa Fe, Taos & Albuquerque
Scandinavia
Scotland
Seattle & Portland
Shanghai
Singapore & Malaysia
South Africa
Southeast Asia
South Florida
South Pacific
Spain
Sweden
Switzerland
Texas
Thailand
Tokyo
Toronto
Tuscany & Umbria
USA
Utah
Vancouver & Victoria
Vermont, New Hampshire & Maine
Vienna & the Danube Valley
Virgin Islands
Virginia
Walt Disney World & Orlando
Washington, D.C.
Washington State

FROMMER'S® DOLLAR-A-DAY GUIDES

Australia from $50 a Day
California from $70 a Day
Caribbean from $70 a Day
England from $70 a Day
Europe from $70 a Day

Florida from $70 a Day
Hawaii from $70 a Day
Ireland from $60 a Day
Italy from $70 a Day
London from $85 a Day

New York from $80 a Day
Paris from $80 a Day
San Francisco from $60 a Day
Washington, D.C., from $70 a Day

FROMMER'S® PORTABLE GUIDES

Acapulco, Ixtapa & Zihuatanejo
Alaska Cruises & Ports of Call
Amsterdam
Australia's Great Barrier Reef
Bahamas
Baja & Los Cabos
Berlin
Boston
California Wine Country
Charleston & Savannah
Chicago

Dublin
Hawaii: The Big Island
Hong Kong
Houston
Las Vegas
London
Los Angeles
Maine Coast
Maui
Miami
New Orleans
New York City
Paris

Phoenix & Scottsdale
Portland
Puerto Rico
Puerto Vallarta, Manzanillo & Guadalajara
San Diego
San Francisco
Seattle
Sydney
Tampa & St. Petersburg
Vancouver
Venice
Washington, D.C.

FROMMER'S® NATIONAL PARK GUIDES

Family Vacations in the National Parks
Grand Canyon

National Parks of the American West
Rocky Mountain
Yellowstone & Grand Teton

Yosemite & Sequoia/ Kings Canyon
Zion & Bryce Canyon

FROMMER'S® MEMORABLE WALKS

Chicago	New York	San Francisco
London	Paris	Washington, D.C.

FROMMER'S® GREAT OUTDOOR GUIDES

Arizona & New Mexico	Northern California	Southern New England
New England	Southern California & Baja	Vermont & New Hampshire

FROMMER'S® BORN TO SHOP GUIDES

Born to Shop: France	Born to Shop: Italy	Born to Shop: New York
Born to Shop: Hong Kong, Shanghai & Beijing	Born to Shop: London	Born to Shop: Paris

FROMMER'S® IRREVERENT GUIDES

Amsterdam	Los Angeles	Seattle & Portland
Boston	Manhattan	Vancouver
Chicago	New Orleans	Walt Disney World
Las Vegas	Paris	Washington, D.C.
London	San Francisco	

FROMMER'S® BEST-LOVED DRIVING TOURS

America	France	New England
Britain	Germany	Scotland
California	Ireland	Spain
Florida	Italy	Western Europe

THE UNOFFICIAL GUIDES®

Bed & Breakfasts in California	Golf Vacations in the Eastern U.S.	New Orleans
Bed & Breakfasts in New England	The Great Smoky & Blue Ridge Mountains	New York City
Bed & Breakfasts in the Northwest	Inside Disney	Paris
Bed & Breakfasts in Southeast	Hawaii	San Francisco
Beyond Disney	Las Vegas	Skiing in the West
Branson, Missouri	London	Southeast with Kids
California with Kids	Mid-Atlantic with Kids	Walt Disney World
Chicago	Mini Las Vegas	Walt Disney World for Grown-ups
Cruises	Mini-Mickey	Walt Disney World for Kids
Disneyland	New England with Kids	Washington, D.C.
Florida with Kids		World's Best Diving Vacations

SPECIAL-INTEREST TITLES

Frommer's Britain's Best Bed & Breakfasts and Country Inns
Frommer's France's Best Bed & Breakfasts and Country Inns
Frommer's Italy's Best Bed & Breakfasts and Country Inns
Frommer's Caribbean Hideaways
Frommer's Adventure Guide to Australia & New Zealand
Frommer's Adventure Guide to Central America
Frommer's Adventure Guide to India & Pakistan
Frommer's Adventure Guide to South America
Frommer's Adventure Guide to Southeast Asia
Frommer's Adventure Guide to Southern Africa
Frommer's Gay & Lesbian Europe
Frommer's Exploring America by RV
Hanging Out in England

Hanging Out in Europe
Hanging Out in France
Hanging Out in Ireland
Hanging Out in Italy
Hanging Out in Spain
Israel Past & Present
Frommer's The Moon
Frommer's New York City with Kids
The New York Times' Guide to Unforgettable Weekends
Places Rated Almanac
Retirement Places Rated
Frommer's Road Atlas Britain
Frommer's Road Atlas Europe
Frommer's Washington, D.C., with Kids
Frommer's What the Airlines Never Tell You